The Editor

JAMES PETHICA has taught at Williams College and at the University of Richmond. Currently a Fellow at the Oakley Center for the Humanities and Social Sciences, Williams College, he is at work on the authorized biography of Lady Gregory.

D0141077

A NORTON CRITICAL EDITION

YEATS'S POETRY, DRAMA, AND PROSE

※

AUTHORITATIVE TEXTS

CONTEXTS

CRITICISM

Selected and Edited by

JAMES PETHICA

WILLIAMS COLLEGE

W • W • NORTON & COMPANY • *New York* • *London*

for
Warwick and Deirdre

Every effort has been made to contact the copyright holders for each of the selections.
Rights holders of any selections not credited should contact W. W. Norton &
Company, Inc., 500 Fifth Avenue, New York, NY 10110, in order for a correction
to be made in the next reprinting of our work.

The text of this book is composed in Electra
with the display set in Bernhard Modern.
Composition by PennSet, Inc.
Manufacturing by R.R. Donnelley
Book design by Antonina Krass.

Library of Congress Cataloging-in-Publication Data
Yeats, W. B. (William Butler), 1865–1939.
[Selections. 1999]
Yeats's poetry, drama, and prose : criticism / selected and edited by James Pethica.
p. cm. — (A Norton critical edition)
Includes bibliographical references and index.

ISBN 0-393-97497-9 (pbk.)

1. Ireland—Literary collections. 2. Yeats, W. B.(William Butler),
1865–1939–Criticism and interpretation. 3. Ireland—In literature. I. Pethica, James.
II. Title.

PR5902.P48   1999
821'.8—dc21   99-051816

W. W. Norton & Company, Inc., 500 Fifth Avenue, New York, N.Y. 10110
www.wwnorton.com

W. W. Norton & Company Ltd., Castle House, 75/76 Wells Street,
London W1T 3QT

1 2 3 4 5 6 7 8 9 0

Contents

Criticism

Introduction

William Butler Yeats's unusual creative potential was readily apparent as a young man, especially to his Irish contemporaries. Reviewing his first collection of poetry—*The Wanderings of Oisin and Other Poems* (1889), published when Yeats was just twenty-three—Oscar Wilde found himself hardly able to "resist the fascinating temptation of recklessly prophesying a fine future for its author," notwithstanding his cautious recognition that "Books of poetry by young writers are usually promissory notes that are never met" (see p. 321). During his late twenties, and especially with the publication of *Poems* (1895), Yeats securely established himself as the most promising poet of his generation. By 1909, with the death of Swinburne, he was able to consider himself "King of the Cats,"[1] and the young Ezra Pound, newly arrived in England, was seeking him out as "the only living man whose work has more than a most temporary interest."[2] More remarkable than his steady rise to eminence, though, was Yeats's staying power. The advent of High Modernism around 1913 briefly made it look as if he would soon be no more than a relic from an earlier age—writing formally patterned lyrics in an era of free verse, and remaining essentially Romantic in his celebrations of the artist-hero at a time when artistic impersonality was in vogue—but his work continued to grow in power, and his output actually increased, with over a third of his poems being written after he was awarded the Nobel Prize in 1923. The energy and urgency of the writings he completed in his seventies, when ill health made it clear he had little time to live, particularly continue to surprise first-time readers. Rather than resting on his laurels, Yeats sought out controversy in his last years, becoming more strident in his politics and his artistic judgments, and more determined in his desire not to fade into repetition, silence, or irrelevance in the way he considered Wordsworth—"withering into eighty years, honoured and empty-witted" (p. 287)—had done. "You think it horrible that lust and rage / Should dance attendance upon my old age;" he remarks in "The Spur," written in 1938: "They were not such a plague when I was young; / What else have I to spur me into song?" (p. 119).

Yeats came to adulthood when the British Empire was seemingly at the height of its power. Ireland was still a British colony, governed by a Protestant Ascendancy landlord class that had only recently seen its dominance begin to be challenged, and the ornate aesthetic of pre-Raphaelitism and late Victorianism dominated in the arts. His death in 1939 came just months before the outbreak of World War II, in a world in which technological, social, and political change had transformed the nature of daily life. British economic and military primacy was long gone; Ireland was partitioned, with the South now a republic and effectively a Catholic state; the fundamental credos of Victorian belief and social hierarchy seemed to have been swept away by the conflagration of World War I; and avant-garde experimentalism predominated in art

---

1. See Joseph Hone, *W. B. Yeats 1865–1939* (New York: St. Martin's Press, 1962), p. 230.
2. See James Longenbach, *Stone Cottage* (Oxford: Oxford University Press, 1988), p. 13.

and literature. Yeats's success in remaining a major poetic force across the five decades between the publication of his first and his last collections of poetry stemmed in large part from his often contentious engagement with the aesthetic, political, and cultural shifts of his era, but most of all from his uncanny accompanying ability to constantly evolve and renew himself as a writer.

His work falls into several phases. The early writings, culminating in the poems of *The Wind Among the Reeds* (1899) and the play *The Shadowy Waters* (1900), are typically ornate, visionary, and escapist. The figure of the artist or poet is omnipresent here, questing, like Shelley's Alastor, for an eternal beauty he hopes may be found in a mystical love. But that love repeatedly proves incompatible with ordinary reality, and, like Shelley's hero, the poet or lover in early Yeats is almost invariably doomed, either to die, to be marginalized, or simply to retreat from view to distant islands or into the obscurity of the woods. In reaction against scientific rationalism, Yeats in these years privileged imagination above all else, repeatedly asserting that "the arts are founded on the life beyond the world" (p. 265). He hoped to find in folklore and heroic mythology a source of inspiration that could both animate a new sense of Irish identity and confirm the "ancient supremacy of imagination" (p. 262). "The arts by brooding upon their own intensity have become religious" he wrote in 1897, "and are seeking . . . to create a sacred book" (p. 266). By 1903 he had begun to distance himself from this aesthetic, briskly dismissing his earlier writings as "too lyrical, too full of aspirations after remote things, too full of desires."[3] This forceful self-criticism is often regarded as marking a radical break in his work, but while it certainly signaled his intention to turn from the expression of "disembodied beauty"[4] toward a more active engagement with the known and the tangible, it involved continuity as well as departure: the dismissal defines his early writings as "too" lyrical and "too" desiring of remote things, but it falls well short of rejecting outright either the lyrical mode or his interest in the unseen. Yeats had in fact been aware of the dangers of his tendency toward mystical abstraction from the first, fretting to Katharine Tynan as early as 1888 that his work tended to "cloud and foam."[5] Much of his best early poetry indeed turns on what would become and remain a characteristic Yeatsian tension deriving from this awareness: a tension between desire for the visionary or unseen, and the impulse to counter its insubstantiality with the flawed but vital realm of the actual. The faeries in his 1886 poem "The Stolen Child" (pp. 8–10), for instance, seductively and rhythmically call on both the child and the reader to turn away from a world that is "anxious" and "full of weeping," yet the poem also recognizes that the alternative world the faeries offer may be dangerous and deceptive. The title emphasizes that the child and its volition are being literally "stolen," and in the third stanza hints of malevolence or evil emerge when the faeries seem to revel in causing "unquiet dreams" in the "slumbering trout." The last stanza, by contrast, pointedly reminds us that the quotidian world ("the calves on the warm hillside; / Or the kettle on the hob") has a comforting and reliable side to it, for all its faults. The poem seems well aware, then, that to succumb to the glamour of the visionary world involves a potentially dangerous credulity or loss of self-consciousness, and that succumbing may be merely an easy evasion of the need to come to terms with the known. Yeats's most popular early poem, "The Lake Isle of Innisfree," first published in 1890, revisits this tension more

3. Yeats to John Quinn, May 15, 1903. *The Collected Letters of W. B. Yeats, Volume III: 1901–1904*, ed. John Kelly and Ronald Schuchard (Oxford: Clarendon Press, 1994), p. 372.
4. Yeats to George Russell, May 14, 1903. Ibid., p. 369.
5. Yeats to Katharine Tynan, September 1888. *The Collected Letters of W. B. Yeats, Volume I: 1865–1895*, ed. John Kelly and Eric Domville (Oxford: Clarendon Press, 1986), p. 98.

personally in its investigation of his longing for an escape from the "gray" pavements of metropolitan London to an Irish retreat where he might live alone in a restorative and natural peace (p. 15). The cadence and rhythmic force of the poem quickly convince the reader of the intensity of Yeats's longing, and its rich evocations of sounds and color conjure up an alluring image of the island as a place that seems, like the faery world, to transcend the flawed urban realm of crowds and commerce. But the speaker's longing in the poem is tellingly static. The poem closes, as it begins, with an expression of forceful intent to reach Innisfree—"I will arise and go now"—yet the poet has signally failed to move, even though there is no overt indication of anything preventing him from doing so. The poem thus manages to suggest the speaker knows on some level that the vision he longs for is idealized, and that to actually go to Innisfree would be a form of evasion, and perhaps not as satisfying in reality as in reverie.

For Yeats, as for many other artists and thinkers, the beginning of the new century and the death of Queen Victoria in 1901 served as a call to modernize. Symptomatically, Sigmund Freud postdated the title page of *The Interpretation of Dreams* by a year to 1900, so that his first major work could be part of the new dispensation rather than of the old century. Recalling the end of the decadent nineties and what he called the "Tragic" generation, Yeats would reflect that "in 1900 everybody got down off his stilts; henceforth nobody drank absinthe with his black coffee; nobody went mad; nobody committed suicide."[6] Changes in his style and his aesthetic—changes he called for directly in 1903, as we have seen—did not emerge immediately, or in such neat response to historical forces as we may restrospectively like to imagine, but a new focus on action and engagement with the ordinary came gradually to replace or at least complicate the abstraction and introspection that had predominated in his earlier work. The plays *Cathleen ni Houlihan*, written with Lady Gregory in 1901, and *On Baile's Strand*, first drafted in 1902, typify the emerging change, being written mainly in prose rather than the pentameter verse typical of Yeats's earlier drama. In the first of these plays he deliberately sought to "get down out of that high window of dramatic verse" in an effort to replicate real "country speech,"[7] while the action of *On Baile's Strand*, he hoped, foreshadowed the emergence of "a less dream-burdened will" in his writing.[8] As if to epitomize how deliberately he was moving beyond the extravagant aestheticism of the nineties, Yeats issued his 1903 volume *In the Seven Woods* as a slim and almost defiantly plain book, its pale blue covers devoid of ornament—in striking contrast to the form of his 1890s collections of poems, almost all of which were bound in dark blue covers tooled in gilt with intricate occult designs.

The new volume haltingly marked the beginning of a transitional phase that would continue until around 1917, in which Yeats would seek with increasing determination to strip his poetry of ornament and abstraction. "A Coat" (p. 52), first published in 1914, concisely articulates his new aims. The poem proposes that his old style, having become overly elaborate, like a "coat . . . Covered with embroideries," needs to be cast away and replaced by directness and simplicity. The poem's own form deliberately models the desired change. Its opening four lines offer perfect rhymes, with the elaborate polysyllabic pairing of "embroideries/mythologies" prominently positioned so as to evoke

6. Introduction to *The Oxford Book of Modern Verse* (Oxford: Clarendon Press, 1936) p. xi.
7. *The Variorum Edition of the Plays* of W. B. Yeats, ed. Russell Alspach (London: Macmillan, 1966), p. 232.
8. *The Variorum Edition of the Poems of W. B. Yeats*, ed. Peter Allt and Russell Alspach (New York: Macmillan, 1966), p. 814.

the manner of his early lyrics. This gives way in line 5, however, to a chain of awkward, simpler, off-rhymes ("throat/it/naked"), with the drab and flat-sounding monosyllabic word "it" being used three times, as if to dramatize and insist on the virtues of the new minimalism Yeats seeks. The poem closes with the resolute declaration that "there's more enterprise / In walking naked." But this goal of stripping and renewal was not easily achieved. "Adam's Curse" (p. 32), written in 1902, and the most important poem to be included in the new collection, is representative of the contradictions and challenges inherent in the stylistic and aesthetic self-renovation to which Yeats aspired. On the one hand, the poem calls for extreme artifice to produce a writing that will seem only "a moment's thought"—an artifice apparent in its simulation of ordinary speech, its disguise of its meter and rhyme scheme through heavy enjambments, and in the unobtrusive but telling off-rhymes ("enough/love"; "poetry/maybe") that would thereafter be a signature of Yeats's style. This seems, on the face of it, a massive shift from the way poems such as "He wishes for the Cloths of Heaven" and "He thinks of those who have Spoken Evil of his Beloved" (pp. 28–29) had deliberately called attention to their own intricacy, and defiantly claimed or aspired to have the power to persuade or influence. Yet on the other hand, for all its innovation and its protestation that "the old high way of love" is now an "idle trade," "Adam's Curse" remains resolutely within the tradition of love poetry it suggests is now redundant. The poet's closing expression of weariness and dejection seems at first glance to reflect a new self-knowledge and the emergence of a new realism in the face of a world apparently unimpressed by his poetry. Yet the poem takes evident pride in its claim that having to "articulate sweet sounds" skillfully is to "work harder" even than those doing manual labor. Rather than turning from an unrequited and seemingly hopeless love, the poet makes his own failure his subject matter, and, in this, "Adam's Curse" represents a fundamental continuation of the emotional dynamic at the heart of Yeats's earlier love poems. The lover no longer simply withdraws to the woods or to Innisfree, or imagines his own death, but he is still centered on the art of love poetry and his continuing quest for love, and he remains resolutely marginalized from "the noisy set / Of bankers, schoolmasters and clergymen" and the ordinary realms of commerce, thought, and belief they represent.

The 1903 marriage of Yeats's beloved, Maud Gonne, to Major John Mac-Bride complicated and accelerated the evolution of his aesthetic in this transitional period. Shocked by the news, he wrote almost no poetry for five years, concentrating instead on playwriting and on founding and directing the Abbey Theatre. The practical demands of the Abbey—"Theatre business, management of men" (p. 38)—and the constant need to revise his own and others' plays to make them more effective in performance served to toughen Yeats. So did a five month lecture-tour of the United States over the winter of 1903–04, which honed his skills as a public speaker and left him financially secure for the first time in his life. On his return he was a changed man, writing dismissively of the "sentimental sadness" and "introspection" of his early lyrics, and declaring the need for "athletic joy" in his work.[9] Novelist George Moore recalled him having acquired "a paunch, a huge stride, and an immense fur overcoat" (p. 325) in his travels, and also detected a seismic shift in the poet's politics, with a new, aristocratic disdain for the Irish middle classes suddenly dominating. The protests against John Synge's *The Playboy of the Western World* in 1907, years of controversy over Hugh Lane's effort to found a gallery

---

9. Yeats to George Russell, April 1904. *The Collected Letters of W. B. Yeats. Volume III: 1901–1904*, ed. John Kelly and Ronald Schuchard (Oxford: Clarendon Press, 1994), pp. 577–78.

of modern art in Dublin, and Yeats's increasing recognition that support for the arts in Ireland was severely limited combined to further fuel this shift. Around 1907 his writings begin to take on an increasingly bitter tone and to reflect an increasingly hieratic notion of art. "Ireland is passing through a crisis of the mind greater than any she has known since [the 1840s]," he wrote in 1907 in an essay that condemns the uniform thinking of the masses and extols "the right of the individual mind to see the world in its own way" (p. 279). Traveling in Italy that summer with his closest friend and patron, Lady Gregory, Yeats immersed himself in the art and culture of the Renaissance, and he returned to Ireland deeply convinced that for art to flourish there required either an aristocratic tradition, in which wealthy patrons follow their own tastes and cultivate genius accordingly, or a nonmaterialistic rural culture, in which "countrymen" generate "beautiful stories and beliefs, because they have nothing to lose" (p. 281). The importance of aristocratic daring and of rooted tradition, and the competing dangers of "ill-breeding" (p. 252) and the narrow-minded materialism of the marketplace became his constant themes in this period, and they would remain so throughout his career.

These ideological shifts register powerfully in Yeats's poems between 1908 and 1913 in the form of his increasingly direct engagement with contemporary politics. The threat posed to Lady Gregory's estate (and by extension to all aristocratic "big houses") by rent reform in 1909 inspired "Upon a House shaken by the Land Agitation" (p. 40), in which he laments that redistribution of the estate's wealth will make poorer houses "sturdier" only by destroying an accomplished governing class. His increasing bitterness and sense of marginalization from the mainstream of contemporary Ireland spurred the 1913 collection *Poems Written in Discouragement*, including "September 1913" (pp. 44–45)—his first poem to be titled with a date—in which Yeats charges that the idealism of an earlier generation has been lost, and that crass materialism and narrow religious orthodoxy now prevail in Ireland. Such stark "contemporary" poems emphasize how far he had traveled by 1913 from the ornate, visionary mode of his earliest lyrics. Yet the central tensions that animate him imaginatively in these later poems are less changed than his new subject matter initially suggests. An ideal world—now the Ireland of his own youth or the cultured courts of the Italian Renaissance, rather than the realm of the faeries or an imagined Innisfree—is still set as a desirable image against which the actual world—now contemporary Ireland—falls short. In Yeats's love poetry of the period, too, an underlying familiarity remains. Although Maud Gonne's marriage to John MacBride seemed to have ended any likelihood of Yeats ever marrying her, he continued to devote a significant portion of his effort to love poetry in which she is his central iconic inspiration. Although he and Gonne were both approaching fifty, he continued to dwell on her former beauty, portraying himself in "Fallen Majesty" as a devoted courtier who records "what's gone" (p. 50). Ezra Pound, otherwise generally admiring of Yeats's self-modernization, regarded such works as backward-looking and imaginatively stagnant, and in 1912 he made the bold move of altering some of the older man's poems, without permission, before their publication in the magazine *Poetry*. Although initially affronted, Yeats soon forgave Pound and seems to have responded attentively to his call for greater precision and realism in his writing. In the opening poem of *Responsibilities*, dated January 1914, Yeats asks "Pardon" from his ancestors that "for a barren passion's sake" he has reached "close on forty-nine" with "no child" (p. 42). "Lines Written in Dejection," written in 1915, engages frontally the possibility that he had become imaginatively barren, too. The poem expresses his resolve to "endure" the stark, revealing brightness of "the embittered sun," but also his fear that the banishment of the "heroic" mythology that had been the dominant source of his inspiration will leave him with "nothing" (p. 61). His play *At the Hawk's Well*, written in 1916, powerfully dramatizes this fear of bankruptcy, featuring an old man who realizes that he has wasted his life in waiting for the waters of immortality to rise in a dried-up well, and a young man who seems destined to repeat his mistakes. Perhaps most revealingly of all, Yeats chose to end *Reveries Over Childhood and Youth*, his first volume of autobiography, completed in 1914, with the following plangent declaration:

> For some months now I have lived with my own youth and childhood, not always writing indeed but thinking of it almost every day, and I am sorrowful and disturbed. It is not that I have accomplished too few of my plans, for I am not ambitious; but when I think of all the books I have read, and of the wise words I have heard spoken, and of the anxiety I have given to parents and grandparents, and of the hopes that I have had, all life weighed in the scales of my own life seems to me a preparation for something that never happens. (p. 219)

He had spent the greater part of his adult life believing that he lived in an age when revelation or apocalyse was imminent, and he had pursued the study of the occult since his youth, believing that a poet should be able to draw on quasi-magical powers to make language evoke higher spiritual realities. But now, with age already beckoning, it seemed that his efforts had been vain.

These fears were soon to be swept away, and the "trembling of the veil of the Temple"[1] that Yeats had hoped for since the 1890s would unexpectedly occur. As had been the case with Maud Gonne's marriage in 1903, a series of real-world events intruded to accelerate and complicate the emergence of a new phase in his work. On Easter Monday 1916, a force of some 700 Nationalists proclaimed an Irish Republic, seized key sites in Dublin, and held out against British forces for six days before surrendering. For Yeats, who believed himself to be in tune with his country's political life, the Rising came as a complete surprise. Like most Irish observers he was initially unreceptive to the rebellion and deplored its use of force, but the execution of fifteen of the Rising's leaders by the British in the wake of their surrender dramatically changed his conception of what had occurred. "I had no idea that any public event could so deeply move me," he wrote to Lady Gregory; "At the moment I feel that all the work of years has been overturned."[2] "Easter, 1916" (pp. 73–75) embodies his extraordinary, conflicted poetic response: a sense of loss over the deaths of the leaders, many of whom he had known personally; apocalyptic excitement at the "terrible beauty" their self-sacrifice had generated; a feeling that his own "work of years" had proved useless; a related, emerging desire now to be the interpreter of events and the maker of new national master myths; admiration for the leaders' heroism, competing with a sense of jealousy at their courage; contempt for what he saw as their fanaticism and single-mindedness, combined with humble acknowledgment of the incredible impact it had produced; and, most of all, utter uncertainty as to whether the Rising had really been necessary, and as to how it would affect the future course of Ireland. And while the Rising brought sharply into question all that Yeats had achieved and aspired to as an Irish writer and cultural critic, it also

---

1. As a young man, Yeats had recorded a saying by French symbolist poet Stéphane Mallarmé (1842–1898) that his era was troubled by "the trembling of the veil of the Temple" (an allusion to Matthew 27.51), and he used the phrase as the title for the second volume of his *Autobiographies*.
2. Yeats to Lady Gregory, May 11, 1916. *The Letters of W. B. Yeats*, ed. Allan Wade (New York: Macmillan, 1955), p. 613.

brought new crisis into his personal life, since John MacBride was one of the executed leaders, and his death now revived the possibility of Yeats marrying Maud Gonne. During a three-month stay with her in France that summer he proposed, was refused, and then unsuccessfully began to court her twenty-two-year-old daughter, Iseult. Returning to Ireland, he began "The Wild Swans at Coole," perhaps his finest self-elegy — a meditation on his seeming barrenness, his sense of age, and his loss of visionary energy. The following year he proposed to Iseult, but was refused, and then, in a decisive rebound, he proposed to and was accepted by George Hyde-Lees, twenty-seven years his junior, whom he had known for some years but had never previously courted.

The marriage would quickly result in an "incredible experience" (p. 298). A few days after the wedding, sensing her new husband's guilt at having married more out of determination than for love, George Yeats attempted automatic writing — a process in which the writer suspends the conscious mind and allows the hand to move across paper at the behest of outside forces. Random scribbles are the usual result, but George Yeats, either deliberately or by psychic gift, generated coherent messages that seemed to come from spirits. When these spirits began to respond to Yeats's questions, he quickly resolved to "spend what remained of life explaining and piecing together those scattered sentences," only to be met with the message that his unknown instructors had come "to give you metaphors for poetry" (p. 298).

Influenced by these events, the period around 1917 marks the beginning of what is generally thought of as "great" Yeats. His 1919 edition of *The Wild Swans at Coole* reflects the shift, with the gloomy uncertainty and sense of creative barrenness that prevailed in many of the poems of 1913–17 giving way to a renewed joy in and celebration of the power of vision and imagination. "Ego Dominus Tuus" (pp. 66–68) completed a few weeks after his marriage and in the first flush of excitement over the automatic writing, epitomizes the change, with "Hic" — one aspect of Yeats's self — cautioning against the delusion of seeking revelation, only to be soundly rejected by "Ille" (quickly dubbed "Willie" by some of Yeats's friends), who insists that he will quest for the antiself who alone can "disclose / All that I seek." Dialogic poems such as this proliferate in his canon after 1917, serving as a forum for the dramatization of his inner debates. Characteristically for Yeats — for whom assertion almost always led quickly to qualification and complication — the certainty of choice evident in "Ego Dominus Tuus" would gradually give way to more taut and intellectually stringent forms of self-debate over the relationship between the worlds of action and thought, life and art.

The Anglo-Irish War of 1919–21 and the Irish Civil War that followed posed a particularly acute challenge to his new certainty in the power of imagination and in the value of the discipline and withdrawal from ordinary human activities needed to reach spiritual perfection. From his vantage point at Thoor Ballylee, a Norman tower in County Galway that he restored and used intermittently as a summer home from 1917 onward, Yeats was torn between a desire for active engagement in events and the wish to turn away from a violence that seemed to be negating everything he had worked for over the years. As in the wake of the Easter Rising, his wish to take an active role in shaping Ireland's future competed with uncertainty as to whether taking sides in the conflict would be either justifiable or beneficial. "Meditations in Time of Civil War" (pp. 86–91) majestically wrestles with this uncertainty, with Yeats vacillating between the knowledge that to turn away would mean a willful evasion of the facts — such as the corpse of a "dead young soldier" being taken past his window — and disgust at the recurring "rage" of war and its fanatic excesses. This basic tension is counterpointed by the poem's opening speculation as to whether violence is in fact a precondition for art and hence, paradoxically, desirable. If so, Yeats suggests, then intellectual distance such as his own, and the aestheticism that wealth allows (whether in a Renaissance court or an Irish "big house"), might be a source of sterility—with "slippered Contemplation" leading to effete inaction and indecision, rather than to erudition or truth. The poem closes with Yeats turning away from engagement, in favor of a withdrawal into the tower of the self and the renewed pursuit of "abstract joy," but it is a decision clearly freighted with regret. Life in all its richness (as well as its brutality) is only to be found outside the tower—in the form of the fertile honey bees and birds who live in its masonry, in the moor-hen guiding its young chicks on the stream running by, and of course in the soldiers, whose willingness to fight gives them a vitality Yeats clearly envies—whereas the intellectual realm within is described as the "cold snows of a dream."

The choice explored in "Meditations in Time of Civil War" would be revisited and reconsidered in "A Dialogue of Self and Soul," "Vacillation," "Sailing to Byzantium," and numerous other poems written during Yeats's prime, as he strove for progressively more complex explorations and formulations of the central tensions in his work. In the poems of the 1920s, vacillation becomes a dominant mode, with neither the choice of withdrawal from the world in favor of spiritual discipline, nor the choice of engagement with the realm of the physical, providing satisfaction for long. In "The Double Vision of Michael Robartes," the closing poem of *The Wild Swans at Coole*, Michael Robartes is granted a revelation that seems to promise the possibility of his reaching ultimate truth; in "Michael Robartes and the Dancer," which comes next in *Collected Poems*, however, he reappears as an aged pedant whose supposed erudition fails to persuade in the face of the Dancer's seemingly simple questions. But Robartes's vision in the earlier of the two poems introduces an image—of a girl dancing—that would be central for Yeats during the next decade. The girl dances between statues of a Sphinx—a figure for inscrutability and the control of the intellect—and a Buddha—for Yeats, a figure for the control of the emotions. The unself-conscious girl of the vision achieves a perfection of motion and physical beauty that seems to offer a momentary balance between the needs of the mind and the needs of the body; her dancing is thus a figure for art itself as a possible source of balance or synthesis between the realms of the real and the ideal, and between the competing needs of mind and body. Her motion offers a pattern that is simultaneously both artless, since it is instinctive rather than planned, and artful, in the sense that it is elaborate and manages to engage and please both the mind and the senses. The possibility of accommodation between mind and body is perhaps most forcibly signaled in the poem in lines that figure the mind itself as if physically moving yet seeming at the same time to reach the stasis of eternity: "Mind moved yet seemed to stop / As 'twere a spinning top" (p. 69).

Yeats's poetry of the 1920s repeatedly seeks an art that might achieve this condition—the "death-in-life and life-in-death" of "Byzantium" (p. 108)—and that might transcend, if only momentarily, the inevitable continuing conflict between thought and action, mind and body, vision and reality. He had always been attentive to the way a single poem's meanings were reinflected or enriched by its positioning within a sequence, but from *The Tower* (1928) onward he designed his volumes ever more carefully to construct larger dialogic structures than individual poems could allow. Most of the poems of *The Tower*, for instance, espouse the form of withdrawal enacted in "Meditations in Time of Civil War," highlighting the limitations and imperfections of ordinary life, and the dangers of the "sensual music" (p. 80) of the realm of the physical. *The Tower* closes with the speaker of "All Souls' Night" refusing to tell his racial "stocks" (p. 316). Given his oligarchic beliefs, Yeats was inevitably fascinated with the rise of fascism in the early 1930s, and he briefly flirted with the Irish Blueshirt movement. In this latter enthusiasm, however, Yeats's support was only temporary, since he was eventually able to discriminate between the rhetoric of leadership by the strong, and the unpleasant realities of the fascist movement's practice. The poems of his last two or three years continue to signal their distaste with the debased condition of contemporary culture, but they also reflect increasing ironic distance from the rage and intolerance that generated that distaste. The speaker of "Politics," for instance, which Yeats placed as the final poem in his canon, is ultimately unable to keep his mind fixed on contemporary politics and the prospect of war (p. 130). At the sight of a young girl, the wish that he could be young again sweeps all other thoughts away. In Yeats's final play, *Purgatory*, the Old Man kills his only son — like himself, a "bastard" born of a coupling initiated without regard for the perpetuation of social caste or culture — rather than have him "pass pollution on" (p. 174). Yeats's drafts of the play, however, show his initial identification with the Old Man being progressively complicated and subverted, and in the finished play the killing of the Boy is a moment of apocalyptic rupture that brings horror rather than revelation.[3] In destroying the remnants of his own lineage, the Old Man merely compounds the crime he considers his mother has committed, and his closing plea that the "misery of the living and the remorse of the dead" be appeased remains unanswered, leaving him in a living purgatory that parallels the spiritual purgatory to which he believes his mother has been condemned. Rather than railing against current political leaders, Yeats's last poems tend instead to evoke heroic figures from the past, holding these up as images of a nobility and power now lost. Dead friends feature prominently here, alongside imagined figures such as the resolute soldiers of "The Black Tower" or the warrior-hero Cuchulain in "Cuchulain Comforted."

Elegy is indeed the dominant mode of Yeats's final volumes, *New Poems* (1938) and *Last Poems and Two Plays* (1939), in which the process of celebrating and mourning iconic figures from his own past complements poems that reflect more directly on his own inexorable decline and impending death. What is perhaps most impressive in these poems is the "tragic joy" (p. 114) they seek to express, with Yeats aspiring to reach, and sing, a "transfiguring" gaiety (p. 115) amidst his own decline and the decay he saw around him. This quality, much of the time, redeems or offsets the harsher didactic or vainglorious tendencies also present in his late work. The imperiousness of "Under Ben Bulben," for instance, is counterpointed by the optimism of "Lapis Lazuli," just as its hubris is counterpointed by the humility of "The Circus Animals' Desertion." With its antithetical implications, the phrase "tragic joy" was doubtless intended to evoke Yeats's resonant earlier coinage "terrible beauty" in "Easter, 1916" as well as the conflicted self-debates characteristic of his work of that earlier period. In these last writings Yeats is again at his best when his feelings are at their most conflicted, and when his poetry serves as means of self-discovery, rather than self-assertion. As he had written in 1917, in what was perhaps his most incisive moment of self-criticism:

> We make out of the quarrel with others, rhetoric, but of the quarrel with ourselves, poetry. Unlike the rhetoricians, who get a confident voice from remembering the crowd they have won or may win, we sing amid our uncertainty. (p. 285)

---

3. See Introduction, Sandra Siegel, ed., *W. B. Yeats: Purgatory: Manuscript Materials* (Ithaca: Cornell University Press, 1986).

"mummy truths"—he asserts that "No living man can drink from the whole wine" (p. 101)—and instead preferring the silence of a spiritual quest that is figured as deathly. Most of the poems in *The Winding Stair* (1933), by contrast, proclaim a renewed commitment to the messy and painful, but vital, struggles of ordinary life. In "Crazy Jane talks with the Bishop," for instance, Jane rejects the limiting morality of the Church and specifically condemns any form of spirituality that might deny the vitality of the body and its desires: "For nothing can be sole or whole / That has not been rent" (p. 112). The underlying dialogic conflict between the volumes adds intellectual urgency and rhetorical force to Yeats's effort in individual poems to arrive at some form of synthesis such as that briefly offered by the dancer's perfection. At the same time, his work of the period increasingly problematizes the prospect of arriving at such a synthesis. The celebrated close of "Among School Children," in particular, asks how one can ever distinguish clearly between experience and meaning, between transient performance and enduring pattern, between the artist's self and the creation he or she creates:

> O body swayed to music, O brightening glance,
> How can we know the dancer from the dance?   (p. 98)

Apocalyptic rupture or violence is increasingly seen as a necessary precondition for revelation in the poems of this period, but as in poems such as "The Second Coming" and "Leda and the Swan" Yeats is torn between excitement at the possibility of revelation and horror at the destruction and barbarism that accompany it.

The publication of *The Collected Poems of W. B. Yeats* in November 1933 marked the first collected edition of his poetry that Yeats had issued since 1908. The process of preparing this and the companion volume *Collected Plays*, published in 1934, together with his work toward two deluxe editions of his collected writings planned for the collectors' market, must inevitably have set him thinking more urgently about the final form his creative canon would take. Following Lady Gregory's death in May 1932 he wrote almost no new poetry for nearly two years, and as had been the case at turning points earlier in his life, he briefly feared his inspiration had dried up. The end of this barren period coincided closely with his decision to undergo a Steinach "rejuvenation" operation—a vasectomy, a procedure thought at that time to increase the production of male hormones—in May 1934. Following the operation he had a remarkable burst of creative energy. Over the next four-and-a-half years he would compose more than seventy new lyrics and four new plays, edit *The Oxford Book of Modern Verse*, issue a revised edition of his occult-philosophical text *A Vision* (based on the automatic writing), complete his autobiography, and write a substantial number of essays—the work that constitutes "late" Yeats.

His writing in this final phase is marked by an urgent desire to fight bodily decline and find fresh incentives to create, even if it requires rage or "foolish" (p. 113) passion. With Ireland evolving in directions he increasingly found distasteful, politics and the state of contemporary civilization provided much of the motivation he needed. The hieratic, aristocratic strain that had begun to emerge since around 1904 now reached its height, resulting in numerous poems of complaint against the "degeneration" (p. 316) he saw proliferating as a result of democracy. In "Under Ben Bulben," he scorns "the sort now growing up / All out of shape from toe to top" as being "Base-born products of base beds" (p. 124); in the reactionary 1939 pamphlet *On the Boiler*, he went so far as to extol the merits of eugenics as a way of improving Ireland's

A Note on the Texts

The development of Yeats's poetic, as broadly described in the Introduction, involved stylistic and aesthetic self-renovations more elaborate than merely the sporadic castings-off he himself evoked in "Adam's Curse" or "A Coat," in which he rejects older work as worn out or flawed, and resolves to find a new style or more powerful insight. Yeats was an inveterate reviser of his writings, and the textual history of his poems is consequently one of almost unrivaled instability. Rarely satisfied with the first form in which his poems were printed, he would habitually engage in a phase of significant revision in the period immediately after their initial publication. Typically he published new poems first in journal printings, then would make changes for their first appearance in a book. Between 1903 and 1938, these first book printings were mainly in limited editions issued by the Cuala Press, and he usually took the opportunity to make further revisions in the trade editions that followed. This initial process of revision generally took between a few months and three or four years for the majority of the poems in Yeats's canon, and it would result—in the main— in texts with which he was largely satisfied, and which would be subject to only incremental minor revisions in subsequent printings.

But in addition to this generic pattern—a pattern that reflects Yeats's constant investment in his craft—he also engaged in a second, more remarkable, process of textual revision. Following major evolutions in his poetic, or when given the opportunity to take stock of his achievement when preparing collected editions, he would compulsively revise his earlier writings so as to reshape the trajectory of his entire oeuvre. While many poems remained unchanged during these phases, others were rewritten substantially, and new poems were sometimes added to existing sequences or others dropped. This habit of retroactive reshaping was pronounced from early on in his career. In *Poems* (1895), for instance, Yeats presented "all the writer cares to preserve out of his previous volumes of verse"—a process that involved him omitting half the poems included in *The Wanderings of Oisin and Other Poems* (1889), significantly revising most of the remainder, and positioning them *after* the poems retained from his later volume *The Countess Kathleen and Various Legends and Lyrics* (1892).[1] In new editions of *Poems* in 1899 and 1901 incremental further revisions followed, and changes were also introduced in some of the numerous later editions. In the final printing of the volume—in 1927, thirty-two years after the first edition—Yeats carried out another major retroactive reshaping, now placing the poems derived from the 1889 volume *before* those derived from the 1892 volume, a shift he had recently made in the 1925 volume *Early Poems and Stories*. As he acknowledged in a prefatory note to *Poems* (1927), his early poetry was hence, even after nearly four decades, still in some sense a work in progress:

1. Preface, *Poems* (London: T. Fisher Unwin, 1895), p. v; reprinted in *The Variorum Edition of the Poems of W. B. Yeats*, ed. Peter Allt and Russell K. Alspach (London: Macmillan, 1966), p. 845 (hereafter *VP*). For the omissions, see Allan Wade, *A Bibliography of the Writings of W. B. Yeats*, 3rd ed., revised by Russell K. Alspach (London: Rupert Hart-Davis, 1968), pp. 21–27, 35–37.

This volume contains what is, I hope, the final text of the poems of my youth; and yet it may not be, seeing that in it are not only the revisions from my 'Early Poems and Stories,' published last year, but quite new revisions on which my heart is greatly set. One is always cutting out the dead wood.[2]

And so indeed it would prove, with further new revisions being introduced as he prepared copy-text for *Collected Poems* (1933) and again, later in the 1930s, as he planned collected editions of his work projected for the British and American collectors' markets. For Yeats, as Warwick Gould has observed, "publication" was thus always merely "a moment in the history of composition" rather than the absolute fulfillment of an authorial intention.[3] Yeats himself was fully conscious of this. In a short verse included in his *Collected Works* of 1908, responding to the frustration of some of his readers at his habit of changing lines they loved (and also preparing them for the many new changes they would find), he asserted that revision was essential to his sense of self and that the changing poet and his changing textual self-representations were inextricably connected:

> The friends that have it I do wrong
> When ever I remake a song,
> Should know what issue is at stake:
> It is myself that I remake.[4]

For more than three decades, editions and selections of Yeats's poetry routinely followed the texts presented in *The Poems of W. B. Yeats* (1949)—the so-called definitive edition prepared posthumously by Yeats's widow and Thomas Mark, his longtime reader and adviser from the Macmillan publishing house. The publication of *The Poems: A New Edition* in 1983, however—edited by Richard Finneran, whose work highlights the shortcomings of the 1949 volume—has ushered in a period of intense debate about Yeats's final intentions for his poetic canon. The arrangements offered in subsequent collected editions have consequently varied widely in terms of their choice of copy-texts, the sequence the poems are presented in, and numerous other matters. All these editions, however, have aimed to represent the best possible "final" texts of the poems. The complex earlier textual histories of individual poems have been available only in *The Variorum Edition of the Poems of W. B. Yeats*, last revised in 1966, a volume that itself privileges Yeats's "final" texts, since it presents earlier versions as variant readings in a critical apparatus subordinated to those texts.

Given the increasing recognition of the importance of Yeats's habits of revision, and that his texts are highly contingent on the historical circumstances of their publication, an unquestioned privileging of Yeats's "final" texts has now become problematic. To print texts of the poems of the 1880s and early 1890s as presented by Yeats in, say, *Collected Poems* (1933) manifestly offers a "Yeats" as reconceived more than two decades after he first wrote those poems. "The Sorrow of Love" and "The Lamentation of the Old Pensioner" as rewritten in 1925, for instance (see pp. 16, 20), bear little stylistic or thematic connection either with those poems as they appeared before 1925, or with the poet's work pre-1895 generally. To include only the latest versions of such poems in any selected or collected edition of Yeats's poems thus reflects

2. Preface to *Poems* (1927); reprinted in *VP*, p. 848.
3. "W. B. Yeats and the Resurrection of the Author," *The Library* 16.2 (June 1994): 108–09.
4. Untitled, in volume 2 of *The Collected Works in Verse and Prose of William Butler Yeats* (Stratford-on-Avon: A. H. Bullen, 1908); reprinted in *VP*, p. 778.

his "final" aims, but in so doing it unavoidably misrepresents the chronological development of his aesthetic, presenting the reader with poems rewritten under the influence of Modernism, and under the influence of political events of the 1920s, as if they are "early" Yeats.

Given that this Norton Critical Edition is likely to be used predominantly by readers concerned with the chronological course of Yeats's development as a poet—how his style and subject matter evolved from decade to decade, for instance—as well as those concerned with the historical aspects of his place within the canon of late-nineteenth- and early-twentieth-century poetry—how he responds to the challenge of Modernism, for instance—the texts of the poems given here are drawn from relatively early printings in which Yeats's "initial" phase of revisions is substantially finished, but before significant later incremental or "retroactive" revisions had begun. Copy-texts are generally taken from first trade printings and predominantly date to within two or three years of first publication of a given poem. For *New Poems* (1938), the final collection of his poems published in Yeats's lifetime, I have followed the Cuala Press first printing, as no trade edition appeared before his death. For the poems published posthumously in *Last Poems and Two Plays* (1939), I draw on journal printings for which Yeats is known to have corrected proofs, or, for the few poems that were not printed during his life, on the surviving drafts. Given the unusually complex textual history of Yeats's earliest poems, I have taken *Poems* (1895) as copy-text, but I have additionally included some paradigmatic earlier and later versions of a few poems, so that the reader may judge the extent of Yeats's stylistic and intellectual shifts in his revisions: these include both the 1889 and 1895 versions of "Ephemera" and the 1892 and 1925 versions of "The Sorrow of Love," amongst others. Variant versions of "The Scholars" dating from 1915 and 1929 are also presented as a symptomatic example of a major revision of a poem from a later period. The choice of *Poems* (1895) as copy-text for the early poems in this volume also restores to view the highly patterned layouts characteristic of Yeats's early career, in which lines are frequently indented to accentuate the rhyme schemes of the poems. After 1901, his poems appeared only in flush-left format—whether as a deliberate part of his effort to move away from his own 1890s ornateness in the early years of the century (as described in the Introduction) or in more general response to the practices of the publishing marketplace is as yet unclear. Regardless, the shift certainly significantly modifies the visual appearance on the page of early poems such as "The Stolen Child" and consequently also modifies the experience of reading them. While no selection can adequately represent the complex aesthetic of Yeats's early poems, particularly given his care in exploiting elements as diverse as binding and page layout to augment and complicate the content and sequencing of the poems themselves, restoration of the patterned layouts of the 1890s offers at least a modest step toward a more attentive representation of his early aesthetic.

Dates in the Text

To stress further the chronological specificity of Yeats's texts, the date of first publication of each poem is given in square brackets to the left under the text, with the date of the printing reproduced in this Norton Critical Edition given to the right. (In those few instances where the version printed here is the first published version, a single date is given on the right.) An asterisk next to the first date indicates that a title change or substantial revisions occurred between that first printing and the printing given here; while an asterisk next to the second date likewise indicates that significant changes were made in subsequent printings. Readers are urged to consult the Bibliographical Appendix in this volume (pp. 495–510) for a brief account of such changes, and of the textual history of individual poems and the collections in which they appear. Yeats himself included dates under a number of his poems — in *Poems* (1895), for instance, and with increasing frequency after 1912. His positioning of these authorial dates varied considerably during his career between centered and indented left or right. For this Norton Critical Edition, these dates are regularized in a position centered under the poems. Yeats's practice in dating his collections of poems was also variable. In *Collected Poems* (1933), for instance, the poems from *The Green Helmet* are dated 1910 (which accords with the first Cuala Press and trade editions of the collection), whereas in *Later Poems* (1922) they are dated 1912 (which accords with the revised and enlarged trade edition of the volume); poems from *The Winding Stair*, by contrast, are dated 1932, which accords with neither the 1929 volume of that name nor the 1933 volume *The Winding Stair and Other Poems*. In this Norton Critical Edition, I consequently regularize the dates following titles to reflect the first published appearance of those titles, with the exception of "Crossways" and "The Rose" — titles adopted in 1895 — for which I give the dates of first publication of the volumes from which these collections were predominantly selected.

The selection of copy-texts for the plays and prose printed here was informed by a similar editorial strategy to that used for the poems, and relatively early printings again predominate. The complete history of Yeats's textual revisions and rearrangements of the sequences and contexts in which he published can be charted by consulting Allan Wade's *Bibliography of the Writings of W. B. Yeats* and Allt and Alspach's *The Variorum Edition of the Poems of W. B. Yeats*.

The titles of poems are reproduced in this volume as they appear in the copy-texts. In the few instances in which Yeats later revised a title, that later title is offered in square brackets. Details of earlier titles abandoned by Yeats are given in the Bibliographical Appendix.

JAMES PETHICA

Acknowledgments

My particular thanks to Ronald Schuchard and to Stephen Parrish, for suggesting and encouraging my work on this volume; and to Carol Bemis, Marian Johnson, Kate Lovelady, and Ben Reynolds at Norton, for their care, patience, and expertise in every aspect of seeing it through the press under tight deadlines.

All scholars in the field of Yeats studies are indebted to the pioneering bibliographical and textual work of the late Allan Wade, Peter Allt, and Russell Alspach. The annotation, bibliographical detail, and much else in this volume also owe greatly to the broader canon of critical and textual work on Yeats generated over the past few decades. Of the many scholars whose work has assisted and enabled the preparation of this volume, I would like to thank especially the following: Richard Finneran, Warwick Gould, George Mills Harper, A. Norman Jeffares, John Kelly, and William H. O'Donnell.

My thanks, also, to the following friends and scholars whose timely assistance of one sort or another was both welcome and much appreciated: Deborah Brothers, Wayne Chapman, Paula Consolini, Margaret Mills Harper, Jim Mahon, Lucy McDiarmid, Paul Park, Louis Schwartz, Colin Smythe, Anita Sokolsky, and Deirdre Toomey.

My last and best thanks, as always, go to Alison Case, without whose love of Yeats—and of me—this project would not have been completed.

Acknowledgments

The Texts of the
POEMS

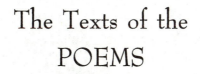

From *Crossways* (1889)

The Song of the Happy Shepherd

The woods of Arcady[1] are dead,
And over is their antique joy;
Of old the world on dreaming fed;
Gray Truth is now her painted toy;
Yet still she turns her restless head: 5
But O, sick children of the world,
Of all the many changing things
In dreary dancing past us whirled,
To the cracked tune that Chronos[2] sings,
Words alone are certain good.   10
Where are now the warring kings,
Word be-mockers?—By the Rood[3]
Where are now the warring kings?
An idle word is now their glory,
By the stammering schoolboy said,   15
Reading some entangled story:
The kings of the old time are fled.
The wandering earth herself may be
Only a sudden flaming word,
In clanging space a moment heard,   20
Troubling the endless reverie.

Then no wise worship dusty deeds,
Nor seek—for this is also sooth[4] —
To hunger fiercely after truth,
Lest all thy toiling only breeds   25
New dreams, new dreams; there is no truth,
Saving in thine own heart. Seek, then,
No learning from the starry men,[5]
Who follow with the optic glass[6]
The whirling ways of stars that pass—   30
Seek, then, for this is also sooth,
No word of theirs—the cold star-bane[7]

---

1. The pastoral paradise of classical Greek literature, here used as an image of an imaginative Eden now swept aside by the "Gray Truth" of scientific rationalism.
2. Greek for "time" (and also the father of the Greek gods).
3. The cross on which Christ was crucified.
4. Truth.
5. Astronomers.
6. Telescope.
7. Star poison.

Has cloven and rent their hearts in twain,
And dead is all their human truth.
Go gather by the humming sea   35
Some twisted, echo-harbouring shell,
And to its lips thy story tell,
And they thy comforters will be,
Rewording in melodious guile
Thy fretful words a little while,   40
Till they shall singing fade in ruth,[8]
And die a pearly brotherhood;
For words alone are certain good:
Sing then, for this is also sooth.

I must be gone—there is a grave   45
Where daffodil and lily wave,
And I would please the hapless faun,[9]
Buried under the sleepy ground,
With mirthful songs before the dawn.
His shouting days with mirth were crowned;   50
And still I dream he treads the lawn,
Walking ghostly in the dew,
Pierced by my glad singing through,
My songs of old earth's dreamy youth:
But ah! she dreams not now—dream thou!   55
For fair are poppies[1] on the brow:
Dream, dream, for this is also sooth.

                    1885.

[1885*]   [1895]

The Sad Shepherd

There was a man whom Sorrow named his friend,
  And he, of his high comrade Sorrow dreaming,
  Went walking with slow steps along the gleaming
And humming sands, where windy surges wend:
And he called loudly to the stars to bend   5
  From their pale thrones and comfort him, but they
  Among themselves laugh on and sing alway:
And then the man whom Sorrow named his friend
Cried out, *Dim sea, hear my most piteous story!*
  The sea swept on and cried her old cry still,   10
  Rolling along in dreams from hill to hill;
He fled the persecution of her glory

---

8. Sadness.
9. In classical mythology, a creature half goat and half man.
1. The source of opium, hence a traditional symbol for sleep and dreams.

And, in a far-off, gentle valley stopping,
   Cried all his story to the dewdrops glistening,
   But naught they heard, for they are always listening,   15
The dewdrops, for the sound of their own dropping.
And then the man whom Sorrow named his friend
   Sought once again the shore, and found a shell
   And thought, *I will my heavy story tell*
Till my own words, re-echoing, shall send   20
Their sadness through a hollow, pearly heart;
   And my own tale again for me shall sing,
   And my own whispering words be comforting
And lo! my ancient burden may depart.
Then he sang softly nigh the pearly rim;   25
   But the sad dweller[1] by the sea-ways lone
   Changed all he sang to inarticulate moan
Among her wildering whirls, forgetting him.

1885.

[1886*]   [1895]

The Cloak, the Boat, and the Shoes

'What do you make so fair and bright?'

'I make the cloak of Sorrow:
   'O, lovely to see in all men's sight
'Shall be the cloak of Sorrow,
   'In all men's sight.'   5

'What do you build with sails for flight?'

'I build a boat for Sorrow,
   'O, swift on the seas all day and night
'Saileth the rover Sorrow,
   'All day and night.'   10

'What do you weave with wool so white?'

'I weave the shoes of Sorrow,
   'Soundless shall be the footfall light
'In all men's ears of Sorrow,
   'Sudden and light.'   15

[1885*]   [1895]

---

1. The shell.

The Indian to His Love

The island dreams under the dawn
    And great boughs drop tranquillity;
The peahens dance on a smooth lawn,
    A parrot sways upon a tree,
    Raging at his own image in the dim enamelled sea.   5

Here we will moor our lonely ship
    And wander ever with woven hands,
Murmuring softly lip to lip,
    Along the grass, along the sands,
    Murmuring gently how far off are the unquiet lands: 10

How we alone of mortals are
    Hid under quiet boughs apart,
While our love grows an Indian star,
    A meteor of the burning heart,
    One with the glimmering tide, the wings that glimmer   15
        and gleam and dart;

The great boughs, and the burnished dove
    That moans and sighs a hundred days:
How when we die our shades will rove,
    Where eve has hushed the feathered ways,
    And drop a vapoury footfall in the water's drowsy blaze.   20

                    1886.

[1886*]   [1895]

The Falling of the Leaves

Autumn is over the long leaves that love us,
    And over the mice in the barley sheaves;
Yellow the leaves of the rowan above us,
    And yellow the wet wild-strawberry leaves.

The hour of the waning of love has beset us,   5
    And weary and worn are our sad souls now;
Let us part, ere the season of passion forget us,
    With a kiss and a tear on thy drooping brow.

[1889*]   [1895]

Ephemera [1889 version]

An Autumn Idyl

"Your eyes that once were never weary of mine
Lie now half hidden under pendulous lids,
Veiled in a dreamy sorrow for their love
That wanes." "Ah, wistful voice," replied the other,
"Though our sad love is fading, let us yet   5
Stand by the border of the lake once more,
Together in that hour of gentleness
When the poor tired child, passion, falls asleep.
How far away the stars seem, and how far
Is our first kiss, and ah, how old my heart!"   10
Pensive they paced among the faded leaves,
While slowly answered he whose hand held hers—
"Often has passion worn our wandering hearts,
Earth's aliens. Why so sorrowful? Our souls
Shall warm their lives at many a rustling flame."   15

The woods were round them, and the yellow leaves
Fell like faint meteors in the gloom, and once
A rabbit old and lame limped down the path—
Autumn was over him—and now they stood
On the lone border of the sullen lake.   20
Turning, he saw that she had thrust dead leaves,
Gathered in silence, dewy as her eyes,
In bosom and hair.
                        Then he: "Let us not mourn
That we are tired, for other loves await us.
Hate on and love through unrepining hours.   25
Before us lies eternity; our souls
Are love, and a continual farewell."

He spake once more and fondled with his lips
That word of the soul's peace—"Eternity."

The little waves that walked in evening whiteness,   30
Glimmering in her drooped eyes, saw her lips move
And whisper, "The innumerable reeds
I know the word they cry, 'Eternity!'
And sing from shore to shore, and every year
They pine away and yellow and wear out,   35
And ah, they know not, as they pine and cease,
Not they are the eternal—'tis the cry."

[1889*]

Ephemera [1895 version]

'Your eyes that once were never weary of mine
'Are bowed in sorrow under pendulous lids,
'Because our love is waning.'
                    And then she:
'Although our love is waning, let us stand
'By the lone border of the lake once more,   5
'Together in that hour of gentleness
'When the poor tired child, Passion, falls asleep:
'How far away the stars seem, and how far
'Is our first kiss, and ah, how old my heart!'

Pensive they paced along the faded leaves,   10
While slowly he whose hand held hers replied:
'Passion has often worn our wandering hearts.'

The woods were round them, and the yellow leaves
Fell like faint meteors in the gloom, and once
A rabbit old and lame limped down the path;   15
Autumn was over him: and now they stood
On the lone border of the lake once more:
Turning, he saw that she had thrust dead leaves
Gathered in silence, dewy as her eyes,
In bosom and hair.
                    'Ah, do not mourn,' he said,   20
'That we are tired, for other loves await us:
'Hate on and love through unrepining hours;
'Before us lies eternity; our souls
'Are love, and a continual farewell.'

[1895]

The Stolen Child[1]

Where dips the rocky highland
  Of Slewth Wood[2] in the lake,
There lies a leafy island
  Where flapping herons wake
The drowsy water rats;   5
There we've hid our faery vats
Full of berries,
And of reddest stolen cherries.
Come away, O human child!
To the waters and the wild   10

1. In Irish folklore, the faeries were thought to steal human children to be their companions.
2. A wood bordering Lough Gill, County Sligo, Ireland.

With a faery, hand in hand,
For the world's more full of weeping than you
   can understand.

    Where the wave of moonlight glosses
      The dim gray sands with light,
    Far off by furthest Rosses[3]   15
      We foot it all the night,
    Weaving olden dances,
    Mingling hands and mingling glances
      Till the moon has taken flight;
    To and fro we leap   20
      And chase the frothy bubbles,
      While the world is full of troubles
    And is anxious in its sleep.
Come away, O human child!
To the waters and the wild   25
With a faery, hand in hand,
For the world's more full of weeping than you
   can understand.

    Where the wandering water gushes
      From the hills above Glen-Car,[4]
    In pools among the rushes   30
      That scarce could bathe a star,
    We seek for slumbering trout,
      And whispering in their ears
        Give them unquiet dreams;
    Leaning softly out   35
      From ferns that drop their tears
      Over the young streams.
Come away, O human child!
To the waters and the wild
With a faery, hand in hand,   40
For the world's more full of weeping than you
   can understand.

    Away with us he's going,
      The solemn-eyed:
    He'll hear no more the lowing
      Of the calves on the warm hillside;   45
    Or the kettle on the hob
      Sing peace into his breast,
    Or see the brown mice bob
      Round and round the oatmeal chest.
For he comes, the human child,   50
To the waters and the wild

---

3. Rosses Point, a sandy peninsula and village about eight miles northeast of the town of Sligo, associated by Yeats with supernatural activity. See "Drumcliff and Rosses," p. 179.
4. A valley and lake in the mountains north of Sligo town.

> With a faery, hand in hand,
> From a world more full of weeping than he
>   can understand.

[1886]   [1895]

To an Isle in the Water

Shy one, shy one,
  Shy one of my heart,
She moves in the firelight
  Pensively apart.

She carries in the dishes,   5
  And lays them in a row.
To an isle in the water
  With her would I go.

She carries in the candles,   10
  And lights the curtained room;
Shy in the doorway
  And shy in the gloom;

And shy as a rabbit,
  Helpful and shy.
To an isle in the water   15
  With her would I fly.

[1889]   [1895]

Down by the Salley Gardens[1]

Down by the salley[2] gardens my love and I did meet;
She passed the salley gardens with little snow-white feet.
She bid me take love easy, as the leaves grow on the tree;
But I, being young and foolish, with her would not agree.

In a field by the river my love and I did stand,   5
And on my leaning shoulder she laid her snow-white hand.
She bid me take life easy, as the grass grows on the weirs;
But I was young and foolish, and now am full of tears.

[1889]   [1895]

---

1. "This is an attempt to reconstruct an old song from three lines imperfectly remembered by an old peasant woman in the village of Ballysodare, Sligo, who often sings them to herself " (Yeats's note, 1889).
2. Willow. Willows were grown along the banks of the Ballysodare River, Sligo, to provide thatch for houses.

The Meditation of the Old Fisherman[1]

You waves, though you dance by my feet like children at play,
    Though you glow and you glance, though you purr and you dart;
In the Junes that were warmer than these are, the waves were more
      gay,
    When I was a boy with never a crack in my heart.

The herring are not in the tides as they were of old;   5
    My sorrow! for many a creak gave the creel[2] in the cart
That carried the take to Sligo town to be sold,
    When I was a boy with never a crack in my heart.

And ah, you proud maiden, you are not so fair when his oar
    Is heard on the water, as they were, the proud and apart,   10
Who paced in the eve by the nets on the pebbly shore,
    When I was a boy with never a crack in my heart.

[1886*]   [1895]

1. "This poem is founded upon some things a fisherman said to me when out fishing in Sligo Bay" (Yeats's note, 1895).
2. Wicker basket.

From *The Rose*[1] (1892)

To the Rose upon the Rood[2] of Time

Red Rose, proud Rose, sad Rose of all my days!
Come near me, while I sing the ancient ways:
Cuhoollin battling with the bitter tide;[3]
The Druid,[4] *gray, wood nurtured, quiet-eyed,*
Who cast round Fergus dreams, and ruin untold;[5]   5
And thine own sadness, whereof stars, grown old
In dancing silver sandalled on the sea,
Sing in their high and lonely melody.
Come near, that no more blinded by man's fate,
I find under the boughs of love and hate,   10
In all poor foolish things that live a day,
Eternal Beauty wandering on her way.

Come near, come near, come near—Ah, leave me still
A little space for the rose-breath to fill!
Lest I no more hear common things that crave;   15
The weak worm hiding down in its small cave,
The field mouse running by me in the grass,
And heavy mortal hopes that toil and pass;
But seek alone to hear the strange things said
By God to the bright hearts of those long dead,   20
And learn to chaunt a tongue, men do not know.
Come near—I would, before my time to go,
Sing of old Eri[6] *and the ancient ways:*
Red Rose, proud Rose, sad Rose of all my days.

[1892]   [1895]

---

1. The rose was a key symbol for Yeats in the 1890s, representing eternal and spiritual beauty, and it was central to the iconography of the Order of the Golden Dawn, an occult and Rosicrucian society into which he was initiated in 1890. His notes in *Poems* (1895) also alert readers to the traditional usage of the rose as a symbol of love and, in Ireland, as a symbol of the nation.
2. The cross on which Christ was crucified.
3. "Cuchulain" in all printings from 1904. Cuchulain was the warrior hero of the Ulster cycle of Irish tales. Late in life, Cuchulain killed an unknown young warrior who had challenged him, who proved to be his own son. Afterward he was enchanted by Druids to fight with the ocean waves for several days of madness, lest in his grief he should kill his own companions. Yeats's play *On Baile's Strand* (see p. 141) focuses on this story.
4. The Druids were priest-seers in ancient Ireland.
5. "He was once king of all Ireland, but gave up his throne that he might live at peace hunting in the woods" *Poems* (1895). Fergus's decision was inspired by the influence of a Druid.
6. Ancient Ireland.

12

Fergus and the Druid[1]

FERGUS

The whole day have I followed in the rocks,
And you have changed and flowed from shape to shape.
First as a raven on whose ancient wings
Scarcely a feather lingered, then you seemed
A weasel moving on from stone to stone,   5
And now at last you wear a human shape—
A thin gray man half lost in gathering night.

DRUID

What would you, king of the proud Red Branch kings?[2]

FERGUS

This would I say, most wise of living souls:
Young subtle Concobar[3] sat close by me   10
When I gave judgment, and his words were wise,
And what to me was burden without end,
To him seemed easy, so I laid the crown
Upon his head to cast away my care.

DRUID

What would you, king of the proud Red Branch kings?   15

FERGUS

I feast amid my people on the hill,
And pace the woods, and drive my chariot wheels
In the white border of the murmuring sea;
And still I feel the crown upon my head.

DRUID

What would you?   20

FERGUS

                    I would be no more a king,
But learn the dreaming wisdom that is yours.

DRUID

Look on my thin gray hair and hollow cheeks,
And on these hands that may not lift the sword,
This body trembling like a wind-blown reed.
No maiden loves me, no man seeks my help,   25
Because I be not of the things I dream.

---

1. See notes on "To the Rose upon the Rood of Time" (p. 12).
2. The Red Branch warriors served the king of Ulster.
3. "Conchubar" in later printings. He was Fergus's stepson, who succeeded him as king of Ulster.

FERGUS

A wild and foolish labourer is a king,
To do and do and do, and never dream.

DRUID

Take, if you must, this little bag of dreams;
Unloose the cord, and they will wrap you round.   30

FERGUS

I see my life go dripping like a stream
From change to change; I have been many things—
A green drop in the surge, a gleam of light
Upon a sword, a fir-tree on a hill,
An old slave grinding at a heavy quern,[4]   35
A king sitting upon a chair of gold,
And all these things were wonderful and great;
But now I have grown nothing, being all,
And the whole world weighs down upon my heart—
Ah! Druid, Druid, how great webs of sorrow   40
Lay hidden in the small slate-coloured thing!

[1892]   [1895]

The Rose of the World[1]

Who dreamed that beauty passes like a dream?
    For these red lips, with all their mournful pride,
    Mournful that no new wonder may betide,
Troy passed away[2] in one high funeral gleam,
    And Usna's children[3] died.   5

We and the labouring world are passing by:
    Amid men's souls, that waver and give place,
    Like the pale waters in their wintry race,
Under the passing stars, foam of the sky,
    Lives on this lonely face.   10

4. A hand-mill for grinding corn.
1. Yeats first met Irish Nationalist and celebrated beauty Maud Gonne (1866–1953) in 1889. He proposed to her several times over the next decade but was repeatedly refused, and he retained hopes of marrying her until as late as 1916, when his final proposal was rejected. This poem was written to her, and she would be an enduring subject in and inspiration for his poetry.
2. The Trojan city of Troy was beseiged for ten years and finally destroyed by the Greeks following the abduction of Helen, wife of King Menelaus of Sparta, by Paris, son of King Priam of Troy. Yeats associated his beloved, Maud Gonne, with Helen of Troy in a number of poems.
3. In Irish legend, Usna's sons were Naoise, Ainnle, and Ardan. Naoise, accompanied by his two brothers, eloped with Deirdre, whom Conchubar (see note to "Fergus and the Druid," p. 13) had chosen to be his queen. On being lured back to Ireland, the three brothers were killed, despite Conchubar's promise that they would not be harmed.

Bow down, archangels, in your dim abode:
Before you were, or any hearts to beat,
Weary and kind one lingered by His seat;
He made the world to be a grassy road
Before her wandering feet.   15

[1892]   [1895]

The Lake Isle of Innisfree[1]

I will arise and go now, and go to Innisfree,
And a small cabin build there, of clay and wattles[2] made;
Nine bean rows will I have there, a hive for the honey bee,
And live alone in the bee-loud glade.

And I shall have some peace there, for peace comes dropping slow,   5
Dropping from the veils of the morning to where the cricket sings;
There midnight's all a glimmer, and noon a purple glow,
And evening full of the linnet's wings.

I will arise and go now, for always night and day
I hear lake water lapping with low sounds by the shore;   10
While I stand on the roadway, or on the pavements gray,
I hear it in the deep heart's core.

[1890]   [1895]

The Pity of Love

A pity beyond all telling
Is hid in the heart of love:
The folk who are buying and selling;
The clouds on their journey above;
The cold wet winds ever blowing;   5
And the shadowy hazel grove
Where mouse-gray waters are flowing,
Threaten the head that I love.

[1892]   [1895]

1. In his autobiography (*Four Years: 1887–1891*) Yeats recalled that "when walking through Fleet Street [in London in 1888] very homesick I heard a little tinkle of water and saw a fountain in a shop-window which balanced a little ball upon its jet, and began to remember lake water. From the sudden remembrance came my poem 'Innisfree', my first lyric with anything in its rhythm of my own music." Innisfree (from Inis Fraoigh: "Heather Island") is a small island in Lough Gill, Sligo.
2. Twigs or branches interwoven to form a wall or roof that could then be plastered with clay.

The Sorrow of Love [1895 version]

The quarrel of the sparrows[1] in the eaves,
   The full round moon and the star-laden sky,
And the loud song of the ever-singing leaves,
   Had hid away earth's old and weary cry.

And then you came with those red mournful lips,   5
   And with you came the whole of the world's tears,
And all the sorrows of her labouring ships,
   And all the burden of her myriad years.

And now the sparrows warring in the eaves,
   The curd-pale moon, the white stars in the sky,   10
And the loud chaunting of the unquiet leaves,
   Are shaken with earth's old and weary cry.

[1892]   [1895*]

The Sorrow of Love [1925 version][1]

The brawling of a sparrow in the eaves,
   The brilliant moon and all the milky sky,
And all that famous harmony of leaves,
   Had blotted out man's image and his cry.

A girl arose that had red mournful lips   5
And seemed the greatness of the world in tears,
Doomed like Odysseus[2] and the labouring ships
And proud as Priam[3] murdered with his peers;

Arose, and on the instant clamorous eaves,
A climbing moon upon an empty sky,   10
And all that lamentation of the leaves,
Could but compose man's image and his cry.

[1925]

---

1. In classical literature, often used as symbols of sexual desire.
1. Yeats revised this poem heavily for *Early Poems and Stories* in 1925, in which it is one of several described as being made "altogether new."
2. Greek hero, whose central part in the seige of Troy and whose ten-year journey back to Ithaca are told in Homer's *Odyssey*.
3. King of Troy, killed after its fall.

When You are Old[1]

When you are old and gray and full of sleep,
    And nodding by the fire, take down this book,
    And slowly read, and dream of the soft look
Your eyes had once, and of their shadows deep;

How many loved your moments of glad grace,   5
    And loved your beauty with love false or true;
    But one man loved the pilgrim soul in you,
And loved the sorrows of your changing face.

And bending down beside the glowing bars
    Murmur, a little sad, *From us fled Love*;   10
    He paced upon the mountains far above,
And hid his face amid a crowd of stars.

[1892]   [1895]

The White Birds[1]

I would that we were, my beloved, white birds on the foam
    of the sea!
We tire of the flame of the meteor, before it can fade and flee;
And the flame of the blue star of twilight, hung low on the
    rim of the sky,
Has awaked in our hearts, my beloved, a sadness that may
    not die.

A weariness comes from those dreamers, dew dabbled, the lily   5
    and rose;
Ah, dream not of them, my beloved, the flame of the meteor
    that goes,
Or the flame of the blue star that lingers hung low in the fall
    of the dew:
For I would we were changed to white birds on the wandering
    foam: I and you!

I am haunted by numberless islands, and many a Danaan shore,
Where Time would surely forget us, and Sorrow come near us   10
    no more;

1. Adapted from (though not a translation of) "Quand Vous Serez Bien Vielle," a sonnet by Pierre de Ronsard (1524–1585).
1. "The birds of fairyland are said to be white as snow. The Danaan Islands are the islands of the fairies" (Yeats's note, 1892). Yeats also noted that "the Danaan shore is, of course, *Tier-nan-oge*, or fairyland." Tir na nOg ("The Country of the Young") was the legendary paradise where mortals could enjoy everlasting youth.

Soon far from the rose and the lily, and fret of the flames would
    we be,
Were we only white birds, my beloved, buoyed out on the foam
    of the sea!

[1892]   [1895]

[Who Goes with Fergus?][1]

Who will go drive with Fergus now,
  And pierce the deep wood's woven shade,
    And dance upon the level shore?
Young man, lift up your russet brow,
  And lift your tender eyelids, maid,   5
    And brood on hopes and fears no more.

And no more turn aside and brood
  Upon Love's bitter mystery;
    For Fergus rules the brazen cars,[2]
And rules the shadows of the wood,   10
  And the white breast of the dim sea
    And all dishevelled wandering stars.

[1892]   [1895*]

The Dedication to a Book of Stories
selected from the Irish Novelists [1895 version]

There was a green branch hung with many a bell[1]
  When her own people ruled in wave-worn Eri;[2]
  And from its murmuring greenness, calm of faery,
A Druid[3] kindness, on all hearers fell.

It charmed away the merchant from his guile,   5
  And turned the farmer's memory from his cattle,
  And hushed in sleep the roaring ranks of battle,
For all who heard it dreamed a little while.

Ah, Exiles wandering over many seas,
  Spinning at all times Eri's good to-morrow![4]   10
  Ah, world-wide Nation, always growing Sorrow!
I also bear a bell branch full of ease.

---

1. See note on "To the Rose upon the Rood of Time" (p. 12).
2. Chariots.
1. "A legendary branch whose shaking cast all men into a gentle sleep" (Yeats's note, 1895).
2. (In later printings, "Eire") Ireland.
3. The Druids were priest-seers in ancient Ireland.
4. Telling stories of a time in which Ireland will be free.

I tore it from green boughs winds tossed and hurled,
   Green boughs of tossing always, weary, weary!
   I tore it from the green boughs of old Eri,   15
The willow of the many-sorrowed world.

Ah, Exiles, wandering over many lands!
   My bell branch murmurs: the gay bells bring laughter,
   Leaping to shake a cobweb from the rafter;
The sad bells bow the forehead on the hands.   20

A honeyed ringing: under the new skies
   They bring you memories of old village faces;
   Cabins gone now, old well-sides, old dear places;
And men who loved the cause that never dies.[5]

[1891*]   [1895*]

The Dedication to a Book of Stories selected from the Irish Novelists [1925 version][1]

There was a green branch hung with many a bell
When her own people ruled this tragic Eire;
And from its murmuring greenness, calm of faery,
A Druid kindness, on all hearers fell.

It charmed away the merchant from his guile,   5
And turned the farmer's memory from his cattle,
And hushed in sleep the roaring ranks of battle;
And all grew friendly for a little while.

Ah, Exiles wandering over lands and seas,
And planning, plotting always that some morrow   10
May set a stone upon ancestral Sorrow!
I also bear a bell branch full of ease.

I tore it from green boughs winds tore and tossed
Until the sap of summer had grown weary!
I tore it from the barren boughs of Eire,   15
That country where a man can be so crossed;

Can be so battered, badgered and destroyed
That he's a loveless man: gay bells bring laughter,
That shakes a mouldering cobweb from the rafter;
And yet the saddest chimes are best enjoyed.   20

5. Ireland's freedom.
1. Yeats revised this poem in the wake of the civil war that had followed on Irish independence, at
   a time when he was disillusioned with both the cause of Irish Nationalism and prospects for
   cultural and spiritual renewal in Ireland.

Gay bells or sad, they bring you memories
Of half-forgotten innocent old places:
We and our bitterness have left no traces
On Munster[2] grass and Connemara[3] skies.

[1925]

The Lamentation of the Old Pensioner[1] [1895 version]

I had a chair at every hearth,
   When no one turned to see,
With 'Look at that old fellow there,
   'And who may he be?'
And therefore do I wander now,   5
   And the fret lies on me.

The road-side trees keep murmuring.
   Ah, wherefore murmur ye,
As in the old days long gone by,
   Green oak and poplar tree?   10
The well-known faces are all gone:
   And the fret lies on me.

[1890*]   [1895*]

The Lamentation of the Old Pensioner[1] [1925 version]

Although I shelter from the rain
Under a broken tree,
My chair was nearest to the fire
In every company,
That talked of love or politics   5
E'er time transfigured me.

Though lads are making pikes again
For some conspiracy,
And crazy rascals rage their fill
At human tyranny;   10
My contemplations are of time
That has transfigured me.

2. The southwestern of Ireland's four provinces.
3. The western region of County Galway, bordering the Atlantic Ocean.
1. Yeats noted that this poem was "little more than a translation into verse of the very words of an old Wicklow peasant" (*Poems*, 1895).
1. See note 1 to 1925 version of "The Dedication to a Book of Stories selected from the Irish Novelists" (p. 19).

There's not a woman turns her face
Upon a broken tree,
And yet the beauties that I loved   15
Are in my memory;
I spit into the face of Time
That has transfigured me.

[1925]

To Ireland in the Coming Times

Know, that I would accounted be
True brother of that company,
Who sang to sweeten Ireland's wrong,
Ballad and story, rann[1] and song;
Nor be I any less of them,   5
Because the red-rose-bordered hem
Of her,[2] whose history began
Before God made the angelic clan,
Trails all about the written page;
For in the world's first blossoming age   10
The light fall of her flying feet
Made Ireland's heart begin to beat;
And still the starry candles flare
To help her light foot here and there;
And still the thoughts of Ireland brood   15
Upon her holy quietude.

Nor may I less be counted one
With Davis, Mangan, Ferguson,[3]
Because to him, who ponders well,
My rhymes more than their rhyming tell   20
Of the dim wisdoms old and deep,
That God gives unto man in sleep.
For the elemental beings go
About my table to and fro.
In flood and fire and clay and wind,   25
They huddle from man's pondering mind;
Yet he who treads in austere ways
May surely meet their ancient gaze.
Man ever journeys on with them
After the red-rose-bordered hem.   30

1. A verse of a poem in Irish.
2. A personification of the spiritual beauty that preoccupied Yeats in his occult studies at this time.
3. The most popular poets of nineteenth-century Ireland. Thomas Davis (1814–1845), a founder of the Nationalist newspaper *The Nation* and a member of the Young Ireland movement; James Clarence Mangan (1803–1849); and Sir Samuel Ferguson (1810–1886), whose use of Irish legends in his poetry particularly influenced Yeats's early work.

Ah, faeries, dancing under the moon,
A Druid land, a Druid tune!

While still I may, I write for you
The love I lived, the dream I knew.
From our birthday, until we die,   35
Is but the winking of an eye;
And we, our singing and our love,
The mariners of night above,
And all the wizard things that go
About my table to and fro,   40
Are passing on to where may be,
In truth's consuming ecstasy,
No place for love and dream at all;
For God goes by with white foot-fall.
I cast my heart into my rhymes,   45
That you, in the dim coming times,
May know how my heart went with them
After the red-rose-bordered hem.

[1892*]   [1895]

From *The Wind Among the Reeds* (1899)

The Hosting of the Sidhe[1]

The host is riding from Knocknarea[2]
And over the grave of Clooth-na-bare;[3]
Caolte[4] tossing his burning hair
And Niamh[5] calling *Away, come away:*
Empty your heart of its mortal dream.   5
The winds awaken, the leaves whirl round,
Our cheeks are pale, our hair is unbound,
Our breasts are heaving, our eyes are a-gleam,
Our arms are waving, our lips are apart;
And if any gaze on our rushing band,   10
We come between him and the deed of his hand,
We come between him and the hope of his heart.
The host is rushing 'twixt night and day,
And where is there hope or deed as fair?
Caolte tossing his burning hair,   15
And Niamh calling *Away, come away.*

[1893*]   [1906]

The Lover tells of the Rose in his Heart

All things uncomely and broken, all things worn out and old,
The cry of a child by the roadway, the creak of a lumbering cart,
The heavy steps of the ploughman, splashing the wintry mould,[1]

1. "The powerful and wealthy called the gods of ancient Ireland the Tuatha de Danaan, or the Tribes of the Goddess Danu, but the poor called them, and still sometimes call them, the Sidhe [pronounced "Shee"]. . . . Sidhe is also Gaelic for wind" (Yeats's note, 1899).
2. A mountain overlooking Sligo Bay, topped by a cairn reputed to be the burial site of Queen Maeve of the Sidhe.
3. "Clooth-na-Bare . . . 'went all over the world, seeking a lake deep enough to drown her faery life, of which she had grown weary . . . until, at last, she found the deepest water in the world in little Lough Ia, on top of the bird mountain, in Sligo' " (Yeats's note, 1899).
4. Caoilte MacRonain was the favorite warrior of Fionn Mac Cumhaill, or Finn MacCool, the central figure of the Fenian cycle of Irish mythology, a warrior and poet whose followers were known as the Fianna.
5. A faery woman (daughter of Aengus, god of love) who enchanted Finn's son, Oisin, and spirited him away from the human world for three hundred years.
1. Soil.

Are wronging your image that blossoms a rose in the deeps of my
    heart.

The wrong of unshapely things is a wrong too great to be told;   5
I hunger to build them anew and sit on a green knoll apart,
With the earth and the sky and the water, remade, like a casket of gold
For my dreams of your image that blossoms a rose in the deeps of my
    heart.

[1892*]   [1906]

The Fisherman [The Fish]

Although you hide in the ebb and flow
Of the pale tide when the moon has set,
The people of coming days will know
About the casting out of my net,
And how you have leaped times out of mind   5
Over the little silver cords,
And think that you were hard and unkind,
And blame you with many bitter words.

[1898*]   [1906*]

The Song of Wandering Aengus[1]

I went out to the hazel wood,
Because a fire was in my head,
And cut and peeled a hazel wand,
And hooked a berry to a thread;
And when white moths were on the wing,   5
And moth-like stars were flickering out,
I dropped the berry in a stream
And caught a little silver trout.

When I had laid it on the floor
I went to blow the fire a-flame,   10
But something rustled on the floor,
And some one called me by my name:
It had become a glimmering girl
With apple blossom in her hair
Who called me by my name and ran   15
And faded through the brightening air.

Though I am old with wandering
Through hollow lands and hilly lands,

---

1. "The god of youth, beauty, and poetry. He reigned in Tir-nan-Oge, the country of the young"
(Yeats's note, 1895).

I will find out where she has gone,
And kiss her lips and take her hands; 20
And walk among long dappled grass,
And pluck till time and times are done,
The silver apples of the moon,
The golden apples of the sun.

[1897*]   [1906]

The Lover mourns for the Loss of Love[1]

Pale brows, still hands and dim hair,
I had a beautiful friend
And dreamed that the old despair
Would end in love in the end:
She looked in my heart one day   5
And saw your image was there;
She has gone weeping away.

[1898*]   [1906]

He reproves the Curlew

O, curlew, cry no more in the air,
Or only to the waters in the West;
Because your crying brings to my mind
Passion-dimmed eyes and long heavy hair
That was shaken out over my breast: 5
There is enough evil in the crying of wind.

[1896*]   [1906]

He remembers Forgotten Beauty

When my arms wrap you round I press
My heart upon the loveliness
That has long faded from the world;
The jewelled crowns that kings have hurled
In shadowy pools, when armies fled;   5
The love-tales wrought with silken thread
By dreaming ladies upon cloth
That has made fat the murderous moth;
The roses that of old time were
Woven by ladies in their hair,   10

1. In *Memoirs* (pp. 230–32), Yeats describes his first affair, with novelist Olivia Shakespear (1863–1938), in 1896–97, and its ending when she realized that his love for Maud Gonne remained unbroken.

The dew-cold lilies ladies bore
Through many a sacred corridor
Where such gray clouds of incense rose
That only the gods' eyes did not close:
For that pale breast and lingering hand   15
Come from a more dream-heavy land,
A more dream-heavy hour than this;
And when you sigh from kiss to kiss
I hear white Beauty sighing, too,
For hours when all must fade like dew   20
But flame on flame, deep under deep,
Throne over throne, where in half sleep
Their swords upon their iron knees
Brood her high lonely mysteries.

[1896*]   [1906]

A Poet to his Beloved

I bring you with reverent hands
The books of my numberless dreams;
White woman that passion has worn
As the tide wears the dove-gray sands,
And with heart more old than the horn   5
That is brimmed from the pale fire of time:
White woman with numberless dreams
I bring you my passionate rhyme.

[1896*]   [1906]

He gives his Beloved certain Rhymes

Fasten your hair with a golden pin,
And bind up every wandering tress;
I bade my heart build these poor rhymes:
It worked at them, day out, day in,
Building a sorrowful loveliness   5
Out of the battles of old times.

You need but lift a pearl-pale hand,
And bind up your long hair and sigh;
And all men's hearts must burn and beat;
And candle-like foam on the dim sand,   10
And stars climbing the dew-dropping sky,
Live but to light your passing feet.

[1896*]   [1906]

To my Heart, bidding it have no Fear

Be you still, be you still, trembling heart;
Remember the wisdom out of the old days:
Him who trembles before the flame and the flood,
And the winds that blow through the starry ways,
Let the starry winds and the flame and the flood   5
Cover over and hide, for he has no part
With the proud, majestical multitude.

[1896*]   [1906*]

The Cap and Bells[1]

The jester walked in the garden:
The garden had fallen still;
He bade his soul rise upward
And stand on her window-sill.

It rose in a straight blue garment,   5
When owls began to call:
It had grown wise-tongued by thinking
Of a quiet and light footfall;

But the young queen would not listen;
She rose in her pale night gown;   10
She drew in the heavy casement
And pushed the latches down.

He bade his heart go to her,
When the owls called out no more;
In a red and quivering garment   15
It sang to her through the door.

It had grown sweet-tongued by dreaming,
Of a flutter of flower-like hair;
But she took up her fan from the table
And waved it off on the air.   20

"I have cap and bells," he pondered,
"I will send them to her and die;"
And when the morning whitened
He left them where she went by.

She laid them upon her bosom,   25
Under a cloud of her hair,

---

1. Traditionally worn by a jester or fool.

And her red lips sang them a love song:
Till stars grew out of the air.

She opened her door and her window,
And the heart and the soul came through, 30
To her right hand came the red one,
To her left hand came the blue.

They set up a noise like crickets,
A chattering wise and sweet,
And her hair was a folded flower 35
And the quiet of love in her feet.

[1894*]   [1906]

He hears the Cry of the Sedge

I wander by the edge
Of this desolate lake
Where wind cries in the sedge[1]
Until the axle break
That keeps the stars in their round, 5
And hands hurl in the deep
The banners of East and West,
And the girdle of light is unbound,
Your breast will not lie by the breast
Of your beloved in sleep. 10

[1898*]   [1906]

He thinks of those who have Spoken Evil of his Beloved

Half close your eyelids, loosen your hair,
And dream about the great and their pride;
They have spoken against you everywhere,
But weigh this song with the great and their pride;
I made it out of a mouthful of air, 5
Their children's children shall say they have lied.

[1898*]   [1906]

1. Grass.

The Lover pleads with his Friend for Old Friends

Though you are in your shining days,
Voices among the crowd
And new friends busy with your praise,
Be not unkind or proud,
But think about old friends the most: 5
Time's bitter flood will rise,
Your beauty perish and be lost
For all eyes but these eyes.

[1897*]   [1906]

He wishes his Beloved were Dead

Were you but lying cold and dead,
And lights were paling out of the West,
You would come hither, and bend your head,
And I would lay my head on your breast;
And you would murmur tender words,   5
Forgiving me, because you were dead:
Nor would you rise and hasten away,
Though you have the will of the wild birds,
But know your hair was bound and wound
About the stars and moon and sun: 10
O would beloved that you lay
Under the dock-leaves in the ground,
While lights were paling one by one.

[1898*]   [1906]

He wishes for the Cloths of Heaven

Had I the heavens' embroidered cloths,
Enwrought with golden and silver light,
The blue and the dim and the dark cloths
Of night and light and the half light,
I would spread the cloths under your feet: 5
But I, being poor, have only my dreams;
I have spread my dreams under your feet;
Tread softly because you tread on my dreams.

[1899*]   [1906]

From *In the Seven Woods*[1] (1903)

In the Seven Woods

I have heard the pigeons of the Seven Woods
Make their faint thunder, and the garden bees
Hum in the lime tree flowers; and put away
The unavailing outcries and the old bitterness
That empty the heart. I have forgot awhile   5
Tara uprooted,[2] and new commonness
Upon the throne and crying about the streets
And hanging its paper flowers from post to post,[3]
Because it is alone of all things happy.
I am contented for I know that Quiet   10
Wanders laughing and eating her wild heart
Among pigeons and bees, while that Great Archer,[4]
Who but awaits His hour to shoot, still hangs
A cloudy quiver over Parc-na-Lee.[5]

August, 1902

[1903]   [1906]

The Arrow

I thought of your beauty, and this arrow,
Made out of a wild thought, is in my marrow.
There's no man may look upon her, no man;
As when newly grown to be a woman,
Blossom pale, she pulled down the pale blossom   5
At the moth hour and hid it in her bosom.[1]

1. The "seven woods" of the title are at Coole Park, Galway, the estate of Yeats's close friend, collaborator, and patron, Lady Gregory (1852–1932).
2. Yeats had cosigned a letter to the London *Times* in June 1902 protesting the destruction caused by excavations made at the Hill of Tara, County Meath, traditionally the seat of the ancient Irish kings.
3. The coronation of King Edward VII and Queen Alexandra was celebrated in Dublin with street decorations.
4. Usually glossed as Sagittarius, but possibly Cupid, given Yeats's placement of "The Arrow" as the following poem.
5. One of the seven woods of Coole.
1. Yeats lastingly associated apple blossoms with his first meeting with Maud Gonne. See also "The Song of Wandering Aengus" (p. 24).

30

This beauty's kinder, yet for a reason
I could weep that the old is out of season.

[1903] [1906]

The Folly of Being Comforted

One that is ever kind[1] said yesterday:
"Your well beloved's hair has threads of grey,
And little shadows come about her eyes;
Time can but make it easier to be wise,
Though now it's hard, till trouble is at an end; 5
And so be patient, be wise and patient, friend."
But heart, there is no comfort, not a grain;
Time can but make her beauty over again,
Because of that great nobleness of hers;
The fire that stirs about her, when she stirs 10
Burns but more clearly. O she had not these ways,
When all the wild summer was in her gaze.
O heart! O heart! if she'd but turn her head,
You'd know the folly of being comforted.

[1902] [1906]

Never Give all the Heart

Never give all the heart, for love
Will hardly seem worth thinking of
To passionate women if it seem
Certain, and they never dream
That it fades out from kiss to kiss; 5
For everything that's lovely is
But a brief, dreamy, kind delight.
Oh! never give the heart outright,
For they, for all smooth lips can say,
Have given their hearts up to the play; 10
And who could play it well enough
If deaf and dumb and blind with love?
He that made this knows all the cost,
For he gave all his heart and lost.[1]

[1905] [1906]

1. Probably Lady Gregory.
1. Maud Gonne had married Irish Nationalist John MacBride (1865–1916) in February 1903. Yeats was devastated, and in the five years that followed he wrote only three poems, of which this is one and "O Do Not Love Too Long" (p. 34) another.

Adam's Curse

We sat together at one summer's end,
That beautiful mild woman,[1] your close friend,
And you and I, and talked of poetry.

I said: "A line will take us hours maybe;
Yet if it does not seem a moment's thought,   5
Our stitching and unstitching has been naught.
Better go down upon your marrow bones
And scrub a kitchen pavement, or break stones
Like an old pauper, in all kinds of weather;
For to articulate sweet sounds together   10
Is to work harder than all these, and yet
Be thought an idler by the noisy set
Of bankers, schoolmasters, and clergymen
The martyrs call the world."

               That woman then
Murmured with her young voice, for whose mild sake   15
There's many a one shall find out all heartache
In finding that it's young and mild and low:
"There is one thing that all we women know,
Although we never heard of it at school —
That we must labour to be beautiful."   20

I said: "It's certain there is no fine thing
Since Adam's fall but needs much labouring.[2]
There have been lovers who thought love should be
So much compounded of high courtesy
That they would sigh and quote with learned looks   25
Precedents out of beautiful old books;
Yet now it seems an idle trade enough."

We sat grown quiet at the name of love;
We saw the last embers of daylight die,
And in the trembling blue-green of the sky   30
A moon, worn as if it had been a shell
Washed by time's waters as they rose and fell
About the stars, and broke in days and years.

I had a thought for no one's but your ears;
That you were beautiful, and that I strove   35
To love you in the old high way of love;
That it had all seemed happy, and yet we'd grown
As weary hearted as that hollow moon.

[1902]   [1906]

1. Maud Gonne's sister, Kathleen Pilcher (1868–1919).
2. Expulsion from the Garden of Eden obliged Adam to work for a living.

Red Hanrahan's Song about Ireland

The old brown thorn trees break in two high over Cummen
    Strand,[1]
Under a bitter black wind that blows from the left hand;
Our courage breaks like an old tree in a black wind and dies,
But we have hidden in our hearts the flame out of the eyes
Of Cathleen, the daughter of Houlihan.[2]   5

The wind has bundled up the clouds high over Knocknarea,
And thrown the thunder on the stones for all that Maeve[3] can say.
Angers that are like noisy clouds have set our hearts abeat;
But we have all bent low and low and kissed the quiet feet
Of Cathleen, the daughter of Houlihan.   10

The yellow pool has overflowed high up on Clooth-na-Bare,[4]
For the wet winds are blowing out of the clinging air;
Like heavy flooded waters our bodies and our blood
But purer than a tall candle before the Holy Rood[5]
Is Cathleen, the daughter of Houlihan.   15

[1894*]   [1906]

The Old Men Admiring Themselves in the Water

       I heard the old, old men say,
       "Everything alters,
       And one by one we drop away."
       They had hands like claws, and their knees
       Were twisted like the old thorn trees   5
       By the waters.
       I heard the old, old men say,
       "All that's beautiful drifts away
       Like the waters."

       [1903]   [1906]

---

1. On the northwest shore of Sligo Bay.
2. A traditional figure for Ireland. Maud Gonne had played the title role in Yeats and Lady Gregory's play *Cathleen ni Houlihan* in 1902, and Yeats long associated her with Cathleen.
3. Knocknarea, a mountain overlooking Sligo Bay, is topped by a cairn reputed to be the burial place of Queen Maeve of the Sidhe.
4. A mythological figure who, having grown weary of life, drowned herself in a small lake on a mountain in Sligo (see also p. 23, notes to "The Hosting of the Sidhe"). Here, Yeats appears to associate the mountain itself with her name.
5. Cross.

O Do Not Love Too Long

Sweetheart, do not love too long:
I loved long and long,
And grew to be out of fashion
Like an old song.

All through the years of our youth[1]   5
Neither could have known
Their own thought from the other's,
We were so much at one.

But, O in a minute she changed—[2]
O do not love too long,   10
Or you will grow out of fashion
Like an old song.

[1905*]   [1908]

---

1. Yeats had first met Maud Gonne in 1889, when he was twenty-three and she twenty-two.
2. Gonne's marriage in 1903 came as a complete surprise to Yeats.

From *The Green Helmet and Other Poems* (1910)

His Dream

I swayed upon the gaudy stern
The butt end of a steering oar,
And everywhere that I could turn
Men ran upon the shore.

And though I would have hushed the crowd   5
There was no mother's son but said,
"What is the figure in a shroud
Upon a gaudy bed?"

And fishes bubbling to the brim
Cried out upon that thing beneath,   10
It had such dignity of limb,
By the sweet name of Death.

Though I'd my finger on my lip,
What could I but take up the song?
And fish and crowd and gaudy ship   15
Cried out the whole night long,

Crying amid the glittering sea,
Naming it with ecstatic breath,
Because it had such dignity
By the sweet name of Death.   20

[1908*]   [1912]

A Woman Homer Sung[1]

If any man drew near
When I was young,
I thought, "He holds her[2] dear,"
And shook with hate and fear.

---

1. Homer was a Greek poet of c. eighth century B.C.E., whose *Iliad* tells of the Trojan War, caused by the abduction of Helen of Troy.
2. Maud Gonne.

But oh, 'twas bitter wrong   5
If he could pass her by
With an indifferent eye.

Whereon I wrote and wrought,
And now, being gray,
I dream that I have brought   10
To such a pitch my thought
That coming time can say,
"He shadowed in a glass
What thing her body was."

For she had fiery blood   15
When I was young,
And trod so sweetly proud
As 'twere upon a cloud,
A woman Homer sung,
That life and letters seem   20
But an heroic dream.

[1910]   [1912]

The Consolation [Words]

I had this thought awhile ago,
"My darling cannot understand
What I have done, or what would do
In this blind bitter land."[1]

And I grew weary of the sun   5
Until my thoughts cleared up again,
Remembering that the best I have done
Was done to make it plain;

That every year I have cried, "At length
My darling understands it all,   10
Because I have come into my strength,
And words obey my call."

That had she done so who can say
What would have shaken from the sieve?
I might have thrown poor words away   15
And been content to live.

[1910]   [1912*]

---

1. Yeats's resistance to using his art as a form of Irish Nationalist propaganda was a recurrent source
of difference between him and Maud Gonne.

No Second Troy

Why should I blame her that she filled my days
With misery, or that she would of late
Have taught to ignorant men most violent ways,
Or hurled the little streets upon the great,[1]
Had they but courage equal to desire?   5
What could have made her peaceful with a mind
That nobleness made simple as a fire,
With beauty like a tightened bow, a kind
That is not natural in an age like this,
Being high and solitary and most stern?   10
Why, what could she have done being what she is?
Was there another Troy for her to burn?[2]

[1910]   [1912]

Reconciliation

Some may have blamed you that you took away
The verses that could move them on the day
When, the ears being deafened, the sight of the eyes blind
With lightning you went from me,[1] and I could find
Nothing to make a song about but kings,   5
Helmets, and swords, and half-forgotten things
That were like memories of you—but now
We'll out, for the world lives as long ago;
And while we're in our laughing, weeping fit,
Hurl helmets, crowns, and swords into the pit.   10
But, dear, cling close to me; since you were gone,
My barren thoughts have chilled me to the bone.

[1910]   [1912]

The Fascination of What's Difficult

The fascination of what's difficult
Has dried the sap out of my veins, and rent
Spontaneous joy and natural content
Out of my heart. There's something ails our colt[1]

1. Yeats had begun to grow increasingly critical of Maud Gonne's support for physically direct, and sometimes violent, forms of Nationalist action. As his own politics became increasingly anti-democratic, he also had progressively less sympathy for her populist views.
2. Troy was destroyed by the Greeks at the end of the Trojan War.
1. The day of Gonne's marriage to John MacBride.
1. Pegasus, the winged horse of Greek mythology, was able to fly to heaven and is thus associated with poetry.

That must, as if it had not holy blood,   5
Nor on an Olympus[2] leaped from cloud to cloud,
Shiver under the lash, strain, sweat and jolt
As though it dragged road metal. My curse on plays
That have to be set up in fifty ways,
On the day's war with every knave and dolt,   10
Theatre business,[3] management of men.
I swear before the dawn comes round again
I'll find the stable and pull out the bolt.

[1910]   [1912]

A Drinking Song

Wine comes in at the mouth
And love comes in at the eye;
That's all we shall know for truth
Before we grow old and die.
I lift the glass to my mouth,   5
I look at you, and I sigh.

[1910]   [1912]

The Coming of Wisdom with Time

Though leaves are many, the root is one;
Through all the lying days of my youth
I swayed my leaves and flowers in the sun;
Now I may wither into the truth.

[1910*]   [1912]

On hearing that the Students of our New University have joined the Ancient Order of Hibernians and the Agitation against Immoral Literature[1]

Where, where but here have Pride and Truth,
That long to give themselves for wage,

2. A mountain in Greece, regarded as the home of the gods in classical mythology.
3. Yeats, who had cofounded the Abbey Theatre in 1904, had come to find his time dominated by its business.
1. University College, founded in Dublin in 1908 as the Royal University of Ireland, though technically nondenominational, was widely regarded as the "Catholic" university. It was "new" in contrast to the traditionally Protestant Trinity College, founded in 1591. Enrollment in the Ancient Order of Hibernians, a Catholic and broadly Nationalist organization begun as an American-Irish society in New York in 1836, was at its peak in Ireland in 1912. Yeats regarded the order as synonymous with sectarianism, masonic-style jobbery, and middle-class narrow-mindedness, and hence he saw the enthusiasm of students at the new university for its campaigns against supposed immorality as a symptom of the lack of idealism and imagination in contemporary Ireland.

To shake their wicked sides at youth
Restraining reckless middle-age.

[1912*]

To a Poet, who would have me Praise certain Bad Poets, Imitators of His and Mine

You[1] say, as I have often given tongue
In praise of what another's said or sung,
'Twere politic to do the like by these;
But where's the wild dog that has praised his fleas?

[1910*]   [1912]

The Mask

'Put off that mask of burning gold
With emerald eyes.'
'O no, my dear, you make so bold
To find if hearts be wild and wise,
And yet not cold.'   5

'I would but find what's there to find,
Love or deceit.'
'It was the mask engaged your mind,
And after set your heart to beat,
Not what's behind.'   10

'But lest you are my enemy,
I must enquire.'
'O no, my dear, let all that be,
What matter, so there is but fire
In you, in me?'   15

[1910*]   [1913]

1. Probably Irish poet and artist George Russell (1867–1935), whose literary circle still wrote in what Yeats considered an overly ornate 1890s style.

Upon a House shaken by the Land Agitation[1]

How should the world be luckier if this house,[2]
Where passion and precision have been one
Time out of mind, became too ruinous
To breed the lidless eye[3] that loves the sun?
And the sweet laughing eagle thoughts that grow   5
Where wings have memory of wings, and all
That comes of the best knit to the best? Although
Mean roof-trees[4] were the sturdier for its fall,
How should their luck run high enough to reach
The gifts that govern men,[5] and after these   10
To gradual Time's last gift, a written speech
Wrought of high laughter, loveliness and ease?

[1910*]   [1912]

All Things can Tempt Me

All things can tempt me from this craft of verse:
One time it was a woman's face, or worse—
The seeming needs of my fool-driven land;
Now nothing but comes readier to the hand
Than this accustomed toil. When I was young,   5
I had not given a penny for a song
Did not the poet sing it with such airs
That one believed he had a sword upstairs;
Yet would be now, could I but have my wish,
Colder and dumber and deafer than a fish.   10

[1909*]   [1912]

The Young Man's Song [Brown Penny]

I whispered, "I am too young,"
And then, "I am old enough,"
Wherefore I threw a penny

1. The relationship between Irish landlords and their tenants had been tense since the Land War of 1879–82, during which boycotting campaigns orchestrated by Nationalists had brought about significant reform of tenants' rights. After 1903, Land courts increasingly controlled the level of rents. Lady Gregory, who prided herself on the way the Coole estate had avoided evictions and on its long history of peaceful relations with its tenants, was in 1909 confronted with the prospect of substantially reduced income when several of her tenants applied to the Land courts to have their rents lowered.
2. Coole Park.
3. Eagles were thought to be the only creatures able to look at the sun without blinking, and they are hence for Yeats a symbol of aristocratic confidence.
4. Cottages and other poorer dwellings.
5. Lady Gregory's husband, Sir William Gregory (1817–1892), had been governor of Ceylon in the 1870s.

To find out if I might love;
"Go and love, go and love, young man,   5
If the lady be young and fair,"
Ah, penny, brown penny, brown penny,
I am looped in the loops of her hair.

Oh love is the crooked thing,
There is nobody wise enough   10
To find out all that is in it,
For he would be thinking of love
Till the stars had run away,
And the shadows eaten the moon;
Ah, penny, brown penny, brown penny,   15
One cannot begin it too soon.

[1910]   [1912*]

From *Responsibilities* (1914)

[Introductory Rhymes]

Pardon, old fathers, if you still remain
Somewhere in ear-shot for the story's end,
Old Dublin merchant 'free of ten and four'[1]
Or trading out of Galway into Spain;
And country scholar, Robert Emmet's friend,[2]   5
A hundred-year-old memory to the poor;
Traders or soldiers who have left me blood
That has not passed through any huxter's loin,
Pardon, and you that did not weigh the cost,
Old Butlers when you took to horse and stood   10
Beside the brackish waters of the Boyne
Till your bad master blenched and all was lost;[3]
You merchant skipper[4] *that leaped overboard*
After a ragged hat in Biscay Bay,
You most of all, silent and fierce old man[5]   15
Because you were the spectacle that stirred
My fancy, and set my boyish lips to say
'Only the wasteful virtues earn the sun';
Pardon that for a barren passion's sake,[6]
Although I have come close on forty-nine   20
I have no child, I have nothing but a book,
Nothing but that to prove your blood and mine.

January 1914.

[1914*]   [1916]

---

1. Probably Yeats's paternal great-great-grandfather, Benjamin Yeats (d. 1795), a linen merchant listed as being "free of the six and ten per cent tax" at the Dublin Custom House.
2. John Yeats (d. 1846), Yeats's great-grandfather, was a friend of the Irish patriot Robert Emmet, who was executed in 1803 after leading a rebellion.
3. Yeats at this point thought his ancestors had fought on the side of James II, whose Catholic forces suffered terminal defeat at the battle of the Boyne in 1690 at the hands of William of Orange's Protestant forces. Yeats later revised the lines on finding that his ancestors had in fact fought on the Williamite side.
4. Yeats's maternal great-grandfather, William Middleton (d. 1832).
5. Yeats's maternal grandfather, William Pollexfen (d. 1892).
6. His love for Maud Gonne.

42

To a Wealthy Man who promised a Second Subscription to the Dublin Municipal Gallery if it were proved the People wanted Pictures[1]

You gave but will not give again
Until enough of Paudeen's pence
By Biddy's[2] halfpennies have lain
To be 'some sort of evidence,'
Before you'll put your guineas down,   5
That things it were a pride to give
Are what the blind and ignorant town
Imagines best to make it thrive.
What cared Duke Ercole,[3] that bid
His mummers[4] to the market place,   10
What th' onion-sellers thought or did
So that his Plautus[5] set the pace
For the Italian comedies?
And Guidobaldo,[6] when he made
That grammar school of courtesies   15
Where wit and beauty learned their trade
Upon Urbino's windy hill,
Had sent no runners to and fro
That he might learn the shepherds' will.
And when they drove out Cosimo,[7]   20
Indifferent how the rancour ran,
He gave the hours they had set free
To Michelozzo's[8] latest plan
For the San Marco Library,
Whence turbulent Italy should draw   25
Delight in Art whose end is peace,

---

1. An important collection of Impressionist and other paintings had been offered to the Dublin Municipal Gallery in 1907 by Sir Hugh Lane (d. 1915) on condition that a suitable new building be provided for them. Controversy erupted over the proposed site, over Lane's preferred choice of architect, Englishman Sir Edwin Lutyens, and over the value of committing public funds toward an art gallery. In response, Lane eventually bequeathed the collection to the London National Gallery, but just before his death he added an unsigned codicil to his will reverting the gift to Dublin. The codicil was treated as invalid by the British government, and the paintings remained in London for several decades before an arrangement to share them was finally reached. Yeats's disgust at the Dublin municipality's failure to meet the terms of Lane's gift resulted in a sequence of bitter lyrics, *Poems Written in Discouragement* (1913), in which he attacks the narrow-mindedness of the Irish commercial classes.
2. Diminutives of Patrick (Paídín; usually anglicized as "Paddy") and Bridget, common Irish (Catholic) names, frequently used contemptuously as generic names for the Irish poor.
3. Duke Ercole de l'Este (1431–1505) of Ferrara, Italy, renowned for his patronage of the arts.
4. Actors.
5. Titus Plautus (c. 254–184 B.C.E.), Roman comic playwright.
6. Duke Guidobaldo di Montefeltro (1472–1508) of Urbino, Italy, renowned for the refinement and accomplishment of his court.
7. Cosimo de Medici (1389–1464), the first of the famous family to rule Florence, and a celebrated patron of the arts, was exiled to Venice briefly in 1433.
8. Michelozzo de Bartolomeo (1396–1472), an architect, went to Venice with Cosimo in 1433 and returned to Florence with him in triumph the following year. He designed the Library of St. Mark's, Florence.

In logic and in natural law
By sucking at the dugs[9] of Greece.

Your open hand but shows our loss,
For he knew better how to live.   30
Let Paudeens play at pitch and toss,
Look up in the sun's eye and give
What the exultant heart calls good
That some new day may breed the best.
Because you gave, not what they would   35
But the right twigs for an eagle's nest!

                    December 1912.

    [1913*]   [1916]

September 1913

What need you,[1] being come to sense,
But fumble in a greasy till[2]
And add the halfpence to the pence
And prayer to shivering prayer, until
You have dried the marrow from the bone;   5
For men were born to pray and save:
Romantic Ireland's dead and gone,
It's with O'Leary[3] in the grave.

Yet they were of a different kind
The names that stilled your childish play,   10
They have gone about the world like wind,
But little time had they to pray
For whom the hangman's rope was spun,
And what, God help us, could they save:
Romantic Ireland's dead and gone,   15
It's with O'Leary in the grave.

Was it for this the wild geese[4] spread
The grey wing upon every tide;
For this that all that blood was shed,
For this Edward Fitzgerald[5] died,   20
And Robert Emmet[6] and Wolfe Tone,[7]
All that delirium of the brave;

9. Breasts.
1. The people of Ireland.
2. Cash register.
3. John O'Leary (1830–1907), Irish Nationalist who greatly influenced Yeats in his youth.
4. Irishmen who had emigrated to serve in the armies of Spain, France, and Austria, during the
   period of anti-Catholic penal laws passed after 1691, which prevented Catholics from holding
   commissions in the British military.
5. Lord Edward Fitzgerald (1763–1798), a leader of the 1798 Irish Rising.
6. Robert Emmet (1778–1803), leader of an abortive Irish Nationalist revolt in 1803.
7. Theobald Wolfe Tone (1763–1798), a leader of the 1798 Rising.

Romantic Ireland's dead and gone,
It's with O'Leary in the grave.

Yet could we turn the years again,   25
And call those exiles as they were,
In all their loneliness and pain
You'd cry 'Some woman's yellow hair
Has maddened every mother's son':
They weighed so lightly what they gave,   30
But let them be, they're dead and gone,
They're with O'Leary in the grave.

[1913*]   [1916]

To A Friend whose Work has come to Nothing

Now all the truth is out,
Be secret and take defeat[1]
From any brazen throat,
For how can you compete,
Being honour bred, with one[2]   5
Who, were it proved he lies,
Were neither shamed in his own
Nor in his neighbours' eyes?
Bred to a harder thing
Than Triumph, turn away   10
And like a laughing string
Whereon mad fingers play
Amid a place of stone,
Be secret and exult,
Because of all things known   15
That is most difficult.

[1913]   [1916]

Paudeen

Indignant at the fumbling wits, the obscure spite
Of our old Paudeen in his shop, I stumbled blind
Among the stones and thorn trees, under morning light;
Until a curlew cried and in the luminous wind
A curlew answered; and suddenly thereupon I thought   5
That on the lonely height where all are in God's eye,

1. Lady Gregory, for whom the poem was written, had energetically supported her nephew Sir Hugh
   Lane's plans for a Dublin Municipal Gallery of Art.
2. Probably William Martin Murphy (1844–1919), proprietor of two popular and influential Dublin
   newspapers that had attacked Hugh Lane's proposals for the Municipal Gallery.

There cannot be, confusion of our sound forgot,
A single soul that lacks a sweet crystaline cry.

[1913]   [1916]

The Three Beggars

'Though to my feathers in the wet,
I have stood here from break of day,
I have not found a thing to eat
For only rubbish comes my way.
Am I to live on lebeen-lone[1]?'   5
Muttered the old crane of Gort.[2]
'For all my pains on lebeen-lone.'

King Guari[3] walked amid his court
The palace-yard and river-side
And there to three old beggars said: 10
'You that have wandered far and wide
Can ravel out what's in my head.
Do men who least desire get most,
Or get the most who most desire?'
A beggar said: 'They get the most   15
Whom man or devil cannot tire,
And what could make their muscles taut
Unless desire had made them so.'
But Guari laughed with secret thought,
'If that be true as it seems true,   20
One of you three is a rich man,
For he shall have a thousand pounds
Who is first asleep, if but he can
Sleep before the third noon sounds.'
And thereon merry as a bird,   25
With his old thoughts King Guari went
From river-side and palace-yard
And left them to their argument.
'And if I win,' one beggar said,
'Though I am old I shall persuade   30
A pretty girl to share my bed';
The second: 'I shall learn a trade';
The third: 'I'll hurry to the course
Among the other gentlemen,
And lay it all upon a horse';   35
The second: 'I have thought again:
A farmer has more dignity.'
One to another sighed and cried:

1. Minnow's food; from the Irish "libin" (a minnow) and "lon" (food).
2. A small market town in County Galway, close to Lady Gregory's estate at Coole Park.
3. King Guaire of Connacht (d. 663) was famous for his hospitality.

The exorbitant dreams of beggary,
That idleness had borne to pride, 40
Sung through their teeth from noon to noon;
And when the second twilight brought
The frenzy of the beggars' moon
They closed their blood-shot eyes for naught.
One beggar cried: 'You're shamming sleep.' 45
And thereupon their anger grew
Till they were whirling in a heap.

They'd mauled and bitten the night through
Or sat upon their heels to rail,
And when old Guari came and stood 50
Before the three to end this tale,
They were commingling lice and blood.
'Time's up,' he cried, and all the three
With blood-shot eyes upon him stared.
'Time's up,' he cried, and all the three 55
Fell down upon the dust and snored.

'Maybe I shall be lucky yet,
Now they are silent,' said the crane.
'Though to my feathers in the wet
I've stood as I were made of stone 60
And seen the rubbish run about,
It's certain there are trout somewhere
And maybe I shall take a trout
If but I do not seem to care.'

[1913]   [1916]

Beggar to Beggar Cried

'Time to put off the world and go somewhere
And find my health again in the sea air,'
Beggar to beggar cried, being frenzy-struck,
'And make my soul[1] before my pate[2] is bare.'

'And get a comfortable wife and house 5
To rid me of the devil in my shoes,'
Beggar to beggar cried, being frenzy-struck,
'And the worse devil that is between my thighs.'

'And though I'd marry with a comely lass,
She need not be too comely—let it pass,' 10
Beggar to beggar cried, being frenzy-struck,
'But there's a devil in a looking-glass.'

1. Prepare oneself spiritually for death.
2. Head.

'Nor should she be too rich, because the rich
Are driven by wealth as beggars by the itch,'
Beggar to beggar cried, being frenzy-struck,   15
'And cannot have a humorous happy speech.'

'And there I'll grow respected at my ease,
And hear amid the garden's nightly peace,'
Beggar to beggar cried, being frenzy-struck,
'The wind-blown clamour of the barnacle-geese.'   20

[1914]   [1916]

I

The Witch

Toil and grow rich,
What's that but to lie
With a foul witch
And after, drained dry,
To be brought   5
To the chamber where
Lies one long sought
With despair.

[1914]   [1916]

II

The Peacock

What's riches to him
That has made a great peacock
With the pride of his eye?
The wind-beaten, stone-grey,
And desolate Three-rock[1]   5
Would nourish his whim.
Live he or die
Amid wet rocks and heather,
His ghost will be gay
Adding feather to feather   10
For the pride of his eye.

[1914]   [1916]

1. Possibly Three Rock Mountain, which overlooks Dublin.

To a Child Dancing in the Wind

I

Dance there upon the shore;
What need have you[1] to care
For wind or water's roar?
And tumble out your hair
That the salt drops have wet;   5
Being young you have not known
The fool's triumph, nor yet
Love lost as soon as won,
Nor the best labourer dead[2]
And all the sheaves to bind.   10
What need have you to dread
The monstrous crying of wind?

[1912*]   [1916]

[Two Years Later]

II

Has no one said those daring
Kind eyes should be more learn'd?
Or warned you how despairing   15
The moths are when they are burned,
I could have warned you, but you are young,
So we speak a different tongue.

O you will take whatever's offered
And dream that all the world's a friend,   20
Suffer as your mother suffered,[3]
Be as broken in the end.
But I am old and you are young,
And I speak a barbarous tongue.

[1914*]   [1916*]

1. Iseult Gonne (1894–1954), Maud Gonne's daughter, aged eighteen when lines 1–12 were first published and twenty when the lines 13–24 were first published.
2. Probably playwright John Synge (1871–1909), Yeats's codirector at the Abbey Theatre, whose death Yeats saw as a great blow to the possibility of artistic imagination triumphing over the philistinism of the middle classes in Ireland.
3. Maud Gonne's marriage to John MacBride had been short and unhappy, and she sued for divorce in early 1905, citing his drunkenness and a sexual assault on her half-sister. Their separation lastingly damaged her standing as an Irish Nationalist since it offended Catholics who deplored divorce and since MacBride, celebrated in Dublin for leading the Irish Brigade in the Boer War, managed to retain widespread sympathy among influential Nationalists.

Fallen Majesty

Although crowds gathered once if she[1] but showed her face,
And even old men's eyes grew dim, this hand alone,
Like some last courtier at a gypsy camping place,
Babbling of fallen majesty, records what's gone.

The lineaments, a heart that laughter has made sweet,   5
These, these remain, but I record what's gone. A crowd
Will gather, and not know it walks the very street
Whereon a thing once walked that seemed a burning cloud.

[1912]   [1916]

Friends

Now must I these three praise—
Three women that have wrought
What joy is in my days;
One[1] that no passing thought,
Nor those unpassing cares,   5
No, not in these fifteen
Many times troubled years,
Could ever come between
Heart and delighted heart;
And one[2] because her hand   10
Had strength that could unbind
What none can understand,
What none can have and thrive,
Youth's dreamy load, till she
So changed me that I live   15
Labouring in ecstasy.
And what of her[3] that took
All till my youth was gone
With scarce a pitying look?
How should I praise that one?   20
When day begins to break
I count my good and bad,
Being wakeful for her sake,
Remembering what she had,
What eagle look[4] still shows,   25

1. Maud Gonne, whose beauty in her youth had been celebrated.
1. Probably Olivia Shakespear (1867–1938), with whom Yeats had an affair in 1896–97 and who remained until her death one of his closest friends in his London social circle.
2. Probably Lady Gregory, whose financial patronage and emotional support of Yeats, and whose creative contribution to his work as a collaborator and advisor, were crucial to his success in the years after their first meeting in the 1890s.
3. Maud Gonne.
4. Eagles were thought to be the only creatures able to look at the sun without blinking, and they are hence for Yeats a symbol of aristocratic confidence.

While up from my heart's root
So great a sweetness flows
I shake from head to foot.

[1912]   [1916*]

The Cold Heaven

Suddenly I saw the cold and rook-delighting Heaven
That seemed as though ice burned and was but the more ice,
And thereupon imagination and heart were driven
So wild that every casual thought of that and this
Vanished, and left but memories, that should be out of season   5
With the hot blood of youth, of love crossed long ago;
And I took all the blame out of all sense and reason,
Until I cried and trembled and rocked to and fro,
Riddled with light. Ah! when the ghost begins to quicken,
Confusion of the death-bed over, is it sent   10
Out naked on the roads, as the books say, and stricken
By the injustice of the skies for punishment?

[1912]   [1916]

I

The Magi[1]

Now as at all times I can see in the mind's eye,
In their stiff, painted clothes, the pale unsatisfied ones
Appear and disappear in the blue depth of the sky
With all their ancient faces like rain-beaten stones,
And all their helms of silver hovering side by side,   5
And all their eyes still fixed, hoping to find once more,
Being by Calvary's turbulence[2] unsatisfied,
The uncontrollable mystery on the bestial floor.

[1914]   [1916]

1. The wise men who came to Bethlehem to seek the baby Jesus.
2. The crucifixion of Jesus, which took place on Calvary.

II

The Dolls[1]

A doll in the doll-maker's house
Looks at the cradle and bawls:
'That[2] is an insult to us.'
But the oldest of all the dolls
Who had seen, being kept for show,   5
Generations of his sort,
Out-screams the whole shelf: 'Although
There's not a man can report
Evil of this place,
The man and the woman bring   10
Hither to our disgrace,
A noisy and filthy thing.'
Hearing him groan and stretch
The doll-maker's wife is aware
Her husband has heard the wretch,   15
And crouched by the arm of his chair,
She murmurs into his ear,
Head upon shoulder leant:
'My dear, my dear, oh dear,
It was an accident.'   20

[1914]   [1916]

A Coat

I made my song a coat
Covered with embroideries
Out of old mythologies[1]
From heel to throat;
But the fools caught it,   5
Wore it in the world's eye
As though they'd wrought it.
Song, let them take it
For there's more enterprise
In walking naked.   10

[1914]   [1916]

1. Yeats linked "The Magi" and "The Dolls" by numbering them as above until 1933, but even after deleting the numbers he retained a note stressing their connection and emphasizing that the Magi were "complementary forms of those enraged dolls."
2. A baby born to the doll-maker's wife.
1. A reference to the prominent use of Irish legends in his early work.

[Closing Rhymes]

While I, from that reed-throated whisperer
Who comes at need, although not now as once
A clear articulation in the air
But inwardly, surmise companions
Beyond the fling of the dull ass's hoof,[1]   5
—Ben Jonson's phrase—and find when June is come
At Kyle-na-no[2] *under that ancient roof*
A sterner conscience and a friendlier home,
I can forgive even that wrong of wrongs,
Those undreamt accidents that have made me   10
—Seeing that Fame has perished this long while
Being but a part of ancient ceremony—
Notorious, till all my priceless things
Are but a post the passing dogs defile.

[1914*]   [1916*]

---

1. Irish novelist George Moore (1852–1933), formerly a friend of and collaborator with Yeats and Lady Gregory, had recently published chapters from a forthcoming volume of his autobiography that treated both Yeats and Lady Gregory harshly. Yeats's phrase dismissing Moore's vulgarity echoes a line from "An Ode to Himself " by Ben Jonson (1572–1637).
2. One of the seven woods of Lady Gregory's Coole Park estate.

From *The Wild Swans at Coole*
(1917)

The Wild Swans at Coole

The trees are in their autumn beauty,
The woodland paths[1] are dry,
Under the October twilight the water
Mirrors a still sky;
Upon the brimming water among the stones   5
Are nine and fifty swans.

The nineteenth Autumn has come upon me
Since I first made my count;[2]
I saw, before I had well finished,
All suddenly mount   10
And scatter wheeling in great broken rings
Upon their clamorous wings.

I have looked upon those brilliant creatures,
And now my heart is sore.
All's changed since I, hearing at twilight,   15
The first time on this shore,
The bell-beat of their wings above my head,
Trod with a lighter tread.[3]

Unwearied still, lover by lover,
They paddle in the cold,   20
Companionable streams or climb the air;
Their hearts have not grown old;
Passion or conquest, wander where they will,
Attend upon them still.

---

1. In the seven woods of Lady Gregory's Coole Park estate.
2. Yeats first stayed at Coole Park in 1897, and he had spent a significant part of each year since then (usually much of the summer) as Lady Gregory's guest.
3. The poem was begun shortly after Yeats's return from France in autumn 1916, during which he proposed to Maud Gonne for the last time and was again refused. At age fifty-one he was contemplating the prospect of never marrying and having children. The poem was also written in the wake of the upheavals caused by the Easter Rising of 1916.

But now they drift on the still water   25
Mysterious, beautiful;
Among what rushes will they build,
By what lake's edge or pool
Delight men's eyes when I awake some day
To find they have flown away?   30

[1917]   [1919]

In Memory of Major Robert Gregory[1]

1

Now that we're almost settled in our house[2]
I'll name the friends that cannot sup with us
Beside a fire of turf in th' ancient tower,
And having talked to some late hour
Climb up the narrow winding stair[3] to bed: 5
Discoverers of forgotten truth
Or mere companions of my youth,
All, all are in my thoughts to-night being dead.

2

Always we'd have the new friend meet the old
And we are hurt if either friend seem cold,   10
And there is salt to lengthen out the smart
In the affections of our heart,
And quarrels are blown up upon that head;
But not a friend that I would bring
This night can set us quarrelling,   15
For all that come into my mind are dead.

3

Lionel Johnson[4] comes the first to mind,
That loved his learning better than mankind,
Though courteous to the worst; much falling he
Brooded upon sanctity   20
Till all his Greek and Latin learning seemed
A long blast upon the horn that brought
A little nearer to his thought
A measureless consummation that he dreamed.

1. Lady Gregory's only child, Robert, was killed in action as an airman on the Italian front in January 1918.
2. Yeats had married Georgie Hyde-Lees in October 1917, and they were waiting for renovations to be completed on a Norman tower, close to Coole Park, that Yeats had bought earlier that year. He named the property Thoor Ballylee, preferring a version of the Irish word "tor" to the English "tower" or "castle."
3. Thoor Ballylee had a spiral stone staircase, soon to become a key symbol in Yeats's poetry.
4. Irish poet and critic (d. 1902). Yeats had dedicated *The Rose* to him.

4

And that enquiring man John Synge[5] comes next,   25
That dying chose the living world for text
And never could have rested in the tomb
But that, long travelling, he had come
Towards nightfall upon certain set apart
In a most desolate stony place,[6]   30
Towards nightfall upon a race
Passionate and simple like his heart.

5

And then I think of old George Pollexfen,[7]
In muscular youth well known to Mayo men
For horsemanship at meets or at racecourses,   35
That could have shown how purebred horses
And solid men, for all their passion, live
But as the outrageous stars incline
By opposition, square and trine;[8]
Having grown sluggish and contemplative.   40

6

They were my close companions many a year,
A portion of my mind and life, as it were,
And now their breathless faces seem to look
Out of some old picture-book;
I am accustomed to their lack of breath,   45
But not that my dear friend's dear son,
Our Sidney[9] and our perfect man,
Could share in that discourtesy of death.

7

For all things the delighted eye now sees
Were loved by him; the old storm-broken trees   50
That cast their shadows upon road and bridge;
The tower set on the stream's edge;
The ford where drinking cattle make a stir
Nightly, and startled by that sound
The water-hen[1] must change her ground;   55
He might have been your heartiest welcomer.

5. Playwright (d. 1909) and cofounder of the Abbey Theatre with Yeats and Lady Gregory.
6. The Aran Islands, off the coast of Galway, where Synge had found a rich Irish-speaking peasant
   culture that inspired his plays and his volume *The Aran Islands*.
7. Yeats's maternal uncle (d. 1910), who had shared his interest in astrology.
8. Astrological terms used to describe the position of heavenly bodies that are, respectively, 180, 90,
   and 120 degrees apart.
9. Philip Sidney (1554–1586), Elizabethan poet, courtier, and soldier, and an example of the "Renaissance man," since he excelled in a number of widely different spheres.
1. A water bird, more commonly known as a moor-hen.

8

When with the Galway foxhounds he would ride
From Castle Taylor to the Roxborough[2] side
Or Esserkelly plain, few kept his pace;
At Mooneen[3] he had leaped a place   60
So perilous that half the astonished meet
Had shut their eyes, and where was it
He rode a race without a bit?
And yet his mind outran the horses' feet.

9

We dreamed that a great painter[4] had been born   65
To cold Clare rock and Galway rock and thorn,
To that stern colour and that delicate line
That are our secret discipline
Wherein the gazing heart doubles her might.
Soldier, scholar, horseman, he,   70
And yet he had the intensity
To have published all to be a world's delight.

10

What other could so well have counselled us
In all lovely intricacies of a house
As he that practised or that understood   75
All work in metal or in wood,
In moulded plaster or in carven stone?
Soldier, scholar, horseman, he,
And all he did done perfectly
As though he had but that one trade alone.   80

11

Some burn damp fagots, others may consume
The entire combustible world in one small room
As though dried straw, and if we turn about
The bare chimney is gone black out
Because the work had finished in that flare.   85
Soldier, scholar, horseman, he,
As 'twere all life's epitome.
What made us dream that he could comb grey hair?

12

I had thought, seeing how bitter is that wind
That shakes the shutter, to have brought to mind   90
All those that manhood tried, or childhood loved

2. Properties neighboring Coole Park. Roxborough, the estate of Lady Gregory's family (the Persses),
was her birthplace.
3. Places within a few miles of Coole.
4. Gregory studied art after graduating from Oxford and had held several exhibitions.

Or boyish intellect approved,
With some appropriate commentary on each;
Until imagination brought
A fitter welcome; but a thought   95
Of that late death took all my heart for speech.

[1918]   [1919]

An Irish Airman Foresees his Death

I[1] know that I shall meet my fate
Somewhere among the clouds above;
Those that I fight[2] I do not hate,
Those that I guard I do not love;[3]
My country is Kiltartan Cross,[4]   5
My countrymen Kiltartan's poor,
No likely end could bring them loss
Or leave them happier than before.
Nor law, nor duty bade me fight,
Nor public man, nor cheering crowds,   10
A lonely impulse of delight
Drove to this tumult in the clouds;
I balanced all, brought all to mind,
The years to come seemed waste of breath,
A waste of breath the years behind   15
In balance with this life, this death.

[1919]   [1920]

Men Improve with the Years

I am worn out with dreams;
A weather-worn, marble triton[1]
Among the streams;
And all day long I look
Upon this lady's beauty   5
As though I had found in book
A pictured beauty,
Pleased to have filled the eyes
Or the discerning ears,
Delighted to be but wise,   10
For men improve with the years;

1. Robert Gregory.
2. The Germans and the Austrians.
3. The English. Gregory served in the British Royal Flying Corps, enlisting as a volunteer in 1915.
   Military conscription was not ordered in Ireland until early 1918, and Nationalists were strongly
   opposed to Irish involvement in what they saw as "England's war." Yeats's wording stresses that
   Gregory did not choose to fight out of allegiance to Britain.
4. The crossroads village nearest to Coole Park.
1. Tritons were sea-gods in Greek legend.

And yet and yet
Is this my dream, or the truth?
O would that we had met
When I had my burning youth;   15
But I grow old among dreams,
A weather-worn, marble triton
Among the streams.

[1917]   [1919]

The Living Beauty[1]

I'll say and maybe dream I have drawn content—
Seeing that time has frozen up the blood,
The wick of youth being burned and the oil spent—
From beauty that is cast out of a mould
In bronze, or that in dazzling marble appears,   5
Appears, and when we have gone is gone again,
Being more indifferent to our solitude
Than 'twere an apparition. O heart, we are old,
The living beauty is for younger men,
We cannot pay its tribute of wild tears.   10

[1918]   [1919*]

A Song

I thought no more was needed
Youth to prolong
Than dumb-bell and foil[1]
To keep the body young.
Oh, who could have foretold   5
That the heart grows old?

Though I have many words,
What woman's satisfied,
I am no longer faint
Because at her side?   10
Oh, who could have foretold
That the heart grows old?

1. In 1933, lines 1–3 were revised to read:
    I bade, because the wick and oil are spent
    And frozen are the channels of the blood,
    My discontented heart to draw content
Yeats had proposed to Maud Gonne's daughter Iseult in summer 1917 and had been refused.
1. Yeats took lessons in fencing from Ezra Pound during the winter of 1913–14, as part of a new regimen of exercise.

I have not lost desire
But the heart that I had,
I thought 'twould burn my body   15
Laid on the death-bed.
But who could have foretold
That the heart grows old?

[1918]   [1919*]

The Scholars [1919 version]

Bald heads forgetful of their sins,
Old, learned, respectable bald heads
Edit and annotate the lines
That young men, tossing on their beds,
Rhymed out in love's despair   5
To flatter beauty's ignorant ear.

They'll cough in the ink to the world's end;
Wear out the carpet with their shoes
Earning respect; have no strange friend;
If they have sinned nobody knows.   10
Lord, what would they say
Should their Catullus[1] walk that way?

[1915]   [1919*]

The Scholars [1929 version]

Bald heads forgetful of their sins,
Old, learned, respectable bald heads
Edit and annotate the lines
That young men, tossing on their beds,
Rhymed out in love's despair   5
To flatter beauty's ignorant ear.

All shuffle there; all cough in ink;
All wear the carpet with their shoes;
All think what other people think;
All know the man their neighbour knows.   10
Lord, what would they say
Did their Catullus walk that way?

[1929]

---

1. A Roman poet of the first century B.C.E., notorious for his erotic love poems.

Lines Written in Dejection

When have I last looked on
The round green eyes and the long wavering bodies
Of the dark leopards of the moon?[1]
All the wild witches those most noble ladies,
For all their broom-sticks and their tears,   5
Their angry tears, are gone.
The holy centaurs[2] of the hills are vanished;
I have nothing but the embittered sun;[3]
Banished heroic mother moon and vanished,
And now that I have come to fifty years   10
I must endure the timid sun.

[1917*]   [1920]

On Woman

May God be praised for woman
That gives up all her mind,
A man may find in no man
A friendship of her kind
That covers all he has brought   5
As with her flesh and bone,
Nor quarrels with a thought
Because it is not her own.

Though pedantry denies
It's plain the Bible means   10
That Solomon[1] grew wise
While talking with his queens
Yet never could, although
They say he counted grass,
Count all the praises due   15
When Sheba[2] was his lass,
When she the iron wrought, or
When from the smithy fire
It shuddered in the water:
Harshness of their desire   20
That made them stretch and yawn,
Pleasure that comes with sleep,

---

1. The moon was a symbol of subjectivity for Yeats and hence associated with the mythology, romanticism, and imagination of his earlier poetry.
2. In Greek mythology, horses with the head and torso of humans.
3. A symbol of objectivity for Yeats, and hence of the refusal or failure of imagination.
1. King of the Hebrews (c. 972–932 B.C.E.), proverbially a man of extraordinary wisdom.
2. See Kings 10.1–13, which describe the visit of Sheba, a queen of Arabia, to Solomon, her testing him with "hard questions" and (elliptically mentioned) their desire for one another. In several poems postdating "On Woman," Sheba is associated with Yeats's wife, and Solomon with Yeats himself.

Shudder that made them one.
What else He give or keep
God grant me—no, not here,   25
For I am not so bold
To hope a thing so dear
Now I am growing old,
But when if the tale's true
The Pestle of the moon   30
That pounds up all anew
Brings me to birth again—
To find what once I had
And know what once I have known,
Until I am driven mad,   35
Sleep driven from my bed,
By tenderness and care,
Pity, an aching head,
Gnashing of teeth, despair;
And all because of some one   40
Perverse creature of chance,
And live like Solomon
That Sheba led a dance.

[1916]   [1919]

The Fisherman

Although I can see him still
The freckled man who goes
To a grey place on a hill
In grey Connemara[1] clothes
At dawn to cast his flies,   5
It's long since I began
To call up to the eyes
This wise and simple man.
All day I'd looked in the face
What I had hoped 'twould be   10
To write for my own race
And the reality;
The living men that I hate,
The dead man that I loved,
The craven man in his seat,   15
The insolent unreproved
And no knave brought to book
Who has won a drunken cheer,
The witty man and his joke
Aimed at the commonest ear,   20
The clever man who cries
The catch-cries of the clown,

---

1. A region in western Ireland, known for its homespun tweed cloth.

The beating down of the wise
And great Art beaten down.[2]

Maybe a twelvemonth since   25
Suddenly I began,
In scorn of this audience
Imagining a man,
And his sun-freckled face,
And grey Connemara cloth,   30
Climbing up to a place
Where stone is dark under froth,
And the down turn of his wrist
When the flies drop in the stream;
A man who does not exist,   35
A man who is but a dream;
And cried, 'Before I am old
I shall have written him one
Poem maybe as cold
And passionate as the dawn.'   40

[1916]   [1919]

The People

'What have I earned for all that work,' I said,
'For all that I have done[1] at my own charge?
The daily spite of this unmannerly town,[2]
Where who has served the most is most defamed,
The reputation of his lifetime lost   5
Between the night and morning. I might have lived,
And you know well how great the longing has been,
Where every day my footfall should have lit
In the green shadow of Ferrara[3] wall;
Or climbed among the images of the past—   10
The unperturbed and courtly images—
Evening and morning, the steep street of Urbino[4]
To where the duchess[5] and her people talked
The stately midnight through until they stood
In their great window looking at the dawn;   15

2. The attacks on John Synge's plays; on Hugh Lane (d. 1915), the art dealer whose gift of modern
paintings to the Dublin Municipal Gallery of Art on condition that a new gallery be built to
house them had roused controversy; and more recently on Lady Gregory, along with the financial
troubles of the poorly attended Abbey Theatre in Dublin, had gradually deepened Yeats's pessi-
mism about the possibilities for imaginative literature in contemporary Ireland.
1. Yeats was the principal force behind the Irish literary movement, the founding of the Abbey
Theatre, and many other Irish cultural enterprises.
2. Dublin.
3. See note 3 to "To a Wealthy Man . . ." (p. 43).
4. See note 6 to "To a Wealthy Man . . ." (p. 43).
5. Duchess Elisabetta Gonzaga (1471–1526), who, according to Castiglione's *The Book of the Courtier*, talked with her courtiers through the night unaware of how late it was, so great was their
intellectual excitement.

I might have had no friend that could not mix
Courtesy and passion into one like those
That saw the wicks grow yellow in the dawn;
I might have used the one substantial right
My trade allows: chosen my company,   20
And chosen what scenery had pleased me best.'
Thereon my phoenix[6] answered in reproof,
'The drunkards, pilferers of public funds,
All the dishonest crowd I had driven away,
When my luck changed and they dared meet my face,   25
Crawled from obscurity, and set upon me
Those I had served and some that I had fed;
Yet never have I, now nor any time,
Complained of the people.'

               All I could reply
Was: 'You, that have not lived in thought but deed,   30
Can have the purity of a natural force,
But I, whose virtues are the definitions
Of the analytic mind, can neither close
The eye of the mind nor, keep my tongue from speech.'
And yet, because my heart leaped at her words,   35
I was abashed, and now they come to mind
After nine years, I sink my head abashed.

[1916*]   [1919]

Broken Dreams

There is grey in your hair.[1]
Young men no longer suddenly catch their breath
When you are passing;
But maybe some old gaffer mutters a blessing
Because it was your prayer   5
Recovered him upon the bed of death.
For your sole sake—that all heart's ache have known,
And given to others all heart's ache,
From meagre girlhood's putting on
Burdensome beauty—for your sole sake   10
Heaven has put away the stroke of her doom,
So great her portion in that peace you make
By merely walking in a room.

Your beauty can but leave among us
Vague memories, nothing but memories.   15
A young man when the old men are done talking

---

6. The phoenix is a mythological bird reputed to be able to rise from its own ashes with renewed
   youth; here a figure for Maud Gonne.
1. Maud Gonne was in her early fifties when the poem was written.

Will say to an old man, 'Tell me of that lady
The poet stubborn with his passion sang us
When age might well have chilled his blood.'

Vague memories, nothing but memories,   20
But in the grave all, all, shall be renewed.
The certainty that I shall see that lady
Leaning or standing or walking
In the first loveliness of womanhood,
And with the fervour of my youthful eyes,   25
Has set me muttering like a fool.

You are more beautiful than any one
And yet your body had a flaw:
Your small hands were not beautiful,
And I am afraid that you will run   30
And paddle to the wrist
In that mysterious, always brimming lake
Where those that have obeyed the holy law
Paddle and are perfect; leave unchanged
The hands that I have kissed   35
For old sakes' sake.

The last stroke of midnight dies.
All day in the one chair
From dream to dream and rhyme to rhyme I have ranged
In rambling talk with an image of air: 40
Vague memories, nothing but memories.

[1917]   [1919]

The Balloon of the Mind

Hands do what you're bid;
Bring the balloon of the mind
That bellies and drags in the wind
Into its narrow shed.

[1917]   [1919]

On being asked for a War Poem

I think it better that in times like these[1]
A poet keep his mouth shut, for in truth
We have no gift to set a statesman right;
He has had enough of meddling who can please

1. World War I began in August 1914 and continued until 1918.

A young girl in the indolence of her youth,   5
Or an old man upon a winter's night.

[1916*]   [1919]

Ego Dominus Tuus[1]

HIC

On the grey sand beside the shallow stream
Under your old wind-beaten tower, where still
A lamp burns on beside the open book
That Michael Robartes[2] left, you walk in the moon
And though you have passed the best of life still trace   5
Enthralled by the unconquerable delusion
Magical shapes.

ILLE

By the help of an image
I call to my own opposite, summon all
That I have handled least, least looked upon.

HIC

And I would find myself and not an image.   10

ILLE

That is our modern hope and by its light
We have lit upon the gentle, sensitive mind
And lost the old nonchalance of the hand;
Whether we have chosen chisel, pen or brush
We are but critics, or but half create   15
Timid, entangled, empty and abashed
Lacking the countenance of our friends.

HIC

And yet
The chief imagination of Christendom
Dante Alighieri so utterly found himself
That he has made that hollow face of his   20
More plain to the mind's eye than any face
But that of Christ.

ILLE

And did he find himself
Or was the hunger that had made it hollow

---

1. In the *Vita Nuova*, Dante Alighieri (1265–1321) tells of a vision in which a "lord of terrible aspect" says to him, "Ego Dominus Tuus" ("I am your master"). "Hic" and "Ille" are Latin pronouns meaning "the one" and "the other."
2. An invented character who features in Yeats's early stories, some poems in *The Wind Among the Reeds*, and his philosophical text *A Vision* (1925/1937).

A hunger for the apple on the bough
Most out of reach? and is that spectral image   25
The man that Lapo and that Guido[3] knew?
I think he fashioned from his opposite
An image that might have been a stony face,
Staring upon a bedouin's horse-hair roof
From doored and windowed cliff, or half upturned   30
Among the coarse grass and the camel dung.
He set his chisel to the hardest stone.
Being mocked by Guido for his lecherous life
Derided and deriding, driven out
To climb that stair and eat that bitter bread,   35
He found the unpersuadable justice, he found
The most exalted lady loved by a man.

HIC

Yet surely there are men who have made their art
Out of no tragic war, lovers of life,
Impulsive men that look for happiness   40
And sing when they have found it.

ILLE

                  No not sing,
For those that love the world serve it in action,
Grow rich, popular and full of influence,
And should they paint or write still it is action:
The struggle of the fly in marmalade.   45
The rhetorician would deceive his neighbours,
The sentimentalist himself; while art
Is but a vision of reality.
What portion in the world can the artist have
Who has awakened from the common dream   50
But dissipation and despair?

HIC

          And yet
No one denies to Keats[4] love of the world;
Remember his deliberate happiness.

ILLE

His art is happy but who knows his mind?
I see a schoolboy when I think of him   55
With face and nose pressed to a sweet-shop window,
For certainly he sank into his grave
His senses and his heart unsatisfied,
And made—being, poor, ailing and ignorant,
Shut out from all the luxury of the world,   60

---

3. Italian poets Lapo Gianni (c. 1270–c. 1330) and Guido Calvacanti (c. 1230–1300) were friends of Dante's.
4. John Keats (1795–1821), English Romantic poet.

The coarse-bred son of a livery stable-keeper—
Luxuriant song.

HIC

       Why should you leave the lamp
Burning alone beside an open book.
And trace these characters upon the sands?
A style is found by sedentary toil   65
And by the imitation of great masters.

ILLE

Because I seek an image not a book.
Those men that in their writings are most wise
Own nothing but their blind, stupefied hearts.
I call to the mysterious one who yet   70
Shall walk the wet sands by the edge of the stream
And look most like me, being indeed my double,
And prove of all imaginable things
The most unlike, being my anti-self,
And standing by these characters disclose   75
All that I seek; and whisper it as though
He were afraid the birds, who cry aloud
Their momentary cries before it is dawn,
Would carry it away to blasphemous men.

[1917]   [1919]

The Double Vision of Michael Robartes

I

On the grey rock of Cashel[1] the mind's eye
Has called up the cold spirits that are born
When the old moon is vanished from the sky
And the new still hides her horn.

Under blank eyes and fingers never still   5
The particular is pounded till it is man,
When had I my own will?
Oh, not since life began.

Constrained, arraigned, baffled, bent and unbent
By these wire-jointed jaws and limbs of wood,   10
Themselves obedient,
Knowing not evil and good;

1. The Rock of Cashel, County Tipperary, Ireland, an ecclesiastical site on a dramatic rocky outcrop
that includes the ruins of a chapel built in the twelfth century by Cormac McCarthy.

Obedient to some hidden magical breath.
They do not even feel, so abstract are they,
So dead beyond our death,   15
Triumph that we obey.

II

On the grey rock of Cashel I suddenly saw
A Sphinx[2] with woman breast and lion paw,
A Buddha,[3] hand at rest,
Hand lifted up that blest;   20
And right between these two a girl at play
That it may be had danced her life away,
For now being dead it seemed
That she of dancing dreamed.

Although I saw it all in the mind's eye   25
There can be nothing solider till I die;
I saw by the moon's light
Now at its fifteenth night.

One lashed her tail; her eyes lit by the moon
Gazed upon all things known, all things unknown,   30
In triumph of intellect
With motionless head erect.

That other's moonlit eyeballs never moved,
Being fixed on all things loved, all things unloved,
Yet little peace he had   35
For those that love are sad.

Oh, little did they care who danced between,
And little she by whom her dance was seen
So that she danced. No thought,
Body perfection brought,   40

For what but eye and ear silence the mind
With the minute particulars of mankind?
Mind moved yet seemed to stop
As 'twere a spinning-top.

In contemplation had those three so wrought   45
Upon a moment, and so stretched it out
That they, time overthrown,
Were dead yet flesh and bone.

2. In Greek mythology, the Sphinx typically has a lion's body, the head and bust of a woman, and wings. Originally monstrous, the Sphinx in later Greek mythology is a messenger of the gods.
3. Gautama Siddhartha (c. 562–c. 483 B.C.E.), known as "the Buddha," founder of Buddhism.

III

I knew that I had seen, had seen at last
That girl my unremembering nights hold fast   50
Or else my dreams that fly,
If I should rub an eye,

And yet in flying fling into my meat
A crazy juice that makes the pulses beat
As though I had been undone   55
By Homer's Paragon[4]

Who never gave the burning town a thought;
To such a pitch of folly I am brought,
Being caught between the pull
Of the dark moon and the full,   60

The commonness of thought and images
That have the frenzy of our western seas.
Thereon I made my moan,
And after kissed a stone,

And after that arranged it in a song   65
Seeing that I, ignorant for so long,
Had been rewarded thus
In Cormac's ruined house.

[1919]

---

4. Helen of Troy.

From *Michael Robartes and the Dancer* (1921)

Michael Robartes[1] and the Dancer

He

Opinion is not worth a rush;
In this altar-piece[2] the knight,
Who grips his long spear so to push
That dragon through the fading light,
Loved the lady; and it's plain   5
The half-dead dragon was her thought
That every morning rose again
And dug its claws and shrieked and fought.
Could the impossible come to pass
She would have time to turn her eyes,   10
Her lover thought, upon the glass
And on the instant would grow wise.

She

You mean they argued.

He

Put it so;
But bear in mind your lover's wage
Is what your looking-glass can show,   15
And that he will turn green with rage
At all that is not pictured there.

She

May I not put myself to College?

He

Go pluck Athena[3] by the hair;
For what mere book can grant a knowledge   20
With an impassioned gravity
Appropriate to that beating breast,
That vigorous thigh, that dreaming eye?
And may the devil take the rest.

1. See note 2 to "Ego Dominus Tuus" (p. 66)
2. Depicting Saint George and the dragon.
3. Greek goddess of wisdom, usually figured as virginal.

She

And must no beautiful woman be   25
Learned like a man?

He

                    Paul Veronese[4]
And all his sacred company
Imagined bodies all their days,
By the lagoon[5] you love so much,
For proud, soft, ceremonious proof   30
That all must come to sight and touch;
While Michael Angelo's Sistine roof[6]
His Morning and his Night disclose
How sinew that has been pulled tight,
Or it may be loosened in repose,   35
Can rule by supernatural right
Yet be but sinew.

She

                    I have heard said
There is great danger in the body.

He

Did God in portioning wine and bread
Give man His thought or His mere body?   40

She

My wretched dragon is perplexed.

He

I have principles to prove me right.
It follows from this Latin text
That blest souls are not composite,
And that all beautiful women may   45
Live in uncomposite blessedness,
And lead us to the like—if they
Will banish every thought, unless
The lineaments that please their view,
When the long looking-glass is full,   50
Even from the foot-sole think it too.

She

They say such different things at school.

                                    [1920]

4. Venetian painter Paolo Caliari (1528–1588), known as "Veronese," since he was born in Verona.
5. At Venice.
6. Italian artist Michelangelo Buonarroti (1475–1564), who painted the ceiling of the Sistine Chapel in Rome.

Easter, 1916[1]

I have met them at close of day
Coming with vivid faces
From counter or desk among grey
Eighteenth-century houses.
I have passed with a nod of the head   5
Or polite meaningless words,
Or have lingered awhile and said
Polite meaningless words,
And thought before I had done
Of a mocking tale or a gibe   10
To please a companion
Around the fire at the club,
Being certain that they and I
But lived where motley[2] is worn:
All changed, changed utterly: 15
A terrible beauty is born.

That woman's days[3] were spent
In ignorant good will,
Her nights in argument
Until her voice grew shrill.   20
What voice more sweet than hers
When young and beautiful,
She rode to harriers?
This man[4] had kept a school
And rode our winged horse;   25
This other[5] his helper and friend
Was coming into his force;
He might have won fame in the end,
So sensitive his nature seemed,
So daring and sweet his thought.   30
This other man[6] I had dreamed
A drunken, vain-glorious lout.
He had done most bitter wrong
To some who are near my heart,
Yet I number him in the song;   35
He, too, has resigned his part

1. The poem responds to the Easter Rising of 1916, during which an Irish Republic was proclaimed and a force of some 700 Volunteers seized key sites in Dublin and held out against British forces for six days before surrendering. In the two weeks following, fifteen of the Rising's leaders were executed. The Rising was planned for the Easter period deliberately to evoke Christ's death and resurrection: many of its leaders expected to die, and they hoped their sacrifice would bring new life to Ireland.
2. The particolored clothes traditionally worn by jesters.
3. Countess Constance Markievicz, née Gore-Booth (d. 1927), whom Yeats had known since the 1890s, was initially sentenced to death for her part in the Easter Rising but was later given amnesty and released in 1917.
4. Patrick Pearse (1879–1916), who had taught at St. Enda's School in Dublin and was a poet.
5. Thomas MacDonagh (1878–1916), poet and critic.
6. John MacBride (1865–1916), whose marriage to Maud Gonne was short and unhappy.

In the casual comedy;
He, too, has been changed in his turn,
Transformed utterly:
A terrible beauty is born.   40

Hearts with one purpose alone
Through summer and winter seem
Enchanted to a stone
To trouble the living stream.
The horse that comes from the road,   45
The rider, the birds that range
From cloud to tumbling cloud,
Minute by minute they change;
A shadow of cloud on the stream
Changes minute by minute;   50
A horse-hoof slides on the brim,
And a horse plashes within it
Where long-legged moor-hens dive,
And hens to moor-cocks call.
Minute by minute they live: 55
The stone's in the midst of all.

Too long a sacrifice
Can make a stone of the heart.
O when may it suffice?
That is heaven's part, our part   60
To murmur name upon name,
As a mother names her child
When sleep at last has come
On limbs that had run wild.
What is it but nightfall?   65
No, no, not night but death;
Was it needless death after all?
For England may keep faith[7]
For all that is done and said.
We know their dream;[8] enough   70
To know they dreamed and are dead;
And what if excess of love
Bewildered them till they died?
I write it out in a verse—
MacDonagh and MacBride   75
And Connolly[9] and Pearse
Now and in time to be,
Wherever green is worn,

---

7. A bill granting Home Rule to Ireland was passed in 1913, but its implementation was suspended after the outbreak of World War I.
8. Of Ireland's political independence from Britain.
9. James Connolly (1870–1916), a trade union organizer and commandant general of the Easter Rising.

Are changed, changed utterly:
A terrible beauty is born.   80

September 25, 1916.

[1916*]   [1922]

On a Political Prisoner

She[1] that but little patience knew,
From childhood on, had now so much
A grey gull lost its fear and flew
Down to her cell and there alit,
And there endured her fingers' touch   5
And from her fingers ate its bit.

Did she in touching that lone wing
Recall the years before her mind
Became a bitter, an abstract thing,
Her thought some popular enmity: 10
Blind and leader of the blind
Drinking the foul ditch where they lie?

When long ago I saw her ride
Under Ben Bulben[2] to the meet,
The beauty of her country-side   15
With all youth's lonely wildness stirred,
She seemed to have grown clean and sweet
Like any rock-bred, sea-borne bird:

Sea-borne, or balanced on the air
When first it sprang out of the nest   20
Upon some lofty rock to stare
Upon the cloudy canopy,
While under its storm-beaten breast
Cried out the hollows of the sea.

[1920]   [1922]

1. Countess Markievicz (see note 3 to "Easter, 1916," p. 73), who was imprisoned again in 1918–19 for her Republican activities.
2. A mountain north of Sligo.

The Second Coming

Turning and turning in the widening gyre[1]
The falcon cannot hear the falconer;
Things fall apart; the centre cannot hold;
Mere anarchy[2] is loosed upon the world,
The blood-dimmed tide is loosed, and everywhere   5
The ceremony of innocence is drowned;
The best lack all conviction, while the worst
Are full of passionate intensity.

Surely some revelation is at hand;
Surely the Second Coming[3] is at hand.   10
The Second Coming! Hardly are those words out
When a vast image out of Spiritus Mundi[4]
Troubles my sight: somewhere in sands of the desert
A shape with lion body and the head of a man,[5]
A gaze blank and pitiless as the sun,   15
Is moving its slow thighs, while all about it
Reel shadows of the indignant desert birds.
The darkness drops again; but now I know
That twenty centuries of stony sleep
Were vexed to nightmare by a rocking cradle,   20
And what rough beast, its hour come round at last,
Slouches towards Bethlehem[6] to be born?

[1920]   [1922]

A Prayer for my Daughter

Once more the storm is howling and half hid
Under this cradle-hood and coverlid
My child[1] sleeps on. There is no obstacle
But Gregory's wood[2] and one bare hill
Whereby the haystack and roof-levelling wind,   5

1. A term used by Yeats to describe a spiraling motion that forms a cone. In a note to the poem he defined the forces of history in terms of gyres: "the end of an age, which always receives the revelation of the character of the next age, is represented by the coming of one gyre to its place of greatest expansion and of the other to that of its greatest contraction. At the present moment the life gyre is sweeping outward, unlike that before the birth of Christ." Yeats's model sees as imminent the end of a Christian, subjective age, and the beginning of an objective age.
2. The poem was written in 1919, in the wake of World War I and the Russian Revolution, and with the Anglo-Irish War looming.
3. In the Revelation to John, Christ's Second Coming is heralded by the arrival of the Beast of the Apocalypse.
4. Yeats glossed this term as "a general storehouse of images which have ceased to be a property of any personality or spirit."
5. A sphinxlike beast, associated by Yeats with objectivity.
6. The place of Christ's birth.
1. Yeats's first child, Anne, born in February 1919.
2. Lady Gregory's estate at Coole Park was about three miles from Yeats's tower at Thoor Ballylee, where the poem was written.

Bred on the Atlantic, can be stayed;
And for an hour I have walked and prayed
Because of the great gloom that is in my mind.

I have walked and prayed for this young child an hour
And heard the sea-wind scream upon the tower, 10
And under the arches of the bridge, and scream
In the elms above the flooded stream;
Imagining in excited reverie
That the future years had come,
Dancing to a frenzied drum, 15
Out of the murderous innocence of the sea.

May she be granted beauty and yet not
Beauty to make a stranger's eye distraught,
Or hers before a looking-glass, for such,
Being made beautiful overmuch, 20
Consider beauty a sufficient end,
Lose natural kindness and maybe
The heart-revealing intimacy
That chooses right and never find a friend.

Helen[3] being chosen found life flat and dull 25
And later had much trouble from a fool,
While that great Queen,[4] that rose out of the spray,
Being fatherless could have her way
Yet chose a bandy-legged smith[5] for man.
It's certain that fine women eat 30
A crazy salad with their meat
Whereby the Horn of Plenty[6] is undone.

In courtesy I'd have her chiefly learned;
Hearts are not had as a gift but hearts are earned
By those that are not entirely beautiful; 35
Yet many, that have played the fool
For beauty's very self, has charm made wise,
And many a poor man that has roved,
Loved and thought himself beloved,
From a glad kindness cannot take his eyes.[7] 40

May she become a flourishing hidden tree
That all her thoughts may like the linnet[8] be,
And have no business but dispensing round

---

3. Helen, wife of King Menelaus of Sparta, was abducted by Paris, son of King Priam of Troy, and this precipitated the Trojan War.
4. Aphrodite, the Greek goddess of love, was born out of the sea and thus had no father.
5. Hephaestus, god of fire and metalwork, who was lame.
6. Zeus, king of the gods in Greek mythology, was suckled as a child by a goat. She gave him one of her horns, which flowed with ambrosia and nectar. The overflowing horn, or cornucopia, is thus a traditional image of plenty.
7. Yeats had married "sensibly" in October 1917 after finally abandoning his decades-long love for Maud Gonne.
8. A small bird.

Their magnanimities of sound,
Nor but in merriment begin a chase,   45
Nor but in merriment a quarrel.
Oh, may she live like some green laurel
Rooted in one dear perpetual place.

My mind, because the minds that I have loved,
The sort of beauty that I have approved,   50
Prosper but little, has dried up of late,
Yet knows that to be choked with hate
May well be of all evil chances chief.
If there's no hatred in a mind
Assault and battery of the wind   55
Can never tear the linnet from the leaf.

An intellectual hatred is the worst,
So let her think opinions are accursed.
Have I not seen the loveliest woman born
Out of the mouth of Plenty's horn,   60
Because of her opinionated mind
Barter that horn and every good
By quiet natures understood
For an old bellows full of angry wind?

Considering that, all hatred driven hence,   65
The soul recovers radical innocence
And learns at last that it is self-delighting,
Self-appeasing, self-affrighting,
And that its own sweet will is heaven's will;
She can, though every face should scowl   70
And every windy quarter howl
Or every bellows burst, be happy still.

And may her bride-groom bring her to a house
Where all's accustomed, ceremonious;
For arrogance and hatred are the wares   75
Peddled in the thoroughfares.
How but in custom and in ceremony
Are innocence and beauty born?
Ceremony's a name for the rich horn,
And custom for the spreading laurel tree.   80

June 1919.

[1919]   [1922]

To be Carved on a Stone at Thoor Ballylee

I, the poet William Yeats,
With old mill boards and sea-green slates,
And smithy work from the Gort[1] forge,
Restored this tower for my wife George;[2]
And may these characters remain   5
When all is ruin once again.

[1921*]   [1922]

---

1. Thoor Ballylee is about four miles north of the small town of Gort, County Galway.
2. Georgie Hyde-Lees (1892–1968).

From *The Tower* (1928)

Sailing to Byzantium

I

That is no country[1] for old men. The young
In one another's arms, birds in the trees,
—Those dying generations—at their song,
The salmon-falls, the mackerel-crowded seas,
Fish flesh or fowl, commend all summer long   5
Whatever is begotten born and dies.
Caught in that sensual music all neglect
Monuments of unaging intellect.

II

An aged man is but a paltry thing,
A tattered coat upon a stick, unless   10
Soul clap its hands and sing, and louder sing
For every tatter in its mortal dress,
Nor is there singing school but studying
Monuments of its own magnificence;
And therefore I have sailed the seas and come   15
To the holy city of Byzantium.[2]

III

O sages standing in God's holy fire
As in the gold mosaic of a wall,[3]
Come from the holy fire, perne in a gyre,[4]
And be the singing masters of my soul.   20
Consume my heart away; sick with desire
And fastened to a dying animal
It knows not what it is; and gather me
Into the artifice of eternity.

1. Ireland.
2. Chosen as capital of the Roman Empire by Emperor Constantine, who renamed it Constantinople in 330. For Yeats it was the image of an ideal city, where, briefly, "religious, aesthetic and practical life were one."
3. Yeats saw the friezes at the church of S. Apollinare Nuova at Ravenna in 1907; they depict early Christian martyrs being burned.
4. Turn in a spiral. See note 1 to "The Second Coming" (p. 76).

IV

Once out of nature I shall never take   25
My bodily form from any natural thing,
But such a form as Grecian goldsmiths make
Of hammered gold and gold enamelling
To keep a drowsy emperor awake;[5]
Or set upon a golden bough to sing   30
To lords and ladies of Byzantium
Of what is past, or passing, or to come.

1927

[1927]   [1928]

The Tower

I

What shall I do with this absurdity—
O heart, O troubled heart—this caricature,
Decrepit age that has been tied to me
As to a dog's tail?
            Never had I more
Excited, passionate, fantastical   5
Imagination, nor an ear and eye
That more expected the impossible—
No, not in boyhood when with rod and fly,
Or the humbler worm, I climbed Ben Bulben's[1] back
And had the livelong summer day to spend.   10
It seems that I must bid the Muse[2] go pack,
Choose Plato and Plotinus[3] for a friend
Until imagination, ear and eye,
Can be content with argument and deal
In abstract things; or be derided by   15
A sort of battered kettle at the heel.

II

I pace upon the battlements and stare
On the foundations of a house, or where
Tree, like a sooty finger, starts from the earth;
And send imagination forth   20
Under the day's declining beam, and call
Images and memories

---

5. "I have read somewhere that in the Emperor's palace at Byzantium was a tree made of gold and silver, and artificial birds that sang" (Yeats's note).
1. A mountain north of Sligo.
2. There were nine Muses in Greek mythology, credited with inspiring the arts, but the term is most often used to refer to the Muse of poetry.
3. The Greek philosopher Plato (c. 429–c. 348 B.C.E.) distinguished between universal, unchanging forms and the transient, warning that man is prone to mistake sense impressions for reality. The Roman philosopher Plotinus (c. 205–70 B.C.E.) was a neoplatonist.

From ruin or from ancient trees,
For I would ask a question of them all.

Beyond that ridge lived Mrs. French, and once   25
When every silver candlestick or sconce
Lit up the dark mahogany and the wine,
A serving man that could divine
That most respected lady's every wish,
Ran and with the garden shears   30
Clipped an insolent farmer's ears
And brought them in a little covered dish.[4]

Some few remembered still when I was young
A peasant girl[5] commended by a song,
Who'd lived somewhere upon that rocky place,   35
And praised the colour of her face,
And had the greater joy in praising her,
Remembering that, if walked she there,
Farmers jostled at the fair
So great a glory did the song confer.   40

And certain men, being maddened by those rhymes,
Or else by toasting her a score of times,
Rose from the table and declared it right
To test their fancy by their sight;
But they mistook the brightness of the moon   45
For the prosaic light of day—
Music had driven their wits astray—
And one was drowned in the great bog of Cloone.

Strange, but the man who made the song was blind,[6]
Yet, now I have considered it, I find   50
That nothing strange; the tragedy began
With Homer that was a blind man,
And Helen has all living hearts betrayed.[7]
O may the moon and sunlight seem
One inextricable beam,   55
For if I triumph I must make men mad.

And I myself created Hanrahan[8]
And drove him drunk or sober through the dawn
From somewhere in the neighbouring cottages.

4. An event that occurred in 1778, recounted in Sir Jonah Barrington's *Personal Sketches of His Own Times* (1827, 1832).
5. Mary Hynes of Ballylee, a noted beauty.
6. Anthony Raftery (c. 1784–1835), an Irish poet and fiddler who wrote the song "Mary Hynes."
7. The parallel between Raftery and Homer, a Greek poet of c. eighth century B.C.E.—both blind and both writing of the impact of a beautiful woman—is here extended to Yeats himself, through his familiar association of Helen of Troy with Maud Gonne. Homer's *Iliad* tells of the Trojan War, caused by the abduction of the renowned beauty Helen by Paris, son of the king of Troy.
8. The itinerant poet in several early Yeats stories and poems; he is put under an enchantment in the story "Red Hanrahan" and thereby loses his sweetheart.

Caught by an old man's juggleries 60
He stumbled, tumbled, fumbled to and fro
And had but broken knees for hire
And horrible splendour of desire;
I thought it all out twenty years ago:

Good fellows shuffled cards in an old bawn[9]; 65
And when that ancient ruffian's turn was on
He so bewitched the cards under his thumb
That all, but the one card, became
A pack of hounds and not a pack of cards,
And that he changed into a hare. 70
Hanrahan rose in frenzy there
And followed up those baying creatures towards—

O towards I have forgotten what—enough!
I must recall a man that neither love
Nor music nor an enemy's clipped ear 75
Could, he was so harried, cheer;
A figure that has grown so fabulous
There's not a neighbour left to say
When he finished his dog's day:
An ancient bankrupt master of this house. 80

Before that ruin came, for centuries,
Rough men-at-arms, cross-gartered to the knees
Or shod in iron, climbed the narrow stairs,
And certain men-at-arms there were
Whose images, in the Great Memory stored, 85
Come with loud cry and panting breast
To break upon a sleeper's rest
While their great wooden dice beat on the board.

As I would question all, come all who can;
Come old, necessitous, half-mounted[1] man; 90
And bring beauty's blind rambling celebrant;
The red man[2] the juggler sent
Through God-forsaken meadows; Mrs. French,
Gifted with so fine an ear;
The man drowned in a bog's mire, 95
When mocking muses chose the country wench.

Did all old men and women, rich and poor,
Who trod upon these rocks or passed this door,
Whether in public or in secret rage
As I do now against old age? 100
But I have found an answer in those eyes

9. A yard or pasture, often fortified.
1. The "bankrupt" master of line 80, unable to afford a fully equipped horse.
2. Red Hanrahan.

That are impatient to be gone;
Go therefore; but leave Hanrahan
For I need all his mighty memories.

Old lecher with a love on every wind   105
Bring up out of that deep considering mind
All that you have discovered in the grave,
For it is certain that you have
Reckoned up every unforeknown, unseeing
Plunge, lured by a softening eye,   110
Or by a touch or a sigh,
Into the labyrinth of another's being;

Does the imagination dwell the most
Upon a woman won or woman lost?
If on the lost, admit you turned aside   115
From a great labyrinth out of pride,
Cowardice, some silly over-subtle thought
Or anything called conscience once;
And that if memory recur, the sun's
Under eclipse and the day blotted out.   120

III

It is time that I wrote my will;
I choose upstanding men,
That climb the streams until
The fountain leap, and at dawn
Drop their cast at the side   125
Of dripping stone; I declare
They shall inherit my pride,
The pride of people that were
Bound neither to Cause nor to State,
Neither to slaves that were spat on,   130
Nor to the tyrants that spat,
The people of Burke and of Grattan[3]
That gave, though free to refuse—
Pride, like that of the morn,
When the headlong light is loose,   135
Or that of the fabulous horn,
Or that of the sudden shower
When all streams are dry,
Or that of the hour
When the swan must fix his eye   140
Upon a fading gleam,
Float out upon a long

3. Irish politician and writer Edmund Burke (1729–1797) fought for an Irish parliament free from English control. Irish politician Henry Grattan (1746–1820) fought for Catholic Emancipation and legislative independence for Ireland. Yeats here chooses as his exemplary men two Protestants who regarded themselves as Irish rather than English, yet who (like Yeats himself at this point in his life) were separated from the Catholic majority of the Irish people by both their religion and their class status.

Last reach of glittering stream
And there sing his last song.
And I declare my faith;   145
I mock Plotinus' thought
And cry in Plato's teeth,
Death and life were not
Till man made up the whole,
Made lock, stock and barrel   150
Out of his bitter soul,
Aye, sun and moon and star, all,
And further add to that
That, being dead, we rise,
Dream and so create   155
Translunar Paradise.
I have prepared my peace
With learned Italian things[4]
And the proud stones of Greece,
Poet's imaginings   160
And memories of love,
Memories of the words of women,
All those things whereof
Man makes a superhuman,
Mirror-resembling dream.   165

As at the loophole[5] there,
The daws chatter and scream,
And drop twigs layer upon layer.
When they have mounted up,
The mother bird will rest   170
On their hollow top,
And so warm her wild nest.

I leave both faith and pride
To young upstanding men
Climbing the mountain side,   175
That under bursting dawn
They may drop a fly;
Being of that metal made
Till it was broken by
This sedentary trade.   180

Now shall I make my soul
Compelling it to study
In a learned school
Till the wreck of body
Slow decay of blood,   185
Testy delirium
Or dull decrepitude,

4. Such as the writings of Dante and the art and culture achieved by the courts of the Renaissance.
5. A narrow opening in the tower's wall.

Or what worse evil come—
The death of friends, or death
Of every brilliant eye   190
That made a catch in the breath—
Seem but the clouds of the sky
When the horizon fades;
Or a bird's sleepy cry
Among the deepening shades.   195

1926

[1927]   [1928]

Meditations in Time of Civil War[1]

I

ANCESTRAL HOUSES

Surely among a rich man's flowering lawns,
Amid the rustle of his planted hills,
Life overflows without ambitious pains;
And rains down life until the basin spills,
And mounts more dizzy high the more it rains   5
As though to choose whatever shape it wills
And never stoop to a mechanical,
Or servile shape, at others' beck and call.

Mere dreams, mere dreams! Yet Homer had not sung
Had he not found it certain beyond dreams   10
That out of life's own self-delight had sprung
The abounding glittering jet; though now it seems
As if some marvellous empty sea-shell flung
Out of the obscure dark of the rich streams,
And not a fountain, were the symbol which   15
Shadows the inherited glory of the rich.

Some violent bitter man, some powerful man
Called architect and artist in, that they,
Bitter and violent men, might rear in stone
The sweetness that all longed for night and day,   20
The gentleness none there had ever known;
But when the master's buried mice can play,
And maybe the great-grandson of that house,
For all its bronze and marble, 's but a mouse.

1. The Irish Civil War was fought in 1922–23 between supporters of the new Irish Free State
government and Republicans who rejected the terms of the Anglo-Irish Treaty, ratified in January
1922. Republicans objected particularly to the partition of Ireland that took place as a result of
the treaty.

Oh what if gardens where the peacock strays 25
With delicate feet upon old terraces,
Or else all Juno[2] from an urn displays
Before the indifferent garden deities;
Oh what if levelled lawns and gravelled ways
Where slippered Contemplation finds his ease 30
And Childhood a delight for every sense,
But take our greatness with our violence!

What if the glory of escutcheoned[3] doors,
And buildings that a haughtier age designed,
The pacing to and fro on polished floors 35
Amid great chambers and long galleries, lined
With famous portraits of our ancestors;
What if those things the greatest of mankind,
Consider most to magnify, or to bless,
But take our greatness with our bitterness! 40

II

MY HOUSE

An ancient bridge, and a more ancient tower,[4]
A farmhouse that is sheltered by its wall,
An acre of stony ground,
Where the symbolic rose can break in flower,
Old ragged elms, old thorns innumerable, 5
The sound of the rain or sound
Of every wind that blows;
The stilted water-hen
Crossing stream again
Scared by the splashing of a dozen cows; 10

A winding stair, a chamber arched with stone,
A grey stone fireplace with an open hearth,
A candle and written page.
Il Penseroso's Platonist[5] toiled on
In some like chamber, shadowing forth 15
How the daemonic rage
Imagined everything.
Benighted travellers
From markets and from fairs
Have seen his midnight candle glimmering. 20

Two men have founded here. A man-at-arms
Gathered a score of horse and spent his days

2. Queen of the gods in Roman mythology, often depicted with peacocks, symbols of immortality.
3. Having on it a shield with armorial family bearings.
4. Thoor Ballylee.
5. The 1632 poem "Il Penseroso" ("the pensive man") by John Milton (1608–1674) features a scholar who aspires to work in "some high lonely tower" where he can "unsphere / The spirit of Plato, to unfold / What worlds, or what vast regions hold / The immortal mind that has forsook / Her mansion in this fleshly nook."

In this tumultuous spot,
Where through long wars and sudden night alarms
His dwindling score and he seemed cast-a-ways   25
Forgetting and forgot;
And I, that after me
My bodily heirs may find,
To exalt a lonely mind,
Befitting emblems of adversity.   30

III

MY TABLE

Two heavy tressels, and a board
Where Sato's gift, a changeless sword,[6]
By pen and paper lies,
That it may moralise
My days out of their aimlessness.   5
A bit of an embroidered dress
Covers its wooden sheath.
Chaucer[7] had not drawn breath
When it was forged. In Sato's house,
Curved like new moon, moon luminous   10
It lay five hundred years.
Yet if no change appears
No moon; only an aching heart
Conceives a changeless work of art.
Our learned men have urged   15
That when and where 'twas forged
A marvellous accomplishment,
In painting or in pottery, went
From father unto son
And through the centuries ran   20
And seemed unchanging like the sword.
Soul's beauty being most adored,
Men and their business took
The soul's unchanging look;
For the most rich inheritor,   25
Knowing that none could pass heaven's door
That loved inferior art,
Had such an aching heart
That he, although a country's talk
For silken clothes and stately walk,   30
Had waking wits; it seemed
Juno's peacock screamed.[8]

---

6. Yeats was given an ancient ceremonial sword in 1920 by Junzo Sato, then a Japanese consul to the United States.
7. Geoffrey Chaucer (c. 1340–1400), English poet.
8. See note 2 to "Ancestral Houses" (p. 87). In Yeats's A *Vision*, a peacock's scream signals the end of a civilization.

IV

MY DESCENDANTS

Having inherited a vigorous mind
From my old fathers I must nourish dreams
And leave a woman and a man[9] behind
As vigorous of mind, and yet it seems
Life scarce can cast a fragrance on the wind,   5
Scarce spread a glory to the morning beams,
But the torn petals strew the garden plot;
And there's but common greenness after that.

And what if my descendants lose the flower
Through natural declension of the soul,   10
Through too much business with the passing hour,
Through too much play, or marriage with a fool?
May this laborious stair and this stark tower
Become a roofless ruin that the owl
May build in the cracked masonry and cry   15
Her desolation to the desolate sky.

The Primum Mobile[1] that fashioned us
Has made the very owls in circles move;
And I, that count myself most prosperous,
Seeing that love and friendship are enough,   20
For an old neighbour's[2] friendship chose the house
And decked and altered it for a girl's love,[3]
And know whatever flourish and decline
These stones remain their monument and mine.

V

THE ROAD AT MY DOOR

An affable Irregular,[4]
A heavily built Falstaffan[5] man,
Comes cracking jokes of civil war
As though to die by gunshot were
The finest play under the sun.   5

A brown Lieutenant and his men,
Half dressed in national uniform,[6]

9. His children, Anne (b. 1919) and Michael (b. 1921).
1. The outermost sphere in Ptolemaic astrology, thought to revolve around the earth, carrying the spheres of fixed stars and planets with it: hence, seen as the source of motion.
2. Lady Gregory's.
3. George Hyde-Lees, whom Yeats married in 1917.
4. A member of the Irish Republican Army and hence on the Republican side against the Anglo-Irish Treaty.
5. John Falstaff, a fat, humorous knight in several of Shakespeare's plays.
6. These Free State soldiers had obviously not been fully issued with the new uniforms of the provisional government.

Stand at my door, and I complain
Of the foul weather, hail and rain,
A pear tree broken by the storm.   10

I count those feathered balls of soot[7]
The moor-hen guides upon the stream,
To silence the envy in my thought;
And turn towards my chamber, caught
In the cold snows of a dream.   15

VI

THE STARE'S NEST BY MY WINDOW[8]

The bees build in the crevices
Of loosening masonry, and there
The mother birds bring grubs and flies.
My wall is loosening; honey-bees
Come build in the empty house of the stare.   5

We are closed in, and the key is turned
On our uncertainty; somewhere
A man is killed, or a house burned,
Yet no clear fact to be discerned:
Come build in the empty house of the stare.   10

A barricade of stone or of wood;
Some fourteen days of civil war;
Last night they trundled down the road
That dead young soldier in his blood:
Come build in the empty house of the stare.   15

We had fed the heart on fantasies,
The heart's grown brutal from the fare,
More substance in our enmities
Than in our love; oh, honey-bees
Come build in the empty house of the stare.   20

VII

I SEE PHANTOMS OF HATRED AND OF THE HEART'S FULLNESS
AND OF THE COMING EMPTINESS

I climb to the tower top and lean upon broken stone,
A mist that is like blown snow is sweeping over all,
Valley, river, and elms, under the light of a moon
That seems unlike itself, that seems unchangeable,
A glittering sword out of the east. A puff of wind   5
And those white glimmering fragments of the mist sweep by.

7. The moor-hen's chicks.
8. Yeats explained that "in the West of Ireland we call a starling a stare."

Frenzies bewilder, reveries perturb the mind;
Monstrous familiar images swim to the mind's eye.

'Vengeance upon the murderers,' the cry goes up,
'Vengeance for Jacques Molay.'[9] In cloud-pale rags, or in lace,   10
The rage driven, rage tormented, and rage hungry troop,
Trooper belabouring trooper, biting at arm or at face,
Plunges towards nothing, arms and fingers spreading wide
For the embrace of nothing; and I, my wits astray
Because of all that senseless tumult, all but cried   15
For vengeance on the murderers of Jacques Molay.[1]

Their legs long delicate and slender, aquamarine their eyes,
Magical unicorns bear ladies on their backs,
The ladies close their musing eyes. No prophecies,
Remembered out of Babylonian almanacs,   20
Have closed the ladies' eyes, their minds are but a pool
Where even longing drowns under its own excess;
Nothing but stillness can remain when hearts are full
Of their own sweetness, bodies of their loveliness.

The cloud-pale unicorns, the eyes of aquamarine,   25
The quivering half-closed eyelids, the rags of cloud or of lace,
Or eyes that rage has brightened, arms it has made lean,
Give place to an indifferent multitude, give place
To brazen hawks. Nor self-delighting reverie,
Nor hate of what's to come, nor pity for what's gone,   30
Nothing but grip of claw, and the eye's complacency,
The innumerable clanging wings that have put out the moon.

I turn away and shut the door, and on the stair
Wonder how many times I could have proved my worth
In something that all others understand or share;   35
But oh, ambitious heart had such a proof drawn forth
A company of friends, a conscience set at ease,
It had but made us pine the more. The abstract joy,
The half read wisdom of daemonic images,
Suffice the ageing man as once the growing boy.   40

1923

[1923*]   [1928]

---

9. Grand Master of the Knights Templars, a monastic-military society founded to protect pilgrims and the interests of Christianity; he was burnt at the stake in 1207, nominally for heresy but more likely as a way of curtailing the power of the Templars, who were finally outlawed by the Pope in 1312.
1. Yeats saw those who called for vengeance for Molay as a "fit symbol for those who labour from hatred, and so for sterility in various kinds."

Nineteen Hundred and Nineteen[1]

I

Many ingenious lovely things are gone
That seemed sheer miracle to the multitude,
Protected from the circle of the moon
That pitches common things about. There stood
Amid the ornamental bronze and stone   5
An ancient image made of olive wood—[2]
And gone are Phidias' famous ivories
And all the golden grasshoppers and bees.[3]

We too had many pretty toys when young;
A law indifferent to blame or praise,   10
To bribe or threat; habits that made old wrong
Melt down, as it were wax in the sun's rays;
Public opinion ripening for so long
We thought it would outlive all future days.
O what fine thought we had because we thought   15
That the worst rogues and rascals had died out.

All teeth were drawn, all ancient tricks unlearned,
And a great army but a showy thing;
What matter that no cannon had been turned
Into a ploughshare; parliament and king   20
Thought that unless a little powder burned
The trumpeters might burst with trumpeting
And yet it lack all glory; and perchance
The guardsmen's drowsy chargers would not prance.

Now days are dragon-ridden, the nightmare   25
Rides upon sleep: a drunken soldiery
Can leave the mother, murdered at her door,
To crawl in her own blood,[4] and go scot-free;
The night can sweat with terror as before
We pieced our thoughts into philosophy,   30
And planned to bring the world under a rule,
Who are but weasels fighting in a hole.

He who can read the signs nor sink unmanned
Into the half-deceit of some intoxicant
From shallow wits; who knows no work can stand,   35

1. The poem was inspired by atrocities during the Anglo-Irish War of 1919–21, when vicious reprisals were enacted by British forces, notably by the violent "Black and Tans," against Nationalists fighting for Irish independence.
2. A statue of the goddess Athena that had stood on the Acropolis in Athens.
3. The sculptor Phidias (c. 490–c. 423 B.C.E.) made important statues for Athens; the Greek historian Thucydides (c. 460–c. 400 B.C.E.) wrote of Athenian women using golden grasshoppers as broaches and fastenings.
4. In a particularly vicious killing, a Gort woman was killed outside her house by passing Black and Tans in November 1920.

Whether health, wealth or peace of mind were spent
On master work of intellect or hand,
No honour leave its mighty monument,
Has but one comfort left: all triumph would
But break upon his ghostly solitude.   40

But is there any comfort to be found?
Man is in love and loves what vanishes,
What more is there to say? That country round
None dared admit, if such a thought were his,
Incendiary or bigot could be found   45
To burn that stump on the Acropolis,
Or break in bits the famous ivories
Or traffic in the grasshoppers or bees?

II

When Loie Fuller's Chinese dancers[5] enwound
A shining web, a floating ribbon of cloth,   50
It seemed that a dragon of air
Had fallen among dancers, had whirled them round
Or hurried them off on its own furious path;
So the platonic year
Whirls out new right and wrong,   55
Whirls in the old instead;
All men are dancers and their tread
Goes to the barbarous clangour of gong.

III

Some moralist or mythological poet
Compares the solitary soul to a swan;[6]   60
I am satisfied with that,
Satisfied if a troubled mirror show it
Before that brief gleam of its life be gone,
An image of its state;
The wings half spread for flight,   65
The breast thrust out in pride
Whether to play, or to ride
Those winds that clamour of approaching night.

A man in his own secret meditation
Is lost amid the labyrinth that he has made   70
In art or politics;
Some platonist affirms that in the station
Where we should cast off body and trade
The ancient habit sticks,
And that if our works could   75

5. American dancer Loie Fuller (1862–1928) toured with a group of dancers (in fact Japanese, not
Chinese) who used whirling draperies in their dances.
6. English Romantic poet Percy Bysshe Shelley (1792–1822) in *Prometheus Unbound*.

But vanish with our breath
That were a lucky death,
For triumph can but mar our solitude.

The swan has leaped into the desolate heaven:
That image can bring wildness, bring a rage   80
To end all things, to end
What my laborious life imagined, even
The half imagined, the half written page;
O but we dreamed to mend
Whatever mischief seemed   85
To afflict mankind, but now
That winds of winter blow
Learn that we were crack-pated when we dreamed.

IV

We, who seven years ago
Talked of honour and of truth,   90
Shriek with pleasure if we show
The weasel's twist, the weasel's tooth.

V

Come let us mock at the great
That had such burdens on the mind
And toiled so hard and late   95
To leave some monument behind,
Nor thought of the levelling wind.

Come let us mock at the wise;
With all those calendars whereon
They fixed old aching eyes,   100
They never saw how seasons run,
And now but gape at the sun.

Come let us mock at the good
That fancied goodness might be gay,
And sick of solitude   105
Might proclaim a holiday:
Wind shrieked—and where are they?

Mock mockers after that
That would not lift a hand maybe
To help good, wise or great   110
To bar that foul storm out, for we
Traffic in mockery.

VI

Violence upon the roads: violence of horses;
Some few have handsome riders, are garlanded

On delicate sensitive ear or tossing mane,   115
But wearied running round and round in their courses
All break and vanish, and evil gathers head:
Herodias' daughters[7] have returned again
A sudden blast of dusty wind and after
Thunder of feet, tumult of images,   120
Their purpose in the labyrinth of the wind;
And should some crazy hand dare touch a daughter
All turn with amorous cries, or angry cries,
According to the wind, for all are blind.
But now wind drops, dust settles; thereupon   125
There lurches past, his great eyes without thought
Under the shadow of stupid straw-pale locks,
That insolent fiend Robert Artisson[8]
To whom the love-lorn Lady Kyteler brought
Bronzed peacock feathers, red combs of her cocks.   130

1919

[1921*]   [1928]

A Prayer for my Son

Bid a strong ghost stand at the head
That my Michael[1] may sleep sound,
Nor cry, nor turn in the bed
Till his morning meal come round;
And may departing twilight keep   5
All dread afar till morning's back,
That his mother may not lack
Her fill of sleep.

Bid the ghost have sword in fist:
Some there are, for I avow   10
Such devilish things exist,
Who have planned his murder for they know
Of some most haughty deed or thought
That waits upon his future days,
And would through hatred of the bays[2]   15
Bring that to nought.

Though You[3] can fashion everything
From nothing every day, and teach
The morning stars to sing,

---

7. In a note on Irish faeries, Yeats explained that they "journey in whirling wind, the winds that were called the dance of the daughters of Herodias in the Middle Ages."
8. The incubus of Dame Alice Kyteler, who was condemned for witchcraft in 1324. Yeats described him as "an evil spirit much run after in Kilkenny at the start of the fourteenth century."
1. Michael Yeats, born in August 1921.
2. Probably the bay wreaths associated with success.
3. Christ.

You have lacked articulate speech   20
To tell Your simplest want, and known,
Wailing upon a woman's knee,
All of that worst ignominy
Of flesh and bone;

And when through all the town there ran   25
The servants of Your enemy,
A woman and a man,
Unless the Holy Writings lie,
Hurried through the smooth and rough
And through the fertile and waste,   30
Protecting, till the danger past,
With human love.[4]

[1922]   [1928]

Leda and the Swan[1]

A sudden blow: the great wings beating still
Above the staggering girl, her thighs caressed
By the dark webs, her nape caught in his bill,
He holds her helpless breast upon his breast.

How can those terrified vague fingers push   5
The feathered glory from her loosening thighs?
And how can body, laid in that white rush
But feel the strange heart beating where it lies?

A shudder in the loins engenders there
The broken wall, the burning roof and tower   10
And Agamemnon[2] dead.
                      Being so caught up,
So mastered by the brute blood of the air,
Did she put on his knowledge with his power
Before the indifferent beak could let her drop?

                    1923

[1924*]   [1928]

4. Mary and Joseph fled from Bethlehem to Egypt after the birth of Jesus, having been warned that King Herod would try to kill him. See Matthew 2.1–21.
1. In Greek mythology, Zeus, in the form of a swan, raped Leda, a mortal. From the union, Castor, Pollux, and Helen were born. Helen's abduction was later the cause of the Trojan War. For Yeats, this union between a god and a mortal was a violent annunciation that ushered in Greek civilization, just as the Annunciation to Mary ushered in the Christian era.
2. Leader of the Greek army that besieged Troy.

Among School Children

I

I walk through the long schoolroom questioning,
A kind old nun in a white hood replies;
The children learn to cipher and to sing,
To study reading-books and history,
To cut and sew, be neat in everything 5
In the best modern way—the children's eyes
In momentary wonder stare upon
A sixty year old smiling public man.[1]

II

I dream of a Ledæan[2] body, bent
Above a sinking fire, a tale that she 10
Told of a harsh reproof, or trivial event
That changed some childish day to tragedy—
Told, and it seemed that our two natures blent
Into a sphere from youthful sympathy,
Or else, to alter Plato's parable, 15
Into the yolk and white of the one shell.[3]

III

And thinking of that fit of grief or rage
I look upon one child or t'other there
And wonder if she stood so at that age—
For even daughters of the swan can share 20
Something of every paddler's heritage—
And had that colour upon cheek or hair
And thereupon my heart is driven wild:
She stands before me as a living child.

IV

Her present image floats in to the mind— 25
Did quattrocento[4] finger fashion it
Hollow of cheek as though it drank the wind
And took a mass of shadows for its meat?
And I though never of Ledæan kind
Had pretty plumage once—enough of that, 30
Better to smile on all that smile, and show
There is a comfortable kind of old scarecrow.

1. Yeats had visited a Montessori school in Waterford in 1926 in his capacity as a Free State senator enquiring into Irish education.
2. Yeats associated Maud Gonne with Leda's daughter, Helen of Troy (see note 1 to "Leda and the Swan," p. 96).
3. In Plato's *Symposium*, Aristophanes argues that man was once spherical and androgynous until divided by Zeus into man and woman, like the cutting of an egg, and that love is an attempt to regain that feeling of oneness that existed before the division took place.
4. An unspecified artist of the fifteenth century.

V

What youthful mother, a shape upon her lap
Honey of generation had betrayed,
And that must sleep, shriek, struggle to escape   35
As recollection or the drug decide,
Would think her son, did she but see that shape
With sixty or more winters on its head,
A compensation for the pang of his birth,
Or the uncertainty of his setting forth?   40

VI

Plato thought nature but a spume that plays
Upon a ghostly paradigm of things;
Solider Aristotle played the taws
Upon the bottom of a king of kings;[5]
World-famous golden-thighed Pythagoras   45
Fingered upon a fiddle stick or strings[6]
What a star sang and careless Muses heard:
Old clothes upon old sticks to scare a bird.

VII

Both nuns and mothers worship images,
But those the candles light are not as those   50
That animate a mother's reveries,
But keep a marble or a bronze repose.
And yet they too break hearts—O Presences
That passion, piety or affection knows,
And that all heavenly glory symbolise—   55
O self-born mockers of man's enterprise;

VIII

Labour is blossoming or dancing where
The body is not bruised to pleasure soul,
Nor beauty born out of its own despair,
Nor blear-eyed wisdom out of midnight oil.   60
O chestnut tree, great rooted blossomer,
Are you the leaf, the blossom or the bole?
O body swayed to music, O brightening glance,
How can we know the dancer from the dance?

[1927]   [1928]

---

5. The Greek philosopher Aristotle (384–322 B.C.E.), himself a pupil of Plato, later tutored Alexander
   the Great (356–323 B.C.E.). Taws were small strips of leather: here meaning, presumably, a whip.
6. Greek mathematician and philosopher (sixth century B.C.E.), credited with discovering the mathematical nature of musical intervals.

All Souls'[1] Night

An Epilogue to 'A Vision'[2]

Midnight has come and the great Christ Church[1] Bell,
And many a lesser bell, sound through the room;
And it is All Souls' Night,[3]
And two long glasses brimmed with muscatel
Bubble upon the table. A ghost may come;   5
For it is a ghost's right,
His element is so fine
Being sharpened by his death,
To drink from the wine-breath
While our gross palates drink from the whole wine.   10

I need some mind that, if the cannon sound
From every quarter of the world, can stay
Wound in mind's pondering,
As mummies in the mummy-cloth are wound;
Because I have a marvellous thing to say,   15
A certain marvellous thing
None but the living mock,
Though not for sober ear;
It may be all that hear
Should laugh and weep an hour upon the clock.   20

H—'s[4] the first I call. He loved strange thought
And knew that sweet extremity of pride
That's called platonic love,
And that to such a pitch of passion wrought
Nothing could bring him, when his lady died,   25
Anodyne for his love.
Words were but wasted breath;
One dear hope had he:
The inclemency
Of that or the next winter would be death.   30

Two thoughts were so mixed up I could not tell
Whether of her or God he thought the most,
But think that his mind's eye,
When upward turned, on one sole image fell;
And that a slight companionable ghost,   35
Wild with divinity,
Had so lit up the whole

1. Catholic feast-day (November 2) on which the dead still suffering in Purgatory are remembered and prayed for.
2. Yeats's philosophical and occult work *A Vision*, first published in 1925.
3. Christ Church College, Oxford. Yeats was living in Oxford when he wrote the poem.
4. William Horton (1864–1919), mystical painter. Yeats supplied his name in printings of the poem from 1933 on.

Immense miraculous house,
The Bible promised us,
It seemed a gold-fish swimming in a bowl.   40

On Florence Emery[5] I call the next,
Who finding the first wrinkles on a face
Admired and beautiful,
And knowing that the future would be vexed
With 'minished beauty, multiplied commonplace,   45
Preferred to teach a school,
Away from neighbour or friend
Among dark skins, and there
Permit foul years to wear
Hidden from eyesight to the unnoticed end.[6]   50

Before that end much had she ravelled out
From a discourse in figurative speech
By some learned Indian
On the soul's journey. How it is whirled about,
Wherever the orbit of the moon can reach,   55
Until it plunge into the sun;
And there, free and yet fast
Being both Chance and Choice,
Forget its broken toys
And sink into its own delight at last.   60

And I call up MacGregor[7] from the grave,
For in my first hard springtime we were friends,
Although of late estranged.
I thought him half a lunatic, half knave,
And told him so, but friendship never ends;   65
And what if mind seem changed,
And it seem changed with the mind,
When thoughts rise up unbid
On generous things that he did
And I grow half contented to be blind.   70

He had much industry at setting out,
Much boisterous courage, before loneliness
Had driven him crazed;
For meditations upon unknown thought
Make human intercourse grow less and less;   75
They are neither paid nor praised.
But he'd object to the host,
The glass because my glass;
A ghost-lover he was

5. Florence Farr Emery (1869–1917); a close friend of Yeats's from the mid-1890s, she acted in some of his plays, toured with him reciting his poems, and was a co-member with him of the Golden Dawn, an occult society.
6. Emery left England in 1912 to teach in Ceylon.
7. MacGregor Mathers (1854–1918), a fellow occultist. He and Yeats quarreled over Golden Dawn matters in 1900.

And may have grown more arrogant being a ghost. 80

But names are nothing. What matter who it be,
So that his elements have grown so fine
The fume of muscatel
Can give his sharpened palate ecstasy
No living man can drink from the whole wine. 85
I have mummy truths to tell
Whereat the living mock,
Though not for sober ear,
For maybe all that hear
Should laugh and weep an hour upon the clock. 90

Such thought—such thought have I that hold it tight
Till meditation master all its parts,
Nothing can stay my glance
Until that glance run in the world's despite
To where the damned have howled away their hearts, 95
And where the blessed dance;
Such thought, that in it bound
I need no other thing
Wound in mind's wandering,
As mummies in the mummy-cloth are wound. 100

[1921*]   [1928]

From *The Winding Stair and Other Poems* (1933)

In Memory of Eva Gore-Booth and Con Markiewicz

The light of evening, Lissadell,[1]
Great windows open to the south,
Two girls in silk kimonos, both
Beautiful, one a gazelle.
But a raving autumn shears   5
Blossom from the summer's wreath;
The older[2] is condemned to death,
Pardoned, drags out lonely years
Conspiring among the ignorant.
I know not what the younger dreams—   10
Some vague Utopia[3]—and she seems,
When withered old and skeleton-gaunt,
An image of such politics.
Many a time I think to seek
One or the other out and speak   15
Of that old Georgian mansion, mix
Pictures of the mind, recall
That table and the talk of youth,
Two girls in silk kimonos, both
Beautiful, one a gazelle.   20

Dear shadows,[4] now you know it all,
All the folly of a fight
With a common wrong or right.
The innocent and the beautiful
Have no enemy but time;   25
Arise and bid me strike a match
And strike another till time catch;
Should the conflagration climb,
Run till all the sages know.

1. The home of the Gore-Booths, overlooking Sligo Bay. Yeats had known the Gore-Booth sisters, Eva (1870–1926) and Constance (1868–1927), since 1893. Yeats stayed at Lissadell briefly in 1894, and he was drawn to the "gazelle-like beauty" Eva, who wrote poetry.
2. Con Markiewicz, initially sentenced to death for her part in the 1916 Easter Rising but later given amnesty and released in 1917. She was elected to the Irish Dáil (Parliament) shortly before her death.
3. Eva was active as a trade union organizer and campaigner for women's suffrage.
4. Both the sisters had recently died.

We the great gazebo built,   30
They convicted us of guilt;
Bid me strike a match and blow.

October 1927

[1929*]   [1933]

A Dialogue of Self and Soul

I

My Soul. I summon to the winding ancient stair;[1]
  Set all your mind upon the steep ascent,
  Upon the broken, crumbling battlement,
  Upon the breathless starlit air,
  Upon the star that marks the hidden pole;   5
  Fix every wandering thought upon
  That quarter where all thought is done:
  Who can distinguish darkness from the soul?

My Self. The consecrated blade upon my knees
  Is Sato's ancient blade,[2] still as it was,   10
  Still razor-keen, still like a looking-glass
  Unspotted by the centuries;
  That flowering, silken, old embroidery, torn
  From some court-lady's dress and round
  The wooden scabbard bound and wound,   15
  Can, tattered, still protect, faded adorn.

My Soul. Why should the imagination of a man
  Long past his prime remember things that are
  Emblematical of love and war?
  Think of ancestral night that can,   20
  If but imagination scorn the earth
  And intellect its wandering
  To this and that and t'other thing,
  Deliver from the crime of death and birth.

My Self. Montashigi,[3] third of his family, fashioned it   25
  Five hundred years ago, about it lie
  Flowers from I know not what embroidery—
  Heart's purple—and all these I set
  For emblems of the day against the tower
  Emblematical of the night,   30
  And claim as by a soldier's right
  A charter to commit the crime once more.

1. The winding stair of Yeats's tower at Thoor Ballylee.
2. A ceremonial sword given to Yeats in 1920 by Junzo Sato, a Japanese consul to the United States.
3. Sato's sword was made by Bishu Motoshigi, a Japanese artisan working in the late fourteenth century.

My Soul. Such fullness in that quarter overflows
And falls into the basin of the mind
That man is stricken deaf and dumb and blind,   35
For intellect no longer knows
Is from the *Ought,* or *Knower* from the *Known*—
That is to say, ascends to Heaven;
Only the dead can be forgiven;
But when I think of that my tongue's a stone.   40

II

My Self. A living man is blind and drinks his drop.
What matter if the ditches are impure?
What matter if I live it all once more?
Endure that toil of growing up;
The ignominy of boyhood; the distress   45
Of boyhood changing into man;
The unfinished man and his pain
Brought face to face with his own clumsiness;

The finished man among his enemies?—
How in the name of Heaven can he escape   50
That defiling and disfigured shape
The mirror of malicious eyes
Casts upon his eyes until at last
He thinks that shape must be his shape?
And what's the good of an escape   55
If honour find him in the wintry blast?

I am content to live it all again
And yet again, if it be life to pitch
Into the frog-spawn of a blind man's ditch,
A blind man battering blind men;   60
Or into that most fecund ditch of all,
The folly that man does
Or must suffer, if he woos
A proud woman not kindred of his soul.

I am content to follow to its source   65
Every event in action or in thought;
Measure the lot; forgive myself the lot!
When such as I cast out remorse
So great a sweetness flows into the breast
We must laugh and we must sing,   70
We are blest by everything,
Everything we look upon is blest.

[1929]   [1933]

Blood and the Moon

I

Blessed be this place,[1]
More blessed still this tower;
A bloody, arrogant power
Rose out of the race
Uttering, mastering it,   5
Rose like these walls from these
Storm-beaten cottages—
In mockery I have set
A powerful emblem up,
And sing it rhyme upon rhyme   10
In mockery of a time
Half dead at the top.

II

Alexandria's was a beacon tower, and Babylon's
An image of the moving heavens, a log-book of the sun's journey
    and the moon's;[2]
And Shelley[3] had his towers, thought's crowned powers he called
    them once.   15

I declare this tower is my symbol; I declare
This winding, gyring, spiring treadmill of a stair is my ancestral
    stair;
That Goldsmith and the Dean, Berkeley and Burke[4] have travelled
    there.

Swift beating on his breast in sibylline frenzy blind
Because the heart in his blood-sodden breast had dragged him
    down into mankind,   20
Goldsmith deliberately sipping at the honey-pot of his mind,

And haughtier-headed Burke that proved the State a tree,
That this unconquerable labyrinth of the birds, century after century,
Cast but dead leaves to mathematical equality;

---

1. Yeats's property at Thoor Ballylee.
2. The Pharos, a lighthouse built at Alexandria by King Ptolemy II in the second century B.C.E., was one of the Seven Wonders of the World. Babylon, the chief city of ancient Mesopotamia, was renowned as a center for the study of astrology and astronomy.
3. The English Romantic poet Percy Bysshe Shelley refers to "thought's crowned powers" in *Prometheus Unbound* (1820), IV, l. 103.
4. Yeats's pantheon of eighteenth-century Irish creators: Oliver Goldsmith (1728–1774), writer; Jonathan Swift (1667–1745), writer and Dean of St. Patrick's Cathedral, Dublin; George Berkeley (1685–1753), philosopher; and Edmund Burke (1729–1797), philosopher and politician.

And God-appointed Berkeley that proved all things a dream,   25
That this pragmatical, preposterous pig of a world, its farrow that
    so solid seem,
Must vanish on the instant if the mind but change its theme;

Saeva Indignatio[5] and the labourer's hire,
The strength that gives our blood and state magnanimity of its
    own desire;
Everything that is not God consumed with intellectual fire.   30

III

The purity of the unclouded moon
Has flung its arrowy shaft upon the floor.
Seven centuries have passed and it is pure;
The blood of innocence has left no stain.
There, on blood-saturated ground, have stood   35
Soldier, assassin, executioner,
Whether for daily pittance or in blind fear
Or out of abstract hatred, and shed blood,
But could not cast a single jet thereon.
Odour of blood on the ancestral stair!   40
And we that have shed none must gather there
And clamour in drunken frenzy for the moon.

IV

Upon the dusty, glittering windows cling,
And seem to cling upon the moonlit skies,
Tortoiseshell butterflies, peacock butterflies: 45
A couple of night-moths are on the wing.
Is every modern nation like the tower,
Half dead at the top? No matter what I said,
For wisdom is the property of the dead,
A something incompatible with life; and power,   50
Like everything that has the stain of blood,
A property of the living; but no stain
Can come upon the visage of the moon
When it has looked in glory from a cloud.

[1928]   [1933]

Coole Park, 1929

I meditate upon a swallow's flight,
Upon an aged woman[1] and her house,
A sycamore and lime tree lost in night
Although that western cloud is luminous,

5. "Savage indignation"; a phrase from the (Latin) epitaph Swift wrote for his own tombstone.
1. Lady Gregory of Coole Park, who died in May 1932.

Great works constructed there in nature's spite   5
For scholars and for poets after us,
Thoughts long knitted into a single thought,
A dance-like glory that those walls begot.

There Hyde[2] before he had beaten into prose
That noble blade the Muses buckled on,   10
There one[3] that ruffled in a manly pose
For all his timid heart, there that slow man,
That meditative man, John Synge,[4] and those
Impetuous men, Shaw Taylor and Hugh Lane,[5]
Found pride established in humility,   15
A scene well set and excellent company.

They came like swallows and like swallows went,
And yet a woman's powerful character
Could keep a swallow to its first intent;
And half a dozen in formation there,   20
That seemed to whirl upon a compass-point,
Found certainty upon the dreaming air,
The intellectual sweetness of those lines
That cut through time or cross it withershins.

Here, traveller, scholar, poet, take your stand   25
When all those rooms and passages are gone,
When nettles wave upon a shapeless mound
And saplings root among the broken stone,
And dedicate—eyes bent upon the ground,
Back turned upon the brightness of the sun   30
And all the sensuality of the shade—
A moment's memory to that laurelled head.[6]

[1931*]   [1933]

The Choice

The intellect of man is forced to choose
Perfection of the life, or of the work,
And if it take the second must refuse
A heavenly mansion, raging in the dark.

---

2. Douglas Hyde (1860–1949), Irish translator, folklorist, and poet, founder of the Gaelic League (which sought to promote the Irish language), and first president of Ireland (1938–45). In Yeats's view, Hyde had subordinated his creative skills to his work for the Gaelic League.
3. Yeats himself, an insecure young poet at the time of his first visit to Coole.
4. Playwright (d. 1909) and cofounder of the Abbey Theatre with Yeats and Lady Gregory.
5. John Shawe-Taylor (1866–1911), Lady Gregory's nephew, was the force behind a conference in 1903 that had settled the most vexed aspects of the Irish land question. Hugh Lane (d. 1915), also a nephew of Lady Gregory, was the preeminent Irish art dealer of his time and a decisive patron of Irish art, most notably in pressing for the development of the Dublin Municipal Gallery.
6. As Yeats anticipated, Coole was demolished after Lady Gregory's death.

When all that story's finished, what's the news?   5
In luck or out the toil has left its mark:
That old perplexity an empty purse,
Or the day's vanity, the night's remorse.

[1932*]   [1933]

Byzantium

The unpurged images of day recede;
The Emperor's drunken soldiery are abed;
Night resonance recedes, night-walkers' song
After great cathedral gong;
A starlit or a moonlit dome disdains   5
All that man is,
All mere complexities,
The fury and the mire of human veins.

Before me floats an image, man or shade,
Shade more than man, more image than a shade;   10
For Hades' bobbin[1] bound in mummy-cloth
May unwind the winding path;
A mouth that has no moisture and no breath
Breathless mouths may summon;
I hail the superhuman;   15
I call it death-in-life and life-in-death.

Miracle, bird or golden handiwork,
More miracle than bird or handiwork,
Planted on the starlit golden bough,
Can like the cocks of Hades crow,   20
Or, by the moon embittered, scorn aloud
In glory of changeless metal
Common bird or petal
And all complexities of mire or blood.

At midnight on the Emperor's pavement flit   25
Flames that no faggot feeds, nor steel has lit,
Nor storm disturbs, flames begotten of flame,
Where blood-begotten spirits come
And all complexities of fury leave,
Dying into a dance,   30
An agony of trance,
An agony of flame that cannot singe a sleeve.

---

1. Hades was god of the underworld—the realm of the dead—in Greek mythology; the underworld itself is usually referred to as Hades. In Plato's *Republic* one of the speakers refers to a "spindle" that holds together the universe and transmits its motion: the "bobbin" here perhaps refers to this idea.

Astraddle on the dolphin's mire and blood,[2]
Spirit after spirit! The smithies break the flood,
The golden smithies of the Emperor!   35
Marbles of the dancing floor
Break bitter furies of complexity,
Those images that yet
Fresh images beget,
That dolphin-torn, that gong-tormented sea.   40

1930

[1932]   [1933]

Vacillation

I

Between extremities
Man runs his course;
A brand, or flaming breath,
Comes to destroy
All those antinomies[1]   5
Of day and night;
The body calls it death,
The heart remorse.
But if these be right
What is joy?   10

II

A tree there is that from its topmost bough
Is half all glittering flame and half all green
Abounding foliage moistened with the dew;
And half is half and yet is all the scene;
And half and half consume what they renew,   15
And he that Attis'[2] image hangs between
That staring fury and the blind lush leaf
May know not what he knows, but knows not grief.

III

Get all the gold and silver that you can,
Satisfy ambition, or animate   20
The trivial days and ram them with the sun,
And yet upon these maxims meditate:

2. In ancient mythology, dolphins were thought to carry the souls of the dead to the Isles of the Blessed.
1. Contradictions.
2. A vegetation god in Greek mythology. The earth-goddess Cybele caused him to castrate himself, so as to prevent him from marrying someone else. After his death he was transformed into a pine tree.

All women dote upon an idle man
Although their children need a rich estate;
No man has ever lived that had enough   25
Of children's gratitude or woman's love.

No longer in Lethean[3] foliage caught
Begin the preparation for your death
And from the fortieth winter by that thought
Test every work of intellect or faith   30
And everything that your own hands have wrought,
And call those works extravagance of breath
That are not suited for such men as come
Proud, open-eyed and laughing to the tomb.

                        IV

My fiftieth year had come and gone,   35
I sat, a solitary man,
In a crowded London shop,
An open book and empty cup
On the marble table-top.

While on the shop and street I gazed   40
My body of a sudden blazed;
And twenty minutes more or less
It seemed, so great my happiness,
That I was blessèd and could bless.

                        V

Although the summer sunlight gild   45
Cloudy leafage of the sky,
Or wintry moonlight sink the field
In storm-scattered intricacy,
I cannot look thereon,
Responsibility so weighs me down.   50

Things said or done long years ago,
Or things I did not do or say
But thought that I might say or do,
Weigh me down, and not a day
But something is recalled,   55
My conscience or my vanity appalled.

                        VI

A rivery field spread out below,
An odour of the new-mown hay
In his nostrils, the great lord of Chou[4]

---

3. The waters of Lethe, a river in Hades, caused forgetfulness.
4. Probably the Chinese author and statesman Chou-Kung (d. 1105 B.C.E.).

Cried, casting off the mountain snow,   60
'Let all things pass away.'

Wheels by milk-white asses drawn
Where Babylon or Nineveh[5]
Rose; some conqueror drew rein
And cried to battle-weary men,   65
'Let all things pass away.'

From man's blood-sodden heart are sprung
Those branches of the night and day
Where the gaudy moon is hung.
What's the meaning of all song?   70
'Let all things pass away.'

VII

The Soul. Seek out reality, leave things that seem.
The Heart. What, be a singer born and lack a theme?
The Soul. Isaiah's coal,[6] what more can man desire?
The Heart. Struck dumb in the simplicity of fire!   75
The Soul. Look on that fire, salvation walks within.
The Heart. What theme had Homer but original sin?

VIII

Must we part, Von Hügel,[7] though much alike, for we
Accept the miracles of the saints and honour sanctity?
The body of Saint Teresa[8] lies undecayed in tomb,   80
Bathed in miraculous oil, sweet odours from it come,
Healing from its lettered slab. Those self-same hands[9] perchance
Eternalised the body of a modern saint that once
Had scooped out Pharaoh's mummy.[1] I—though heart might
      find relief
Did I become a Christian man and choose for my belief   85
What seems most welcome in the tomb—play a predestined part.
Homer is my example and his unchristened heart.
The lion and the honeycomb,[2] what has Scripture said?
So get you gone, Von Hügel, though with blessings on your head.

1932

[1932*]   [1933]

5. See note 2 to "Blood and the Moon" (p. 105); Nineveh was the capital of the Assyrian Empire.
6. In Isaiah 6.6–7, the prophet is purified when an angel touches a fiery coal to his lips.
7. Friedrich von Hügel (1852–1925), Catholic philosopher who stressed the mystical elements in religion.
8. The embalmed body of St. Teresa (1515–1582), a Spanish Carmelite nun, was believed to have remained miraculously undecayed.
9. Of the embalmers.
1. The Egyptian pharaohs were embalmed and mummified.
2. In Judges 14.5–14, Samson kills a lion, then later finds a honeycomb in the carcass. From this he makes a riddle: "Out of the eater came something to eat. / Out of the strong came something sweet."

From Words for Music Perhaps

VI

CRAZY JANE TALKS WITH THE BISHOP

I met the Bishop on the road
And much said he and I.
'Those breasts are flat and fallen now,
Those veins must soon be dry;
Live in a heavenly mansion,   5
Not in some foul sty.'

'Fair and foul are near of kin,
And fair needs foul,' I cried.
'My friends are gone, but that's a truth
Nor grave nor bed denied,   10
Learned in bodily lowliness
And in the heart's pride.

'A woman can be proud and stiff
When on love intent;
But Love has pitched his mansion in   15
The place of excrement;
For nothing can be sole or whole
That has not been rent.'

[1933]

From A Woman Young and Old

I

FATHER AND CHILD[1]

She hears me strike the board and say
That she is under ban
Of all good men and women,
Being mentioned with a man
That has the worst of all bad names;   5
And thereupon replies
That his hair is beautiful,
Cold as the March wind his eyes.

[1929]   [1933]

---

1. Yeats's daughter, Anne, was about ten years old when the poem was first published, and its last lines were inspired by her words of praise for a boy she knew.

From *A Full Moon in March*
(1935)

A Prayer for Old Age

God guard me from those thoughts men think
In the mind alone;
He that sings a lasting song
Thinks in a marrow-bone;

From all that makes a wise old man   5
That can be praised of all;
O what am I that I should not seem
For the song's sake a fool?

I pray—for fashion's word is out
And prayer comes round again—   10
That I may seem, though I die old,
A foolish, passionate man.

[1934*]   [1935]

From Supernatural Songs

9. THE FOUR AGES OF MAN

He with body waged a fight,
But body won; it walks upright.

Then he struggled with the heart;
Innocence and peace depart.

Then he struggled with the mind;   5
His proud heart he left behind.

Now his wars on God begin;
At stroke of midnight God shall win.

[1934]   [1935]

113

From *New Poems* (1938)

The Gyres[1]

The gyres! the gyres! Old Rocky Face[2] look forth;
Things thought too long can be no longer thought
For beauty dies of beauty, worth of worth,
And ancient lineaments are blotted out.
Irrational streams of blood[3] are staining earth;　　　　　5
Empedocles[4] has thrown all things about;
Hector[5] is dead and there's a light in Troy;
We that look on but laugh in tragic joy.

What matter though numb nightmare ride on top
And blood and mire the sensitive body stain?　　　　　10
What matter? Heave no sigh, let no tear drop,
A greater, a more gracious time has gone;
For painted forms or boxes of make-up
In ancient tombs I sighed, but not again;
What matter? Out of Cavern comes a voice　　　　　15
And all it knows is that one word "Rejoice."

Conduct and work grow coarse, and coarse the soul,
What matter! Those that Rocky Face holds dear,
Lovers of horses and of women, shall
From marble of a broken sepulchre　　　　　20
Or dark betwixt the polecat and the owl,
Or any rich, dark nothing disinter
The workman, noble and saint, and all things run
On that unfashionable gyre again.

[1938]

---

1. See note 1 to "The Second Coming" (p. 76).
2. Probably not a specific allusion, but implying an ancient seer.
3. World War II seemed inevitable as Yeats was writing.
4. Greek philosopher (c. 490–430 B.C.E.) who propounded a theory of four basic elements of matter: earth, air, fire, and water.
5. Oldest son of King Priam of Troy, killed by Achilles during the Trojan War.

Lapis Lazuli[1]

(For Harry Clifton)

I have heard that hysterical women say
They are sick of the palette and fiddle-bow,
Of poets that are always gay,
For everybody knows or else should know
That if nothing drastic is done   5
Aeroplane and Zeppelin[2] will come out,
Pitch like King Billy bomb-balls in
Until the town lie beaten flat.[3]

All perform their tragic play,
There struts Hamlet, there is Lear,   10
That's Ophelia, that Cordelia;
Yet they, should the last scene be there
The great stage curtain about to drop,
If worthy their prominent part in the play,
Do not break up their lines to weep.   15
They know that Hamlet and Lear are gay;
Gaiety transfiguring all that dread.
All men have aimed at, found and lost;
Black out; Heaven blazing into the head:
Tragedy wrought to its uttermost.   20
Though Hamlet rambles and Lear rages,
And all the drop scenes drop at once
Upon a hundred thousand stages,
It cannot grow by an inch or an ounce.

On their own feet they came, or on shipboard,   25
Camel-back, horse-back, ass-back, mule-back,
Old civilisations put to the sword.
Then they and their wisdom went to rack:
No handiwork of Calimachus[4]
Who handled marble as if it were bronze,   30
Made draperies that seemed to rise
When sea-wind swept the corner, stands;
His long lamp chimney shaped like the stem
Of a slender palm, stood but a day;
All things fall and are built again   35
And those that build them again are gay.

---

1. Yeats had been given a carving made of lapis lazuli for his seventieth birthday by the young
   English writer Harry Clifton (1908–1978).
2. Zeppelin airships bombed London during World War I, and they are here emblematic of the
   rising political tension in Europe.
3. At the battle of the Boyne (1690), William of Orange defeated the forces of James II, thereby
   ensuring Protestant supremacy in England and Ireland. Yeats is presumably also alluding to the
   imperialist aims of Kaiser Wilhelm (1859–1941), emperor of Germany during World War I.
4. Greek sculptor of the fifth century B.C.E.

Two Chinamen, behind them a third,
Are carved in Lapis Lazuli,
Over them flies a long-legged bird
A symbol of longevity;   40
The third, doubtless a serving-man
Carries a musical instrument.

Every discolouration of the stone,
Every accidental crack or dent
Seems a water-course or an avalanche,   45
Or lofty slope where it still snows
Though doubtless plum or cherry-branch
Sweetens the little half-way house
Those Chinamen climb towards, and I
Delight to imagine them seated there;   50
There, on the mountain and the sky,
On all the tragic scene they stare;
One asks for mournful melodies;
Accomplished fingers begin to play;
Their eyes mid many wrinkles, their eyes,   55
Their ancient, glittering eyes, are gay.

[1938]   [1938]

Imitated from the Japanese[1]

A most astonishing thing
Seventy years have I lived;

(Hurrah for the flowers of Spring
For Spring is here again.)

Seventy years have I lived   5
No ragged beggar man,
Seventy years have I lived,
Seventy years man and boy,
And never have I danced for joy.

[1938]

What Then?

His chosen comrades thought at school
He must grow a famous man;
He thought the same and lived by rule,

1. Yeats commented to a friend that this poem was inspired by a Japanese haiku poem in praise of spring.

All his twenties crammed with toil;
"*What then?*" *sang Plato's ghost,*[1] "*what then?*"   5

Everything he wrote was read,
After certain years he won
Sufficient money for his need,
Friends that have been friends indeed;
"*What then?*" *sang Plato's ghost, "what then?*"   10

All his happier dreams came true—
A small old house, wife, daughter, son,
Grounds where plum and cabbage grew,
Poets and Wits about him drew;
"*What then?*" *sang Plato's ghost, "what then?*"   15

"The work is done," grown old he thought,
"According to my boyish plan;
Let the fools rage, I swerved in nought,
Something to perfection brought;"
But louder sang that ghost "What then?"   20

[1937]   [1938]

Beautiful Lofty Things

Beautiful lofty things; O'Leary's noble head;[1]
My father[2] upon the Abbey stage, before him a raging crowd.
"This Land of Saints," and then as the applause died out,
"Of plaster Saints;" his beautiful mischievous head thrown back.
Standish O'Grady[3] supporting himself between the tables   5
Speaking to a drunken audience high nonsensical words;
Augusta Gregory seated at her great ormolu table
Her eightieth winter approaching; "Yesterday he threatened my life,
I told him that nightly from six to seven I sat at this table
The blinds drawn up;"[4] Maud Gonne at Howth station waiting   10
     a train,
Pallas Athene[5] in that straight back and arrogant head:
All the Olympians;[6] a thing never known again.

[1938]

1. The Greek philosopher Plato (c. 428–c. 348 B.C.E.) was a germinal figure for Yeats because of both his advocacy of abstract idealism and the dialogic form of his works.
1. John O'Leary (1830–1907), Irish Nationalist, who greatly influenced Yeats in his youth.
2. John Butler Yeats (1839–1922) spoke in defense of playwright John M. Synge at an explosively contentious 1907 debate at the Abbey Theatre in the wake of the protests over Synge's *The Playboy of the Western World*.
3. Irish historian and novelist (1866–1928), often regarded as the figure who spurred the Irish Literary Revival though his *History of Ireland* (1878, 1880), which made much Irish heroic mythology available for a wider audience.
4. Lady Gregory was threatened by a tenant in 1922 and responded defiantly.
5. Greek goddess of wisdom: a virgin goddess who was born, in full armor, from the head of Zeus.
6. The gods in Greek mythology, who dwelt on Mount Olympus.

Come Gather Round Me Parnellites[1]

Come gather round me Parnellites
And praise our chosen man,
Stand upright on your legs awhile,
Stand upright while you can,
For soon we lie where he is laid   5
And he is underground;
Come fill up all those glasses
And pass the bottle round.

And here's a cogent reason
And I have many more,   10
He fought the might of England
And saved the Irish poor,
Whatever good a farmer's got
He brought it all to pass;[2]
And here's another reason,   15
That Parnell loved a lass.

And here's a final reason,
He was of such a kind
Every man that sings a song
Keeps Parnell in his mind   20
For Parnell was a proud man,
No prouder trod the ground,
And a proud man's a lovely man
So pass the bottle round.

The Bishops and the Party[3]   25
That tragic story made,
A husband that had sold his wife
And after that betrayed;[4]
But stories that live longest
Are sung above the glass,   30
And Parnell loved his country
And Parnell loved his lass.

[1937]   [1938]

1. Charles Stewart Parnell (1846–1891) was the leader of the Irish Parliamentary Party from 1880; his skill in uniting the Irish constituency gave him the balance of power in the British Parliament. He was stripped of his leadership in 1890 after his affair with Kitty O'Shea, wife of another Irish politician, was made public.
2. Parnell's leadership of the Irish Land League, which organized tenants in collective action against landlords and advocated boycotting campaigns, had brought about significant reform of tenants' rights, and paved the way for systematic land reform in Ireland.
3. Parnell's affair with Kitty O'Shea was condemned from Irish pulpits, as well as by the majority of his own party.
4. William O'Shea had known about Parnell's affair with his wife for several years but kept silent until 1889, preferring to tolerate the situation with the aim of furthering his political career and later hoping that Parnell would pay him to allow his wife an uncontested divorce.

The Great Day

Hurrah for revolution and more cannon shot;
A beggar upon horseback lashes a beggar upon foot;
Hurrah for revolution and cannon come again,
The beggars have changed places but the lash goes on.

[1938]   [1938]

Parnell[1]

Parnell came down the road, he said to a cheering man;
"Ireland shall get her freedom and you still break stone."

[1938]   [1938]

The Spur

You think it horrible that lust and rage
Should dance attendance upon my old age;
They were not such a plague when I was young;
What else have I to spur me into song?

[1938]   [1938]

The Municipal Gallery Re-visited[1]

I

Around me the images[2] of thirty years;
An ambush; pilgrims at the water-side;
Casement[3] upon trial, half hidden by the bars,
Guarded; Griffith[4] staring in hysterical pride;
Kevin O'Higgins'[5] countenance that wears   5
A gentle questioning look that cannot hide

1. See note 1 to "Come Gather Round Me Parnellites" (p. 118).
1. The Dublin Municipal Gallery of Modern Art.
2. The paintings on display in the gallery. The poem describes or responds to a number of actual paintings in the gallery.
3. Roger Casement (1864–1916) joined the Irish Volunteers in 1913 and went to Germany in 1914 to seek military support for Ireland. He was arrested soon after landing in Ireland from a German U-boat in 1916, tried for high treason, and hanged.
4. Arthur Griffith (1872–1922), Irish newspaper editor and leader of the Sinn Fein movement. Briefly head of the Free State government just before his death.
5. Minister of Justice in the Free State government, assassinated in 1927. Yeats regarded him as the "finest intellect in Irish public life."

A soul incapable of remorse or rest;
A revolutionary soldier kneeling to be blessed.

II

An Abbot or Archbishop with an upraised hand
Blessing the Tricolour.[6] "This is not" I say   10
"The dead Ireland of my youth, but an Ireland
The poets have imagined, terrible and gay."
Before a woman's portrait suddenly I stand;
Beautiful and gentle in her Venetian way.
I met her all but fifty years ago   15
For twenty minutes in some studio.

III

Heart smitten with emotion I sink down
My heart recovering with covered eyes;
Wherever I had looked I had looked upon
My permanent or impermanent images;   20
Augusta Gregory's son;[7] her sister's son,
Hugh Lane,[8] "onlie begetter" of all these;
Hazel Lavery living and dying,[9] that tale
As though some ballad singer had sung it all.

IV

Mancini's portrait of Augusta Gregory,[1]   25
"Greatest since Rembrandt," according to John Synge;
A great ebullient portrait certainly;
But where is the brush that could show anything
Of all that pride and that humility,
And I am in despair that time may bring   30
Approved patterns of women or of men
But not that selfsame excellence again.

V

My mediaeval knees lack health until they bend,
But in that woman, in that household[2] where
Honour had lived so long, all lacking found.   35
Childless I thought "my children may find here

6. The national flag of Ireland.
7. Robert Gregory (1881–1918).
8. Lady Gregory's nephew and an eminent art dealer (d. 1915). Lane was the "onlie begetter" (a
   phrase from Shakespeare's dedication of his *Sonnets* to his patron) because of his many gifts to
   the Dublin Municipal Gallery.
9. Wife of the Irish painter Sir John Lavery (1856–1941). She died in 1935, and his paintings of her
   in the gallery include the "dying" portrait *It is finished — The Unfinished Harmony*.
1. Lady Gregory's portrait was painted in 1908 by the Italian artist Antonio Mancini (1852–1930).
2. Lady Gregory's home at Coole Park.

Deep-rooted things," but never foresaw its end,[3]
And now that end has come I have not wept;
No fox can foul the lair the badger swept.

VI

(An image out of Spenser[4] and the common tongue)   40
John Synge, I and Augusta Gregory thought
All that we did, all that we said or sang
Must come from contact with the soil, from that
Contact everything Antaeus-like grew strong.[5]
We three alone in modern times had brought   45
Everything down to that sole test again,
Dream of the noble and the beggarman.

VII

And here's John Synge himself,[6] that rooted man
"Forgetting human words," a grave deep face.
You that would judge me do not judge alone   50
This book or that, come to this hallowed place
Where my friends' portraits hang and look thereon;
Ireland's history in their lineaments trace;
Think where man's glory most begins and ends
And say my glory was I had such friends.   55

[1937*]   [1938]

---

3. Coole had been sold to the Forestry Commission in 1927 and was now vacant; it would be demolished in 1942.
4. Yeats here echoes lines from "The Ruins of Time" by Edmund Spenser (c. 1552–1599).
5. Antaeus, a giant and son of Earth and Poseidon in Greek mythology, grew stronger whenever he touched the earth.
6. A portrait of Synge in the gallery, by Yeats's father, John Butler Yeats.

From *Last Poems* (1939)

Under Ben Bulben[1]

I

Swear by what the Sages spoke
Round the Mareotic Lake
That the Witch of Atlas knew,[2]
Spoke and set the cocks a-crow.

Swear by those horsemen, by those women,   5
Complexion and form prove superhuman,
That pale, long-visaged company
That airs an immortality
Completeness of their passions won;
Now they ride the wintry dawn   10
Where Ben Bulben sets the scene.

Here's the gist of what they mean.

II

Many times man lives and dies
Between his two eternities,
That of race and that of soul,   15
And ancient Ireland knew it all.
Whether man die in his bed
Or the rifle knocks him dead,
A brief parting from those dear
Is the worst man has to fear.   20
Though grave-diggers' toil is long,
Sharp their spades, their muscle strong,
They but thrust their buried men
Back in the human mind again.

---

1. A mountain north of Sligo.
2. The region around Lake Mareotis, south of Alexandria, was a center for the rise of monasticism in the fourth century. "The Witch of Atlas" is a poem by Percy Bysshe Shelley (1792–1822).

III

You that Mitchel's prayer have heard   25
"Send war in our time, O Lord!"[3]
Know that when all words are said
And a man is fighting mad,
Something drops from eyes long blind
He completes his partial mind,   30
For an instant stands at ease,
Laughs aloud, his heart at peace,
Even the wisest man grows tense
With some sort of violence
Before he can accomplish fate   35
Know his work or choose his mate.

IV

Poet and sculptor do the work
Nor let the modish painter shirk
What his great forefathers did,
Bring the soul of man to God,   40
Make him fill the cradles right.

Measurement began our might:
Forms a stark Egyptian thought,
Forms that gentler Phidias[4] wrought.

Michaelangelo left a proof   45
On the Sistine Chapel roof,[5]
Where but half-awakened Adam
Can disturb globe-trotting Madam
Till her bowels are in heat
Proof that there's a purpose set   50
Before the secret-working mind:
Profane perfection of mankind.

Quattro-cento[6] put in paint,
On backgrounds for a God or Saint,
Gardens where a soul's at ease;   55
The soul's perfection is from peace;[7]   55a
Where everything that meets the eye
Flowers and grass and cloudless sky

---

3. John Mitchel (1815–1875), Irish Nationalist, included this prayer in his *Jail Journal* (1854), since times of war and difficulty for England were traditionally thought to provide opportunity for Irish Nationalists.
4. Greek sculptor (c. 490–c. 423 B.C.E.) who made important statues for Athens.
5. Italian artist Michelangelo Buonarroti (1475–1564) painted the ceiling of the Sistine Chapel in Rome.
6. An unspecified artist of the fifteenth century.
7. See Bibliographical Appendix, p. 506.

Resemble forms that are, or seem
When sleepers wake and yet still dream,
And when it's vanished still declare, 60
With only bed and bedstead there,
That Heavens had opened.

                    Gyres run on;
When that greater dream had gone
Calvert and Wilson, Blake and Claude[8]
Prepared a rest for the people of God, 65
Palmer's phrase,[9] but after that
Confusion fell upon our thought.

V

Irish poets learn your trade,
Sing whatever is well made,
Scorn the sort now growing up 70
All out of shape from toe to top,
Their unremembering hearts and heads
Base-born products of base beds.
Sing the peasantry, and then
Hard-riding country gentlemen, 75
The holiness of monks, and after
Porter-drinkers' randy laughter;
Sing the lords and ladies gay
That were beaten into the clay
Through seven heroic centuries; 80
Cast your mind on other days
That we in coming days may be
Still the indomitable Irishry.

VI

Under bare Ben Bulben's head
In Drumcliff churchyard Yeats is laid,[1] 85
An ancestor was rector there[2]
Long years ago; a church stands near,
By the road an ancient Cross.
No marble, no conventional phrase,
On limestone quarried near the spot 90
By his command these words are cut:

8. Edward Calvert (1799–1883), English artist known for his visionary themes; Richard Wilson (1714–1782), landscape artist; William Blake (1757–1827), English mystical poet and artist; Claude Lorrain (1600–1682), French artist.
9. English visionary artist Samuel Palmer (1805–1881) once described Blake's engravings as giving a glimpse of "that rest which remaineth to the people of God."
1. Drumcliff churchyard in Sligo is overlooked by Ben Bulben. Yeats, who knew he was dying, wanted to be buried there, surrounded by the landscape he grew up in.
2. Yeats's great-grandfather, John Yeats (d. 1846), was rector of Drumcliff church.

Cast a cold eye
On life, on death.
Horseman, pass by![3]

[1939]

The Black Tower

Say that the men of the old black tower
Though they but feed as the goatherd feeds
Their money spent, their wine gone sour,
Lack nothing that a soldier needs,
That all are oath-bound men   5
Those banners come not in.

There in the tomb stand the dead upright
But winds come up from the shore
They shake when the winds roar
Old bones upon the mountain shake.   10

Those banners come to bribe or threaten
Or whisper that a man's a fool
Who when his own right king's forgotten
Cares what king sets up his rule.
If he died long ago   15
Why do you dread us so?

There in the tomb drops the faint moonlight
But wind comes up from the shore
They shake when the winds roar
Old bones upon the mountain shake.   20

The tower's old cook that must climb and clamber
Catching small birds in the dew of the morn
When we hale men lie stretched in slumber
Swears that he hears the king's great horn
But he's a lying hound   25
Stand we on guard oath-bound.

There in the tomb the dark grows blacker
But wind comes up from the shore
They shake when the winds roar
Old bones upon the mountain shake.   30

[1939]

3. Yeats died and was buried in France in 1939 but was reinterred at Drumcliff in 1948, with his tombstone bearing this epitaph.

Long-legged Fly

That civilisation may not sink
Its great battle lost,
Quiet the dog, tether the pony
To a distant post.
Our master Caesar is in the tent   5
Where the maps are spread,
His eyes fixed upon nothing,
A hand under his head.

Like a long-legged fly upon the stream
His mind moves upon silence.   10

That the topless towers[1] be burnt
And men recall that face,[2]
Move most gently if move you must
In this lonely place.
She thinks, part woman, three parts a child,   15
That nobody looks; her feet
Practice a tinker shuffle
Picked up on the street.

Like a long-legged fly upon the stream
Her mind moves upon silence.   20

That girls at puberty may find
The first Adam in their thought,
Shut the door of the Pope's chapel,
Keep those children out.
There on that scaffolding reclines   25
Michael Angelo.
With no more sound than the mice make
His hand moves to and fro.

Like a long-legged fly upon the stream
His mind moves upon silence.   30

[1939]

High Talk

Processions that lack high stilts have nothing that catches the eye.
What if my great-granddad had a pair that were twenty foot high,
And mine were but fifteen foot, no modern stalks upon higher,
Some rogue of the world stole them to patch up a fence or a fire.

1. Of Troy.
2. Helen of Troy.

Because piebald ponies, led bears, caged lions, make but poor shows,   5
Because children demand Daddy-long-legs upon his timber toes,
Because women in the upper stories demand a face at the pane
That patching old heels they may shriek, I take to chisel and plane.

Malachi Stilt-Jack am I, whatever I learned has run wild,
From collar to collar, from stilt to stilt, from father to child.   10

All metaphor, Malachi, stilts and all. A barnacle goose
Far up in the stretches of night; night splits and the dawn breaks
      loose;
I, through the terrible novelty of light, stalk on, stalk on;
Those great sea-horses bare their teeth and laugh at the dawn.

                                                          [1938]

Man and the Echo

MAN

In a cleft that's christened Alt[1]
Under broken stone I halt
At the bottom of a pit
That broad noon has never lit,
And shout a secret to the stone.   5
All that I have said and done,
Now that I am old and ill,
Turns into a question till
I lie awake night after night
And never get the answers right.   10
Did that play of mine[2] send out
Certain men the English shot?
Did words of mine put too great strain
On that woman's reeling brain?[3]
Could my spoken words have checked   15
That whereby a house lay wrecked?[4]
And all seems evil until I
Sleepless would lie down and die.

ECHO

Lie down and die.

1. Probably a deep rocky chasm on the side of Knocknarea in Sligo.
2. *Cathleen ni Houlihan* (see p. 133), the nationalist play Yeats wrote with Lady Gregory and first produced with Maud Gonne in the title role in 1902.
3. Margot Ruddock (1907–1951), a young poet with whom Yeats had a brief affair in the 1930s, and who subsequently suffered a breakdown.
4. Probably Coole Park, vacant since Lady Gregory's death in 1932 and soon to be demolished.

MAN

       That were to shirk
The spiritual intellect's great work   20
And shirk it in vain. There is no release
In a bodkin or disease,
Nor can there be a work so great
As that which cleans man's dirty slate.
While man can still his body keep   25
Wine or love drug him to sleep,
Waking he thanks the Lord that he
Has body and its stupidity,
But body gone he sleeps no more
And till his intellect grows sure   30
That all's arranged in one clear view
Pursues the thoughts that I pursue,
Then stands in judgment on his soul,
And, all work done, dismisses all
Out of intellect and sight   35
And sinks at last into the night.

ECHO

Into the night.

MAN

      O rocky voice
Shall we in that great night rejoice?
What do we know but that we face
One another in this place?   40
But hush, for I have lost the theme
Its joy or night seem but a dream;
Up there some hawk or owl has struck
Dropping out of sky or rock,
A stricken rabbit is crying out   45
And its cry distracts my thought.

[1939]

The Circus Animals' Desertion

I

I sought a theme and sought for it in vain,
I sought it daily for six weeks or so.
Maybe at last being but a broken man
I must be satisfied with my heart, although
Winter and summer till old age began   5
My circus animals[1] were all on show,

1. His poetic metaphors and themes.

Those stilted boys, that burnished chariot,
Lion and woman and the Lord knows what.

II

What can I but enumerate old themes,
First that sea-rider Usheen[2] led by the nose   10
Through three enchanted islands, allegorical dreams,
Vain gaiety, vain battle, vain repose,
Themes of the embittered heart, or so it seems,
That might adorn old songs or courtly shows;
But what cared I that set him on to ride,   15
I, starved for the bosom of his fairy bride.

And then a counter-truth filled out its play,
"The Countess Cathleen" was the name I gave it,
She, pity-crazed, had given her soul away
But masterful Heaven had intervened to save it.[3]   20
I thought my dear must her own soul destroy
So did fanaticism and hate enslave it,
And this brought forth a dream and soon enough
This dream itself had all my thought and love.

And when the Fool and Blind Man stole the bread   25
Cuchullain fought the ungovernable sea;[4]
Heart mysteries there, and yet when all is said
It was the dream itself enchanted me:
Character isolated by a deed
To engross the present and dominate memory.   30
Players and painted stage took all my love
And not those things that they were emblems of.

III

Those masterful images because complete
Grew in pure mind but out of what began?
A mound of refuse or the sweepings of a street,   35
Old kettles, old bottles, and a broken can,
Old iron, old bones, old rags, that raving slut
Who keeps the till. Now that my ladder's gone
I must lie down where all the ladders start
In the foul rag and bone shop of the heart.   40

[1939]

---

2. Yeats's long poem *The Wanderings of Oisin* (1889), his first significant success as a writer, recounts
   how an immortal, Niamh, falls in love with Oisin (or Usheen) and brings him to faeryland.
3. Yeats wrote this play (first published in 1892) for Maud Gonne. The titular character sells her
   soul to the devil in order to buy food for the starving Irish poor during a famine.
4. Characters in Yeats's 1903 play *On Baile's Strand* (see p. 141) in which the legendary Irish warrior
   Cuchulain fights with the waves after learning that he has killed his own son.

Politics

"In our time the destiny of man presents its meanings in political terms."
—THOMAS MANN.[1]

How can I, that girl standing there,
My attention fix
On Roman or on Russian
Or on Spanish politics,[2]
Yet here's a travelled man that knows   5
What he talks about,
And there's a politician
That has both read and thought,
And maybe what they say is true
Of war and war's alarms,   10
But O that I were young again
And held her in my arms.

[1939]

---

1. Yeats drew this quotation from German writer Thomas Mann (1875–1955) from the essay "Public Speech and Private Speech in Poetry" by American writer Archibald MacLeish (1892–1982), which praised Yeats's language as "public."
2. The volatile situation across Europe meant war was an almost certain prospect as the poem was written.

The Texts of the
PLAYS

Cathleen ni Houlihan[1]

PETER GILLANE
MICHAEL GILLANE, his Son, going to be married
PATRICK GILLANE, a lad of twelve, Michael's Brother
BRIDGET GILLANE, Peter's Wife
DELIA CAHEL, engaged to MICHAEL
THE POOR OLD WOMAN
Neighbours

SCENE: *Interior of a cottage close to Killala,[2] in 1798.* BRIDGET
is standing at a table undoing a parcel. PETER *is sitting at one
side of the fire,* PATRICK *at the other.*

PETER   What is that sound I hear?
PATRICK   I don't hear anything. [*He listens.*] I hear it now. It's like cheer-
ing. [*He goes to the window and looks out.*] I wonder what they are
cheering about. I don't see anybody.
PETER   It might be a hurling[3] match.
PATRICK   There's no hurling to-day. It must be down in the town the
cheering is.
BRIDGET   I suppose the boys must be having some sport of their own.
Come over here, Peter, and look at Michael's wedding-clothes.
PETER [*Shifts his chair to table.*]   Those are grand clothes, indeed.
BRIDGET   You hadn't clothes like that when you married me, and no coat
to put on of a Sunday any more than any other day.
PETER   That is true, indeed. We never thought a son of our own would
be wearing a suit of that sort for his wedding, or have so good a place
to bring a wife to.
PATRICK [*Who is still at the window.*]   There's an old woman coming
down the road. I don't know, is it here she's coming?
BRIDGET   It will be a neighbour coming to hear about Michael's wedding.
Can you see who it is?
PATRICK   I think it is a stranger, but she's not coming to the house. She's
turned into the gap that goes down where Murteen and his sons are
shearing sheep. [*He turns towards* BRIDGET.] Do you remember what
Winny of the Cross Roads was saying the other night about the strange
woman that goes through the country whatever time there's war or trouble coming?

1. Written collaboratively with Lady Gregory in 1901 and first produced in 1902. Cathleen ni Houlihan: a traditional figure for Ireland, also referred to as the Shan van vocht (Irish: "the Poor Old
   Woman"). In the original production of the play, the title role was played by Maud Gonne.
2. Site in County Mayo of the landing of French troops under General Joseph Humbert in 1798 to
   support an abortive Irish uprising. The failure of the uprising led directly to the Act of Union of
   1800, which abolished the independent Irish parliament. Yeats, with Maud Gonne, had in 1898
   been one of the organizers of the centennial commemorations of the uprising, which helped to
   raise Nationalist feelings in Ireland.
3. Traditional Irish sport similar to field hockey.

BRIDGET　Don't be bothering us about Winny's talk, but go and open the door for your brother. I hear him coming up the path.

PETER　I hope he has brought Delia's fortune[4] with him safe, for fear her people might go back on the bargain and I after making it. Trouble enough I had making it.

[PATRICK *opens the door and* MICHAEL *comes in.*]

BRIDGET　What kept you, Michael? We were looking out for you this long time.

MICHAEL　I went round by the priest's house to bid him be ready to marry us to-morrow.

BRIDGET　Did he say anything?

MICHAEL　He said it was a very nice match, and that he was never better pleased to marry any two in his parish than myself and Delia Cahel.

PETER　Have you got the fortune, Michael?

MICHAEL　Here it is.

[*He puts bag on table and goes over and leans against the chimney-jamb.* BRIDGET, *who has been all this time examining the clothes, pulling the seams and trying the lining of the pockets, etc., puts the clothes on the dresser.*]

PETER　[*Getting up and taking the bag in his hand and turning out the money.*]　Yes, I make the bargain well for you, Michael. Old John Cahel would sooner have kept a share of this a while longer. "Let me keep the half of it till the first boy is born," says he. "You will not," says I. "Whether there is or is not a boy, the whole hundred pounds must be in Michael's hands before he brings your daughter in the house." The wife spoke to him then, and he gave in at the end.

BRIDGET　You seem well pleased to be handling the money, Peter.

PETER　Indeed, I wish I had had the luck to get a hundred pounds, or twenty pounds itself, with the wife I married.

BRIDGET　Well, if I didn't bring much I didn't get much. What had you the day I married you but a flock of hens and you feeding them, and a few lambs and you driving them to the market at Ballina. [*She is vexed and bangs a jug on the dresser.*] If I brought no fortune I worked it out in my bones, laying down the baby, Michael that is standing there now, on a stook of straw, while I dug the potatoes, and never asking big dresses or anything but to be working.

PETER　That is true, indeed. [*He pats her arm.*]

BRIDGET　Leave me alone now till I ready the house for the woman that is to come into it.

PETER　You are the best woman in Ireland, but money is good, too. [*He begins handling the money again and sits down.*] I never thought to see so much money within my four walls. We can do great things now we have it. We can take the ten acres of land we have a chance of since Jamsie Dempsey died, and stock it.[5] We will go to the fair of Ballina to

---

4. Dowry.
5. *Take:* become tenants on. *Stock it:* put sheep or cattle on the land.

buy the stock. Did Delia ask any of the money for her own use, Michael?

MICHAEL   She did not, indeed. She did not seem to take much notice of it, or to look at it at all.

BRIDGET   That's no wonder. Why would she look at it when she had yourself to look at, a fine, strong young man, it is proud she must be to get you; a good steady boy that will make use of the money, and not be running through it or spending it on drink like another.

PETER   It's likely Michael himself was not thinking much of the fortune either, but of what sort the girl was to look at.

MICHAEL   [*Coming over towards the table.*]   Well, you would like a nice comely girl to be beside you, and to go walking with you. The fortune only lasts for a while, but the woman will be there always.

PATRICK   [*Turning round from the window.*]   They are cheering again down in the town. May be they are landing horses from Enniscrone.[6] They do be cheering when the horses take the water well.

MICHAEL   There are no horses in it. Where would they be going and no fair at hand? Go down to the town, Patrick, and see what is going on.

PATRICK   [*Opens the door to go out, but stops for a moment on the threshold.*]   Will Delia remember, do you think, to bring the greyhound pup she promised me when she would be coming to the house?

MICHAEL   She will surely.

[PATRICK *goes out leaving the door open.*]

PETER   It will be Patrick's turn next to be looking for a fortune, but he won't find it so easy to get it and he with no place of his own.[7]

BRIDGET   I do be thinking sometimes, now things are going so well with us, and the Cahels such a good back to us in the district, and Delia's own uncle a priest, we might be put in the way of making Patrick a priest some day, and he so good at his books.

PETER   Time enough, time enough, you have always your head full of plans, Bridget.

BRIDGET   We will be well able to give him learning, and not to send him tramping the country like a poor scholar that lives on charity.

MICHAEL   They're not done cheering yet.

[*He goes over to the door and stands there for a moment putting up his hand to shade his eyes.*]

BRIDGET   Do you see anything?

MICHAEL   I see an old woman coming up the path.

BRIDGET   Who is it, I wonder. It must be the strange woman Patrick saw a while ago.

MICHAEL   I don't think it's one of the neighbours anyway, but she has her cloak over her face.

---

6. Enniscrone, County Sligo, is on the eastern side of Killala Bay. Taking horses across the bay to Killala, on the western side, would save a journey of several miles.
7. The farm and its stock would traditionally pass to the eldest son, making him a more desirable match in marriage and able to marry sooner and demand a higher dowry from his wife's family than a younger son could.

BRIDGET   It might be some poor woman heard we were making ready for the wedding and came to look for her share.

PETER   I may as well put the money out of sight. There is no use leaving it out for every stranger to look at.

[*He goes over to a large box in the corner, opens it and puts the bag in and fumbles at the lock.*]

MICHAEL   There she is, father! [*An* OLD WOMAN *passes the window slowly, she looks at* MICHAEL *as she passes.*] I'd sooner a stranger not to come to the house the night before my wedding.

BRIDGET   Open the door, Michael; don't keep the poor woman waiting.

[*The* OLD WOMAN *comes in.* MICHAEL *stands aside to make way for her.*]

OLD WOMAN   God save all here!

PETER   God save you kindly!

OLD WOMAN   You have good shelter here.

PETER   You are welcome to whatever shelter we have.

BRIDGET   Sit down there by the fire and welcome.

OLD WOMAN [*Warming her hands.*]   There is a hard wind outside.

[MICHAEL *watches her curiously from the door,* PETER *comes over to the table.*]

PETER   Have you travelled far to-day?

OLD WOMAN   I have travelled far, very far, there are few have travelled so far as myself, and there's many a one that doesn't make me welcome. There was one that had strong sons I thought were friends of mine, but they were shearing their sheep, and they wouldn't listen to me.

PETER   It's a pity indeed for any person to have no place of their own.

OLD WOMAN   That's true for you indeed, and it's long I'm on the roads since I first went wandering.

BRIDGET   It is a wonder you are not worn out with so much wandering.

OLD WOMAN   Sometimes my feet are tired and my hands are quiet, but there is no quiet in my heart. When the people see me quiet, they think old age has come on me and that all the stir has gone out of me. But when the trouble is on me I must be talking to my friends.

BRIDGET   What was it put you wandering?

OLD WOMAN   Too many strangers in the house.[8]

BRIDGET   Indeed you look as if you'd had your share of trouble.

OLD WOMAN   I have had trouble indeed.

BRIDGET   What was it put the trouble on you?

OLD WOMAN   My land that was taken from me.

PETER   Was it much land they took from you?

OLD WOMAN   My four beautiful green fields.[9]

---

8. A phrase traditionally used to refer to the English colonial presence in Ireland, though here, as with many other expressions used by the Old Woman, the Gillanes appear to take it literally.
9. A traditional reference to four provinces of Ireland—Munster, Leinster, Ulster, and Connacht.

PETER [*Aside to* BRIDGET.]   Do you think could she be the widow Casey that was put out of her holding[1] at Kilglass a while ago?

BRIDGET   She is not. I saw the widow Casey one time at the market in Ballina, a stout fresh woman.

PETER [*To* OLD WOMAN.]   Did you hear a noise of cheering, and you coming up the hill?

OLD WOMAN   I thought I heard the noise I used to hear when my friends came to visit me. [*She begins singing half to herself.*]

> I will go cry with the woman,
> For yellow-haired Donough is dead,
> With a hempen rope for a neckcloth,
> And a white cloth on his head,—[2]

MICHAEL [*Coming from the door.*]   What is that you are singing, ma'am?

OLD WOMAN   Singing I am about a man I knew one time, yellow-haired Donough, that was hanged in Galway. [*She goes on singing, much louder.*]

> I am come to cry with you, woman,
> My hair is unwound and unbound;
> I remember him ploughing his field,
> Turning up the red side of the ground,
>
> And building his barn on the hill
> With the good mortared stone;
> O! we'd have pulled down the gallows
> Had it happened in Enniscrone!

MICHAEL   What was it brought him to his death?

OLD WOMAN   He died for love of me: many a man has died for love of me.

PETER [*Aside to* BRIDGET.]   Her trouble has put her wits astray.

MICHAEL   Is it long since that song was made? Is it long since he got his death?

OLD WOMAN   Not long, not long. But there were others that died for love of me a long time ago.

MICHAEL   Were they neighbours of your own ma'am?

OLD WOMAN   Come here beside me and I'll tell you about them. [MICHAEL *sits down beside her at the hearth.*] There was a red man of the O'Donnells from the north, and a man of the O'Sullivans from the south, and there was one Brian that lost his life at Clontarf by the sea,[3] and there were a great many in the west, some that died hundreds of years ago, and there are some that will die to-morrow.

MICHAEL   Is it in the west that men will die to-morrow?

1. Evicted from the land on which she was a tenant.
2. In an article published shortly after the first performance of *Cathleen ni Houlihan*, Yeats indicated that the verses Cathleen sings here were "suggested to me by some old Gaelic folk-song." His source was probably the ballad "Fair-haired Donagh," published by Lady Gregory in an article on "West Irish Folk Ballads" in the *Monthly Review*, October 1902.
3. "Red" Hugh O'Donnell (1571–1602) and Donal O'Sullivan Beare (1560–1618) both fought against English colonial forces in Ireland. Brian Boru, high king of Ireland, was killed at the battle of Clontarf in 1014 in the course of defeating Danish invading forces.

OLD WOMAN   Come nearer, nearer to me.

BRIDGET   Is she right, do you think? Or is she a woman from the north?[4]

PETER   She doesn't know well what she's talking about, with the want and the trouble she has gone through.

BRIDGET   The poor thing, we should treat her well.

PETER   Give her a drink of milk and a bit of the oaten cake.

BRIDGET   Maybe we should give her something along with that, to bring her on her way. A few pence, or a shilling itself, and we with so much money in the house.

PETER   Indeed I'd not begrudge it to her if we had it to spare, but if we go running through what we have, we'll soon have to break the hundred pounds, and that would be a pity.

BRIDGET   Shame on you, Peter. Give her the shilling, and your blessing with it, or our own luck will go from us.

[PETER goes to the box and takes out a shilling.]

BRIDGET [To the OLD WOMAN.]   Will you have a drink of milk?

OLD WOMAN   It is not food or drink that I want.

PETER [Offering the shilling.]   Here is something for you.

OLD WOMAN   That is not what I want. It is not silver I want.

PETER   What is it you would be asking for?

OLD WOMAN   If any one would give me help he must give me himself, he must give me all.

[PETER goes over to the table staring at the shilling in his hand in a bewildered way, and stands whispering to BRIDGET.]

MICHAEL   Have you no man of your own, ma'am?

OLD WOMAN   I have not. With all the lovers that brought me their love, I never set out the bed for any.

MICHAEL   Are you lonely going the roads, ma'am?

OLD WOMAN   I have my thoughts and I have my hopes.

MICHAEL   What hopes have you to hold to?

OLD WOMAN   The hope of getting my beautiful fields back again; the hope of putting the strangers out of my house.

MICHAEL   What way will you do that, ma'am?

OLD WOMAN   I have good friends that will help me. They are gathering to help me now. I am not afraid. If they are put down to-day they will get the upper hand to-morrow. [She gets up.] I must be going to meet my friends. They are coming to help me, and I must be there to welcome them. I must call the neighbours together to welcome them.

MICHAEL   I will go with you.

BRIDGET   It is not her friends you have to go and welcome, Michael; it is the girl coming into the house you have to welcome. You have plenty to do, it is food and drink you have to bring to the house. The woman that is coming home is not coming with empty hands; you would not

---

4. From Ulster; also a colloquialism for a woman with otherworldly power (a woman of the Sidhe or a witch).

have an empty house before her. [*To the* OLD WOMAN.] Maybe you don't know, ma'am, that my son is going to be married to-morrow.

OLD WOMAN   It is not a man going to his marriage that I look to for help.

PETER [*To* BRIDGET.]   Who is she, do you think, at all?

BRIDGET   You did not tell us your name yet, ma'am.

OLD WOMAN   Some call me the Poor Old Woman, and there are some that call me Cathleen, the daughter of Houlihan.

PETER   I think I knew someone of that name once. Who was it, I wonder? It must have been some one I knew when I was a boy. No, no, I remember, I heard it in a song.

OLD WOMAN [*Who is standing in the doorway.*]   They are wondering that there were songs made for me; there have been many songs made for me. I heard one on the wind this morning. [*She sings.*]

> Do not make a great keening[5]
> When the graves have been dug to-morrow.
> Do not call the white-scarfed riders
> To the burying that shall be to-morrow.
> Do not spread food to call strangers
> To the wakes that shall be to-morrow;
> Do not give money for prayers
> For the dead that shall die to-morrow . . .

they will have no need of prayers, they will have no need of prayers.

MICHAEL   I do not know what that song means, but tell me something I can do for you.

PETER   Come over to me, Michael.

MICHAEL   Hush, father, listen to her.

OLD WOMAN   It is a hard service they take that help me. Many that are red-cheeked now will be pale-cheeked; many that have been free to walk the hills and the bogs and the rushes, will be sent to walk hard streets in far countries; many a good plan will be broken; many that have gathered money will not stay to spend it; many a child will be born, and there will be no father at its christening to give it a name. They that had red cheeks will have pale cheeks for my sake; and for all that, they will think they are well paid.

[*She goes out, her voice is heard outside singing.*]

> They shall be remembered for ever,
> They shall be alive for ever,
> They shall be speaking for ever,
> The people shall hear them for ever.

BRIDGET [*To* PETER.]   Look at him, Peter; he has the look of a man that has got the touch.[6] [*Raising her voice.*] Look here, Michael, at the wedding-clothes. Such grand clothes as these are. You have a right to fit them on now, it would be a pity tomorrow if they did not fit. The boys

---

5. A wailing cry for the dead, traditional at Irish burials until the late nineteenth century.
6. Been enchanted by otherworldly power.

would be laughing at you. Take them, Michael, and go into the room and fit them on. [*She puts them on his arm.*]

MICHAEL   What wedding are you talking of? What clothes will I be wearing to-morrow?

BRIDGET   These are the clothes you are going to wear when you marry Delia Cahel to-morrow.

MICHAEL   I had forgotten that.

[*He looks at the clothes and turns towards the inner room, but stops at the sound of cheering outside.*]

PETER   There is the shouting come to our own door. What is it has happened?

[*Neighbours come crowding in,* PATRICK *and* DELIA *with them.*]

PATRICK   There are ships in the Bay; the French are landing at Killala!

[PETER *takes his pipe from his mouth and his hat off, and stands up. The clothes slip from* MICHAEL'*s arm.*]

DELIA   Michael! [*He takes no notice.*] Michael! [*He turns towards her.*] Why do you look at me like a stranger?

[*She drops his arm.* BRIDGET *goes over towards her.*]

PATRICK   The boys are all hurrying down the hillsides to join the French.

DELIA   Michael won't be going to join the French.

BRIDGET [*To* PETER.]   Tell him not to go, Peter.

PETER   It's no use. He doesn't hear a word we're saying.

BRIDGET   Try and coax him over to the fire.

DELIA   Michael! Michael! You won't leave me! You won't join the French, and we going to be married!

[*She puts her arms about him, he turns towards her as if about to yield.*]

OLD WOMAN'*s voice outside.*

> They shall be speaking for ever,
> The people shall hear them for ever.

[MICHAEL *breaks away from* DELIA *and goes towards* Neighbours *at the door.*]

MICHAEL   Come, we have no time to lose; we must follow her.

[MICHAEL *and the* Neighbours *go out.*]

PETER [*To* PATRICK, *laying a hand on his arm.*]   Did you see an old woman going down the path?

PATRICK   I did not, but I saw a young girl, and she had the walk of a queen.

On Baile's Strand[1]

CUCHULAIN, the King of Muirthemne
CONCHUBAR, the High King of Ulad
DAIRE, a King
FINTAIN, a blind man
BARACH, a fool
A Young Man
Young Kings and old Kings

SCENE: *A great hall at Dundealgan; not "Cuchulain's great ancient house," but an assembly house nearer to the sea. A big door at the back, and through the door misty light as of sea mist. There are many chairs on either side raised one above another, tier above tier. One of these chairs, which is turned towards the front of the stage, is bigger than the others. An elaborate cloak lies on a chair at the other side. Somewhere at the back there is a table with flagons of ale upon it and drinking horns. There is a small door at one side of the hall. A* FOOL *and* BLIND MAN *come in through the door at the back. They wear patched and ragged clothes, and the* BLIND MAN *leans upon a staff.*

FOOL   What a clever man you are, though you are blind! There's nobody with two eyes in his head that is as clever as you are. Who but you could have thought that the henwife sleeps every day a little at noon! I would never be able to steal anything if you didn't tell me where to look for it. And what a good cook you are! You take the fowl out of my hands after I have stolen it, and you pluck it, and put it into the big pot at the fire there, and I can go out and run races with the witches at the edge of the waves and get an appetite; and when I've got it, there's the hen waiting inside for me done to the turn!

BLIND MAN [*Who is feeling about with his stick.*]   Done to the turn.

FOOL [*Putting his arm round* BLIND MAN'*s neck.*]   Come now, I'll have a leg and you'll have a leg, and we'll draw lots for the wish-bone. I'll be praising you—I'll be praising you while we're eating it—for your good plans and for your good cooking. There's nobody in the world like you, Blind Man. Come, come—wait a minute—I shouldn't have closed the door. There are some that look for me, and I wouldn't let them find me. Don't tell it to any body, Blind Man. There are some that follow

---

1. First published in 1903 and produced at the Abbey Theatre in 1904. The play was revised extensively after early productions, and the text given here dates from 1907. The play is based on a story from the *Tain Bó Cualnge* ("Cattle Raid of Cooley"), the central narrative of the Ulster cycle of Irish mythology. Yeats drew on Lady Gregory's version of the *Tain*, published in 1902 as *Cuchulain of Muirthemne*, and particularly on her chapter "The Only Son of Aoife," which recounts how Queen Aoife of Scotland, having been defeated in battle by Cuchulain—the central warrior hero of the Ulster cycle—became his lover. After he left her soon afterward, she bore a child, Conlaoch, whom she raised as a warrior with the aim of revenging herself against Cuchulain. Conchubar was the king of Ulster, and thus chief of the Red Branch warriors (of whom Cuchulain was one). Baile's Strand is near Dundalk (Dundealgan) in County Louth, Ulster.

me: Boann[2] herself out of the river, and Fand[3] out of the deep sea—witches they are, and they come by in the wind and they cry, "Give a kiss, Fool, give a kiss!" That's what they cry. That's wide enough; all the witches can come in now. I wouldn't have them beat at the door and say, "Where is the Fool? Why has he put a lock on the door?" Maybe they'll hear the bubbling of a pot and come in and sit on the ground —but we won't give them any of the fowl—let them go back to the sea, let them go back to the sea.

BLIND MAN [*Feeling legs of chair with his hands.*]   Ah! [*Then in a louder voice as he feels the back of it.*] Ah—ah!

FOOL   Why do you say "ah—ah"?

BLIND MAN   I know the big chair. It is to-day the High King Conchubar is coming. They have brought out his chair. He is going to be Cuchulain's master in earnest from this day out. It is that he's coming for.

FOOL   He must be a great man to be Cuchulain's master.

BLIND MAN   So he is. He is a great man. He is over all the rest of the kings of Ireland.

FOOL   Cuchulain's master! I thought Cuchulain could do anything he liked.

BLIND MAN   So he did, so he did; but he ran too wild, and Conchubar is coming to-day to put an oath upon him that will stop his rambling and make him as biddable as a house dog and keep him always at his hand. He will sit in this chair and put the oath upon him. [*He sits in chair.*]

FOOL   How will he do that?

BLIND MAN   You have no wits to understand such things. He will sit up in this chair, and he'll say, "Take the oath, Cuchulain; I bid you take the oath. Do as I tell you. What are your wits compared with mine? And what are your riches compared with mine? And what sons have you to pay your debts and to put a stone over you when you die? Take the oath, I tell you; take a strong oath."

FOOL [*Crumpling himself up and whining.*]   I will not—I'll take no oath—I want my dinner.

BLIND MAN   Hush! hush! It is not done yet.

FOOL   You said it was done to a turn.

BLIND MAN   Did I, now! Well, it might be done and not done. The wings might be white, but the legs might be red; the flesh might stick hard to the bones and not come away in the teeth . . . but believe me, Fool, it will be well done before you put your teeth in it.

FOOL   My teeth are growing long with the hunger.

BLIND MAN   I'll tell you a story. The kings have story tellers while they are waiting for their dinner. I will tell you a story with a fight in it, a story with a champion in it, and a ship and a queen's son that has his mind set on killing somebody that you and I know.

FOOL   Who is that? Who is he coming to kill?

BLIND MAN   Wait, now, till you hear. When you were stealing the fowl I

---

2. A water goddess.
3. The wife of Manannan Mac Lir, god of the sea.

was lying in a hole in the sand, and I heard three men coming with a shuffling sort of noise. They were wounded and groaning.

FOOL   Go on, tell me about the fight.

BLIND MAN   There had been a fight, a great fight, a tremendous great fight. A young man had landed on the shore, the guardians of the shore had asked his name and he had refused to tell it,[4] and he had killed one and others had run away.

FOOL   That's enough. Come on, now, to the fowl. I wish it was bigger. I wish it was as big as a goose.

BLIND MAN   Hush! I haven't told you all. I know who that young man is. I heard the men who were running away say he had red hair, that he came from Aoife's country, that he was coming to kill Cuchulain.

FOOL   Nobody could do that.

[*To a tune.*]

> Cuchulain has killed kings,
> Kings and sons of kings,
> Dragons out of the water,
> And witches out of the air,

Bocanachs and Bananachs[5] and people of the woods.

BLIND MAN   Hush! hush!

FOOL   [*Still singing.*]

> Witches that steal the milk,
> Fomor[6] that steal the children,
> Hags that have heads like hares,
> Hares that have claws like witches,
> All riding a cock-horse.

[*Spoken.*]

Out of the very bottom of the bitter black North.

BLIND MAN   Hush, I say!

FOOL   Does Cuchulain know that he is coming to kill him?

BLIND MAN   How would he know that with his head in the clouds? He doesn't care for common fighting. Why would he put himself out, and nobody in it but that young man? Now, if it were a white fawn that might turn into a queen before morning—

FOOL   Come to the fowl. I wish it was as big as a pig. A fowl with goose-grease and pig's crackling.

BLIND MAN   No hurry, no hurry. I know whose son it is. I wouldn't tell anybody else, but I will tell you. A secret is better to you than your dinner. You like being told secrets.

FOOL   Tell me the secret.

BLIND MAN   That young man is Aoife's son. . . . I am sure it is Aoife's son;

---

4. Aoife (see note 1, p. 141) had put her son under bonds not to reveal his name and also to accept all challenges no matter what the risk.
5. Female and male goblins.
6. In a note to *Poems* (1895), Yeats wrote that "Fomoroh means from under the sea, and is the name of the gods of night and death and cold."

it is borne in upon me that it is Aoife's son. You have often heard me talking of Aoife, the great woman fighter Cuchulain got the mastery over in the North?

FOOL　I know, I know. She is one of those cross queens that live in hungry Scotland.

BLIND MAN　I am sure it is her son. I was in Aoife's country for a long time.

FOOL　That was before you were blinded for putting a curse upon the wind.

BLIND MAN　There was a boy in her house that had her own red colour on him, and everybody said he was to be brought up to kill Cuchulain, that she hated Cuchulain. She used to put a helmet on a pillar stone and call it Cuchulain and set him casting at it. . . . There is a step outside—Cuchulain's step.

[CUCHULAIN *passes by in the mist outside the big door.*]

FOOL　Where is Cuchulain going?

BLIND MAN　He is going to meet Conchubar, that has bidden him to take the oath.

FOOL　Ah! an oath, Blind Man. . . . How can I remember so many things at once? Who is going to take an oath?

BLIND MAN　Cuchulain is going to take an oath to Conchubar, who is High King.

FOOL　What a mix-up you make of everything, Blind Man! You were telling me one story, and now you are telling me another story. How can I understand things, when they begin to happen, if you mix up everything at the beginning?—Wait till I settle it out. [*Takes off shoes.*] There now, there's Cuchulain, and there is the young man that is coming to kill him, and Cuchulain doesn't know. But where's Conchubar? [*Takes bag from side.*] That's Conchubar with all his riches.—Cuchulain—Conchubar—the Young Man.—And where's Aoife? [*Throws up cap.*] There is Aoife, high up on the mountains in high hungry Scotland. [*Begins putting on shoes.*] Maybe it's not true after all. Maybe it was your own making up. It's many a time you cheated me before with your lies. Come to the cooking-pot, my stomach is pinched and rusty. Would you have it be creaking like a gate?

BLIND MAN　I tell you it's true. And more than that is true. If you listen to what I say you'll forget your stomach.

FOOL　I won't!

BLIND MAN　Listen. I know who the young man's father is, but I won't say; I would be afraid to say. . . . Ah, Fool, you would forget everything if you could know who the young man's father is!

FOOL　Who is it? Tell me now, quick, or I'll shake you. Come, out with it, or I'll shake you!

[*A murmur of voices in the distance.*]

BLIND MAN　Wait, wait, there's somebody coming. . . . It is Cuchulain is coming. He's coming back with the High King. Go and ask Cuchulain.

He'll tell you. It's little you'll care about the cooking-pot when you have asked Cuchulain that.

[BLIND MAN *goes out by side door.*]

FOOL   I'll ask him. Cuchulain will know. He was in Aoife's country. [*Going towards door at back.*] I'll ask him. [*Turns and goes to door at side.*] But no, I won't ask him. I would be afraid. [*Going up towards door and back again.*] Yes, I will ask him.—What harm in asking?—The blind man said I was to ask him.—[*Going to door at side again.*] No, no; I'll not ask him.—He might kill me.—I have but killed hens and geese and pigs. He has killed kings. [*Goes up again almost to door at back.*] Who says I'm afraid? I'm not afraid; I'm no coward. I'll ask him.—No, no, Cuchulain, I'm not going to ask you. [*Running to door at side.*]

> He has killed kings,
> Kings, and the sons of kings,
> Dragons out of the water,
> And witches out of the air,

Bocanachs and Bananachs and people of the wood.

[*He runs out, the last words being heard outside.* CUCHULAIN *and* CON-CHUBAR *enter through the big door at the back. While they are still outside* CUCHULAIN's *voice is heard raised in anger. He is a dark man, something over forty years of age.* CONCHUBAR *is much older, though not feeble-looking.*]

CUCHULAIN   Because I have killed men without your bidding,
And have rewarded others at my own pleasure,
Because of half a score of trifling things,
You lay this oath upon me; and now—and now
You add another pebble to the heap,
And I must be your man, wellnigh your bondsman,
Because a youngster out of Aoife's country
Has found the shore ill guarded.
CONCHUBAR   He came to land
While you were somewhere out of sight and hearing;
Hunting or dancing with your wild companions.
CUCHULAIN   He can be driven out. I'll not be bound.
I'll dance or hunt, or quarrel or make love,
Wherever or whenever I've a mind to.
If time had not put water in your blood
You never would have thought it.
CONCHUBAR   I would leave
A strong and settled country to my children.
CUCHULAIN   And I must be obedient in all things;
Give up my will to yours, go where you please,
Come where you will, sit at the council-board
Among the unshapely bodies of old men!
I, whose mere name has kept this country safe,
I, that in early days have driven out

Maeve of Cruachan[7] and the northern pirates,
The hundred kings of Sorcha[8] and the kings
Out of the Garden in the East of the World!
Must I that held you on the throne, when all
Had pulled you from it, swear obedience
As if I were some cattle-raising king?
Are my shins speckled with the heat of the fire,
Or have my hands no skill but to make figures
Upon the ashes with a stick? Am I
So slack and idle that I need a whip
Before I serve you?

CONCHUBAR   No, no whip, Cuchulain.
But every day my children come and say:
"This man is growing harder to endure.
How can we be at safety with this man,
That nobody can buy or bid or bind?
We shall be at his mercy when you are gone.
He burns the earth as if it were a fire,
And time can never touch him."

CUCHULAIN   And so the tale
Grows finer yet, and I am to obey
Whatever child you set upon the throne
As if it were yourself!

CONCHUBAR   Most certainly.
I am High King, my son shall be High King;
And you, for all the wildness of your blood,
And though your father came out of the sun,
Are but a little king, and weigh but light
In anything that touches government,
If put into the balance with my children,

CUCHULAIN   It's well that we should speak our minds out plainly,
For when we die we shall be spoken of
In many countries. We in our young days
Have seen the heavens like a burning cloud
Brooding upon the world, and being more
Than men can be, now that cloud's lifted up,
We should be the more truthful, Conchubar.
I do not like your children. They have no pith,
No marrow in their bones, and will lie soft
Where you and I lie hard.

CONCHUBAR   You rail at them
Because you have no children of your own.

CUCHULAIN   I think myself most lucky that I leave
No pallid ghost or mockery of a man
To drift and mutter in the corridors
Where I have laughed and sung.

---

7. Queen of Connacht in Irish mythology, who held court at Cruachan in County Roscommon.
8. Part of the underworld in Irish mythology.

CONCHUBAR   That is not true,
For all your boasting of the truth between us,
For there is none that having house and lands,
That have been in the one family,
And called by the one name for centuries,
But is made miserable if he know
They are to pass into a stranger's keeping,
As yours will pass.
CUCHULAIN   The most of men feel that;
But you and I leave names upon the harp.
CONCHUBAR   You play with arguments as lawyers do,
And put no heart in them. I know your thoughts,
For we have slept under the one cloak and drunk
From the one wine cup. I know you to the bone.
I have heard you cry—aye, in your very sleep—
"I have no son!" and with such bitterness
That I have gone upon my knees and prayed
That it might be amended.
CUCHULAIN   For you thought
That I should be as biddable as others
Had I their reason for it; but that's not true,
For I would need a weightier argument
Than one that marred me in the copying,
As I have that clean hawk out of the air,
That as men say begot this body of mine
Upon a mortal woman.[9]
CONCHUBAR   Now as ever
You mock at every measurable hope,
And would have nothing or impossible things.
What eye has ever looked upon the child
Would satisfy a mind like that?
CUCHULAIN   I would leave
My house and name to none that would not face
Even myself in battle.
CONCHUBAR   Being swift of foot,
And making light of every common chance,
You should have overtaken on the hills
Some daughter of the air, or on the shore
A daughter of the Country-under-Wave.[1]
CUCHULAIN   I am not blasphemous.
CONCHUBAR   Yet you despise
Our queens, and would not call a child your own
If one of them had borne him.
CUCHULAIN   I have not said it.
CONCHUBAR   Ah, I remember I have heard you boast,

---

9. Cuchulain was the son of Conchubar's sister, Dechtire, and Lugh, prince of the Sidhe.
1. In Irish folklore, spirits and faeries were associated with land, air, and water, and, as Yeats noted,
   the "favourite dwelling of the faeries," Tier-nan-Og, was said by some to be "an underwater land."

When the ale was in your blood, that there was one
In Scotland, where you had learned the trade of war,
That had a stone-pale cheek and red-brown hair,
And that although you had loved other women,
You'd sooner that fierce woman of the camp
Bore you a son than any queen among them.

CUCHULAIN   You call her a fierce woman of the camp;
But having lived among the spinning-wheels,
You'd have no woman near that would not say,
"Ah, how wise!" "What will you have for supper?"
"What shall I wear that I may please you, sir?"
And keep that humming through the day and night
Forever. A fierce woman of the camp!—
But I am getting angry about nothing.
You have never seen her. Ah, Conchubar, had you seen her,
With that high, laughing, turbulent head of hers
Thrown backward, and the bow-string at her ear,
Or sitting at the fire with those grave eyes
Full of good counsel as it were with wine,
Or when love ran through all the lineaments
Of her wild body—although she had no child,
None other had all beauty, queen or lover,
Or was so fitted to give birth to kings.

CONCHUBAR   There's nothing I can say but drifts you farther
From the one weighty matter. That very woman—
For I know well that you are praising Aoife—
Now hates you, and will leave no subtilty
Unknotted that might run into a noose
About your throat, no army in idleness
That might bring ruin on this land you serve.

CUCHULAIN   No wonder in that—no wonder at all in that.
I never have known love but as a kiss
In the mid-battle, and a difficult truce
Of oil and water, candles and dark night,
Hillside and hollow, the hot-footed sun,
And the cold sliding, slippery-footed moon—
A brief forgiveness between opposites
That have been hatreds for three times the age
Of this long-'stablished ground.

CONCHUBAR   Listen to me:
Aoife makes war on us, and every day
Our enemies grow greater and beat the walls
More bitterly, and you within the walls
Are every day more turbulent; and yet
When I would speak about these things, your mind
Runs as it were a swallow on the wind.
Look at the door, and what men gather there—
Old counsellors that steer the land with me

And younger kings, the dancers and harp-players
That follow in your tumults, and all these
Are held there by the one anxiety.
Will you be bound into obedience,
And so make this land safe for them and theirs?
You are but half a king, and I but half.
I need your might of hand and burning heart,
And you my wisdom.

[*Outside the door in the blue light of the sea mist are many old and
young kings; amongst them are three women, two of whom carry a bowl
full of fire. The third woman puts from time to time fragrant herbs into
the fire so that it flickers up into brighter flame.*]

CUCHULAIN [*Going near to the door.*]
                              Nestlings of a high nest,
Hawks that have followed me into the air
And looked upon the sun, we'll out of this
And sail upon the wind once more. This king
Would have me take an oath to do his will,
And having listened to his tune from morning,
I will no more of it. Run to the stable
And set the horses to the chariot-pole,
And send a messenger to the harp-players.
We'll find a level place among the woods
And dance awhile.
A YOUNG KING   Cuchulain, take the oath.
There is none here that would not have you take it.
CUCHULAIN   You'd have me take it? Are you of one mind?
THE KINGS   All, all, all, all!
A KING   Do what the High King bids you.
CONCHUBAR   There is not one but dreads this turbulence,
   Now that they are settled men.
CUCHULAIN   Are you so changed,
   Or have I grown more dangerous of late?
   But that's not it. I understand it all.
   It's you that have changed. You've wives and children now,
   And for that reason cannot follow one
   That lives like a bird's flight from tree to tree—
   It's time the years put water in my blood
   And drowned the wildness of it, for all's changed,
   But that unchanged.—I'll take what oath you will:
   The moon, the sun, the water, light, or air,
   I do not care how binding.
CONCHUBAR [*Who has seated himself in his great chair.*]
                              On this fire
That has been lighted from your hearth and mine,
The older men shall be my witnesses,
The younger yours. The holders of the fire

Shall purify the thresholds of the house
With waving fire, and shut the outer door,
According to old custom, and sing rhyme
That has come down from the old law-makers
To blow the witches out. Considering
That the wild will of man could by oath be bound,
But that a woman's could not, they bid us sing
Against the will of woman at its wildest
In the shape-changers that run upon the wind.

[*The song of the* WOMEN.]

May this fire have driven out
The shape-changers that can put
Ruin on a great king's house
Until all be ruinous.
Names whereby a man has known
The threshold and the hearthstone,
Gather on the wind and drive
Women none can kiss and thrive,
For they are but whirling wind,
Out of memory and mind.
They would make a prince decay
With light images of clay
Planted in the running wave;
Or, for many shapes they have,
They would change them into hounds
Until he had died of his wounds,
Though the change were but a whim;
Or they'd hurl a spell at him,
That he follow with desire
Bodies that can never tire
Or grow kind, for they anoint
All their bodies joint by joint
With a miracle-working juice
That is made out of the grease
Of the ungoverned unicorn;
But the man is thrice forlorn,
Emptied, ruined, wracked, and lost,
That they follow, for at most
They will give him kiss for kiss
While they murmur "After this
Hatred may be sweet to the taste;"
Those wild hands that have embraced
All his body can but shove
At the burning wheel of love
Till the side of hate comes up.
Therefore, in this ancient cup
May the sword-blades drink their fill
Of the home-brew there, until
They will have for master none
But the threshold and hearthstone.

[*After* "Memory and mind" *their words die away to a murmur, but are loud again at* "Therefore in." *The others do not speak when these words are loud.*]

CUCHULAIN [*Speaking while they are singing.*]
I'll take and keep this oath, and from this day
I shall be what you please, my nestlings.
Yet I had thought you one of those that praised
Whatever life could make the pulse run quickly,
Even though it were brief, and though you held
That a free gift was better than a forced;
But that's all over.—I will keep it, too.
I never gave a gift and took it again.
If the wild horse should break the chariot-pole
It would be punished. Should that be in the oath?—

[*Two of the women, still singing, crouch in front of him holding the bowl over their heads. He spreads his hands over the flame.*]

I swear to be obedient in all things
To Conchubar, and to uphold his children.
CONCHUBAR   We are one being, as these flames are one.
I give my wisdom, and I take your strength.
Now thrust the swords in the flame, and pray
That they may serve the threshold and the hearthstone
With faithful service.

[*The* KINGS *kneel in a semicircle before the two women and* CUCHULAIN, *who thrusts his sword in the flame. They all put the points of their swords in the flame. The third woman is at the back near the big door.*]

CUCHULAIN   O pure glittering ones,
That should be more than wife or friend or mistress,
Give us the enduring will, the unquenchable hope,
The friendliness of the sword!—

[*The song grows louder, and the last words ring out clearly. There is a loud knocking at the door, and a cry of* "Open! open!"]

CONCHUBAR   Some king that has been loitering on the way.
Open the door, for I would have all know
That the oath's finished, and Cuchulain bound
And that the swords are drinking up the flame.

[*The door is opened by the third woman, and a* YOUNG MAN *with a drawn sword enters.*]

YOUNG MAN   I am of Aoife's army.

[*The* KINGS *rush towards him.* CUCHULAIN *throws himself between.*]

CUCHULAIN   Put up your swords.
He is but one. Aoife is far away.

YOUNG MAN   I have come alone into the midst of you
  To weigh this sword against Cuchulain's sword.
CONCHUBAR   And are you noble? for if of common seed
  You cannot weigh your sword against his sword
  But in mixed battle.
YOUNG MAN   I am under bonds
  To tell my name to no man; but it's noble.
CONCHUBAR   But I would know your name, and not your bonds.
  You cannot speak in the Assembly House
  If you are not noble.
FIRST KING   Answer the High King!
YOUNG MAN   I will give no other proof than the hawk gives—
  That it's no sparrow!

  [*He is silent for a moment, then speaks to all.*]

          Yet look upon me, kings.
  I too am of that ancient seed, and carry
  The signs about this body and in these bones.
CUCHULAIN   To have shown the hawk's grey feather is enough,
  And you speak highly, too. Give me that helmet!
  I'd thought they had grown weary sending champions.
  That sword and belt will do. This fighting's welcome.
  The High King there has promised me his wisdom;
  But the hawk's sleepy till its well-beloved
  Cries out amid the acorns, or it has seen
  Its enemy like a speck upon the sun.
  What's wisdom to the hawk, when that clear eye
  Is burning nearer up in the high air!

  [*Looks hard at* YOUNG MAN; *then comes down steps and
  grasps the* YOUNG MAN *by his shoulder.*]

Hither into the light!   [*To* CONCHUBAR.]
          The very tint
Of her that I was speaking of but now.
Not a pin's difference.   [*To* YOUNG MAN.]
          You are from the North,
Where there are many that have that tint of hair—
Red-brown, the light red-brown. Come nearer, boy,
For I would have another look at you.
There's more likeness—a pale, a stone-pale cheek.
What brought you, boy? Have you no fear of death!
YOUNG MAN   Whether I live or die is in the Gods' hands.
CUCHULAIN   That is all words, all words; a young man's talk.
  I am their plough, their harrow, their very strength;
  For he that's in the sun begot this body
  Upon a mortal woman, and I have heard tell
  It seemed as if he had outrun the moon,
  That he must follow always through waste heaven,
  He loved so happily. He'll be but slow

To break a tree that was so sweetly planted.
Let's see that arm! I'll see it if I like.
That arm had a good father and a good mother,
But it is not like this.

YOUNG MAN   You are mocking me!
You think I am not worthy to be fought.
But I'll not wrangle but with this talkative knife.

CUCHULAIN   Put up your sword; I am not mocking you.
I'd have you for my friend; but if it's not
Because you have a hot heart and a cold eye,
I cannot tell the reason. [*To* CONCHUBAR.] He has got her fierceness,
And nobody is as fierce as those pale women.
And I will keep him with me, Conchubar,
That he may set my memory upon it
When the day's fading.
                    You will stop with us,
And we will hunt the deer and the wild bulls;
And, when we have grown weary, light our fires
Between the wood and water, or on some mountain
Where the shape-changers of the morning come.
The High King there would make a mock of me
Because I did not take a wife among them.
Why do you hang your head? It's a good life.
The head grows prouder in the light of the dawn,
And friendship thickens in the murmuring dark,
Where the spare hazels meet the wool-white foam.
But I can see there's no more need for words,
And that you'll be my friend from this day out.

CONCHUBAR   He has come hither, not in his own name,
But in Queen Aoife's name; and has challenged us
In challenging the foremost man of us all.

CUCHULAIN   Well, well, what matter!

CONCHUBAR   You think it does not matter,
And that a fancy lighter than the air,
A whim of the moment has more matter in it,
For having none that shall reign after you,
You cannot think, as I do, who would leave
A throne too high for insult.

CUCHULAIN   Let your children
Re-mortar their inheritance as we have,
And put more muscle on. I'll give you gifts,
But I'd have something too—that arm-ring, boy.
We'll have this quarrel out when you are older.

YOUNG MAN   There is no man I'd sooner have my friend
Than you, whose name has gone about the world
As if it had been the wind; but Aoife'd say
I had turned coward.

CUCHULAIN   I will give you gifts,
That Aoife'll know, and all her people know,

To have come from me. [*Showing cloak which is on a chair.*]
                My father gave me this.
He came to try me, rising up at dawn
Out of the cold dark of the rich sea.
He challenged me to battle, but before
My sword had touched his sword, told me his name,
Gave me this cloak, and vanished. It was woven
By women of the Country-under-Wave
Out of the fleeces of the sea. O! tell her
I was afraid, or tell her what you will.
No; tell her that I heard a raven croak
On the north side of the house, and was afraid.
CONCHUBAR   Some witch of the air has troubled Cuchulain's mind.
CUCHULAIN   No witchcraft. His head is like a woman's head
   I had a fancy for.
CONCHUBAR   A witch of the air
Can make a leaf confound us with memories.
They ride upon the wind and hurl the spells
That make us nothing, out of the invisible wind.
They have gone to school to learn the trick of it.
CUCHULAIN   No, no, there's nothing out of common here;
   The winds are innocent. That arm-ring, boy!
A KING   If I've your leave, I'll take this challenge up.
ANOTHER KING   No, give it me, High King, for that wild Aoife
   Has carried off my slaves.
ANOTHER KING   No, give it me,
   For she has harried me in house and herd.
ANOTHER KING   I claim this fight.
OTHER KINGS [*Together.*]   And I! and I! and I!
CUCHULAIN   Back! back! Put up your swords! put up your swords!
   There's none alive that shall accept a challenge
   I have refused. Laegaire put up your sword!
YOUNG MAN   No, let them come! If they've a mind for it,
   I'll try it out with any two together.
CUCHULAIN   That's spoken as I'd have spoken at your age.
   But you are in my house. Whatever man
   Would fight with you shall fight it out with me.
   They're dumb, they're dumb? How many of you
      would meet   [*Draws sword.*]
This mutterer, this old whistler, this sand-piper,
This edge that's greyer than the tide, this mouse
That's gnawing at the timbers of the world,
This, this—? Boy, I would meet them all in arms
If I'd a son like you. He would avenge me
When I have withstood for the last time the men
Whose fathers, brothers, sons, and friends I have killed
Upholding Conchubar, when the four provinces
Have gathered with the ravens over them.
But I'd need no avenger. You and I

Would scatter them like water from a dish.

YOUNG MAN We'll stand by one another from this out.
  Here is the ring.

CUCHULAIN   No, turn and turn about.
  But my turn's first, because I am the older.   [*Spreading out cloak.*]
  Nine queens out of the Country-under-Wave
  Have woven it with the fleeces of the sea,
  And they were long embroidering at it. Boy,
  If I had fought my father, he'd have killed me
  As certainly as if I had a son,
  And fought with him, I should be deadly to him,
  For the old fiery fountains are far off,
  And every day there is less heat o' the blood.

CONCHUBAR [*In a loud voice.*] No more of that; I will not have this
    friendship.
  Cuchulain is my man, and I forbid it.
  He shall not go unfought, for I myself——

CUCHULAIN I will not have it.

CONCHUBAR   You lay commands on me?

CUCHULAIN [*Seizing* CONCHUBAR.] You shall not stir, High King; I'll
    hold you there.

CONCHUBAR Witchcraft has maddened you.

THE KINGS [*Shouting.*]   Yes, witchcraft! witchcraft!

FIRST KING Some witch has worked upon your mind, Cuchulain.
  The head of that young man seemed like a woman's
  You had a fancy for. Then of a sudden
  You laid your hands on the High King himself.

[*He has taken his hands from the* HIGH KING. *He stands as if he were
dazed.*]

CUCHULAIN And laid my hands on the High King himself.

CONCHUBAR Some witch is floating in the air above us.

CUCHULAIN Yes, witchcraft, witchcraft. Witches of
    the air.   [*To* YOUNG MAN.]
  Why did you? Who was it set you to this work?
  Out! out, I say! for now it's sword on sword!

YOUNG MAN But . . . but I did not.

CUCHULAIN   Out, I say! out! out!

[YOUNG MAN *goes out followed by* CUCHULAIN. *The* KINGS *follow them
out with confused cries, and words one can hardly hear because of the
noise. Some cry,* "Quicker, quicker!" "Why are you so long at the
door?" "We'll be too late!" "Have they begun to fight?" *and so on; and
one, it may be,* "I saw him fight with Ferdia!"[2] *Their voices drown
each other. The three women are left alone.*]

---

2. Cuchulain's fight with Ferdia, son of Daire, who had been his childhood friend and whom he
regretfully kills, takes several days, and it forms one of the central chapters of the *Tain.*

FIRST WOMAN   I have seen, I have seen.
SECOND WOMAN   What do you cry aloud?
FIRST WOMAN   The ever-living have shown me what's to come.
THIRD WOMAN   How? Where?
FIRST WOMAN   In the ashes of the bowl.
SECOND WOMAN   While you were holding it between your hands?
THIRD WOMAN   Speak quickly!
FIRST WOMAN   I saw Cuchulain's roof-tree
Leap into fire, and the walls split and blacken.
SECOND WOMAN   Cuchulain has gone out to die.
THIRD WOMAN   O! O!
SECOND WOMAN   Who could have thought that one so great as he
Should meet his end at this unnoted sword!
FIRST WOMAN   Life drifts between a Fool and a Blind Man
To the end, and nobody can know his end.
SECOND WOMAN   Come, look upon the quenching of this greatness.

[*The other two go to the door, but they stop for a moment upon the threshold and wail.*]

FIRST WOMAN   No crying out, for there'll be need of cries
And knocking at the breast when it's all finished.

[*The women go out. There is a sound of clashing swords from time to time during what follows. Enter the* FOOL *dragging the* BLIND MAN.]

FOOL   You have eaten it, you have eaten it! You have left me nothing but the bones!

[*He throws* BLIND MAN *down by big chair.*]

BLIND MAN   O, that I should have to endure such a plague! O, I ache all over! O, I am pulled to pieces! This is the way you pay me all the good I have done you!

FOOL   You have eaten it! You have told me lies. I might have known you had eaten it when I saw your slow, sleepy walk. Lie there till the kings come. O, I will tell Conchubar and Cuchulain and all the kings about you!

BLIND MAN   What would have happened to you but for me, and you without your wits? If I did not take care of you, what would you do for food and warmth?

FOOL   You take care of me! You stay safe, and send me into every kind of danger. You sent me down the cliff for gull's eggs while you warmed your blind eyes in the sun; and then you ate all that were good for food. You left me the eggs that were neither egg nor bird. [BLIND MAN *tries to rise;* FOOL *makes him lie down again.*] Keep quiet now, till I shut the door. There is some noise outside—a high vexing noise, so that I can't be listening to myself. [*Shuts the big door.*] Why can't they be quiet! why can't they be quiet! [BLIND MAN *tries to get away.*] Ah! you would get away, would you! [*Follows* BLIND MAN *and brings him back.*] Lie there! lie there! No, you won't get away! Lie there till the kings come. I'll tell them all about you. I will tell it all. How you sit warming yourself, when you have made me light a fire of sticks, while I sit blowing it with my mouth. Do you not always make me take the windy side of the bush when it blows, and the rainy side when it rains?

BLIND MAN   O, good Fool! listen to me. Think of the care I have taken of you. I have brought you to many a warm hearth, where there was a good welcome for you, but you would not stay there; you were always wandering about.

FOOL   The last time you brought me in it was not I who wandered away, but you that got put out because you took the crubeen[3] out of the pot when nobody was looking. Keep quiet, now!

CUCHULAIN [*Rushing in.*]   Witchcraft! There is no witchcraft on the earth, or among the witches of the air, that these hands cannot break.

FOOL   Listen to me Cuchulain. I left him turning the fowl at the fire. He ate it all, though I had stolen it. He left me nothing but the feathers.

CUCHULAIN   Fill me a horn of ale!

BLIND MAN   I gave him what he likes best. You do not know how vain this Fool is. He likes nothing so well as a feather.

FOOL   He left me nothing but the bones and feathers. Nothing but the feathers, though I had stolen it.

CUCHULAIN   Give me that horn! Quarrels here, too! [*Drinks.*] What is there between you two that is worth a quarrel? Out with it!

BLIND MAN   Where would he be but for me? I must be always thinking —thinking to get food for the two of us, and when we've got it, if the moon is at the full or the tide on the turn, he'll leave the rabbit in the snare till it is full of maggots, or let the trout slip back through his hands into the stream.

[*The* FOOL *has begun singing while the* BLIND MAN *is speaking.*]

[*Sings.*]

When you were an acorn on the tree top,
    Then was I an eagle cock;
Now that you are a withered old block,
    Still am I an eagle cock.

BLIND MAN   Listen to him now. That's the sort of talk I have to put up with day out, day in.

[*The* FOOL *is putting the feathers into his hair.* CUCHULAIN *takes a handful of feathers out of a heap the* FOOL *has on the bench beside him, and out of the* FOOL's *hair, and begins to wipe the blood from his sword with them.*]

FOOL   He has taken my feathers to wipe his sword. It is blood that he is wiping from his sword.

CUCHULAIN [*Goes up to door at back and throws away feathers.*]   They are standing about his body. They will not awaken him for all his witchcraft.

BLIND MAN   It is that young champion that he has killed. He that came out of Aoife's country.

_____
3. Pig's foot.

CUCHULAIN   He thought to have saved himself with witchcraft.

FOOL   That blind man there said he would kill you. He came from Aoife's country to kill you. That blind man said they had taught him every kind of weapon that he might do it. But I always knew that you would kill him.

CUCHULAIN   [*To the* BLIND MAN.]   You knew him, then?

BLIND MAN   I saw him, when I had my eyes, in Aoife's country.

CUCHULAIN   You were in Aoife's country?

BLIND MAN   I knew him and his mother there.

CUCHULAIN   He was about to speak of her when he died.

BLIND MAN   He was a queen's son.

CUCHULAIN   What queen? what queen? [*Seizes* BLIND MAN, *who is now sitting upon the bench.*] Was it Scathach[4]? There were many queens. All the rulers there were queens.

BLIND MAN   No, not Scathach.

CUCHULAIN   It was Uathach, then? Speak! speak!

BLIND MAN   I cannot speak; you are clutching me too tightly. [CUCHULAIN *lets him go.*] I cannot remember who it was. I am not certain. It was some queen.

FOOL   He said a while ago that the young man was Aoife's son.

CUCHULAIN   She? No, no! She had no son when I was there.

FOOL   That blind man there said that she owned him for her son.

CUCHULAIN   I had rather he had been some other woman's son. What father had he? A soldier out of Alba? She was an amorous woman—a proud, pale, amorous woman.

BLIND MAN   None knew whose son he was.

CUCHULAIN   None knew! Did you know, old listener at doors?

BLIND MAN   No, no; I knew nothing.

FOOL   He said a while ago that he heard Aoife boast that she'd never but the one lover, and he the only man that had overcome her in battle. [*Pause.*]

BLIND MAN   Somebody is trembling, Fool! The bench is shaking. Why are you trembling? Is Cuchulain going to hurt us? It was not I who told you, Cuchulain.

FOOL   It is Cuchulain who is trembling. It is Cuchulain who is shaking the bench.

BLIND MAN   It is his own son he has slain.

CUCHULAIN   'Twas they that did it, the pale windy people.
Where? where? where? My sword against the thunder!
But no, for they have always been my friends;
And though they love to blow a smoking coal
Till it's all flame, the wars they blow aflame
Are full of glory, and heart-uplifting pride,
And not like this. The wars they love awaken
Old fingers and the sleepy strings of harps.
Who did it, then? Are you afraid? speak out?
For I have put you under my protection,

---

4. Scathach of Alba (an ancient term for Scotland, where Aoife was born and raised) trained Cuchulain in arms as a young man. Uathach, her daughter, had been Cuchulain's lover.

And will reward you well. Dubthach the Chafer[5]?
He'd an old grudge. No, for he is with Maeve.
Laegaire did it! Why do you not speak?
What is this house? [*Pause.*] Now I remember all.

[*Comes before* CONCHUBAR'S *chair, and strikes out with his sword as if* CONCHUBAR *was sitting upon it.*]

'Twas you who did it—you who sat up there
With your old rod of kingship, like a magpie
Nursing a stolen spoon. No, not a magpie,
A maggot that is eating up the earth!
Yes, but a magpie, for he's flown away.
Where did he fly to?

BLIND MAN   He is outside the door.

CUCHULAIN   Outside the door?

BLIND MAN   Between the door and the sea.

CUCHULAIN   Conchubar, Conchubar! the sword into your heart!

[*He rushes out. Pause.* FOOL *creeps up to the big door and looks after him.*]

FOOL   He is going up to King Conchubar. They are all about the young man. No, no, he is standing still. There is a great wave going to break, and he is looking at it. Ah! now he is running down to the sea, but he is holding up his sword as if he were going into a fight. [*Pause.*] Well struck! well struck!

BLIND MAN   What is he doing now!

FOOL   O! he is fighting the waves.[6]

BLIND MAN   He sees King Conchubar's crown on every one of them.

FOOL   There, he has struck at a big one! He has struck the crown off it; he has made the foam fly. There again, another big one!

BLIND MAN   Where are the kings! What are the kings doing?

FOOL   They are shouting and running down to the shore, and the people are running out of the houses. They are all running.

BLIND MAN   You say they are running out of the houses? There will be nobody left in the houses. Listen, Fool!

FOOL   There, he is down! He is up again. He is going into the deep water. There is a big wave. It has gone over him. I cannot see him now. He has killed kings and giants, but the waves have mastered him, the waves have mastered him!

BLIND MAN   Come here, Fool!

FOOL   The waves have mastered him.

BLIND MAN   Come here!

FOOL   The waves have mastered him.

BLIND MAN   Come here, I say!

---

5. Dubthach "the Backbiter" was a Red Branch warrior who deserted to join Queen Maeve.
6. Conchubar asked the Druids to enchant Cuchulain so that he would fight the sea, to prevent him from killing his companions in his rage.

FOOL [*Coming towards him, but looking backward towards the door.*] What is it?

BLIND MAN There will be nobody in the houses. Come this way; come quickly! The ovens will be full. We will put our hands into the ovens.

[*They go out.*]

At the Hawk's Well[1]

THREE MUSICIANS (their faces made up to resemble masks)
THE GUARDIAN OF THE WELL (with face made up to resemble a mask)
AN OLD MAN (wearing a mask)
A YOUNG MAN (wearing a mask)

The Time—the Irish Heroic Age

The stage is any bare space before a wall against which stands a patterned screen. A drum and a gong and a zither have been laid close to the screen before the play begins. If necessary, they can be carried in, after the audience is seated, by the FIRST MUSICIAN, *who also can attend to the lights if there is any special lighting. We had two lanterns upon posts—designed by Mr. Dulac[2]—at the outer corners of the stage, but they did not give enough light, and we found it better to play by the light of a large chandelier. Indeed I think, so far as my present experience goes, that the most effective lighting is the lighting we are most accustomed to in our rooms. These masked players seem stranger when there is no mechanical means of separating them from us. The* FIRST MUSICIAN *carries with him a folded black cloth and goes to the centre of the stage towards the front and stands motionless, the folded cloth hanging from between his hands. The two musicians enter and, after standing a moment at either side of the stage, go towards him and slowly unfold the cloth, singing as they do so:*

> I call to the eye of the mind
> A well long choked up and dry
> And boughs long stripped by the wind,
> And I call to the mind's eye
> Pallor of an ivory face,   5
> Its lofty dissolute air,
> A man climbing up to a place
> The salt sea wind has swept bare.

1. By 1916, Yeats had become disaffected with the prospects for a popular Irish theater at the Abbey, and he was writing plays intended for private performance in drawing rooms. The stylized setting, action, and dialogue, and the use of masks, show the influence of Japanese Noh drama, to which Yeats had been introduced by Ezra Pound. *At the Hawk's Well* was first performed for a privately invited audience in April 1916, and first published in 1917. Its narrative, inspired by though not part of the Cuchulain stories of the *Tain Bó Cualnge*, takes place well before the action portrayed in *On Baile's Strand* (see note 1, p. 141).
2. Artist Edmund Dulac (1882–1953) designed the masks, costumes, and some other properties for the first production of the play.

*As they unfold the cloth, they go backward a little so that the
stretched cloth and the wall make a triangle with the* FIRST
MUSICIAN *at the apex supporting the centre of the cloth. On
the black cloth is a gold pattern suggesting a hawk. The* SEC-
OND *and* THIRD MUSICIANS *now slowly fold up the cloth again,
pacing with a rhythmic movement of the arms towards the* FIRST
MUSICIAN *and singing:*

> What were his life soon done!
> Would he lose by that or win?   10
> A mother that saw her son
> Doubled over a speckled shin,
> Cross-grained with ninety years,
> Would cry, "How little worth
> Were all my hopes and fears   15
> And the hard pain of his birth!"

*The words "a speckled shin" are familiar to readers of Irish
legendary stories in descriptions of old men bent double over
the fire. While the cloth has been spread out, the* GUARDIAN OF
THE WELL *has entered and is now crouching upon the ground.
She is entirely covered by a black cloak. The three musicians
have taken their places against the wall beside their instruments
of music; they will accompany the movements of the players
with gong or drum or zither.*

FIRST MUSICIAN [*Singing.*]

> The boughs of the hazel shake,
> The sun goes down in the west.

SECOND MUSICIAN [*Singing.*]

> The heart would be always awake,
> The heart would turn to its rest.   20

[*They now go to one side of the stage rolling up the cloth. A* GIRL *has
taken her place by a square blue cloth representing a well. She is
motionless.*]

FIRST MUSICIAN [*Speaking.*]
  Night falls;
  The mountain-side grows dark;
  The withered leaves of the hazel
  Half-choke the dry bed of the well;
  The guardian of the well is sitting   25
  Upon the old grey stone at its side,
  Worn out from raking its dry bed,
  Worn out from gathering up the leaves.
  Her heavy eyes
  Know nothing, or but look upon stone.   30
  The wind that blows out of the sea
  Turns over the heaped-up leaves at her side;

They rustle and diminish.
SECOND MUSICIAN.   I am afraid of this place.
BOTH MUSICIANS [*Singing.*]

35

"Why should I sleep," the heart cries,
"For the wind, the salt wind, the sea wind
Is beating a cloud through the skies;
I would wander always like the wind."

[*An* OLD MAN *enters through the audience.*]

FIRST MUSICIAN [*Speaking.*]
That old man climbs up hither,
Who has been watching by his well   40
These fifty years.
He is all doubled up with age;
The old thorn-trees are doubled so
Among the rocks where he is climbing.

[*The* OLD MAN *stands for a moment motionless by the side of the stage
with bowed head. He lifts his head at the sound of a drum tap. He
goes towards the front of the stage moving to the taps of the drum. He
crouches and moves his hands as if making a fire. His movements, like
those of the other persons of the play, suggest a marionette.*]

FIRST MUSICIAN [*Speaking.*]
He has made a little heap of leaves;   45
He lays the dry sticks on the leaves
And, shivering with cold, he has taken up
The fire-stick and socket from its hole.
He whirls it round to get a flame;
And now the dry sticks take the fire   50
And now the fire leaps up and shines
Upon the hazels and the empty well.

MUSICIANS [*Singing.*]

"O wind, O salt wind, O sea wind!"
Cries the heart, "it is time to sleep;
Why wander and nothing to find?
Better grow old and sleep."

OLD MAN [*Speaking.*]
Why don't you speak to me? Why don't you say
"Are you not weary gathering those sticks?
Are not your fingers cold?" You have not one word,
While yesterday you spoke three times. You said: 60
"The well is full of hazel leaves." You said:
"The wind is from the west." And after that:
"If there is rain it's likely there'll be mud."
To-day you are as stupid as a fish,
No, worse, worse, being less lively and as dumb.   65

[*He goes nearer.*]

Your eyes are dazed and heavy. If the Sidhe[3]
Must have a guardian to clean out the well
And drive the cattle off, they might choose somebody
That can be pleasant and companionable
Once in the day. Why do you stare like that?   70
You had that glassy look about the eyes
Last time it happened. Do you know anything?
It is enough to drive an old man crazy
To look all day upon these broken rocks,
And ragged thorns, and that one stupid face,   75
And speak and get no answer.
YOUNG MAN [*Who has entered through the audience during the last speech.*]
                                    Then speak to me,
For youth is not more patient than old age;
And though I have trod the rocks for half a day
I cannot find what I am looking for.
OLD MAN   Who speaks?
Who comes so suddenly into this place   80
Where nothing thrives? If I may judge by the gold
On head and feet and glittering in your coat,
You are not of those who hate the living world.
YOUNG MAN   I am named Cuchulain, I am Sualtam's son.
OLD MAN   I have never heard that name.   85
CUCHULAIN   It is not unknown.
I have an ancient house beyond the sea.
OLD MAN   What mischief brings you hither, you are like those
Who are crazy for the shedding of men's blood,
And for the love of women?
YOUNG MAN   A rumour has led me,
A story told over the wine towards dawn.   90
I rose from table, found a boat, spread sail
And with a lucky wind under the sail
Crossed waves that have seemed charmed, and found this shore.
OLD MAN   There is no house to sack among these hills
Nor beautiful woman to be carried off.   95
YOUNG MAN   You should be native here, for that rough tongue
Matches the barbarous spot. You can, it may be,
Lead me to what I seek, a well wherein
Three hazels drop their nuts and withered leaves,
And where a solitary girl keeps watch   100
Among grey boulders. He who drinks, they say,
Of that miraculous water lives for ever.
OLD MAN   And are there not before your eyes at the instant
Grey boulders and a solitary girl
And three stripped hazels?   105
YOUNG MAN   But there is no well.

3. Name (pronounced "Shee") for immortal beings or faeries in Irish folklore.

OLD MAN Can you see nothing yonder?
YOUNG MAN   I but see
   A hollow among stones half-full of leaves.
OLD MAN And do you think so great a gift is found
   By no more toil than spreading out a sail,
   And climbing a steep hill? Oh, folly of youth,   110
   Why should that hollow place fill up for you,
   That will not fill for me? I have lain in wait
   For more than fifty years to find it empty,
   Or but to find the stupid wind of the sea
   Drive round the perishable leaves.   115
YOUNG MAN   So it seems
   There is some moment when the water fills it.
OLD MAN A secret moment that the holy shades
   That dance upon the desolate mountain know,
   And not a living man, and when it comes
   The water has scarce plashed before it is gone.   120
YOUNG MAN I will stand here and wait. Why should the luck.
   Of Sualtam's son desert him now? For never
   Have I had long to wait for anything.
OLD MAN No! Go from this accursed place, this place
   Belongs to me, that girl there and those others,[4]   125
   Deceivers of men.
YOUNG MAN   And who are you who rail
   Upon those dancers that all others bless?
OLD MAN One whom the dancers cheat. I came like you
   When young in body and in mind, and blown
   By what had seemed to me a lucky sail.   130
   The well was dry, I sat upon its edge,
   I waited the miraculous flood, I waited
   While the years passed and withered me away.
   I have snared the birds for food and eaten grass
   And drunk the rain, and neither in dark nor shine   135
   Wandered too far away to have heard the plash,
   And yet the dancers have deceived me. Thrice
   I have awakened from a sudden sleep
   To find the stones were wet.
YOUNG MAN   My luck is strong,
   It will not leave me waiting, nor will they   140
   That dance among the stones put me asleep;
   If I grow drowsy I can pierce my foot.
OLD MAN No, do not pierce it, for the foot is tender,
   It feels pain much. But find your sail again
   And leave the well to me, for it belongs   145
   To all that's old and withered.
YOUNG MAN   No, I stay.

---

4. The Sidhe, associated with dangerous enchantments.

[*The* GIRL *gives the cry of the hawk.*]

There is that bird again.
OLD MAN   There is no bird.
YOUNG MAN   It sounded like the sudden cry of a hawk,
But there's no wing in sight. As I came hither
A great grey hawk swept down out of the sky,   150
And though I have good hawks, the best in the world
I had fancied, I have not seen its like. It flew
As though it would have torn me with its beak,
Or blinded me, smiting with that great wing.
I had to draw my sword to drive it off,   155
And after that it flew from rock to rock.
I pelted it with stones, a good half-hour,
And just before I had turned the big rock there
And seen this place, it seemed to vanish away.
Could I but find a means to bring it down   160
I'd hood it.[5]
OLD MAN   The woman of the Sidhe herself,
The mountain witch, the unappeasable shadow,
She is always flitting upon this mountain-side,
To allure or to destroy. When she has shown
Herself to the fierce women of the hills   165
Under that shape they offer sacrifice
And arm for battle. There falls a curse
On all who have gazed in her unmoistened eyes;
So get you gone while you have that proud step
And confident voice, for not a man alive   170
Has so much luck that he can play with it.
Those that have long to live should fear her most,
The old are cursed already. That curse may be
Never to win a woman's love and keep it;
Or always to mix hatred in the love;   175
Or it may be that she will kill your children,
That you will find them, their throats torn and bloody,
Or you will be so maddened that you kill them
With your own hand.
YOUNG MAN   Have you been set down there
To threaten all who come, and scare them off?   180
You seem as dried up as the leaves and sticks,
As though you had no part in life.

[GIRL *gives hawk cry again.*]
              That cry!
There is that cry again. That woman made it,
But why does she cry out as the hawk cries?
OLD MAN   It was her mouth, and yet not she, that cried.   185
It was that shadow cried behind her mouth;

---

5. Captured hawks were hooded (had their eyes covered) as part of the process of taming them.

And now I know why she has been so stupid
All the day through, and had such heavy eyes.
Look at her shivering now, the terrible life
Is slipping through her veins. She is possessed.   190
Who knows whom she will murder or betray
Before she awakes in ignorance of it all,
And gathers up the leaves! But they'll be wet;
The water will have come and gone again;
That shivering is the sign. Oh, get you gone,   195
At any moment now I shall hear it bubble.
If you are good you will leave it. I am old,
And if I do not drink it now, will never;
I have been watching all my life and maybe
Only a little cupful will bubble up.   200

YOUNG MAN   I'll take it in my hands. We shall both drink,
And even if there are but a few drops,
Share them.

OLD MAN   But swear that I may drink the first;
The young are greedy, and if you drink the first
You'll drink it all. Ah, you have looked at her;   205
She has felt your gaze and turned her eyes on us;
I cannot bear her eyes, they are not of this world,
Nor moist, nor faltering; they are no girl's eyes.

[*He covers his head. The* GUARDIAN OF THE WELL *throws off her cloak
and rises. Her dress under the cloak suggests a hawk.*]

YOUNG MAN   Why do you gaze upon me with the eyes of a hawk?
I am not afraid of you, bird, woman, or witch.   210

[*He goes to the side of the well, which the Guardian of the Well has
left.*]

Do what you will, I shall not leave this place
Till I have grown immortal like yourself.

[*He has sat down, the* GIRL *has begun to dance, moving like a hawk.
The* OLD MAN *sleeps. The dance goes on for some time.*]

FIRST MUSICIAN [*Singing or half-singing*]

        O God protect me
        From a horrible deathless body
        Sliding through the veins of a sudden.   215

[*The dance goes on for some time. The* YOUNG MAN *rises slowly.*]

FIRST MUSICIAN [*Speaking.*]
The madness has laid hold upon him now,
For he grows pale and staggers to his feet.

[*The dance goes on.*]

YOUNG MAN   Run where you will,
Grey bird, you shall be perched upon my wrist,
Some were called queens and yet have been perched there.   220

[*The dance goes on.*]

FIRST MUSICIAN [*Speaking.*]
  I have heard water plash; it comes, it comes;
  It glitters among the stones and he has heard the plash;
  Look, he has turned his head.

    [*The Hawk has gone out. The* YOUNG MAN *drops his spear as if in a dream and goes out.*]

MUSICIANS [*Singing.*]
        He has lost what may not be found
        Till men heap his burial mound   225
        And all the history ends.
        He might have lived at his ease,
        An old dog's head on his knees,
        Among his children and friends.

  [*The* OLD MAN *creeps up to the well.*]

OLD MAN   The accursed shadows have deluded me,   230
  The stones are dark and yet the well is empty;
  The water flowed and emptied while I slept;
  You have deluded me my whole life through.
  Accursed dancers, you have stolen my life.
  That there should be such evil in a shadow.   235
YOUNG MAN [*Entering.*]
  She has fled from me and hidden in the rocks.
OLD MAN   She has but led you from the fountain. Look!
  The stones and leaves are dark where it has flowed,
  Yet there is not a drop to drink.

  [*The* MUSICIANS *cry "Eofe!" "Eofe!"*[6] *and strike gong.*]

YOUNG MAN   What are those cries?
  What is that sound that runs along the hill?   240
  Who are they that beat a sword upon a shield?
OLD MAN   She has roused up the fierce women of the hills,
  Eofe, and all her troop, to take your life,
  And never till you are lying in the earth,
  Can you know rest.
YOUNG MAN   The clash of arms again!   245
OLD MAN   Oh, do not go! The mountain is accursed;
  Stay with me, I have nothing more to lose,
  I do not now deceive you.
YOUNG MAN   I will face them.

---

6. Other printings give "Aoife." Cuchulain defeats Queen Aoife of Scotland, briefly becomes her lover, and leaves her pregnant with a child, Conlaoch, whom Cuchulain later kills (see note 1, p. 141), unaware of his identity.

[*He goes out no longer as if in a dream, but shouldering his spear and calling.*]

He comes! Cuchulain, son of Sualtam, comes!

[*The* MUSICIANS *stand up, one goes to centre with folded cloth. The others unfold it. While they do so they sing. During the singing, and while hidden by the cloth, the* OLD MAN *goes out. When the play is performed with Mr. Dulac's music, the Musicians do not rise or unfold the cloth till after they have sung the words "a bitter life."*]

[*Songs for the unfolding and folding of the cloth.*]

> Come to me, human faces,   250
> Familiar memories;
> I have found hateful eyes
> Among the desolate places,
> Unfaltering, unmoistened eyes.
>
> Folly alone I cherish,   255
> I choose it for my share,
> Being but a mouthful of air,
> I am content to perish,
> I am but a mouthful of sweet air.
>
> O lamentable shadows,   260
> Obscurity of strife,
> I choose a pleasant life,
> Among indolent meadows;
> Wisdom must live a bitter life.

[*They then fold up the cloth, again singing.*]

> "The man that I praise,"   265
> Cries out the empty well,
> "Lives all his days
> Where a hand on the bell
> Can call the milch cows
> To the comfortable door of his house.   270
> Who but an idiot would praise
> Dry stones in a well?"
>
> "The man that I praise,"
> Cries out the leafless tree,
> "Has married and stays   275
> By an old hearth, and he
> On naught has set store
> But children and dogs on the floor.
> Who but an idiot would praise
> A withered tree?"   280

[*They go out.*]

Purgatory[1]

A ruined house and a bare tree in the background.

BOY   Half door,[2] hall door
    Hither and thither day and night
    Hill or hollow, shouldering this pack.
    Hearing you talk.
OLD MAN   Study that house.
    I think about its jokes and stories;   5
    I try to remember what the butler
    Said to a drunken gamekeeper
    In mid-October, but I cannot,
    If I cannot, none living can.
    Where are the jokes and stories of a house   10
    Its threshold gone to patch a pig-sty?
BOY   So you have come this path before?
OLD MAN   The moonlight falls upon the path,
    The shadow of a cloud upon the house
    And that's symbolical; study that tree,   15
    What is it like?
BOY   A silly old man.
OLD MAN   It's like—no matter what it's like.
    I saw it a year ago stripped bare as now,
    I saw it fifty years ago[3]
    Before the thunder-bolt had riven it,   20
    Green leaves, ripe leaves, leaves thick as butter,
    Fat, greasy life. Stand there and look,
    Because there is somebody in that house.

[*The boy puts down pack and stands in the doorway.*]

BOY   There's nobody here.
OLD MAN   There's somebody there.
BOY   The floor is gone, the windows gone,   25
    And where there should be roof there's sky,
    And here's a bit of an egg-shell thrown
    Out of a jackdaw's nest.
OLD MAN   But there are some
    That do not care what's gone, what's left;
    The souls in Purgatory that come back   30
    To habitations and familiar spots.
BOY   Your wits are out again.

---

1. First produced at the Abbey Theatre, Dublin, in August 1938. First published, after Yeats's death, in *Last Poems and Two Plays* (1939). In Catholic belief, Purgatory is a place of suffering in which the souls of the dead are purified of their sin.
2. A door divided into two sections, the upper of which can be left open to let in air and light.
3. The richness the Old Man recalls is of the period before the demise of the Protestant landowning class in Ireland.

OLD MAN   Re-live
   Their transgressions, and that not once
   But many times, they know at last
   The consequence of those transgressions   35
   Whether upon others, or upon themselves;
   Upon others, others may bring help
   For when the consequence is at an end
   The dream must end; upon themselves
   There is no help but in themselves   40
   And in the mercy of God
BOY   I have had enough!
   Talk to the jackdaws, if talk you must.
OLD MAN   Stop! Sit there upon that stone.
   That is the house where I was born.
BOY   The big old house that was burnt down?   45
OLD MAN   My mother that was your grand-dam owned it,
   This scenery and this countryside,
   Kennel and stable, horse and hound—
   She had a horse at the Curragh,[4] and there met
   My father, a groom in a training stable,   50
   Looked at him and married him.
   Her mother never spoke to her again,
   And she did right.
BOY   What's right and wrong?
   My grand-dad got the girl and the money.
OLD MAN   Looked at him and married him,   55
   And he squandered everything she had.
   She never knew the worst, because
   She died in giving birth to me,
   But now she knows it all, being dead.
   Great people lived and died in this house;   60
   Magistrates, colonels, members of Parliament,
   Captains and Governors, and long ago
   Men that had fought at Aughrim and the Boyne.[5]
   Some that had gone on government work
   To London or to India, came home to die,   65
   Or came from London every spring
   To look at the May-blossom in the park.
   They had loved the trees that he cut down
   To pay what he had lost at cards
   Or spent on horses, drink and women;   70
   Had loved the house, had loved all
   The intricate passages of the house,
   But he killed the house; to kill a house
   Where great men grew up, married, died,
   I here declare a capital offence.   75

4. Renowned Irish center for racing and horse-breeding, in County Kildare.
5. At the battle of the Boyne in 1690 and then at Aughrim, Galway, in 1691, the English forces of
   William of Orange defeated the Irish, Catholic forces of James II, thereby ensuring Protestant,
   English control of Ireland.

BOY   My God, but you had luck. Grand clothes,
    And maybe a grand horse to ride.
OLD MAN   That he might keep me upon his level
    He never sent me to school, but some
    Half-loved me for my half of her,   80
    A gamekeeper's wife taught me to read,
    A Catholic curate taught me Latin.
    There were old books and books made fine
    By eighteenth century French binding, books
    Modern and ancient, books by the ton.   85
BOY   What education have you given me?
OLD MAN   I gave the education that befits
    A bastard that a pedlar got
    Upon a tinker's daughter in a ditch.
    When I had come to sixteen years old   90
    My father burned down the house when drunk.
BOY   But that is my age,[6] sixteen years old.
    At the Puck Fair.[7]
OLD MAN   And everything was burnt;
    Books, library, all were burnt.
BOY   Is what I have heard upon the road the truth,   95
    That you killed him in the burning house?
OLD MAN   There's nobody here but our two selves?
BOY   Nobody, Father.
OLD MAN   I stuck him with a knife,
    That knife that cuts my dinner now,
    And after that I left him in the fire;   100
    They dragged him out, somebody saw
    The knife-wound but could not be certain
    Because the body was all black and charred.
    Then some that were his drunken friends
    Swore they would put me upon trial,   105
    Spoke of quarrels, a threat I had made.
    The gamekeeper gave me some old clothes,
    I ran away, worked here and there
    Till I became a pedlar on the roads,
    No good trade, but good enough   110
    Because I am my father's son,
    Because of what I did or may do.
    Listen to the hoof beats! Listen, Listen!
BOY   I cannot hear a sound.
OLD MAN   Beat! Beat!
    This night is the anniversary   115
    Of my mother's wedding night,
    Or of the night wherein I was begotten.
    My father is riding from the public house
    A whiskey bottle under his arm.

6. The Irish Free State was approximately sixteen years old when the play was first produced and
   published.
7. A fair held annually in County Kerry, Ireland, at which a goat is crowned king.

[*A window is lit showing a young girl.*]

Look at the window; she stands there   120
Listening, the servants are all in bed,
She is alone, he has stayed late
Bragging and drinking in the public house.
BOY   There's nothing but an empty gap in the wall.
You have made it up. No, you are mad!   125
You are getting madder every day.
OLD MAN   It's louder now because he rides
Upon a gravelled avenue
All grass to-day. The hoof beat stops,
He has gone to the other side of the house,   130
Gone to the stable, put the horse up.
She has gone down to open the door.
This night she is no better than her man
And does not mind that he is half drunk,
She is mad about him. They mount the stairs   135
She brings him into her own chamber.
And that is the marriage chamber now.
The window is dimly lit again.

Do not let him touch you! It is not true
That drunken men cannot beget   140
And if he touch he must beget
And you must bear his murderer.
Deaf! Both deaf! If I should throw
A stick or stone they would not hear;
And that's a proof my wits are out.   145
But there's a problem: she must live
Through everything in exact detail,
Driven to it by remorse, and yet
Can she renew the sexual act
And find no pleasure in it, and if not,   150
If pleasure and remorse must both be there
Which is the greater?
                    I lack schooling.
Go fetch Tertullian;[8] he and I
Will ravel all that problem out
Whilst those two lie upon the mattress   155
Begetting me.
                    Come back! Come back!
And so you thought to slip away,
My bag of money between your fingers,
And that I could not talk and see!
You have been rummaging in the pack.   160

[*The light in the window has faded out.*]

---

8. Christian theologian (c. 160–c. 220) who argued that both pleasure and remorse continue in the soul after death.

BOY You never gave me my right share.

OLD MAN And had I given it, young as you are
You would have spent it upon drink.

BOY What if I did? I had a right
To get it and spend it as I chose.   165

OLD MAN Give me that bag and no more words.

BOY I will not.

OLD MAN I will break your fingers.

[*They struggle for the bag. In the struggle it drops, scattering the money. The* OLD MAN *staggers but does not fall. They stand looking at each other.*]

BOY What if I killed you? You killed my grand-dad
Because you were young and he was old.
Now I am young and you are old.   170

[*A window is lit up, a man is seen pouring whiskey into a glass.*]

OLD MAN [*Staring at window.*] Better looking, those sixteen years—

BOY What are you muttering?

OLD MAN   Younger—and yet
She should have known he was not her kind.

BOY What are you saying? Out with it!

[OLD MAN *points to window.*]

My God the window is lit up   175
And somebody stands there, although
The floorboards are all burnt away.

OLD MAN The window is lit up because my father
Has come to find a glass for his whiskey.
He leans there like some tired beast.   180

BOY A dead, living, murdered man.

OLD MAN Then the bride sleep fell upon Adam:[9]
Where did I read those words?
                              And yet
There's nothing leaning in the window
But the impression upon my mother's mind,   185
Being dead she is alone in her remorse.

BOY A body that was a bundle of old bones
Before I was born. Horrible! Horrible! [*He covers his eyes.*]

OLD MAN That beast there would know nothing being nothing.
If I should kill a man under the window,   190
He would not even turn his head. [*He stabs the boy.*]
My father and my son on the same jack-knife!
That finishes—there—there—there—

[*He stabs again and again. The window grows dark.*]

9. The poem "Eden Bower" (1870), by English painter and poet Dante Gabriel Rossetti (1828–1882), includes the lines "Yea, where the bride-sleep fell upon Adam / (Alas the hour!) / None shall hear when the storm-wind whistles / Through roses choked among thorns and thistles." "Bride-sleep" implies postcoital sleep.

"Hush-a-bye baby, thy father's a knight,
Thy mother a lady, lovely and bright."   195
No, that is something that I read in a book
And if I sing it must be to my mother,
And I lack rhyme.

[*The stage has grown dark except where the tree stands in white light.*]

Study that tree.
It stands there like a purified soul,
All cold, sweet, glistening light.   200
Dear mother, the window is dark again
But you are in the light because
I finished all that consequence.
I killed that lad for he was growing up,
He would soon take some woman's fancy,   205
Beget and pass pollution on.
I am a wretched foul old man
And therefore harmless. When I have stuck
This old jack-knife into a sod
And pulled it out all bright again,   210
And picked up all the money that he dropped
I'll to a distant place, and there
Tell my old jokes among new men.

[*He cleans the knife and begins to pick up money.*]

Hoof beats! Dear God
How quickly it returns—beat—beat—   215
Her mind cannot hold up that dream.
Twice a murderer and all for nothing,
And she must animate that dead night
Not once but many times!
            O God!
Release my mother's soul from its dream!   220
Mankind can do no more. Appease
The misery of the living and the remorse of the dead.

THE CURTAIN FALLS

The Texts of
THE PROSE

Prose Fiction and Folklore Writings

From *The Celtic Twilight*[1] (1893)

This Book

Next to the desire, which every artist feels, to create for himself a little world out of the beautiful, pleasant, and significant things of this marred and clumsy universe, I have desired to show in a vision something of the face of Ireland to any of my own people who care for things of this kind. I have therefore written down accurately and candidly much that I have heard and seen, and, except by way of commentary, nothing that I have merely imagined. I have, however, been at no pains to separate my own beliefs from those of the peasantry, but have rather let my men and women, dhouls[2] and faeries, go their way unoffended or defended by any argument of mine. The things a man has heard and seen are threads of life, and if he pull them carefully from the confused distaff[3] of memory, any who will can weave them into whatever garments of belief please them best. I too have woven my garment like another, but I shall try to keep warm in it, and shall be well content if it do not unbecome me.

Hope and Memory have one daughter and her name is Art, and she has built her dwelling far from the desperate field where men hang out their garments upon forked boughs to be banners of battle. O beloved daughter of Hope and Memory, be with me for a little.

W. B. YEATS

---

1. In his 1893 review-essay "The Message of the Folk-lorist" (see pp. 262–63), Yeats wrote that "Folklore is at once the Bible, the Thirty-nine Articles, and the Book of Common Prayer, and wellnigh all the great poets have lived by its light." *The Celtic Twilight*, a collection of folklore from the region around Sligo, Yeats's childhood home, reflects his enthusiasm for the cultural and imaginative traditions he found still flourishing in the west of Ireland. Such folklore, he believed, could play a crucial role in inspiring creative work for the Irish Revival, and it would promote a distinctively Irish racial and cultural mythology in opposition to what he saw as the "Gray Truth" of late nineteenth-century scientific rationalism and the bourgeois commercialism of England. His title for the volume, which refers to the twilight of morning rather than the dusk of evening, reflects his hope for the dawning of a new imaginative era in Ireland. In collaboration with Lady Gregory, whose own career as a folklorist was inspired by reading *The Celtic Twilight*, Yeats issued a revised and enlarged edition of the volume in 1902, in which the new material is drawn from the Galway region around Lady Gregory's home at Coole Park.
2. Devils or demons.
3. A rod from which material is unwound as it is spun into thread.

Belief and Unbelief

There are some doubters even in the western villages. One woman told me last Christmas that she did not believe either in hell or in ghosts. Hell she thought was merely an invention got up by the priest to keep people good; and ghosts would not be permitted, she held, to go 'trapsin about the earth' at their own free will; 'but there are faeries,' she added, 'and little leprechauns, and water-horses,[1] and fallen angels.' I have met also a man with a mohawk tattooed upon his arm, who held exactly similar beliefs and unbeliefs. No matter what one doubts one never doubts the faeries, for, as the man with the mohawk on his arm said to me, 'they stand to reason.' Even the official mind does not escape this faith.

A little girl who was at service in the village of Grange,[2] close under the seaward slopes of Ben Bulben, suddenly disappeared one night about three years ago. There was at once great excitement in the neighbourhood, because it was rumoured that the faeries had taken her. A villager was said to have long struggled to hold her from them, but at last they prevailed, and he found nothing in his hands but a broomstick.[3] The local constable was applied to, and he at once instituted a house-to-house search, and at the same time advised the people to burn all the *bucalauns* (ragweed) on the field she vanished from, because *bucalauns* are sacred to the faeries. They spent the whole night burning them, the constable repeating spells the while. In the morning the little girl was found, the story goes, wandering in the field. She said the faeries had taken her away a great distance, riding on a faery horse. At last she saw a big river, and the man who had tried to keep her from being carried off was drifting down it—such are the topsy-turvydoms of faery glamour—in a cockle-shell. On the way her companions had mentioned the names of several people who were about to die shortly in the village.

Perhaps the constable was right. It is better doubtless to believe much unreason and a little truth than to deny for denial's sake truth and unreason alike, for when we do this we have not even a rush candle to guide our steps, not even a poor sowlth[4] to dance before us on the marsh, and must needs fumble our way into the great emptiness where dwell the misshapen dhouls. And after all, can we come to so great evil if we keep a little fire on our hearths, and in our souls, and welcome with open hand whatever of excellent come to warm itself, whether it be man or phantom, and do not say too fiercely, even to the dhouls themselves. 'Be ye gone'? When all is said and done, how do we not know but that our own unreason may be better than another's truth? for it has been warmed on our hearths and in our souls, and is ready for the wild bees of truth to hive in it, and make their sweet honey. Come into the world again, wild bees, wild bees!

---

1. In an 1888 preface listing the various types of fairies and ghosts seen by the Irish peasantry, Yeats included "the Augh-iska, the Water-horse" as a type of monster, adding "but whether these be animals, fairies, or spirits, I know not."
2. A village about eight miles north of Sligo, close to the mountain Ben Bulben.
3. As Yeats wrote in his *Fairy and Folk Tales of the Irish Peasantry* (1888), "Sometimes the fairies fancy mortals, and carry them away into their own country, leaving instead some sick fairy child, or a log of wood."
4. A formless, luminous ghost or spirit.

Drumcliff and Rosses[1]

Drumcliff and Rosses were, are, and ever shall be, please Heaven! places of unearthly resort. I have lived near by them and in them, time after time, and have gathered thus many a crumb of faery lore. Drumcliff is a wide green valley, lying at the foot of Ben Bulben, the mountain in whose side the square white door swings open at nightfall to loose the faery riders on the world. The great St. Columba[2] himself was the builder of many of the old ruins in the valley, climbed the mountains on one noted occasion to get nearer heaven with his prayers. Rosses is a little sea-dividing, sandy plain, covered with short grass, like a green table-cloth, and lying in the foam midway between the round cairn-headed Knocknarea[3] and 'Ben Bulben, famous for hawks':

> 'But for Ben Bulben and Knocknarea
> Many a poor sailor'd be cast away,'

as the rhyme goes.[4]

At the northern corner of Rosses is a little promontory of sand and rocks and grass: a mournful, haunted place. No wise peasant would fall asleep under its low cliff, for he who sleeps here may wake 'silly,' the 'good people'[5] having carried off his soul. There is no more ready short-cut to the dim kingdom than this plovery headland, for, covered and smothered now from sight by mounds of sand, a long cave goes thither 'full of gold and silver, and the most beautiful parlours and drawing-rooms.' Once, before the sand covered it, a dog strayed in, and was heard yelping vainly deep underground in a fort far inland. These forts or raths, low circular ditches made before history began, cover all Rosses and all Columkille.[6] The one where the dog yelped has, like most others, an underground beehive chamber in the midst. Once when I was poking around there, an unusually intelligent and 'reading' peasant who had come with me, and waited outside, knelt down by the opening, and whispered in a timid voice, 'Are you all right, sir?' I had been some little while underground, and he feared I had been carried off like the dog.

No wonder he was afraid, for the fort has long been circled by ill-boding rumours. It is on the ridge of a small hill, on whose northern slope lie a few stray cottages. One night a farmer's young son came from one of them and saw the fort all flaming, and ran towards it, but the 'glamour'[7] fell on him, and he sprang on to a fence, cross-legged, and commenced beating it with a stick, for he imagined the fence was a horse, and that all night

---

1. Drumcliff, a village four miles north of Sligo. Yeats's great-grandfather, John Yeats, had been rector of Drumcliff Church. Rosses Point, a sandy peninsula and village about seven miles north-west of Sligo; Yeats's maternal relatives the Middletons and the Pollexfens owned much of the land in this area when he was young.
2. Saint Columba (521–597), also known as Columcille, missionary and poet and founder of monastic settlements in Ireland.
3. A mountain west of Sligo, topped by a cairn reputed to be the burial place of Maeve, a mythological queen of Connacht.
4. Ships coming into Sligo had to navigate a difficult channel on the south side of Rosses Point.
5. A colloquial phrase used to refer to the faeries or Sidhe, since it was believed that speaking ill of the unseen might bring bad luck. They were also sometimes referred to as "the Gentry."
6. The area around the estuary at the northeastern end of Rosses Point, named after St. Columcille.
7. Faery enchantment.

long he went on the most wonderful ride through the country. In the morning he was still beating his fence, and they carried him home, where he remained a simpleton for three years before he came to himself again. A little later a farmer tried to level the fort. His cows and horses died, and all manner of trouble overtook him, and finally he himself was led home, and left useless with 'his head on his knees by the fire to the day of his death.'

A few hundred yards southwards of the northern angle of Rosses is another angle having also its cave, though this one is not covered with sand. About twenty years ago a brig was wrecked near by, and three or four fishermen were put to watch the deserted hulk through the darkness. At midnight they saw sitting on a stone at the cave's mouth two red-capped fiddlers fiddling with all their might. The men fled. A great crowd of villagers rushed down to the cave to see the strange musicians, but the creatures had gone.

To the wise peasant the green hills and woods round him are full of never-fading mystery. When the aged countrywoman stands at her door in the evening, and, in her own words, 'looks at the mountains and thinks of the goodness of God,' God is all the nearer, because the pagan powers are not far: because northward in Ben Bulben, famous for hawks, the white square door swings open at sundown, and those wild unchristian riders rush forth upon the fields, while southward the White Lady[8] still wanders under the broad cloud night-cap of Knocknarea. How may she doubt these things, even though the priest shakes his head at her? Did not a herd-boy, no long while since, see the White Lady? She passed so close that the skirt of her dress touched him. 'He fell down, and was dead three days.' But this is merely the small gossip of faerydom—the little stitches that join this world and the other.

One night as I sat eating Mrs. H——'s soda-bread, her husband told me a longish story, much the best of all I heard in Rosses. Those creatures, the 'good people,' love to repeat themselves, and many a poor man from Fin M'Coul[9] to our own days has happened on some such adventure.

'In the times when we used to travel by the canal,' said my entertainer, 'I was coming down from Dublin. When we came to Mullingar[1] the canal ended, and I began to walk, and stiff and fatigued I was after the slowness. I had some friends with me, and now and then we walked, now and then we rode in a cart. So on till we saw some girls milking cows, and stopped to joke with them. After a while we asked them for a drink of milk. "We have nothing to put it in here," they said, "but come to the house with us." We went home with them, and sat round the fire talking. After a while the others went, and left me, loth to stir from the good fire. I asked the girls for something to eat. There was a pot on the fire, and they took the meat out and put it on a plate, and told me to eat only the meat that came off the head. When I had eaten, the girls went out, and I did not

8. A ghost.
9. Fionn mac Cumhaill, or Finn MacCool, the central figure of the Fenian cycle of Irish mythology, a warrior and poet whose followers were known as the Fianna.
1. Town in County Westmeath, close to midway between Sligo and Dublin, and connected to Dublin by the Royal Canal.

see them again. It grew darker and darker, and there I still sat, loth as ever to leave the good fire, and after a while two men came in, carrying between them a corpse. When I saw them coming I hid behind the door. Says one to the other, putting the corpse on the spit, "Who'll turn the spit?" Says the other, "Michael H——, come out of that and turn the meat." I came out all of a tremble, and began turning the spit. "Michael H——," says the one who spoke first, "If you let it burn we'll have to put you on the spit instead;" and on that they went out. I sat there trembling and turning the corpse till towards midnight. The men came again, and the one said it was burnt, and the other said it was done right. But having fallen out over it, they both said they would do me no harm that time; and, sitting by the fire, one of them cried out: "Michael H——, can you tell me a story?" "Divil a one," said I. On which he caught me by the shoulder, and put me out like a shot. It was a wild blowing night. Never in all my born days did I see such a night—the darkest night that ever came out of the heavens. I did not know where I was for the life of me. So when one of the men came after me and touched me on the shoulder, with a "Michael H——, can you tell me a story now?" "I can," says I. In he brought me; and putting me by the fire, says: "Begin." I have no story but the one," says I, "that I was sitting here, and you two men brought in a corpse and put it on the spit, and set me turning it." "That will do," says he; "ye may go in there and lie down on the bed." And I went, nothing loth; and in the morning where was I but in the middle of a green field!'

'Drumcliff' is a great place for omens. Before a prosperous fishing season a herring-barrel appears in the midst of a storm-cloud; and at a place called Columkille's Strand[2]—a place of marsh and mire—on a moonlight night an ancient boat, with St. Columba himself, comes floating in from sea: a portent of a brave harvesting. They have their dread portents too. Some few seasons ago a fisherman saw, far on the horizon, renowned Hy Brazel,[3] where he who touches shall find no more labour or care, nor cynic laughter, but shall go walking about under shadiest boscage,[4] and enjoy the conversation of Cuchullin[5] and his heroes. A vision of Hy Brazel forebodes national troubles.

Drumcliff and Rosses are chokeful of ghosts. By bog, road, rath, hillside, sea-border they gather in all shapes: headless women, men in armour, shadow hares, fire-tongued hounds, whistling seals, and so on. A whistling seal sank a ship the other day. At Drumcliff there is a very ancient graveyard. *The Annals of the Four Masters*[6] have this verse about a soldier names Denadhach, who died in 871: 'A pious soldier of the race of Con lies under hazel crosses at Drumcliff.' Not very long ago an old woman, turning to go into the churchyard at night to pray, saw standing before her a man in armour, who asked her where she was going. It was the 'pious soldier of the race of Con,' says local wisdom, still keeping watch, with

---

2. A beach.
3. Also known as the "Happy Islands," the paradise of ancient Irish mythology, reputed to be sometimes seen as a phantom island in the distance.
4. A thicket or grove.
5. The warrior hero of the Ulster cycle of Irish mythology.
6. A compilation of Irish historical records made in the seventeenth century. Yeats here cites an entry for the year 817, in which the soldier's name is more usually translated as "Dunadhach."

his ancient piety, over the graveyard. Again, the custom is still common hearabouts of sprinkling the doorstep with the blood of a chicken on the death of a very young child, thus (as belief is) drawing into the blood the evil spirits from the too weak soul. Blood is a great gatherer of 'supernaturals.' To cut your hand on a stone on going into a fort is said to be very dangerous.

There is no more curious ghost in Drumcliff or Rosses than the snipeghost. There is a bush behind a house in a village that I know well: for excellent reasons I do not say whether in Drumcliff or Rosses or on the slope of Ben Bulben, or even on the plain round Knocknarea. There is a history concerning the house and the bush. A man once lived there who found on the quay of Sligo a package containing three hundred pounds in notes. It was dropped by a foreign sea captain. This my man knew, but said nothing. It was money for freight, and the sea captain, not daring to face his owners, committed suicide in mid-ocean. Shortly afterwards my man died. His soul could not rest. At any rate, strange sounds were heard round his house, though that had grown and prospered since the freight money. The wife was often seen by those still alive out in the garden praying at the bush I have spoken of,—the shade of the departed appearing there at times. The bush remains to this day: once portion of a hedge, it now stands by itself, for no one dare put spade or pruning-knife about it. As to the strange sounds and voices, they did not cease till a few years ago, when, during some repairs, a snipe flew out of the solid plaster and away; the troubled ghost, say the neighbours, of the note-finder was at last dislodged.

My forebears and relations have lived near Rosses and Drumcliff these many years. A few miles northward I am wholly a stranger, and can find nothing. When I ask for stories of the faeries, my answer is some such as was given me by a woman who lives near a white stone fort—one of the few stone ones in Ireland—under the seaward angle of Ben Bulben: 'They always mind their own affairs and I always mind mine:' for it is dangerous to talk of the creatures. Only friendship for yourself or knowledge of your forbears will loosen these cautious tongues. My friend, 'the sweet Harp-String'[7] (I give no more than his Irish name for fear of gaugers[8])—the best of all our folk-tale hunters—seems to have the science of unpacking the stubbornest heart, but then he supplies the *potheen*-makers[9] with grain from his own fields. Besides, he is descended from a noted Gaelic magician who raised the 'dhoul' in Great Eliza's century,[1] and he has a kind of prescriptive right to hear tell of all kind of other-world creatures. They are almost relations of his, if all folk say concerning the parentage of magicians be true.

7. Folklorist, translator, and poet Douglas Hyde (1860–1949), known by the pseudonym An Craoibhin Aoibhinn ("the pleasant little branch"). Yeats regarded his *Beside the Fire* (1890) as "the one quite perfect book of Irish folklore."
8. Government agents who sought out illegally produced liquor.
9. Distillers of illicit spirits.
1. "Great Eliza" was Elizabeth I, queen of England from 1558 to 1603. Hyde's first Irish ancestors came to Ireland in the sixteenth century, but the "magician" is untraced.

From *The Celtic Twilight* (1902)

'Dust hath closed Helen's Eye'[1]

I

I have been lately to a little group of houses, not many enough to be called a village, in the barony of Kiltartan[2] in County Galway, whose name, Ballylee,[3] is known through all the west of Ireland. There is the old square castle, Ballylee, inhabited by a farmer and his wife, and a cottage where their daughter and their son-in-law live, and a little mill with an old miller, and old ash-trees throwing green shadows upon a little river and great stepping-stones. I went there two or three times last year to talk to the miller about Biddy Early,[4] a wise woman that lived in Clare some years ago, and about her saying, 'There is a cure for all evil between the two mill-wheels of Ballylee,' and to find out from him or another whether she meant the moss between the running waters or some other herb. I have been there this summer, and I shall be there again before it is autumn, because Mary Hynes, a beautiful woman whose name is still a wonder by turf fires, died there sixty years ago; for our feet would linger where beauty has lived its life of sorrow to make us understand that it is not of the world. An old man brought me a little way from the mill and the castle, and down a long, narrow boreen[5] that was nearly lost in brambles and sloe bushes, and he said, 'That is the little old foundation of the house, but the most of it is taken for building walls, and the goats have ate those bushes that are growing over it till they've got cranky, and they won't grow any more. They say she was the handsomest girl in Ireland, her skin was like dribbled snow'—he meant driven snow, perhaps,—'and she had blushes in her cheeks. She had five handsome brothers, but all are gone now!' I talked to him about a poem in Irish, Raftery,[6] a famous poet, made about her, and how it said, 'there is a strong cellar in Ballylee.' He said the strong cellar was the great hole where the river sank underground, and he brought me to a deep pool, where an otter hurried away under a grey boulder, and told me that many fish came up out of the dark water at early morning 'to taste the fresh water coming down from the hills.'

I first heard of the poem from an old woman who lives about two miles further up the river, and who remembers Raftery and Mary Hynes. She says, 'I never saw anybody so handsome as she was, and I never will till I die,' and that he was nearly blind, and had 'no way of living but to go round and to mark some house to go to, and then all the neighbours

1. From the song "Adieu, Farewell Earth's Bliss" in the comic play *Summer's Last Will and Testament* (1600) by dramatist Thomas Nashe (1567–1601).
2. A neighborhood surrounding the crossroads village nearest to Lady Gregory's home at Coole Park.
3. Yeats first visited Ballylee, about three miles from Coole Park, in 1896. He would buy the "old square castle" in 1917, and spent several summers there.
4. A renowned wise woman and herb healer/witch doctor (1798–1874), who had lived near Feakle, County Clare.
5. "Boirin" (Irish), a lane.
6. Anthony Raftery (c. 1784–1835), Irish poet and fiddler. His songs included "Mary Hynes," celebrating the Ballylee woman.

would gather to hear. If you treated him well he'd praise you, but if you did not, he'd fault you in Irish. He was the greatest poet in Ireland, and he'd make a song about that bush if he chanced to stand under it. There was a bush he stood under from the rain, and he made verses praising it, and then when the water came through he made verses dispraising it.'[7] She sang the poem to a friend[8] and to myself in Irish, and every word was audible and expressive, as the words in a song were always, as I think, before music grew too proud to be the garment of words, flowing and changing with the flowing and changing of their energies. The poem is not as natural as the best Irish poetry of the last century, for the thoughts are arranged in a too obviously traditional form, so the old poor half-blind man who made it has to speak as if he were a rich farmer offering the best of everything to the woman he loves, but it has naïve and tender phrases. The friend that was with me has made some of the translation, but some of it has been made by the country people themselves. I think it has more of the simplicity of the Irish verses than one finds in most translations.

'Going to Mass by the will of God,
The day came wet and the wind rose;
I met Mary Hynes at the cross of Kiltartan,
And I fell in love with her then and there.

I spoke to her kind and mannerly,
As by report was her own way;
And she said, "Raftery, my mind is easy,
You may come to-day to Ballylee."

When I heard her offer I did not linger,
When her talk went to my heart my heart rose.
We had only to go across the three fields,
We had daylight with us to Ballylee.

The table was laid with glasses and a quart measure,
She had fair hair, and she sitting beside me;
And she said, "Drink, Raftery, and a hundred welcomes,
There is a strong cellar in Ballylee."

O star of light and O sun in harvest,
O amber hair, O my share of the world,
Will you come with me upon Sunday
Till we agree together[9] before all the people?

I would not grudge you a song every Sunday evening,
Punch on the table, or wine if you would drink it,
But, O King of Glory, dry the roads before me,
Till I find the way to Ballylee.

7. Raftery's poem "Seanchus no caisimirt na Sgeiche" ("The History of the Bush").
8. Lady Gregory.
9. Exchange marriage vows.

There is sweet air on the side of the hill
When you are looking down upon Ballylee;
When you are walking in the valley picking nuts and blackberries,
There is music of the birds in it and music of the Sidhe.

What is the worth of greatness till you have the light
Of the flower of the branch that is by your side?
There is no god to deny it or to try and hide it,
She is the sun in the heavens who wounded my heart.

There was no part of Ireland I did not travel,
From the rivers to the tops of the mountains,
To the edge of Lough Greine[1] whose mouth is hidden,
And I saw no beauty but was behind hers.

Her hair was shining, and her brows were shining too;
Her face was like herself, her mouth pleasant and sweet.
She is the pride, and I give her the branch,
She is the shining flower of Ballylee.

It is Mary Hynes, the calm and easy woman,
Has beauty in her mind and in her face.
If a hundred clerks were gathered together,
They could not write down a half of her ways.'

An old weaver, whose son is supposed to go away among the Sidhe (the faeries) at night, says, 'Mary Hynes was the most beautiful thing ever made. My mother used to tell me about her, for she'd be at every hurling,[2] and wherever she was she was dressed in white. As many as eleven men asked her in marriage in one day, but she wouldn't have any of them. There was a lot of men up beyond Kilbecanty[3] one night sitting together drinking, and talking of her, and one of them got up and set out to go to Ballylee and see her; but Cloon Bog[4] was open then, and when he came to it he fell into the water, and they found him dead there in the morning. She died of the fever that was before the famine.'[5] Another old man says he was only a child when he saw her, but he remembered that 'the strongest man that was among us, one John Madden, got his death of the head of her, cold he got crossing rivers in the night-time to get to Ballylee.' This is perhaps the man the other remembered, for tradition gives the one thing many shapes. There is an old woman who remembers her, at Derrybrien[6] among the Echtge hills, a vast desolate place, which has changed little since the old poem said, 'the stag upon the cold summit of Echtge hears the cry of the wolves,' but still mindful of many poems and of the dignity

1. A lake now known as Lough Graney, at the foot of the Slieve Aughty Mountains, about nine miles southeast of Ballylee.
2. A traditional Irish sport similar to field hockey.
3. A village three miles south of Ballylee.
4. An area (later drained) bordering the Turra River, about a mile south of Ballylee.
5. The Great Irish Famine of 1845–49.
6. A village about twelve miles east of Coole Park, in the Slieve Aughty Mountains, which run north-south from southern County Galway into County Clare.

of ancient speech. She says, 'The sun and the moon never shone on anybody so handsome, and her skin was so white that it looked blue, and she had two little blushes on her cheeks.' And an old wrinkled woman who lives close by Ballylee, and has told me many tales of the Sidhe, says, 'I often saw Mary Hynes, she was handsome indeed. She had two bunches of curls beside her cheeks, and they were the colour of silver. I saw Mary Molloy that was drowned in the river beyond, and Mary Guthrie that was in Ardrahan,[7] but she took the sway of them both, a very comely creature. I was at her wake[8] too—she had seen too much of the world. She was a kind creature. One day I was coming home through that field beyond, and I was tired, and who should come out but the Poisin Glegeal[9] (the shining flower), and she gave me a glass of new milk.' This old woman meant no more than some beautiful bright colour by the colour of silver, for though I knew an old man—he is dead now—who thought she might know 'the cure for all the evils in the world,' that the Sidhe knew, she has seen too little gold to know its colour. But a man by the shore at Kinvara,[1] who is too young to remember Mary Hynes, says, 'Everybody says there is no one at all to be seen now so handsome; it is said she had beautiful hair, the colour of gold. She was poor, but her clothes every day were the same as Sunday, she had such neatness. And if she went to any kind of a meeting, they would all be killing one another for a sight of her, and there was a great many in love with her, but she died young. It is said that no one that has a song made about them will ever live long.'

Those who are much admired are, it is held, taken by the Sidhe, who can use ungoverned feeling for their own ends, so that a father, as an old herb doctor told me once, may give his child into their hands, or a husband his wife. The admired and desired are only safe if one says 'God bless them' when one's eyes are upon them. The old woman that sang the song thinks, too, that Mary Hynes was 'taken,' as the phrase is, 'for they have taken many that are not handsome, and why would they not take her? And people came from all parts to look at her, and maybe there were some that did not say "God bless her." ' An old man who lives by the sea at Duras[2] has as little doubt that she was taken, 'for there are some living yet can remember her coming to the pattern[3] there beyond, and she was said to be the handsomest girl in Ireland.' She died young because the gods loved her, for the Sidhe are the gods, and it may be that the old saying,[4] which we forget to understand literally, meant her manner of death in old times. These poor countrymen and countrywomen in their beliefs, and in their emotions, are many years nearer to that old Greek world, that set beauty beside the fountain of things, than are our men of learning. She 'had seen too much of the world'; but these old men and women, when

---

7. A village five miles north of Ballylee.
8. Irish funeral ceremony, traditionally involving music and drinking.
9. An Pósaidh Glégeal (The Bright Posy), the name given to Mary Hynes by Anthony Raftery in his poem about her.
1. A village on the coast about eight miles west of Ballylee.
2. A property on the coast about ten miles west of Ballylee, owned by a friend of Lady Gregory's.
3. A "pattern," or "patron," is a festival in honor of a saint.
4. "Those whom the Gods love die young."

they tell of her, blame another and not her, and though they can be hard, they grow gentle as the old men of Troy grew gentle when Helen passed by on the walls.[5]

The poet who helped her to so much fame has himself a great fame throughout the west of Ireland. Some think that Raftery was half blind, and say, 'I saw Raftery, a dark man, but he had sight enough to see her,' or the like, but some think he was wholly blind, as he may have been at the end of his life. Fable makes all things perfect in their kind, and her blind people must never look on the world and the sun. I asked a man I met one day, when I was looking for a pool *na mna Sidhe*[6] where women of faery have been seen, how Raftery could have admired Mary Hynes so much if he had been altogether blind? He said, 'I think Raftery was altogether blind, but those that are blind have a way of seeing things, and have the power to know more, and to feel more, and to do more, and to guess more than those that have their sight, and a certain wit and a certain wisdom is given to them.' Everybody, indeed, will tell you that he was very wise, for was he not only blind but a poet? The weaver whose words about Mary Hynes I have already given, says, 'His poetry was the gift of the Almighty, for there are three things that are the gift of the Almighty—poetry and dancing and principles. That is why in the old times an ignorant man coming down from the hillside would be better behaved and have better learning than a man with education you'd meet now, for they got it from God;' and a man at Coole[7] says, 'When he put his finger to one part of his head, everything would come to him as if it was written in a book;' and an old pensioner at Kiltartan says, 'He was standing under a bush one time, and he talked to it, and it answered him back in Irish. Some say it was the bush that spoke, but it must have been an enchanted voice in it, and it gave him the knowledge of all the things of the world. The bush withered up afterwards, and it is to be seen on the roadside now between this and Rahasine.'[8] There is a poem of his about a bush, which I have never seen, and it may have come out of the cauldron of fable in this shape.

A friend of mine met a man once who had been with him when he died, but the people say that he died alone, and one Maurteen Gillane told Dr. Hyde[9] that all night long a light was seen streaming up to heaven from the roof of the house where he lay, and 'that was the angels who were with him'; and all night long there, was a great light in the hovel, 'and that was the angels who were waking him. They gave that honour to him because he was so good a poet, and sang such religious songs.' It may be that in a few years Fable, who changes mortalities to immortalities in her cauldron, will have changed Mary Hynes and Raftery to perfect symbols of the sorrow of beauty and of the magnificence and penury of dreams.

1900.

5. The city of Troy was beseiged and finally destroyed by the Greeks in the twelfth century B.C.E., following the abduction of Helen, wife of King Menelaus of Sparta, by Paris, son of King Priam of Troy.
6. "Of the faery woman" (Irish).
7. Coole Park, Lady Gregory's estate.
8. An estate, now known as Rahasane House, nine miles north of Ballylee.
9. Folklorist and poet Douglas Hyde (1860–1949).

II

When I was in a northern town awhile ago I had a long talk with a man who had lived in a neighbouring country district when he was a boy. He told me that when a very beautiful girl was born in a family that had not been noted for good looks, her beauty was thought to have come from the Sidhe, and to bring misfortune with it. He went over the names of several beautiful girls that he had known, and said that beauty had never brought happiness to anybody. It was a thing, he said, to be proud of and afraid of. I wish I had written out his words at the time, for they were more picturesque than my memory of them.

1902.

Enchanted Woods

I

Last summer, whenever I had finished my day's work, I used to go wandering in certain roomy woods,[1] and there I would often meet an old countryman, and talk to him about his work and about the woods, and once or twice a friend[2] came with me to whom he would open his heart more readily than to me. He had spent all his life lopping away the witch elm and the hazel and the privet and the hornbeam from the paths, and had thought much about the natural and supernatural creatures of the wood. He has heard the hedgehog—'grainne oge,'[3] he calls him—'grunting like a Christian,' and is certain that he steals apples by rolling about under an apple tree until there is an apple sticking to every quill. He is certain too that the cats, of whom there are many in the woods, have a language of their own—some kind of old Irish. He says, 'Cats were serpents, and they were made into cats at the time of some great change in the world. That is why they are hard to kill, and why it is dangerous to meddle with them. If you annoy a cat it might claw or bite you in a way that would put poison in you, and that would be the serpent's tooth.' Sometimes he thinks they change into wild cats, and then a nail grows on the end of their tails; but these wild cats are not the same as the marten cats, who have been always in the woods. The foxes were once tame, as the cats are now, but they ran away and became wild. He talks of all wild creatures except squirrels—whom he hates—with what seems an affectionate interest, though at times his eyes will twinkle with pleasure as he remembers how he made hedgehogs unroll themselves when he was a boy, by putting a wisp of burning straw under them.

I am not certain that he distinguishes between the natural and supernatural very clearly. He told me the other day that foxes and cats like, above all, to be in the 'forths' and lisses[4] after nightfall; and he will certainly pass from some story about a fox to a story about a spirit with less change of voice than when he is going to speak about a marten cat—a rare beast

1. The woods of Coole Park.
2. Lady Gregory.
3. "Graineog" (Irish for hedgehog).
4. Fords and forts.

now-a-days. Many years ago he used to work in the garden, and once they put him to sleep in a garden-house where there was a loft full of apples, and all night he could hear people rattling plates and knives and forks over his head in the loft. Once, at any rate, he has seen an unearthly sight in the woods. He says, 'One time I was out cutting timber over in Inchy,[5] and about eight o'clock one morning when I got there I saw a girl picking nuts, with her hair hanging down over her shoulders, brown hair, and she had a good, clean face, and she was tall and nothing on her head, and her dress no way gaudy but simple, and when she felt me coming she gathered herself up and was gone as if the earth had swallowed her up. And I followed her and looked for her, but I never could see her again from that day to this, never again.' He used the word clean as we would use words like fresh or comely.

Others too have seen spirits in the Enchanted Woods. A labourer told us of what a friend of his had seen in a part of the woods that is called Shanwalla, from some old village that was before the wood.[6] He said, 'One evening I parted from Lawrence Mangan in the yard, and he went away through the path in Shanwalla, an' bid me good-night. And two hours after, there he was back again in the yard, an' bid me light a candle that was in the stable. An' he told me that when he got into Shanwalla, a little fellow about as high as his knee, but having a head as big as a man's body, came beside him and led him out of the path an' round about, and at last it brought him to the lime-kiln, and then it vanished and left him.'

A woman told me of a sight that she and others had seen by a certain deep pool in the river. She said, 'I came over the stile from the chapel, and others along with me; and a great blast of wind came and two trees were bent and broken and fell into the river, and the splash of water out of it went up to the skies. And those that were with me saw many figures, but myself I only saw one, sitting there by the bank where the trees fell. Dark clothes he had on, and he was headless.'

A man told me that one day, when he was a boy, he and another boy went to catch a horse in a certain field, full of boulders and bushes of hazel and creeping juniper and rock-roses, that is where the lake side is for a little clear of the woods. He said to the boy that was with him, 'I bet a button that if I fling a pebble on to that bush it will stay on it,' meaning that the bush was so matted the pebble would not be able to go through it. So he took up 'a pebble of cow-dung, and as soon as it hit the bush there came out of it the most beautiful music that ever was heard.' They ran away, and when they had gone about two hundred yards they looked back and saw a woman dressed in white, walking round and round the bush. 'First it had the form of a woman, and then of a man, and it was going round the bush.'

II

I often entangle myself in arguments more complicated than even those paths of Inchy as to what is the true nature of apparitions, but at other

---

5. Inchy Wood, one of the seven woods of Coole.
6. Shanwalla Wood (probably from "sean bóthar": old road), one of the seven woods of Coole.

times I say as Socrates said when they told him a learned opinion about a nymph of the Ilissus, 'The common opinion is enough for me.'[7] I believe when I am in the mood that all nature is full of people whom we cannot see, and that some of these are ugly or grotesque, and some wicked or foolish, but very many beautiful beyond any one we have ever seen, and that these are not far away when we are walking in pleasant and quiet places. Even when I was a boy I could never walk in a wood without feeling that at any moment I might find before me somebody or something I had long looked for without knowing what I looked for. And now I will at times explore every little nook of some poor coppice with almost anxious footsteps, so deep a hold has this imagination upon me. You too meet with a like imagination, doubtless, somewhere, wherever your ruling stars will have it, Saturn driving you to the woods, or the Moon, it may be, to the edges of the sea.[8] I will not of a certainty believe that there is nothing in the sunset, where our forefathers imagined the dead following their shepherd the sun, or nothing but some vague presence as little moving as nothing. If beauty is not a gateway out of the net we were taken in at our birth, it will not long be beauty, and we will find it better to sit at home by the fire and fatten a lazy body or to run hither and thither in some foolish sport than to look at the finest show that light and shadow ever made among green leaves. I say to myself, when I am well out of that thicket of argument, that they are surely there, the divine people, for only we who have neither simplicity nor wisdom have denied them, and the simple of all times and the wise men of ancient times have seen them and even spoken to them. They live out their passionate lives not far off, as I think, and we shall be among them when we die if we but keep our natures simple and passionate. May it not even be that death shall unite us to all romance, and that some day we shall fight dragons among blue hills, or come to that whereof all romance is but

> 'Foreshadowings mingled with the images
> Of man's misdeeds in greater days than these,'

as the old men thought in *The Earthly Paradise*[9] when they were in good spirits.

1902.

By the Roadside

Last night I went to a wide place on the Kiltartan[1] road to listen to some Irish songs. While I waited for the singers an old man sang about that country beauty who died so many years ago, and spoke of a singer he had

---

7. From the dialogue *Phaedrus*, by Greek philosopher Plato (c. 429–347 B.C.E.). Questioned by Phaedrus as to which of the many stories about the abduction of the nymph Orithyia from the banks of the river Ilissus is correct, the philosopher Socrates responds by saying common opinion is good enough for him, as he would rather save his energies for perfecting his knowledge of himself.
8. The influence of the planet Saturn was traditionally thought to produce gloom and a desire for silence or solitude; the Moon was associated with the sea, through its influence on the tides.
9. From the epilogue poem that follows "The Doom of King Acrisius" in *The Earthly Paradise* by William Morris (1834–1896).
1. A crossroads village close to Lady Gregory's home at Coole Park.

known who sang so beautifully that no horse would pass him, but must turn its head and cock its ears to listen. Presently a score of men and boys and girls, with shawls over their heads, gathered under the trees to listen. Somebody sang *Sa Muirnín Díles*, and then somebody else *Jimmy Mo Mílestór*, mournful songs of separation, of death, and of exile. Then some of the men stood up and began to dance, while another lilted the measure they danced to, and then somebody sang *Eiblín a Rúin*,[2] that glad song of meeting which has always moved me more than other songs, because the lover who made it sang it to his sweetheart under the shadow of a mountain I looked at every day through my childhood.[3] The voices melted into the twilight, and were mixed into the trees, and when I thought of the words they too melted away, and were mixed with the generations of men. Now it was a phrase, now it was an attitude of mind, an emotional form, that had carried my memory to older verses, or even to forgotten mythologies. I was carried so far that it was as though I came to one of the four rivers, and followed it under the wall of Paradise to the roots of the trees of knowledge and of life. There is no song or story handed down among the cottages that has not words and thoughts to carry one as far, for though one can know but a little of their ascent, one knows that they ascend like medieval genealogies through unbroken dignities to the beginning of the world. Folk art is, indeed, the oldest of the aristocracies of thought, and because it refuses what is passing and trivial, the merely clever and pretty, as certainly as the vulgar and insincere, and because it has gathered into itself the simplest and most unforgetable thoughts of the generations, it is the soil where all great art is rooted. Wherever it is spoken by the fireside, or sung by the roadside, or carved upon the lintel, appreciation of the arts that a single mind gives unity and design to, spreads quickly when its hour is come.

In a society that has cast out imaginative tradition, only a few people—three or four thousand out of millions—favoured by their own characters and by happy circumstance, and only then after much labour, have understanding of imaginative things, and yet 'the imagination is the man himself.' The churches in the Middle Age won all the arts into their service because men understood that when imagination is impoverished, a principal voice—some would say the only voice—for the awakening of wise hope and durable faith, and understanding charity, can speak but in broken words, if it does not fall silent. And so it has always seemed to me that we, who would re-awaken imaginative tradition by making old songs live again, or by gathering old stories into books, take part in the quarrel of Galilee.[4] Those who are Irish and would spread foreign ways,[5] which, for all but a few, are ways of spiritual poverty, take part also. Their part is

---

2. "Sa Mhuirnín Dílis" ("My Own Beloved"), the lament of a returning soldier who finds his beloved "Eileen Og" is dead; "Jimmy Mo Mílestór" ("Jimmy My Thousand Treasures"), the lament of a young woman whose lover has gone overseas; and "Eiblín a Rúin" ("Eileen My Love"), a song ascribed to the seventeenth-century Carlow poet Cearbhall O Daliagh (O'Daly).

3. O Daliagh reputedly won the hand of his love by singing "Eiblín a Rúin" to her. Yeats's Introduction to *Fairy and Folk Tales of the Irish Peasantry* (1888) shows that he thought O'Daly was a Sligo poet, and that the event thus occurred near Ben Bulben Mountain.

4. The region of the Holy Land associated with Jesus and the emergence of Christianity.

5. English culture, which Yeats at this point associated with a sterile bourgeois commercialism, and with the "Gray Truth" of scientific rationalism.

with those who were of Jewry, and yet cried out, 'If thou let this man go thou art not Cæsar's friend.'[6]

1901.

From *The Secret Rose* (1897)

The Crucifixion of the Outcast

A man, with thin brown hair and a pale face, half ran, half walked, along the road that wound from the south to the Town of the Shelly River.[1] Many called him Cumhal, the son of Cormac, and many called him the Swift, Wild Horse; and he was a gleeman,[2] and he wore a short particoloured doublet, and had pointed shoes, and a bulging wallet. Also he was of the blood of the Ernaans,[3] and his birth-place was the Field of Gold; but his eating and sleeping places were the four provinces of Eri,[4] and his abiding place was not upon the ridge of the earth. His eyes strayed from the Abbey tower of the White Friars and the town battlements to a row of crosses which stood out against the sky upon a hill a little to the eastward of the town, and he clenched his fist, and shook it at the crosses. He knew they were not empty, for the birds were fluttering about them; and he thought how, as like as not, just such another vagabond as himself was hanged on one of them; and he muttered; 'If it were hanging or bowstringing, or stoning or beheading, it would be bad enough. But to have the birds pecking your eyes and the wolves eating your feet! I would that the red wind of the Druids[5] had withered in his cradle the soldier of Dathi,[6] who brought the tree of death out of barbarous lands, or that the lightning, when it smote Dathi at the foot of the mountain, had smitten him also, or that his grave had been dug by the green-haired and green-toothed merrows[7] deep at the roots of the deep sea.'

While he spoke, he shivered from head to foot, and the sweat came out upon his face, and he knew not why, for he had looked upon many crosses. He passed over two hills and under the battlemented gate, and then round by a left-hand way to the door of the Abbey. It was studded with great nails, and when he knocked at it, he roused the lay brother who was the porter, and of him he asked a place in the guest-house. Then the lay brother took a glowing turf on a shovel, and led the way to a big and naked outhouse strewn with very dirty rushes; and lighted a rush-candle fixed between two of the stones of the wall, and set the glowing turf upon the hearth and gave him two unlighted sods[8] and a wisp of straw, and showed him a blanket hanging from a nail, and a shelf with a loaf of bread and a

---

6. John 19.12, in which the Jews urge the reluctant Pontius Pilate to condemn Jesus, thereby participating in their own submission to Roman rule.
1. Identified as Sligo in later printings of this story.
2. A traveling poet or musician.
3. A descendant of Erannan, one of the Milesians, the last of the mythological conquerors of Ireland.
4. Ulster, Leinster, Connacht, and Munster, Ireland's four ancient regions.
5. Priest-seers in ancient Ireland.
6. A Connacht king of the fourth century, whom Yeats credited with having first brought the Cross to Ireland from Christian Europe in Druid times. He died in the Alps and was brought back to Ireland for burial.
7. Mermaids.
8. Sods of turf, with which to make a fire.

jug of water, and a tub in a far corner. Then the lay brother left him and went back to his place by the door. And Cumhal the son of Cormac began to blow upon the glowing turf, that he might light the two sods and the wisp of straw; but his blowing profited him nothing, for the sods and the straw were damp. So he took off his pointed shoes, and drew the tub out of the corner with the thought of washing the dust of the highway from his feet; but the water was so dirty that he could not see the bottom. He was very hungry, for he had not eaten all that day; so he did not waste much anger upon the tub, but took up the black loaf, and bit into it, and then spat out the bite, for the bread was hard and mouldy. Still he did not give way to his wrath, for he had not drunken these many hours; having a hope of heath beer or wine at his day's end, he had left the brooks untasted, to make his supper the more delightful. Now he put the jug to his lips, but he flung it from him straightway, for the water was bitter and ill-smelling. Then he gave the jug a kick, so that it broke against the opposite wall, and he took down the blanket to wrap it about him for the night. But no sooner did he touch it than it was alive with skipping fleas. At this, beside himself with anger, he rushed to the door of the guest-house, but the lay brother, being well accustomed to such outcries, had locked it on the outside; so Cumhal emptied the tub and began to beat the door with it, till the lay brother came to the door, and asked what ailed him, and why he woke him out of sleep. 'What ails me!' shouted Cumhal, 'are not the sods as wet as the sands of the Three Headlands? and are not the fleas in the blanket as many as the waves of the sea and as lively? and is not the bread as hard as the heart of a lay brother who has forgotten God? and is not the water in the jug as bitter and as ill-smelling as his soul? and is not the foot-water the colour that shall be upon him when he has been charred in the Undying Fires?' The lay brother saw that the lock was fast, and went back to his niche, for he was too sleepy to talk with comfort. And Cumhal went on beating at the door, and presently he heard the lay brother's foot once more, and cried out at him, 'O cowardly and tyrannous race of friars, persecutors of the bard[9] and the gleeman, haters of life and joy! O race that does not draw the sword and tell the truth! O race that melts the bones of the people with cowardice and with deceit!'

'Gleeman,' said the lay brother, 'I also make rhymes; I make many while I sit in my niche by the door, and I sorrow to hear the bards railing upon the friars. Brother, I would sleep, and therefore I make known to you that it is the head of the monastery, our gracious Coarb, who orders all things concerning the lodging of travellers.'

'You may sleep,' said Cumhal, 'I will sing a bard's curse on the Coarb.' And he set the tub upside down under the window, and stood upon it, and began to sing in a very loud voice. The singing awoke the Coarb, so that he sat up in bed and blew a silver whistle until the lay brother came to him. 'I cannot get a wink of sleep with that noise,' said the Coarb. 'What is happening?'

'It is a gleeman,' said the lay brother, 'who complains of the sods, of

9. Poet.

the bread, of the water in the jug, of the foot-water, and of the blanket. And now he is singing a bard's curse upon you, O brother Coarb, and upon your father and your mother, and your grandfather and your grandmother, and upon all your relations.'

'Is he cursing in rhyme?'

'He is cursing in rhyme, and with two assonances[1] in every line of his curse.'

The Coarb pulled his night-cap off and crumpled it in his hands, and the circular brown patch of hair in the middle of his bald head looked like an island in the midst of a pond, for in Connaught[2] they had not yet abandoned the ancient tonsure for the style then coming into use.[3] 'If we do not somewhat,' he said, 'he will teach his curses to the children in the street, and the girls spinning at the doors, and to the robbers on the mountain of Gulben.'[4]

'Shall I go then,' said the other, 'and give him dry sods, a fresh loaf, clean water in a jug, clean foot-water, and a new blanket, and make him swear by the blessed St. Benignus,[5] and by the sun and moon, that no bond be lacking, not to tell his rhymes to the children in the street, and the girls spinning at the doors, and the robbers on the mountain of Gulben?'

'Neither our blessed Patron nor the sun and the moon would avail at all,' said the Coarb: 'for to-morrow or the next day the mood to curse would come upon him, or a pride in those rhymes would move him, and he would teach his lines to the children, and the girls, and the robbers. Or else he would tell another of his craft how he fared in the guest-house, and he in his turn would begin to curse, and my name would wither. For learn there is no steadfastness of purpose upon the roads, but only under roofs, and between four walls. Therefore I bid you go and awaken Brother Kevin, Brother Dove, Brother Little Wolf, Brother Bald Patrick, Brother Bald Brandon, Brother James and Brother Peter. And they shall take the man, and bind him with ropes, and dip him in the river that he may cease to sing. And in the morning, lest this but make him curse the louder, we will crucify him.'

'The crosses are all full,' said the lay brother.

'Then we must make another cross. If we do not make an end of him another will, for who can eat and sleep in peace while men like him are going about the world? Ill should we stand before blessed St. Benignus, and sour would be his face when he comes to judge us at the Last Day, were we to spare an enemy of his when we had him under our thumb! Brother, the bards and the gleemen are an evil race, ever cursing and ever stirring up the people, and immoral and immoderate in all things, and

---

1. Assonance is the repetition of a vowel sound, and here it signals that Hanrahan is making formal, carefully crafted verse, of a kind that the abbott of the monastery might expect to be memorized and thus make Hanrahan's curses widely known.
2. The western province of Ireland, which includes Sligo.
3. The "ancient" practice described here was replaced by the shaving of the top of the head and leaving the rest of the head unshaven.
4. Ben Bulben, a mountain overlooking the town of Sligo.
5. A fifth-century Irish chief who was converted to Christianity by Saint Patrick, became his most devoted follower, and evangelized County Clare and Connacht.

heathen in their hearts, always longing after the Son of Lir, and Angus, and Bridget, and the Dagda, and Dana the Mother,[6] and all the false gods of the old days; always making poems in praise of those kings and queens of the demons, Finvaragh of the Hill in the Plain, and Red Aodh of the Hill of the Shee, and Cleena of the Wave, and Eiveen of the Grey Rock, and him they call Don of the Vats of the Sea;[7] and railing against God and Christ and the blessed Saints.' While he was speaking he crossed himself, and when he had finished he drew the nightcap over his ears, to shut out the noise, and closed his eyes, and composed himself to sleep.

The lay brother found Brother Kevin, Brother Dove, Brother Little Wolf, Brother Bald Patrick, Brother Bald Brandon, Brother James and Brother Peter sitting up in bed, and he made them get up. Then they bound Cumhal, and they dragged him to the river, and they dipped him in it at the place which was afterwards called Buckley's Ford.

'Gleeman,' said the lay brother, as they led him back to the guest-house, 'why do you ever use the wit which God has given you to make blasphemous and immoral tales and verses? For such is the way of your craft. I have, indeed, many such tales and verses well nigh by rote, and so I know that I speak true! And why do you praise with rhyme those demons, Finvaragh, Red Aodh, Cleena, Eiveen and Don? I, too, am a man of great wit and learning, but I ever glorify our gracious Coarb, and Benignus our Patron, and the princes of the province. My soul is decent and orderly, but yours is like the wind among the salley gardens.[8] I said what I could for you, being also a man of many thoughts, but who could help such a one as you?'

'My soul, friend,' answered the gleeman, 'is indeed like the wind, and it blows me to and fro, and up and down, and puts many things into my mind and out of my mind, and therefore am I called the Swift, Wild Horse.' And he spoke no more that night, for his teeth were chattering with the cold.

The Coarb and the friars came to him in the morning, and bade him get ready to be crucified, and led him out of the guest-house. And while he still stood upon the step a flock of great grass-barnacles[9] passed high above him with clanking cries. He lifted his arms to them and said, 'O great grass-barnacles, tarry a little, and mayhap my soul will travel with you to the waste places of the shore and to the ungovernable sea!' At the gate a crowd of beggars gathered about them, being come there to beg from any traveller or pilgrim who might have spent the night in the guest-house. The Coarb and the friars led the gleeman to a place in the woods at some distance, where many straight young trees were growing, and they

---

6. Manannan Mac Lir was the mythological Irish god of the sea; Aengus, the Irish god of love; Bridget, a goddess from the valley of the Boyne, a river that runs into the Irish sea at Drogheda; the Dagda was father of Aengus; the faeries were known in Ireland as the "Tuatha de Danaan," or literally, "the people of the Goddess Dana."

7. Finvara, king of the Sidhe (pronounced "Shee," the Irish faeries), was believed to live on Cruachmaa or Knockma, a hill near Tuam, Galway; Red Aodh, or "Red Hugh," also of the Sidhe at Cruachmaa; Cleena or Clion, a goddess associated with the bay of Glandore, Cork; Aoibheal ("Eiveen" in Yeats's Anglicization), a goddess associated with the coast of County Clare; Donn of the Vats, a god associated with an island off the County Cork coast.

8. Gardens where willows were grown, for use in making thatching for roofs.

9. Wild geese.

made him cut one down and fashion it to the right length, while the beggars stood round them in a ring, talking and gesticulating. The Coarb then bade him cut off another and shorter piece of wood, and nail it upon the first. So there was his cross for him; and they put it upon his shoulder, for his crucifixion was to be on the top of the hill where the others were. A half-mile on the way he asked them to stop and see him juggle for them: for he knew, he said, all the tricks of Angus the Subtle-Hearted. The old friars were for pressing on, but the young friars would see him: so he did many wonders for them, even to the drawing of live frogs out of his ears. But after a while they turned on him, and said his tricks were dull and a shade unholy, and set the cross on his shoulders again. Another half-mile on the way, and he asked them to stop and hear him jest for them, for he knew, he said, all the jests of Conan the Bald,[1] upon whose back a sheep's wool grew. And the young friars, when they had heard his merry tales, again bade him take up his cross, for it ill became them to listen to such follies. Another half-mile on the way, he asked them to stop and hear him sing the story of White-Breasted Deirdre,[2] and how she endured many sorrows, and how the sons of Usna died to serve her. And the young friars were mad to hear him, but when he had ended, they grew angry, and beat him for waking forgotten longings in their hearts. So they set the cross upon his back, and hurried him to the hill.

When he was come to the top, they took the cross from him, and began to dig a hole to stand it in, while the beggars gathered round, and talked among themselves. 'I ask a favour before I die,' says Cumhal.

'We will grant you no more delays,' says the Coarb.

'I ask no more delays, for I have drawn the sword, and told the truth, and lived my vision, and am content.'

'Would you then confess?'

'By sun and moon, not I; I ask but to be let eat the food I carry in my wallet. I carry food in my wallet whenever I go upon a journey, but I do not taste of it unless I am well-nigh starved. I have not eaten now these two days.'

'You may eat, then,' says the Coarb, and he turned to help the friars dig the hole.

The gleeman took a loaf and some strips of cold fried bacon out of his wallet and laid them upon the ground. 'I will give a tithe to the poor,' says he, and he cut a tenth part from the loaf and the bacon. 'Who among you is the poorest?' And thereupon was a great clamour, for the beggars began the history of their sorrows and their poverty, and their yellow faces swayed like the Shelly River when the floods have filled it with water from the bogs.

He listened for a little, and, says he, 'I am myself the poorest, for I have travelled the bare road, and by the glittering footsteps of the sea; and the

1. A warrior and satirist of the Fianna, in the Fenian cycle of Irish mythology. When a magician stuck his head to the floor his companions tugged him free, but his hair and scalp were pulled off in the process. To hide his baldness, a sheep's skin was grafted onto his head.
2. In the Ulster cycle of Irish mythology, Deirdre was chosen by Conchubar, king of Ulster, to be his queen, but she eloped with Naoise, son of Usna, accompanied by his two brothers, Ainnle and Ardan. On being lured back to Ireland by Conchubar with a promise that they would not be harmed, the three brothers were promptly killed, and Deirdre, grief-stricken, took her own life.

tattered doublet of particoloured cloth upon my back and the torn pointed shoes upon my feet have ever irked me, because of the towered city full of noble raiment[3] which was in my heart. And I have been the more alone upon the roads and by the sea, because I heard in my heart the rustling of the rose-bordered dress of her[4] who is more subtle than Angus, the Subtle-Hearted, and more full of the beauty of laughter than Conan the Bald, and more full of the wisdom of tears than White-Breasted Deirdre, and more lovely than a bursting dawn to them that are lost in the darkness. Therefore, I award the tithe to myself; but yet, because I am done with all things, I give it unto you.'

So he flung the bread and the strips of bacon among the beggars, and they fought with many cries until the last scrap was eaten. But meanwhile the friars nailed the gleeman to his cross, and set it upright in the hole, and shovelled the earth in at the foot, and trampled it level and hard. So then they went away, but the beggars stared on, sitting round the cross. But when the sun was sinking, they also got up to go, for the air was getting chilly. And as soon as they had gone a little way, the wolves, who had been showing themselves on the edge of a neighbouring coppice, came nearer, and the birds wheeled closer and closer. 'Stay, outcasts, yet a little while,' the crucified one called in a weak voice to the beggars, 'and keep the beasts and the birds from me.' But the beggars were angry because he had called them outcasts, so they threw stones and mud at him, and went their way. Then the wolves gathered at the foot of the cross, and the birds flew lower and lower. And presently the birds lighted all at once upon his head and arms and shoulders, and began to peck at him, and the wolves began to eat his feet. 'Outcasts,' he moaned, 'have you also turned against the outcast?'

The Old Men of the Twilight

At the place, close to the Dead Man's Point, at the Three Headlands, where the disused pilot-house looks out to sea through two round windows like eyes,[1] a mud cottage stood in the last century. It also was a watchhouse, for a certain old Michael Bruen, who had been a smuggler in his day, and was still the father and grandfather of smugglers, lived there, and when, under the shadow of night, a tall schooner crept over the bay, from Roughley of the Children of Byrne,[2] it was his business to hang a horn lanthorn in the southern window, that the news might travel to Dorren's Island, and from thence, by another horn lanthorn, to the village of the Headlands.[3] But for this glimmering of messages, he had little communion with mankind, for he was very old, and had no thought for anything, but for the making of his soul, at the foot of the Spanish crucifix of carved oak that hung by his chimney, or bent double over the rosary of stone beads brought to him in a cargo of silks and laces out of France. One

3. Clothing.
4. The Rose, an occult symbol of Beauty for Yeats in the 1890s, and also a figure for Ireland.
1. On Rosses Point, Sligo. The ruins of the pilot-house still stand.
2. A headland across Sligo Bay to the west of Rosses Point.
3. Presumably to what is now known as Coney Island, in the estuary opposite Lower Rosses Point, and thence to the village of Rosses.

night he had watched hour after hour, because a gentle and favourable wind was blowing, and *La Mère de Miséricorde*[4] was much overdue; and he was about to lie down upon his heap of straw, seeing that the dawn was whitening the east, and that the schooner would not dare to round Roughley of the Children of Byrne and swing at anchor by the second Headland, except under the shadow of night; when he saw a long line of herons flying slowly from Dorren's Island and towards the pools which lie, half choked with reeds, behind the Headlands. He had never before seen herons flying over the sea, for they are shore-keeping birds, and partly because this had startled him out of his drowsiness, and more because the long delay of the schooner kept his cupboard empty, he took down his rusty shot-gun, of which the barrel was tied on with a piece of string, and followed them towards the pools.

When he came close enough to hear the sighing of the rushes in the outermost pool, the morning was grey over the world, so that the tall rushes, the still waters, the vague clouds, the thin mist lying among the sand-heaps, seemed carved out of an enormous pearl. In a little he came upon the herons, of whom there were a great number, standing with lifted legs in the shallow water; and crouching down behind a bank of rushes, looked to the priming of his gun, and bent for a moment over his rosary to murmur: 'Patron Patrick, let me shoot a heron; made into a pie it will support me for nearly four days, for I no longer eat as in my youth. If you keep me from missing I will say a rosary to you every night until the pie is eaten.' Then he lay down, and, resting his gun upon a large stone, turned towards a heron which stood upon a bank of smooth grass over a little stream that flowed into the pool; for he feared to take the rheumatism by wading, as he would have to do if he shot one of those which stood in the water. But when he looked along the barrel the heron was gone, and, to his wonder and terror, a man of infinitely great age and infirmity stood in its place. He lowered the gun, and the heron stood there with bent head and motionless feathers, as though it had slept from the beginning of the world. He raised the gun, and no sooner did he look along the iron than that enemy of all enchantment brought the old man again before him, only to vanish when he lowered the gun for the second time. He laid the gun down, and crossed himself three times, and said a *Paternoster* and an *Ave Maria*[5] and muttered half aloud: 'Some enemy of God and of my patron is standing upon the smooth place and fishing in the blessed water,' and then aimed very carefully and slowly and with an exultant heart. He fired, and when the smoke had gone saw an old man, huddled upon the grass and a long line of herons flying with clamour towards the sea. He went round a bend of the pool, and coming to the little stream looked down on a figure wrapped in faded clothes of black and green of an ancient pattern and spotted with blood. He shook his head at the sight of so great a wickedness. Suddenly the clothes moved and an arm was stretched upwards towards the rosary which hung about his neck, and long wasted fingers almost touched the cross. He started back, crying: 'Wizard,

4. Mother of Mercy (French): a boat's name.
5. The prayers "Our Father" and "Hail Mary."

I will let no wicked thing touch my blessed beads;' and the sense of a great danger just evaded made him tremble.

'If you listen to me,' replied a voice so faint that it was like a sigh, 'you will know that I am not a wizard, and you will let me kiss the cross before I die.'

'I will listen to you,' he answered, 'but I will not let you touch my blessed beads,' and sitting on the grass a little way from the dying man, he reloaded his gun and laid it across his knees and composed himself to listen.

'I know not how many generations ago we, who are now herons, were the men of learning of the King Leaghaire;[6] we neither hunted, nor went to battle, nor listened to the Druids[7] preaching by their grey stones, and even love, if it came to us at all, was but a transitory fire. The Druids and the poets told us, many and many a time, of a new Druid Patrick;[8] and most among them were fierce against him, while a few held his doctrine merely the doctrine of the gods set out in new symbols, and were for giving him welcome; but we yawned in the midst of their tale. At last they came crying that he was coming to the liss[9] of the king and fell to their dispute, but we would listen to neither party, for we were busy with a dispute about the merits of the Great and of the Little Metre;[1] nor were we disturbed when they passed our door with staves of enchantment under their arms, travelling towards the forest to contend against his coming, nor when they returned after nightfall with torn robes and despairing cries; for the click, click! of our knives filled us with peace and our dispute filled us with joy; nor even when in the morning crowds passed us to hear the strange Druid preaching the commandments of his God. The crowds passed, and one, who had laid down his knife to yawn and stretch himself, heard a voice speaking far off, and knew that the Druid Patrick was preaching within the liss of the king; but our hearts were deaf, and we carved and disputed and read, and laughed a thin laughter together. In a little we heard many feet coming towards the house, and presently two tall figures stood in the door, the one in white, the other in a crimson robe; like a great lily and a heavy poppy; and we knew the Druid Patrick and our King Leaghaire. We laid down the slender knives and bowed before the king, but when the black and green robes had ceased to rustle, it was not the loud rough voice of King Leaghaire that spoke to us, but a strange voice in which there was a rapture as of one speaking from behind a battlement of Druid flame: "I preached the commandments of the Maker of the world," it said: "within the liss of the king and from the centre of the earth to the windows of Heaven there was a great silence, so that the eagle floated with unmoving wings in the white air, and the fish with unmoving fins in the dim water, while the linnets and the wrens and the sparrows stilled their ever-trembling tongues in the heavy boughs, and the clouds were like white marble, and the rivers became their motionless mirrors, and the shrimps

---

6. Probably Loegaire Mac Neill, a fifth-century king of Ireland, who was converted to Christianity by Saint Patrick.
7. Priest-seers of ancient Ireland.
8. Saint Patrick (c. 385–c. 461), who introduced Christianity into Druidic Ireland.
9. Fort.
1. Metrical forms in poetry.

in the far-off sea pools were still, enduring eternity in patience, although it was hard." And as he named these things, it was like a king numbering his people. "But your slender knives went click, click! upon the oaken staves, and, all else being silent, the sound shook the angels with anger. O, little roots, nipped by the winter, who do not wake although the summer pass above you with innumerable feet. O, men who have no part in love, who have no part in song, who have no part in wisdom, but dwell with the shadows of memory where the feet of angels cannot touch you as they pass over your heads, where the hair of demons cannot sweep about you as they pass under your feet, I lay upon you a curse, and change you to an example for ever and ever; you shall become grey herons and stand pondering in grey pools and flit over the world in that hour when it is most full of sighs, having forgotten the flame of the stars and not yet perceived the flame of the sun; and you shall preach to the other herons until they also are like you, and are an example for ever and ever; and your deaths shall come to you by chance and unforeseen that no fire of certainty may visit your hearts." '

The voice of the old man of learning became still, but the voteen[2] bent over his gun with his eyes upon the ground, trying in vain to understand something of this tale; and he had so bent for no little while, had not a tug at his rosary made him start out of his dream. The old man of learning had crawled along the grass, and was now trying to draw the cross down low enough for his lips to reach it.

'You must not touch my blessed beads,' cried the voteen, and struck the long withered fingers with the barrel of his gun. He need not have trembled, for the old man fell back upon the grass with a sigh and was still. He bent down and began to consider the black and green clothes, for his fear had begun to pass when he came to understand that he had something the man of learning wanted and pleaded for, and now that the blessed beads were safe, it was nearly all gone; and surely, he thought, if that ample cloak, and that little tight-fitting cloak under it, were warm and goodly, St. Patrick would take the enchantment out of them and leave them fit for human use. Unhappily the black and green clothes fell away wherever his fingers touched them, and while this was a new wonder, a slight wind blew over the pool and crumbled the old man of learning and all his ancient gear into a little heap of dust, and then made the little heap less and less until there was nothing but the smooth green grass.

From *Stories of Red Hanrahan* (1904)

The Twisting of the Rope

Hanrahan was walking the roads one time near Kinvara[1] at the fall of day, and he heard the sound of a fiddle from a house a little way off the roadside. He turned up the path to it, for he never had the habit of passing by any place where there was music or dancing or good company, without

2. A devotee or very religious person.
1. A village on the coast, County Galway.

going in. The man of the house was standing at the door, and when Hanrahan came near he knew him and he said:—'A welcome before you, Hanrahan, you have been lost to us this long time.' But the woman of the house came to the door and she said to her husband: 'I would be as well pleased for Hanrahan not to come in to-night, for he has no good name now among the priests, or with women that mind themselves, and I wouldn't wonder from his walk if he has a drop of drink taken.' But the man said: 'I will never turn away Hanrahan of the poets from my door,' and with that he bade him enter.

There were a good many neighbours gathered in the house, and some of them remembered Hanrahan; but some of the little lads that were in the corners had only heard of him, and they stood up to have a view of him, and one of them said: 'Is not that Hanrahan that had the school, and that was brought away by Them?'[2] But his mother put her hand over his mouth and bade him be quiet and not be saying things like that. 'For Hanrahan is apt to grow wicked,' she said, 'if he hears talk of that story, or if anyone goes questioning him.' One or another called out then, asking him for a song, but the man of the house said it was no time to ask him for a song, before he had rested himself; and he gave him whiskey in a glass, and Hanrahan thanked him and wished him good health and drank it off.

The fiddler was tuning his fiddle for another dance, and the man of the house said to the young men, they would all know what dancing was when they saw Hanrahan dance, for the like of it had never been seen since he was there before. Hanrahan said he would not dance, he had better use for his feet now, travelling as he was through the five provinces of Ireland. Just as he said that, there came in at the half door[3] Oona, the daughter of the house, having a few bits of bog deal from Connemara[4] in her arms for the fire. She threw them on the hearth and the flame rose up, and showed her to be very comely and smiling, and two or three of the young men rose up and asked for a dance. But Hanrahan crossed the floor and brushed the others away, and said it was with him she must dance, after the long road he had travelled before he came to her. And it is likely he said some soft word in her ear, for she said nothing against it, and stood out with him, and there were little blushes in her cheeks. Then other couples stood up, but when the dance was going to begin, Hanrahan chanced to look down, and he took notice of his boots that were worn and broken, and the ragged grey socks showing through them; and he said angrily it was a bad floor, and the music no great things, and he sat down in the dark place beside the hearth. But if he did, the girl sat down there with him.

The dancing went on, and when that dance was over another was called for, and no one took much notice of Oona and Red Hanrahan for a while, in the corner where they were. But the mother grew to be uneasy, and

2. In the story "Red Hanrahan," Yeats tells of Hanrahan's enchantment by the Sidhe (pronounced "Shee"), immortal beings or faeries in Irish folklore.
3. A door divided into two sections, the upper of which can be left open to let in air and light.
4. Wood recovered from ancient peat-bogs in the western province of Ireland; it is renowned for its excellence as firing.

she called to Oona to come and help her to set the table in the inner room. But Oona that had never refused her before, said she would come soon, but not yet, for she was listening to whatever he was saying in her ear. The mother grew yet more uneasy then, and she would come nearer them, and let on to be stirring the fire or sweeping the hearth, and she would listen for a minute to hear what the poet was saying to her child. And one time she heard him telling about white-handed Deirdre,[5] and how she brought the sons of Usnach to their death; and how the blush in her cheeks was not so red as the blood of kings' sons that was shed for her, and her sorrows had never gone out of mind; and he said it was maybe the memory of her that made the cry of the plover on the bog as sorrowful in the ear of the poets as the keening[6] of young men for a comrade. And there would never have been that memory of her, he said, if it was not for the poets that had put her beauty in their songs. And the next time she did not well understand what he was saying, but as far as she could hear, it had the sound of poetry though it was not rhymed, and this is what she heard him say: 'The sun and the moon are the man and the girl, they are my life and your life, they are travelling and ever travelling through the skies as if under the one hood. It was God made them for one another. He made your life and my life before the beginning of the world, he made them that they might go through the world, up and down, like the two best dancers that go on with the dance up and down the long floor of the barn, fresh and laughing, when all the rest are tired out and leaning against the wall.'

The old woman went then to where her husband was playing cards, but he would take no notice of her, and then she went to a woman of the neighbours and said: 'Is there no way we can get them from one another?' and without waiting for an answer she said to some young men that were talking together: 'What good are you when you cannot make the best girl in the house come out and dance with you? And go now the whole of you,' she said, 'and see can you bring her away from the poet's talk.' But Oona would not listen to any of them, but only moved her hand as if to send them away. Then they called to Hanrahan and said he had best dance with the girl himself, or let her dance with one of them. When Hanrahan heard what they were saying he said: 'That is so, I will dance with her, there is no man in the house must dance with her but myself.'

He stood up with her then, and led her out by the hand, and some of the young men were vexed, and some began mocking at his ragged coat and his broken boots. But he took no notice, and Oona took no notice, but they looked at one another as if all the world belonged to themselves alone. But another couple that had been sitting together like lovers stood out on the floor at the same time, holding one another's hands and moving their feet to keep time with the music. But Hanrahan turned his back on them as if angry, and in place of dancing he began to sing, and as he sang he held her hand, and his voice grew louder, and the mocking of the

5. See p. 196, n. 2.
6. A wailing cry of lamentation for the dead.

young men stopped, and the fiddle stopped, and there was nothing heard but his voice that had in it the sound of the wind. And what he sang was a song he had heard or had made one time in his wanderings on Slieve Echtge[7] and the words of it as they can be put into English were like this:

> I heard under a ragged hollow wood,
> A queen-woman dressed out in silver, cry
> When the sun looked out of his golden hood,
> O that none ever loved but you and I!
>
> O hurry to the water amid the trees,
> For there the tall deer and his leman[8] cry
> When they have but looked upon their images,
> O that none ever loved but you and I!
>
> O hurry to the ragged wood for there
> I will drive out the deer and moon and cry—
> O my share of the world, O yellow hair,
> No one has ever loved but you and I!

And while he was singing it Oona moved nearer to him, and the colour had gone from her cheek, and her eyes were not blue now, but grey with the tears that were in them, and anyone that saw her would have thought she was ready to follow him there and then from the west to the east of the world.

But one of the young men called out: 'Where is that country he is singing about? Mind yourself, Oona, it is a long way off, you might be a long time on the road before you would reach to it.' And another said: 'It is not to the Country of the Young[9] you will be going if you go with him, but to Mayo[1] of the bogs.' Oona looked at him then as if she would question him, but he raised her hand in his hand, and called out between singing and shouting: 'It is very near us that country is, it is on every side; it may be on the bare hill behind it is, or it may be in the heart of the wood.' And he said out very loud and clear: 'In the heart of the wood; oh, death will never find us in the heart of the wood. And will you come with me there, Oona?' he said.

But while he was saying this the two old women had gone outside the door, and Oona's mother was crying, and she said: 'He has put an enchantment on Oona. Can we not get the men to put him out of the house?'

'That is a thing you cannot do,' said the other woman, 'for he is a poet of the Gael,[2] and you know well if you would put a poet of the Gael out

---

7. Slieve Aughty, a range of low mountains that runs north-south from southern County Galway into County Clare.
8. Lover.
9. In Irish mythology, Tir na nOg ("the Country of the Young") was the paradise where mortals could enjoy everlasting youth.
1. The most westerly region of Connacht.
2. The people of Ireland, particularly those who held to the Irish language.

of the house, he would put a curse on you that would wither the corn in the fields and dry up the milk of the cows, if it had to hang in the air seven years.'

'God help us,' said the mother, 'and why did I ever let him into the house at all, and the wild name he has!'

'It would have been no harm at all to have kept him outside, but there would great harm come upon you if you put him out by force. But listen to the plan I have to get him out of the house by his own doing, without anyone putting him from it at all.'

It was not long after that the two women came in again, each of them having a bundle of hay in her apron. Hanrahan was not singing now, but he was talking to Oona very fast and soft, and he was saying: 'The house is narrow but the world is wide, and there is no true lover that need be afraid of night or morning or sun or stars or shadows of evening, or any earthly thing.' 'Hanrahan,' said the mother then, striking him on the shoulder, 'will you give me a hand here for a minute.' 'Do that, Hanrahan,' said the woman of the neighbours; 'and help us to make this hay into a rope, for you are ready with your hands, and a blast of wind has loosened the thatch on the haystack.'

'I will do that for you,' said he, and he took the little stick in his hands, and the mother began giving out the hay, and he twisting it, but he was hurrying to have done with it, and to be free again. The women went on talking and giving out the hay, and encouraging him, and saying what a good twister of a rope he was, better than their own neighbours or than anyone they had ever seen. And Hanrahan saw that Oona was watching him, and he began to twist very quick and with his head high, and to boast of the readiness of his hands, and the learning he had in his head, and the strength in his arms. And as he was boasting, he went backward, twisting the rope always till he came to the door that was open behind him, and without thinking he passed the threshold and was out on the road. And no sooner was he there than the mother made a sudden rush, and threw out the rope after him, and she shut the door and the half door and put a bolt upon them.

She was well pleased when she had done that, and laughed out loud, and the neighbours laughed and praised her. But they heard him beating at the door, and saying words of cursing outside it, and the mother had but time to stop Oona that had her hand upon the bolt to open it. She made a sign to the fiddler then, and he began a reel, and one of the young men asked no leave but caught hold of Oona and brought her into the thick of the dance. And when it was over and the fiddle had stopped, there was no sound at all of anything outside, but the road was as quiet as before.

As to Hanrahan, when he knew he was shut out and that there was neither shelter nor drink nor a girl's ear for him that night, the anger and the courage went out of him, and he went on to where the waves were beating on the strand.

He sat down on a big stone, and he began swinging his right arm and singing slowly to himself, the way he did always to hearten himself when every other thing failed him. And whether it was that time or another time he made the song that is called to this day 'The Twisting of the Rope,'[3] and that begins, 'What was the dead cat that put me in this place,' is not known.

But after he had been singing a while, mist and shadows seemed to gather about him, sometimes coming out of the sea, and sometimes moving upon it. It seemed to him that one of the shadows was the queen-woman he had seen in her sleep at Slieve Echtge;[4] not in her sleep now, but mocking, and calling out to them that were behind her: 'He was weak, he was weak, he had no courage.' And he felt the strands of the rope in his hand yet, and went on twisting it, but it seemed to him as he twisted, that it had all the sorrows of the world in it. And then it seemed to him as if the rope had changed in his dream into a great water-worm that came out of the sea, and that twisted itself about him, and held him closer and closer, and grew from big to bigger till the whole of the earth and skies were wound up in it, and the stars themselves were but the shining of the ridges of its skin. And then he got free of it, and went on, shaking and unsteady, along the edge of the strand, and the grey shapes were flying here and there around him. And this is what they were saying: 'It is a pity for him that refuses the call of the daughters of the Sidhe,[5] for he will find no comfort in the love of the women of the earth to the end of life and time, and the cold of the grave is in his heart for ever. It is death he has chosen; let him die, let him die, let him die.'

The Death of Hanrahan

Hanrahan, that was never long in one place, was back again among the villages that are at the foot of Slieve Echtge, Illeton and Scalp and Bally-lee,[1] stopping sometimes in one house and sometimes in another, and finding a welcome in every place for the sake of the old times and of his poetry and his learning. There was some silver and some copper money in the little leather bag under his coat, but it was seldom he needed to take anything from it, for it was little he used, and there was not one of the people that would have taken payment from him. His hand had grown heavy on the blackthorn[2] he leaned on, and his cheeks were hollow and worn, but so far as food went, potatoes and milk and a bit of oaten cake, he had what he wanted of it; and it is not on the edge of so wild and boggy a place as Echtge a mug of spirits would be wanting, with the taste of the turf smoke on it. He would wander about the big wood at Kinadife, or he would sit through many hours of the day among the rushes about Lake Belshragh,[3] listening to the streams from the hills, or watching the

---

3. A popular anonymous nineteenth-century song, "Casadh an tSugáin" ("The Twisting of the Rope"), which begins "Nach é an cat marbh chas ann na h-áitesi mé" ("What mortal conflict drove me here to roam"), with "cat/cait" taken either as English "cat" or as "strife/conflict."
4. In Yeats's earlier story "Red Hanrahan," Hanrahan is enchanted and sees a vision of a queen of the Sidhe.
5. Immortal beings or faeries in Irish folklore (pronounced "Shee").
1. Hamlets at the foot of the Slieve Aughty Mountains in County Galway, all within a few miles of Lady Gregory's estate at Coole Park.
2. A walking stick, cut from a blackthorn bush.
3. Places northeast of Coole. Lough Belsrah, as it is now known, is close to the summit of one of the Slieve Aughty peaks.

shadows in the brown bog pools; sitting so quiet as not to startle the deer that came down from the heather to the grass and the tilled fields at the fall of night. As the days went by it seemed as if he was beginning to belong to some world out of sight and misty, that has for its mearing[4] the colours that are beyond all other colours and the silences that are beyond all silences of this world. And sometimes he would hear coming and going in the wood music that when it stopped went from his memory like a dream; and once in the stillness of midday he heard a sound like the clashing of many swords, that went on for a long time without any break. And at the fall of night and at moonrise the lake would grow to be like a gateway of silver and shining stones, and there would come from its silence the faint sound of keening[5] and of frightened laughter broken by the wind, and many pale beckoning hands.

He was sitting looking into the water one evening in harvest time, thinking of all the secrets that were shut into the lakes and the mountains, when he heard a cry coming from the south, very faint at first, but getting louder and clearer as the shadow of the rushes grew longer, till he could hear the words: 'I am beautiful, I am beautiful; the birds in the air, the moths under the leaves, the flies over the water look at me, for they never saw anyone so beautiful as myself. I am young, I am young: look upon me, mountains; look upon me, perishing woods, for my body will shine like the white waters when you have been hurried away. You and the whole race of men, and the race of the beasts and the race of the fish and the winged race are dropping like a candle that is nearly burned out, but I laugh out aloud because I am in my youth.' The voice would break off from time to time, as if tired, and then it would begin again, calling out always the same words: 'I am beautiful, I am beautiful.' Presently the bushes at the edge of the little lake trembled for a moment, and a very old woman forced her way among them, and passed by Hanrahan, walking with very slow steps. Her face was of the colour of earth, and more wrinkled than the face of any old hag that was ever seen, and her grey hair was hanging in wisps, and the rags she was wearing did not hide her dark skin that was roughened by all weathers. She passed by him with her eyes wide open, and her head high, and her arms hanging straight beside her, and she went into the shadow of the hills towards the west.

A sort of dread came over Hanrahan when he saw her, for he knew her to be one Winny Byrne, that went begging from place to place crying always the same cry, and he had often heard that she had once such wisdom that all the women of the neighbours used to go looking for advice from her, and that she had a voice so beautiful that men and women would come from every part to hear her sing at a wake or a wedding; and that the Others, the great Sidhe, had stolen her wits one Samhain[6] night many years ago, when she had fallen asleep on the edge of a rath,[7] and had seen in her dreams the servants of Echtge of the hills.

And as she vanished away up the hillside, it seemed as if her cry, 'I am

4. Boundary.
5. A wailing cry of lamentation, usually for the dead.
6. An ancient Celtic festival held on the eve of November 1, marking the beginning of winter.
7. A hill fort.

beautiful, I am beautiful,' was coming from among the stars in the heavens.

There was a cold wind creeping among the rushes, and Hanrahan began to shiver, and he rose up to go to some house where there would be a fire on the hearth. But instead of turning down the hill as he was used, he went on up the hill, along the little track that was may be a road and may be the dry bed of a stream. It was the same way Winny had gone, and it led to the little cabin where she stopped when she stopped in any place at all. He walked very slowly up the hill, as if he had a great load on his back, and at last he saw a light a little to the left, and he thought it likely it was from Winny's house it was shining, and he turned from the path to go to it. But clouds had come over the sky, and he could not well see his way, and after he had gone a few steps his foot slipped and he fell into a bog drain, and though he dragged himself out of it, holding on to the roots of the heather, the fall had given him a great shake, and he felt better fit to lie down than to go travelling. But he had always great courage, and he made his way on, step by step, till at last he came to Winny's cabin, that had no window, but the light was shining from the door. He thought to go into it and to rest for a while, but when he came to the door he did not see Winny inside it, but what he saw was four old grey-haired women playing cards, but Winny herself was not among them. Hanrahan sat down on a heap of turf beside the door, for he was tired out and out, and had no wish for talking or for card-playing, and his bones and his joints aching the way they were. He could hear the four women talking as they played, and calling out their hands. And it seemed to him that they were saying, like the strange man[8] in the barn long ago: 'Spades and Diamonds, Courage and Power. Clubs and Hearts, Knowledge and Pleasure.' And he went on saying those words over and over to himself; and whether or not he was in his dreams, the pain that was in his shoulder never left him. And after a while the four women in the cabin began to quarrel, and each one to say the other had not played fair, and their voices grew from loud to louder, and their screams and their curses, till at last the whole air was filled with the noise of them around and above the house, and Hanrahan, hearing it between sleep and waking, said: 'That is the sound of the fighting between the friends and the illwishers of a man that is near his death. And I wonder,' he said, 'who is the man in this lonely place that is near his death.'

It seemed as if he had been asleep a long time, and he opened his eyes, and the face he saw over him was the old wrinkled face of Winny of the Cross Roads. She was looking hard at him, as if to make sure he was not dead, and she wiped away the blood that had grown dry on his face with a wet cloth, and after a while she partly helped him and partly lifted him into the cabin, and laid him down on what served her for a bed. She gave him a couple of potatoes from a pot on the fire, and what served him better, a mug of spring water. He slept a little now and again, and sometimes he heard her singing to herself as she moved about the house, and so the night wore away. When the sky began to brighten with the dawn

---

8. Featured in Yeats's story "Red Hanrahan."

he felt for the bag where his little store of money was, and held it out to her, and she took out a bit of copper and a bit of silver money, but she let it drop again as if it was nothing to her, maybe because it was not money she was used to beg for, but food and rags; or maybe because the rising of the dawn was filling her with pride and a new belief in her own great beauty. She went out and cut a few armfuls of heather, and brought it in and heaped it over Hanrahan, saying something about the cold of the morning, and while she did that he took notice of the wrinkles in her face, and the greyness of her hair, and the broken teeth that were black and full of gaps. And when he was well covered with the heather she went out of the door and away down the side of the mountain, and he could hear her cry, 'I am beautiful, I am beautiful,' getting less and less as she went, till at last it died away altogether.

Hanrahan lay there through the length of the day, in his pains and his weakness, and when the shadows of the evening were falling he heard her voice again coming up the hillside, and she came in and boiled the potatoes and shared them with him the same way as before. And one day after another passed like that, and the weight of his flesh was heavy about him. But little by little as he grew weaker he knew there were some greater than himself in the room with him, and that the house began to be filled with them; and it seemed to him they had all power in their hands, and that they might with one touch of the hand break down the wall the hardness of pain had built about him, and take him into their own world. And sometimes he could hear voices, very faint and joyful, crying from the rafters or out of the flame on the hearth, and other times the whole house was filled with music that went through it like a wind. And after a while his weakness left no place for pain, and there grew up about him a great silence like the silence in the heart of a lake, and there came through it like the flame of a rushlight, the faint joyful voices, ever and always.

One morning he heard music somewhere outside the door, and as the day passed it grew louder and louder until it drowned the faint joyful voices, and even Winny's cry upon the hillside at the fall of evening. About midnight and in a moment, the walls seemed to melt away and to leave his bed floating on a pale misty light that shone on every side as far as the eye could see; and after the first blinding of his eyes he saw that it was full of great shadowy figures rushing here and there.

At the same time the music came very clearly to him, and he knew that it was but the continual clashing of swords.

'I am after my death,' he said, 'and in the very heart of the music of Heaven. O Cherubim and Seraphim,[9] receive my soul!'

At his cry the light where it was nearest to him filled with sparks of yet brighter light, and he saw that these were the points of swords turned towards his heart; and then a sudden flame, bright and burning like God's love or God's hate, swept over the light and went out and he was in darkness. At first he could see nothing, for all was as dark as if there was black bog earth about him, but all of a sudden the fire blazed up as if a wisp of straw had been thrown upon it. And as he looked at it, the light

9. Angels.

was shining on the big pot that was hanging from a hook, and on the flat stone where Winny used to bake a cake now and again, and on the long rusty knife she used to be cutting the roots of the heather with, and on the long blackthorn stick he had brought into the house himself. And when he saw those four things, some memory came into Hanrahan's mind, and strength came back to him, and he rose sitting up in the bed, and he said very loud and clear: 'The Cauldron, the Stone, the Sword, the Spear. What are they? Who do they belong to? And I have asked the question this time,' he said.

And then he fell back again, weak, and the breath going from him.

Winny Byrne, that had been tending the fire, came over then, having her eyes fixed on the bed; and the faint laughing voices began crying out again, and a pale light, grey like a wave, came creeping over the room, and he did not know from what secret world it came. He saw Winny's withered face and her withered arms that were grey like crumbled earth, and weak as he was he shrank back farther towards the wall. And then there came out of the mud-stiffened rags arms as white and as shadowy as the foam on a river, and they were put about his body, and a voice that he could hear well but that seemed to come from a long way off said to him in a whisper: 'You will go looking for me no more upon the breasts of women.'

'Who are you?' he said then.

'I am one of the lasting people, of the lasting unwearied Voices, that make my dwelling in the broken and the dying and those that have lost their wits; and I came looking for you, and you are mine until the whole world is burned out like a candle that is spent. And look up now,' she said, 'for the wisps that are for our wedding are lighted.'

He saw then that the house was crowded with pale shadowy hands, and that every hand was holding what was sometimes like a wisp lighted for a marriage, and sometimes like a tall white candle for the dead.

When the sun rose on the morning of the morrow Winny of the Cross Roads rose up from where she was sitting beside the body, and began her begging from townland to townland, singing the same song as she walked, 'I am beautiful, I am beautiful. The birds in the air, the moths under the leaves, the flies over the water look at me. Look at me, perishing woods, for my body will be shining like the lake water after you have been hurried away. You and the whole race of men, and the race of the beasts, and the race of the fish, and the winged race, are wearing away like a candle that has been burned out. But I laugh out loud, because I am in my youth.'

She did not come back that night or any night to the cabin, and it was not till the end of two days that the turf cutters going to the bog found the body of Red Owen Hanrahan, and gathered men to wake him and women to keen him, and gave him a burying worthy of so great a poet.

Autobiographical Writings

From *Reveries Over Childhood and Youth* (1916)

My first memories are fragmentary and isolated and contemporaneous, as though one remembered vaguely some early day of the Seven Days.[1] It seems as if time had not yet been created, for all are connected with emotion and place and without sequence.

I remember sitting upon somebody's knee, looking out of a window at a wall covered with cracked and falling plaster, but what wall I do not remember, and being told that some relation once lived there. I am looking out of another window in London. It is at Fitzroy Road.[2] Some boys are playing in the road and among them a boy in uniform, a telegraph boy perhaps. When I ask who the boy is, a servant tells me that he is going to blow the town up, and I go to sleep in terror.[3]

After that come memories of Sligo, where I live with my grandparents.[4] I am sitting on the ground looking at a mastless toy boat with the paint rubbed and scratched, and I say to myself in great melancholy, "it is further away than it used to be," and while I am saying it I am looking at a long scratch in the stern, for it is especially the scratch which is further away. Then one day at dinner my great-uncle William Middleton[5] says, "we should not make light of the troubles of children. They are worse than ours, because we can see the end of our trouble and they can never see any end," and I feel grateful for I know that I am very unhappy and have often said to myself, "when you grow up, never talk as grown-up people do of the happiness of childhood." I may have already had the night of misery when, having prayed for several days that I might die, I had begun to be afraid that I was dying and prayed that I might live. There was no reason for my unhappiness. Nobody was unkind, and my grandmother has still after so many years my gratitude and my reverence. The house was so big that there was always a room to hide in, and I had a red pony and

1. The seven days of the creation of the world, as recounted in Genesis.
2. Yeats's parents rented a house at 23 Fitzroy Road, near Regent's Park, London, between July 1867 and July 1873, though Yeats himself spent only part of this period there.
3. In December 1867, a Fenian bomb killed fifteen people at Clerkenwell, London. The Fenian Brotherhood (also known as the Irish Republican Brotherhood), a militant Irish Nationalist movement established in 1858, was determined to end English rule in Ireland, by force if necessary. Yeats's memory perhaps recalls the tension resulting from this and other Fenian campaigns of 1867 and 1868.
4. Yeats spent his summers between 1868 and 1874, most of 1872–74, and some other substantial periods of time as a child at "Merville," the Sligo home of his maternal grandparents, William Pollexfen (1811–1892) and Susan Middleton Pollexfen (1819–1892).
5. William Middleton (1820–1882), brother of Yeats's maternal grandmother.

FROM *REVERIES OVER CHILDHOOD AND YOUTH*

a garden where I could wander, and there were two dogs to follow at my
heels, one white with some black spots on his head and the other with
long black hair all over him. I used to think about God and fancy that I
was very wicked, and one day when I threw a stone and hit a duck in the
yard by mischance and broke its wing, I was full of wonder when I was
told that the duck would be cooked for dinner and that I should not be
punished.

*   *   *

I can only remember my grandmother punishing me once. I was playing
in the kitchen and a servant in horseplay pulled my shirt out of my trousers
in front just as my grandmother came in and I, accused of I knew not
what childish indecency, was given my dinner in a room by myself. But I
was always afraid of my uncles and aunts, and once the uncle who had
taken the crowbar to the bully found me eating lunch which my grandmother had given me and reproved me for it and made me ashamed. We
breakfasted at nine and dined at four and it was considered self-indulgent
to eat anything between meals; and once an aunt told me that I had reined
in my pony and struck it at the same moment that I might show it off as
I rode through the town, and I, because I had been accused of what I
thought a very dark crime, had a night of misery. Indeed I remember little
of childhood but its pain. I have grown happier with every year of life as
though gradually conquering something in myself, for certainly my mis-
eries were not made by others but were a part of my own mind.

*   *   *

IV

Because I had found it hard to attend to anything less interesting than my
thoughts, I was difficult to teach. Several of my uncles and aunts had tried
to teach me to read, and because they could not, and because I was much
older than children who read easily, had come to think, as I have learnt
since, that I had not all my faculties.[6] But for an accident they might have
thought it for a long time. My father was staying in the house and never
went to church,[7] and that gave me the courage to refuse to set out one
Sunday morning. I was often devout, my eyes filling with tears at the
thought of God and of my own sins, but I hated church. My grandmother
tried to teach me to put my toes first to the ground because I suppose I
stumped on my heels and that took my pleasure out of the way there.
Later on when I had learnt to read I took pleasure in the words of the
hymn, but never understood why the choir took three times as long as I
did in getting to the end; and the part of the service I liked, the sermon

6. Yeats had been unable to read until he was seven years old.
7. John Butler Yeats (1839–1922) had married Susan Middleton Pollexfen (1841–1900) in 1863; he
was called to the Irish bar in 1865 but quit the following year to become an artist. He had lost
belief in Christianity under the influence of the utilitarian and humanist views of English philosopher John Stuart Mill (1806–1873) and French philospher and social theorist Auguste Comte
(1798–1857), and he became and remained a sceptical positivist.

and passages of the Apocalypse and Ecclesiastes,[8] were no compensation for all the repetitions and for the fatigue of so much standing. My father said if I would not go to church he would teach me to read. I think now that he wanted to make me go for my grandmother's sake and could think of no other way. He was an angry and impatient teacher and flung the reading book at my head, and next Sunday I decided to go to church. My father had, however, got interested in teaching me, and only shifted the lesson to a week-day till he had conquered my wandering mind. My first clear image of him was fixed on my imagination, I believe, but a few days before the first lesson. He had just arrived from London and was walking up and down the nursery floor. He had a very black beard and hair, and one cheek bulged out with a fig that was there to draw the pain out of a bad tooth. One of the nurses (a nurse had come from London with my brothers and sisters) said to the other that a live frog, she had heard, was best of all. Then I was sent to a dame school[9] kept by an old woman who stood us in rows and had a long stick like a billiard cue to get at the back rows. My father was still at Sligo when I came back from my first lesson and asked me what I had been taught. I said I had been taught to sing, and he said, "sing then" and I sang

> "Little drops of water,
> Little grains of sand,
> Make the mighty ocean,
> And the pleasant land."

high up in my head. So my father wrote to the old woman that I was never to be taught to sing again, and afterwards other teachers were told the same thing.

* * *

My father's unbelief had set me thinking about the evidences of religion and I weighed the matter perpetually with great anxiety, for I did not think I could live without religion. All my religious emotions were, I think, connected with clouds and cloudy glimpses of luminous sky, perhaps because of some bible picture of God's speaking to Abraham or the like. At least I can remember the sight moving me to tears. One day I got a decisive argument for belief. A cow was about to calve, and I went to the field where the cow was with some farm-hands who carried a lantern, and next day I heard that the cow had calved in the early morning. I asked everybody how calves were born, and because nobody would tell me, made up my mind that nobody knew. They were the gift of God, that much was certain, but it was plain that nobody had ever dared to see them come, and children must come in the same way. I made up my mind that when I was a man, I would wait up till calf or child had come. I was certain there would be a cloud and a burst of light and God would bring the calf in the cloud out of the light. That thought made me content until a boy

8. The book of Revelations, in the New Testament, tells of the Apocalypse and Judgment Day. Ecclesiastes, in the Old Testament, recounts the teachings of King David and includes long sections of verse.
9. A private school for young children, usually run by one woman.

of twelve or thirteen, who had come on a visit for the day, sat beside me in a hay-loft and explained all the mechanism of sex. He had learnt all about it from an elder boy whose pathic[1] he was (to use a term he would not have understood) and his description, given as I can see now, as if he were telling of any other fact of physical life, made me miserable for weeks. After the first impression wore off, I began to doubt if he had spoken truth, but one day I discovered a passage in the encyclopedia, though I only partly understood its long words, that confirmed what he had said. I did not know enough to be shocked at his relation to the elder boy, but it was the first breaking of the dream of childhood.

My realization of death came when my father and mother and my two brothers and my two sisters were on a visit. I was in the Library when I heard feet running past and heard somebody say in the passage that my younger brother, Robert, had died.[2] He had been ill for some days. A little later my sister and I sat at the table, very happy, drawing ships with their flags half-mast high. We must have heard or seen that the ships in the harbour had their flags at half-mast. Next day at breakfast I heard people telling how my mother and the servant had heard the banshee[3] crying the night before he died. It must have been after this that I told my grandmother I did not want to go with her when she went to see old bed-ridden people because they would soon die.

IX

My father read out to me, for the first time, when I was eight or nine years old. Between Sligo and Rosses Point,[4] there is a tongue of land covered with coarse grass that runs out into the sea or the mud according to the state of the tide. It is the place where dead horses are buried. Sitting there, my father read me "The Lays of Ancient Rome."[5] It was the first poetry that had moved me after the stable-boy's "Orange Rhymes."[6] Later on he read me "Ivanhoe" and "The Lay of the Last Minstrel,"[7] and they are still vivid in the memory. I re-read "Ivanhoe" the other day, but it has all vanished except Gurth, the swineherd, at the outset and Friar Tuck and his venison pasty, the two scenes that laid hold of me in childhood. "The Lay of the Last Minstrel" gave me a wish to turn magician[8] that competed for years with the dream of being killed upon the sea-shore. When I first went to school, he tried to keep me from reading boys' papers, because a paper, by its very nature, as he explained to me, had to be made for the

1. Homosexual partner (with the implication of being a passive or unwilling one).
2. Robert Corbet Yeats (1870–1873) died in Sligo of croup.
3. From "bean sidhe" (Irish: fairy woman). As Yeats described it, "an attendant fairy that follows the old families, and none but them, and wails before a death."
4. Rosses Point, a sandy peninsula and village about seven miles northwest of Sligo.
5. A volume of poems (1842) about heroic events and episodes in Roman history, by the English historian and poet Thomas Macaulay (1800–1859).
6. Poems celebrating the victory of the Protestant William of Orange (1650–1702) over the Catholic forces of King James at the battle of the Boyne in 1690.
7. A novel (1820) by Sir Walter Scott (1771–1832), and a long dramatic poem (1805), also by Scott.
8. Scott's poem, told by an old wandering mistrel who lives in an age when his profession has been all but erased by puritanism, tells of a goblin page who steals a wizard's book of spells, but who is unable to control them fully; an enchantress; and the fate of two old families. Its thematic linkages of poetry and magic were particularly appealing to Yeats.

average boy or man and so could not but thwart one's growth. He took away my paper and I had not courage to say that I was but reading and delighting in a prose re-telling of the Iliad.[9] But after a few months, my father said he had been too anxious and became less urgent about my lessons and less violent if I had learnt them badly, and he ceased to notice what I read. From that on I shared the excitement which ran through all my fellows on Wednesday afternoons when the boys' papers were published, and I read endless stories I have forgotten as completely as Grimm's Fairy Tales[1] that I read at Sligo, and all of Hans Andersen except the Ugly Duckling[2] which my mother had read to me and to my sisters. I remember vaguely that I liked Hans Andersen better than Grimm because he was less homely, but even he never gave me the knights and dragons and beautiful ladies that I longed for. I have remembered nothing that I read, but only those things that I heard or saw. When I was ten or twelve my father took me to see Irving play Hamlet, and did not understand why I preferred Irving to Ellen Terry,[3] who was, I can now see, the idol of himself and his friends. I could not think of her, as I could of Irving's Hamlet, as but myself, and I was not old enough to care for feminine charm and beauty. For many years Hamlet was an image of heroic self-possession for the poses of youth and childhood to copy, a combatant of the battle within myself. My father had read me the story of the little boy murdered by the Jews in Chaucer and the tale of Sir Topaz,[4] explaining the hard words, and though both excited me, I had liked Sir Topaz best and been disappointed that it left off in the middle. As I grew older, he would tell me plots of Balzac's novels, using incident or character as an illustration for some profound criticism of life. Now that I have read all the Comédie Humaine, certain pages have an unnatural emphasis, straining and overbalancing the outline, and I remember how in some suburban street, he told me of Lucien de Rubempré, or of the duel after the betrayal of his master, and how the wounded Lucien had muttered "so much the worse" when he heard someone say that he was not dead.[5]

I now can but share with a friend my thoughts and my emotions, and there is a continual discovery of difference, but in those days, before I had found myself, we could share adventures. When friends plan and do together, their minds become one mind and the last secret disappears. I was useless at games. I cannot remember that I ever kicked a goal or made a run, but I was a mine of knowledge when I and the athlete and those two notoriously gentlemanly boys—theirs was the name that I remember without a face—set out for Richmond Park, for Coomb Wood or Twyford

---

9. The epic poem by Greek poet Homer, dating from around the eighth century B.C.E.
1. Fairy tales collected by Jacob and Karl Grimm, German folklorists and philologists, first published in 1812–15.
2. A story (1843) by Danish writer Hans Christian Andersen (1805–1875).
3. Henry Irving (1838–1905), celebrated English actor; and Ellen Terry (1848–1928), his leading lady for more than two decades.
4. In "The Prioress's Tale" and "The Tale of Sir Topaz" in Geoffrey Chaucer's *Canterbury Tales* (written in the 1380s).
5. French novelist Honoré de Balzac (1799–1850), who called his collected fiction *La Comédie Humaine* (The Human Comedy). The scene recalled here is from *A Distinguished Provincial in Paris.*

Abbey[6] to look for butterflies and moths and beetles. Sometimes to-day I meet people at lunch or dinner whose address will sound familiar and I remember of a sudden how a game-keeper chased me from the plantation behind their house, and how I have turned over the cow-dung in their paddock in the search for some rare beetle believed to haunt the spot. The athlete was our watchman and our safety. He would suggest, should we meet a carriage on the drive, that we take off our hats and walk on as though about to pay a call. And once when we were sighted by a game-keeper at Coomb Wood, he persuaded the eldest of the brothers to pretend to be a school-master taking his boys for a walk, and the keeper, instead of swearing and threatening the law, was sad and argumentative. No matter how charming the place, (and there is a little stream in a hollow where Wimbledon Common flows into Coomb Wood that is pleasant in the memory,) I knew that those other boys saw something I did not see. I was a stranger there. There was something in their way of saying the names of places that made me feel this.

XIV

The great event of a boy's life is the awakening of sex. He will bathe many times a day, or get up at dawn and having stripped leap to and fro over a stick laid upon two chairs and hardly know, and never admit, that he had begun to take pleasure in his own nakedness, nor will he understand the change until some dream discovers it. He may never understand at all the greater change in his mind.

It all came upon me when I was close upon seventeen like the bursting of a shell. Somnambulistic country-girls, when it is upon them, throw plates about or pull them with long hairs in simulation of the polter-geist,[7] or become mediums for some genuine spirit-mischief, surrendering to their desire of the marvellous. As I look backward, I seem to discover that my passions, my loves and my despairs, instead of being my enemies, a disturbance and an attack, became so beautiful that I must be constantly alone to give them my whole attention. I notice that, for the first time as I run through my memory, what I saw when alone is more vivid than what I did or saw in company.

A herd had shown me a cave some hundred and fifty feet below the cliff[8] path and a couple of hundred above the sea, and told me how an evicted tenant called Macrom, dead some fifteen years, had lived there many years, and shown me a rusty nail in the rock which had served perhaps to hold up some wooden protection from wind and weather. Here I stored a tin of cocoa and some biscuits, and instead of going to my bed, would slip out on warm nights and sleep in the cave on the excuse of catching moths. One had to pass over a rocky ledge, safe enough for anyone with a fair head, yet seeming, if looked at from above, narrow and

6. Places in southern England.
7. A type of ghost credited with moving objects around.
8. On Howth Head, on the north side of Dublin Bay. The Yeats family lived at Howth between 1881 and early 1884.

sloping; and a remonstrance from a stranger who had seen me climbing along it doubled my delight in the adventure. When however, upon a bank holiday, I found lovers in my cave, I was not content with it again till I heard of alarm among the fishing boats, because the ghost of Macrom had been seen a little before the dawn, stooping over his fire in the cave-mouth. I had been trying to cook eggs, as I had read in some book, by burying them in the earth under a fire of sticks.

At other times, I would sleep among the rhododendrons and rocks in the wilder part of the grounds of Howth Castle. After a while my father said I must stay in-doors half the night, meaning that I should get some sleep in my bed; but I, knowing that I would be too sleepy and comfortable to get up again used to sit over the kitchen fire till half the night was gone. Exaggerated accounts spread through the school, and sometimes when I did not know a lesson some master would banter me. My interest in science began to fade away, and presently I said to myself, "it has all been a misunderstanding." I remembered how soon I tired of my specimens, and how little I knew after all my years of collecting, and I came to believe that I had gone through so much labour because of a text, heard for the first time in St. John's Church in Sligo. I wanted to be certain of my own wisdom by copying Solomon, who had knowledge of hyssop and of tree.[9] I still carried my green net but I began to play at being a sage, a magician or a poet. I had many idols, and now as I climbed along the narrow ledge I was Manfred[1] on his glacier, and now I thought of Prince Athanase and his solitary lamp, but I soon chose Alastor[2] for my chief of men and longed to share his melancholy, and maybe at last to disappear from everybody's sight as he disappeared drifting in a boat along some slow-moving river between great trees. When I thought of women they were modelled on those in my favourite poets and loved in brief tragedy, or like the girl in "The Revolt of Islam,"[3] accompanied their lovers through all manner of wild places, lawless women without homes and without children.

XV

My father's influence upon my thoughts was at its height. We went to Dublin by train every morning, breakfasting in his studio. He had taken a large room with a beautiful 18th century mantel-piece in a York Street tenement house, and at breakfast he read passages from the poets, and always from the play or poem at its most passionate moment. He never read me a passage because of its speculative interest, and indeed did not care at all for poetry where there was generalisation or abstraction however impassioned. * * * He did not care even for a fine lyric passage unless one felt some actual man behind its elaboration of beauty, and he was always looking for the lineaments of some desirable, familiar life. When

9. See I Kings 4.33. Solomon, a king of ancient Israel, was considered the wisest man of his era.
1. The title character of the dramatic poem *Manfred* by English poet Lord Byron (1788–1824).
2. In "Prince Athanase: A Fragment" (1818) by Percy Bysshe Shelley (1792–1822), Prince Athanase roves the world searching for perfect love. The eponymous poet-magician in Shelley's "Alastor, or the Spirit of Solitude" (1816) drifts out of view to meet death; Yeats here evokes, in particular, lines 515–24 of the poem.
3. Shelley's "The Revolt of Islam" (1818).

the spirits sang their scorn of Manfred I was to judge by Manfred's answer "O sweet and melancholy voices"[4] that they could not, even in anger, put off their spiritual sweetness. He thought Keats a greater poet than Shelley, because less abstract, but did not read him, caring little, I think, for any of that most beautiful poetry which has come in modern times from the influence of painting. All must be an idealisation of speech, and at some moment of passionate action or somnambulistic reverie. I remember his saying that all contemplative men were in a conspiracy to overrate their state of life, and that all writers were of them, excepting the great poets. Looking backwards, it seems to me that I saw his mind in fragments, which had always hidden connections I only now begin to discover. He disliked the Victorian poetry of ideas, and Wordsworth but for certain passages or whole poems. He described one morning over his breakfast how in the shape of the head of a Wordsworthian scholar, an old and greatly respected clergyman whose portrait he was painting, he had discovered all the animal instincts of a prize-fighter. He despised the formal beauty of Raphael,[5] that calm which is not an ordered passion but an hypocrisy, and attacked Raphael's life for its love of pleasure and its self-indulgence. In literature he was always pre-Raphaelite, and carried into literature principles that, while the Academy was still unbroken, had made the first attack upon academic form.[6] He no longer read me anything for its story, and all our discussion was of style.

XXV

It was only when I began to study psychical research and mystical philosophy that I broke away from my father's influence. He had been a follower of John Stuart Mill[7] and had grown to manhood with the scientific movement. In this he had never been of Rossetti's[8] party who said that it mattered to nobody whether the sun went round the earth or the earth round the sun. But through this new research, this reaction from popular science, I had begun to feel that I had allies for my secret thought.

Once when I was in Dowden's[9] drawing-room a servant announced my late head-master. I must have got pale or red, for Dowden with some ironical, friendly remark, brought me into another room and there I stayed, until the visitor was gone. A few months later, when I met the head-master again I had more courage. We chanced upon one another in the street and he said, "I want you to use your influence with so-and-so, for he is giving all his time to some sort of mysticism and he will fail in his examination." I was in great alarm, but I managed to say something about the children of this world being wiser than the children of light. He went

4. In Act I, scene 1 of *Manfred*.
5. Raffaello Raphael (1483–1520), Italian painter of the Renaissance period.
6. The pre-Raphaelite Brotherhood, a group of artists and writers first constituted in 1848, sought inspiration from the Middle Ages. Their work challenged the authority of the British Academy of Arts, the main arbiter of artistic taste at the time.
7. John Stuart Mill (1806–1873), English philosopher whose mix of empiricism and utilitarianism was enriched by his eloquent humanist definition of and defense of the freedoms of the individual against the claims of state and society.
8. Dante Gabriel Rossetti (1828–1882), English pre-Raphaelite painter.
9. Edward Dowden (1843–1913), professor of English literature at Trinity College, Dublin; he and Yeats's father had been friends since their student days.

off with a brusque "good morning." I do not think that even at that age I would have been so grandiloquent but for my alarm. He had, however, aroused all my indignation.

My new allies and my old had alike sustained me. "Intermediate examinations," which I had always refused, meant money for pupil and for teacher, and that alone. My father had brought me up never when at school to think of the future or of any practical result. I have even known him to say, "when I was young, the definition of a gentleman was a man not wholly occupied in getting on." And yet this master wanted to withdraw my friend from the pursuit of the most important of all the truths. My friend,[1] now in his last year at school, was a show boy, and had beaten all Ireland again and again, but now he and I were reading Baron Reichenbach on Odic Force[2] and manuals published by the Theosophical Society. We spent a good deal of time in the Kildare Street Museum[3] passing our hands over the glass-cases, feeling or believing we felt the Odic Force flowing from the big crystals. We also found pins blindfolded and read papers on our discoveries to the Hermetic Society[4] that met near the roof in York Street. I had, when we first made our society, proposed for our consideration that whatever the great poets had affirmed in their finest moments was the nearest we could come to an authoritative religion, and that their mythology, their spirits of water and wind were but literal truth. I had read "Prometheus Unbound"[5] with this thought in mind and wanted help to carry my study through all literature. I was soon to vex my father by defining truth as "the dramatically appropriate utterance of the highest man." And if I had been asked to define the "highest" man, I would have said perhaps, "we can but find him as Homer found Odysseus when he was looking for a theme."

✻   ✻   ✻

XXX

Someone at the Young Ireland Society[6] gave me a newspaper that I might read some article or letter. I began idly reading verses describing the shore of Ireland as seen by a returning, dying emigrant. My eyes filled with tears and yet I knew the verses were badly written—vague, abstract words such as one finds in a newspaper. I looked at the end and saw the name of some political exile who had died but a few days after his return to Ireland. They had moved me because they contained the actual thoughts of a man at a passionate moment of life, and when I met my father I was full of the discovery. We should write out our own thoughts in as nearly as possible the language we thought them in, as though in a letter to an intimate

---

1. Charles Johnston (1867–1931), Yeats's friend since their school days.
2. The German physicist Carl von Reichenbach (1788–1869) studied "vital forces" including animal magnetism, auras, and light purportedly emanating from crystals. His *Letters on Od and Magnetism* was published in 1852.
3. In Dublin.
4. A group founded by Yeats and friends in 1885 for the study of theosophy and spiritual forces.
5. A poetic drama by Shelley.
6. A Dublin Nationalist society, founded in 1885, which drew its inspiration from the Young Ireland patriotic movement of the 1840s, and which aimed to promote Irish nationalism via Irish literature.

friend. We should not disguise them in any way; for our lives give them force as the lives of people in plays give force to their words. Personal utterance, which had almost ceased in English literature, could be as fine an escape from rhetoric and abstraction as drama itself. My father was indignant, almost violent, and would hear of nothing but drama. "Personal utterance was only egotism." I knew it was not, but as yet did not know how to explain the difference. I tried from that on to write out of my emotions exactly as they came to me in life, not changing them to make them more beautiful, and to rid my syntax of all inversions and my vocabulary of literary words, and that made it hard to write at all. It meant rejecting the words or the constructions that had been used over and over because they flow most easily into rhyme and measure. Then, too, how hard it was to be sincere, not to make the emotion more beautiful and more violent or the circumstance more romantic. "If I can be sincere and make my language natural, and without becoming discursive, like a novelist, and so indiscreet and prosaic," I said to myself, "I shall, if good luck or bad luck make my life interesting, be a great poet; for it will be no longer a matter of literature at all." Yet when I re-read those early poems which gave me so much trouble, I find little but romantic convention, unconscious drama. It is so many years before one can believe enough in what one feels even to know what the feeling is.

XXXIII

For some months now I have lived with my own youth and childhood, not always writing indeed but thinking of it almost every day, and I am sorrowful and disturbed. It is not that I have accomplished too few of my plans, for I am not ambitious; but when I think of all the books I have read, and of the wise words I have heard spoken, and of the anxiety I have given to parents and grandparents, and of the hopes that I have had, all life weighed in the scales of my own life seems to me a preparation for something that never happens.

From *The Trembling of the Veil* (1922)

From Book I. Four Years: 1887–1891

VI

My first meeting with Oscar Wilde was an astonishment.[1] I never before heard a man talking with perfect sentences, as if he had written them all over night with labour and yet all spontaneous. There was present that night at Henley's,[2] by right of propinquity or of accident, a man full of the secret spite of dulness, who interrupted from time to time, and always to check or disorder thought; and I noticed with what mastery he was

---

1. Yeats first met Oscar Wilde (1854–1900), playwright, poet, and critic, in September 1888.
2. William Henley (1849–1903), poet and editor, was an important early encourager of Yeats's work, and he published many of Yeats's reviews and articles in the journals the *Scots Observer*, the *National Observer*, and the *New Review* in the 1880s and 1890s.

foiled and thrown. I noticed, too, that the impression of artificiality that I think all Wilde's listeners have recorded came from the perfect rounding of the sentences and from the deliberation that made it possible. That very impression helped him, as the effect of metre, or of the antithetical prose of the seventeenth century, which is itself a true metre, helped its writers, for he could pass without incongruity from some unforeseen, swift stroke of wit to elaborate reverie. I heard him say a few nights later: "Give me The Winter's Tale, 'Daffodils that come before the swallow dare' but not King Lear. What is King Lear but poor life staggering in the fog?" and the slow cadence, modulated with so great precision, sounded natural to my ears. That first night he praised Walter Pater's Essays on the Renaissance:[3] "It is my golden book; I never travel anywhere without it; but it is the very flower of decadence: the last trumpet should have sounded the moment it was written." "But," said the dull man, "would you not have given us time to read it?" "Oh no," was the retort, "there would have been plenty of time afterwards—in either world." I think he seemed to us, baffled as we were by youth, or by infirmity, a triumphant figure, and to some of us a figure from another age, an audacious Italian fifteenth century figure. A few weeks before I had heard one of my father's friends, an official in a publishing firm that had employed both Wilde and Henley as editors, blaming Henley who was "no use except under control" and praising Wilde, "so indolent but such a genius"; and now the firm became the topic of our talk. "How often do you go to the office?" said Henley. "I used to go three times a week," said Wilde, "for an hour a day but I have since struck off one of the days." "My God," said Henley, "I went five times a week for five hours a day and when I wanted to strike off a day they had a special committee meeting." "Furthermore," was Wilde's answer, "I never answered their letters. I have known men come to London full of bright prospects and seen them complete wrecks in a few months through a habit of answering letters." He too knew how to keep our elders in their place, and his method was plainly the more successful, for Henley had been dismissed. "No he is not an aesthete," Henley commented later, being somewhat embarrassed by Wilde's Pre-Raphaelite entanglement; "one soon finds that he is a scholar and a gentleman." And when I dined with Wilde a few days afterwards he began at once, "I had to strain every nerve to equal that man at all"; and I was too loyal to speak my thought: "You and not he said all the brilliant things." He like the rest of us had felt the strain of an intensity that seemed to hold life at the point of drama. He had said on that first meeting "The basis of literary friendship is mixing the poisoned bowl"; and for a few weeks Henley and he became close friends till, the astonishment of their meeting over, diversity of character and ambition pushed them apart, and, with half the cavern helping, Henley began mixing the poisoned bowl for Wilde. Yet Henley never wholly lost that first admiration, for after Wilde's downfall[4] he said to me: "Why

3. *Studies in the History of the Renaissance* (1873) by Walter Pater (1839–1894) was a key influence on Wilde's aestheticism.
4. Wilde was convicted of sodomy in 1895, and sentenced to prison. He left England after his release and died soon after in France.

did he do it? I told my lads to attack him and yet we might have fought under his banner."

XX

I generalized a great deal and was ashamed of it. I thought that it was my business in life to be an artist and a poet, and that there could be no business comparable to that. I refused to read books, and even to meet people who excited me to generalization, but all to no purpose. I said my prayers much as in childhood, though without the old regularity of hour and place, and I began to pray that my imagination might somehow be rescued from abstraction, and become as preoccupied with life as had been the imagination of Chaucer.[5] For ten or twelve years more I suffered continual remorse, and only became content when my abstractions had composed themselves into picture and dramatization. My very remorse helped to spoil my early poetry, giving it an element of sentimentality through my refusal to permit it any share of an intellect which I considered impure. Even in practical life I only very gradually began to use generalizations, that have since become the foundation of all I have done, or shall do, in Ireland. For all I know all men may have been so timid, for I am persuaded that our intellects at twenty contain all the truths we shall ever find, but as yet we do not know truths that belong to us from opinions, caught up in casual irritation or momentary fantasy. As life goes on we discover that certain thoughts sustain us in defeat, or give us victory, whether over ourselves or others, and it is these thoughts, tested by passion, that we call convictions. Among subjective men (in all those, that is, who must spin a web out of their own bowels) the victory is an intellectual daily recreation of all that exterior fate snatches away, and so that fate's antithesis; while what I have called "the mask" is an emotional antithesis to all that comes out of their internal nature. We begin to live when we have conceived life as tragedy.

XXI

A conviction that the world was now but a bundle of fragments possessed me without ceasing. I had tried this conviction on the Rhymers,[6] thereby plunging into greater silence an already too silent evening. * * * I had been put into a rage by the followers of Huxley, Tyndall, Carolus Duran, and Bastien-Lepage,[7] who not only asserted the unimportance of subject whether in art or literature, but the independence of the arts from one another. Upon the other hand I delighted in every age where poet and artist confined themselves gladly to some inherited subject matter known

5. English poet Geoffrey Chaucer (c. 1343–1400), author of *The Canterbury Tales*.
6. The Rhymers' Club, a group of young poets and writers who met regularly in a London pub in the early 1890s to discuss literature. Through the club, Yeats met most of the promising poets of his generation.
7. Yeats's representatives of the nineteenth-century scientific rationalism and realism he deplored. Biologist Thomas Huxley (1825–1895) supported the theory of evolution and originated the word "agnostic"; scientist John Tyndall (1820–1893) popularized the study of science via his lectures; Charles Duran (1837–1917), known as Carolus-Duran, and Jules Bastien-Lepage (1848–1884) were both French realist painters.

to the whole people, for I thought that in man and race alike there is something called "unity of being" using that term as Dante used it when he compared beauty in the Convito to a perfectly proportioned human body.[8] My father, from whom I had learned the term, preferred a comparison to a musical instrument so strung that if we touch a string all the strings murmur faintly. There is not more desire, he had said, in lust than in true love, but in true love desire awakens pity, hope, affection, admiration, and, given appropriate circumstance, every emotion possible to man. When I began, however, to apply this thought to the state and to argue for a law-made balance among trades and occupations my father displayed at once the violent free trader and propagandist of liberty. I thought that the enemy of this unity was abstraction, meaning by abstraction not the distinction but the isolation of occupation, or class or faculty—

> "Call down the hawk from the air
> Let him be hooded, or caged,
> Till the yellow eye has grown mild,
> For larder and spit are bare,
> The old cook enraged,
> The scullion gone wild."[9]

I knew no mediaeval cathedral, and Westminster, being a part of abhorred London, did not interest me, but I thought constantly of Homer and Dante and the tombs of Mausolus and Artemesia,[1] the great figures of King and Queen and the lesser figures of Greek and Amazon, Centaur[2] and Greek. I thought that all art should be a Centaur finding in the popular lore its back and its strong legs.

*   *   *

From Book II. Ireland after Parnell

X

I was at Sligo when I received a letter from John O'Leary,[1] saying that I could do no more in Dublin, for even the younger men had turned against me,[2] were "jealous," his letter said, though what they had to be jealous of, God knows. He said further that it was all my own fault, that he had warned me what would happen if I lived on terms of intimacy with those I tried to influence. I should have kept myself apart and alone. It was all true; through some influence from an earlier generation, from Walt Whit-

---

8. Yeats appears to conflate references in *Il Convito* (treatises III and IV), by Italian poet Dante Alighieri (1265–1321).
9. The opening stanza of Yeats's poem "The Hawk," first published in 1916.
1. The tomb built for Mausolus, king of Caria in the fourth century B.C.E., by order of his widow, Artemisia, was one of the Seven Wonders of the World.
2. In Greek mythology, a horse with the head and torso of a human.
1. Irish Nationalist (1830–1907) who greatly influenced Yeats in his youth.
2. Yeats had clashed publicly with Charles Gavan Duffy (1816–1903), a founder of the Nationalist newspaper the *Nation* and a member of the Young Ireland movement of the 1840s, over the New Irish Library, a project to disseminate Irish books to country branches of the National Literary Society, Dublin. Yeats's effort to prevent Duffy from choosing books for their patriotic rather than intellectual merits had cost him support in Nationalist circles.

man,[3] perhaps, I had sat talking in public bars, had talked late into the night at many men's houses, showing all my convictions to men that were but ready for one, and used conversation to explore and discover among men who looked for authority. I did not yet know that intellectual freedom and social equality are incompatible; and yet, if I had, could hardly have lived otherwise, being too young for silence. The trouble came from half a dozen obscure young men, who having nothing to do attended every meeting,[4] and were able to overturn a project, that seemed my only bridge to other projects, including a travelling theatre. We had planned small libraries of Irish literature in connexion with our country branches, we collected books and money, sending a lecture to every branch, and taking half the proceeds of that lecture to buy books. Maud Gonne,[5] whose beauty could draw a great audience in any country town, had been the lecturer, the scheme was very nearly self-supporting, and six or seven bundles of books, chosen after much disputation by John O'Leary, J. F. Taylor,[6] and myself, had been dispatched to some six or seven branches. "The country will support this work," Taylor had said somewhere on some public platform, "because we are the most inflammable people on God's earth," his harsh voice giving almost a quality of style to Carlylian[7] commonplace; but we are also a very jealous people. The half a dozen young men, if a little jealous of me, were still more jealous of those country branches which were getting so much notice, and where there was so much of that peasant mind their schoolmasters had taught them to despise. One must be English or Irish, they would have said. I returned to find a great box of books appropriated for some Dublin purpose and the whole scheme abandoned. I know that it was a bitter moment because I remember with gratitude, words spoken not to my ear, but for my ear, by a young man who had lately joined our Society, Mr Stephen McKenna,[8] now well-known amongst scholars for his distinguished translations of Plotinus, and I seem to remember that I lost through anger what gift of persuasion I may possess, and that I was all the more helpless because I felt that even the best of us disagreed about everything at heart.

I began to feel that I needed a hostess more than a society, and that I was not to find for years to come. I tried to persuade Maud Gonne to be that hostess; but her social life was in Paris, and she had already formed a new ambition, the turning of French public opinion against England. Without intellectual freedom there can be no agreement, and in Nationalist Dublin there was not—indeed there still is not—any society where a man is heard by the right ears, but never overheard by the wrong, and where he speaks his whole mind gaily, and is not the cautious husband of a part; where fantasy can play before matured into conviction, where life can shine and ring, and lack utility. Mere life lacking the protection of

3. American poet (1819–1892) whose faith in social democracy and competing belief in the power of individual imagination against society's restrictions were central to his writings.
4. Of the National Literary Society, Dublin, which Yeats had been instrumental in founding, and which had first proposed the publishing of the New Irish Library.
5. Yeats's beloved (1865–1953); she was an active Irish Nationalist.
6. John Francis Taylor (1850–1902), barrister, promoter of the Irish language, and a notable orator.
7. Thomas Carlyle (1795–1881), historian.
8. Irish critic and journalist (1872–1934), and translator of the work of Roman neo-Platonist philosopher Plotinus (205–70 B.C.E.).

wealth or rank, or some beauty's privilege of caprice cannot choose its company, taking up and dropping men, merely because it likes, or dislikes, their manners and their looks, and in its stead opinion crushes and rends, and all is hatred and bitterness: wheel biting upon wheel, a roar of steel or iron tackle, a mill of argument grinding all things down to mediocrity. If as I think minds and metals correspond, the goldsmiths of Paris foretold the French Revolution when they substituted steel for that unserviceable gold in the manufacture of the more expensive jewel work, and made those large, flat steel buttons for men of fashion whereby the card players were able to cheat by studying the reflections of the cards.

XII

When I look back upon my Irish propaganda of those years, I can see little but its bitterness. I never met with, or but met to quarrel with, my father's old family acquaintance; or with acquaintance I myself might have found, and kept, among the prosperous educated class, who had all the great appointments at University or Castle[9]; and this I did by deliberate calculation. If I must attack so much that seemed sacred to Irish nationalist opinion, I must, I knew, see to it that no man suspect me of doing it to flatter Unionist opinion. Whenever I got the support of some man who belonged by birth and education to University or Castle, I would say, "Now you must be baptized of the gutter." I chose Royal visits especially for demonstrations of disloyalty,[1] rolling up with my own hands the red carpet spread by some elderly Nationalist, softened or weakened by time, to welcome Viceroyalty; and threatened, if the London Society drank to the King's health, that my friends and I would demonstrate against it by turning our glasses upside down; and was presently to discover that one can grow impassioned and fanatical about opinions, which one has chosen as one might choose a side upon the football field; and I thought many a time of the pleasant Dublin houses that would never ask me to dine; and the still pleasanter houses with trout-streams near at hand, that would never ask me upon a visit. I became absurdly sensitive, glancing about me in certain public places, the private view of our Academy, or the like, to discover imagined enemies; and even now, after twenty or thirty years, I feel at times that I have not recovered my natural manner. Yet it was in those pleasant houses, among the young men and the young girls, that we were to make our converts. When we loathe ourselves or our world, if that loathing but turn to intellect, we see self or world and its anti-self as in one vision; when loathing remains but loathing, it consumes itself away, till at last we turn to its mechanical opposite. Popular Nationalism and Unionism so changed into one another, being each but the other's headache. The Nationalist abstractions were like the fixed ideas of some hysterical woman, a part of the mind turned into stone, and all the rest a seething and burning; and Unionist Ireland had re-acted from that seething

9. Dublin Castle, symbol of British and Protestant Ascendancy power in Ireland.
1. Yeats made various displays of "disloyalty" in the late 1890s, including writing letters to the press during Royal visits to Ireland, and refusing to enter "Official" residences such as the Chief Secretary's Lodge in Dublin.

and burning to a cynical indifference, and from those fixed ideas to what-ever might bring the most easy and obvious success.

From *Memoirs*

From *Autobiography*[1]

VI

I was greatly troubled because I was making no money. I should have gone to the art schools, but with my memories of the Dublin art schools I put off the day. I wanted to do something that would bring in money at once, for my people were poor and I saw my father sometimes sitting over the fire in great gloom, and yet I had no money-making faculty. Our neigh-bour, York Powell,[2] at last offered to recommend me for the sub-editorship of, I think, [the] *Manchester Courier*. I took some days to think it over; it meant an immediate income, but it was a Unionist paper. At last I told my father that I could not accept and he said, 'You have taken a great weight off my mind.' My father suggested that I should write a story and, partly in London and partly in Sligo, where I stayed with my uncle George Pollexfen,[3] I wrote *Dhoya*,[4] a fantastic tale of the heroic age. My father was dissatisfied and said he meant a story with real people, and I began *John Sherman*, putting into it my memory of Sligo and my longing for it. While writing it I was going along the Strand and, passing a shop window where there was a little ball kept dancing by a jet of water, I remembered waters about Sligo and was moved to a sudden emotion that shaped itself into 'The Lake Isle of Innisfree'.

X

I was twenty-three years old when the troubling of my life began.[5] I had heard from time to time in letters from Miss O'Leary, John O'Leary's old sister,[6] of a beautiful girl who had left the society of the Viceregal Court for Dublin nationalism.[7] In after years I persuaded myself that I felt pre-monitory excitement at the first reading of her name. Presently she drove

---

1. Reprinted with the permission of Scribner, a division of Simon & Schuster, from *The Memoirs of W. B. Yeats*, edited by Denis Donoghue. © 1972 by Michael Butler Yeats and Anne Yeats. See also the excerpt from this text on pp. 250–54 of this volume. Yeats completed a private manuscript "Autobiography," which covers approximately the period 1887–1898, around 1916. He drew on portions of this material for use in his published *Autobiographies*, but the manuscript in its entirety was only published posthumously in 1972. Extracts from this text are included here, amidst the selections from *Autobiographies*, so as to fit the chronological sequence of Yeats's life.
2. Frederick York Powell (1850–1904), from 1894 a professor of history at Oxford.
3. Yeats's maternal uncle (1838–1910), with whom he stayed often in the 1890s, and who shared his interest in the occult.
4. A story published in one volume along with the novella *John Sherman*, under the pseudonym "Ganconagh," in 1891.
5. Yeats first met Maud Gonne on January 30, 1889.
6. Ellen O'Leary (1831–1889), poet and, like her brother, an Irish Nationalist.
7. Though the daughter of a British army captain, and of considerable means, Maud Gonne had converted to nationalism after witnessing evictions in Ireland in the late 1880s, and she had ceased to attend social events at the Viceregal Court, symbol of British political authority in Ireland.

up to our house in Bedford Park[8] with an introduction from John O'Leary
to my father. I had never thought to see in a living woman so great beauty.
It belonged to famous pictures, to poetry, to some legendary past. A complexion like the blossom of apples, and yet face and body had the beauty
of lineaments which Blake[9] calls the highest beauty because it changes
least from youth to age, and a stature so great that she seemed of a divine
race. Her movements were worthy of her form, and I understood at last
why the poet of antiquity, where we would but speak of face and form,
sings, loving some lady, that she paces like a goddess. I remember nothing
of her speech that day except that she vexed my father by praise of war,
for she too was of the Romantic movement and found those uncontro-
vertible Victorian reasons, that seemed to announce so prosperous a future,
a little grey. As I look backward, it seems to me that she brought into my
life in those days—for as yet I saw only what lay upon the surface—the
middle of the tint, a sound as of a Burmese gong, an overpowering tumult
that had yet many pleasant secondary notes.

She asked [me] to dine with her that evening in her rooms in Ebury
Street, and I think that I dined with her all but every day during her stay
in London of perhaps nine days, and there was something so exuberant
in her ways that it seemed natural she should give her hours in overflowing
abundance. She had heard of me from O'Leary; he had praised me, and
it was natural that she should give and take without stint. She lived surrounded by cages of innumerable singing birds and with these she always
travelled, it seemed, taking them even upon short journeys, and they and
she were now returning to Paris where their home was.

She spoke to me of her wish for a play that she could act in Dublin.
Somebody had suggested Todhunter's[1] *Helena in Troas*, but he had refused. I told her of a story I had found when compiling my *Fairy and Folk
Tales of the Irish Peasantry*, and offered to write for her the play I have
called *The Countess Cathleen*.[2]

*   *   *

She, like myself, had received the political tradition of Davis with an
added touch of hardness and heroism from the hand of O'Leary, and when
she spoke of William O'Brien,[3] [who] was in jail making a prolonged
struggle against putting on the prison clothes, she said, 'There was a time
when men sacrificed their lives for their country, but now they sacrifice
their dignity.' But mixed with this feeling for what is permanent in human
life there was something declamatory, Latin in a bad sense, and perhaps
even unscrupulous. She spoke of her desire for power, apparently for its
own sake, and when we talked of politics spoke much of mere effective-

---

8. The Yeats family had moved to Bedford Park, London, in 1888.
9. William Blake (1757–1827), visionary English poet. Yeats here evokes a passage from Blake's
   Descriptive Catalogue (1809).
1. Irish writer John Todhunter (1839–1916), a friend of Yeats's father's.
2. Yeats's play, about a woman who sells her soul during a famine so as to prevent peasants from
   selling their souls, was not produced publicly until 1899. The source tale, which he had believed
   to be Irish, seems to have originated in France.
3. Thomas Davis (1814–1845), a founder of the Nationalist newspaper the *Nation* and leader of the
   Young Ireland movement; William O'Brien (1852–1928), journalist and founder of the Nationalist
   journal *United Ireland*, was imprisoned for Land League agitations.

ness, or the mere winning of this or that election. Her two and twenty years had taken some colour, I thought, from French Boulangist[4] adventurers and journalist *arrivistes* of whom she had seen too much, and [she] already had made some political journey into Russia in their interest. I was full of that thought of the 'Animula Vagula' chapter, I had heard it at the feet of a young Brahmin[5] in Dublin, 'Only the means can justify the end.' She meant her ends to be unselfish, but she thought almost any means justified in their success. We were seeking different things: she, some memorable action for final consecration of her youth, and I, after all, but to discover and communicate a state of being. Perhaps even in politics it would in the end be enough to have lived and thought passionately and have, like O'Leary, a head worthy of a Roman coin.

I spoke much of my spiritual philosophy. How important it all seemed to me; what would I not have given that she might think exactly right on all those great questions of the day? All is but faint to me beside a moment when she passed before a window, dressed in white, and rearranged a spray of flowers in a vase. Twelve years afterwards I put that impression into verse: ('she pulled down the pale blossom'. Quote):

> [Blossom pale, she pulled down the pale blossom
> At the moth hour and hid it in her bosom.][6]

I felt in the presence of a great generosity and courage, and of a mind without peace, and when she and all her singing birds had gone my melancholy was not the mere melancholy of love. I had what I thought was a 'clairvoyant' perception but was, I can see now, but an obvious deduction of an awaiting immediate disaster. I was compiling for an American publisher a selection from the Irish novelists,[7] and I can remember that all the tribulations of their heroes but reminded me of that dread. They too, according to a fashion of the writers of early Victoria, had been so often thrown without father or mother or guardian amid a world of deception, and they too, in their different way, were incurably romantic. I was in love but had not spoken of love and never meant to speak, and as the months passed I grew master of myself again. 'What wife could she make,' I thought, 'what share could she have in the life of a student?'

XII

A few months later I was again in Ireland and I heard that she was in Dublin. I called and waited for her at a little hotel in Nassau Street, which no longer exists, in a room overlooking the College Park. At the first sight of her as she came through the door, her great height seeming to fill it, I was overwhelmed with emotion, an intoxication of pity. She did not seem to have any beauty, her face was wasted, the form of the bones showing,

4. Yeats was unaware at the beginning of his friendship with Maud Gonne that she was the mistress of French politician Lucien Millevoye (1850–1918), a supporter of Georges Boulanger (1837–1891), a radical French reformist politician.
5. In the mid-1880s Yeats met the Indian adept and sage Mohini Chatterjee (1858–1936), who introduced him to *Marius the Epicurean* (which includes the chapter "Anima Vagula") by Walter Pater (1839–1894).
6. From Yeats's poem "The Arrow" (see pp. 30–31).
7. *Representative Irish Tales*, published in 1891.

and there was no life in her manner. As our talk became intimate, she hinted at some unhappiness, some disillusionment.[8] The old hard resonance had gone and she had become gentle and indolent. I was in love once more and no longer wished to fight against it. I no longer thought what kind of wife would this woman make, but of her need for protection and for peace.

Yet I left Dublin next day to stay somewhere in Orange Ulster with the brilliant student of my old Dublin school, Charles Johnston,[9] and spent a week or ten days with him and his elder brother, making fire balloons. We made the fire balloons of tissue paper and then chased them over the countryside, our chase becoming longer and longer as our skill in manufacture improved. I was not, it seems—not altogether—captive; but presently came from her a letter touching a little upon her sadness, and telling of a dream of some past life. She and I had been brother and sister somewhere on the edge of the Arabian desert, and sold together into slavery. She had an impression of some long journey and of miles upon miles of the desert sand. I returned to Dublin at once, and that evening, but a few minutes after we had met, asked her to marry me.[1] I remember a curious thing. I had come into the room with that purpose in my mind, and hardly looked at her or thought of her beauty. I sat there holding her hand and speaking vehemently. She did not take away her hand for a while. I ceased to speak, and presently as I sat in silence I felt her nearness to me and her beauty. At once I knew that my confidence had gone, and an instant later she drew her hand away. No, she could not marry—there were reasons— she would never marry; but in words that had no conventional ring she asked for my friendship. We spent the next day upon the cliff paths at Howth[2] and dined at a little cottage near the Baily Lighthouse, where her old nurse lived, and I overheard the old nurse asking if we were engaged to be married. At the day's end I found I had spent ten shillings, which seemed to me a very great sum.

I saw her day after day. I read her my unfinished *The Countess Cathleen*, and I noticed that she became moved at the passage, 'the joy of losing joy, of ceasing all resistance'—

> [there is a kind of joy
> In casting hope away, in losing joy,
> In ceasing all resistance.][3]

and thought, she is burdened by a sense of responsibility for herself. I told her after meeting her in London I had come to understand the tale of a woman selling her soul to buy food for a starving people as a symbol of all souls who lose their peace, or their fineness, or any beauty of the spirit in political service, but chiefly of her soul that had seemed so incapable

8. Gonne was under strain both from her complicated personal life, at this point concealed from Yeats and other Irish friends, and from the demands of her political campaigning.
9. Charles Johnston (1867–1931), a friend of Yeats's since their school days, and a fellow theosophist. Yeats stayed with him near Downpatrick in Northern Ireland in July 1891.
1. This proposal took place in August 1891.
2. Howth Head, on the north side of Dublin Bay. The Yeats family had lived at Howth between 1881 and early 1884.
3. These lines are spoken by one of the demons in the play, as he reflects on the various motivations that make people choose to sell their souls to him.

of rest. For the moment she had no political work nor plan of any, and we saw each other continually. Suddenly she was called back to France, and she told me in confidence that she had joined a secret political society and though she had come to look upon its members as self-seekers and adventurers she could not disobey this, the first definite summons it had sent to her. I stayed on in Ireland, probably at Sligo with my uncle, George Pollexfen, finishing *The Countess Cathleen* that had become but the symbolical song of my pity. Then came a letter of wild sorrow. She had adopted a little child, she told me, some three years ago, and now this child had died.[4] Mixed into her incoherent grief were accounts of the death bird that had pecked at the nursery window the day when it was taken ill, and how at sight of the bird she had brought doctor after doctor.

XXIII

I was tortured by sexual desire and had been for many years. I have often said to myself that some day I would put it all down in a book that some young man of talent might not think as I did that my shame was mine alone. It began when I was fifteen years old. I had been bathing, and lay down in the sun on the sand on the Third Rosses[5] and covered my body with sand. Presently the weight of the sand began to affect the organ of sex, though at first I did not know what the strange, growing sensation was. It was only at the orgasm that I knew, remembering some boy's description or the description in my grandfather's encyclopedia. It was many days before I discovered how to renew that wonderful sensation. From that on it was a continual struggle against an experience that almost invariably left me with exhausted nerves. Normal sexual intercourse does not affect me more than other men, but that, though never frequent, was plain ruin. It filled me with loathing of myself; and yet at first pride and perhaps, a little, lack of obvious opportunity, and now love kept me in unctuous celibacy. When I returned to London in my twenty-seventh year I think my love seemed almost hopeless,[6] and I knew that my friends had all mistresses of one kind or another and that most, at need, went home with harlots. Henley,[7] indeed, mocked at any other life. I had never since childhood kissed a woman's lips. At Hammersmith I saw a woman of the town walking up and down in the empty railway station. I thought of offering myself to her, but the old thought came back, 'No, I love the most beautiful woman in the world.'

XXV

On my return from France came a performance of my play and it had a measure of success, keeping the stage in part perhaps from the kindness

---

4. As Yeats later learned, the child, Georges (1890–1891), was in fact Maud Gonne's own, by her lover Lucien Millevoye. He died of meningitis.
5. At Rosses Point (see p. 179, n. 1).
6. Yeats returned to London in October 1891.
7. William Henley (1849–1903), poet and editor, and an important early encourager of Yeats's work.

of the management, my friend Florence Farr, for nearly seven weeks.[8] Presently the member of the Rhymers' Club introduced me to the lady I had seen between the two famous novelists, and a friendship I hope to keep till death began. In this book I cannot give her her real name—Diana Vernon[9] sounds pleasantly in my ears and will suit her as well as any other. When I went to see her she said, 'So-and-so seemed disinclined to introduce us; after I saw your play I made up my mind to write to you if [I] could not meet you otherwise.' She had profound culture, a knowledge of French, English, and Italian literature, and seemed always at leisure. Her nature was gentle and contemplative, and she was content, it seems, to have no more of life than leisure and the talk of her friends. Her husband, whom I saw but once, was much older and seemed a little heavy, a little without life. As yet I did not know how utterly estranged they were. I told her of my love sorrow, indeed it was my obsession, never leaving by day or night.

XXX

I had received while at Sligo many letters from Diana Vernon, kind letters that gave me a sense of half-conscious excitement. I remember after one such letter asking some country woman to throw the tea leaves for me and my disappointment at the vagueness of the oracle. (I think Mary Battle, my uncle's second-sighted servant, was again ill and away.) She was to tell me later on that my letters were unconscious love-letters, and I was taken by surprise at the description. I do not know how long after my return the conversation that was to decide so much in my life took place. I had found the Rhymer who had introduced me[1] under the influence of drink, speaking vaguely and with vague movements, and while we were speaking this recent memory came back. She spoke of her pagan life in a way that made me believe that she had had many lovers and loathed her life. I thought of that young man so nearly related. Here is the same weakness, I thought; two souls so distinguished and contemplative that the common world seems empty. What is there left but sanctity, or some satisfying affection, or mere dissipation?—'Folly the comforter,' some Elizabethan had called it. Her beauty, dark and still, had the nobility of defeated things, and how could it help but wring my heart? I took a fortnight to decide what I should do.

I was poor and it would be a hard struggle if I asked her [to] come away, and perhaps after all I would but add my tragedy to hers, for she might return to that evil life. But, after all, if I could not get the woman I loved, it would be a comfort even but for a little while to devote myself to another. No doubt my excited senses had their share in the argument,

---

8. *The Land of Heart's Desire* was first produced at the Avenue Theatre in London in March 1894. Florence Farr Emery (1860–1917) acted in the play and was also nominally the sponsor of the production. She and Yeats were comembers of the occult society The Golden Dawn until 1902, and she appeared frequently with Yeats in the first decade of the new century in their experiments of speaking verse accompanied by a psaltery (stringed instrument).
9. Yeats was introduced to novelist Olivia Shakespear (1863–1938), whose identity he conceals here, in early 1894. "Diana Vernon" is the heroine of Walter Scott's novel *Rob Roy*.
1. Lionel Johnson (1867–1902), Olivia Shakespear's cousin.

but it was an unconscious one. At the end of the fortnight I asked her to leave home with me. She became very gay and joyous and a few days later praised me [for] what she thought my beautiful tact in giving at the moment but a brother's kiss. Doubtless at the moment I was exalted above the senses, and yet I do not [think] I knew any better way of kissing, for when on our first railway journey together—we were to spend the day at Kew[2]—she gave me the long passionate kiss of love I was startled and a little shocked.

Presently I told something of my thoughts during that fortnight, and she [was] perplexed and ashamed that I should have had such imagination of her. Her wickedness had never gone further than her own mind; I would be her first lover. We decided that we should be but friends till she could leave her home for mine, but agreed to wait until her mother, a very old woman, had died. We decided to consult each a woman friend that we might be kept to these resolutions, as sponsors of our adventure, and for nearly a year met in railway carriages and at picture galleries and occasionally at her house. * * *

       *   *   *

* * * For a short time, a few months I think, I shared a flat with Arthur Symons in the Temple.[3] Symons knew I had such a friend and plan, but did [not] know her name. He indeed met my friend somewhere in society and asked if he might call, and came back with her praises. At last she and her sponsor were to come to tea. I do not think I had asked Symons, for I went myself to buy the cake. As I came home with the parcel I began to think of Maud Gonne till my thought was interrupted by my finding the door locked. I had forgotten the key and I went off in a great fuss to find a locksmith and found instead a man who climbed along the roof and in at an attic window.

That night at twelve o'clock I said to Symons, who had just come in, 'Did I ever tell you about Maud Gonne?' and till two or three in the morning I spoke of my love for her. Of all the men I have known he was the best listener; he could listen as a woman listens, never meeting one's thought as a man does with a rival thought, but taking up what one said and changing [it], giving it as it were flesh and bone.[4] A couple of days later I got a wild letter from Maud Gonne, who was in Dublin. 'Was I ill? Had some accident happened?' On a day that was, I found, the day I had had those guests and lost the key, I had walked into the room in her hotel where she was sitting with friends. At first she thought I was really there, but presently on finding that no one else saw me knew that it was my ghost. She told me to return at twelve that night and I vanished. At twelve I had stood, dressed in some strange, priest-like costume, at her bedside and brought her soul away, and we had wandered round the cliffs [of] Howth where we had been together years before. I remember one phrase

2. Kew Gardens, London.
3. Yeats lived with poet and critic Arthur Symons (1865–1945) at Fountain Court, the Temple, London, for about four months from October 1895.
4. See Yeats's poem "On Woman" (pp. 61–62).

very clearly, 'It was very sad, and all the seagulls were asleep.' All my old love had returned and began to struggle with the new.

Presently I was asked to call and see my friend's sponsor. She condemned our idea of going away from home. There were various arguments that I cannot recall without perhaps, against my will, revealing Diana Vernon's true name. My sponsor came to see me and used the same arguments, and both, people of the world, advised us to live together without more ado. Then Diana Vernon tried to get a separation from the husband who had for her, she believed, aversion or indifference. 'He ceased to pay court to me from the day of our marriage,' she had said. He was deeply distressed and became ill, and she gave up the project and said to me, 'It will be kinder to deceive him.' Our senses were engaged now, and though we spoke of parting it was but to declare it impossible. I took my present rooms at Woburn Buildings[5] and furnished them very meagrely with such cheap furniture as I could throw away without regret as I grew more prosperous. She came with me to make every purchase, and I remember an embarrassed conversation in the presence of some Tottenham Court [Road] shop man upon the width of the bed—every inch increased the expense.

At last she came to me in I think January of my thirtieth year, and I was impotent from nervous excitement. The next day we met at the British Museum—we were studying together—and I wondered that there seemed no change in me or in her. A week later she came to me again, and my nervous excitement was so painful that it seemed best but to sit over our tea and talk. I do not think we kissed each other except at the moment of her leaving. She understood instead of, as another would, changing liking for dislike—was only troubled by my trouble. My nervousness did not return again and we had many days of happiness. It will always be a grief to me that I could not give the love that was her beauty's right, but she was too near my soul, too salutary and wholesome to my inmost being. All our lives long, as da Vinci says,[6] we long, thinking it is but the moon that we long [for], for our destruction, and how, when we meet [it] in the shape of a most fair woman, can we do less than leave all others for her? Do we not seek our dissolution upon her lips?

My liaison lasted but a year, interrupted by one journey to Italy upon her part and by one of mine also to Paris. I had a struggle to earn my living, and that made it harder for me, I was so often preoccupied when she came. Then Maud Gonne wrote to me; she was in London and would I come to dine? I dined with her and my trouble increased—she certainly had no thought of the mischief she was doing. And at last one morning instead of reading much love poetry, as my way was to bring the right mood round, I wrote letters. My friend found my mood did not answer hers and burst into tears. 'There is someone else in your heart,' she said. It was the breaking between us for many years.[7]

5. Yeats moved to rented rooms at 18 Woburn Buildings, near the Euston Road, London, in early 1896, and this would remain his address until after his marriage in 1917.
6. Leonardo da Vinci (1452–1519), Italian artist.
7. The liaison and its ending are evoked in Yeats's poem "The Lover mourns for the Loss of Love" (see p. 25).

XXXVI

* * *

I have a memory, full of self-mockery, of the Jubilee riot of 1897.[8] Maud
Gonne had promised a then small Labour leader, James Connolly,[9] since
executed for his part in the rebellion of 1916, to speak at his Socialist
society, meaning one of the small regular meetings. When we arrived in
Dublin for some meeting of the council,[1] she found the streets placarded
with an announcement of a Socialist meeting in Dame Street, and her
name as that of the principal speaker. She was not a Socialist, and had
never spoken in Dublin to an open-air meeting, and wrote to refuse. I
was with her when Connolly called. If she refused, he was ruined, for nobody would believe that he had ever had a promise. She was firm and
he went away, but his despair was so deep that I softened her heart afterwards. She drove to the house he lived in on a car, and came back with
a pathetic account of his wife and his four children and their one
room.

The next day there was a great crowd in Dame Street, and while Maud
Gonne was speaking an old woman kept waving a miniature before her
face, a portrait of a martyr of the great rebellion,[2] a treasure of some
household in a shrine, and calling out, 'I was in it before she was born.'
Maud Gonne told how the day before was the anniversary, when she was
accustomed to decorate the graves of the martyrs,[3] and that the custodian
of some graveyard—St Michan's perhaps—had refused her admission because it was Queen Victoria's Jubilee. She said then, speaking slowly in a
low voice that yet seemed to go through the whole crowd, 'Must the graves
of our dead go undecorated because Victoria has her Jubilee?' and the
whole crowd went wild.

That evening there was a meeting of our council in the City Hall, and
when we came out after it the crowds were waiting for us all round the
Hall. We were going to the National Club in Rutland Square, and they
came too. Outside the National Club a magic lantern was to show on a
white screen statistics of evictions, deaths from starvation, etc., during Victoria's reign. Somewhere in front of us was a mock funeral Maud Gonne
devised, a coffin with 'The British Empire' printed upon it, and black flags
with the names of all those who had been hanged for treason during
Queen Victoria's reign. Presently they began breaking windows where
there were decorations. Maud Gonne was walking with a joyous face; she
had taken all those people into her heart. I knew she would not interfere.
I knew her principle. If a crowd does anything illegal and you try to stop
it, you may succeed, but you are certain to seem to have done it to keep
from danger yourself. I tried to speak and could only whisper. I had spoken
too much through a disorderly debate at the council, and my voice had

8. Irish Nationalists organized major demonstrations against the celebration of Queen Victoria's
   diamond jubilee (the sixtieth year of her reign) in Dublin in June 1897.
9. Connolly (1870–1916), a trade union organizer, was Commander of the 1916 Irish Rising.
1. Yeats was a member of the Executive Council of the '98 Centenary Association, a Nationalist organization that promoted the commemoration and celebration of the 1798 Irish
   Rebellion.
2. The Nationalist Rebellion of 1798.
3. Those executed after the 1798 Rebellion.

gone. Then I too resigned myself and felt the excitement of the moment, that joyous irresponsibility and sense of power.

At the National Club she and I were given tea, and I settled down to a long table, as I believed, on which I had been writing all day upon some subject in no way connected with politics. Thereupon a man more excited than I have ever seen anybody or ever shall see anybody ran in calling out, 'Oh, it is awful; it is awful. Police are batoning the people outside. It is awful,' and so on. Maud Gonne got [up] and said she was going out and somebody else said she would be hurt. I told them to lock the door and keep her in. My brain was not working quickly; I remember regretting my tea, which was getting cold. She was perhaps right to be angry when I refused to let her out unless she explained what she meant to do. 'How do I know till I get out?' she said. I offered to go out myself if she would not try to get out when the door was opened, though what I could have done with my whisper I do not know, but she would make no promise. Later on she told me that I had made her do the only cowardly thing of her life. That night I went to all the newspaper offices and took responsibility for my action. My memory is that two hundred people were taken to hospital and that one old woman was killed.

XL

On a visit to Dr Hyde I had seen the Castle Rock, as it was called, in Lough Key.[4] There is this small island entirely covered by what was a still habitable but empty castle. The last man who had lived there had been Dr Hyde's father who, when a young man, lived there for a few weeks. All round were the wooded and hilly shores, a place of great beauty. I believed that the castle could be hired for little money, and had long been dreaming of making it an Irish Eleusis or Samothrace.[5] An obsession more constant than anything but my love itself was the need of mystical rites— a ritual system of evocation and meditation—to reunite the perception of the spirit, of the divine, with natural beauty. I believed that instead of thinking of Judea as holy we should [think] our own land holy, and most holy where most beautiful. Commerce and manufacture had made the world ugly; the death of pagan nature-worship had robbed visible beauty of its inviolable sanctity. I was convinced that all lonely and lovely places were crowded with invisible beings and that it would be possible to communicate with them. I meant to initiate young men and women in this worship, which would unite the radical truths of Christianity to those of a more ancient world, and to use the Castle Rock for their occasional retirement from the world.

For years to come it was in my thought, as in much of my writing, to seek also to bring again in[to] imaginative life the old sacred places— Slievenamon, Knocknarea[6]—all that old reverence that hung—above all—

4. Near Hyde's home in County Roscommon.
5. Eleusis: a town in Greece where sacred ancient Greek rituals known as Eleusinian Mysteries originated. Samothrace: an island in the Aegean, likewise the birthplace of a highly ritualistic religious cult.
6. Slievenamon, a mountain in County Tipperary, and Knocknarea, a mountain in County Sligo, were both associated with the ancient gods of Ireland and with the Sidhe (see p. 205, n. 5).

about conspicuous hills. But I wished by my writings and those of the school I hoped to found to have a secret symbolical relation to these mysteries, for in that way, I thought, there will be a greater richness, a greater claim upon the love of the soul, doctrine without exhortation and rhetoric. Should not religion hide within the work of art as God is within His world, and how can the interpreter do more than whisper? I did not wish to compose rites as if for the theatre. They must in their main outline be the work of invisible hands.

My own seership was, I thought, inadequate; it was to be Maud Gonne's work and mine. Perhaps that was why we had been thrown together. Were there not strange harmonies amid discord? My outer nature was passive— but for her I should never perhaps have left my desk—but I knew my spiritual nature was passionate, even violent. In her all this was reversed, for it was her spirit only that was gentle and passive and full of charming fantasy, as though it touched the world only with the point of its finger. When I had first met her I had used as a test the death symbol, imagining it in my own mind, but not wishing to alarm her had asked that it should take the form not of a human but of a dog's skull. She said, 'I see a figure holding out its hand with a skull on it. No, there is a bruise on the hand, but I was compelled to say it was a skull.' I, who could not influence her actions, could dominate her inner being. I could therefore use her clairvoyance to produce forms that would arise from both minds, though mainly seen by one, and escape therefore from what is mere[ly] personal. There would be, as it were, a spiritual birth from the soul of a man and a woman. I knew that the incomprehensible life could select from our memories and, I believed, from the memory of the race itself; could realize of ourselves, beyond personal predilection, all it required, of symbol and of myth. I believed we were about to attain a revelation.

Maud Gonne entirely shared these ideas, and I did not doubt that in carrying them out I should win her for myself. Politics were merely a means of meeting, but this was a link so perfect that [it] would restore at once, even [after] a quarrel, the sense of intimacy. At every moment of leisure we obtained in vision long lists of symbols. Various trees corresponded to cardinal points, and the old gods and heroes took their places gradually in a symbolic fabric that had for its centre the four talismans of the Tuatha de Danaan,[7] the sword, the stone, the spear and the cauldron, which related themselves in my mind with the suits of the Tarot. George Pollexfen,[8] though already an old man, shared my plans, and his slow and difficult clairvoyance added certain symbols. He and Maud Gonne only met once—in politics he was an extreme Unionist—but he and she worked with each other's symbols and I did much of the work in his house. The forms became very continuous in my thoughts, and when AE came to stay at Coole[9] he asked who was the white jester he had seen about the corridors. It was a form I associated with the god Aengus.[1]

---

7. The Tuatha de Danaan (the Tribes of the Goddess Danu) were the ancient gods of Ireland.
8. See p. 225, n. 3.
9. "A.E." was the pseudonym of Yeats's friend, Irish artist and poet George Russell (1867–1935). Coole Park was Lady Gregory's estate in County Galway.
1. The god of love in Irish mythology.

It was a time of great personal strain and sorrow. Since my mistress[2] had left me, no other woman had come into my life, and for nearly seven years none did. I was tortured by sexual desire and disappointed love. Often as I walked in the woods at Coole it would have been a relief to have screamed aloud. When desire became an unendurable torture, I would masturbate, and that, no matter how moderate I was, would make me ill. It never occured to me to seek another love. I would repeat to myself again and again the last confession of Lancelot, and indeed it was my greatest pride, 'I have loved a queen beyond measure and exceeding long.'[3] I was never before or since so miserable as in those years that followed my first visit to Coole.[4] In the second as during the first visit my nervous system was worn out. The toil of dressing in the morning exhausted me, and Lady Gregory began to send me cups of soup when I was called.

Instead of the work which I could not make myself do, I began with her that great collection of faery belief which is now passing through the press.[5] I lived amid mystery. It seemed as if these people possessed an ancient knowledge. Ah, if we could but speak face to face with those they spoke to. 'That old man,' Lady Gregory said to me of an old man who passed us in the wood, 'may have the mystery of the ages.' I began to have visions and dreams full of wisdom or beauty. Much of my thought since is founded upon certain sentences that came in this way. Once I asked when going to sleep what was the explanation of those curious tales of people 'away', of which Lady Gregory [and] I had so many. In all these tales some man, woman, or child was believed to be carried off bodily by the faery world, a changeling, some old man or woman perhaps, or perhaps [a] mere heap of shavings bewitched into their likeness, being left instead. I awoke enough to know that I lay in bed and had the familiar objects round, but to hear a strange voice speaking through my lips: 'We make an image of him who sleeps, and it is not him who sleeps but it is like him who sleeps, and we call it Emmanuel.'[6]

I was crossing one afternoon a little stream, and as I leaped I felt an emotion very strange to me—for all my thoughts were pagan—a sense of utter dependence on the divine will. It was over in an instant, and I said to myself, 'That is the way Christians feel.' That night I seemed to wake in my bed to hear a voice saying, 'The love of God for every soul is infinite, for every soul is unique; no other soul can satisfy the same need in God.' At other times I received fragments of poems, partly hearing and partly seeing. I saw in a dream a young shepherdess among many goats and sheep. Somebody passed and spoke the name of some young man whom she had never seen. In my dream she stood up and said good-bye to each goat and sheep by name, and set out upon a journey. While I saw I seemed to hear also at moments the words [of] the poem, but only one sentence remained with me: 'She had but just heard his name, and yet it seemed as if he had long lain between her arms.'

2. Olivia Shakespear.
3. From Malory's *Morte d'Arthur*. Lancelot loved Queen Guinevere, wife of King Arthur.
4. Yeats first stayed at Coole in the summer of 1897.
5. Lady Gregory's *Visions and Beliefs in the West of Ireland* (1920).
6. See Matthew 1.18–25.

Sometimes as I awoke marvellous illuminated pages seemed to be held before [me], with symbolic pictures that seemed profound, but when I tried to read the text all would vanish or but a sentence remain. I remember, 'The secret of the world is so simple that it could be written on a blade of grass with the juice of a berry'; and 'The rivers of Eden are in the midst of our rivers.' Sometimes when I lay in bed seeming awake, but always on my back as one lies when in nightmare, but with a feeling of wonder and delight, I would see forms at my bedside: once a fair woman who said she was Aedain,[7] and both man and woman; and once a young boy and a young girl dressed in olive green, with sad, gentle faces; once my mother holding a cup in her hand; once a woman with an Elizabethan ruff.

A sexual dream was very rare, I neither then nor at any other time told the woman I loved to come to me [in] such a dream; I think I surrounded her with too great reverence and fear. One night I heard a voice, while I lay on my back, say I would be shown a secret, the secret of life and of death, but I must not speak of it. The room seemed to brighten and as I looked towards the foot of the bed I saw that it was changed into precious stones and yet these stones had a familiar look—they reminded me of the raised glass fruit on the bottles of lime-juice in my childhood. I never associated this growing brightness with sex, until all became suddenly dark and I found I had emitted seed.

I dreamed that I was lying on my back in a great stone trough in a great round house. I knew it was an initiation, and a wind was blowing over [me], I think from the feet up. Round me stood forms I could not see, and certain currents of influence were being directed through my eyes and various points of my body. These influences were painful. I heard a voice say, 'We are doing this to find out if it is worth going on doing this.' I knew my fitness for initiation was being questioned. Another night I thought I was taken out of my body and into a world of light, and while in this light, which was also complete happiness, I was told I would now be shown the passage of the soul at its incarnation. I saw the mystic elements gather about my soul in a certain order, a whole elaborate process, but the details vanished as I awoke. Little remained but a sentence I seemed to have spoken to myself: 'Beauty is becoming beautiful objects, and truth is becoming truths.'

I found I could call dreams by my symbols, though I think the most profound came unsought, and I would go to sleep, say with a spray of apple blossoms on my pillow. Sometimes, when I had gone to sleep with the endeavour to send my soul to that of Maud Gonne, using some symbol, which I forget, I would wake dreaming of a shower of precious stones. Sometimes she would have some corresponding experience in Paris and upon the same night, but always with more detail. I thought we became one in a world of emotion eternalized by its own intensity and purity, and that this world had for its symbol precious stones. No physical, sexual sensation ever accompanied these dreams and I noticed that once the excitement of the genital ceased, a visionary form, that of Aedain, approached.

---

7. Probably Etain, a queen of the Sidhe in Irish mythology.

I tried to describe some vision to Lady Gregory, and to my great surprise could not. I felt a difficulty in articulation and became confused. I had wanted to tell her of some beautiful sight, and could see no reason for this. I remembered then what I had read of mystics not being always [able] to speak, and remembered some tale of a lecturer on mysticism having to stop in the middle of a sentence. Even to this moment, though I can sometimes speak without difficulty, I am more often unable to. I am a little surprised that I can write what I please.

XLIII

I joined Maud Gonne from time to time, once at Belfast,[8] where she [had] gone on some political mission, sometimes at Paris, often in Dublin. In Dublin I never went to the same hotel, fearing to compromise her, though she often laughed at my scruple. Once she complained that she saw too much of me. 'I do not say,' she said, 'that the crowds are in love with me, but they would hate anybody who was.' But I never failed to get my letter saying when we could meet. One morning[9] I woke in my hotel somewhere near Rutland Square[1] with the fading vision of her face bending over mine and the knowledge that she had just kissed me. I joined her after breakfast in the Nassau Hotel. We were to spend the day together and visit in the afternoon the old Fenian leader, James Stephens.[2] She said, 'Had you a strange dream last night?' I said, 'I dreamed this morning for the first time in my life that you kissed me.' She made no answer, but late that night when dinner was over and I was about to return home she said, 'I will tell you now what happened. When I fell asleep last night I saw standing at my bedside a great spirit. He took me to a great throng of spirits, and you were among them. My hand was put into yours and I was told that we were married. After that I remember nothing.' Then and there for the first time with the bodily mouth, she kissed me.

The next day I found her sitting very gloomily over the fire. 'I should not have spoken to you in that way,' she said, 'for I can never be your wife in reality.' I said, 'Do you love anyone else?' and she said 'No' but added that there was somebody else, and that she had to be a moral nature for two. Then bit by bit came out the story of her life, things I had heard all twisted awry by scandal, and disbelieved.

She had met in the South of France the French Boulangist deputy, Millevoye,[3] while staying with a relative in her nineteenth year, and had at once and without any urging on his part fallen in love with him. She then returned to Dublin where her father had a military command. She had sat one night over the fire thinking over her future life. She longed to have control over her own life, and chance discovery of some book on magic among her father's books had made her believe that the Devil, if she prayed to him, might help her. He was rather a real personage to her,

8. A city in Northern Ireland.
9. In December 1898.
1. In Dublin (and since renamed Parnell Square).
2. Irish Nationalist (1825–1901), wounded in the 1848 Rising, and founder of the Irish Republican Brotherhood ("the Fenians") in 1853.
3. See p. 227, n. 4.

for in her earlier girlhood she had wanted to join a convent. She asked the Devil to give her control of her own life and offered in return her soul. At that moment the clock struck twelve, and she felt of a sudden that the prayer had been heard and answered. Within a fortnight her father died suddenly, and she was stricken with remorse.

She had control of her life now, and when she was of age settled in Paris, and after some months became Millevoye's mistress. She was often away from him, for sexual love soon began to repel her, but was for all that very much in love. Then he failed her in various ways. But [she] gave me no coherent account and when I asked some questions clenched her hands together and said it was not well to speak of such things. He had, I discovered, at one time urged her to become the mistress of one man to help his political projects, and that she had refused. Then a little boy was born, the adopted child I had been told of—she thought that sexual love was only justified by children. If the boy had not died, she would have broken with Millevoye altogether and lived in Ireland. As it was, after its death she had thought of breaking with him, and had engaged herself for a week to someone else—I thought, I may have had that poor betrothal for my reward—but had broken it off. The idea came to her that the lost child might be reborn, and she had gone back to Millevoye, in the vault under the memorial chapel. A girl child was born, now two years old.[4] Since the child's birth, I understood her to say amid so much broken speech, she and Millevoye had lived apart.

But she was necessary to him, 'She did not know what would happen to him if her influence was not there.' I wonder as I write these words if I rightly understood, if she had not [in] mind some service he might fall from, to a political ideal. I thought at the time that [she] was appeasing a troubled conscience by performing to the last tittle every duty, and Lady Gregory confirmed me later in this thought. And in all that followed I was careful to touch [her] as one might a sister. If she was to come to me, it must be from no temporary passionate impulse, but with the approval of her conscience. Many a time since then, as I lay awake at night, have I accused myself of acting, not as I thought from a high scruple, but from a dread of moral responsibility, and my thoughts have gone round and round, as do miserable thoughts, coming to no solution.

A little later, how many days I do not remember, we were sitting together when she said, 'I hear a voice saying, "You are about to receive the initiation of the spear." ' We became silent; a double vision unfolded itself, neither speaking till all was finished. She thought herself a great stone statue through which passed flame, and I felt myself becoming flame and mounting up through and looking out of the eyes of a great stone Minerva.[5] Were the beings which stand behind human life trying to unite us, or had we brought it by our own dreams? She was now always very emotional, and would kiss me very tenderly, but when I spoke of marriage on the eve of her leaving said, 'No, it seems to me impossible.' And then,

4. Iseult Gonne (1894–1954).
5. The virginal warrior and goddess of wisdom in Roman mythology (known as Athena to the Greeks).

with clenched hands, 'I have a horror and terror of physical love.' Lady
Gregory was in Venice, but had come home at once on receiving from
me an incoherent letter. She offered me money to travel, and told me not
to leave Maud Gonne till I had her promise of marriage, but I said, 'No,
I am too exhausted; I can do no more.'

From *The Trembling of the Veil* (1922)

From Book III. Hodos Chameliontos[1]

XXI

Now that I am old and settled and have many birds—the canaries have
just hatched out four nestlings—I have before me the problem that Locke[2]
waved aside. As I gave them an artificial nest, a hollow vessel like a saucer,
they had no need of that skill the wild bird shows, each species having its
own preference among lichen, or moss; but they could sort out wool and
hair and a certain soft white down that I found under a big tree. They
would twist a stem of grass till it was limber, and would wind all about
the centre of the nest, and when the four grey eggs were laid, the mother
bird knew how to turn them over from time to time, that they might be
warmed evenly; and how long she must leave them uncovered, that the
white might not be dried up, and when to return that the growing bird
might not take cold. Then the young birds, even when they had all their
feathers, were very still as compared with the older birds, as though any
habit of movement would disturb the nest or make them tumble out. One
of them would now and again pass on the food that he had received from
his mother's beak to some other nestling. The father had often pecked the
mother bird before the eggs were laid, but now, until the last nestling was
decently feathered, he took his share in the feeding, and was very peace-
able, and it was only when the young could be left to feed themselves that
he grew jealous, and had to be put into another cage.

When I watch my child who is not yet three years old, I can see so
many signs of knowledge from beyond her own mind; why else should
she be so excited when a little boy passes outside the window, and take so
little interest in a girl; why should she put a cloak about her, and look
over her shoulder to see it trailing upon the stairs, as she will some day
trail a dress; and why, above all, as she lay against her mother's side, and
felt the unborn child moving within, did she murmur "Baby, baby"?[3]

When a man writes any work of genius, or invents some creative action,
is it not because some knowledge or power has come into his mind from
beyond his mind? It is called up by an image, as I think; all my birds'

---

1. Yeats described himself as having been in the 1890s "lost in that region a cabbalistic manuscript
   . . . had warned me of; astray upon the Path of the Chamelion, upon Hodos Chameliontos."
2. John Locke (1632–1704), English empiricist philosopher, who argued that all knowledge derives
   from sensation.
3. Anne Yeats was born in February 1919; Michael Yeats, in August 1921.

adventures started when I hung a little saucer at one side of the cage, and at the other a bundle of hair and grass; but our images must be given to us, we cannot choose them deliberately.

XXII

I know now that revelation is from the self, but from the age-long memoried self, that shapes the elaborate shell of the mollusc and the child in the womb, that teaches the birds to make their nest; and that genius is a crisis that joins that buried self for certain moments to our trivial daily self. There are, indeed, personifying spirits that we had best call but gates and gate-keepers, because through their dramatic power they bring our souls to crisis, to Mask and Image, caring not a straw whether we be Juliet going to her wedding, or Cleopatra to her death;[4] for in their eyes nothing has weight but passion. We have dreamed a foolish dream these many centuries in thinking that they value a life of contemplation, for they scorn that more than any possible life, unless it be but a name for the worst crisis of all. They have but one purpose, to bring their chosen man to the greatest obstacle he may confront without despair. They contrived Dante's banishment,[5] and snatched away his Beatrice,[6] and thrust Villon into the arms of harlots, and sent him to gather cronies at the foot of the gallows,[7] that Dance and Villon might through passion become conjoint to their buried selves, turn all to Mask and Image, and so be phantoms in their own eyes. In great lesser writers like Landor and like Keats[8] we are shown that Image and that Mask as something set apart; Andromeda and her Perseus but not the sea-dragon;[9] but in a few in whom we recognize supreme masters of tragedy, the whole contest is brought into the circle of their beauty. Such masters, Villon and Dante, let us say, would not, when they speak through their art, change their luck; yet they are mirrored in all the suffering of desire. The two halves of their nature are so completely joined that they seem to labour for their objects, and yet to desire whatever happens, being at the same instant predestinate and free, creation's very self. We gaze at such men in awe; because we gaze not at a work of art, but at the re-creation of the man through that art, the birth of a new species of man, and it may even seem that the hairs of our heads stand up; because that birth, that re-creation, is from terror. Had not Dante and Villon understood that their fate wrecked what life could not rebuild, had they lacked their vision of Evil, had they cherished any species of optimism, they could but have found a false beauty, or some momentary instinctive beauty, and suffered no change at all, or but changed as do the wild creatures, or from devil well to devil sick, and so go round the clock.

4. In Shakespeare's plays *Romeo and Juliet* and *Anthony and Cleopatra*.
5. Poet Dante Alighieri (1265–1321) was banished from Florence, his home since birth, in 1302, for supporting the cause of the city's independence from Papal control. He never returned, and his exile, one of the pivotal events of his adult life, was a key influence on his later poetry.
6. Dante's beloved, who died when she and Dante were in their mid-twenties.
7. French poet François Villon (c. 1431–post-1463), whose adult life combined literature and crime. He was pardoned from death sentences three times, and banished from France in 1463.
8. Walter Savage Landor (1775–1821), English writer; John Keats (1795–1821), English Romantic poet.
9. In Greek legend, Perseus, son of Zeus, prevents Andromeda from being sacrificed to a sea monster.

They and their sort alone earn contemplation, for it is only when the intellect has wrought the whole of life to drama, to crisis, that we may live for contemplation, and yet keep our intensity.

And these things are true also of nations, but the Gate-keepers who drive the nation to war or anarchy that it may find its Image are different from those who drive individual men, though I think at times they work together. And as I look backward upon my own writing, I take pleasure alone in those verses where it seems to me I have found something hard, cold, some articulation of the image, which is the opposite of all that I am in my daily life, and all that my country is; yet man or nation can no more make Mask or Image than the seed can be made by the soil into which it is cast.

ILLE
What portion in the world can the artist have,
Who has awakened from the common dream,
But dissipation and despair?

HIC
And yet
No one denies to Keats, love of the world.
Remember his deliberate happiness.

ILLE
His art is happy, but who knows his mind?
I see a schoolboy, when I think of him,
With face and nose pressed to a sweet-shop window.
For certainly he sank into his grave
His senses and his heart unsatisfied,
And made, being poor, ailing, and ignorant,
Shut out from all the luxury of the world,
Luxurious song.[1]

From Book IV. The Tragic Generation

XLII

I am certain of one date, for I have gone to much trouble to get it right. I met John Synge[1] for the first time in the autumn of 1896 when I was one and thirty, and he four and twenty. I was at the Hotel Corneille[2] instead of my usual lodging, and why I cannot remember for I thought it expensive. Synge's biographer says that you boarded there for a pound a week,[3] but I was accustomed to cook my own breakfast and dine at an anarchist restaurant in the Boulevard St Jacques for little over a shilling. Someone, whose name I forget, told me there was a poor Irishman at the top of the house, and presently introduced us. Synge had come lately from

1. From Yeats's poem "Ego Dominus Tuus" (see pp. 67–68).
1. John Millington Synge (1871–1909), playwright and cofounder, with Yeats and Lady Gregory, of the Abbey Theatre.
2. In Paris.
3. Maurice Bourgeois, in *John Millington Synge and the Irish Theatre* (1913).

Italy, and had played his fiddle to peasants in the Black Forest;[4] six months of travel upon fifty pounds; and was now reading French literature and writing morbid and melancholy verse. He told me that he had learned Irish at Trinity College,[5] so I urged him to go to the Aran Islands and find a life that had never been expressed in literature, instead of a life where all had been expressed. I did not divine his genius, but I felt he needed something to take him out of his morbidity and melancholy. Perhaps I would have given the same advice to any young Irishman who knew Irish, for I had been that summer upon Inishmaan and Inishmore, and was full of the subject.[6] My friends and I had landed from a fishing boat to find ourselves among a group of islanders, one of whom offered to bring us to the oldest man upon Inishmaan. He brought us to an old man who said, speaking very slowly, "If any gentleman has done a crime, we'll hide him. There was a gentleman that killed his father, and I had him in my own house six months till he got away to America."

From that on I saw much of Synge, and brought him to Mme Gonne's, under whose persuasion perhaps he joined the Young Ireland Society of Paris, the name we gave to half a dozen Parisian Irish, but resigned after a few months because "it wanted to stir up Continental nations against England, and England will never give us freedom until she feels she is safe," the one political sentence I ever heard him speak. Over a year was to pass before he took my advice and settled for a while in an Aran Cottage, and became happy, having escaped at last, as he wrote "from the squalor of the poor and the nullity of the rich." I almost forget the prose and verse he showed me in Paris, though I read it all through again when after his death I decided at his written request what was to be published and what not. Indeed I have but a vague impression, as of a man trying to look out of a window and blurring all that he sees by breathing upon the glass. According to my lunar parable he was a man of the twenty-third phase,[7] a man whose subjective lives—for a constant return to our life is a part of my dream—were over, who must not pursue an image but fly from it, all that subjective dreaming that had once been power and joy now corrupting within him. He had to take the first plunge into the world beyond himself, that first plunge away from oneself that is always pure technique, delight in doing, not because one would or should, but merely because one can.

He once said to me "a man has to bring up his family and be as virtuous as is compatible with so doing, and if he does more than that he is a Puritan; a dramatist has to express his subject and to find as much beauty as is compatible with that, and if he does more he is an aesthete." That is to say, he was consciously objective. Whenever he tried to write drama without dialect he wrote badly, and he made several attempts, because only through dialect could he escape self-expression, see all that he did

4. A region in southwest Germany.
5. In Dublin.
6. Yeats had visited the Aran Islands (Inishmore, Inishmaan, and Inishere), off the west coast of Ireland, in summer 1896. The island culture was at that time little disturbed by visitors, and almost exclusively Irish-speaking.
7. In Yeats's philosophical text *A Vision* (1925/1937), personalities are categorized according to phases of the moon.

from without, allow his intellect to judge the images of his mind as if they had been created by some other mind. His objectivity was however technical only, for in those images paraded all the desires of his heart. He was timid, too shy for general conversation, an invalid[8] and full of moral scruple, and he was to create now some ranting braggadocio, now some tipsy hag full of poetical speech, and now some young man or girl full of the most abounding health. He never spoke an unkind word, had admirable manners, and yet his art was to fill the streets with rioters, and to bring upon his dearest friends enmities that may last their lifetime.[9]

No mind can engender till divided into two, but that of a Keats or a Shelley falls into an intellectual part that follows, and a hidden emotional flying image, whereas in a mind like that of Synge the emotional part is dreaded and stagnant, while the intellectual part is a clear mirror like technical achievement.

But in writing of Synge I have run far ahead for in 1896 he was but one picture among many. I am often astonished when I think that we can meet unmoved some person, or pass some house, that in later years is to bear a chief part in our lives. Should there not be some flutter of the nerve or stopping of the heart like that of Macgregor[1] experienced at the first meeting with a phantom?

From Book V. The Stirring of the Bones

VI

*   *   *

A couple of weeks after my vision,[1] Lady Gregory whom I had met once in London for a few minutes,[2] drove over to Tullyra and after Symons'[3] return to London, I stayed at her house. When I saw her great woods on the edge of a lake, I remembered the saying about avoiding woods and living near the water. Had this new friend come because of my invocation, or had the saying been but prevision and my invocation no act of will, but prevision also? Were those unintelligible words—"avoid woods because they concentrate the solar ray"—but a dream confusion, an attempt to

8. Synge died from Hodgkin's disease, following years of undiagnosed illness.
9. Synge's *The Playboy of the Western World* caused rioting during its first production at the Abbey Theatre in 1907 and, after Synge's death, during the Abbey's American tours, due to its supposed immorality. The play's portrayal of a rural Irish community that idealizes a young peasant thought to have killed his father, and whose young women compete for his attention, comically subverts the popular contemporary notion of Ireland as pure and pious. Yeats and Lady Gregory endured long-term hostility from some Catholics and Nationalists due to their championship of the play.
1. Samuel "MacGregor" Mathers (1854–1918), occultist who told Yeats that he experienced quasi-electric shocks when meeting phantoms.
1. In an earlier section of this memoir, Yeats describes a vision of "a galloping centaur, and . . . a naked woman of incredible beauty, standing upon a pedestal and shooting an arrow at a star," experienced while staying at Tullyra Castle, home of Edward Martyn, Irish playwright and patron, nearby Lady Gregory's home at Coole Park.
2. Yeats met Lady Gregory (1852–1932) briefly in London in 1894, and the acquaintance was renewed permanently during his travels in Ireland in summer 1896. A widow who was seeking to involve herself in the Irish literary movement, she quickly became his patron, closest friend, and close collaborator on folklore writings and plays. Yeats would spend several months at Coole each year for some two decades.
3. Yeats toured Ireland with poet and critic Arthur Symons (1865–1945) in summer 1896.

explain symbolically an actual juxtaposition of wood and water? I could not say nor can I now. I was in poor health, the strain of youth had been greater than it commonly is, even with imaginative men, who must always I think find youth bitter, and I had lost myself besides as I had done periodically for years, upon *Hodos Camelionis*.[4] The first time was in my eighteenth or nineteenth year, when I tried to create a more multitudinous dramatic form, and now I had got there through a novel that I could neither write nor cease to write which had *Hodos Camelionis* for its theme.[5] My chief person was to see all the modern visionary sects pass before his bewildered eyes, as Flaubert's St Anthony saw the Christian sects,[6] and I was as helpless to create artistic, as my chief person to create philosophic order. It was not that I do not love order, or that I lack capacity for it, but that, and not in the arts and the thought only, I outrun my strength. It is not so much that I choose too many elements, as that the possible unities themselves seem without number, like those angels, that in Henry More's paraphrase of the Schoolman's problem, dance spurred and booted upon the point of a needle.[7] Perhaps fifty years ago I had been in less trouble, but what can one do when the age itself has come to *Hodos Camelionis*?

Lady Gregory seeing that I was ill brought me from cottage to cottage to gather folk-belief tales of the fairies and the like and wrote down herself what we had gathered, considering that this work, in which one let others talk, and walked about the fields so much, would lie, to use a country phrase "Very light upon the mind." She asked me to return there the next year, and for years to come I was to spend my summers at her house. When I was in good health again, I found myself indolent, partly because I was affrighted by that impossible novel, and asked her to send me to my work every day at eleven, and at some other hour to my letters, rating me with idleness if need be, and I doubt if I should have done much with my life but for her firmness and her care. After a time though not very quickly, I recovered industry, though it has only been of late years that I have found it possible to face an hour's verse-writing without a preliminary struggle and much putting off.

Certain woods at Sligo, the woods above Dooney Rock, and those above the waterfall at Ben Bulben, though I shall never perhaps walk there again, are so deep in my affections that I dream about them at night; and yet the woods at Coole, though they do not come into my dream are so much more knitted to my thought, that when I am dead they will have I am persuaded, my longest visit. When we are dead according to my belief, we live our lives backward for a certain number of years, treading the paths that we have trodden, growing young again, even childish again, till some attain an innocence that is no longer a mere accident of nature, but the human intellect's crowning achievement.

4. See p. 240, n. 1.
5. *The Speckled Bird*, which Yeats never completed to his satisfaction.
6. In the novel *The Temptation of Saint Anthony* (1874) by French writer Gustave Flaubert (1821–1880).
7. English philosopher Henry More (1614–1687), a Platonist who later turned to occult and mystical interests, addresses the traditional question—how many angels can fit on the tip of a needle—in his work *The Immortality of the Soul* (1659).

*　*　*

L

On the sea-coast at Duras a few miles from Coole an old French count Florimond de Bastero[t] lived for certain months in every year;[8] Lady Gregory and I talked over my project of an Irish Theatre[9] looking out upon the lawn of his house, watching a large flock of ducks that was always gathered for his arrival from Paris, and that would be a very small flock if indeed it were a flock at all when he set out for Rome in the autumn. I told her that I had given up my project because it was impossible to get the few pounds necessary for a start in little halls, and she promised to collect or give the money necessary. That was her first great service to the Irish intellectual movement. She reminded me the other day that when she first asked me what she could do to help our movement I suggested nothing, and certainly I no more foresaw her genius than I foresaw that of John Synge, nor had she herself foreseen it. Our theatre had been established before she wrote or had any ambition to write, and yet her little comedies have merriment and beauty, an unusual combination,[1] and those two volumes where the Heroic Tales are arranged and translated in an English so simple and so noble, may do more than other books to deepen Irish imagination.[2] They contain our ancient literature, are something better than our Mabinogion,[3] are almost our Morte d'Arthur.[4] It is more fitting however that in a book of memoirs I should speak of her personal influence, and especially as no witness to it is likely to arise better qualified to speak. If that influence were lacking Ireland would be greatly impoverished, so much has been planned out in the library or among the woods at Coole, for it was there that John Shawe-Taylor[5] found the independence from class and family that made him summon the conference between landlord and tenant that brought land purchase, and it was there that Hugh Lane[6] formed those Irish ambitions that led to his spending many thousands and gathering much ingratitude; and where, but for that conversation at Florimond de Bastero[t]'s, had been the genius of Synge?[7]

    I have written these words instead of leaving all to posterity, and though my friend's ear seems indifferent to praise or blame, that young men to

8. A property on the coast about nine miles west of Coole Park, owned by Florimonde de Basterot (1836–1904), a French aristocrat with Irish family connections, and a good friend of Lady Gregory's.
9. Dissatisfied with English productions of his work, and wishing to spur an Irish dramatic revival, Yeats had begun to lay plans for productions in Ireland.
1. Lady Gregory excelled in writing one-act comic plays.
2. Lady Gregory's translations of the Irish epics in *Cuchulain of Muirthemne* (1902) and *Gods and Fighting Men* (1904).
3. Epic Welsh tales dating from around the twelfth century.
4. The Arthurian legends, as published by Thomas Malory (d. 1471).
5. Lady Gregory's nephew (1866–1911), who had been the force behind a conference in 1903 that had settled the most vexed aspects of the Irish land question.
6. Also a nephew of Lady Gregory's (d. 1915); he was the preeminent Irish art dealer of his time, and a decisive patron of Irish art, most notably in pressing for the development of the Dublin Municipal Gallery.
7. Yeats's conversation with Lady Gregory at Duras spawned the Irish Literary Theatre, which in turn precipitated the Abbey Theatre, which produced and promoted all of Synge's plays.

whom recent events are often more obscure than those long past, may learn what debts they owe and to what creditor.

From *Dramatis Personae*, 1896–1902 (1935)

VI

I must have spent the summer of 1897 at Coole. I was involved in a miserable love affair, that had but for one brief interruption absorbed my thoughts for years past, and would for some years yet.[1] My devotion might as well have been offered to an image in a milliner's window, or to a statue in a museum, but romantic doctrine had reached its extreme development. Dowson[2] was in love with a girl in an Italian restaurant, courted her for two years; at first she was too young, then he too disreputable; she married the waiter and his life went to wreck. Sober, he looked on no woman; drunk, he picked the cheapest whore. 'He did not even want them clean,' said a friend. 'I have been faithful to thee, Cynara, in my fashion.'[3] My health was giving way, my nerves had been wrecked. Finding that I could not work, and thinking the open air salutary, Lady Gregory brought me from cottage to cottage collecting folk-lore. Every night she wrote out what we had heard in the dialect of the cottages. She wrote, if memory does not deceive me, two hundred thousand words, discovering that vivid English she was the first to use upon the stage. My object was to find actual experience of the supernatural, for I did not believe, nor do I now, that it is possible to discover in the text-books of the schools, in the manuals sold by religious booksellers, even in the subtle reverie of saints, the most violent force in history. I have described elsewhere our discovery that when we passed the door of some peasant's cottage, we passed out of Europe as that word is understood. 'I have longed,' she said once, 'to turn Catholic, that I might be nearer to the people, but you have taught me that paganism brings me nearer still.' Yet neither she nor those peasants were pagans. Christianity begins to recognise the validity of experiences that preceded its birth and were, in some sense, shared by its founders. When later she asked me to annotate and introduce her book, *Visions and Beliefs*,[4] I began a study of 'Spiritualism' not only in its scientific form but as it is found among the London poor, and discovered that there was little difference except that the experience of the cottagers was the richer. Requiring no proof that we survive the grave, they could turn to what was dramatic or exciting and, though more ignorant than the townsmen, lacked vulgarity. Do the cottagers still live that mysterious life? Has it been driven away by exciting tales of ambush and assassination or has it become more inaccessible? When I was yet a very young man Sligo people told me whatever I

1. His unrequited love for Maud Gonne, interrupted only by his relationship with Olivia Shakespear in 1896–97 (see pp. 230–32).
2. Poet Ernest Dowson (1867–1900), a fellow member with Yeats of The Rhymers' Club, and one of what Yeats termed "The Tragic Generation."
3. The refrain in Dowson's poem "Non Sum Qualis Eram Bonae Sub Regno Cynarae" ("I am not as I was when kind Cynara ruled me"). The poem's title comes from the first ode from Book IV of the *Odes* by Roman poet and satirist Horace (65–8 B.C.E.).
4. *Visions and Beliefs in the West of Ireland* (1920).

asked, because all knew my mother's father, and some still remembered my father's grandfather. The people of South Galway did the same because Lady Gregory was my friend; an old witch-doctor in Clare said to us both: 'I have told you now what I have not told my own wife'; but if a stranger, or a neighbour that might mock, questioned them, they would say that all such things had long disappeared through the influence of the school. Once when I heard an old shepherd at Doneraile, where I spent a few days, give Lord Castletown[5] such an answer, I said: 'Has anybody ever gone from here to consult Biddy Earley?'[6]—a famous Clare witch—and in a moment the man's face became excited; he himself had stood at the roadside, watching spirits playing hurley in a field, until one came and pulled the cap over his eyes. What he saw, what he did not see but thought he saw, does not concern me here, being but a part of that traditional experience which I have discussed only too much elsewhere. That experience is my obsession, as Coole and its history, her hope that her son or her grandson[7] might live there, were Lady Gregory's.

XV

I saw Moore daily, we were at work on *Diarmuid and Grania*.[8] Lady Gregory thought such collaboration would injure my own art, and was perhaps right. Because his mind was argumentative, abstract, diagrammatic, mine sensuous, concrete, rhythmical, we argued about words. In later years, through much knowledge of the stage, through the exfoliation of my own style, I learnt that occasional prosaic words gave the impression of an active man speaking. In dream poetry, in *Kubla Khan*, in *The Stream's Secret*,[9] every line, every word, can carry its unanalysable, rich associations; but if we dramatise some possible singer or speaker we remember that he is moved by one thing at a time, certain words must be dull and numb. Here and there in correcting my early poems I have introduced such numbness and dullness, turned, for instance, 'the curd-pale moon' into the 'brilliant moon,' that all might seem, as it were, remembered with indifference, except some one vivid image. When I began to rehearse a play I had the defects of my early poetry; I insisted upon obvious all-pervading rhythm. Later on I found myself saying that only in those lines or words where the beauty of the passage came to its climax, must rhythm be obvious. * * *

5. Yeats visited Donerail Court, Cork, home of Bernard Fitzpatrick (1849–1937), 2nd Baron Castle-town, in September 1897. Castletown was a prime mover in the Pan-Celtic movement, and an early sponsor of the Irish literary movement.
6. A renowned wise woman and herb healer/witch doctor (1798–1874) who had lived near Feakle, Clare.
7. Her son, Robert Gregory (1881–1918); her grandson, Richard Gregory (1909–1981). Coole was left empty after Lady Gregory's death in 1932, and later demolished.
8. Yeats collaborated stormily with novelist George Moore (1852–1933) on *Diarmuid and Grania*, a play based on a story from the Fenian cycle of Irish mythology. The play was produced in 1901 but remained unpublished until 1951.
9. "Kubla Khan": a poem by Samuel Taylor Coleridge (1772–1834); "Stream's Secret": a poem by Dante Gabriel Rossetti (1828–1882).

XXIII

During these first years Lady Gregory was friend and hostess, a centre of peace, an adviser who never overestimated or underestimated trouble, but neither she nor we thought her a possible creator. And now all in a moment, as it seemed, she became the founder of modern Irish dialect literature. When her husband died she had sold her London house, hiring instead a small flat in Queen Anne's Mansions, lived most of the year at Coole, cutting down expenses that her son might inherit an unencumbered estate. In early life she had written two or three articles, such as many clever fashionable women write, more recently had edited her husband, Sir William Gregory's, *Autobiography*[1] and Mr. *Gregory's Letter-Box*, a volume of letters to Richard Gregory, Irish Under-Secretary at the beginning of the nineteenth century, from Palmerston, Wellesley, many famous men, drawn from the Coole archives.[2] Some slight desire to create had been put aside until her son reached manhood; but now he had left the university and she was fifty. I told her that Alfred Nutt[3] had offered to supply me with translations of the Irish heroic cycles if I would pick the best versions and put my English upon them, attempting what Malory had done for the old French narratives.[4] I told her that I was too busy with my own work. Some days later she asked if I would object to her attempting it, making or finding the translations herself. An eminent Trinity College professor had described ancient Irish literature as 'silly, religious, or indecent,' and she thought such work necessary for the dignity of Ireland. 'We work to add dignity to Ireland' was a favourite phrase of hers. I hesitated, I saw nothing in her past to fit her for that work; but in a week or two she brought a translation of some heroic tale, what tale I cannot now remember, in the dialect of the neighbourhood, where one discovers the unemphatic cadence, the occasional poignancy of Tudor English. Looking back, *Cuchulain of Muirthemne* and *Gods and Fighting Men* at my side, I can see that they were made possible by her past; semi-feudal Roxborough,[5] her inherited sense of caste, her knowledge of that top of the world where men and women are valued for their manhood and their charm, not for their opinions, her long study of Scottish Ballads, of Percy's *Reliques*,[6] of the *Morte d'Arthur*. If she had not found those tales, or finding them had not found the dialect of Kiltartan,[7] that past could not, as it were, have drawn itself together, come to birth as present personality.

1. Lady Gregory completed and edited the unfinished autobiography of Sir William Gregory (1816–1892), who had been governor of Ceylon in the 1870s, in 1894.
2. Sir William's grandfather, Mr. William (not Richard) Gregory (1762–1840), had been under-secretary for Ireland 1813–30. Lady Gregory's selections from his correspondence with Lord Palmerston (English secretary of war 1809–28, and later prime minister of Britain, 1855–58 and 1859–65) and Arthur Wellesley, duke of Wellington (lord lieutenant of Ireland 1821–28, and prime minister of Britain 1828–30 and 1834), were published in 1898 as Mr. *Gregory's Letter-Box*.
3. Alfred Nutt (1856–1910), manager of the Nutt publishing house.
4. Thomas Malory (d. 1471), compiler of the Arthurian legends in the *Morte d'Arthur*. Lady Gregory's work resulted in her *Cuchulain of Muirthemne* (1902).
5. Lady Gregory's childhood home in County Galway.
6. *Reliques of Ancient English Poetry* (1765), a collection of English and Scottish ballads by Thomas Percy (1729–1811).
7. The crossroads village nearest to Lady Gregory's home at Coole Park. The dialect style she developed, which relies heavily on English replications of Irish syntactical constructions, was widely known as "Kiltartan" speech.

Sometimes in her letters, in her books when she wrote ordinary English, she was the late-Victorian woman turning aside from reality so what seems pleasing, or to a slightly sentimental persiflage[8] as to a form of politeness —in society, to discover 'eternity glaring,' as Carlyle did when he met Charles Lamb[9] for the first time, is scarcely in good taste—but in her last years, when speaking in her own character, she seemed always her greater self. A writer must die every day he lives, be reborn, as it is said in the Burial Service, an incorruptible self, that self opposite of all that he has named 'himself.' George Moore, dreading the annihilation of an impersonal bleak realism, used life like a medieval ghost making a body for itself out of drifting dust and vapour; and have I not sung in describing guests at Coole—'There one that ruffled in a manly pose, For all his timid heart'[1]—that one myself? Synge was a sick man picturing energy, a doomed man picturing gaiety; Lady Gregory, in her life much artifice, in her nature much pride, was born to see the glory of the world in a peasant mirror.

From *Memoirs*

From Journal (1909, published 1972)

5

To keep these notes natural and useful to me in my life I must keep one note from leading on to another. To do that is to surrender oneself to literature. Every note must first have come as a casual thought, then it will be my life. If Christ or Buddha or Socrates had written, they would have surrendered life for a logical process.[1]

8

I have had a curious breakdown of some sort.[2] I had been working hard, and suddenly I found I could not use my mind on any serious subject. Yet at this moment I cannot tell if the whole thing was not a slight indisposition brought on by too much smoking heightened by that kind of nervous fright I get from time to time: the fear of losing my inspiration by absorption in outer things. The poet's enemies are those industries that make a good citizen. A poet is a good citizen turned inside out. * * *

10

Today the thought came to me that PIAL[3] never really understands my plans, or nature, or ideas. Then came the thought, what matter? How

---

8. Lightweight conversation.
9. Historian Thomas Carlyle (1795–1881) recalled in *Reminiscences* (1881) that the conversation of essayist Charles Lamb (1775–1834) was like "diluted insanity."
1. From Yeats's poem "Coole Park, 1929" (see pp. 106–07).
1. In *Estrangement* (1926), Yeats revised this line to read: "Neither Christ nor Buddha nor Socrates wrote a book, for to do that is to exchange life for a logical process."
2. Yeats was under immense strain in January 1909, managing the Abbey Theatre single-handedly.
3. The initials of the identifying motto ("Per Ignem ad Lucem": "Through Fire to Light") adopted by Maud Gonne on becoming a member of the occult society The Golden Dawn.

much of the best I have done and still do is but the attempt to explain myself to her?[4] If she understood, I should lack a reason for writing, and one never can have too many reasons for doing what is so laborious.

42

Lady Gregory is planting trees; for a year they have taken up much of her time. Her grandson will be fifty years old before they can be cut.[5] We artists, do not we also plant trees and it is only after some fifty years that we are of much value? Every day I notice some new analogy between [the] long-established life of the well-born and the artist's life. We come from the permanent things and create them, and instead of old blood we have old emotions and we carry in our head that form of society which aristocracies create now and again for some brief moment at Urbino or Versailles.[6] We too despise the mob and suffer at its hands and when we are happiest we have some little post in the house of Duke Frederick[7] where we watch the proud dreamless world with humility, knowing that our kingdom is invisible and that at the first breath of ambition our dreams vanish. If we do not see daily beautiful life at which we look as old men and women do at young children, we become theorists—thinkers as it is called—or else give ourselves to strained emotions, to some overflow of sentiment 'sighing after Jerusalem in the regions of the grave'.[8] How can we sing without our bush of whins,[9] our clump of heather, and does not Blake say that it takes a thousand years to create a flower?[1]

43

Perhaps we may find in the spectacle of some beautiful woman our Ferrara,[2] our Urbino. Perhaps that is why we have no longer any poetry but the poetry of love.

50   (On 6 and 7 of month ☌ ☌ ♃ p)[3]

Feb. 4 [1909]. This morning I got a letter telling me of Lady Gregory's illness.[4] I did not recognize her son's writing at first, and my mind wandered, I suppose because I am not well. I thought my mother was ill and that my sister was asking me to come at once: then I remembered that my

4. See Yeats's poem "The Consolation" ["Words"], p. 36.
5. Richard Gregory (1909–1981), Lady Gregory's first grandchild, had been born on January 6, 1909.
6. The fifteenth- and sixteenth-century court of Urbino, Italy, was renowned for its artistic refinement and accomplishment. Versailles, the ornate palace of the French royalty, was begun by Louis XIV in 1662.
7. Frederick, duke of Urbino (c. 1417–1482).
8. A misquotation of a line from an engraving in *Jerusalem* by William Blake (1757–1827), English poet, painter, engraver, and mystic: "They inquire after Jerusalem in the regions of the dead."
9. Furze or gorse.
1. "To create a little flower is the labour of ages": from Blake's *The Marriage of Heaven and Hell* (1791).
2. Duke Ercole de l'Este (1431–1505) of Ferrara in Italy was renowned for his patronage of the arts.
3. Astrological symbols: Mars in conjunction with Jupiter, progressed. Yeats was presumably calculating the celestial influences affecting Lady Gregory's condition.
4. Lady Gregory suffered a cerebral hemorrhage that nearly killed her.

mother died years ago[5] and that more than kin was at stake. She has been to me mother, friend, sister and brother. I cannot realize the world without her—she brought to my wavering thoughts steadfast nobility. All day the thought of losing her is like a conflagration in the rafters. Friendship is all the house I have.

64

Feb. 13 [1909]. There is no wisdom without indolence. Nobody running at full speed has either a head or a heart.

66

One thought must be continually pressed upon all free souls—here in Ireland above all—to resist ill-breeding in thought as our fathers in their more leisurely lives—alike in country poverty, where most of all they brooded over this one thing, or in great houses—resisted ill-breeding in manners. These are associated, and even though we be called the worst names, the hardest to bear, we must keep the fountains pure. Education, newspapers, a thousand impersonalities have filled the world with the imitation of what once was gold—an imitation worse than the ill-manners of the parvenu, for he would have preferred the gold had he found it. We have everywhere now counterfeit that is thought better, instead of merely more obtainable, than true metal.

82   *Ne se vend*[6]

March 7 [1909]. In spite of myself my mind dwells more and more on ideas of class. Ireland has grown sterile, because power has passed to men who lack the training which requires a certain amount of wealth to ensure continuity from generation to generation, and to free the mind in part from other tasks. A gentleman is for one thing a man whose principal ideas are not connected with his personal needs and his personal success. In old days he was a clerk or a noble, that is to say, he had freedom because of inherited wealth and position, or because of a personal renunciation. The names are different today, and I would put the artist and the scholar in the category of the clerk, yet personal renunciation is not now sufficient or the *hysterica passio*[7] of Ireland would be inspiration, or perhaps it is sufficient but is impossible without inherited culture. For without culture or holiness, which is always the gift of a very few, a man may renounce wealth or any other external thing but he cannot renounce hatred, envy, jealousy, revenge. Culture is the sanctity of the intellect.

86

A mind without traditional culture, moral or literary, is only powerful in hate. A clever man unhelped by a synthetic social ideal, or the remnant

---

5. Yeats's mother, Susan Pollexfen Yeats (1841–1900), had been an invalid for the last dozen years of her life after suffering a stroke in 1887.
6. Not for sale (French).
7. Hysteria. The phrase is used in *King Lear*, Act II, scene 4.

of it which lives on as culture in certain social regions, becomes an executioner. Ricketts[8] said this to me a year ago: 'Artists begin to hesitate to
accept public tasks because the almost certain attack may ruin their reputation.' In Ireland, where the cultivated remnant has no power on public
opinion, what is a little true of all modern states becomes a portent, a
prophecy of what is to come.

87

I cry out continually against my life. I have sleepless nights, thinking of
the time that I must take from my poetry, from the harvest of the Lord—
last night I could not sleep—and yet perhaps I must do all these things
that I may set myself into a life of action, so as to express not the traditional
poet but that forgotten thing, the normal active man.

105

March 18 [1909]. I dare say that these notes, if some chance eye light on
them, may seem morbid; but they help me to understand myself, and I
remember hearing a man of science once argue that all progress is at the
outset 'pathological'. I know that I have already made moral gains.

The pain others give us passes away in their later kindness; the pain of
one's own blunders, especially when they hurt one's vanity, never passes
away. One's own acts are isolated and one act does not buy absolution for
another. They are always present before a strangely abstract judgment. One
is never a unity, a personality: to oneself, small acts of years ago are so
painful in the memory that often one starts at the presence a little below
'the threshold of consciousness' of a thought that remains unknown. It
sheds a vague light like that of the moon before it rises, or after its setting.
Vanity is so intimately associated with one's spiritual identity that the errors
or what hurt it, above all if they came from it, are more painful in the
memory than serious sins, and yet I do not think this means that one is
very vain. The harm one does to others is lost in changing events and
passes away, and so is healed by time, unless it was very great. Looking
back, I find only one offence which is as painful to me as a hurt to vanity.
It was done to a man who died shortly after.[9] Because of his death it has
not been touched by the transforming hand—tolerant Nature has not rescued it from Justice.

107

I think all happiness depends on having the energy to assume the mask
of some other self, that all joyous or creative life is a rebirth as something
not oneself, something created in a moment and perpetually renewed in
playing a game like that of a child where one loses the infinite pain of
self-realization, a grotesque or solemn painted face put on that one may

8. Charles Ricketts (1866–1931), artist and designer.
9. Yeats details the incident in *Memoirs*. As a young man he had nominated into a Dublin society
   a friend who was then charged an initiation fee he could not afford. Yeats remained silent though
   he knew the fee should not be charged.

hide from the terrors of judgment, an imaginative Saturnalia[1] that makes one forget reality. Perhaps all the sins and energies of the world are but the world's flight from an infinite blinding beam.

198

Last night, walking home late, I felt as I passed the canal bridge a desire to throw a ring which I value more than anything I possess, because of her that gave it, into the canal. It passed off in a moment or two, but it was almost as strong as the desire I felt when at San Marino to throw myself from the cliff.[2] Once when I was walking in a wood with a dear friend,[3] holding an axe in my hand, the impulse had for a moment a homicidal form, which passed off the moment I held the axe by the head instead of the handle. My father says that when he is on the top of an omnibus and another passes he wants to jump from one to the other. Is there violent madness at the root of every mind, waiting for some breaking of the leash?

221

Oh masters of life, give me confidence in something, even if it be but in my own reason. I can never believe in anything else now, for I have accused the impulses of too many sins. I know that reason is almost a blasphemous thing, a claim to an infinity of being while we are limited social creatures, half artificial. Twenty, no, a hundred times if I had acted upon impulse and against reason I should have created a finer world[*] of rights and wrongs, a more personal and passionate life than impersonal reason could give. Reason is the stopping of the pendulum, a kind of death. Life is a perpetual injustice.

[*]Yes, but I should have gone from my world. The passionate man must believe he obeys his reason.

From *Pages from a Diary Written in Nineteen Hundred and Thirty* (1944)

x

A poet whose free verse I have admired[1] rejects God and every kind of unity, calls the ultimate reality anarchy, means by that word something which for lack of metaphysical knowledge he cannot define. He thinks, however, that a baptismal and marriage service and some sort of ceremo-

---

1. The festival of the god Saturn, observed in December in Roman times.
2. Yeats traveled through Italy with Lady Gregory in spring 1907. No other record of this incident seems to have survived. Other entries in this journal show that Yeats feared he had inherited a predisposition to nervous breakdown and possible madness from his mother; several of his Pollexfen relatives spent time in mental institutions.
3. Presumably Lady Gregory, while in the woods at Coole.
1. Ezra Pound (1885–1972). Pound and Yeats were both living at Rapallo, Italy, in the winter of 1929–30.

nial preparation for death are necessary, and that the Churches should stick to these and be content.

He now writes in the traditional forms because they satisfy a similar need. But why stop at the metrical forms? It has always seemed to me that all great literature at its greatest intensity displays the sage, the lover, or some image of despair, and that these are traditional attitudes. * * *

XXI

I think that two conceptions, that of reality as a congeries of beings, that of reality as a single being, alternate in our emotion and in history, and must always remain something that human reason, because subject always to one or the other, cannot reconcile. I am always, in all I do, driven to a moment which is the realisation of myself as unique and free, or to a moment which is the surrender to God of all that I am. I think that there are historical cycles wherein one or the other predominates, and that a cycle approaches where all shall [be] as particular and concrete as human intensity permits. Again and again I have tried to sing that approach—*The Hosting of the Sidhe*, 'O sweet everlasting voices', and those lines about. 'The lonely, majestical multitude'[2]—and have almost understood my intention. Again and again with remorse, a sense of defeat, I have failed when I would write of God, written coldly and conventionally. Could those two impulses, one as much a part of truth as the other, be reconciled, or if one or the other could prevail, all life would cease.

XXV

The other day Gogarty[3] wrote that John[4] wanted to do a 'serious portrait'. I replied that 'I would think it a great honour'. And to-day I have been standing in front of the hotel mirror noticing certain lines about my mouth and chin marked strongly by shadows cast from a window on my right, and have wondered if John would not select those very lines and lay great emphasis upon them, and, if some friend complain that he has obliterated what good looks I have, insist that those lines show character, and perhaps that there are no good looks but character. In those lines I see the marks of recent illness, marks of time, growing irresolution, perhaps some faults that I have long dreaded; but then my character is so little myself that all my life it has thwarted me. It has affected my poems, my true self, no more than the character of a dancer affects the movement of the dance. When I was painted by John years ago, and saw for the first time the portrait (or rather the etching taken from it) now in a Birmingham gallery, I shuddered.

Always particular about my clothes, never dissipated, never unshaven except during illness, I saw myself there an unshaven, drunken bar-tender, and then I began to feel John had found something that he liked in me,

2. Poems from *The Wind Among the Reeds* (1899): "The Hosting of the Sidhe" (see p. 23), "The Everlasting Voices," and "To my Heart, bidding it have no Fear" (see p. 27).
3. Oliver St. John Gogarty (1878–1957), surgeon, writer, and fellow senator with Yeats in the early years of the Irish Free State.
4. Augustus John (1867–1961), artist. Yeats had sat for John in 1907, the result making him, he thought, look like a "gypsy." This proposed new sitting took place at Gogarty's hotel in the west of Ireland in 1930. Confirming Yeats's fears, the new portrait stressed his age.

something closer than character, and by that very transformation made it visible. He had found Anglo-Irish solitude, a solitude I have made for my self, an outlawed solitude.

XL

THREE ESSENTIALS

I would found literature on the three things which Kant[5] thought we must postulate to make life livable—Freedom, God, Immortality. The fading of these three before 'Bacon, Newton, Locke'[6] has made literature decadent. Because Freedom is gone we have Stendhal's 'mirror dawdling down a lane';[7] because God has gone we have realism, the accidental, because Immortality is gone we can no longer write those tragedies which have always seemed to me alone legitimate—those that are a joy to the man who dies. Recent Irish literature has only delighted me in so far as it implies one or the other, in so far as it has been a defiance of all else, in so far as it has created those extravagant characters and emotions which have always arisen spontaneously from the human mind when it sees itself exempt from death and decay, responsible to its source alone.

James Joyce differs from Arnold Bennett and Galsworthy,[8] let us say, because he can isolate the human mind and its vices as if in eternity. So could Synge,[9] so could O'Casey till he caught the London contagion in *The Silver Tassie* and changed his mountain into a mouse.[1] The movement began with A.E.'s first little verses made out of the Upanishads,[2] and my *Celtic Twilight*,[3] a bit of ornamental trivial needlework sewn on a prophetic fury got by Blake and Boehme.[4] James Stephens has read the *Tain* in the light of the *Veda* but the time is against him and he is silent.[5]

5. German philosopher Immanuel Kant (1724–1804), whose *Critique of Judgement* (1790) investigates the ethics of purposiveness.
6. Yeats's representative figures for the triumph of scientific rationalism over imagination and mysticism: English philosopher Francis Bacon (1561–1626) emphasized scientific induction, insisting on empirical facts and evidence to uphold a given thesis; mathematician Isaac Newton (1642–1727) expounded the basic laws of motion; English empiricist philosopher John Locke (1632–1704) argued that all knowledge derives from sensation.
7. Pseudonym of French novelist Henri Marie Beyle (1783–1842). Yeats's quotation is from the epigraph to chapter 13 of *The Red and the Black* (1831) and refers to the realist method of the novel.
8. James Joyce (1882–1941), Irish novelist, who is here contrasted with the Edwardian English realists Arnold Bennett (1867–1931) and John Galsworthy (1867–1933).
9. John Millington Synge (1871–1909), playwright and cofounder, with Yeats and Lady Gregory, of the Abbey Theatre.
1. Sean O'Casey (1880–1964) was the most successful Irish playwright of the 1920s, but he left Ireland after his experimental expressionist play *The Silver Tassie* (1928) was rejected at the Abbey Theatre by Yeats and Lady Gregory.
2. "A.E." was the pseudonym of Yeats's friend, Irish artist, poet, and mystic George Russell (1867–1935), whose verse was much influenced by the Hindu Upanishads, mystical writings dating from around 300 B.C.E.
3. Yeats's volume of folklore writings (1893, revised and enlarged 1902), which stressed imagination over science.
4. Yeats here enlists visionary English poet William Blake (1757–1827) and German mystic Jacob Boehme (1575–1624), whose work speculates on the origins of being, as forefathers of his own belief in the primacy of imagination.
5. Yeats regarded James Stephens (1882–1950) as one of the most promising younger Irish writers because of his privileging of imagination and his knowledge of folk tradition and mythology; the *Tain Bó Cualgne* (The Cattle Raid of Cooley) is from the Ulster cycle of Irish mythology, dating from around 700–800 C.E.; the Veda is the sacred ancient literature of Hinduism.

*   *   *

The first nation that can affirm the three convictions affirmed by Kant as free powers—*i.e.* without associations of language, dogma, and ritual—will be able to control the moral energies of the soul.

*   *   *

NOVEMBER 18TH

Science, separated from philosophy, is the opium of the suburbs.

Critical Writings

Hopes and Fears for Irish Literature[1] (1892)

When I come over here from London or cross over to London I am always struck afresh by the difference between the cultivated people in England and the cultivated people—alas! too few—here in Ireland. They could not differ more if they were divided from each other by a half score of centuries. I am thinking especially of the men of my own age, though not entirely of them. In England amongst the best minds art and poetry are becoming every day more entirely ends in themselves, and all life is made more and more but so much fuel to feed their fire. It is partly the influence of France that is bringing this about. In France a man may do anything he pleases, he may spend years in prison even, like Verlaine,[2] and the more advanced of the young men will speak well of him if he have but loved his art sincerely, and they will worship his name as they worship Verlaine's if he have but made beautiful things and added a little to the world's store of memorable experiences. The influence of France is every year pervading more completely English literary life. The influence of that school which calls itself, in the words of its leader, Verlaine, a school of the sunset, or by the term which was flung at it "as a reproach, and caught up, as a battle cry," Decadence is now the dominating thing in many lives. Poetry is an end in itself; it has nothing to do with thought, nothing to do with philosophy, nothing to do with life, nothing to do with anything but the music of cadence, and beauty of phrase. This is the new doctrine of letters. I well remember the irritated silence that fell upon a noted gathering[3] of the younger English imaginative writers once, when I tried to explain a philosophy of poetry in which I was profoundly interested, and to show the dependence, as I conceived it, of all great art and literature upon conviction and upon heroic life. To them literature had ceased to be the handmaid of humanity, and become instead a terrible queen, in

---

1. Published in *United Ireland* in October 1892, this article reflects the growing tension between Yeats's aspirations for a distinctively Irish literature and his continuing investment in the Decadent and "Art for Art's sake" aesthetics current in 1890s England. Having broken with the Arnoldian idea that art should be "a criticism of life," he here resists the idea that Irish writing should be animated by Nationalist convictions and aims and tries to find a middle ground between a purely literary art that has "ceased to be the handmaid of humanity" and an art that is merely didactic or utilitarian and hence commonplace or careless.
2. Paul Verlaine (1844–1896), French poet and aesthete who had spent two years in prison after shooting his lover, poet Arthur Rimbaud (1854–1891), and who promoted the aesthetic of "Art for Art's sake."
3. The Rhymers' Club, a group of young poets and writers who met regularly in a London pub in the early 1890s to discuss literature.

whose services the stars rose and set, and for whose pleasure life stumbles along in the darkness. There is a good deal to be said in favour of all this. Never before, perhaps, were men so anxious to write their best—as they conceive that best—and so entirely loth to bow to the prejudices of the multitude. There is much to be said even for Verlaine, for he who writes well and lives badly is usually of more service to the world at large than he who writes badly and lives well, and he is always better than the crowd who do both indifferently. But one thing cannot be said. It is not possible to call a literature produced in this way the literature of energy and youth. The age which has produced it is getting old and feeble, and sits in the chimney-corner carving all manner of curious and even beautiful things upon the staff that can no longer guide its steps. Here in Ireland we are living in a young age, full of hope and promise—a young age which has only just begun to make its literature. It was only yesterday that it cut from the green hillside the staff which is to help its steps upon the long road. There is no carving upon the staff, the rough bark is still there, and the knots are many upon its side.

When I talk to people of literary ambition here in Ireland, I find them holding that literature must be the expression of conviction, and be the garment of noble emotion and not an end in itself. I found them most interested in the literary forms that give most opportunity for the display of great characters and great passions. Turning to our literature I find that such forms are plenty, often absolutely crude and uninteresting, as in the case of M'Carthy's "Fardiah," and Joyce's "Blanid;" occasionally crude and interesting, like Joyce's "Deirdre," and Ferguson's "Congal;" and once or twice beyond all praise and all imitation like Ferguson's "Conary," and his better known "Vengeance of the Welshmen of Tirawley."[4] But side by side with this robustness and rough energy of ours there goes most utter indifference to art, the most dire carelessness, the most dreadful intermixture of the commonplace. I have before me a letter from a young man in a remote part of Ireland asking an opinion about some verses and telling me, as if it was a special merit, that he did them at great speed, two columns in an hour, I think. I have not yet read his poems; but it is obvious that good poetry cannot be done in this fashion. There is a printed letter of John Francis O'Donnell's, in which he claims to have written I know not how many columns of verse and prose in two or three days.[5] Yet, he who would write a memorable song must be ready to give often days to a few lines, and be ready, perhaps, to pay for it afterwards with certain other days of dire exhaustion and depression, and, if he would be remembered when he is in his grave, he must give to his art the devotion the Crusaders of old gave to their cause and be content to be alone among men, apart

4. "Ferdiah: An Episode from the *Táin Bó Chuailgne*" by Denis MacCarthy (1817–1882); "Blanid" and "Deirdre" by Patrick Weston Joyce (1827–1914); the epic poem "Congal" and "The Vengeance of the Welshmen of Tirawley" by Sir Samuel Ferguson (1810–1886). Yeats here picks out writers using Irish mythological and heroic material as the inspiration for their work. Joyce specialized in collecting and publishing Irish folk songs. Ferguson was in Yeats's view the most accomplished Irish poet post-1850. See note 3 to "To Ireland in the Coming Times," p. 21.
5. Yeats had reviewed the collected poems of John O'Donnell (1837–1874), negatively, the previous year.

alike from their joys and their sorrows, having for companions the multitude of his dreams and for reward the kingdom of his pride. He who would belong to things eternal must for the most part renounce his allotted place amid the things of time. Here in Ireland the art of living interests us greatly, and the art of writing but little. We seek effectiveness rather than depth. We produce good correspondents, good journalists, and good talkers, and few profound and solitary students. "You Irish people," said a witty woman to me once, "will never have a future because you have a present." "We are," said a famous Irishman to me, "too poetical to be poets, we are the greatest talkers since the Greeks, we are a nation of brilliant failures."[6] I no more complain of this absorption in mere living than I complain of the narrow devotion to mere verbal beauty of the newest generation of literary men in France and England. We have the limitations of dawn. They have the limitations of sunset. We also in the coming centuries will grow into the broad noon and pass on at last into twilight and darkness.

Can we but learn a little of their skill, and a little of their devotion to form, a little of their hatred of the commonplace and the banal, we may make all these restless energies of ours alike the inspiration and the theme of a new and wonderful literature. We have behind us in the past the most moving legends and a history full of lofty passions. If we can but take that history and those legends and turn them into dramas, poems, and stories full of the living soul of the present, and make them massive with conviction and profound with reverie, we may deliver that new great utterance for which the world is waiting. Men are growing tired of mere subtleties of form, self-conscious art and no less self-conscious simplicity. But if we are to do this we must study all things Irish, until we know the peculiar glamour that belongs to this nation, and how to distinguish it from the glamour of other countries and other races. "Know thyself" is a true advice for nations as well as for individuals. We must know and feel our national faults and limitations no less than our national virtues, and care for things Gaelic and Irish, not because we hold them better than things Saxon and English, but because they belong to us, and because our lives are to be spent among them, whether they be good or evil. Whether the power that lies latent in this nation is but the seed of some meagre shrub or the seed from which shall rise the vast and spreading tree is not for us to consider. It is our duty to care for that seed and tend it until it has grown to perfection after its kind.

6. In *The Trembling of the Veil*, Yeats ascribes this saying to Oscar Wilde (1854–1900), playwright, poet, and critic.

The De-Anglicising of Ireland[1] (1892)

December 17, 1892

TO THE EDITOR OF *UNITED IRELAND*

Dear Sir—I agree with every word you said last week about Dr. Hyde's lecture, and, like many another, am deeply grateful to you for your reprint of it in the current number. Without going as far as some enthusiastic members of Dr. Hyde's audience, whom I heard call it the most important utterance of its kind since '48,[2] I will say that it seems to me the best possible augury for the success of the movement we are trying to create. Its learning, its profound sincerity, its passionate conviction, are all pledges that the President of the National Literary Society,[3] at any rate, will go the whole journey with us, come foul or fair weather. At the same time there was a good deal in Dr. Hyde's lecture which would have depressed me had I agreed with it. He seemed to have the bulk of his hopes for the "de-Anglicising" of Ireland upon the revival, or, at any rate, the preservation, of the Gaelic language, and at the same time to pronounce it "impossible to find either men or money" to carry out the one scheme he held capable of doing this. Alas, I fear he spoke the truth, and that the Gaelic language will soon be no more heard, except here and there in remote villages, and on the wind-beaten shores of Connaught.

Is there, then, no hope for the de-Anglicising of our people? Can we not build up a national tradition, a national literature, which shall be none the less Irish in spirit from being English in language? Can we not keep the continuity of the nation's life, not by trying to do what Dr. Hyde has practically pronounced impossible, but by translating or retelling in English, which shall have an indefinable Irish quality of rhythm and style, all that is best of the ancient literature? Can we not write and persuade others to write histories and romances of the great Gaelic men of the past, from the son of Nessa to Owen Roe,[4] until there has been made a golden bridge between the old and the new?

America, with no past to speak of, a mere "parvenue" among nations, is creating a national literature which in its most characteristic products differs almost as much from English literature as does the literature of

---

1. In December 1892, Douglas Hyde (see p. 107, n. 2) had delivered a seminal speech on "The Necessity for De-Anglicizing Ireland" that called on the Irish people to reverse the process of English cultural colonization by reviving the Irish language and returning to Irish customs, sports, manners, and habits of dress. The speech spurred the foundation of the Gaelic League, which promoted the use of Irish, in 1893. Yeats, who spoke no Irish, and who drew much of his imaginative inspiration from English literary models, was consequently anxious about the cultural separatism implied in Hyde's program. His call here for an Irish literature in English that "shall have an indefinable Irish quality of rhythm and style," and which should be based on heroic Irish narratives, characterizes his early promotion of a distinctive tradition of Irish literature written in English.
2. The Irish rebellion of 1848 arose out of the patriotic "Young Ireland" movement, which, like Hyde's speech, called for allegiance to a distinctively Irish cultural identity.
3. The National Literary Society was established in Dublin in 1892, with Hyde as president. Yeats helped to found it and was one of its most energetic members.
4. Nessa's son was Conchubar, king of Ulster in the Ulster cycle of Irish tales; Owen Roe O'Neill (1590–1649) was commander of Irish forces in the Ulster Rebellion of 1642. He won a series of brilliant victories against the English, but disagreements with his own allies prevented him from winning overall victory, and his death ended resistance to Cromwell's conquest of Ireland.

France. Walt Whitman, Thoreau, Bret Harte, and Cable,[5] to name no more, are very American, and yet America was once an English colony. It should be more easy for us, who have in us that wild Celtic blood, the most un-English of all things under heaven, to make such a literature. If we fail it shall not be because we lack the materials, but because we lack the power to use them. But we are not failing. Mr. Hyde, Lady Wilde in her recent books, and Mr. Curtin, and the editor of the just-published "Vision of M'Comaile,"[6] are setting before us a table spread with strange Gaelic fruits, from which an ever-growing band of makers of song and story shall draw food for their souls. Nor do we lack creative artists either. Has not Miss Tynan given us her "Legends and Lyrics," Miss Barlow her "Irish Idylls," Miss Lawless her "Grania," and Mr. O'Grady his wonderful and incomparable "Fin and his Companions,"[7] within the last year or two? Let us make these books and the books of our older writers known among the people and we will do more to de-Anglicise Ireland than by longing to recall the Gaelic tongue and the snows of yester year. Let us by all means prevent the decay of that tongue where we can, and preserve it always among us as a learned language to be a fountain of nationality in our midst, but do not let us base upon it our hopes of nationhood. When we remember the majesty of Cuchullin and the beauty of sorrowing Deirdre we should not forget that it is that majesty and that beauty which are immortal, and not the perishing tongue that first told of them.—

Yours, & c., W. B. Yeats.

From The Message of the Folk-lorist (1893)

In one of his unpublished watercolour illustrations to Young's "Night Thoughts," William Blake has drawn a numberless host of spirits and fairies affirming the existence of God.[1] Out of every flower and every grass-blade comes a little creature lifting its right hand above its head. It is possible that the books of folk-lore, coming in these later days from almost every country in the world, are bringing the fairies and the spirits to our study tables that we may witness a like affirmation, and see innumerable hands lifted testifying to the ancient supremacy of imagination. Imagination is God in the world of art, and may well desire to have us come to

5. Poet Walt Whitman (1819–1892); essayist and poet Henry David Thoreau (1817–1862), author of *Walden* (1854); poet and short-story writer Bret Harte (1836–1902); and novelist George Washington Cable (1844–1925).
6. Lady Jane Wilde (1824–1896), Oscar Wilde's mother, had published *Ancient Legends, Mystic Charms, and Superstitions of Ireland* in 1887; anthropologist Jeremiah Curtin (1835–1906) had published *Myths and Folk-Lore of Ireland* in 1890; "M'Comail" is probably a misreading for *The Vision of MacConglinne*, a twelfth-century Irish poem that had been recently published by Kuno Meyer (1858–1919).
7. *Ballads and Lyrics* (1891) by poet and novelist Katharine Tynan (1859–1931), a close friend of Yeats at this time; *Irish Idylls* (1892), stories of Irish life, by Jane Barlow (1857–1917); *Grania* (1892), a novel set on the Aran Islands, by Emily Lawless (1845–1913); and *Finn and His Companions* (1892) by Standish James O'Grady (1846–1928), whose popularizations of Irish mythology were a germinal influence on the Irish Literary Revival.
1. Subsequently published in *William Blake's Designs for Edward Young's 'Night Thoughts'* (Oxford, 1980).

an issue with the atheists who would make us "realists," "naturalists," or the like.

Folk-lore is at once the Bible, the Thirty-nine Articles, and the Book of Common Prayer, and well-nigh all the great poets have lived by its light. Homer, Aeschylus, Sophocles, Shakespeare, and even Dante, Goethe, and Keats, were little more than folk-lorists with musical tongues.[2] The root-stories of the Greek poets are told to-day at the cabin fires of Donegal; the Slavonian peasants tell their children now, as they did a thousand years before Shakespeare was born, of the spirit prisoned in the cloven pine;[3] the Swedes had need neither of Dante nor Spenser to tell them of the living trees that cry or bleed if you break off a bough; and through all the long backward and abysm of time, Faust, under many names, has signed the infernal compact, and girls at St. Agnes' Eve have waited for visions of their lovers to come to them "upon the honeyed middle of the night." It is only in these latter decades that we have refused to learn of the poor and the simple, and turned atheists in our pride. The folk-lore of Greece and Rome lasted us a long time; but having ceased to be a living tradition, it became both worn out and unmanageable, like an old servant. We can now no more get interest in the gods of Olympus than we can in the stories told by the showman of a travelling waxwork company. For lack of those great typical personages who flung the thunderbolts or had serpents in their hair, we have betaken ourselves in a hurry to the poetry of cigarettes and black coffee, of absinthe, and the skirt dance, or are trying to persuade the lecture and the scientific book to look, at least to the eye, like the old poems and dramas and stories that were in the ages of faith long ago. But the countless little hands are lifted and the affirmation has begun.

✻   ✻   ✻

The greatest poets of every nation have drawn from stories like this,[4] symbols and events to express the most lyrical, the most subjective moods. ✻ ✻ ✻ Shakespeare and Keats had the folk-lore of their own day, while Shelley had but mythology; and a mythology which has been passing for long through literary minds without any new influx from living tradition loses all the incalculable instructive and convincing quality of the popular traditions. No conscious invention can take the place of tradition, for he who would write a folk tale, and thereby bring a new life into literature, must have the fatigue of the spade in his hands and the stupor of the fields in his heart. Let us listen humbly to the old people telling their stories, and perhaps God will send the primitive excellent imagination into the midst of us again. Why should we be either 'naturalists' or 'realists'? Are not those little right hands lifted everywhere in affirmation?

---

2. Yeats in this paragraph highlights the use of folkloric material in the writings of Homer, Greek poet of the eighth century B.C.E.; Greek tragedian Aeschylus (c. 525–c. 456 B.C.E.); Greek tragedian Sophocles (c. 496–405 B.C.E.); Italian poet Dante Alighieri (1265–1321) in the *Inferno*; German poet and dramatist Johann Wolfgang von Goethe (1749–1832) in *Faust* (1808–1832); English Romantic poet John Keats (1795–1821) in "The Eve of St. Agnes" (1819); and English poet Edmund Spenser (c. 1552–1599).
3. The spirit Ariel is freed from a cloven pine in Shakespeare's *The Tempest*.
4. The article is a review of *The Ghost World* (1893) by T. F. Dyer (1848–1928).

From The Celtic Element in Literature[1] (1898)

I

Ernest Renan described what he held to be Celtic characteristics in *The Poetry of the Celtic Races*.[2] I must repeat the well-known sentences: 'No race communed so intimately as the Celtic race with the lower creation, or believed it to have so big a share of moral life.' The Celtic race had 'a realistic naturalism,' 'a love of Nature for herself, a vivid feeling for her magic, commingled with the melancholy a man knows when he is face to face with her, and thinks he hears her communing with him about his origin and his destiny.' 'It has worn itself out in mistaking dreams for realities,' and 'compared with the classical imagination the Celtic imagination is indeed the infinite contrasted with the finite.' 'Its history is one long lament, it still recalls its exiles, its flights across the seas.' 'If at times it seems to be cheerful, its tear is not slow to glisten behind the smile. Its songs of joy end as elegies; there is nothing to equal the delightful sadness of its national melodies.' Matthew Arnold, in *The Study of Celtic Literature*, has accepted this passion for nature, this imaginativeness, this melancholy, as Celtic characteristics, but has described them more elaborately. The Celtic passion for nature comes almost more from a sense of her 'mystery' than of her 'beauty,' and it adds 'charm and magic' to nature, and the Celtic imaginativeness and melancholy are alike 'a passionate, turbulent, indomitable reaction against the despotism of fact.' The Celt is not melancholy, as Faust or Werther[3] are melancholy, from 'a perfectly definite motive,' but because of something about him 'unaccountable, defiant and titanic.' How well one knows these sentences, better even than Renan's, and how well one knows the passages of prose and verse which he uses to prove that wherever English literature has the qualities these sentences describe, it has them from a Celtic source. Though I do not think any of us who write about Ireland have built any argument upon them, it is well to consider them a little, and see where they are helpful and where they are hurtful. If we do not, we may go mad some day, and the enemy root up our rose-garden and plant a cabbage-garden instead. * * *

IV

Matthew Arnold asks how much of the Celt must one imagine in the ideal man of genius. I prefer to say, how much of the ancient hunters and fishers and of the ecstatic dancers among hills and woods must one imagine in the ideal man of genius? Certainly a thirst for unbounded emotion and a wild melancholy are troublesome things in the world, and do not make

---

1. This essay constitutes Yeats's most important early attempt to define a distinctively Irish imaginative tradition and to rebut both scientific rationalism and the influential characterizations of Irishness that had been promoted by English poet and critic Matthew Arnold (1822–1888) in his essays *On the Study of Celtic Literature* (1867).
2. Published in 1854, by French historian Ernest Renan (1823–1892).
3. The central characters of the play *Faust* (1808–32) and the novel *The Sorrows of Young Werther* (1774), both by German poet and dramatist Johann Wolfgang von Goethe (1749–1832).

its life more easy or orderly, but it may be the arts are founded on the life beyond the world, and that they must cry in the ears of our penury until the world has been consumed and become a vision. Certainly, as Samuel Palmer wrote, 'Excess is the vivifying spirit of the finest art, and we must always seek to make excess more abundantly excessive.'[4] Matthew Arnold has said that if he were asked 'where English got its turn for melancholy and its turn for natural magic,' he 'would answer with little doubt that it got much of its melancholy from a Celtic source, with no doubt at all that from a Celtic source it got nearly all its natural magic.'

I will put this differently and say that literature dwindles to a mere chronicle of circumstance, or passionless fantasies, and passionless meditations, unless it is constantly flooded with the passions and beliefs of ancient times, and that of all the fountains of the passions and beliefs of ancient times in Europe, the Slavonic, the Finnish, the Scandinavian, and the Celtic, the Celtic alone has been for centuries close to the main river of European literature. It has again and again brought 'the vivifying spirit' 'of excess' into the arts of Europe. Ernest Renan has told how the visions of purgatory seen by pilgrims to Lough Derg[5]—once visions of the pagan under-world, as the boat made out of a hollow tree that bore the pilgrim to the holy island were alone enough to prove—gave European thought new symbols of a more abundant penitence; and had so great an influence that he has written, 'It cannot be doubted for a moment that to the number of poetical themes Europe owes to the genius of the Celt is to be added the framework of the divine comedy.'[6]

A little later the legends of Arthur and his table, and of the Holy Grail, once it seems the cauldron of an Irish God, changed the literature of Europe, and, it may be, changed, as it were, the very roots of man's emotions by their influence on the spirit of chivalry and on the spirit of romance; and later still Shakespeare found his Mab, and probably his Puck, and one knows not how much else of his faery kingdom, in Celtic legend; while at the beginning of our own day Sir Walter Scott gave Highland legends and Highland excitability so great a mastery over all romance that they seem romance itself.[7]

In our own time Scandinavian tradition, because of the imagination of Richard Wagner and of William Morris and of the earlier and, as I think, greater Heinrich Ibsen,[8] has created a new romance, and through the imagination of Richard Wagner, become all but the most passionate element in the arts of the modern world. There is indeed but one other

---

4. A dictum by visionary English artist Samuel Palmer (1805–1881).
5. St. Patrick's Purgatory is an island in Lough Derg, County Donegal, Ireland, where Catholic pilgrims come to undergo rigorous penitence, doing without food and sleep as they complete a fixed cycle of prayers.
6. The *Divina Commedia* by Italian poet Dante Alighieri (1265–1321), long regarded as one of the germinal literary texts of Western civilization.
7. Scottish novelist and poet Sir Walter Scott (1771–1832), whose work frequently treats Scottish highland themes and settings.
8. German composer Richard Wagner (1813–1883), whose epic operas Yeats saw as inspiring examples of "national" use of myth and legend; poet and designer William Morris (1834–1896), whose revival of Medieval and Arthurian themes and models Yeats admired as a young man, and who also translated Icelandic heroic literature; and Norwegian dramatist Henrik Ibsen (1828–1906), whose prose realist style Yeats generally disliked, but whose resistance to convention and to censorship he admired.

element as passionate, the still unfaded legends of Arthur and of the Holy Grail; and now a new fountain of legends, and, as I think, a more abundant fountain than any in Europe, is being opened, the fountain of Gaelic legends; the tale of Deirdre, who alone among women who have set men mad was at once the white flame and the red flame, wisdom and loveliness; the tale of the Sons of Tuireann, with its unintelligible mysteries, an old Grail Quest as I think; the tale of the four children changed into four swans, and lamenting over many waters; the tale of the love of Cuchulain for an immortal goddess, and his coming home to a mortal woman in the end; the tale of his many battles at the ford with that dear friend he kissed before the battles, and over whose dead body he wept when he had killed him; the tale of his death and of the lamentations of Emer; the tale of the flight of Grainne with Diarmuid, strangest of all tales of the fickleness of woman, and the tale of the coming of Oisin out of faeryland, and of his memories and lamentations. 'The Celtic movement,' as I understand it, is principally the opening of this fountain, and none can measure of how great importance it may be to coming times, for every new fountain of legends is a new intoxication for the imagination of the world. It comes at a time when the imagination of the world is as ready, as it was at the coming of the tales of Arthur and of the Grail, for a new intoxication.[9] The reaction against the rationalism of the eighteenth century has mingled with a reaction against the materialism of the nineteenth century, and the symbolical movement, which has come to perfection in Germany in Wagner, in England in the Pre-Raphaelites, in France in Villiers de l'Isle-Adam, and Mallarmé, and in Maeterlinck, and has stirred the imagination of Ibsen and D'Annunzio, is certainly the only movement that is saying new things.[1] The arts by brooding upon their own intensity have become religious, and are seeking, as I think Verhaeren[2] has said, to create a sacred book. They must, as religious thought has always done, utter themselves through legends; and the Sclavonic and Finnish legends tell of strange woods and seas, and the Scandinavian legends are held by a great master, and tell also of strange woods and seas, and the Welsh legends are held by almost as many great masters as the Greek legends, while the Irish legends move among known woods and seas, and have so much of a new beauty, that they may well give the opening century its most memorable symbols.

---

9. Yeats here evokes key narratives from the Ulster and Fenian cycles of Irish legend. He had already drawn on the Middle Irish dialogues of Saint Patrick and Oisin in his 1889 poem "The Wanderings of Oisin," and he would respond to other legendary material mentioned here in plays such as *Diarmuid and Grania* (1901), *Deirdre* (1907), and *The Only Jealousy of Emer* (1921), amongst other works.
1. Yeats had seen the poetic play *Axël* by French Symbolist Villiers de l'Isle Adam (1838–1889) in Paris in 1894, and it exerted a profound influence, inspiring work such as his own play *The Shadowy Waters* (1900); he had been introduced to the work of French Symbolist poet Stéphane Mallarmé (1842–1898) by Arthur Symons (1865–1945) in the early 1890s; his enthusiasm for Belgian dramatist Maurice Maeterlinck (1862–1949) and for Italian writer Gabriele d'Annunzio (1863–1938) was short-lived.
2. Emile Verhaeren (1855–1916), Belgian poet, whom Yeats had met briefly in early 1898.

The Irish Literary Theatre[1] (1899)

Norway has a great and successful school of contemporary drama, and Spain and Germany, though they have an admiration for bad work, which Norway has not, have good dramatists whom they admire. Elsewhere— and there is no difference of opinion on this matter among men of letters—vulgarity and triviality have an almost perfect possession of the theatre. Now and then a play is better than the others, and when it is nearly as good as a good, but still ephemeral novel, the critics, who are not men of letters, call it a great play, and common playgoers believe them, because "it does not accuse them of want of wit," being but the image of a passing fashion. One finds the literary drama alone, when some great work, old enough to be a national superstition, is revived with scenery and costume so elaborate that nobody need listen to the words unless he likes, or in little and unexpensive theatres which associations of men of letters hire from time to time that they may see upon the stage—the plays of Henrik Ibsen, Maurice Maeterlinck, Gerard Hauptmann, Jose Echegaray,[2] or of some less famous dramatist who has written, in the only way literature can be written, to express a dream which has taken possession of his mind. These associations, the Theatre Libre and the Independent Theatre[3] especially, have, in the face of violent opposition, trained actors who have become famous, and had a powerful influence even upon those plays, which are written to please as many people as possible that they may make as much money as possible. We are about to attempt in Dublin what has been done in London and Paris, and we will, if we have even the smallest success, produce every Spring a play or two founded upon some Irish subject. We believe that common playgoers will not dislike us very much, certainly nothing like as much as they dislike those who make similar attempts in other countries, and that they will come in time to like us; for even if they do not understand that we offer them plays written in a more sincere spirit than plays which are written to please as many people as possible, they will understand that we are writing about the country in which they live, and re-telling those ancient, heroic tales which are chief among its treasures. We believe, too, that the people who read books and have ceased to go to the theatre will find out about us gradually, as they have found out about similar attempts in other countries, and will come to see our plays, and will even stay a little longer in town for their sake. There is no feeling, except religious feeling, which moves masses of men so powerfully as national feeling, and upon this, more widely spread among all classes in Ireland to-day than at any time this century, we build our principal hopes. It will give us just that help which men of letters have

1. Yeats had announced plans for the Irish Literary Theatre in summer 1897. This essay formed part of his campaign to draw attention to and cultivate an audience for it.
2. Gerhart Hauptmann (1862–1946), German dramatist who introduced Ibsen-influenced realist methods to Germany; José Echegaray (1833–1916), Spanish dramatist, and Nobel laureate in 1904.
3. French actor-manager André Antoine (1858–1943) founded the Theatre Libre in Paris in 1887 to play Ibsenite drama, and this had been the inspiration for the Independent Theatre in London, founded in 1891 by J. T. Grein (1862–1935).

lacked for similar attempts elsewhere, and keep us out of the shadow of dilletantism. About six weeks ago an anonymous play in four acts about an old Irish story and a musical play with words by a nun, and about an old Irish story, were acted in Letterkenny before enthusiastic audiences. I have no way of knowing whether these plays had literary merit, but I am certain that their audiences did not find in them, or expect to find in them, that superficial appeal to the nerves and to vulgar appetites which has made sincere drama impossible in the ordinary modern theatre. They appealed to the national feeling, and because all feeling is more or less imaginative, were understood, as plays were understood before modern vulgarity began its inventions. Although we have for the moment decided to produce no plays not upon Irish subjects, we know that when Irish literature is more developed Irishmen will utter the personality of their country, no matter what subjects they write about. When they have learned their lesson, when they have come to understand the country they live in, they will write admirably about other countries. All literature and all art is national. The Eastern poets, Homer and the Greek dramatists, the writers of the Icelandic Sagas, Dante, Shakespeare in "King Lear" and in the historical plays, Goethe in "Faust," the only one among his works which has moved the imagination of the world, and Ibsen at almost all times, have written about the history and legends of their own countries. Shakespeare, Calderon, Milton,[4] in writing of the history and legends of other countries, have written out of emotions and thoughts that came to them because of their profound sympathy with the life about them. Egyptian art differs from Greek, Dutch art differs from Italian, French art differs from English, because they have come out of different nationalities. The curious imaginative sterility of what are called the Irish educated classes has its source in that spirit of antagonism to the life about them, which until recently has cut them off from the foundations of literature, and left their imaginations cold and conventional. That small minority, which from time to time, has divided itself from its class, has been so fruitful in imagination that one understands how much evil has been worked by a bad theory and how great the flood may be once the flood-gates have been lifted. Victor Hugo has said that in the theatre the mob became a people,[5] and, though this could be perfectly true only of ancient times when the theatre was a part of the ceremonial of religion, I have some hope that, if we have enough success to go on from year to year, we may help to bring a little ideal thought into the common thought of our times. The writers, on whom we principally depend, have laboured to be citizens, not merely of that passing and modern Ireland of prosaic cynicism and prosaic rivalries which it may be their duty to condemn, but of that eternal and ancient Ireland which has lived from old times in tender and heroic tales and in the unwearied love of many thousand men and women who have been poor in all other things. And they have laboured to write of Irish and all other things, as men should write who have never doubted that all things

4. Pedro Calderón (1600–1681), Spanish dramatist. John Milton (1608–1674), English poet.
5. A paraphrase from *Post-Scriptum de Ma Vie* by French novelist Victor Hugo (1802–1885).

are shadows of spiritual things, and that men may come to the gates of peace by beautiful and august thoughts.

From Irish Language and Irish Literature[1] (1900)

* * * Side by side with the spread of the Irish language, and with much writing in the Irish language, must go on much expression of Irish emotion and Irish thought, much writing about Irish things and people, in the English language, for no man can write well except in the language he has been born and bred to, and no man, as I think, becomes perfectly cultivated except through the influence of that language; and this writing must for a long time to come be the chief influence in shaping the opinions and the emotions of the leisured classes in Ireland in so far as they are concerned with Irish things, and the more sincere it is, the more lofty it is, the more beautiful it is, the more will the general life of Ireland be sweetened by its influence, through its influence over a few governing minds. It will always be too separate from the general life of Ireland to influence it directly, and it was chiefly because I believed this that I differed so strongly in 1892 and 1893 from Sir Charles Gavan Duffy and his supporters, who wished to give such writing an accidental and fleeting popularity by uniting it with politics and economics.[2] I believe that Ireland cannot have a Burns or a Dickens,[3] because the mass of the people cease to understand any poetry when they cease to understand the Irish language, which is the language of their imagination, and because the middle class is the great supporter and originator of the more popular kind of novels, and we have no middle class to speak of; but I believe that we may have a poetry like that of Wordsworth and Shelley and Keats, and a prose like that of Meredith and Pater and Ruskin.[4] There will be a few of all classes who will read this kind of literature, but the rest will read and listen to the songs of some wandering Raftery, or of some poet like Dr. Hyde,[5] who has himself high culture, but makes his songs out of the thoughts and

1. Yeats's difficulties in reconciling the English and Irish aspects of his artistic life—already marked in his 1892 articles "Hopes and Fears for Irish Literature" and "The De-Anglicising of Ireland" (pp. 258–62)—continued to trouble him in the late 1890s and beyond. This article was written in response to the frequent claims of Irish Nationalists that only literature written in the Irish language could be considered truly Irish, with Yeats once more urging that literary merit and imaginative power, rather than narrow ideological concerns, should be the prime consideration in expressing "Irish emotion and Irish thought." The article, published as a letter in the Irish Nationalist paper *The Leader*, is addressed to its editor, D. P. Moran (1869–1936).
2. Yeats had clashed with Charles Gavan Duffy (1816–1903), a founder of the Nationalist newspaper the *Nation* and a member of the Young Ireland movement of the 1840s, over the selection of Irish books for a series to be issued by the New Irish Library. Yeats had pressed for well-written books, and he saw Duffy as choosing titles merely for their didactic Nationalist content.
3. Scottish poet Robert Burns (1759–1796), and English novelist Charles Dickens (1812–1870).
4. English Romantic poets William Wordsworth (1770–1850), Percy Bysshe Shelley (1792–1822), and John Keats (1795–1821); and English writers George Meredith (1828–1909), Walter Pater (1839–1894), and John Ruskin (1819–1900), all particularly admired for their prose style.
5. Folklorist, translator, and poet Douglas Hyde (1860–1949) had published several volumes of Irish folk-poetry, and he was at this point collecting material for *Songs Ascribed to Raftery* (1903), a volume of the work of Anthony Raftery (c. 1784–1835), an itinerant Irish poet and fiddler. Yeats regarded Raftery, the subject of his essay "Dust Hath Closed Helen's Eye" (see pp. 183–87), as one of the last of the traditional Irish folk-poets.

emotions he finds everywhere about him, and out of the circumstances of a life that is kept poetical by a still useful language, or they will go to perdition with their minds stuffed full of English vulgarity; till perhaps a time has come when no Irishman need write in any but his own language.

We can bring that day the nearer by not quarrelling about names, and by not bringing to literary discussion, which needs a delicate and careful temper, the exasperated and violent temper we have learned from a century of political discussion. You have decided, and rightly, considering your purpose, to call all "literature concerning Ireland written in English," "Anglo-Irish literature," and I shall certainly do the same when I would persuade a man that nothing written in English can unite him perfectly to the past and future of his country, but I will certainly call it Irish literature, for short, when I would persuade him that "Farewell to Bally-shannon and the Winding Banks of Erne" should be more to him than "The Absent-Minded Beggar,"[6] or when I am out of temper with all hyphenated words, or with all names that are a mixture of Latin and English. Such things are governed by usage and convenience, and I do not foresee a day when there will not be Englishmen who will call Walt Whitman English literature,[7] and merely because they like him, and Englishmen who will call him American literature, and merely because they dislike him. And I would be sorry to see a day when I should not find a certain beautiful sermon of St. Columbanus, which compares life to a roadway on which we journey for a little while, and to the rising and falling of smoke,[8] in accounts of Irish literature, as well as in accounts of the Latin literature of the Early Church.

Whether we dispute about names or not, the temper of our dispute is perhaps of more importance than the subject, and it is certainly of especial importance when we discuss those among our writers who have any rank, however small, in that great household I have spoken of. Ruskin, Meredith, Pater, Shelley, Keats, Wordsworth, had all to face misunderstanding and misrepresentation, and sometimes contumely, for they spoke to an evil time out of the depths of the heart, and if England had been accustomed to use in literary discussion the coarse methods of political discussion, instead of descending to them in rare moments of excitement, she would not now have that remnant which alone unites her to the England of Shakespeare and Milton. In Ireland, too, it may be those very men, who have made a subtle personal way of expressing themselves, instead of being content with English as it is understood in the newspapers, or who see all things reflected in their own souls, which are from the parent fountain of their race, instead of filling their work with the circumstance of a life which is dominated by England, who may be recognised in the future as

6. Yeats included the ballad "The Winding Banks of Erne" by Irish poet William Allingham (1824–1889) in his *Book of Irish Verse* (1895). He regarded "The Absent-Minded Beggar," a ballad by Rudyard Kipling (1865–1936) that exhorts support for the families of British soldiers fighting in the Boer War, as the epitome of didactic, political, writing and crude British imperialism.
7. Walt Whitman (1819–1892) was at this point beginning to be viewed by European critics as one of the key figures in a distinctively American tradition of poetry. To argue that he was an "English" poet merely on the grounds that he used English, or was an "American" poet merely because he lived and wrote in America, would be crude and redundant, Yeats implies, since the wellsprings of inspiration, rather than language, determine a writer's cultural alignments.
8. From Sermon V of Saint Columbanus (c. 543–615).

most Irish, though their own time entangled in the surfaces of things may often think them lacking in everything that is Irish. The delicate, obscure, mysterious song of my friend, "A.E.,"[9] which has, as I know, comforted the wise and beautiful when dying, but has hardly come into the hands of the middle class—I use the word to describe an attitude of mind more than an accident of birth—and has no obviously Irish characteristics, may be, or rather must be, more Irish than any of those books of stories or of verses which reflect so many obviously Irish characteristics that every newspaper calls them, in the trying phrase of 1845, "racy of the soil"[1] * * *

From The Symbolism of Poetry (1900)

* * *

All writers, all artists of any kind, in so far as they have had any philosophical or critical power, perhaps just in so far as they have been deliberate artists at all, have had some philosophy, some criticism of their art; and it has often been this philosophy, or this criticism, that has evoked their most startling inspiration, calling into outer life some portion of the divine life, or of the buried reality, which could alone extinguish in the emotions what their philosophy or their criticism would extinguish in the intellect. They have sought for no new thing, it may be, but only to understand and to copy the pure inspiration of early times, but because the divine life wars upon our outer life, and must needs change its weapons and its movements as we change ours, inspiration has come to them in beautiful startling shapes. The scientific movements brought with it a literature which was always tending to lose itself in externalities of all kinds, in opinion, in declamation, in picturesque writing, in word-painting, or in what Mr. Symons[1] has called an attempt 'to build in brick and mortar inside the covers of a book'; and now writers have begun to dwell upon the element of evocation, of suggestion, upon what we call the symbolism in great writers.

II

In 'Symbolism in Painting'[2] I tried to describe the element of symbolism that is in pictures and sculpture, and described a little the symbolism in poetry, but did not describe at all the continuous indefinable symbolism which is the substance of all style.

There are no lines with more melancholy beauty than these by Burns—

9. The pseudonym of Yeats's friend, Irish artist and poet George Russell (1867–1935).
1. This phrase, favored by writers of the Young Ireland movement, became ubiquitous as a description of writing that was considered "authentic" in its representations of Irish life.
1. English poet and critic Arthur Symons (1865–1945), who had introduced Yeats to the French Symbolists.
2. An essay first written in 1898, and that preceded "Symbolism in Poetry" when reprinted in *Ideas of Good and Evil* (1903).

> 'The white moon is setting behind the white wave,
>   And Time is setting with me, O!'[3]

and these lines are perfectly symbolical. Take from them the whiteness of
the moon and of the wave, whose relation to the setting of Time is too
subtle for the intellect, and you take from them their beauty. But, when
all are together, moon and wave and whiteness and setting Time and the
last melancholy cry, they evoke an emotion which cannot be evoked by
any other arrangement of colours and sounds and forms. We may call this
metaphorical writing, but it is better to call it symbolical writing, because
metaphors are not profound enough to be moving, when they are not
symbols, and when they are symbols they are the most perfect, because
the most subtle, outside of pure sound, and through them one can best
find out what symbols are. If one begins the reverie with any beautiful
lines that one can remember, one finds they are like those by Burns. Begin
with this line by Blake—

> 'The gay fishes on the wave when the moon sucks up the dew;'[4]

or these lines by Nash—

> 'Brightness falls from the air,
>   Queens have died young and fair,
>   Dust hath closed Helen's eye;'[5]

or these lines by Shakespeare—

> 'Timon hath made his everlasting mansion
>   Upon the beached verge of the salt flood;
>   Who once a day with his embossed froth
>   The turbulent surge shall cover;'[6]

or take some line that is quite simple, that gets its beauty from its place
in a story, and see how it flickers with the light of the many symbols that
have given the story its beauty, as a sword-blade may flicker with the light
of burning towers.

All sounds, all colours, all forms, either because of their preordained
energies or because of long association, evoke indefinable and yet precise
emotions, or, as I prefer to think, call down among us certain disembodied
powers, whose footsteps over our hearts we call emotions; and when sound,
and colour, and form are in a musical relation, a beautiful relation to one
another, they become, as it were, one sound, one colour, one form, and
evoke an emotion that is made out of their distinct evocations and yet is
one emotion. The same relation exists between all portions of every work
of art, whether it be an epic or a song, and the more perfect it is, and the
more various and numerous the elements that have flowed into its perfection, the more powerful will be the emotion, the power, the god it calls

3. From "Open the Door to Me" by Scottish poet Robert Burns (1759–1796), but misquoting
   "white" for "wan."
4. From *Europe, a Prophecy* by English poet William Blake (1757–1827).
5. From the song "Adieu, Farewell Earth's Bliss" in the comic play *Summer's Last Will and Testament* (1600) by English dramatist Thomas Nashe (1567–1601).
6. From Act V, scene 1 of Shakespeare's *Timon of Athens* (1623).

among us. Because an emotion does not exist, or does not become perceptible and active among us, till it has found its expression, in colour or in sound or in form, or in all of these, and because no two modulations or arrangements of these evoke the same emotion, poets and painters and musicians, and in a less degree because their effects are momentary, day and night and cloud and shadow, are continually making and unmaking mankind. It is indeed only those things which seem useless or very feeble that have any power, and all those things that seem useful or strong, armies, moving wheels, modes of architecture, modes of government, speculations of the reason, would have been a little different if some mind long ago had not given itself to some emotion, as a woman gives herself to her lover, and shaped sounds or colours or forms, or all of these, into a musical relation, that their emotion might live in other minds. A little lyric evokes an emotion, and this emotion gathers others about it and melts into their being in the making of some great epic; and at last, needing an always less delicate body, or symbol, as it grows more powerful, it flows out, with all it has gathered, among the blind instincts of daily life, where it moves a power within powers, as one sees ring within ring in the stem of an old tree. * * *

III

The purpose of rhythm, it has always seemed to me, is to prolong the moment of contemplation, the moment when we are both asleep and awake, which is the one moment of creation, by hushing us with an alluring monotony, while it holds us waking by variety, to keep us in that state of perhaps real trance, in which the mind liberated from the pressure of the will is unfolded in symbols. If certain sensitive persons listen persistently to the ticking of a watch, or gaze persistently on the monotonous flashing of a light, they fall into the hypnotic trance; and rhythm is but the ticking of a watch made softer, that one must needs listen, and various, that one may not be swept beyond memory or grow weary of listening; while the patterns of the artist are but the monotonous flash woven to take the eyes in a subtler enchantment. I have heard in meditation voices that were forgotten the moment they had spoken; and I have been swept, when in more profound meditation, beyond all memory but of those things that came from beyond the threshold of waking life. * * * So I think that in the making and in the understanding of a work of art, and the more easily if it is full of patterns and symbols and music, we are lured to the threshold of sleep, and it may be far beyond it, without knowing that we have ever set our feet upon the steps of horn or of ivory.

IV

Besides emotional symbols, symbols that evoke emotions alone,—and in this sense all alluring or hateful things are symbols, although their relations with one another are too subtle to delight us fully, away from rhythm and pattern,—there are intellectual symbols, symbols that evoke ideas alone, or ideas mingled with emotions; and outside the very definite traditions of mysticism and the less definite criticism of certain modern poets, these alone are called symbols. Most things belong to one or another kind, according to the way we speak of them and the companions we give them, for symbols, associated with ideas that are more than fragments of the shadows thrown upon the intellect by the emotions they evoke, are the playthings of the allegorist or the pedant, and soon pass away. If I say 'white' or 'purple' in an ordinary line of poetry, they evoke emotions so exclusively that I cannot say why they move me; but if I say them in the same mood, in the same breath with such obvious intellectual symbols as a cross or a crown of thorns, I think of purity and sovereignty; while innumerable meanings, which are held to one another by the bondage of subtle suggestion, and alike in the emotions and in the intellect, move visibly through my mind, and move invisibly beyond the threshold of sleep, casting lights and shadows of an indefinable wisdom on what had seemed before, it may be, but sterility and noisy violence. It is the intellect that decides where the reader shall ponder over the procession of the symbols, and if the symbols are merely emotional, he gazes from amid the accidents and destinies of the world; but if the symbols are intellectual too, he becomes himself a part of pure intellect, and he is himself mingled with the procession. If I watch a rushy pool in the moonlight, my emotion at its beauty is mixed with memories of the man that I have seen ploughing by its margin, or of the lovers I saw there a night ago; but if I look at the moon herself and remember any of her ancient names and meanings, I move among divine people, and things that have shaken off our mortality, the tower of ivory, the queen of waters, the shining stag among enchanted woods, the white hare sitting upon the hilltop, the fool of faery with his shining cup full of dreams, and it may be 'make a friend of one of these images of wonder,' and 'meet the Lord in the air.'[7] So, too, if one is moved by Shakespeare, who is content with emotional symbols that he may come the nearer to our sympathy, one is mixed with the whole spectacle of the world; while if one is moved by Dante, or by the myth of Demeter,[8] one is mixed into the shadow of God or of a goddess. So, too, one is furthest from symbols when one is busy doing this or that, but the soul moves among symbols and unfolds in symbols when trance, or madness, or deep meditation has withdrawn it from every impulse but its own. * * * [the arts] cannot overcome the slow dying of men's hearts that we call the progress of the world, and lay their hands upon men's heart-strings again, without becoming the garment of religion as in old times.

V

If people were to accept the theory that poetry moves us because of its symbolism, what change should one look for in the manner of our poetry? A return to the way of our fathers, a casting out of descriptions of nature for the sake of nature, of the moral law for the sake of the moral law, a casting out of all anecdotes and of that brooding over scientific opinion that so often extinguished the central flame in Tennyson,[9] and of that

7. From A Vision of the Last Judgement (1810) by William Blake.
8. Goddess of corn in Greek mythology.
9. Alfred, Lord Tennyson (1809–1892), English poet.

vehemence that would make us do or not do certain things; or, in other words, we should come to understand that the beryl stone[1] was enchanted by our fathers that it might unfold the pictures in its heart, and not to mirror our own excited faces, or the boughs waving outside the window. With this change of substance, this return to imagination, this understanding that the laws of art, which are the hidden laws of the world, can alone bind the imagination, would come a change of style, and we would cast out of serious poetry those energetic rhythms, as of a man running, which are the invention of the will with its eyes always on something to be done or undone; and we would seek out those wavering, meditative, organic rhythms, which are the embodiment of the imagination, that neither desires nor hates, because it has done with time, and only wishes to gaze upon some reality, some beauty; nor would it be any longer possible for anybody to deny the importance of form, in all its kinds, for although you can expound an opinion, or describe a thing when your words are not quite well chosen, you cannot give a body to something that moves beyond the senses, unless your words are as subtle, as complex, as full of mysterious life, as the body of a flower or of a woman. The form of sincere poetry, unlike the form of the popular poetry, may indeed be sometimes obscure, or ungrammatical as in some of the best of the Songs of Innocence and Experience,[2] but it must have the perfections that escape analysis, the subtleties that have a new meaning every day, and it must have all this whether it be but a little song made out of a moment of dreamy indolence, or some great epic made out of the dreams of one poet and of a hundred generations whose hands were never weary of the sword.

From Magic (1901)

I

I believe in the practice and philosophy of what we have agreed to call magic, in what I must call the evocation of spirits, though I do not know what they are, in the power of creating magical illusions, in the visions of truth in the depths of the mind when the eyes are closed; and I believe in three doctrines, which have, as I think, been handed down from early times, and been the foundations of nearly all magical practices. These doctrines are—

(1) That the borders of our mind are ever shifting, and that many minds can flow into one another, as it were, and create or reveal a single mind, a single energy.

(2) That the borders of our memories are as shifting, and that our memories are a part of one great memory, the memory of Nature herself.

(3) That this great mind and great memory can be evoked by symbols.

I often think I would put this belief in magic from me if I could, for I have come to see or to imagine, in men and women, in houses, in handicrafts, in nearly all sights and sounds, a certain evil, a certain ugliness,

1. A transparent gemstone, associated with magical properties by Yeats.
2. *Songs of Innocence* (1789) and *Songs of Experience* (1794) by William Blake.

that comes from the slow perishing through the centuries of a quality of mind that made this belief and its evidences common over the world.

VIII

I have now described that belief in magic which has set me all but unwilling among those lean and fierce minds who are at war with their time, who cannot accept the days as they pass, simply and gladly; and I look at what I have written with some alarm, for I have told more of the ancient secret than many among my fellow-students think it right to tell. I have come to believe so many strange things because of experience, that I see little reason to doubt the truth of many things that are beyond my experience; and it may be that there are beings who watch over that ancient secret, as all tradition affirms, and resent, and perhaps avenge, too fluent speech. They say in the Aran Islands[1] that if you speak over-much of the things of Faery your tongue becomes like a stone, and it seems to me, though doubtless naturalistic reason would call it auto-suggestion or the like, that I have often felt my tongue become just so heavy and clumsy. More than once, too, as I wrote this very essay I have become uneasy, and have torn up some paragraph, not for any literary reason, but because some incident or some symbol that would perhaps have meant nothing to the reader, seemed, I know not why, to belong to hidden things. Yet I must write or be of no account to any cause, good or evil; I must commit what merchandise of wisdom I have to this ship of written speech, and after all, I have many a time watched it put out to sea with not less alarm when all the speech was rhyme. We who write, we who bear witness, must often hear our hearts cry out against us, complaining because of their hidden things, and I know not but he who speaks of wisdom may sometimes, in the change that is coming upon the world, have to fear the anger of the people of Faery, whose country is the heart of the world—'The Land of the Living Heart.' Who can keep always to the little pathway between speech and silence, where one meets none but discreet revelations? And surely, at whatever risk, we must cry out that imagination is always seeking to remake the world according to the impulses and the patterns in that great Mind, and that great Memory? Can there be anything so important as to cry out that what we call romance, poetry, intellectual beauty, is the only signal that the supreme Enchanter, or some one in His councils, is speaking of what has been, and shall be again, in the consummation of time?

---

1. Yeats had visited the Aran Islands, off the west coast of Ireland, in summer 1896. The island culture was at that time little disturbed by visitors, and almost exclusively Irish-speaking.

The Reform of the Theatre[1] (1903)

I think the theatre must be reformed in its plays, its speaking, its acting, and its scenery. That is to say, I think there is nothing good about it at present.

1st. We have to write or find plays that will make the theatre a place of intellectual excitement—a place where the mind goes to be liberated as it was liberated by the theatres of Greece and England and France at certain great moments of their history, and as it is liberated in Scandinavia to-day. If we are to do this we must learn that beauty and truth are always justified of themselves, and that their creation is a greater service to our country than writing that compromises either in the seeming service of a cause. We will, doubtless, come more easily to truth and beauty because we love some cause with all but all our heart; but we must remember when truth and beauty open their mouths to speak, that all other mouths should be as silent as Finn bade the son of Lugaidh be in the houses of the great.[2] Truth and beauty judge and are above judgment. They justify and have no need of justification.

Such plays will require, both in writers and audiences, a stronger feeling for beautiful and appropriate language than one finds in the ordinary theatre. St. Beuve[3] has said that there is nothing immortal in literature except style, and it is precisely this sense of style, once common among us, that is hardest for us to recover. I do not mean by style words with an air of literature about them, what is ordinarily called eloquent writing. The speeches of Falstaff are as perfect in their style as the soliloquies of Hamlet. One must be able to make a king of faery or an old countryman or a modern lover speak that language which is his and nobody else's, and speak it with so much of emotional subtlety that the hearer may find it hard to know whether it is the thought or the word that has moved him, or whether these could be separated at all.

If one does not know how to construct, if one cannot arrange much complicated life into a single action, one's work will not hold the attention or linger in the memory, but if one is not in love with words it will lack the delicate movement of living speech that is the chief garment of life; and because of this lack the great realists seem to the lovers of beautiful art to be wise in this generation, and for the next generation, perhaps, but not for all generations that are to come.

2nd. But if we are to restore words to their sovereignty we must make speech even more important than gesture upon the stage.

I have been told that I desire a monotonous chant, but that is not true, for though a monotonous chant may be a safer beginning for an actor

---

1. From *Samhain*, an annual journal issued by Yeats between 1901 and 1904 to promote the Irish Literary Theatre and recent developments in Irish drama, and named after an ancient Celtic festival held on the last night of October, marking the beginning of winter.
2. The chapter "The Best Men of the Fianna" in *Gods and Fighting Men* (1904), Lady Gregory's redaction of the Fenian cycle of Irish mythology, recounts this incident, in which Finn McCool, the central figure of the Fenian cycle, instructs his relative Lughaidh's son, "If you have a mind to be a good champion, be quiet in a great man's house."
3. French critic Charles Augustin Sainte-Beuve (1804–1869).

than the broken and prosaic speech of ordinary recitation, it puts one to sleep none the less. The sing-song in which a child says a verse is a right beginning, though the child grows out of it. An actor should understand how to so discriminate cadence from cadence, and to so cherish the musical lineaments of verse or prose that he delights the ear with a continually varied music. Certain passages of lyrical feeling, or where one wishes, as in the Angel's part in *The Hour Glass*,[4] to make a voice sound like the voice of an immortal, may be spoken upon pure notes which are carefully recorded and learned as if they were the notes of a song. Whatever method one adopts one must always be certain that the work of art, as a whole, is masculine and intellectual, in its sound as in its form.

3rd. We must simplify acting, especially in poetical drama, and in prose drama that is remote from real life like my *Hour Glass*. We must get rid of everything that is restless, everything that draws the attention away from the sound of the voice, or from the few moments of intense expression, whether that expression is through the voice or through the hands; we must from time to time substitute for the movements that the eye sees the nobler movements that the heart sees, the rhythmical movements that seem to flow up into the imagination from some deeper life than that of the individual soul.

4th. Just as it is necessary to simplify gesture that it may accompany speech without being its rival, it is necessary to simplify both the form and colour of scenery and costume. As a rule the background should be but a single colour, so that the persons in the play wherever they stand, may harmonize with it, and preoccupy our attention. In other words it should be thought out not as one thinks out a landscape, but as if it were the background of a portrait, and this is especially necessary on a small stage where the moment the stage is filled the painted forms of the background are broken up and lost. Even when one has to represent trees or hills they should be treated in most cases decoratively, they should be little more than an unobtrusive pattern. There must be nothing unnecessary, nothing that will distract the attention from speech and movement. An art is always at its greatest when it is most human. Greek acting was great because it did everything with the voice, and modern acting may be great when it does everything with voice and movement. But an art which smothers these things with bad painting, with innumerable garish colours, with continual restless mimicries of the surface of life, is an art of fading humanity, a decaying art.

4. A play by Yeats (1903).

On Taking 'The Playboy' to London (1907)

The failure of the audience to understand this powerful and strange work (*The Playboy of the Western World*[1]) has been the one serious failure of our movement, and it could not have happened but that the greater number of those who came to shout down the play were no regular part of our audience at all, but members of parties and societies whose main interests are political. We have been denounced with even greater violence than on the first production of the play for announcing that we should carry it to London. We cannot see that an attack, which we believe to have been founded on a misunderstanding of the nature of literature, should prevent us from selecting, as our custom is, whatever of our best comes within the compass of our players at the time, to show in some English theatres. Nearly all strong and strange writing is attacked on its appearance, and those who press it upon the world may not cease from pressing it, for their justification is its ultimate acceptance. Ireland is passing through a crisis in the life of the mind greater than any she has known since the rise of the Young Ireland party,[2] and based upon a principle which sets many in opposition to the habits of thought and feeling come down from that party, for the seasons change, and need and occupation with them. Many are beginning to recognise the right of the individual mind to see the world in its own way, to cherish the thoughts which separate men from one another, and that are the creators of distinguished life, instead of those thoughts that had made one man like another if they could, and have but succeeded in setting hysteria and insincerity in place of confidence and self-possession. To the Young Ireland writers, who have the ear of Ireland, though not its distracted mind, truth was historical and external and not a self-consistent personal vision, and it is but according to ancient custom that the new truth should force its way amid riot and great anger.

The Play of Modern Manners (1908)

Of all artistic forms that have had a large share of the world's attention, the worst is the play about modern educated people. Except where it is superficial or deliberately argumentative it fills one's soul with a sense of commonness as with dust. It has one mortal ailment. It cannot become impassioned, that is to say, vital, without making somebody gushing and sentimental. Educated and well-bred people do not wear their hearts upon their sleeves, and they have no artistic and charming language except light

1. *The Playboy of the Western World*, by John Millington Synge (1871–1909), playwright and co-founder, with Yeats and Lady Gregory, of the Abbey Theatre, had sparked a storm of protests during its first performances in January 1907 and renewed protests when plans were announced for its inclusion in the Abbey's English tour that summer (see p. 244, n. 9). For Yeats the disputes provided a forum for upholding the idea of artistic freedom, though in practice the tour avoided performing the play in some cities with significant Irish populations.
2. The "Young Ireland" patriotic movement of the 1840s had aimed to promote Irish Nationalism via Irish literature, and in Yeats's view had consequently made the mistake of judging literature by its political orthodoxy rather than by its creative and intellectual merit.

persiflage and no powerful language at all, and when they are deeply moved they look silently into the fireplace. Again and again I have watched some play of this sort with growing curiosity through the opening scene. The minor people argue, chaff one another, hint sometimes at some deeper stream of life just as we do in our houses, and I am content. But all the time I have been wondering why the chief character, the man who is to bear the burden of fate, is gushing, sentimental and quite without ideas. Then the great scene comes and I understand that he cannot be well-bred or self-possessed or intellectual, for if he were he would draw a chair to the fire and there would be no duologue at the end of the third act. Ibsen understood the difficulty and made all his characters a little provincial that they might not put each other out of countenance, and made a leading article sort of poetry, phrases about vine leaves and harps in the air it was possible to believe them using in their moments of excitement, and if the play needed more than that, they could always do something stupid. They could go out and hoist a flag as they do at the end of *Little Eyolf*.[1] One only understands that this manner, deliberately adopted one doubts not, had gone into his soul and filled it with dust, when one has noticed that he could no longer create a man of genius. The happiest writers are those that, knowing this form of play is slight and passing, keep to the surface, never showing anything but the arguments and the persiflage of daily observation, or now and then, instead of the expression of passion, a stage picture, a man holding a woman's hand or sitting with his head in his hands in dim light by the red glow of a fire. It was certainly an understanding of the slightness of the form, of its incapacity for the expression of the deeper sorts of passion, that made the French invent the play with a thesis, for where there is a thesis people can grow hot in argument, almost the only kind of passion that displays itself in our daily life. The novel of contemporary educated life is upon the other hand a permanent form because, having the power of psychological description, it can follow the thought of a man who is looking into the grate.

A Tower on the Apennines (1908)

The other day I was walking towards Urbino,[1] where I was to spend the night, having crossed the Apennines from San Sepolcro, and had come to a level place on the mountain-top near the journey's end. My friends[2] were in a carriage somewhere behind, on a road which was still ascending in great loops, and I was alone amid a visionary fantastic impossible scenery. It was sunset and the stormy clouds hung upon mountain after mountain, and far off on one great summit a cloud darker than the rest glimmered with lightning. Away south upon another mountain a mediaeval tower, with no building near nor any sign of life, rose into the clouds.

1. Play by Norwegian dramatist Henrik Ibsen (1828–1906).
1. Urbino, Italy, renowned for the artistic refinement and accomplishment of its court during the Renaissance.
2. Lady Gregory and her son Robert. Yeats toured Italy with them in early summer 1907.

I saw suddenly in the mind's eye an old man, erect and a little gaunt, standing in the door of the tower, while about him broke a windy light. He was the poet who had at last, because he had done so much for the word's sake, come to share in the dignity of the saint. He had hidden nothing of himself, but he had taken care of 'that dignity . . . the perfection of form . . . this lofty and severe quality . . . this virtue.' And though he had but sought it for the word's sake, or for a woman's praise, it had come at last into his body and his mind. Certainly as he stood there he knew how from behind that laborious mood, that pose, that genius, no flower of himself but all himself, looked out as from behind a mask that other Who alone of all men, the country people say, is not a hair's-breadth more nor less than six feet high.[3] He has in his ears well instructed voices and seeming solid sights are before his eyes, and not, as we say of many a one, speaking in metaphor, but as this were Delphi or Eleusis,[4] and the substance and the voice come to him among his memories which are of women's faces; for was it Columbanus[5] or another that wrote, 'There is one among the birds that is perfect, and one perfect among the fish'?

From Poetry and Tradition (1908)

II

Him who trembles before the flame and the flood,
And the winds that blow through the starry ways;
Let the starry winds and the flame and the flood
Cover over and hide, for he has no part
With the proud, majestical, multitude.[1]

Three types of men have made all beautiful things. Aristocracies have made beautiful manners, because their place in the world puts them above the fear of life, and the countrymen have made beautiful stories and beliefs, because they have nothing to lose and so do not fear, and the artists have made all the rest, because Providence has filled them with recklessness. All these look backward to a long tradition, for, being without fear, they have held to whatever pleased them. The others being always anxious have come to possess little that is good in itself, and are always changing from thing to thing, for whatever they do or have must be a means to something else, and they have so little belief that anything can be an end in itself, that they cannot understand you if you say, 'All the most valuable things are useless.' They prefer the stalk to the flower, and believe that painting and poetry exist that there may be instruction, and love

---

3. Yeats's vision is of the Italian writer Ludovico Ariosto (1474–1533), who had devoted his life to poetry, and whom Yeats imagines here as a man who has achieved what he called "Unity of Being" (see p. 222). The "Mask," Yeats wrote, is "the emotional antithesis to all that comes out of" the internal nature of subjective men.
4. Greek cities: Delphi was the site of the oracle; Eleusis was the origin of the sacred ancient rituals known as the Eleusinian Mysteries.
5. Saint Columbanus (c. 543–615), missionary and poet.
1. From Yeats's poem "To my Heart, bidding it have no Fear" (see p. 27).

that there may be children, and theatres that busy men may rest, and holidays that busy men may go on being busy. At all times they fear and even hate the things that have worth in themselves, for that worth may suddenly, as it were a fire, consume their book of Life, where the world is represented by ciphers and symbols; and before all else, they fear irreverent joy and unserviceable sorrow. It seems to them, that those who have been freed by position, by poverty, or by the traditions of Art, have something terrible about them, a light that is unendurable to eyesight. They complain much of that commandment that we can do almost what we will, if we do it gaily, and think that freedom is but a trifling with the world.

If we would find a company of our own way of thinking, we must go backward to turreted walls, to courts, to high rocky places, to little walled towns, to jesters like that jester of Charles the Fifth who made mirth out of his own death; to the Duke Guidobaldo in his sickness, or Duke Frederick[2] in his strength, to all those who understood that life is not lived at all, if not lived for contemplation or excitement.

Certainly we could not delight in that so courtly thing, the poetry of light love, if it were sad; for only when we are gay over a thing, and can play with it, do we show ourselves its master, and have minds clear enough for strength. The raging fire and the destructive sword are portions of eternity, too great for the eye of man, wrote Blake, and it is only before such things, before a love like that of Tristan and Iseult,[3] before noble or ennobled death, that the free mind permits itself aught but brief sorrow. That we may be free from all the rest, sullen anger, solemn virtue, calculating anxiety, gloomy suspicion, prevaricating hope, we should be reborn in gaiety. Because there is submission in a pure sorrow, we should sorrow alone over what is greater than ourselves, nor too soon admit that greatness, but all that is less than we are should stir us to some joy, for pure joy masters and impregnates; and so to world end, strength shall laugh and wisdom mourn.

From First Principles (1908)

* * *

In 1892, when I started the National Literary Society, and began a movement that was intended to lead up to the establishment of an Irish Dramatic School, the songs and ballads of Young Ireland[1] were used as examples to prove the personal, and therefore Irish art of A. E., Lionel

2. Guidobaldo di Montefeltro (1472–1508), duke of Urbino in Italy; and his father, Frederick (c. 1417–1482), who preceded him as duke, 1474–82. Both were renowned for their patronage of the arts, and for the cultivation and accomplishment of their courts.
3. Tristan and Iseult (or Isolde), the tragic lovers of Arthurian legend, are doomed to love each other after drinking a magic potion, but Iseult is already betrothed and marries another man. On his deathbed, Tristan sends for Iseult, who alone can heal him, but she arrives too late.
1. A patriotic movement founded in 1842 to promote Irish culture and nationalism.

Johnson, Catherine Tynan[2] and myself (see Lionel Johnson's Essay, *Poetry and Politics*) an unIrish thing. And yet those songs and ballads, with the exception of a small number which are partly copied from Gaelic models, and a few, almost all by Mangan, that have a personal style, are imitations of the poetry of Burns and Macaulay and Scott.[3] All literature in every country is derived from models, and as often as not these are foreign models, and it is the presence of a personal element alone that can give it nationality in a fine sense, the nationality of its maker. It is only before personality has been attained that a race struggling towards self-consciousness is the better for having, as in primitive times, nothing but native models, for before this has been attained it can neither assimilate nor reject. It was precisely at this passive moment, attainment approaching but not yet come, that the Irish heart and mind surrendered to England, or rather to what is most temporary in England; and Irish patriotism, content that the names and opinions should be Irish, was deceived and satisfied. It is always necessary to affirm and to reaffirm that nationality is in the things that escape analysis. We discover it, as we do the quality of saltness or sweetness, by the taste, and literature is a cultivation of taste.

※   ※   ※

In most modern countries when the moment has arrived for a personal impulse either for the first time or in some art hitherto external and conventional, the cry has been raised against the writer that he is preaching sexual immorality, for that is the subject upon which the newspapers, at any rate, most desire to see certain opinions always in force, and a view of the world as sexually unexciting as possible always displayed as if it were reality. Balzac in his preface to the *Comédie Humaine*,[4] had to defend himself from this charge, but it is not the burning question with us at present, for politics are our national passion. We have to free our vision of reality from political prepossession, for entangled as it were with all that is exaggerated, lifeless, frozen, in the attitudes of party, there are true thoughts about all those things that Ireland is most interested in, a reverie over the emptiness and the fullness of Irish character which is not less a part of wisdom because politics like art have their exaggerations. We cannot renounce political subjects in renouncing mere opinions, for that pleasure in the finer culture of England, that displeasure in Irish disunions and disorders which are the root of reasoned Unionism, are as certainly high and natural thoughts, as the self-denying enthusiasm that leads Mi-

2. "A.E." was the pseudonym of Yeats's friend, Irish artist and poet George Russell (1867–1935); English poet Lionel Johnson (1867–1902) was drawn to Irish themes under Yeats's influence, publishing *Ireland with Other Poems* in 1897 and the essay "Poetry and Patriotism" in *Poetry and Ireland: Essays by W. B. Yeats and Lionel Johnson*; Irish poet and novelist Katharine Tynan (1859–1931) was one of Yeats's closest friends in the late 1880s.

3. James Clarence Mangan (1803–1849) was the poet of the "Young Ireland" period for whom Yeats had the most enduring regard; Scottish poet Robert Burns (1759–1796), English historian and poet Thomas Macaulay (1800–1859), and Scottish poet and novelist Sir Walter Scott (1771–1832) all used the ballad as a form for writing "national" poetry.

4. French novelist Honoré de Balzac (1799–1850) referred to his collected fiction as *La Comédie Humaine* (the human comedy).

chael Gillane[5] to probable death or exile and Dervorgilla[6] to her remorse, and Patrick Sarsfield of *The White Cockade* to his sense of what a king should be;[7] and we cannot renounce them because politicians believe that one thought or another may help their opponents, any more than Balzac could have refused to write the *Comédie Humaine* because somebody was afraid Madame l'Epicière[8] might run away from her husband.

At the close of my speech at one of the performances we were asked to give to the British Association[9] I used these words:—

"When I was coming up in the train the other day from Galway, I began thinking how unlike your work was to my work, and then suddenly it struck me that it was all the same. A picture arose before my mind's eye: I saw Adam numbering the creatures of Eden; soft and terrible, foul and fair, they all went before him. That, I thought, is the man of science, naming and numbering, for our understanding, everything in the world. But then, I thought, we writers, do we not also number and describe, though with a difference? You are busy with the exterior world, and we with the interior. Science understands that everything must be known in the world our eyes look at; there is nothing too obscure, too common, too vile, to be the subject of knowledge. When a man of science discovers a new species, or a new law, you do not ask the value of the law, or the value of the species, before you do him honour; you leave all that to the judgment of the generations. It is your pride that in you the human race contemplates all things with so pure, so disinterested an eyesight that it forgets its own necessities and infirmities, all its hopes and fears, in the contemplation of truth for the sake of truth, reality for the sake of reality.

"We, on the other hand, are Adams of a different Eden, a more terrible Eden, perhaps, for we must name and number the passions and motives of men. There, too, everything must be known, everything understood, everything expressed; there, also, there is nothing common, nothing unclean; every motive must be followed through all the obscure mystery of its logic. Mankind must be seen and understood in every possible circumstance, in every conceivable situation. There is no laughter too bitter, no irony too harsh for utterance, no passion too terrible to be set before the minds of men. The Greeks knew that. Only in this way can mankind be understood, only when we have put ourselves in all the possible positions of life, from the most miserable to those that are so lofty that we can only speak of them in symbols and in mysteries, will entire wisdom be possible.

5. A young man in Yeats and Lady Gregory's play *Cathleen ni Houlihan* (see pp. 133–40), who goes to fight for Ireland's cause in the 1798 Rising.
6. The central character in Lady Gregory's historical play *Dervorgilla* (1908), who blames herself for bringing the English into Ireland.
7. Patrick Sarsfield (1645?–1693), who features in Lady Gregory's historical play *The White Cockade*, was the most successful commander of Irish forces fighting for King James II against William of Orange in the wars of 1688–91, and he continued to fight heroically after his "bad master" gave up (see Yeats's poem "[Introductory Rhymes]," p. 42). In Lady Gregory's play a craven King James hides to escape capture.
8. "The Grocer's Wife": in other words, a representative type.
9. The Abbey Theatre performed a matinee for the British Association for the Advancement of Science on September 4, 1908, with Yeats giving a speech that outlined the history, and intellectual and dramatic aims, of the theater.

All wise government depends upon this knowledge not less than upon that other knowledge which is your business rather than ours; and we and you alike rejoice in battle, finding the sweetest of all music to be the stroke of the sword."

From *Per Amica Silentia Lunae* (1918)

From Anima Hominis[1]

I

When I come home after meeting men who are strange to me, and sometimes even after talking to women, I go over all I have said in gloom and disappointment. Perhaps I have overstated everything from a desire to vex or startle, from hostility that is but fear; or all my natural thoughts have been drowned by an undisciplined sympathy. My fellow-diners have hardly seemed of mixed humanity, and how should I keep my head among images of good and evil, crude allegories.

But when I shut my door and light the candle, I invite a Marmorean[2] Muse, an art, where no thought or emotion has come to mind because another man has thought or felt something different, for now there must be no reaction, action only, and the world must move my heart but to the heart's discovery of itself, and I begin to dream of eyelids that do not quiver before the bayonet: all my thoughts have ease and joy, I am all virtue and confidence. When I come to put in rhyme what I have found it will be a hard toil, but for a moment I believe I have found myself and not my anti-self. It is only the shrinking from toil perhaps that convinces me that I have been no more myself than is the cat the medicinal grass it is eating in the garden.

* * *

V

We make out of the quarrel with others, rhetoric, but of the quarrel with ourselves, poetry. Unlike the rhetoricians, who get a confident voice from remembering the crowd they have won or may win, we sing amid our uncertainty; and, smitten even in the presence of the most high beauty by the knowledge of our solitude, our rhythm shudders. I think, too, that no fine poet, no matter how disordered his life, has ever, even in his mere life, had pleasure for his end. Johnson and Dowson, friends of my youth, were dissipated men, the one a drunkard, the other a drunkard and mad about women, and yet they had the gravity of men who had found life out and were awakening from the dream; and both, one in life and art and one in art and less in life, had a continual preoccupation with reli-

1. Yeats translated his Latin title, taken from Book II of Virgil's *Aeneid*, as "Through the friendly silences of the moon." "Anima Hominis" (also Latin) means "The Soul of Man."
2. Resembling marble.

gion.[3] Nor has any poet I have read of or heard of or met with been a sentimentalist. The other self, the anti-self or the antithetical self, as one may choose to name it, comes but to those who are no longer deceived, whose passion is reality. The sentimentalists are practical men who believe in money, in position, in a marriage bell, and whose understanding of happiness is to be so busy whether at work or at play, that all is forgotten but the momentary aim. They find their pleasure in a cup that is filled from Lethe's wharf,[4] and for the awakening, for the vision, for the revelation of reality, tradition offers us a different word—ecstasy. An old artist[5] wrote to me of his wanderings by the quays of New York, and how he found there a woman nursing a sick child, and drew her story from her. She spoke, too, of other children who had died: a long tragic story. "I wanted to paint her," he wrote, "if I denied myself any of the pain I could not believe in my own ecstasy." We must not make a false faith by hiding from our thoughts the causes of doubt, for faith is the highest achievement of the human intellect, the only gift man can make to God, and therefore it must be offered in sincerity. Neither must we create, by hiding ugliness, a false beauty as our offering to the world. He only can create the greatest imaginable beauty who has endured all imaginable pangs, for only when we have seen and foreseen what we dread shall we be rewarded by that dazzling unforeseen wing-footed wanderer.[6] We could not find him if he were not in some sense of our being and yet of our being but as water with fire, a noise with silence. He is of all things not impossible the most difficult, for that only which comes easily can never be a portion of our being, "Soon got, soon gone," as the proverb says. I shall find the dark grow luminous, the void fruitful when I understand I have nothing, that the ringers in the tower[7] have appointed for the hymen[8] of the soul a passing bell.

The last knowledge has often come most quickly to turbulent men, and for a season brought new turbulence. When life puts away her conjuring tricks one by one, those that deceive us longest may well be the wine-cup and the sensual kiss, for our Chambers of Commerce and of Commons[9] have not the divine architecture of the body, nor has their frenzy been ripened by the sun. The poet, because he may not stand within the sacred house but lives amid the whirlwinds that beset its threshold, may find his pardon.

XIII

A poet, when he is growing old, will ask himself if he cannot keep his mask and his vision without new bitterness, new disappointment. Could

3. English poet Lionel Johnson (1867–1902) converted to Catholicism in 1891; he died as a result of a drunken fall. English poet Ernest Dowson (1867–1900), also a convert, suffered from extreme sexual infatuations in his last years.
4. Lethe: a river in the underworld in Greek mythology, whose waters bring oblivion.
5. Yeats's father, John Butler Yeats (1839–1922), who lived in New York from 1907 until his death.
6. Hermes, the messenger of the gods in Greek mythology, wears winged sandals.
7. An allusion to the poem "Julian and Maddalo" by Percy Bysshe Shelley (1792–1822).
8. Marriage.
9. The elected legislative chamber of the British Parliament.

he if he would, knowing how frail his vigour from youth up, copy Landor who lived loving and hating, ridiculous and unconquered, into extreme old age, all lost but the favour of his muses?

> The mother of the muses we are taught
> Is memory; she has left me; they remain
> And shake my shoulder urging me to sing.[1]

Surely, he may think, now that I have found vision and mask I need not suffer any longer. He will buy perhaps some small old house where like Ariosto he can dig his garden,[2] and think that in the return of birds and leaves, or moon and sun, and in the evening flight of the rooks he may discover rhythm and pattern like those in sleep and so never awake out of vision. Then he will remember Wordsworth withering into eighty years,[3] honoured and empty-witted, and climb to some waste room and find, forgotten there by youth, some bitter crust.

February 25, 1917.

From Anima Mundi[1]

I

I have always sought to bring my mind close to the mind of Indian and Japanese poets, old women in Connaught, mediums in Soho,[2] lay brothers whom I imagine dreaming in some mediaeval monastery the dreams of their village, learned authors who refer all to antiquity; to immerse it in the general mind where that mind is scarce separable from what we have begun to call "the subconscious"; to liberate it from all that comes of councils and committees, from the world as it is seen from universities or from populous towns; and that I might so believe I have murmured evocations and frequented mediums, delighted in all that displayed great problems through sensuous images, or exciting phrases, accepting from abstract schools but a few technical words that are so old they seem but broken architraves fallen amid bramble and grass, and have put myself to school where all things are seen: A *Tenedo Tacitae per Amica Silentia Lunae*.[3] At one time I thought to prove my conclusions by quoting from diaries where I have recorded certain strange events the moment they happened, but now I have changed my mind—I will but say like the Arab boy that became

1. From "Memory" by Walter Savage Landor (1775–1864), English writer.
2. Italian poet Ludovico Ariosto (1474–1533) retired in 1525 and spent his last years cultivating his garden at Ferrara.
3. English poet William Wordsworth (1770–1850) was made Poet Laureate in 1843, but he wrote little of merit after 1814.
1. "The Soul of the World" (Latin).
2. Yeats attended seances sporadically from his twenties onward, preferring, he later wrote, "poor districts" such as Soho, in London, where the questioners were working class. Connacht, the western region of Ireland that includes Sligo and Galway, was the area where Yeats gathered most of the folklore he published.
3. From Virgil's *Aeneid*: "from Tenedos . . . through the friendly silences of the quiet moon." Tenedos is an island in the Aegean.

Vizier: "O brother, I have taken stock in the desert sand and of the sayings of antiquity."[4]

X

There are two realities, the terrestrial and the condition of fire. All power is from the terrestrial condition, for there all opposites meet and there only is the extreme of choice possible, full freedom. And there the heterogeneous is, and evil, for evil is the strain one upon another of opposites; but in the condition of fire is all music and all rest. Between is the condition of air where images have but a borrowed life, that of memory or that reflected upon them when they symbolise colours and intensities of fire, the place of shades who are "in the whirl of those who are fading," and who cry like those amorous shades in the Japanese play:

> "That we may acquire power
> Even in our faint substance,
> We will show forth even now,
> And though it be but in a dream,
> Our form of repentance."[5]

After so many rhythmic beats the soul must cease to desire its images, and can, as it were, close its eyes.

When all sequence comes to an end, time comes to an end, and the soul puts on the rhythmic or spiritual body or luminous body and contemplates all the events of its memory and every possible impulse in an eternal possession of itself in one single moment. That condition is alone animate, all the rest is phantasy, and from thence come all the passions, and some have held, the very heat of the body.

> Time drops in decay,
> Like a candle burnt out,
> And the mountains and the woods
> Have their day, have their day.
> What one, in the rout
> Of the fire-born moods,
> Has fallen away?[6]

XIV

Awhile they live again those passionate moments, not knowing they are dead, and then they know and may awake or half awake to be our visitors. How is their dream changed as Time drops away and their senses multiply? Does their stature alter, do their eyes grow more brilliant? Certainly the dreams stay the longer, the greater their passion when alive: Helen may

---

4. From "King Wird Khan, his Women and his Wazirs," Night 925 in *A Plain and Literal Translation of the Arabian Nights Entertainments, Now Intituled The Book of the Thousand Nights and a Night* (1885–86), translated by Richard Burton.
5. From the Noh play *Nishikigi*, in *Certain Noble Plays of Japan* (1916), edited by Ezra Pound, and to which Yeats contributed an Introduction.
6. From Yeats's poem "The Moods," first published in 1893.

still open her chamber door to Paris[7] or watch him from the wall, and know she is dreaming but because nights and days are poignant or the stars unreckonably bright. Surely of the passionate dead we can but cry in words Ben Jonson meant for none but Shakespeare: "So rammed" are they "with life they can but grow in life with being."[8]

XXI

When I remember that Shelley calls our minds "mirrors of the fire for which all thirst,"[9] I cannot but ask the question all have asked, "What or who has cracked the mirror?" I begin to study the only self that I can know, myself, and to wind the thread upon the perne[1] again.

At certain moments, always unforeseen, I become happy, most commonly when at hazard I have opened some book of verse. Sometimes it is my own verse when, instead of discovering new technical flaws, I read with all the excitement of the first writing. Perhaps I am sitting in some crowded restaurant, the open book beside me, or closed, my excitement having over-brimmed the page. I look at the strangers near as if I had known them all my life, and it seems strange that I cannot speak to them: everything fills me with affection, I have no longer any fears or any needs; I do not even remember that this happy mood must come to an end. It seems as if the vehicle had suddenly grown pure and far extended and so luminous that one half imagines that the images from *Anima Mundi*, embodied there and drunk with that sweetness, would, as some country drunkard who had thrown a wisp into his own thatch, burn up time.

It may be an hour before the mood passes, but latterly I seem to understand that I enter upon it the moment I cease to hate. I think the common condition of our life is hatred—I know that this is so with me—irritation with public or private events or persons. There is no great matter in forgetfulness of servants, or the delays of tradesmen, but how forgive the ill-breeding of Carlyle, or the rhetoric of Swinburne,[2] or that woman who murmurs over the dinner-table the opinion of her daily paper? And only a week ago last Sunday, I hated the spaniel who disturbed a partridge on her nest, a trout who took my bait and yet broke away unhooked. The books say that our happiness comes from the opposite of hate, but I am not certain, for we may love unhappily. And plainly, when I have closed a book too stirred to go on reading, and in those brief intense visions of sleep, I have something about me that, though it makes me love, is more like innocence. I am in the place where the daemon is, but I do not think he is with me until I begin to make a new personality, selecting among those images, seeking always to satisfy a hunger grown out of conceit with

---

7. The Trojan War was caused by the abduction of Helen, wife of King Menelaus of Sparta, by Paris, son of King Priam of Troy. In some accounts, however, she goes with Paris willingly.
8. From *Poetaster* (1601) by Ben Jonson (1572–1637); in these lines the Roman poet Horace praises his contemporary Virgil (70–19 B.C.E.).
9. Lines 484–85 from Percy Bysshe Shelley's "Adonais."
1. Yeats recalled being told as a child that pern "was another name for the spool, as I was accustomed to call it, on which thread was wound."
2. Yeats's opinions of historian Thomas Carlyle (1795–1881) and poet Algernon Charles Swinburne (1837–1900) derived largely from William Morris (1834–1896), whom he recalled in *Autobiographies* dismissing Swinburne as a "rhetorician" and Carlyle as a writer who needed someone to punch "his head every five minutes."

daily diet; and yet as I write the words "I select," I am full of uncertainty, not knowing when I am the finger, when the clay. Once, twenty years ago, I seemed to awake from sleep to find my body rigid, and to hear a strange voice speaking these words through my lips as through lips of stone: "We make an image of him who sleeps, and it is not him who sleeps, and we call it Emmanuel."[3]

From A People's Theatre (1919)

A Letter to Lady Gregory[1]

I

My dear Lady Gregory:

Of recent years you have done all that is anxious and laborious in the supervision of the Abbey Theatre and left me free to follow my own thoughts. It is therefore right that I address to you this letter, wherein I shall explain, half for your ears, half for other ears, certain thoughts that have made me believe that the Abbey Theatre can never do all we had hoped. We set out to make a "People's Theatre" and in that we have succeeded. But I did not know until very lately that there are certain things, dear to both our hearts, which no "People's Theatre" can accomplish.

VI

I want to create for myself an unpopular theatre and an audience like a secret society where admission is by favour and never to many. Perhaps I shall never create it, for you and I and Synge[2] have had to dig the stone for our statue and I am aghast at the sight of a new quarry, and besides I want so much—an audience of fifty, a room worthy of it (some great dining room or sitting room), half a dozen young men and women who can dance and speak verse or play drum and flute and zither, and all the while instead of a profession I but offer them "an accomplishment." However, there are my Four Plays for Dancers as a beginning, some masks by Mr. Dulac, music by Mr. Dulac and by Mr. Rummell.[3] In most towns one can find fifty people for whom one need not build all on observation and sympathy, because they read poetry for their pleasure and understand the traditional language of passion. I desire a mysterious art, always reminding and half-

3. See Matthew 1.18–25.
1. Augusta Gregory (1852–1932), Yeats's patron and closest friend, with whom he collaborated on plays and folklore writings, had cofounded the Abbey Theatre in Dublin in 1904 and been its codirector with Yeats since then. They had begun the Abbey hoping to reach a wide Irish audience, but Yeats, already frustrated with the demands that running the Abbey made on his time and creative energies (see "The Fascination of What's Difficult," pp. 37–38), began to aspire to a more aristocractic, elitist theater once he encountered the highly ritualistic Noh plays of Japan (see At the Hawk's Well, pp. 160–68).
2. John Millington Synge (1871–1909), playwright and cofounder, with Yeats and Lady Gregory, of the Abbey Theatre.
3. Artist Edmund Dulac (1882–1953) designed the masks and costumes for the first production of Yeats's At the Hawk's Well (1917); musician Walter Rummell composed music for The Dreaming of the Bones (1919), one of the plays included in Yeats's Four Plays for Dancers (1921).

reminding those who understand it of dearly loved things, doing its work by suggestion, not by direct statement, a complexity of rhythm, colour, gesture, not space pervading like the intellect but a memory and a prophecy; a mode of drama Shelley and Keats could have used without ceasing to be themselves and for which even Blake in the mood of The Book of Thel might not have been too obscure.[4] Instead of advertisements in the Press I need a hostess, and even the most accomplished hostess must choose with more than usual care, for I have noticed that city-living cultivated people, those whose names would first occur to her, set great value on painting, which is a form of property, and on music, which is a part of the organization of life, while the lovers of literature, those who read a book many times, are either young men with little means or live far away from big towns.

*   *   *

I know that you consider Ireland alone our business and in that we do not differ, except that I care very little where a play of mine is first played so that it find some natural audience and good players. My rooks may sleep abroad in the fields for a while, but when the winter comes they will remember the way home to the rookery trees. Indeed, I have Ireland especially in mind, for I want to make, or to help some man some day to make, a feeling of exclusiveness, a bond among chosen spirits, a mystery almost, for leisured and lettered people. Ireland has suffered more than England from democracy, for since the Wild Geese fled[5] who might have grown to be leaders in manners and in taste, she has had but political leaders. As a painted figure is defined by its outline and taste by its rejections, I too must reject, and draw a clear outline about the thing I seek; and say that I seek, not a theatre but the theatre's anti-self, an art that can appease all within us that becomes uneasy as the curtain falls and the house breaks into applause.

VII

Meanwhile the Popular Theatre grows always more objective; more and more a reflection of the general mind; more and more a discovery of the simple emotions that make all men kin, clearing itself the while of sentimentality, the wreckage of an obsolete popular culture, seeking always not to feel and to imagine but to understand and to see. Let those who are all personality, who can only feel and imagine, leave it, before their presence become a corruption and turn it from its honesty. The rhetoric of D'Annunzio, the melodrama and spectacle of the later Maeterlinck, are the insincerities of subjectives, who being very able men have learned to hold an audience that is not their natural audience.[6] To be intelligible

---

4. English Romantic poets Percy Bysshe Shelley (1792–1822) and John Keats (1795–1821), and English poet-artist William Blake (1757–1827), author of the mystical and prophetic Book of Thel (1789).
5. Irishmen who emigrated from Ireland during the period of anti-Catholic penal laws passed after 1691.
6. Italian writer and politician Gabriele d'Annunzio (1863–1938) and Belgian dramatist Maurice Maeterlinck (1862–1949), both of whose plays Yeats had briefly admired some years earlier (see p. 266, n. 1).

they are compelled to harden, to externalize and deform. The Popular theatre left to itself will not lack vicissitude and development, for it will pass, though more slowly than the novel which need not carry with it so great a crowd, from the physical objectivity of Fielding and Defoe to the spiritual objectivity of Tolstoi and Dostoevsky,[7] for beyond the whole we reach by unbiassed intellect there is another whole reached by resignation and the denial of self.

*   *   *

From The Bounty of Sweden[1] (1925)

II

*   *   *

Every now and then, when something has stirred my imagination, I begin talking to myself. I speak in my own person and dramatise myself, very much as I have seen a mad old woman do upon the Dublin quays, and sometimes detect myself speaking and moving as if I were still young, or walking perhaps like an old man with fumbling steps. Occasionally, I write out what I have said in verse, and generally for no better reason than because I remember that I have written no verse for a long time. I do not think of my soliloquies as having different literary qualities. They stir my interest, by their appropriateness to the men I imagine myself to be, or by their accurate description of some emotional circumstance, more than by any aesthetic value. When I begin to write I have no object but to find for them some natural speech, rhythm and syntax, and to set it out in some pattern, so seeming old that it may seem all men's speech, and though the labour is very great, I seem to have used no faculty peculiar to myself, certainly no special gift. I print the poem and never hear about it again, until I find the book years after with a page dog-eared by some young man, or marked by some young girl with a violet, and when I have seen that I am a little ashamed, as though somebody were to attribute to me a delicacy of feeling I should but do not possess. What came so easily at first, and amidst so much drama, and was written so laboriously at the last, cannot be counted among my possessions.

On the other hand, if I give a successful lecture, or write a vigorous, critical essay, there is immediate effect; I am confident that on some one point, which seems to me of great importance, I know more than other men, and I covet honour.

---

7. English novelists Henry Fielding (1707–1754) and Daniel Defoe (1660–1731), and Russian novelists Leo Tolstoy (1828–1910) and Fyodor Dostoyevsky (1821–1881).
1. Yeats was awarded the Nobel Prize for Literature in 1923 and went to Stockholm, Sweden, that December for the presentation of the award from the Swedish Royal Academy. His essay recalls that visit.

XII

On Thursday I give my official lecture to the Swedish Royal Academy. I have chosen 'The Irish Theatre' for my subject, that I may commend all those workers, obscure or well-known, to whom I owe much of whatever fame in the world I may possess. If I had been a lyric poet only, if I had not become through this theatre the representative of a public movement, I doubt if the English committees would have placed my name upon that list from which the Swedish Academy selects its prize-winner. They would not have acknowledged a thought so irrelevant, but those dog-eared pages, those pressed violets, upon which the fame of a lyric poet depends at the last, might without it have found no strong voice. I have seen so much beautiful lyric poetry pass unnoticed for years, and indeed at this very moment a little book of exquisite verse lies upon my table, by an author who died a few years ago, whom I knew slightly, and whose work I ignored, for chance had shown me only that part of it for which I could not care.

On my way to the lecture hall I ask an Academician what kind of audience I will have, and he replies, 'An audience of women, a fit audience for a poet'; but there are men as well as women. I had thought it would be difficult to speak to an audience in a language they had learnt at school, but it is exceedingly easy. All I say seems to be understood, and I am conscious of that sympathy which makes a speaker forget all but his own thoughts, and soliloquise aloud. I am speaking without notes and the image of old fellow-workers comes upon me as if they were present, above all of the embittered life and death of one, and of another's laborious, solitary age, and I say, 'When your King gave me medal and diploma, two forms should have stood, one at either side of me, an old woman sinking into the infirmity of age and a young man's ghost. I think when Lady Gregory's name and John Synge's[2] name are spoken by future generations, my name, if remembered, will come up in the talk, and that if my name is spoken first their names will come in their turn because of the years we worked together. I think that both had been well pleased to have stood beside me at the great reception at your Palace, for their work and mine has delighted in history and tradition.' I think as I speak these words of how deep down we have gone, below all that is individual, modern and restless, seeking foundations for an Ireland that can only come into existence in a Europe that is still but a dream.

From Introduction to *The Oxford Book of Modern Verse* (1936)

IX

Eliot has produced his great effect upon his generation because he has described men and women that get out of bed or into it from mere habit;

---

2. Augusta Gregory (1852–1932), Yeats's patron and closest friend, with whom he collaborated on plays and folklore writings, cofounded the Abbey Theatre in Dublin with Yeats and playwright John Millington Synge (1871–1909) in 1904.

in describing this life that has lost heart his own art seems grey, cold, dry.[1] He is an Alexander Pope, working without apparent imagination, producing his effects by a rejection of all rhythms and metaphors used by the more popular romantics rather than by the discovery of his own, this rejection giving his work an unexaggerated plainness that has the effect of novelty. He has the rhythmical flatness of *The Essay on Man*—despite Miss Sitwell's advocacy I see Pope as Blake and Keats saw him[2]—later, in *The Waste Land*, amid much that is moving in symbol and imagery there is much monotony of accent:

> When lovely woman stoops to folly and
> Paces about her room again, alone,
> She smooths her hair with automatic hand,
> And puts a record on the gramophone.[3]

I was affected, as I am by these lines, when I saw for the first time a painting by Manet. I longed for the vivid colour and light of Rousseau and Courbet, I could not endure the grey middle-tint—and even to-day Manet gives me an incomplete pleasure; he had left the procession.[4] Nor can I put the Eliot of these poems among those that descend from Shakespeare and the translators of the Bible. I think of him as satirist rather than poet. Once only does that early work speak in the great manner:

> The host with someone indistinct
> Converses at the door apart,
> The nightingales are singing near
> The Convent of the Sacred Heart,
>
> And sang within the bloody wood
> When Agamemnon cried aloud,
> And let their liquid siftings fall
> To stain the stiff dishonoured shroud.[5]

Not until *The Hollow Men* and *Ash-Wednesday*, where he is helped by the short lines, and in the dramatic poems where his remarkable sense of actor, chanter, scene, sweeps him away, is there rhythmical animation.[6] Two or three of my friends attribute the change to an emotional enrichment from religion, but his religion compared to that of John Gray, Francis Thomp-

1. Yeats's selections from the poetry of T. S. Eliot (1888–1965) in *The Oxford Book of Modern Verse* included "Preludes" (1917) and sections of *The Waste Land* (1922), poems in which moods of urban alienation dominate.
2. English poet Alexander Pope (1688–1744), whose works include "An Essay on Man," wrote in regular meter, typically in rhymed couplets, a style decried by English Romantic poet John Keats (1795–1821) as monotonous. In a biography of Pope published in 1930, writer Edith Sitwell (1887–1964) praised his style as at its best as flawless.
3. Lines 253–56 from *The Waste Land*.
4. Yeats here prefers the work of French painter Henri Rousseau (1844–1910), whose work defied conventional perspective and conventions of color and typically represented exotic or imaginary landscapes or dreamscapes, and of French realist painter Gustave Courbet (1819–1877), to the Impressionism of French painter Eduoard Manet (1832–1883).
5. Lines 33–40 of Eliot's "Sweeney Among the Nightingales" (1919).
6. "The Hollow Men" (1925) and "Ash Wednesday" (1927) reflect the beginning of Eliot's shift from an avant-garde poetry of modern alienation to a poetry motivated by Anglo-Catholicism.

son, Lionel Johnson in *The Dark Angel*, lacks all strong emotion;[7] a New England Protestant by descent, there is little self-surrender in his personal relation to God and the soul. *Murder in the Cathedral* is a powerful stage play because the actor, the monkish habit, certain repeated words, symbolize what we know, not what the author knows. Nowhere has the author explained how Becket and the King differ in aim; Becket's people have been robbed and persecuted in his absence; like the King he demands strong government. Speaking through Becket's mouth Eliot confronts a world growing always more terrible with a religion like that of some great statesman, a pity not less poignant because it tempers the prayer book with the results of mathematical philosophy.

Peace. And let them be, in their exaltation.
They speak better than they know, and beyond your understanding,
They know and do not know, that acting is suffering
And suffering is action. Neither does the actor suffer
Nor the patient act. But both are fixed
In an eternal action, an eternal patience
To which all must consent that it may be willed
And which all must suffer that they may will it,
That the pattern may subsist, for the pattern is the action
And the suffering, that the wheel may turn and still
Be forever still.[8]

X

Ezra Pound has made flux his theme; plot, characterization, logical discourse, seem to him abstractions unsuitable to a man of his generation. He is mid-way in an immense poem in *vers libre* called for the moment *The Cantos*,[9] where the metamorphosis of Dionysus, the descent of Odysseus into Hades,[1] repeat themselves in various disguises, always in association with some third that is not repeated. Hades may become the hell where whatever modern men he most disapproves of suffer damnation, the metamorphosis petty frauds practised by Jews at Gibraltar.[2] The relation of all the elements to one another, repeated or unrepeated, is to become apparent when the whole is finished. There is no transmission through time, we pass without comment from ancient Greece to modern

7. English poet John Gray (1866–1934), once Oscar Wilde's lover, converted to Catholicism in 1890 and wrote many devotional works thereafter; Francis Thompson (1857–1907), once a drug addict, wrote the powerfully spiritual poem "The Hound of Heaven," which, along with "The Dark Angel" by Lionel Johnson (1867–1902), who converted to Catholicism in 1891, Yeats included in *The Oxford Book of Modern Verse*.
8. From the opening speech by Thomas à Becket in Eliot's play *Murder in the Cathedral* (1935). Becket (1118–1170), archbishop of Canterbury from 1162, resisted the effort of King Henry II to subordinate the Church to the State, and he was murdered in 1170 by four knights who acted on Henry's publicly expressed wish to be rid of him.
9. American poet Ezra Pound (1885–1972) acted as a publicist and polemicist for Modernism in poetry, promoting free verse and criticizing the conventions of Victorian verse. He was Yeats's secretary and companion for three winters beginning in 1913–14, and Yeats's neighbor in Rapallo, Italy, in the late 1920s and 1930s. His poetic epic, *The Cantos*, on which he worked until his death, was never fully completed.
1. In Greek mythology, Dionysus, god of the vine (known as Bacchus to the Romans), was caused to go mad by Hera (Juno), queen of the gods. Odysseus visits Hades in Homer's *Odyssey*.
2. Treated in Pound's Canto XXII.

England, from modern England to medieval China; the symphony, the pattern, is timeless, flux eternal and therefore without movement. Like other readers I discover at present merely exquisite or grotesque fragments. He hopes to give the impression that all is living, that there are no edges, no convexities, nothing to check the flow; but can such a poem have a mathematical structure? Can impressions that are in part visual, in part metrical, be related like the notes of a symphony; has the author been carried beyond reason by a theoretical conception? His belief in his own conception is so great that since the appearance of the first Canto I have tried to suspend judgement.

When I consider his work as a whole I find more style than form; at moments more style, more deliberate nobility and the means to convey it than in any contemporary poet known to me, but it is constantly interrupted, broken, twisted into nothing by its direct opposite, nervous obsession, nightmare, stammering confusion; he is an economist, poet, politician, raging at malignants with inexplicable characters and motives, grotesque figures out of a child's book of beasts. This loss of self-control, common among uneducated revolutionists, is rare—Shelley had it in some degree[3]—among men of Ezra Pound's culture and erudition. Style and its opposite can alternate, but form must be full, sphere-like, single. Even where there is no interruption he is often content, if certain verses and lines have style, to leave unbridged transitions, unexplained ejaculations, that make his meaning unintelligible. He has great influence, more perhaps than any contemporary except Eliot, is probably the source of that lack of form and consequent obscurity which is the main defect of Auden, Day Lewis, and their school, a school which, as will presently be seen, I greatly admire.[4] Even where the style is sustained throughout one gets an impression, especially when he is writing in *vers libre*, that he has not got all the wine into the bowl, that he is a brilliant improvisator translating at sight from an unknown Greek masterpiece:

> See, they return; ah, see the tentative
> Movements, and the slow feet,
> The trouble in the pace and the uncertain
> Wavering!
>
> See, they return, one, and by one,
> With fear, as half-awakened;
> As if the snow should hesitate
> And murmur in the wind,
>   and half turn back;
>
> These were the Wing'd-with-awe,
> Inviolable.

3. English Romantic poet Percy Bysshe Shelley (1792–1822), known as "Mad Shelley" in his school days for his independent style, led a life of political activism (urging reform in Britain and supporting the cause of Greek independence from Turkey) and unconventional and impulsive social behavior (eloping twice and relinquishing his right to an inheritance).
4. Yeats included poems by both C. Day Lewis (1904–1972) and W. H. Auden (1907–1973) in *The Oxford Book of Modern Verse*.

Gods of the winged shoe!
With them the silver hounds,
    sniffing the trace of air![5]

XV

I have a distaste for certain poems written in the midst of the great war; they are in all anthologies, but I have substituted Herbert Read's *End of a War* written long after.[6] The writers of these poems were invariably officers of exceptional courage and capacity, one a man constantly selected for dangerous work, all, I think, had the Military Cross; their letters are vivid and humorous, they were not without joy—for all skill is joyful—but felt bound, in the words of the best known, to plead the suffering of their men. In poems that had for a time considerable fame, written in the first person, they made that suffering their own. I have rejected these poems for the same reason that made Arnold withdraw his *Empedocles on Etna* from circulation; passive suffering is not a theme for poetry.[7] In all the great tragedies, tragedy is a joy to the man who dies; in Greece the tragic chorus danced. When man has withdrawn into the quicksilver at the back of the mirror no great event becomes luminous in his mind; it is no longer possible to write *The Persians, Agincourt, Chevy Chase*:[8] some blunderer has driven his car on to the wrong side of the road—that is all.

If war is necessary, or necessary in our time and place, it is best to forget its suffering as we do the discomfort of fever, remembering our comfort at midnight when our temperature fell, or as we forget the worst moments of more painful disease. Florence Farr returning third class from Ireland found herself among Connaught Rangers just returned from the Boer War who described an incident over and over, and always with loud laughter: an unpopular sergeant struck by a shell turned round and round like a dancer wound in his own entrails.[9] That too may be a right way of seeing war, if war is necessary; the way of the Cockney slums, of Patrick Street, of the *Kilmainham Minut*, of *Johnny I hardly knew ye*, of the medieval *Dance of Death*.[1]

---

5. Lines 11–14 of Pound's poem "The Return." Yeats had praised this poem more fulsomely in 1914, soon after its composition.
6. *The End of a War*, by Herbert Read (1893–1968), treating World War I, was published in 1933.
7. English poet and critic Matthew Arnold (1822–1888) withdrew "Empedocles on Etna" from his *Poems* in 1853 because he considered that no enjoyment could be derived from a work in which suffering found no outlet in action.
8. *The Persians* by Greek tragedian Aeschylus (c. 525–c. 456 B.C.E.); "The Ballad of Agincourt" by poet Michael Drayton (1563–1631); and the anonymous "Ballad of Chevy Chase," probably dating from the fifteenth century.
9. Florence Farr Emery (1860–1917), a friend and co-member with Yeats of the occult society The Golden Dawn in the late 1890s, performed frequently with Yeats in the first decade of the new century in their experiments of speaking verse to a psaltery (stringed instrument). The Connaught Rangers, an Irish regiment, fought in the Boer War between England and the Boer Republic in South Africa between 1899 and 1902.
1. The Cockney region of East London and the Patrick Street area in the Liberties of Dublin were both slum districts. "The Kilmainham Minuet" (or "Minut"), referring to Kilmainham Jail in Dublin, and "Johnny, I hardly knew Ye!" are Irish street ballads dating from the eighteenth and nineteenth century respectively. "The Dance of Death" is a medieval masque featuring skeletons or corpses leading living people into the land of the dead.

From A Vision (1937)

From Introduction to "A Vision"

I

The other day Lady Gregory[1] said to me: "You are a much better educated man than you were ten years ago and much more powerful in argument". And I put *The Tower* and *The Winding Stair* into evidence to show that my poetry has gained in self-possession and power. I owe this change to an incredible experience.

II

On the afternoon of October 24th 1917, four days after my marriage, my wife[2] surprised me by attempting automatic writing. What came in disjointed sentences, in almost illegible writing, was so exciting, sometimes so profound, that I persuaded her to give an hour or two day after day to the unknown writer, and after some half-dozen such hours offered to spend what remained of life explaining and piecing together those scattered sentences. "No," was the answer, "we have come to give you metaphors for poetry." The unknown writer took his theme at first from my just published *Per Amica Silentia Lunae*. I had made a distinction between the perfection that is from a man's combat with himself and that which is from a combat with circumstance, and upon this simple distinction he built up an elaborate classification of men according to their more or less complete expression of one type or the other. He supported his classification by a series of geometrical symbols and put these symbols in an order that answered the question in my essay as to whether some prophet could not prick upon the calendar the birth of a Napoleon[3] or a Christ. A system of symbolism, strange to my wife and to myself, certainly awaited expression, and when I asked how long that would take I was told years.

*　*　*

IV

Whenever I received a certain signal (I will explain what it was later), I would get pencil and paper ready. After they had entranced my wife suddenly when sitting in a chair, I suggested that she must always be lying down before they put her to sleep. They seemed ignorant of our surroundings and might have done so at some inconvenient time or place; once when they had given their signal in a restaurant they explained that because we had spoken of a garden they had thought we were in it. Except at the start of a new topic, when they would speak or write a dozen sen-

---

1. Augusta Gregory (1852–1932), Yeats's patron, creative collaborator, and closest friend.
2. Yeats married Georgie Hyde-Lees (1892–1968) on October 20, 1917.
3. Napoleon Bonaparte (1769–1821), emperor of France 1804–14, who conquered much of Europe before being defeated at Waterloo in 1815.

tences unquestioned, I had always to question, and every question to rise out of a previous answer and to deal with their chosen topic. My questions must be accurately worded, and, because they said their thought was swifter than ours, asked without delay or hesitation. I was constantly reproved for vague or confused questions, yet I could do no better, because, though it was plain from the first that their exposition was based upon a single geometrical conception, they kept me from mastering that conception. They shifted ground whenever my interest was at its height, whenever it seemed that the next day must reveal what, as I soon discovered, they were determined to withhold until all was upon paper. * * * I believe that they so changed their theme because, had I grasped their central idea, I would have lacked the patience and the curiosity to follow their application of it, preferring some hasty application of my own. They once told me not to speak of any part of the system, except of the incarnations which were almost fully expounded, because if I did the people I talked to would talk to other people, and the communicators would mistake that misunderstanding for their own thought.

XV

Some will ask whether I believe in the actual existence of my circuits of sun and moon.[4] Those that include, now all recorded time in one circuit, now what Blake called "the pulsation of an artery",[5] are plainly symbolical, but what of those that fixed, like a butterfly upon a pin, to our central date, the first day of our Era, divide actual history into periods of equal length? To such a question I can but answer that if sometimes, overwhelmed by miracle as all men must be when in the midst of it, I have taken such periods literally, my reason has soon recovered; and now that the system stands out clearly in my imagination I regard them as stylistic arrangements of experience comparable to the cubes in the drawing of Wyndham Lewis and to the ovoids in the sculpture of Brancusi.[6] They have helped me to hold in a single thought reality and justice.

From Book I: The Great Wheel

FROM PART I: THE PRINCIPAL SYMBOL

II

* * *

If we think of the vortex attributed to Discord as formed by circles diminishing until they are nothing, and of the opposing sphere attributed to Concord as forming from itself an opposing vortex, the apex of each vortex

4. The main section of *A Vision* describes twenty-eight "Phases of the Moon": lunar phases that Yeats describes as stages or positions on the "Great Wheel" of incarnation.
5. English poet William Blake (1757–1827) uses the phrase in his poem "Time."
6. English painter and novelist Wyndham Lewis (1882–1957) and French-Romanian abstract sculptor Constantine Brancusi (1876–1957): for Yeats, representative contemporary avant-garde artists.

in the middle of the other's base, we have the fundamental symbol of my instructors.

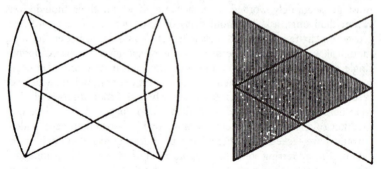

If I call the unshaded cone "Discord" and the other "Concord" and think of each as the bound of a gyre, I see that the gyre of "Concord" diminishes as that of "Discord" increases, and can imagine after that the gyre of "Concord" increasing while that of "Discord" diminishes, and so on, one gyre within the other always. Here the thought of Heraclitus dominates all: "Dying each other's life, living each other's death".[1]

ESSAYS FOR THE SCRIBNER EDITION OF YEATS'S COLLECTED WORKS (1937)[1]

Introduction

I. THE FIRST PRINCIPLE

A poet writes always of his personal life, in his finest work out of its tragedy, whatever it be, remorse, lost love, or mere loneliness; he never speaks directly as to someone at the breakfast table, there is always a phantasmagoria. Dante and Milton[2] had mythologies, Shakespeare the characters of English history or of traditional romance; even when the poet seems most himself, when he is Raleigh and gives potentates the lie,[3] or Shelley 'a nerve o'er which do creep the else unfelt oppressions of this earth,'[4] or Byron when 'the soul wears out the breast' as 'the sword outwears its

---

1. Greek philosopher Heraclitus (fl. 500 B.C.E.) argued that the apparent stability of the world conceals a dynamic tension between opposing forces. Yeats here quotes fragment 67 of Heraclitus's *On Nature* in which "Mortals are immortals and immortals are mortals, the one living the other's death and dying the other's life."
1. The American publishing house Charles Scribner contracted with Yeats in 1936 for a deluxe limited American edition of his collected works, and Yeats completed three introductions intended for the project—a general introduction to his work, and introductions to his plays and to his essays—in 1937. Yeats's death in 1939, and poor market conditions during the war, delayed and eventually caused the abandonment of the edition.
2. Italian poet Dante Alighieri (1265–1321); English poet John Milton (1608–1674).
3. English writer, courtier, soldier, and explorer Walter Ralegh (1552–1618). Yeats refers to line 18 of his poem "The Lie."
4. Lines 449–50 from "Julian and Maddalo" (1819) by English poet Percy Bysshe Shelley (1792–1822).

sheath,'[5] he is never the bundle of accident and incoherence that sits down to breakfast; he has been reborn as an idea, something intended, complete. A novelist might describe his accidence, his incoherence, he must not; he is more type than man, more passion than type. He is Lear, Romeo, Oedipus, Tiresias[6]; he has stepped out of a play, and even the woman he loves is Rosalind, Cleopatra, never The Dark Lady.[7] He is part of his own phantasmagoria and we adore him because nature has grown intelligible, and by so doing a part of our creative power. 'When mind is lost in the light of the Self,' says the Prashna Upanishad, 'it dreams no more; still in the body it is lost in happiness.' 'A wise man seeks in Self,' says the Chandogya Upanishad, 'those that are alive and those that are dead and gets what the world cannot give.'[8] The world knows nothing because it has made nothing, we know everything because we have made everything.

II. SUBJECT-MATTER

It was through the old Fenian leader John O'Leary[9] I found my theme. His long imprisonment, his longer banishment, his magnificent head, his scholarship, his pride, his integrity, all that aristocratic dream nourished amid little shops and little farms, had drawn around him a group of young men; I was but eighteen or nineteen and had already, under the influence of The Faerie Queene and The Sad Shepherd, written a pastoral play, and under that of Shelley's Prometheus Unbound two plays, one staged somewhere in the Caucasus, the other in a crater of the moon;[1] and I knew myself to be vague and incoherent. He gave me the poems of Thomas Davis, said they were not good poetry but had changed his life when a young man, spoke of other poets associated with Davis and The Nation newspaper,[2] probably lent me their books. I saw even more clearly than O'Leary that they were not good poetry. I read nothing but romantic literature; hated that dry eighteenth-century rhetoric; but they had one quality I admired and admire: they were not separated individual men; they spoke or tried to speak out of a people to a people; behind them stretched the generations. I knew, though but now and then as young men know things, that I must turn from that modern literature Jonathan Swift compared to the web a spider draws out of its bowels;[3] I hated and still hate with an ever growing hatred the literature of the point of view. I wanted,

5. Lines 5–6 from "So, We'll Go No More a Roving" by George, Lord Byron (1788–1824).
6. The blind seer in Antigone and Oedipus the King by Greek dramatist Sophocles (c. 496–405 B.C.E.).
7. Rosalind: in Shakespeare's As You Like It; Cleopatra: in Shakespeare's Anthony and Cleopatra; The Dark Lady: the unidentified woman to whom many of Shakespeare's sonnets are addressed.
8. From The Ten Principal Upanishads (1937), translations from the Upanishads (commentaries on Hindu scripture), by Yeats and Shri Purohit Swami.
9. John O'Leary (1830–1907), Irish Nationalist, was exiled for treason-felony in 1865. Yeats met O'Leary soon after his return to Ireland in 1885.
1. Yeats's pastoral play was probably The Island of Statues (1885), which shows the influence of the poem The Faerie Queen by Edmund Spenser (?1552–1599) and the pastoral play The Sad Shepherd by Ben Jonson (1572–1637); the two plays influenced by Shelley's verse drama Prometheus Unbound (1820) were unfinished and never published by Yeats.
2. Thomas Davis (1814–1845), poet and a founder of the Nationalist newspaper the Nation, was a leader of the patriotic "Young Ireland" movement.
3. In The Battle of the Books (1704) by Jonathan Swift (1667–1745), Irish poet, satirist, and clergyman, moderns are represented by the spider, who "Spins and Spits wholly from Himself," ancients by the bee, who travels to collect from the best in nature.

if my ignorance permitted, to get back to Homer,[4] to those that fed at his table. I wanted to cry as all men cried, to laugh as all men laughed, and the Young Ireland poets when not writing mere politics had the same want, but they did not know that the common and its befitting language is the research of a lifetime and when found may lack popular recognition. Then somebody, not O'Leary, told me of Standish O'Grady and his interpretation of Irish legends.[5] O'Leary had sent me to O'Curry,[6] but his unarranged and uninterpreted history defeated my boyish indolence.

A generation before *The Nation* newspaper was founded the Royal Irish Academy had begun the study of ancient Irish literature. That study was as much a gift from the Protestant aristocracy which had created the Parliament as *The Nation* and its school, though Davis and Mitchel were Protestants, was a gift from the Catholic middle classes who were to create the Irish Free State.[7] The Academy persuaded the English Government to finance an ordnance survey on a large scale; scholars, including that great scholar O'Donovan, were sent from village to village recording names and their legends.[8] Perhaps it was the last moment when such work could be well done, the memory of the people was still intact, the collectors themselves had perhaps heard or seen the banshee[9]; the Royal Irish Academy and its public with equal enthusiasm welcome Pagan and Christian; thought the Round Towers a commemoration of Persian fire-worship.[1] There was little orthodoxy to take alarm; the Catholics were crushed and cowed; an honoured great-uncle of mine—his portrait by some forgotten master hangs upon my bedroom wall—a Church of Ireland rector, would upon occasion boast that you could not ask a question he could not answer with a perfectly appropriate blasphemy or indecency. When several counties had been surveyed but nothing published, the Government, afraid of rousing dangerous patriotic emotion, withdrew support; large manuscript volumes remain containing much picturesque correspondence between scholars.

When modern Irish literature began, O'Grady's influence predominated. He could delight us with an extravagance we were too critical to share; a day will come, he said, when Slieve-na-mon will be more famous

4. Greek poet of circa eighth century B.C.E.
5. Irish historian and novelist (1866–1928), often regarded as the figure who spurred the Irish literary Revival though his *History of Ireland* (1878, 1880), which made much Irish heroic mythology available for a wider audience.
6. Irish historian Eugene O'Curry (1796–1862), whose volumes of lectures on *The Manuscript Materials of Ancient Irish History* (1861) and *On the Manners and Customs of the Ancient Irish* (1873) Yeats owned.
7. The first independent Irish Parliament (1782–1801) was controlled by the Anglo-Irish Protestant "Ascendancy" class; the Royal Irish Academy, which promoted the study of Irish history, was founded during its tenure. The Irish Free State government, established in 1922, was Catholic in its majority interest. Irish Nationalist John Mitchel (1815–1875) contributed to the *Nation* until he was exiled from Ireland for treason-felony in 1848.
8. John O'Donovan (1809–1861) and Eugene O'Curry worked on the Irish Ordnance Survey in the early 1830s.
9. From "bean sidhe" (Irish: fairy woman). As Yeats described it, "an attendant fairy that follows the old families, . . . and wails before a death."
1. Pencil-shaped stone towers, most dating from around the seventh and eighth century, are numerous in Ireland, particularly as part of monastic settlements. In the late nineteenth century there was still much debate as to their function and origins.

than Olympus;[2] yet he was no Nationalist as we understood the word, but in rebellion, as he was fond of explaining, against the House of Commons,[3] not against the King. His cousin, that great scholar Hayes O'Grady,[4] would not join our non-political Irish Literary Society because he considered it a Fenian body, but boasted that although he had lived in England for forty years he had never made an English friend. He worked at the British Museum compiling their Gaelic catalogue and translating our heroic tales in an eighteenth-century frenzy; his heroine 'fractured her heart,' his hero 'ascended to the apex of the eminence' and there 'vibrated his javelin,' and afterwards took ship upon 'colossal ocean's superficies.' Both O'Gradys considered themselves as representing the old Irish land-owning aristocracy; both probably, Standish O'Grady certainly, thought that England, because decadent and democratic, had betrayed their order. It was another member of that order, Lady Gregory, who was to do for the heroic legends in *Gods and Fighting Men* and in *Cuchulain of Muirthemne* what Lady Charlotte Guest's *Mabinogion* had done with less beauty and style for those of Wales.[5] Standish O'Grady had much modern sentiment, his style, like that of John Mitchel forty years before, shaped by Carlyle;[6] she formed her style upon the Anglo-Irish dialect of her neighbourhood, an old vivid speech with a partly Tudor[7] vocabulary, a syntax partly moulded by men who still thought in Gaelic.

I had heard in Sligo cottages or from pilots at Rosses Point endless stories of apparitions, whether of the recent dead or of the people of history and legend, of that Queen Maeve whose reputed cairn stands on the mountain over the bay.[8] Then at the British Museum I read stories Irish writers of the 'forties and 'fifties had written of such apparitions, but they enraged me more than pleased because they turned the country visions into a joke. But when I went from cottage to cottage with Lady Gregory and watched her hand recording that great collection she has called *Visions and Beliefs*[9] I escaped disfiguring humour.

Behind all Irish history hangs a great tapestry, even Christianity had to accept it and be itself pictured there. Nobody looking at its dim folds can say where Christianity begins and Druidism ends; 'There is one perfect among the birds, one perfect among the fish, and one among men that is

---

2. Slievenamon, a mountain in County Tipperary, was associated with the ancient gods of Ireland and with the fairies. Mount Olympus was the home of the gods in Greek mythology.
3. The elected legislative chamber of the British Parliament.
4. Standish Hayes O'Grady (1832–1915) compiled the first volume of the *Catalogue of Irish Manuscripts in the British Museum* (not printed until 1926). His *Silva Gadelica* (1892), translations of Irish heroic tales, is quoted largely inaccurately here by Yeats, though the extracts capture O'Grady's turgidity of style appropriately.
5. Lady Gregory's *Cuchulain of Muirthemne* (1902) and *Gods and Fighting Men* (1904) were redactions of the Irish epics; Lady Charlotte Guest (1812–95) translated Welsh heroic tales in *The Mabinogion* (1838–49).
6. English historian and essayist Thomas Carlyle (1795–1881).
7. The period when Henry VII and Henry VIII were kings of England (1485–1547).
8. Rosses Point, a sandy peninsula and village about eight miles northeast of the town of Sligo town in the west of Ireland, was associated by Yeats with supernatural activity. Knocknarea, a mountain overlooking Sligo Bay, is topped by a cairn reputed to be the burial site of Queen Maeve of the Sidhe (see p. 23 and p. 146, n. 7).
9. Lady Gregory's *Visions and Beliefs in the West of Ireland* (1920) included folklore she and Yeats had gathered in the late 1890s in County Galway.

perfect.'[1] I can only explain by that suggestion of recent scholars—Professor Burkitt of Cambridge commended it to my attention—that St. Patrick came to Ireland not in the fifth century but towards the end of the second.[2] The great controversies had not begun; Easter was still the first full moon after the Equinox.[3] Upon that day the world had been created, the Ark rested upon Ararat, Moses led the Israelites out of Egypt; the umbilical cord which united Christianity to the ancient world had not yet been cut, Christ was still the half-brother of Dionysus.[4] A man just tonsured by the Druids[5] could learn from the nearest Christian neighbour to sign himself with the Cross without sense of incongruity, nor would his children acquire that sense. The organised clans weakened Church organisation, they could accept the monk but not the bishop.

A modern man, *The Golden Bough* and *Human Personality*[6] in his head, finds much that is congenial in St. Patrick's Creed as recorded in his Confessions, and nothing to reject except the word 'soon' in the statement that Christ will soon judge the quick and the dead.[7] He can repeat it, believe it even, without a thought of the historic Christ, or ancient Judea, or of anything subject to historical conjecture and shifting evidence; I repeat it and think of 'the Self' in the Upanishads. Into this tradition, oral and written, went in later years fragments of Neo-Platonism,[8] cabbalistic words—I have heard the words 'tetragrammaton agla' in Doneraile[9]—the floating debris of mediaeval thought, but nothing that did not please the solitary mind. Even the religious equivalent for Baroque and Rococo[1] could not come to us as thought, perhaps because Gaelic is incapable of abstraction. It came as cruelty. That tapestry filled the scene at the birth of modern Irish literature, it is there in the Synge of *The Well of the Saints*, in James Stephens, and in Lady Gregory throughout, in all of George Russell that did not come from the Upanishads, and in all but my later poetry.[2]

1. The Druids were priest-prophets in ancient Ireland. Popular lore held that rulers or kings must be perfectly shaped; the phrase was attributed to Saint Columba, a sixth-century Irish saint, by Yeats's contemporary John Rhys.
2. Francis Crawford Burkitt (1864–1935) advanced this supposition in a review he sent Yeats, published in the *Journal of Theological Studies*, July 1932.
3. Burkitt's review observes that the method used in Ireland in the fourth and fifth centuries to calculate the date of Easter was different from the Roman method.
4. The Greek god of wine and fertility, worshipped in orgiastic revelries.
5. Yeats describes the "ancient" (and reputedly Druidic) practice of shaving all but the top of the head in his story "The Crucifixion of the Outcast" (see p. 194). The Roman style of tonsure required the shaving only of the top of the head, with the rest of the head left unshaven.
6. *The Golden Bough: A Study of Magic and Religion* (1890–1915) by English anthropologist and folklorist James Frazer (1854–1941); *Human Personality and Its Survival of Bodily Death* (1903) by Frederic Myers (1843–1901).
7. In his *Confessions*, Saint Patrick (c. 385–c. 461), who introduced Christianity into Druidic Ireland, observes that Christ will "soon" judge the quick (i.e., living) and the dead.
8. Neoplatonism derived, especially among Roman thinkers of the third century, from the work of Greek philosopher Plato (c. 429–347 B.C.E.).
9. The Tetragrammaton, four Hebrew letters that represent the name of God, and Agla, a Hebrew acrostic meaning "You are mighty and eternal, Lord," derive from the Cabala, a mystical theosophy originating in the thirteenth century. Yeats had visited Doneraile in County Cork, Ireland in 1897 (see p. 248, n. 5).
1. The elaborate and ornate styles of the seventeenth and eighteenth centuries, respectively.
2. Yeats here reiterates his beliefs about the "essential" elements necessary for powerful creativity. John Millington Synge (1871–1909), playwright and cofounder, with Yeats and Lady Gregory, of the Abbey Theatre, caused controversy with his treatment of religion in *The Well of the Saints* (1905); Yeats regarded James Stephens (1882–1950) as one of the most promising younger Irish writers in his privileging of imagination and his knowledge of folk tradition and mythology; Irish artist and poet George Russell (1867–1935), Yeats's friend since their youth, shared Yeats's interest in the occult.

Sometimes I am told in commendation, if the newspaper is Irish, in condemnation if English, that my movement perished under the firing squads of 1916; sometimes that those firing squads made our realistic movement possible. If that statement is true, and it is only so in part, for romance was everywhere receding, it is because in the imagination of Pearse and his fellow soldiers the Sacrifice of the Mass had found the Red Branch in the tapestry; they went out to die calling upon Cuchulain:[3]—

> Fall, Hercules, from Heaven in tempests hurled
> To cleanse the beastly stable of this world.[4]

In one sense the poets of 1916 were not of what the newspapers call my school. The Gaelic League, made timid by a modern popularisation of Catholicism sprung from the aspidistra and not from the root of Jesse, dreaded intellectual daring and stuck to dictionary and grammar.[5] Pearse and MacDonagh[6] and others among the executed men would have done, or attempted, in Gaelic what we did or attempted in English.

Our mythology, our legends, differ from those of other European countries because down to the end of the seventeenth century they had the attention, perhaps the unquestioned belief, of peasant and noble alike; Homer belongs to sedentary men, even to-day our ancient queens, our mediaeval soldiers and lovers, can make a pedlar shudder. I can put my own thought, despair perhaps from the study of present circumstance in the light of ancient philosophy, into the mouth of rambling poets of the seventeenth century, or even of some imagined ballad singer of to-day, and the deeper my thought the more credible, the more peasant-like, are ballad singer and rambling poet. Some modern poets contend that jazz and music-hall songs are the folk art of our time, that we should mould our art upon them; we Irish poets, modern men also, reject every folk art that does not go back to Olympus. Give me time and a little youth and I will prove that even 'Johnny, I hardly knew ye'[7] goes back.

Mr. Arnold Toynbee in an annex to the second volume of *The Study of History* describes the birth and decay of what he calls the Far Western Christian culture; it lost at the Synod of Whitby its chance of mastering Europe, suffered final ecclesiastical defeat in the twelfth century with 'the thoroughgoing incorporation of the Irish Christendom into the Roman Church. In the political and literary spheres it lasted unbroken till the seventeenth century.' He then insists that if 'Jewish Zionism and Irish Nationalism succeed in achieving their aims, then Jewry and Irishry will each fit into its own tiny niche . . . among sixty or seventy na-

---

3. Padraic Pearse (1879–1916), executed for his part in the Irish Rising of 1916, had been inspired by the legendary Irish epic stories of Cuchulain, the hero of the Red Branch ("Fenian") warriors, and he had called for blood sacrifice as necessary for Ireland's renewal. The Rising was timed for Easter Monday 1916 to evoke Christ's death and resurrection, celebrated in the Christian Mass.
4. From "Hymnus in Noctem" in *The Shadow of the Night* (1594) by English dramatist George Chapman (c. 1559–1634).
5. The Gaelic League was founded in 1893 to preserve and promote the use of the Irish language. Yeats felt that in trying to be apolitical, it had doomed itself to marginalization. The aspidistra plant is a symbol of middle-class respectability; in the Bible, Jesse is the father of King David.
6. Thomas MacDonagh (1878–1916), Irish poet and critic, executed for his part in the Easter Rising of 1916.
7. An Irish street ballad dating from the late eighteenth century.

tional communities', find life somewhat easier, but cease to be 'the relic of an independent society . . . the romance of Ancient Ireland has at last come to an end . . . Modern Ireland has made up her mind, in our generation, to find her level as a willing inmate in our workaday Western world.'[8]

If Irish literature goes on as my generation planned it, it may do something to keep the 'Irishry' living, nor will the work of the realists hinder, nor the figures they imagine, nor those described in memoirs of the revolution. These last especially, like certain great political predecessors, Parnell, Swift, Lord Edward,[9] have stepped back into the tapestry. It may be indeed that certain characteristics of the 'Irishry' must grow in importance. When Lady Gregory asked me to annotate her *Visions and Beliefs* I began, that I might understand what she had taken down in Galway, an investigation of contemporary spiritualism. For several years I frequented those mediums who in various poor parts of London instruct artisans or their wives for a few pence upon their relations to their dead, to their employers, and to their children; then I compared what she had heard in Galway, or I in London, with the visions of Swedenborg, and, after my inadequate notes had been published, with Indian belief.[1] If Lady Gregory had not said when we passed an old man in the woods, 'That man may know the secret of the ages,' I might never have talked with Shri Purohit Swāmi nor made him translate his Master's travels in Tibet, nor helped him translate the Upanishads.[2] I think I now know why the gamekeeper at Coole[3] heard the footsteps of a deer on the edge of the lake where no deer had passed for a hundred years, and why a certain cracked old priest said that nobody had been to hell or heaven in his time, meaning thereby that the Rath[4] had got them all; that the dead stayed where they had lived, or near it, sought no abstract region of blessing or punishment but retreated, as it were, into the hidden character of their neighbourhood. I am convinced that in two or three generations it will become generally known that the mechanical theory[5] has no reality, that the natural and supernatural are knit together, that to escape a dangerous fanaticism we must study a new science; at that moment Europeans may find something attractive in a Christ posed against a background not of Judaism but of Druidism, not shut off in dead history, but flowing, concrete, phenomenal.

8. From *A Study of History* (1934) by British historian Arnold Toynbee (1889–1975). The Synod of Whitby, which met in 664, regularized Christian practices and rituals in Britain and Ireland to conform to Roman models.
9. Charles Stewart Parnell (1846–1891), the leader of the Irish Parliamentary Party and "uncrowned king" of Ireland, held the balance of power in the British Parliament in the 1880s and pressed the case for Irish Home Rule; Irish Nationalist Lord Edward Fitzgerald (1763–1798) was a leader of the 1798 Irish Rising.
1. Lady Gregory's *Visions and Beliefs in the West of Ireland* (1920) includes the essays "Witches and Wizards and Irish Folk-Lore" and "Swedenborg, Mediums, and the Desolate Places" by Yeats, both dated 1914. Swedish mystic, theologian, and scientist Emanuel Swedenborg (1688–1772) expounded spiritual doctrines based on his visions.
2. Yeats met Indian monk Shri Purohit Swāmi (1882–1941) in 1931 and translated with him *The Ten Principal Upanishads* (1937). Purohit translated and published *The Holy Mountain: Being the Story of a Pigrimage to Lake Amanas and of Initiation on Mount Kailas in Tibet*, by his "master," Bhagwan Shri Hamsa, in 1934.
3. Lady Gregory's estate in County Galway.
4. Raths—ancient forts—were in Ireland associated with spirits and faeries.
5. Newtonian physics and other scientific explanations of the material world.

I was born into this faith, have lived in it, and shall die in it; my Christ, a legitimate deduction from the Creed of St. Patrick as I think, is that Unity of Being Dante compared to a perfectly proportioned human body, Blake's 'Imagination,' what the Upanishads have named 'Self'[6]: nor is this unity distant and therefore intellectually understandable, but imminent, differing from man to man and age to age, taking upon itself pain and ugliness, 'eye of newt, and toe of frog.'[7]

Subconscious preoccupation with this theme brought me A Vision, its harsh geometry an incomplete interpretation. The 'Irishry' have preserved their ancient 'deposit' through wars which, during the sixteenth and seventeenth centuries, became wars of extermination;[8] no people, Lecky said at the opening of his Ireland in the Eighteenth Century, have undergone greater persecution, nor did that persecution altogether cease up to our own day.[9] No people hate as we do in whom that past is always alive, there are moments when hatred poisons my life and I accuse myself of effeminacy because I have not given it adequate expression. It is not enough to have put it into the mouth of a rambling peasant poet. Then I remind myself that though mine is the first English marriage I know of in the direct line, all my family names are English, and that I owe my soul to Shakespeare, to Spenser and to Blake, perhaps to William Morris,[1] and to the English language in which I think, speak, and write, that everything I love has come to me through English; my hatred tortures me with love, my love with hate. I am like the Tibetan monk who dreams at his initiation that he is eaten by a wild beast and learns on waking that he himself is eater and eaten. This is Irish hatred and solitude, the hatred of human life that made Swift write Gulliver and the epitaph upon his tomb,[2] that can still make us wag between extremes and doubt our sanity.

Again and again I am asked why I do not write in Gaelic. Some four or five years ago I was invited to dinner by a London society and found myself among London journalists, Indian students, and foreign political refugees. An Indian paper says it was a dinner in my honour; I hope not; I have forgotten, though I have a clear memory of my own angry mind. I should have spoken as men are expected to speak at public dinners; I should have paid and been paid conventional compliments; then they would speak of the refugees; from that on all would be lively and topical, foreign tyranny would be arraigned, England seem even to those confused Indians the protector of liberty; I grew angrier and angrier; Wordsworth,

6. Yeats evokes Dante's ideas of bodily perfection as expressed in Il Convito (and see also p. 222); Saint Patrick's "Creed" is the second paragraph in his Confessions; in Jerusalem, English poet William Blake (1757–1827) called imagination "the Divine Body of the Lord Jesus."
7. From Macbeth Act IV, scene 1, as the witches add the ingredients to their cauldron.
8. Yeats presumably has in mind here mainly the ruthless conquest of Ireland by Oliver Cromwell (1599–1658) in 1649–51, and the penal laws enforced after the victory of William of Orange over James II of Ireland in 1691. For "deposit" see p. 312, n. 1.
9. A History of Ireland in the Eighteenth Century (1892) by Irish historian William Hartpole Lecky (1838–1903). The Free State government was established in Ireland in 1922, following the Anglo-Irish War of 1919–21 and the Irish Civil War that followed.
1. William Morris (1834–1896), English writer and designer (see also p. 265, n. 8).
2. Swift's Gulliver's Travels (1726) includes a number of allegorical critiques of the culture and politics of his day. Yeats's poem "Swift's Epitaph" is a loose translation of the Latin epitaph on Swift's tomb in St. Patrick's Cathedral, Dublin. The epitaph declares that "savage indignation" can no longer trouble Swift in his tomb, and it urges the reader to imitate Swift, since he served "human liberty."

that typical Englishman, had published his famous sonnet to François Dominique Toussaint, a Santo Domingo Negro:—

> There's not a breathing of the common wind
> That will forget thee[3]

in the year when Emmet conspired and died, and he remembered that rebellion as little as the half hanging and the pitch cap that preceded it by half a dozen years.[4] That there might be no topical speeches I denounced the oppression of the people of India; being a man of letters, not a politician, I told how they had been forced to learn everything, even their own Sanskrit, through the vehicle of English till the first discoverer of wisdom had become bywords for vague abstract facility. I begged the Indian writers present to remember that no man can think or write with music and vigour except in his mother tongue. I turned a friendly audience hostile, yet when I think of that scene I am unrepentant and angry.

I could no more have written in Gaelic than can those Indians write in English; Gaelic is my national language, but it is not my mother tongue.

III. STYLE AND ATTITUDE

Style is almost unconscious. I know what I have tried to do, little what I have done. Contemporary lyric poems, even those that moved me—*The Stream's Secret, Dolores*[5]—seemed too long, but an Irish preference for a swift current might be mere indolence, yet Burns may have felt the same when he read Thomson and Cowper.[6] The English mind is meditative, rich, deliberate; it may remember the Thames valley.[7] I planned to write short lyrics or poetic drama where every speech would be short and concentrated, knit by dramatic tension, and I did so with more confidence because young English poets were at that time writing out of emotion at the moment of crisis, though their old slow-moving meditation returned almost at once. Then, and in this English poetry has followed my lead, I tried to make the language of poetry coincide with that of passionate, normal speech. I wanted to write in whatever language comes most naturally when we soliloquise, as I do all day long, upon the events of our own lives or of any life where we can see ourselves for the moment. I sometimes compare myself with the mad old slum women I hear denouncing and remembering; 'How dare you,' I heard one say of some imaginary suitor, 'and you without health or a home!' If I spoke my thoughts aloud they might be as angry and as wild. It was a long time before I had made

---

3. Lines 11–12 of "To Toussaint l'Overture" by William Wordsworth (1770–1850). L'Overture (1743–1803), a rebel against French rule in Haiti, was imprisoned after protesting the French reinstitution of slavery and died in custody. Yeats notes the hypocrisy of an English poet celebrating the struggle against French tyranny in Haiti while ignoring his own country's brutal repression of Ireland.

4. Irish Nationalist Robert Emmet (1778–1803) was executed for his part in the Irish rebellion of 1803. In the martial law that preceded and followed the Irish Rising of 1798, burning pitch caps were used as a form of torture.

5. "The Stream's Secret" by Dante Gabriel Rossetti (1828–1882) is 234 lines long; "Dolores" by Algernon Charles Swinburne (1837–1909) has 386 lines.

6. Scottish poet James Thomson (1700–1748) and English poet William Cowper (1731–1800) are best known for long poems; Scottish poet Robert Burns (1759–1796), for short lyrics.

7. The Thames River runs west from the heartland of southern England, through London, and then to the sea.

a language to my liking; I began to make it when I discovered some twenty years ago that I must seek, not as Wordsworth thought, words in common use, but a powerful and passionate syntax, and a complete coincidence between period and stanza.[8] Because I need a passionate syntax for passionate subject-matter I compel myself to accept those traditional metres that have developed with the language. Ezra Pound, Turner, Lawrence[9] wrote admirable free verse, I could not. I would lose myself, become joyless like those mad old women. The translators of the Bible, Sir Thomas Browne,[1] certain translators from the Greek when translators still bothered about rhythm, created a form midway between prose and verse that seems natural to impersonal meditation; but all that is personal soon rots; it must be packed in ice or salt. Once when I was in delirium from pneumonia I dictated a letter to George Moore telling him to eat salt because it was a symbol of eternity;[2] the delirium passed, I had no memory of that letter, but I must have meant what I now mean. If I wrote of personal love or sorrow in free verse, or in any rhythm that left it unchanged, amid all its accidence, I would be full of self-contempt because of my egotism and indiscretion, and foresee the boredom of my reader. I must choose a traditional stanza, even what I alter must seem traditional. I commit my emotion to shepherds, herdsmen, camel-drivers, learned men, Milton's or Shelley's Platonist, that tower Palmer drew.[3] Talk to me of originality and I will turn on you with rage. I am a crowd, I am a lonely man, I am nothing. Ancient salt is best packing. The heroes of Shakespeare convey to us through their looks, or through the metaphorical patterns of their speech, the sudden enlargement of their vision, their ecstasy at the approach of death: 'She should have died hereafter,' 'Of many thousand kisses, the poor last,' 'Absent thee from felicity awhile.'[4] They have become God or Mother Goddess, the pelican, 'My baby at my breast,'[5] but all must be cold; no actress has ever sobbed when she played Cleopatra, even the shallow brain of a producer has never thought of such a thing. The supernatural is present, cold winds blow across our hands, upon our faces, the thermometer falls, and because of that cold we are hated by journalists and groundlings. There may be in this or that detail painful tragedy, but in the whole work none. I have heard Lady Gregory say, rejecting some play in the modern manner sent to the Abbey Theatre, 'Tragedy must be

---

8. In his Preface to *Lyrical Ballads* (1800), Wordsworth had called for a poetry drawing on "language really used by men."
9. Yeats included work by American poet Ezra Pound (1885–1972), English poet Walter Turner (1889–1946), and English poet and novelist D. H. Lawrence (1885–1930) in his *Oxford Book of Modern Verse* (1936).
1. Writer and physician (1605–1682) whose prose is elaborately styled.
2. Irish novelist George Moore (1852–1933), with whom Yeats collaborated on the play *Diarmuid and Grania* (produced in 1901). Yeats refers to the medieval belief in salt as "a symbol of eternity" and therefore a "spell against spirits" in his notes to Lady Gregory's *Visions and Beliefs in the West of Ireland* (1920).
3. Milton's 1633 poem "Il Penseroso" ("The Pensive Man") features a scholar who aspires to work in "some high lonely tower" where he can "unsphere / The spirit of Plato, to unfold / What worlds or what vast regions hold / The immortal mind that has forsook / Her mansion in this fleshly nook." In "Prince Athanase: A Fragment" (1817), Shelley's eponymous hero roves the world searching for ideal love. English artist Samuel Palmer (1805–1881) illustrated Milton's "Il Penseroso" with an etching entitled "The Lonely Tower," drawn in 1879.
4. Respectively, from *Macbeth*, Act V, scene 4; *Antony and Cleopatra*, Act IV, scene 15; *Hamlet*, Act V, scene 2.
5. From *Antony and Cleopatra*, Act V, scene 2.

a joy to the man who dies.'[6] Nor is it any different with lyrics, songs, narrative poems; neither scholars nor the populace have sung or read anything generation after generation because of its pain. The maid of honour whose tragedy they sing must be lifted out of history with timeless pattern, she is one of the four Maries,[7] the rhythm is old and familiar, imagination must dance, must be carried beyond feeling into the aboriginal ice. Is ice the correct word? I once boasted, copying the phrase from a letter of my father's, that I would write a poem 'cold and passionate as the dawn.'[8]

When I wrote in blank verse I was dissatisfied; my vaguely mediaeval *Countess Cathleen* fitted the measure, but our Heroic Age went better, or so I fancied, in the ballad metre of *The Green Helmet*.[9] There was something in what I felt about Deirdre, about Cuchulain,[1] that rejected the Renaissance and its characteristic metres, and this was a principal reason why I created in dance plays[2] the form that varies blank verse with lyric metres. When I speak blank verse and analyse my feelings, I stand at a moment of history when instinct, its traditional songs and dances, its general agreement, is of the past. I have been cast up out of the whale's belly[3] though I still remember the sound and sway that came from beyond its ribs, and, like the Queen in Paul Fort's ballad, I smell of the fish of the sea.[4] The contrapuntal structure of the verse, to employ a term adopted by Robert Bridges,[5] combines the past and present. If I repeat the first line of *Paradise Lost* so as to emphasise its five feet I am among the folk singers—'Of mán's fírst dísobédience ánd the frúit,' but speak it as I should I cross it with another emphasis, that of passionate prose—'Of mán's fírst disobédience and the frúit,' or 'Of mán's fírst dísobedience and the frúit'; the folk song is still there, but a ghostly voice, an unvariable possibility, an unconscious norm. What moves me and my hearer is a vivid speech that has no laws except that it must not exorcise the ghostly voice. I am awake and asleep, at my moment of revelation, self-possessed in self-surrender; there is no rhyme, no echo of the beaten drum, the dancing foot, that would overset my balance. When I was a boy I wrote a poem upon dancing that had one good line: 'They snatch with their hands at the sleep of the skies.'[6] If I sat down and thought for a year I would discover that but for certain syllabic limitations, a rejection or acceptance of certain elisions, I must wake or sleep.

6. For Yeats's most forceful expressions of his idea of "tragic joy," see "The Gyres" and "Lapis Lazuli," pp. 114–16.
7. Mary, Queen of Scots (1542–1587), had four maids who served her.
8. In the poem "The Fisherman" (see p. 63).
9. *The Countess Cathleen* (1892, but subsequently revised several times) was written in blank verse; *The Green Helmet* (1910) is in heptameter, giving a sense of underlying ballad meter to its lines, since ballad meter alternates lines of four and three stresses.
1. Yeats's play *Deirdre* (1907) is based on the Ulster cycle of Irish mythology, in which Deirdre is chosen to be high queen of Ulster, elopes with Naoise, and takes her own life when Naoise and his brothers are murdered; Cuchulain is the central warrior hero of the Ulster cycle tales.
2. Such as *At the Hawk's Well* (see pp. 160–68).
3. See Jonah 2.10.
4. In "La Reine á la Mer" ("The Queen in the Sea") by French poet Paul Fort (1872–1960).
5. English poet (1844–1930), Poet Laureate of England 1913–30, who, like Yeats, favored traditional verse forms, commented in his criticism on the inevitable play in poetry between underlying regular meter and the actual rhythms of poetry as spoken.
6. This poem was not published, and apparently not saved.

The Countess Cathleen could speak a blank verse which I had loosened, almost put out of joint, for her need, because I thought of her as mediaeval and thereby connected her with the general European movement. For Deirdre and Cuchulain and all the other figures of Irish legend are still in the whale's belly.

IV. WHITHER?

The young English poets reject dream and personal emotion; they have thought out opinions that join them to this or that political party; they employ an intricate psychology, action in character, not as in the ballads character in action, and all consider that they have a right to the same close attention that men pay to the mathematician and the metaphysician. One of the more distinguished has just explained that man has hitherto slept but must now awake. They are determined to express the factory, the metropolis, that they may be modern.[7] Young men teaching school in some picturesque cathedral town, or settled for life in Capri or in Sicily, defend their type of metaphor by saying that it comes naturally to a man who travels to his work by Tube.[8] I am indebted to a man of this school who went through my work at my request, crossing out all conventional metaphors, but they seem to me to have rejected also those dream associations which were the whole art of Mallarmé.[9] He had topped a previous wave. As they express not what the Upanishads call 'that ancient Self' but individual intellect, they have the right to choose the man in the Tube because of his objective importance. They attempt to kill the whale, push the Renaissance higher yet, out-think Leonardo;[1] their verse kills the folk ghost and yet would remain verse. I am joined to the 'Irishry' and I expect a counter-Renaissance. No doubt it is part of the game to push that Renaissance; I make no complaint; I am accustomed to the geometrical arrangement of history in A Vision, but I go deeper than 'custom' for my convictions. When I stand upon O'Connell Bridge[2] in the half-light and notice that discordant architecture, all those electric signs, where modern heterogeneity has taken physical form, a vague hatred comes up out of my own dark and I am certain that wherever in Europe there are minds strong enough to lead others the same vague hatred rises; in four or five or in less generations this hatred will have issued in violence and imposed some kind of rule of kindred. I cannot know the nature of that rule, for its opposite fills the light; all I can do to bring it nearer is to intensify my hatred. I am no Nationalist, except in Ireland for passing reasons; State and Nation are the work of intellect, and when you consider what comes before and after them they are, as Victor Hugo said of something or other, not worth the blade of grass God gives for the nest of the linnet.[3]

7. Yeats probably has W. H. Auden (1907–1973) in mind here.
8. Probably English writers C. Day Lewis (1904–1972), who taught at Cheltenham Junior School in the early 1930s, and D. H. Lawrence (1885–1930), who lived in Capri and Sicily in 1920–21. The Tube is the London underground railway.
9. French Symbolist poet Stéphane Mallarmé (1842–1898).
1. Italian Renaissance artist and inventor Leonardo da Vinci (1452–1519).
2. O'Connell Bridge crosses the River Liffey in central Dublin.
3. The remark, ascribed to French novelist Victor Hugo (1802–1885), is untraced.

From Introduction to Essays

*   *   *

I have never said clearly that I condemn all that is not tradition, that there is a subject-matter which has descended like that 'deposit' certain philosophers speak of.[1] At the end of his essay upon 'Style' Pater says that a book written according to the principles he has laid down will be well written,[2] but whether it is a great book or not depends upon subject-matter. This subject-matter is something I have received from the generations, part of that compact with my fellow men made in my name before I was born. I cannot break from it without breaking from some part of my own nature, and sometimes it has come to me in supernormal experience; I have met with ancient myths in my dreams, brightly lit; and I think it allied to the wisdom or instinct that guides a migratory bird.

A table of values, heroic joy always, intellectual curiosity and so on— and a public theme: in Japan the mountain scenery of China; in Greece its cyclic tales; in Europe the Christian mythology; this or that national theme. I speak of poets and imaginative writers; the great realistic novelists almost without exception describe familiar scenes and people; realism is always topical, it has for public theme the public itself. Flaubert excused the failure of the principal character in his *Salammbô* by the words 'I could not visit her'.[3] I think of the German actress who said to a reporter, 'To know a man you must talk with him, eat with him, sleep with him. That is how I know Mr. Bernard Shaw.[4] Then too I would have all the arts draw together; recover their ancient association, the painter painting what the poet has written, the musician setting the poet's words to simple airs, that the horseman and the engine-driver may sing them at their work. Nor am I for a changeless tradition. I would rejoice if a rich betrothed man asked Mr T.S. Eliot and the dancer Ninette de Valois[5] to pick a musician and compose a new marriage service, for such a service might restore a lost subject-matter to the imaginative arts and be good for the clergy. I admit other themes, even those that have no tradition; I have never blamed the brothers Caracci [*sic*] for painting the butcher's shop they came from,[6] and why should not that fat, naked woman look like pork? But those themes we share and inherit so long as they engage our emotions come first.

1. The Greek term *paratheke*, meaning "deposit," appears in the New Testament and has been interpreted as "spiritual heritage" or "spiritual tradition."
2. The essay "Style" (1888) by Walter Pater (1839–1894).
3. French novelist Gustave Flaubert (1821–1880) wrote that he did not know whether the eponymous heroine of his novel *Salammbô* (1862) was realistically portrayed, since it was impossible for him to get to know an Oriental woman sufficiently well.
4. English dramatist (1856–1950).
5. Poet, critic, and dramatist T. S. Eliot (1888–1965); and dancer and choreographer Ninette de Valois (1898–1998), who choreographed and danced in productions of Yeats's plays in the late 1920s.
6. Agostino (1557–1602) and Annibale Carracci (1560–1609) and their cousin Lodovico Carracci (1555–1617) were Italian painters; Annibale's oil *Butcher Shop* reputedly depicts them at work as butchers.

When that is no longer possible we are broken off and separate, some sort of dry faggot, and the time has come to read criticism and talk of our point of view. I thought when I was young—Walt Whitman had something to do with it—that the poet, painter and musician should do nothing but express themselves.[7] When the laboratories, pulpits, and newspapers had imposed themselves in the place of tradition the thought was our protection. It may be so still in the provinces, but sometimes when the provinces are out of earshot I may speak the truth. A poet is justified not by the expression of himself, but by the public he finds or creates; a public made by others ready to his hand if he is a mere popular poet, but a new public, a new form of life, if he is a man of genius.

* * *

Introduction to Plays

I

The Theatre for which these plays were written was the creation of seven people: four players, Sara Allgood, her sister Maire O'Neill, girls in a blind factory who joined a patriotic society;[1] William Fay, Frank Fay, an electric light fitter and an accountant's clerk who got up plays at a coffee-house;[2] three writers, Lady Gregory, John Synge,[3] and I. If we all told the story we would all tell it differently. Somewhere among my printed diaries is a note describing how on the same night my two sisters and their servant dreamt the same dream in three different grotesque forms.[4] Once I was in meditation with three students of the supernormal faculties; our instructor had given us the same theme, what, I have forgotten; one saw a ripe fruit, one an unripe, one a lit torch, one an unlit. Science has never thought about the subject and so has no explanation of those parallel streams that make up a great part of history. When I follow back my stream to its source I find two dominant desires: I wanted to get rid of irrelevant movement— the stage must become still that words might keep all their vividness—and I wanted vivid words. When I saw a London play, I saw actors crossing the stage not because the play compelled them, but because a producer said they must do so keep the attention of the audience; and I heard words that had no vividness except what they borrowed from the situation. It seems that I was confirmed in this idea or I found it when I first saw Sarah

7. American poet Walt Whitman (1819–1892); Yeats probably has in mind his poem "Song of Myself."
1. Sara Allgood (1883–1950) and her sister Molly Allgood (1885–1952) (who went by her stage name, "Maire O'Neill") played most of the female lead roles in the first decade of the Abbey Theatre, founded in Dublin in 1904; the "patriotic society" was Inghinidhe na hÉireann ("Daughters of Ireland").
2. William Fay (1872–1947) and his brother Frank Fay (1870–1931) were active in performing plays in Dublin around the turn of the century, and they formed the National Theatre Society, from which the Abbey emerged, with Yeats in 1902.
3. Playwright John Millington Synge (1871–1909) was cofounder and codirector of the Abbey Theatre with Yeats and Lady Gregory (1852–1932).
4. This note is in Yeats's 1909 *Journal*, entry 93.

Bernhardt play in *Phèdre*, and that it was I who converted the players, but I am old, I must have many false memories; perhaps I was Synge's convert. It was certainly a day of triumph when the first act of *The Well of the Saints*[5] held its audience, though the two chief persons sat side by side under a stone cross from start to finish. This rejection of all needless movement first drew the attention of critics. The players still try to preserve it, though audiences accustomed to the cinema expect constant change; perhaps it was most necessary in that first period when the comedies of Lady Gregory, the tragi-comedies of Synge, my own blank-verse plays, made up our repertory, all needing whether in verse or prose an ear attentive to every rhythm.

I hated the existing conventions of the theatre, not because conventions are wrong but because soliloquies and players who must always face the audience and stand far apart when they speak—'dressing the stage' it was called—had been mixed up with too many bad plays to be endurable. Frank Fay agreed, yet he knew the history of all the conventions and sometimes loved them. I would put into his hands a spear instead of a sword because I knew that he would flourish a sword in imitation of an actor in an eighteenth-century engraving. He knew everything, even that Racine at rehearsal made his leading lady speak on musical notes and that Ireland had preserved longer than England the rhythmical utterance of the Shakespearean stage. He was openly, dogmatically, of that school of Talma[6] which permits an actor, as Gordon Craig[7] has said, to throw up an arm calling down the thunderbolts of Heaven, instead of seeming to pick up pins from the floor. Were he living now and both of us young, I would ask his help to elaborate new conventions in writing and representation; for Synge, Lady Gregory, and I were all instinctively of the school of Talma. Do not those tragic sentences, 'shivering into seventy winters,' 'a starved ass braying in the yard,'[8] require convention as much as a blank-verse line? And there are scenes in *The Well of the Saints* which seem to me over-rich in words because the realistic action does not permit that stilling and slowing which turns the imagination in upon itself.

II

I wanted all my poetry to be spoken on a stage or sung and, because I did not understand my own instincts, gave half a dozen wrong or secondary reasons; but a month ago I understood my reasons. I have spent my life in clearing out of poetry every phrase written for the eye, and bringing all

5. French actress Sarah Bernhardt (1844–1923), the greatest tragedienne of her day, excelled in the tragedy *Phèdre* by French dramatist Jean Racine (1639–1699). Synge's *The Well of the Saints* was first produced at the Abbey Theatre in 1905 but drew small audiences and generally unfavorable reviews, being viewed by some critics as an attack on Catholicism. Yeats's admiration for the play endured.

6. French actor François Talma (1762–1826) was notorious for his exaggerated, passionate acting style.

7. Stage designer Edward Gordon Craig (1872–1966) produced sets for Yeats's play *The Hour Glass* and changed Yeats's conception of staging through his invention of moveable screens, which allowed abstract backgrounds and quickly modified stage depths and lighting effects.

8. Yeats misquotes "shivering into seventy years" from Lady Gregory's play *The Workhouse Ward* (1908) and "an old braying jackass strayed upon the rocks" from Synge's *The Playboy of the Western World* (1907).

back to syntax that is for ear alone. Let the eye take delight in the form of the singer and in the panorama of the stage and be content with that. Charles Ricketts[9] once designed for me a black jester costume for the singer, and both he and Craig helped with the panorama, but my audience was for comedy—for Synge, for Lady Gregory, for O'Casey[1]—not for me. I was content, for I knew that comedy was the modern art.

As I altered my syntax I altered my intellect. Browning[2] said that he could not write a successful play because interested not in character in action but in action in character. I had begun to get rid of everything that is not, whether in lyric or dramatic poetry, in some sense character in action; a pause in the midst of action perhaps, but action always its end and theme. 'Write for the ear,' I thought, so that you may be instantly understood as when actor or folk singer stands before an audience. I delight in active men, taking the same delight in soldier and craftsman; I would have poetry turn its back upon all that modish curiosity, psychology—the poetic theme has always been present. I recall an Indian tale: certain men said to the greatest of the sages, 'Who are your Masters?' And he replied, 'The wind and the harlot, the virgin and the child, the lion and the eagle.'[3]

From *On the Boiler*[1] (1939)

From Preliminaries

IV

As I write these words the Abbey Players are finishing a successful American tour.[2] These tours, and Irish songs and novels, when they come from a deeper life than their nineteenth century predecessors, are taking the place of political speakers, political organisations, in holding together the twenty scattered millions conscious of their Irish blood. The attitude towards life of Irish writers and dramatists at this moment will have historical importance. The success of the Abbey Theatre has grown out of a single conviction of its founders: I was the spokesman because I was born arrogant and had learnt an artist's arrogance—"Not what you want but what we want'"—and we were the first modern theatre that said it. I did not speak for John Synge, Augusta Gregory,[3] and myself alone, but for all the dramatists of the theatre. Again and again somebody speaking for our audience, for an influential newspaper or political organisation, has demanded more of this kind of play or less, or none, of that. They have not understood that we cannot, and if we could would not comply; the mo-

---

9. Irish painter and designer Charles Ricketts (1866–1931).
1. Sean O'Casey (1880–1964), the most popular Abbey Theatre dramatist in the 1920s.
2. English poet Robert Browning (1812–1889), in the preface to his play *Strafford* (1837).
3. Untraced.
1. In the opening of *On the Boiler*, Yeats recalls that during his childhood a "mad ship's carpenter" in Sligo had used an old boiler as a soapbox when "denouncing his neighbours."
2. The Abbey Theatre Company toured in the United States from September 1937 to May 1938.
3. John Millington Synge (1871–1909), playwright and cofounder of the Abbey Theatre, with Yeats and Lady Gregory, in 1904.

ment any dramatist has some dramatic sense and applies it to our Irish theme he is played. We may help him with his technique or to clear his mind of the second-hand or the second-rate in their cruder forms, but beyond that we can do nothing. He must find himself and mould his dramatic form to his nature after his own fashion, and that is why we have produced some of the best plays of modern times, and a far greater number of the worst. And what I have said of the dramatists is true of the actors, though there the bad comedians do not reach our principal company. I have seen English producers turn their players into mimics; but all our producers do for theirs, or so it was in my day and I suppose it is still the same, is to help them to understand the play and their own natures.

Yet the theatre has not, apart from this one quality, gone my way or in any way I wanted it to go, and often looking back I have wondered if I did right in giving so much of my life to the expression of other men's genius. According to the Indians a man may do much good yet lose his own soul. Then I say to myself, I have had greater luck than any other modern English-speaking dramatist; I have aimed at tragic ecstasy and here and there in my own work and in the work of my friends I have seen it greatly played. What does it matter that it belongs to a dead art and to a time when a man spoke out of an experience and a culture that were not of his time alone, but held his time, as it were, at arm's length, that he might be a spectator of the ages.

*   *   *

From To-morrow's Revolution

III

* * * Since about 1900 the better stocks have not been replacing their numbers, while the stupider and less healthy have been more than replacing theirs.[1] Unless there is a change in the public mind every rank above the lowest must degenerate, and, as inferior men push up into its gaps, degenerate more and more quickly. The results are already visible in the degeneration of literature, newspapers, amusements (there was once a stock company playing Shakespeare in every considerable town), and, I am convinced, in benefactions like that of Lord Nuffield,[2] a self-made man, to Oxford, which must gradually substitute applied science for ancient wisdom. * * *

1. Yeats's conviction that civilization was declining, and that only aristocratic families rooted in tradition could provide elite future leaders, is reflected broadly in his later writings (see, for instance, *Purgatory*, pp. 169–74, and "Under Ben Bulben," pp. 122–25). In the late 1930s he read many works on eugenics, and this section of *On the Boiler* attempts to offer "scientific" support for his convictions.
2. William Morris (1877–1963), first Viscount Nuffield, the owner of the Morris automobile manufacturing company based in Oxford, gave a large endowment to the Oxford medical school in 1936, and in 1937 he established Nuffield College as a center for political, economic, and social studies.

IV

* * * If some financial re-organisation such as Major Douglas plans,[3] and that better organisation of agriculture and industry which many economists expect, enable everybody without effort to procure all necessities of life and so remove the last check upon the multiplication of the uneducatable masses, it will become the duty of the educated classes to seize and control one or more of those necessities. The drilled and docile masses may submit, but a prolonged civil war seems more likely, with the victory of the skilful, riding their machines as did the feudal knights their armoured horses. During the Great War[4] Germany had four hundred submarine commanders, and sixty per cent. of the damage done was the work of twenty-four men. The danger is that there will be no war, that the skilled will attempt nothing, that the European civilisation, like those older civilisations that saw the triumph of their gangrel[5] stocks, will accept decay. * * *

---

3. Major Clifford Douglas (1879–1952) advocated Social Credit, in which central bank currencies would be replaced by a system of exchangeable credits corresponding to the value of production or services. For Yeats this represented a form of communism.
4. World War I.
5. A Scottish term meaning "vagrant," but seemingly used by Yeats with the subtext of "mongrel."

CRITICISM

Criticism by Yeats's Contemporaries

OSCAR WILDE

[Review of *The Wanderings of Oisin and Other Poems*]†

Books of poetry by young writers are usually promissory notes that are never met. Now and then, however, one comes across a volume that is so far above the average that one can hardly resist the fascinating temptation of recklessly prophesying a fine future for its author. Such a book Mr. Yeats's *Wanderings of Oisin* certainly is. Here we find nobility of treatment and nobility of subject-matter, delicacy of poetic instinct and richness of imaginative resource. Unequal and uneven much of the work must be admitted to be. Mr. Yeats does not try to 'out-baby' Wordsworth, we are glad to say; but he occasionally succeeds in 'out-glittering' Keats, and, here and there, in his book we come across strange crudities and irritating conceits. But when he is at his best he is very good. If he has not the grand simplicity of epic treatment, he has at least something of the largeness of vision that belongs to the epical temper. He does not rob of their stature the great heroes of Celtic mythology. He is very naïve and very primitive and speaks of his giants with the air of a child.

* * *

ARTHUR SYMONS

[Review of *Poems* and *The Wind Among the Reeds*]‡

Mr. Yeats is the only one among the younger English poets who has the whole poetical temperament, and nothing but the poetical temperament. He lives on one plane, and you will find in the whole of his work, with its varying degrees of artistic achievement, no unworthy or trivial mood, no occasional concession to the fatigue of high thinking. It is this continuously poetical quality of mind that seems to me to distinguish Mr. Yeats from the many men of talent, and to place him among the few men

† From *Pall Mall Gazette*, July 12, 1889.
‡ From *The Saturday Review*, May 6, 1899.

321

of genius. A man may indeed be a poet because he has written a single perfect lyric. He will not be a poet of high order, he will not be a poet in the full sense, unless his work, however unequal it may be in actual literary skill, presents this undeviating aspect, as of one to whom the act of writing is no more than the occasional flowering of a mood into speech. And that, certainly, is the impression which remains with one after a careful reading of the revised edition of Mr. Yeats' collected poems and of his new volume of lyrics, 'The Wind among the Reeds', which have appeared almost simultaneously. The big book, now reissued with a cover by a young artist of subtle and delicate talent, Miss Althea Gyles, contains work of many kinds. There is a play, 'The Countess Cathleen', which is to be performed in Dublin next week; and a second play, 'The Land of Heart's Desire', which was performed in London in 1894. 'The Countess Cathleen' is certainly Mr. Yeats' masterpiece. I have but just come from seeing it rehearsed, and the rehearsal has taught me, what I indeed suspected, that it is not only splendid poetry, but, in a very serious sense, a fine acting play. Its visionary ecstasy is firmly embodied in persons whose action is indeed largely a spiritual action, but action which has the lyrical movement of great drama. Here is poetry which is not only heard, but seen; forming a picture, not less than moving to music. And here it is the poetry which makes the drama, or I might say equally the drama which makes the poetry; for the finest writing is always part of the dramatic action, not a hindrance to it, as in almost all the poetical plays of this century. In the long narrative poem contained in the same volume, 'The Wanderings of Oisin', an early work, much rewritten, a far less mature skill has squandered lyrical poetry with a romantic prodigality. Among the lyrics in other parts of the book there are a few which Mr. Yeats has never excelled in a felicity which seems almost a matter of mere luck; there is not a lyric which has not some personal quality of beauty; but we must turn to the new volume to find the full extent of his capacity as a lyric poet.

In the new volume, 'The Wind among the Reeds', in which symbolism extends to the cover, where reeds are woven into a net to catch the wandering sounds, Mr. Yeats becomes completely master of himself and of his own resources. Technically the verse is far in advance of anything he has ever done, and if a certain youthful freshness, as of one to whom the woods were still the only talkers upon earth, has gone inevitably, its place has been taken by a deeper, more passionate, and wiser sense of the 'everlasting voices' which he has come to apprehend, no longer quite joyously, in the crying of birds, the tongues of flame, and the silence of the heart. It is only gradually that Mr. Yeats has learnt to become quite human. Life is the last thing he has learnt, and it is life, an extraordinarily intense inner life, that I find in this book of lyrics, which may seem also to be one long 'hymn to intellectual beauty'.

*　*　*

EZRA POUND

[Review of *Responsibilities*]†

* * * [W]henever I mention Mr. Yeats I am apt to be assailed with questions: "Will Mr. Yeats do anything more?", "Is Yeats in the movement?", "How *can* the chap go on writing this sort of thing?"

And to these inquiries I can only say that Mr. Yeats' vitality is quite unimpaired, and that I dare say he'll do a good deal; and that up to date no one has shown any disposition to supersede him as the best poet in England, or any likelihood of doing so for some time; and that after all Mr. Yeats has brought a new music upon the harp, and that one man seldom leads two movements to triumph, and that it is quite enough that he should have brought in the sound of keening and the skirl of the Irish ballads, and driven out the sentimental cadence with memories of *The County of Mayo* and *The Coolun*; and that the production of good poetry is a very slow matter, and that, as touching the greatest of dead poets, many of them could easily have left that *magnam partem*, which keeps them with us, upon a single quire of foolscap or at most upon two; and that there is no need for a poet to repair each morning of his life to the *Piazza dei Signori* to turn a new sort of somersault; and that Mr. Yeats is so assuredly an immortal that there is no need for him to recast his style to suit our winds of doctrine; and that, all these things being so, there is nevertheless a manifestly new note in his later work that they might do worse than attend to.

"Is Mr. Yeats an Imagiste?" No, Mr. Yeats is a symbolist, but he has written *des Images* as have many good poets before him; so that is nothing against him, and he has nothing against them (*les Imagistes*), at least so far as I know—except what he calls "their devil's metres."

He has written *des Images* in such poems as *Braseal and the Fisherman*; beginning, "Though you hide in the ebb and flow of the pale tide when the moon has set;" and he has driven out the inversion and written with prose directness in such lyrics as, "I heard the old men say everything alters"; and these things are not subject to a changing of the fashions. What I mean by the new note—you could hardly call it a change of style— was apparent four years ago in his *No Second Troy*, beginning, "Why should I blame her," and ending—

> Beauty like a tightened bow, a kind
> That is not natural in any age like this,
> Being high and solitary and most stern?
> Why, what could she have done being what she is?
> Was there another Troy for her to burn?

I am not sure that it becomes apparent in partial quotation, but with the appearance of *The Green Helmet and Other Poems* one felt that the

† From *Poetry* (Chicago) (May 1914): 65–68.

minor note—I use the word strictly in the musical sense—had gone or was going out of his poetry; that he was at such a cross roads as we find in

Voi che intendendo il terzo ciel movete.[1]

And since that time one has felt his work becoming gaunter, seeking greater hardness of outline. I do not say that this is demonstrable by any particular passage. *Romantic Ireland's Dead and Gone* is no better than Red Hanrahan's song about Ireland, but it is harder. Mr. Yeats appears to have seen with the outer eye in *To a Child Dancing on the Shore* (the first poem, not the one printed in this issue). The hardness can perhaps be more easily noted in *The Magi*.

Such poems as *When Helen Lived* and *The Realists* serve at least to show that the tongue has not lost its cunning. On the other hand, it is impossible to take any interest in a poem like *The Two Kings*—one might as well read the *Idyls* of another. *The Grey Rock* is, I admit, obscure, but it outweighs this by a curious nobility, a nobility which is, to me at least, the very core of Mr. Yeats' production, the constant element of his writing.

In support of my prediction, or of my theories, regarding his change of manner, real or intended, we have at least two pronouncements of the poet himself, the first in *A Coat* * * * . The verses, *A Coat*, should satisfy those who have complained of Mr. Yeats' four and forty followers, that they would "rather read their Yeats in the original." Mr. Yeats had indicated the feeling once before with

Tell me, do the wolf-dogs praise their fleas?

which is direct enough in all conscience, and free of the "glamour." I've not a word against the glamour as it appears in Yeats' early poems, but we have had so many other pseudo-glamours and glamourlets and mists and fogs since the nineties that one is about ready for hard light.

And this quality of hard light is precisely what one finds in the beginning of his *The Magi*:

Now as at all times I can see in the mind's eye
In their stiff, painted clothes, the pale unsatisfied ones
Appear and disappear in the blue depth of the sky
With all their ancient faces like rain-beaten stones,
And all their helms of silver hovering side by side.

Of course a passage like that, a passage of *imagisme*, may occur in a poem not otherwise *imagiste*, in the same way that a lyrical passage may occur in a narrative, or in some poem not otherwise lyrical. There have always been two sorts of poetry which are, for me at least, the most "poetic;" they are firstly, the sort of poetry which seems to be music just forcing itself into articulate speech, and, secondly, that sort of poetry which seems as if sculpture or painting were just forced or forcing itself into words. The gulf between evocation and description, in this latter case, is the unbridgeable difference between genius and talent. It is perhaps the highest function of

---

1. Pound here quotes the opening line of Dante's *Il Convivio*: "You who understand fully, move the third heaven."

art that it should fill the mind with a noble profusion of sounds and images, that it should furnish the life of the mind with such accompaniment and surrounding. At any rate Mr. Yeats' work has done this in the past and still continues to do so. * * *

GEORGE MOORE

From *Vale*†

Chapter VII

As soon as the applause died away Yeats, who had lately returned to us from the States with a paunch, a huge stride, and an immense fur overcoat, rose to speak. We were surprised at the change in his appearance, and could hardly believe our ears when, instead of talking to us as he used to do about the old stories come down from generation to generation, he began to thunder like Ben Tillett himself against the middle classes, stamping his feet, working himself into a great passion, and all because the middle classes did not dip their hands into their pockets and give Lane the money he wanted for his exhibition. It is impossible to imagine the hatred which came into his voice when he spoke the words "the middle classes"; one would have thought that he was speaking against a personal foe; but there are millions in the middle classes! And we looked round asking each other with our eyes where on earth our Willie Yeats had picked up such extraordinary ideas. He could hardly have gathered in the United States the ridiculous idea that none but titled and carriage-folk can appreciate pictures. And we asked ourselves why Willie Yeats should feel himself called upon to denounce the class to which he himself belonged essentially: on one side excellent mercantile millers and ship owners, and on the other a portrait painter of rare talent. With so admirable a parentage it did not seem to us necessary that a man should look back for an ancestry, and we had laughed at the story, looking upon it as *ben trovato*, that on one occasion when Yeats was crooning over Æ's fire he had said that if he had his rights he would be Duke of Ormonde, and that Æ had answered, "In any case, Willie, you are overlooking your father,"—a detestable remark to make to a poet in search of an ancestry, and the addition, "Yeats, we both belong to the lower middle classes," was in equally bad taste. Æ, who is usually quick-witted, should have guessed that Yeats's belief in his lineal descent from the great Duke of Ormonde was part of his poetic equipment. * * * He should have remembered that all the romantic poets have sought illustrious ancestry, and rightly, since romantic poetry is concerned only with nobles and castles, gonfalons and oriflammes. * * * My meditation was interrupted by Yeats's voice.

"We have sacrificed our lives for Art; but you, what have you done? What sacrifices have you made?" he asked, and everybody began to search his memory for the sacrifices that Yeats had made, asking himself in what

† From *Vale*, vol. 3 of *Hail and Farewell* (New York: D. Appleton, 1914), pp. 170–73.

prison Yeats had languished, what rags he had worn, what broken victuals he had eaten. As far as anybody could remember, he had always lived very comfortably, sitting down invariably to regular meals, and the old green cloak that was in keeping with his profession of romantic poet he had exchanged for the magnificent fur coat which distracted our attention from what he was saying, so opulently did it cover the back of the chair out of which he had risen. But, quite forgetful of the coat behind him, he continued to denounce the middle classes, throwing his arms into the air, shouting at us, and we thinking not at all of what he was saying, but of a story that had been floating about Dublin for some time. A visitor had come back from Coole telling how he had discovered the poet lying on a sofa in a shady corner, a plate of strawberries on his knee, and three or four adoring ladies serving him with cream and sugar, and how the poet, after wiping his hands on a napkin, had consented to recite some verses, and the verses he recited were these:

> "I said, 'A line will take us hours maybe,
> Yet if it does not seem a moment's thought
> Our stitching and unstitching has been naught.
> Better go down upon your marrow-bones
> And scrub a kitchen pavement, or break stones
> Like an old pauper in all kinds of weather;
> For to articulate sweet sounds together
> Is to work harder than all these and yet
> Be thought an idler by the noisy set
> Of bankers, schoolmasters and clergymen,
> The martyrs call the world.' "[1]

The poet advanced a step or two nearer to the edge of the platform, and stamping his foot he asked again what the middle classes had done for Art, and in a towering rage (the phrase is no mere figure of speech, for he raised himself up to tremendous height) he called upon the ladies and gentlemen that had come to hear my lecture to put their hands in their pockets and give sovereigns to the stewards who were waiting at the doors to receive them, or, better still, to write large checks. We were led to understand that by virtue of our subscriptions we should cease to belong to the middle classes, and having held out this hope to us he retired to his chair and fell back overcome into the middle of the great fur coat, and remained silent until the end of the debate.

* * *

1. From "Adam's Curse," see p. 32.

MARIANNE MOORE

[Review of *The Wild Swans at Coole*]†

For a poet with such a personality as Yeats, it seems almost indecorous to bare it before us, in the midst of our social, political and literary lives. Yeats makes poetry out of the fact that he is a proud, sensitive, cultivated Irishman. He hardly has to make poetry—except the rhymes, which don't matter; he just lets his heart talk, as in the poems about the dying lady.

In a despondent mood, the poet, like some of the admirers of his earlier manner, longs for the leopards of the moon, and complains of the harsh and timid sun. Whatever the lights are of *Ego Dominus Tuus, Presences, Men Improve With Years, The Collarbone of a Hare, The Fisherman, The Hawk*, they shine. The invading hawk too, if not indecorous, is unfair, as unfair as some similarly naive passages in the Bible are:

> What tumbling cloud did you cleave,
> Yellow-eyed hawk of the mind,
> Last evening? that I who had sat
> Dumbfounded before a knave,
> Should give to my friend
> A pretence of wit.

The weighing and measuring, the critical care evidently spent on this thin volume, save the reviewer most of his labor. If the longer poems seem to him, in spite of their shrewdness and spells of passion, somewhat old-fashioned, he is willing to bend to the opinion of the author of the others. One can not but pay reverence to a poet who, after having written poetry for many years, can still be read with the same critical alertness that one would give to the best of the younger poets. And if there is a drooping line here and there, the author is too proud, too able, and too conscientious to arouse misgivings that he will ever bank on his reputation.

* * *

T. S. ELIOT

The Poetry of W. B. Yeats‡

* * *

Certainly, for the younger poets of England and America, I am sure that their admiration for Yeats's poetry has been wholly good. His idiom was too different for there to be any danger of imitation, his opinions too

---

† From *Poetry* (Chicago) (October 1918): 42–43.
‡ From *Southern Review* (Winter 1941/42): 444–50. Reprinted by permission of Faber and Faber Ltd., on behalf of the Estate of T. S. Eliot.

different to flatter and confirm their prejudices. It was good for them to have the spectacle of an unquestionably great living poet, whose style they were not tempted to echo and whose ideas contradicted those in vogue among them. You will not see, in their writing, more than passing evidences of the impression he made, but the work, and the man himself as poet, have been of the greatest significance to them for all that. This may seem to contradict what I have been saying about the kind of poetry that a young poet chooses to admire. But I am really talking about something different. Yeats would not have this influence had he not become a great poet; but the influence of which I speak is due to the figure of the poet himself, to the integrity of his passion for his art and his craft which provided such an impulse for his extraordinary development. When he visited London he liked to meet and talk to younger poets. People have sometimes spoken of him as arrogant and over-bearing. I never found him so; in his conversations with a younger writer I always felt that he offered terms of equality, as to a fellow worker, a practitioner of the same mystery. It was, I think, that, unlike many writers, he cared more for poetry than for his own reputation as a poet or his picture of himself as a poet. Art was greater than the artist: and this feeling he communicated to others; which was why younger men were never ill-at-ease in his company.

This, I am sure, was part of the secret of his ability, after becoming unquestionably the master, to remain always a contemporary. Another is the continual development of which I have spoken. This has become almost a common-place of criticism of his work.

*   *   *

* * * Returning to his earlier poems after making a close acquaintance with the later, one sees, to begin with, that in technique there was a slow and continuous development of what is always the same medium and idiom. And when I say development, I do not mean that many of the early poems, for what they are, are not as beautifully written as they could be. There are some, such as "Who Goes with Fergus?" which are as perfect of their kind as anything in the language. But the best, and the best-known of them, have this limitation: that they are as satisfactory in isolation, as "anthology pieces," as they are in the context of his other poems of the same period.

I am obviously using the term "anthology piece" in a rather special sense. In any anthology, you find some poems which give you complete satisfaction and delight in themselves, such that you are hardly curious who wrote them, hardly want to look further into the work of that poet. There are others, not necessarily so perfect or complete, which make you irresistibly curious to know more of that poet through his other work. Naturally, this distinction applies only to short poems, those in which a man has only been able to put a part of his mind, if it is a mind of any size. With some such you feel at once that the man who wrote them must have had a great deal more to say, in different contexts, of equal interest. Now among all the poems in Yeats's earlier volumes I find only in a line here or there, that sense of a unique personality which makes one sit up in excitement and eagerness to learn more about the author's mind and feelings. The intensity of Yeats's own emotional experience hardly appears. We have sufficient evidence of the intensity of experience of his youth, but it is from the retrospections in some of his later work that we have our evidence.

I have, in early essays, extolled what I called impersonality in art, and it may seem that, in giving as a reason for the superiority of Yeats's later work the greater expression of personality in it, I am contradicting myself. * * * There are two forms of impersonality: that which is natural to the mere skilful craftsman, and that which is more and more achieved by the maturing artist. The first is that of what I have called the "anthology piece," of a lyric by Lovelace or Suckling, or of Campion, a finer poet than either. The second impersonality is that of the poet who, out of intense and personal experience, is able to express a general truth; retaining all the particularity of his experience, to make of it a general symbol. And the strange thing is that Yeats, having been a great craftsman in the first kind, became a great poet in the second. It is not that he became a different man, for, as I have hinted, one feels sure that the intense experience of youth had been lived through—and indeed, without this early experience he could never have attained anything of the wisdom which appears in his later writing. But he had to wait for a later maturity to find expression of early experience; and this makes him, I think, a unique and especially interesting poet.

Consider the early poem which is in every anthology, "When you are old and grey and full of sleep," or "A Dream of Death" in the same volume of 1893. They are beautiful poems, but only craftsman's work, because one does not feel present in them the particularity which must provide the material for the general truth. By the time of the volume of 1904 there is a development visible in a very lovely poem, "The Folly of Being Comforted," and in "Adam's Curse"; something is coming through, and in beginning to speak as a particular man he is beginning to speak for man. This is clearer still in the poem "Peace," in the 1910 volume. But it is not fully evinced until the volume of 1914, in the violent and terrible epistle dedicatory of *Responsibilities*, with the great lines

> Pardon that for a barren passion's sake,
> Although I have come close on forty-nine. . . .

And the naming of his age in the poem is significant. More than half a lifetime to arrive at this freedom of speech. It is a triumph.

*   *   *

The points that I particularly wish to make about Yeats's development are two. The first, on which I have already touched, is that to have accomplished what Yeats did in the middle and later years is a great and permanent example—which poets-to-come should study with reverence—of what I have called Character of the Artist: a kind of moral, as well as intellectual, excellence. The second point, which follows naturally after what I have said in criticism of the lack of complete emotional expression in his early work, is that Yeats is pre-eminently the poet of middle age. By this I am far from meaning that he is a poet only for middle-aged readers:

the attitude towards him of younger poets who write in English, the world over, is enough evidence to the contrary. Now, in theory, there is no reason why a poet's inspiration or material should fail, in middle age or at any time before senility. For a man who is capable of experience finds himself in a different world in every decade of his life; as he sees it with different eyes, the material of his art is continually renewed. But in fact, very few poets have shown this capacity of adaptation to the years. It requires, indeed, an exceptional honesty and courage to face the change. Most men either cling to the experiences of youth, so that their writing becomes an insincere mimicry of their earlier work, or they leave their passion behind, and write only from the head, with a hollow and wasted virtuosity. There is another and even worse temptation: that of becoming dignified, of becoming public figures with only a public existence—coat-racks hung with decorations and distinctions, doing, saying and even thinking and feeling only what they believe the public expects of them. Yeats was not that kind of poet: and it is, perhaps, a reason why young men should find his later poetry more acceptable than older men easily can. For the young can see him as a poet who in his work remained in the best sense always young, who even in one sense became young as he aged. But the old, unless they are stirred to something of the honesty with oneself expressed in the poetry, will be shocked by such a revelation of what a man really is and remains. They will refuse to believe that *they* are like that.

> You think it horrible that lust and rage
> Should dance attendance upon my old age;
> They were not such a plague when I was young:
> What else have I to spur me into song?

These lines are very impressive and not very pleasant, and the sentiment has recently been criticized by an English critic whom I generally respect. But I think he misread them. I do not read them as a personal confession of a man who differed from other men, but of a man who was essentially the same as most other men; the only difference is in the greater clarity, honesty and vigor. To what honest man, old enough, can these sentiments be entirely alien? They can be subdued and disciplined by religion, but who can say that they are dead? Only those to whom the maxim of La Rochefoucauld applies: *Quand les vices nous quittent, nous nous flattons de la créance que c'est nous qui les quittons.* The tragedy of Yeats's epigram is all in the last line.

* * *

* * * There are some poets whose poetry can be considered more or less in isolation, for experience and delight. There are others whose poetry, though giving equally experience and delight, has a larger historical importance. Yeats was one of the latter: he was one of those few whose history is the history of their own time, who are a part of the consciousness of an age which cannot be understood without them. This is a very high position to assign to him: but I believe that it is one which is secure.

MAUD GONNE

Yeats and Ireland†

Yeats's own lines tell Yeats's story better than any can write it—and his story is part of Ireland's story.

A tall lanky boy with deep-set dark eyes behind glasses, over which a lock of dark hair was constantly falling, to be pushed back impatiently by long sensitive fingers, often stained with paint—dressed in shabby clothes that none noticed (except himself, as he confessed long after)—a tall girl with masses of gold-brown hair and a beauty which made her Paris clothes equally unnoticeable, sat figuratively and sometimes literally, at the feet of a thin elderly man, with eagle eyes, whose unbroken will had turned the outrage of long convict imprisonment into immense dignity. He never spoke of that imprisonment. . . . John O'Leary, the master, and his two favourite disciples, William Butler Yeats and Maud Gonne.

* * *

The land of Ireland, we both felt, was powerfully alive and invisibly peopled, and whenever we grew despondent over the weakness of the national movement, we went to it for comfort. If only we could make contact with the hidden forces of the land it would give us strength for the freeing of Ireland. Most of our talk centred round this and it led us both into strange places, from which I, less daring in thought, if more daring in action, than Willie, drew back, lest it might lead me away and not into the heart of Ireland's hidden strength.

One of our early dreams was a Castle of the Heroes. It was to be in the middle of a lake, a shrine of Irish tradition where only those who had dedicated their lives to Ireland might penetrate; they were to be brought there in a painted boat across the lake and might only stay for short periods of rest and inspiration. It was to be built of Irish stone and decorated only with the Four Jewels of the Tuatha de Danaan, with perhaps a statue of Ireland, if any artist could be found great enough to make one, which we doubted.

* * *

Willie loved symbols, to crystallise his thoughts, and he meditated much on them. All trivialities were to be excluded from the Castle of the Heroes; only things combining beauty with utility were to be admitted in its furnishing. In austere comfort those setting forth on some great task for Ireland might through lonely meditation on Ireland harmonise their individual effort with national endeavour.

Our Castle of the Heroes remained a Castle in the Air, but the last time I saw Willie at Riversdale just before he left Ireland for the last time, as

---

† From *Scattering Branches: Tributes to the Memory of W. B. Yeats*, ed. Stephen Gwynn (Macmillan, 1940), pp. 22–28.

we said goodbye, he, sitting in his armchair from which he could rise only with great effort, said, "Maud, we should have gone on with our Castle of the Heroes, we might still do it". I was so surprised that he remembered, I could not reply. The whirlpool of life had sent the current of our activities wide apart. We had quarrelled seriously when he became a Senator of the Free State which voted Flogging Acts against young republican soldiers still seeking to free Ireland from the contamination of the British Empire, and for several years we had ceased to meet. I stood speechless beside him with the song of Red Hanrahan echoing through my mind, "Angers that are like noisy clouds have set our hearts abeat"—"Like heavy flooded waters our bodies and our blood", and I realised that Willie and I still "bent low and low and kissed the quiet feet" and worshipped Her, who is "purer than a tall candle before the Holy Rood".[1]

He is gone, and I am a prisoner of old age waiting for release. The Ireland I live in is very different from the Ireland of our dreams, because our dream is not yet achieved; the quiet island on the lake over which heroes were to row in a painted boat, has no Castle of simple magnificence built to shelter them momentarily from the "bitter black wind" of confusion "which blows from the left hand" though perhaps some behind prison bars may build one deep in their own hearts.

Looking out from my own prison-house I can see the great work for Ireland accomplished by my fellow pupil of long ago.

What if Yeats wrote in a language which is not the language of Ireland that the English worked hard to obliterate? Spirits need no language to transmit their thought, and the Spirit of Ireland spoke through Willie Yeats, telling of unspeakable beauty and of its heroic call. Nations like men are created in God's image, the image of the most Blessed Trinity— the People, the Land and, from their love proceeding, the Spirit of Life, its creative force which alone can make Nations separate entities. In each generation that Spirit chooses its instrument of expression from among the people, and when it speaks through them, their words and acts have extraordinary significance and extraordinary power.

Without Yeats there would have been no Literary Revival in Ireland. Without the inspiration of that Revival and the glorification of beauty and heroic virtue, I doubt if there would have been an Easter Week. They were poets and writers who led Irish youth to die, that Ireland might live; and because of them and their writings, when they were crushed by the brute force of England, the people did not yield as they did after the crushing of the Fenian rising. In 1918 by heroic effort Ireland triumphed over overwhelming force and, filled with spiritual exultation, the people accomplished miracles.

Yeat's aloofness and his intolerance of mediocrity, a spiritual pride which is dangerous, tended to keep him apart from the first person of the National Trinity, the People. He hated crowds, I loved them. His generous desire to help and share my work brought him into contact with crowds and with all sorts of people, men from the country and men from the towns, working for Ireland's freedom. I hardly realised then how important

1. See p. 33.

that contact was to him and sometimes felt guilty at taking so much of his time from his literary work. As we sat together through the boredom of conventions and long committee meetings, where his dominating personality and practical grasp of detail made him a powerful ally, it sometimes seemed like using a fine Toledo blade instead of a loy in the spade-work of political organisation; but I remember Willie's astonished pleasure when, after a meeting, some shy boy would come up and shake his hand because he had read his poems and loved them; I know that contact was good for him. After my marriage and during my long sojourn in France, he lost this contact and became more unaware of the forces working for Ireland's freedom. His search for hidden knowledge had led him so far along strange paths that he at times almost forgot the object of the quest. * * *

Recent Critical and Biographical Studies

RICHARD ELLMANN

The Prelude†

When W. B. Yeats's first section of autobiography, *Reveries over Childhood and Youth*, appeared in 1915, his oldest friend George Russell (AE) complained that this was no autobiography at all, but a chronological arrangement of pictures. 'His memories of his childhood are the most vacant things man ever wrote, pure externalities, well written in a dead kind of way, but quite dull except for the odd flashes. The boy in the book might have become a grocer as well as a poet. Nobody could be astonished if this had been issued as a novel, part one, to find in part two the hero had for some reason given up thinking of literature and become a merchant.' The objection is partly justified; Yeats, for reasons which will become clear later on, found it impossible and not altogether desirable to lay bare the 'foul rag-and-bone shop of the heart.' But the theme that forces its way through the fragmentary pictures is his dependence upon his father and his constant efforts to escape from that dependence. Had Gosse not already taken the title, said a friend who saw the book in manuscript, Yeats might well have called it *Father and Son.*

* * *

For Yeats the problem of revolt against a father whose intellectual domination was so complete was complicated because J. B. Yeats had himself revolted against the standard values of the nineteenth century. The son was thrown into the position of the counter-revolutionary, like the *avantgarde* in Paris today who, wishing to escape the older generation and finding that the older generation was Dadaist, surrealist, and rebellious, is obliged to attack from the point of view of the conservative. Such a position is always difficult for the young. Because of its difficulty, Yeats had a great deal of trouble in finding a basis for self-expression.

From the time that he was old enough to understand his family situation, he saw a father who was affectionate but intellectually dominating, filling the house with his personality and with his opinions, though he

† From *Yeats: The Man and the Masks* (Oxford: Oxford University Press, 1979), pp. 21–24, 62–64, 67–69. Copyright © 1979 by Oxford University Press. Reprinted by permission of Erwin B. Ellmann on behalf of Ellmann Properties.

would have called the latter by some less contentious name. J. B. Yeats had little sense of financial responsibility, and the financial burden was often very trying for the family. 'Perennially hopeful,' as he described himself, he had no mind for business, and would paint or draw all his friends or any 'good head' for nothing. He was always convinced that the solution of his problems was just around the corner; either he was about to master the secret of style or to win an order for a portrait from a wealthy judge. The unfinished portraits that lay about the studio were tributes to his conscientiousness as an artist but not as a good provider.

In the household father and mother afforded a distinct contrast: the man talked all the time and the woman hardly at all. Susan Pollexfen Yeats, the mother, is difficult to describe. She had few opinions about anything, but liked best of all to exchange ghost and fairy stories with some fisherman's wife in the kitchen. Sensitive and deep-feeling but undemonstrative, she always considered her birthplace, the romantic country of Sligo, the most beautiful place in the world, and she passed on the feeling to her children. Places associated with J. B. Yeats, like London and Dublin, had never the same charm for them or for her. She would have been happier had she never left Sligo, for in Dublin and London she never felt at home; nobody in the cities told ghost or fairy stories. Instead she was always ill at ease with her husband's artistic and literary friends, who used a vocabulary to which she was unaccustomed and looked upon life in a theoretical, selective way to which she was unconsciously hostile. Mrs. Yeats had no interest in art, it is said, and never pretended to any; she was never known to have entered her husband's studio. In her quiet way she stood for a different kind of life, where an ignorant peasant had more worth than a knowledgeable artist, and she secured her husband's respect for this point of view as she drew her children's love for her native home. Though not deeply religious, she did not accept J. B. Yeat's scepticism; without objection from him she had her way in taking the children to church, teaching them to say their prayers, and having them confirmed.

The family moved impecuniously between London, Dublin, and Sligo, with Sligo as the principal residence during the first ten years of Yeats's life. The boy must have been aware that his mother's family looked askance upon John Butler Yeats and his profession, suspecting an irresponsible eccentricity in his indifference to money, in his lack of success, and in his search for an intangible goal. The Pollexfens had their faiths from birth; they were Protestants, though not devout, and Unionists, while J. B. Yeats, in spite of his Anglo-Irish upbringing, was a sceptic and a nationalist. In that atmosphere he was out of place, and so was his oldest son, who resembled him.

In a revealing passage in *Reveries*, William Butler Yeats confessed that he remembered little of childhood except its pain. He had from the first an unhappy time of it. His personal appearance was out of the ordinary; he was delicate, with a complexion so dark that he looked foreign or seemed about to die of a liver ailment. People would often think he came from India. His eyesight was bad, and he was eventually to lose the sight of one eye. In an unpublished autobiographical novel he refers to himself in the title, *The Speckled Bird*, and quotes the Bible, ' "Mine inheritance is as the speckled bird, all the birds of heaven are against it." . . . I wonder,' he says, 'why the other birds are so angry.' His awkwardness and physical weakness kept him from being a favorite of the Pollexfens, who were good athletes. To his father's indignation he did not learn to ride well, nor had he the physical courage with which J. B. Yeats made up for his own lack of horsemanship. The Pollexfens began to think Yeats mentally as well as physically defective when they could not teach him how to read.

Seeking refuge from the Pollexfens' disapproval of his awkwardness and from a keen sense of his physical inadequacies, the boy found what he wanted in revery and solitude; he wandered by himself about the Sligo caves and dreamed the days away. He wrote later of these years to the poet Katharine Tynan:

> The place that has really influenced my life most is Sligo. There used to be two dogs there—one smooth-haired, one curly-haired—I used to follow them all day long. I knew all their occupations, when they hunted for rats and when they went to the rabbit-warren. They taught me to dream maybe. Since then I follow my thoughts as I then followed the two dogs—the smooth and the curly—wherever they lead me.

*   *   *

[Yeats and the Occult]

He was still hesitating about becoming a Theosophist when he moved with his family to London in May of 1887. Madame Blavatsky had arrived a month before and within two weeks of her landing had founded a Blavatsky Lodge. Yeats went to call on her with a letter of introduction from Charles Johnston soon after he came to London, and was immediately persuaded to dismiss his doubts and join the lodge. She exercised a peculiar fascination on her visitors, and Yeats, troubled as we have seen by his self-consciousness and lack of spontaneity, and filled with reverence for great personalities, was especially taken with her because she was so fully herself, so 'unforeseen, illogical, incomprehensible.' While with her he escaped from the restlessness of his own mind, as he wrote in the unpublished first draft of his *Autobiographies*, and he was reassured of the validity of his anti-materialist theories by the certainty and erudition with which she expounded them.

True, he was not altogether convinced of her occult powers. When her broken cuckoo clock hooted at him as he entered the house, he examined the mechanism to see if it were a trick. He wondered, too, why she did not refute Hodgson's charges. But these things did not trouble him much, for he saw in her a creature of myth who held in her head all the folklore of the world and much of its wisdom. The slender young Irishman with his enthusiasms and the fat Russian woman with her obsessions found common ground. 'She made upon me an impression of generosity and indulgence,' he wrote later. 'I remember how careful she was that the young men about her should not overwork. I overhead her saying to some rude strangers who had reproved me for talking too much, "No, no, he is very sensitive." ' She readily divined the young man's psychological difficulties. On one occasion, he read a dull speech to the Theosophists, who received it coldly. Madame Blavatsky called him over and said, ' "Give me the manuscript. Now you go back and say your say about it." ' He did so, with the greatest success, and was always grateful to her.

For about a year after her arrival in London Madame Blavatsky discouraged her over-eager followers from plunging too deeply into Theosophical depths, warning them of the danger of black magic. Yeats disregarded her injunction and took Katharine Tynan to a spiritualist séance, where he was so upset by the supernatural phenomena that he lost control of himself and beat his head on the table; for his disobedience Madame Blavatsky severely scolded him on his next visit to her. But in 1888 the Theosophists' demand for magical instruction was so great that she resolved to form an Esoteric Section for the sincerest of her 'chelas.' Yeats was delighted and joined the group soon after it was formed. He was eager to probe more deeply into Theosophical arcana, and he hoped, too, that the Esoteric Section would give him the opportunity of proving to his own satisfaction, and to the satisfaction even of sceptics like his father, that occult phenomena were possible. His friend George Russell characteristically took the opposite position, and wrote from Dublin in great dismay to Madame Blavatsky, warning her of the danger of changing the goal of the Theosophical Society from union with the absolute to 'proving the phenomena of spiritualism, table-rapping, and the evocation of spooks.' In reply, she assured Russell that the Esoteric Section would not practice magic but would undergo that training necessary before magical power might safely be entrusted to a member. One would not learn to perform miracles, only become ready to learn.

The section had strict rules. Members had to take pledges to renounce all vanity, to live a life of abstinence and asceticism, and to devote themselves to the good of their fellow men. In return, the Esoteric Section promised an undreamed-of change in the personality. The psychological development would be immediate and at the beginning not altogether beneficent. All the powerful impulses of the soul, bad as well as good, would rise to the surface; only in this way could evil be expelled and the 'soul be elevated and rendered capable of grasping and making use of the higher knowledge.'

Yeats was of course extremely interested. The bringing to the surface of all the latent possibilities of his being was exactly what he wanted; he needed help to change his personality, to purify himself of timidity, to learn to control others and himself, to become the hero of whom he dreamed. Still strongly under paternal influence, he wanted to find out the 'law of his own being' and liberate his mind from inherited ideas and attitudes. Since his father won the arguments about occultism that they had together, he had lost his confidence, as he later confessed, but now he moved hopefully 'from speculation to the direct experience of the Mystics.'

*   *   *

Several experiments in fact took place; on one occasion the esotericists tried unsuccessfully to raise the ghost of a flower, on another to study the possibility of evoking certain kinds of dreams by sleeping with special symbols under their pillows. No miracles occurred, doubts rose in the minds of other members, and Yeats's committee seemed unlikely to further the Theosophical cause. His last public appearance in the organization was probably in August, 1890, when, with Annie Besant in the chair, he lectured on 'Theosophy and Modern Culture.' Though the lecture was apparently acceptable, the experiments had tried Madame Blavatsky's patience too far. Shortly afterwards her secretary, no doubt with her approval, asked him to resign. The poet regretfully complied.

Notwithstanding his final excommunication, five or six years of Theosophy, three of them years of active membership under the organization's founder, had left their mark on Yeats. He had been brought into contact with a system based on opposition to materialism and on support of secret and ancient wisdom, and was encouraged to believe that he would be able to bring together all the fairy tales and folklore he had heard in childhood, the poetry he had read in adolescence, the dreams he had been dreaming all his life. The Theosophists gave him support because they accepted and incorporated into their system ghosts and fairies, and regarded dreams and symbols as supernatural manifestations. A definition of the fairies such as Yeats made soon after leaving the Society, 'The fairies are the lesser spiritual moods of that universal mind, wherein every mood is a soul and every thought a body,' was entirely in accord with Theosophical doctrine. To the disciples of Madame Blavatsky the spiritual life, which could easily be equated with the imaginative life, was always at hand, always impinging upon matter. On one occasion a small Indian guest at Madame Blavatsky's house created a disturbance by complaining that a big materialist had sat on his astral body, which was reclining near him on the couch. The episode, ridiculous as it is to us and as it was to Yeats, still suggests how matter and spirit were interchangeable and interactive in the Theosophical outlook. It was on this canvas that he would paint.

*   *   *

Yeats was of course aware that her phenomena might well be fraudulent, as he indicated in his 'Esoteric Sections Journal,' but he rightly considered the 'inherent value of the philosophy' to be independent of the phenomena. The occult and religious tradition compounded by Theosophy contained much that was sensible, even profound. It made clear by examples more reputable than those of Madame Blavatsky, that reality could not be facilely explained as the perceptions of five senses and that scientific rationalism had ignored or superficially dismissed many most important matters. What Yeats now hoped to do was to systematize his knowledge, to put his intuitions and those of the great poets and mystics together, to perform experiments and demonstrate the existence of an occult world, to describe that world more exactly and stylistically than Madame Blavatsky had done. He had secured weapons for the attack on materialism. Theosophy had furnished him with shield and sword, and he went forth like Don Quixote, though with some hesitancy, to tilt at the windmills of modern life.

R. F. FOSTER

Two Years: Bedford Park 1887-1889†

* * * [In] WBY's great personal myth January 1889 was not only the month that saw the publication of *The Wanderings of Oisin*. On the 30th 'a hansom drove up to our door at Bedford Park with Miss Maud Gonne', and 'the troubling of my life began'.

'As I look backward,' he wrote long afterwards, 'it seems to me that she brought into my life in those days—for as yet I saw only what lay upon the surface—the middle of the tint, a sound as of a Burmese gong, an over-powering tumult that had yet many pleasant secondary notes.'[1] The 22-year-old English ex-débutante with a passion for Irish nationalism and romantic poetry invaded Bedford Park with an introduction to JBY [John Butler Yeats, W. B. Yeats's father], but 'really to see Willy', as Lolly acidly pointed out. The Yeats girls 'hated her royal sort of smile' and noted that she was wearing slippers;[2] JBY argued politics with her; the whole family was probably impressed by the fact that she extravagantly kept the cab waiting throughout. She told WBY that 'she cried over "Island of Statues" fragment but altogether favoured the enchantress and hated Nachina'. Thus she cast herself precisely as the *fatale*, capricious beauty of whom the poet had dreamt.

He could not but succumb. Writing to Tynan in August 1887 (in response to a desperate appeal for ready-made ideas about the major poets' attitudes to women), he had tried to itemize poetic types of beauty. Swinburne's were 'passionate and gorgious animals', 'Tennisons . . . much more like actual every day people'; the neo-Romantics created 'essentially men's heroines with no seperate life of their own in this different from Brownings'.[3] Maud Gonne, by contrast, was majestic, unearthly, appealing all at once; and her classic beauty came straight out of epic poetry. Immensely tall, bronze-haired, with a strong profile and beautiful skin, she was a *fin de siècle* beauty in Valkyrie mode: both her appearance and her character represented tragic passion. But there was also a vulnerable side, shown to few, which struck an immediate chord with WBY. He at once saw her as a 'goddess', and remembered her standing luminous as 'apple-blossom through which the light falls . . . by a great heap of such blossoms in the

† From *W. B. Yeats: A Life: I: The Apprentice Mage 1865-1914* by Roy F. Foster. Copyright © 1997 by Roy F. Foster. Used by permission of Oxford University Press, Inc., and by permission of the author c/o Rogers, Coleridge & White Ltd.

1. W. B. Yeats, *Memoirs*, ed. Denis Donoghue (London: Macmillan, 1972), p. 40.
2. From a notebook by Yeats's sister Susan Mary ("Lily") Yeats, and a diary by his sister Elizabeth Corbet ("Lolly") Yeats, cited in *The Collected Letters of W. B. Yeats Volume I: 1865-1895*, ed. John Kelly and Eric Domville (Oxford: Clarendon Press, 1986), p. 134.
3. Ibid., p. 30.

window.'[4] In January the blossom must have been almond, not apple: but the image remained,[5] and the recognition. Implicitly, in his work, he had already cast a woman like this for a part in his life.

Yet at the same time there was something curiously self-conscious in his immediate idealization of her: it may have inspired a reflection twenty years later.

> And when we love, if it be in the excitement of youth, do we not also, that the flood may find no stone to convulse, no wall to narrow it, exclude character or the signs of it by choosing that beauty which seems unearthly because the individual woman is lost amid the labyrinth of its lines as though life were trembling into stillness and silence, or at last folding itself away? Some little irrelevance of line, some promise of character to come, may indeed put us at our ease . . . But should it come, as we had dreamed in love's frenzy, to our dying for that woman's sake, we would find that the discord had its value from the tune.[6]

Even as he cast himself into thrall, like a Shelleyan hero, the writer in him was conscious of what he was doing.

DECLAN KIBERD

Revolt into Style—Yeatsian Poetics†

Yeats's notion that *style* might be an agent of redemption is canvassed in the opening two lyrics of his *Collected Poems*. Both the Happy and Sad Shepherd tell the same sad story: but the former's glad heart ensures that it is finally given a melodious inflection, while the latter's gloom distorts the material to "inarticulate moan". *Le style, c'est l'homme*: content is again proven secondary, illustrative, pliable. Real joy derives less from right thinking than from achieved self-expression. Yeats has little to say and much to express: and what he expresses is the unimportance of ideas or content:

> Go gather by the humming sea
> Some twisted, echo-harbouring shell,
> And to its lips thy story tell,
> And they thy comforters will be,
> Recording in melodious guile
> Thy fretful words a little while,
> Till they shall singing fade in ruth

4. W. B. Yeats, *Autobiographies* (London: Macmillan, 1955), p. 123.
5. In a notebook entry of 13 July 1899, at Coole, he recorded his use of apple-blossom as an occult invocation, adding 'the apple blossoms are symbols of dawn and of the air and of the earth and of resurrection in my system and in the poem [*Shadowy Waters*]'.
6. "The Tragic Theatre" from *The Cutting of an Agate*. In *Essays and Introductions* (London: Macmillan, 1961), pp. 243–44.
† Reprinted by permission of the publisher from *Inventing Ireland* by Declan Kiberd, Cambridge, Mass.: Harvard University Press. Copyright © 1995 by Declan Kiberd. Page references to this Norton Critical Edition are given in brackets after the author's original citations.

And die a pearly brotherhood;
For words alone are certain good:
Sing, then, for this is also sooth.[1]

Art may soothe the pain it describes so well: to express an emotion may also be to purge oneself of it. If singing can be truch, then style itself may be the subject. Insofar as man pursues themes, he does not choose them: rather, they choose him:

There was a man whom sorrow named his friend . . .[2]

The danger of a world constructed on a foundation of pure style is self-enclosure, a point illustrated by the imperviousness of the dewdrops to the Sad Shepherd's overture:

But naught they heard, for they are always listening,
The dewdrops, for the sound of their own dropping.

Self-delight has its narcissistic limits, and so the attempt to communicate with a shell proves circular. Again, in "The Indian on God", creativity seems to betoken self-enclosure, each person seeing God as a version of himself. Humans insist on seeing God as human, but Yeats knows that the soul may exist in many other forms. The parrot in "The Indian to His Love" rages at his own image in the enamelled sea, fearing such self-enclosure but seeking the antiself. In the end, there is but one consolation: if pain can be transmuted into art, and assuaged by it, then something has been achieved.

Many of Yeats's early lyrics are written to a "traditional air", as if the style preceded their content; or else they rework traditional themes and images as if redeemed by Yeatsian style. In this manoeuvre, Yeats seems to be hoping to add a little of his own art, just as folktale tellers do before relaunching the story back into the impersonality of tradition: once again, the implication is that he is a sort of "Homer", a name to which such texts may in time be appended. The poet, in seeking to dramatize himself, seems to become pure medium, the poetry evolving more at the instigation of words and rhythms than from the pressure of felt experience. The fear is that he may lose touch with the popular mood "and learn to chaunt a tongue men do not know".[3] Style is, none the less, prioritized, irresistible, a mode of action and power, as against the antithetical world of thought, contemplation, knowledge. Love is given to style, because all dreams yearn to take their appropriate form, whether a man seeking a woman's or a God coveting the earthly. However, the fusion with that form is ever imperfect and incomplete, for, if it were fully achieved, the passionate emotion would be expressed and thereby lost. Many of Yeats's single-sentence "breath-poems" deal, indeed, with expiration, the dying fall into the moment of death.

Some attempt to conceptualize this method is offered in "The Moods": bodiless souls descend into forms, and these constitute the "moods" which

1. W. B. Yeats, *The Collected Poems of W. B. Yeats* (London: Macmillan, 1950), p. 8 [4].
2. Ibid., p. 9 [4].
3. Ibid., p. 35 [12].

impel actions in the world, but the style or mood determines the content of an action. This allows Yeats to respond to the puritan charge of the bad faith implicit in *mimesis* with the counter-claim that art creates, rather than describes, emotions and moods:

> Literature differs from explanatory or scientific writing in being wrought about a mood . . . argument, theory, erudition, observation are merely what Blake calls "little devils who fight for themselves", illusions of our visible passing life, who must be made to serve the moods, or we have no part in eternity.[4]

A style, like a mood, goes fishing for a subject in the unconscious, but, once expressed in an embodied form, the subject—as in "The Song of Wandering Aengus"—may elude human control. The poet's attempt to recapture what he had created—a girl, a nation—is enacted by revision, by the attempt to see again and control all that floated free: but this proves impossible. The elevation of style over subject is possible only in that liminal, twilit world of wavering rhythms and half-said things, wherein the critical faculties are dulled but not annihilated. In these moments, the all-too-present danger is sentimentality.

"The Cap and Bells" is the fullest exploration in the early books of the process. It tells the story of a young queen who will only accept the jester's love (content) after first receiving quite separately its instruments, the cap and bells (form): yet another case of expression becoming the very condition of conceptualization. The jester must lose his powers of creativity, his expressive instruments, before he can be sure of her love. The woman who enables art thus becomes also its enemy, and so the female who castrates *is* art. *He* wants the woman, but she wants the desire of the man, an irreconcilable conflict. Like all pornographers, she substitutes a part for the whole, his instruments for his soul: but, of course, he has already done the same to her, in fetishizing her foot and her hair. While in the pornographic mode, she holds his cap and bells in triumph, and sings while he is castrated. His prophecy is thereby fulfilled: "I will send them to her and die".[5] Self-castrated, he can experience ultimately in death. Only after this death can his soul blend with her body and, at that moment, she also dies, reuniting with her beloved in song. In the hereafter alone are form and content perfectly at one.

It would be possible to read the poem in many other ways—the male, as slave to an unacknowledged *anima*, being compelled to risk all for a full encounter; the Irish artist in England abandoning the court jester's self-castrating role for a more authentic national art; the high price paid by the licensed fool for his plain speaking. But these are already obvious interpretations. The deeper life of the poem bespeaks a poet's ambivalence about his art and his subservience to image and symbol. Again and again, in early love poems, the poet encounters an exacting woman, whose cruelty makes necessary the very art which she then proceeds to jeopardize. No wonder that he may wish the beloved dead in those moments when

4. W. B. Yeats, *Essays and Introductions* (London: Macmillan, 1961), p. 195.
5. Yeats, *The Collected Poems*, p. 71 [27].

she is not killing him. A volume like *The Wind Among the Reeds* is deliberately organized around styles and moods which later, taken in consort, yield up a meaning. For style is here a mode of arrangement.

"Never Give All the Heart" might equally be read as a recommendation to throw energy into form rather than content: in other words, never to say it all in one poem, for, if one does, then *all* is lost in the act of expression. "The painter's brush consumes his dreams" will be one way of putting this; "our love letters wear out our love" another. The half-said thing is dearest, to lovers as well as to poets, since it still leaves them their role; and a passionate lover would, anyway, never wish to suspect that most of the passion was on the other side. Moreover, if one could seem to say it all in one poem, that could only be a dishonest appearance: recall the actress, described in *Autobiographies*, who could best mimic a feeling only after it was all but gone.

This raises the inevitable question about art as bad faith, but perhaps the notion of a false imitation of a true thing is more applicable to performers than to artists. The paradox in "Never Give All the Heart" is bitter and that bitterness is rendered in the jagged syntax and awkward repetitions. On the one hand, there is the need to "act", but on the other there is the impossibility of acting out of deep feeling. The answer is the Mask, a necessary fakery, which, if consciously and confessedly manipulated, is not vulnerable to the charge of bad faith. The Yeatsian/Wildean theory is uncompromising on this point: it is possible to fake a nation into existence via a style, and what is thus created need be no pale imitation but a radical creation. The exemplar for the nation is not to be slavishly imitated, but one who awakens each man and woman to the hero in themselves, "because all life has the same root".[6]

Hence the rigour brought to the discussion of style in "Adam's Curse", the point being that what seems a nonchalant aristocratic mode is actually hard, middle-class work:

> A line will take us hours maybe;
> Yet if it does not seem a moment's thought
> Our stitching and unstitching has been naught.[7]

The poem is itself an example of the method: a conversation-piece built out of the rhythms of an apparently effortless everyday speech. The styles of the outcast groups, of beggar and landless labourer, are recruited to redeem an altogether more sophisticated but threatened aristocratic wisdom, by a writer who wishes to think like a wise man but express himself like the common people. And the reward for such successful articulation is to be thought an idle trifler by the workaday bourgeoisie:

> Better go down upon your marrow-bones
> And scrub a kitchen pavement, or break stones
> Like an old pauper, in all kinds of weather;
> For to articulate sweet sounds together
> Is to work harder than all these, and yet

6. W. B. Yeats, *Plays and Controversies* (London: Macmillan, 1923), p. 161.
7. Yeats, *The Collected Poems*, p. 88 [32].

> Be thought an idler by the noisy set
> Of bankers, schoolmasters, and clergymen
> The martyrs call the world.[8]

Yet a shaped singing style is not just a basis for "self-conquest", but also an escape from the hot-faced bargainers and money-changers, indeed the only answer to the question which its own success raises. In the end, Yeats will conclude that only the styles of the outcast classes can redeem the language of the nation. So, in the poem, he attacks the middle class, bitterly describing poetry in their terms (of work, reward, trade). Even more, he attacks those (including himself) who succumbed to the bourgeois disease of seeking for precedents in books, of imitating approved models rather than looking inside themselves. Of course, it is a functional irony that "Adam's Curse" adds to that tradition of learned love, in which all books become an endless rehearsal for something which never happens, agents of that delayed gratification which is the essence of the Yeatsian life.

That irony underpins many of the poems in *In the Seven Woods*, which seem anxious to extirpate "literary" precedents from a tradition, but end by adding yet another. The rejection of literary models is based, in part, on the knowledge that sometimes even a style can go out of fashion "like an old song": the dire prophecy of the Sad Shepherd may be fulfilled. If "Adam's Curse" established the fundamental affinity between artist and women in their joint labour to be beautiful, "The Mask" echoes the idea in its call for a deliberate regulation of self-giving spontaneity. Masks, like assumed styles, are essential but problematic: they offer not the truth, but a way towards it. The poem suggests that women are seen as images more than as persons, and yet they must with labour maintain both of those aspects. The pretence involved in wearing masks may betoken a courtesy which hinders love, or it may make available the only viable form of expression. The tension between mask and face intrigues the man: however, the woman rightly refuses to remove the mask, for she senses that the truth lies at that unknown point where mask and face, antiself and self, are one.

Since style is the mask from which the whole person may be inferred, so the forms of an art may in time provide the synecdoche for a nation. This utopian idea explains Yeats's yearning for the success of the Dublin Municipal Gallery and for the return to it of the Lane Collection of paintings. If the arts lie dreaming of what is to come, then the renovated content of a free Ireland may emerge when least expected:

> And maybe I will take a trout
> If but I do not seem to care . . .[9]

The terrifying difficulties attendant upon such a creation are traced in "The Magi", whose lines reach forward only to fall back, and whose slow accretion of clauses conveys a rising sense of expectation, reinforced by the thrice-repeated "all", which is yet unfulfilled. Even the opening word

8. Ibid., p. 89 [32].
9. Ibid., p. 126 [47].

"Now" is so qualified by the following phrase as to be annulled; and that technique of self-cancellation persists all through:

> Now as at all times I can see in the mind's eye,
> In their stiff, painted clothes, the pale unsatisfied ones
> Appear and disappear in the blue depth of the sky
> With all their ancient faces like rain-beaten stones,
> And all their helms of silver hovering side by side,
> And all their eyes still fixed, hoping to find once more,
> Being by Calvary's turbulence unsatisfied,
> The uncontrollable mystery on the bestial floor.[1]

"The Magi" is really an anticipatory style looking for an enabling content, a form without a finalizing substance; and this technique of anticlimax will be used with even greater subtlety in the elaborate stanzas of later poems like "In Memory of Robert Gregory" and "Among School Children".

An anticlimax is precisely what "The Magi" accuses Christianity of providing. The unsatisfactory incarnation of the divine in a fallen human body offers some hint of the sufferings implicit in submitting to a single form; and this comes the more appositely in a volume where Yeats deals, for the first time, with the chancy, sordid, reduced realities of an all-too-flawed Ireland. The assumption of form can be a severe experience of humiliation: the self-conquest of the stylist is won only out of an initial degradation. However, the poet, if he were to wait for knowledge, might never begin his quest: and so he must start with the search for a form. William Blake saw the body as satanic, but Christ took that form; likewise, the artist-martyr takes on the weaknesses of the flawed medium which he chooses, before casting it off again. "Incarnation and crucifixion are one",[2] declared Yeats, by which he meant that style and form, pursued outside the self by a poet, are fully known as one only at the moment of death.

By this logic, Synge could never have rested quiet in the tomb, until he had found his antiself on Aran. "In Memory of Major Robert Gregory" not only chronicles such exemplary moments in exemplary lives: it becomes also an instance of that enactment, eluding the artist's intended controls, as the deliberated poem gives way to the authentic one, the manifest to the latent content. The final stanza is an autocritical explanation of the seeming formlessness of the poem:

> I had thought, seeing how bitter is that wind
> That shakes the shutter, to have brought to mind
> All those that manhood tried, or childhood loved
> Or boyish intellect approved,
> With some appropriate commentary on each;
> Until imagination brought
> A fitter welcome; but a thought
> Of that late death took all my heart for speech.[3]

1. Ibid., p. 141 [51].
2. On this see W. B. Yeats, *Autobiographies* (London: Macmillan, 1955), pp. 330–32; Yeats, *Essays and Introductions*, pp. 111–45.
3. Yeats, *The Collected Poems*, pp. 151–52 [57–58].

The very difficulty of enunciating that final line is part of its meaning, for now the poet too endures "lack of breath", with his heart literally in his mouth, blocking utterance. Acknowledging its own redundancy, after a patently ludicrous attempt to tabulate and catalogue elements of a very casual build-up, the poem's baffled silence is in fact the greater tribute, rather like that offered at the end of "The Fisherman", which concludes that the audience for (as well as the content of) a national art has yet to be inferred.

In Yeats's middle period, the Dancer becomes an emblem of pure form, sheer contour, devoid of intellectual content ("opinion"), which is now subsumed by style. What Michael Robartes wishes to see is the supernatural element incarnated in bodily form; but the yearning for "thought" is not so easily denied:

> . . . it's plain
> The half-dead dragon was her thought,
> That every morning rose again
> And dug its claws and shrieked and fought.
> Could the impossible come to pass
> She would have time to turn her eyes,
> Her lover thought, upon the glass
> And on the instant could grow wise.[4]

This represents a phase of womanhood with which the poet fully identifies himself by now, that moment when every rational control is lost and a supernatural visitation becomes possible. It is the moment of second coming and, indeed, the moment of Leda.

*   *   *

DANIEL ALBRIGHT

Yeats's Waves†

I. YEATS'S FIGURES AS REFLECTIONS IN WATER

Most of us, when we read Yeats's poetry, pay close attention to the ravishing *images*—the Japanese sword, the bird made of gold, the old Norman tower. But in some ways the true subject of the poems consists not of these formal particulars, but of a hovering formlessness behind them: Yeats was less concerned with *images* than with the imagination itself, a shapeless matrix of shapes, a retina that could be knuckled into emanating waves of sparks and fields of intenser darkness. Behind all the hard-edged sensuous imagery there is a liquidity, an indistinctness, a swirl. Though

---

4. Ibid., p. 197 [71].

† From *Quantum Poetics: Yeats, Pound, Eliot, and the Science of Modernism* (Cambridge: Cambridge University Press, 1997), pp. 31–34. Copyright © 1997. Reprinted with the permission of Cambridge University Press. Page references to this Norton Critical Edition are given in brackets after the author's original citations.

critics once described Yeats's poems as perfected artifacts, urns of words, no poems are less iconic than Yeats's: they are histories of heaving imaginative processes, standing waves. Let us begin, then, by looking at Yeats's deconstructive power, his methodical erasures of all the poem-particles that his work comprises. Soon we will see that Yeats's dispersed, uniform fields start to oscillate or radiate, to become energized: one of the gyres that govern Yeats's poetry is a rhythm of *image* and imagelessness.

The first critic, to my knowledge, who noted the essential tenuousness of Yeats's imaginative constructions, the themelessness of his poetry, was his (generally hostile) fellow Irishman, Samuel Beckett. In 1934 Beckett announced that poems are written in the empty space between the poet and the world of objects, a world forever beyond the poet's reach. Beckett used Yeats as an example of a modern poet facing this crisis, "the breakdown of the object": "At the centre there is no theme . . . And without a theme there can be no poem, as witness the exclamation of Mr. Yeats's 'fánatic heart': 'What, be a singer born and lack a theme!' ('The Winding Stair' ["Vacillation" VII]). But at the circumference is an iridescence of themes—Oisin, Cuchulain, Maeve" (*Disjecta*, p. 71). * * *

All his life Yeats considered himself, with some justice, an uneducated man. Every great poet works at the outermost edges of his knowledge; but Yeats did not have to travel very far to reach those edges. He liked to see himself as the successor of the illiterate Gaelic beggar-poets, like the historical Anthony Raftery or the imaginary Hanrahan, in touch with secret springs of inspiration. To some extent Yeats's ideal poet is the Fool: "I knew . . . a truly great seer, who . . . saw . . . a white fool sitting by a pool and smiling and watching images of beautiful women floating up from the pool. What else can death be but the beginning of wisdom and power and beauty? and foolishness may be a kind of death" (*Mythologies*, p. 115 [1901]). An empty brain and an empty pool—these are the surfaces on which the most ravishing *images* take shape. Every inflection of personality, every impurity in the medium, interferes with the formation of these pictures. The poet must cultivate folly in order to be fully receptive to the forces outside him that engender poems. Feelings, intensities, grand passions—what Yeats called the Moods—reside not in the poet but in the *Anima Mundi*, the World-Soul, the treasure-house of *symbols*; and the successful poet can so clarify himself, so rid himself of peculiarity, that he becomes a medium for propagation of transcendental forms.

* * *

According to the system of personality described in A *Vision* (1925, 1937), most poets must seek fulfillment by struggling toward their anti-selves. Yeats's own anti-self was the Shepherd, a rude, half-formed, half-awake man only partially disengaged from the matrix of loam, from the rhythm of the seasons. The anti-self of Keats, a poet still closer to ultimate vision, was the Fool. The great poets, then, were sophisticated men who consciously strove for extreme simplicity, self-abandonment to significant *images*. The poet makes himself meaningless in order to become the vehicle of transcendental meanings.

In much of Yeats's work one finds a preoccupation with empty backgrounds. In his earliest poems, creatures—witch, song-bird, parrot—keep staring at their reflections in water:

> Vivien (*looking down into the fountain*). Where moves there any
>   beautiful as I,
> Save, with the little golden greedy carp,
> Gold unto gold, a gleam in its long hair,
> My image yonder?
>   ("Time and the Witch Vivien" [1889], *Variorum Poems*, p. 720)

> While round the shore a million stood
> Like drops of frozen rainbow light,
> And pondered in a soft vain mood
> Upon their shadows in the tide.
>   (*The Wanderings of Oisin* [1889], *Poems*, p. 6).

> A parrot sways upon a tree,
> Raging at his own image in the enamelled sea.
>   ("The Indian to his Love" [1886], *Poems*, p. 40) [6]

According to the Neoplatonic mythology Yeats used, water is the medium for the generation of *images* (*Mythologies*, p. 80 [1902]); and in these early poems water is the medium that generates *images* of self-inquiry, self-approval, self-condemnation. A man is imprisoned in his reflection; and only Death (who defeats the witch Vivien in a chess-game) can break this spectral obsession. According to this water-reflection model, an *image* is not a stable, triumphantly determinate entity: its contours shift with the slightest disturbance of the pool, with the slightest change of the facial expression of the onlooker. Yeats once called the *Anima Mundi* itself a "great pool" (*Mythologies*, p. 352 [1917]); and the *images* extracted from it are simply floating shapes drawn on water.

As Yeats moved away from the doctrine that the proper goal of art is self-expression, toward a colder, more impersonal theory of art, these empty backgrounds started to yield *images* of a different sort. The *images* stiffen, start to behave, at least provisionally, as solid particles of poem-stuff. Narcissus' pool changes into a medium's crystal, in which take shape *images* of ecrie beauty or potency—*images* not necessarily relevant to the poet's personal life: "the beryl stone was enchanted by our father that it might unfold the pictures in its heart, and not to mirror our own excited faces, or the boughs waving outside the window" (*Essays and Introductions*, p. 163 [1900]). The mirror is no longer a slave to chance, bound to reflect the people and objects that happen to be nearby; the mirror has its own private ideas. Around and after the turn of the century, Yeats's work often illustrates the process by which the outer world is dismantled to make room for vision—*Where There is Nothing, There is God*, a title Yeats used for a short story (1896) and for a play (1902), summarizes this process. The search for a Symbolist theatre was largely an experiment in how thoroughly the stage can be evacuated—of furniture, painted scenery, and so forth. And Yeats's poems ("Paudeen" [1913] is a good example) also show a turning-aside from a detailed, ugly background to an empty but pregnant background. Once the landscape is rid of objects and themes, amazing things can happen:

> Now as at all times I can see in the mind's eye,
> In their stiff, painted clothes, the pale unsatisfied ones
> Appear and disappear in the blue depth of the sky.
> ("The Magi" [1914], *Poems*, p. 177) [51]

And in the deliberately preposterous tale Yeats concocted to explain the origin of the occult wisdom in *A Vision*, the diagrams that explicate the universe were traced on the sands of the Arabian desert by the feet of wandering dancers (*A Vision* [1925], pp. 9–11, *A Vision* [1937], p. 19). On another desert landscape, in "The Second Coming" (1920), the shadows of birds start to reel like spots swimming in the eye, and a rough beast begins the slow struggle to get itself born. Such *images* are impressive; but more impressive still is the background on which the *images* are inscribed. Sea, sky, desert—at the world's end Yeats hoped to find a surface large enough and blank enough to be the mirror of ultimate things: "I shall find the dark grow luminous, the void fruitful when I understand I have nothing, that the ringers in the tower have appointed for the hymen of the soul a passing bell" (*Mythologies*, p. 332 [1917]). Every *image* arises out of a void; and every *image* will sink back into a void. An *image* is not immortal: it has a given life-span, and will inevitably recede into imagelessness, as the stuff of art disintegrates into the stuff of criticism and science:

> Science is the criticism of Myth. There would be no Darwin had there been no Book of Genesis, no electron but for the Greek atomic myth; and when the criticism is finished there is not even a drift of ashes on the pyre. Sexual desire dies because every touch consumes the Myth . . . We free ourselves from obsession that we may become nothing. The last kiss is given to the void. (*W. B. Yeats and T. Sturge Moore*, p. 154 [1929])

* * *

JAHAN RAMAZANI

The Elegiac Love Poems: A Woman Dead and Gon(n)e†

Although Yeats later resists it, pathos clearly predominates over other moods in his early work, particularly in the elegiac love lyrics. Since no one is really dying or dead, these poems are elegiac in mode without being formal elegies. * * * To generate their "love," some of the love poems conjure a death. They imagine that the beloved "had died in a strange

† From *Yeats and the Poetry of Death: Elegy, Self-Elegy, and the Sublime* by Jahan Ramazani (New Haven: Yale University Press, 1990), pp. 17–26. Copyright © 1990. Reprinted by permission of Yale University Press. Page references to this Norton Critical Edition are given in brackets after the author's original citations.

place" and that she is "lying cold and dead" in the ground (P^1 42, 72). Surrendering the beloved in effigy, they enact a symbolic rite of presence and absence that resembles not only the fertility rituals Yeats knew from Frazer and other comparative anthropologists but also Freud's famous *fort/ da* game. Like the anthropologist's rituals and the psychoanalyst's game, the elegiac love poems both lament the beloved's death and yet require it as their condition of possibility. Although they are written neither in the group form nor in the querulous tone of many later elegies, the early love lyrics call attention to their aggressive absenting of the beloved, thereby raising one of the questions that haunts elegies like "In Memory of Major Robert Gregory" and "Parnell's Funeral"—namely, whether the elegist in some sense wills the death he mourns. In the early love poems as in the later elegies, Yeats guiltily acknowledges his reliance on thoughts of death to produce poetic mourning.

Lamenting the death that he imaginatively projects, Yeats increases the traditional inaccessibility and absence of the beloved. In this regard he is hardly alone: the dead woman is an aesthetic obsession during the period of his early poetic development. * * *

But if pervasive social and cultural traditions help to define woman as the mute, dead "other"—the absent center around which male love poets elaborate their symbolic rites of mourning—how does Yeats stand apart? To an extraordinary extent, he thematizes his dependence on the beloved's death and absence for the life of his poetry. In the midst of "The Tower," a later sequence that uses the figure of the poet's blindness to reaffirm that the beloved must exist only in the mind's eye, Yeats echoes his earlier question about the woman lost; but this time the question is almost a self-accusation:

> Does the imagination dwell the most
> Upon a woman won or woman lost?[2]   (P 197) [84]

He considers only one possible answer. Sometimes boldly, sometimes subtly, often unknowingly, Yeats's early love lyrics ruminate over their own implicit logic and that of their engendering tradition, even while perpetuating that same logic. The self-analysis in Yeats's love poetry does not "save" it from androcentric culture, but it can help us to probe the connections between that culture's erotic and elegiac poetry.

Because the titles of Yeats's elegiac love lyrics signal their thematic, generic, and psychic structures, these titles themselves deserve consideration for what they suggest about the interrelation between love and mourn-

---

1. W. B. Yeats, *The Poems, Revised*, ed. Richard J. Finneran (New York: Macmillan, 1989).
2. In the next line he also echoes the earlier image of woman as "labyrinth." On the beloved's absence and poetic inspiration in Yeats, see Elizabeth Cullingford, "Yeats and Women: *Michael Robartes and the Dancer*," *Yeats Annual* 4 (1986): 40, and Patricia Yaeger, " 'Because a Fire Was in My Head': Eudora Welty and the Dialogic Imagination," *PMLA* 99 (1984): 959–60. Among works that discuss the representation of women in Yeats, see also Richard Ellmann's preface to the later edition of *Yeats: The Man and the Masks* (New York: Norton, 1979), vii–xxviii; A. Norman Jeffares, "Women in Yeats's Poetry," *The Circus Animals: Essays on W. B. Yeats* (Stanford: Stanford University Press, 1970), 78–102; Gloria Klein, *The Last Courtly Lover: Yeats and the Idea of Woman* (Ann Arbor: UMI Research Press, 1983); Catherine Cavanaugh, *Love and Forgiveness in Yeats's Poetry* (Ann Arbor: UMI Research Press, 1986); and Patrick J. Keane, *Terrible Beauty: Yeats, Joyce, Ireland, and the Myth of the Devouring Female* (Columbia: University of Missouri Press, 1988).

ing in the early Yeats. Proposing a theme for elaboration, titles like "The Pity of Love" and "The Sorrow of Love" thematically commingle desire and melancholy. Other titles guide us into the poems by establishing their genre or subgenre, such as "Two Love Poems" and, strikingly, "An Epitaph" (VP,[3] 154, 170, 123). A third kind of title combines these Victorian conventions of designating the theme and genre of the poem, while offering a brief description of its psychic action. Again love and lament interfuse—for example, "The Lover mourns for the Loss of Love" and, in a title that traces the conversion of elegy into apocalyptic yearning, "He mourns for the Change that has come upon Him and his Beloved, and longs for the End of the World." The verbs in these descriptive titles— *mourns, remembers, longs, wishes,* but also *bids, tells, speaks*—suggest that for the early Yeats mournful love is the wellspring of poetic utterance. In his formal elegies Yeats tries to strip himself of this protracted despondency, a change reflected in the new directness ("In Memory of Alfred Pollexfen") and brevity ("Easter, 1916") of the later titles.[4]

Long before asking the famous question of "The Tower," Yeats begins to suggest that the (male) imagination dwells the most upon a woman lost. The early dream-poem "A Dream of Death" raises the disturbing possibility that many a love lyric may ultimately be, as he had originally entitled the poem, "An Epitaph":

> I dreamed that one had died in a strange place
> Near no accustomed hand;
> And they had nailed the boards above her face,
> The peasants of that land,
> Wondering to lay her in that solitude,
> And raised above her mound
> A cross they had made out of two bits of wood,
> And planted cypress round;
> And left her to the indifferent stars above
> Until I carved these words:
> *She was more beautiful than thy first love,*
> *But now lies under boards.*   (P 42)

The beloved is at first merely an anonymous "one," lost in the solitary landscape, where even the peasants' memorial mound, cross, and cypress cannot save her from the indifference of the stars. Dead, she can be humanized only by the poet: he carves words on the cross that celebrate her beauty (in the earlier version he "wrote" upon the cross). But to idealize her, the poet has had to imagine her dead—inhumed and requiring his rehumanizing "hand." The astonishing image of nailing "boards above her face" is initially displaced onto the agency of the peasants; yet, the poet's own inscription repeats the word *boards,* relating the defacement to his act of writing. The lyric enacts and exaggerates the contradictory move-

---

3. *The Variorum Edition of the Poems of W. B. Yeats,* ed. Peter Allt and Russell K. Alspach (New York: Macmillan, 1966).
4. See the helpful discussions of titles in John Hollander, *Vision and Resonance: Two Senses of Poetic Form* (1975; New Haven: Yale University Press, 1985), 212–26, and Alastair Fowler: *Kinds of Literature: An Introduction to the Theory of Genres and Modes* (Cambridge, Mass.: Harvard University Press, 1982), 92–98.

ments of courtly love poetry, idealizing but defacing the beloved. In a later autobiographical celebration of Maud Gonne, to whom Yeats sent this poem, he rhapsodically invokes a brief moment when "her face, like the face of some Greek statue, showed little thought" and "might outface even Artemisia's sepulchral image," but alas, her face soon resumes its place among the merely living (Au,[5] 242). Embedded within the larger epitaph of the whole lyric, the beloved's two-line epitaph is not really hers at all, particularly if we accept the traditional association of "thy first love" with Yeats's cousin, Laura Johnston, and the second with Maud Gonne. On that reading, the epitaph is not merely a formulaic boast to the passerby; self-reflexive, it is an apostrophe to the poet himself, writing the second love into a comparison between his relationships. The epitaph that the beloved's imagined death has allowed the poet to create is a miniature of the epitaphic process of much love poetry.

Although Frank Kermode calls "the dead face and the dancer . . . the central icon of Yeats and of the whole tradition," we have heard a lot about the dancer, while this dead face has been largely ignored.[6] Perhaps the poem's unsettling representation of the way it and other love lyrics work, burying and idealizing the beloved, is incongruous with our sentimental notions of the early Yeats; but the poem meditates on its own genesis as rigorously, if not as spectacularly, as "Byzantium" does. In its reflection on writing and the dead woman, "A Dream of Death" rivals its predecessors in a troubling line of Romantic love elegies, from Wordsworth's Lucy poems to Dante Gabriel Rossetti's paradoxically entitled The House of Life and Wilde's stilted "Requiescat," a line subsequently resumed by Hardy's Poems of 1912–13.[7] Because the poem is about itself and precisely not about women, because it is indeed about the erasure of women in love poetry, it is about Maud Gonne or Laura Johnston only in the root sense of about—outside. Gonne recalls in her autobiography that, recovering from a serious illness, she received the poem in France: "I was getting steadily better and was greatly amused when Willie Yeats sent me a poem, my epitaph he had written with much feeling."[8] Only imagined to be dead can she inspire such an impassioned love epitaph.

"A Dream of Death" is a poetic representation of a dream-representation of the beloved's death; but if we are hesitant about concluding that it therefore expresses a wish-fulfillment, the title of a companion dream-poem is more direct: "He wishes his Beloved were Dead." In their self-analysis, "A Dream of Death" and "He wishes his Beloved were Dead" share much with Freud's commentary on "Dreams of the Death of Beloved Persons" (Die Traüme von Tod Teurer Personen), a commentary included in another work of the nineties—The Interpretation of Dreams. Indeed, Freud's opus and Yeats's Wind Among the Reeds appeared in the

5. The Autobiography of William Butler Yeats (New York: Macmillan, 1935).
6. Frank Kermode, Romantic Image (1957; London: Routledge and Kegan Paul, 1961), 89.
7. Allen Grossman argues that "Requiescat" is the precursor-poem; see this reading and his general commentary on the early Yeats in Poetic Knowledge in the Early Yeats: A Study of "The Wind Among the Reeds" (Charlottesville: University Press of Virginia, 1969), 154.
8. Maud Gonne MacBride, A Servant of the Queen (London: Victor Gollancz, 1938), 147.

same year (1899). Freud attributes the wish for the loved one's death to a repressed childhood desire that the parent be "gone" *(fort)*, the child, like the adult unconscious, not distinguishing between death and other kinds of absence.[9] Yeats's lyrics reveal less the personal pathology of a necrophiliac than an awareness of unconscious desires—their *materia poetica*. Suggesting that their desire-charged language depends on the imagined absence or death of the loved one, these poems exemplify and highlight the psychological basis of much erotic poetry—perhaps even of Eros itself, at least according to the Lacanian theory of desire. As Lacan remarks in his *Discours de Rome*, "The symbol manifests itself first of all as the murder of the thing [*le meurtre de la chose*], and this death constitutes in the subject the eternalization of his desire."[1]

Aedh, the original speaker of "He wishes his Beloved were Dead," is appropriately enough both a poet and a "God of death" (*VP*, 794):

> Were you but lying cold and dead,
> And lights were paling out of the West,
> You would come hither, and bend your head,
> And I would lay my head on your breast;
> And you would murmur tender words,
> Forgiving me, because you were dead:
> Nor would you rise and hasten away,
> Though you have the will of the wild birds,
> But know your hair was bound and wound
> About the stars and moon and sun:
> O would, beloved, that you lay
> Under the dock-leaves in the ground,
> While lights were paling one by one.   (*P* 72–73) [29]

The disjunction between the two levels of the poem's rhetoric is even more jarring than in "A Dream of Death." The beloved is a dead woman, "lying cold and dead," and she is a divine principle of the cosmos, dispersed in interstellar space. To borrow de Man's terms, she is both a natural image and an emblem.[2] Critics tend to suppress the natural imagery in such poems and perceive only the apotheosis of the dead woman as Sophia, Wisdom, or the holy Shekinah. But the poem shows us that it must "kill" the beloved as natural image in order to transfigure her into a divine

---

9. Freud, *Die Traumdeutung* (Frankfurt am Main: Fischer Taschenbuch Verlag, 1942), 216. Although published in 1899, this work was dated 1900. For Freud's subsequent analysis of his grandson's *fort/da* (gone/there) game, in which the boy mournfully renounces and seeks the mother, see *Beyond the Pleasure Principle*, *The Standard Edition of the Complete Psychological Works of Sigmund Freud*, ed. James Strachey (London: Hogarth Press, 1953–74), 18:14–17.

1. In Lacan's view desire is inextricable from the elegiac language that creates it. See Jacques Lacan, *Speech and Language in Psychoanalysis*, trans. Anthony Wilden (Baltimore: Johns Hopkins University Press, 1981), 84. Schopenhauer anticipates the view that "lack" generates desire, and Yeats echoes him on this point in *Explorations* (New York: Macmillan, 1962), 430; see *The World as Will and Representation*, 2:539.

2. See Paul de Man, "Image and Emblem in Yeats," *Rhetoric of Romanticism*, 145–238. The translation of the beloved into an emblem is what Derrida calls "metaphorization": "the movement of metaphorization . . . is nothing other than a movement of idealization" ("White Mythology: Metaphor in the Text of Philosophy," *Margins of Philosophy*, trans. Alan Bass [Chicago: University of Chicago Press, 1982], 226).

principle of the imagination.[3] Though the beloved in Yeats does differ from the corpses in Poe and Baudelaire, this woman is both a disembodied essence and a cold, dead body, lying in the ground. Yeats even specifies the coarse weeds—dock-leaves—that cover her grave. In the dream-logic of this wish-poem, the poet "wishes his Beloved were Dead" because dead, she would generate language, not her own language but the words he wants to hear: "you would murmur tender words, / Forgiving me, because you were dead." These words forgive *d'outre-tombe* his transgressions, possibly even his having wished her dead. Dead, she would submit to his control, unable to articulate her own desires or to "rise and hasten away." This lover is indeed both poet and "God of death."

Together, the two early dream-poems partially anticipate a view shared by later theorists: that the sign is a carrier not of presence but of death and absence (in spite of Yeats's avowedly mystical theory of the symbol).[4] Thus, Raftery's words seemed to kill Mary Hynes, a young man explains to Yeats in *The Celtic Twilight*: "It is said that no one that has a song made about them will ever live long" (*Myth*,[5] 27). For Yeats, a living woman and the nothingness in a man's song sometimes seem incompatible.[6]

Not all of Yeats's elegiac love poems represent the beloved as dead. If not dead, she may be dying or fallen, thus leaving a space between her present and past selves for the elegiac imagination to fill. Even when she is not dead, it is only the absent self that the poet records, as Yeats reminds us as late as "Fallen Majesty" (1912):

> Although crowds gathered once if she but showed her face,
> And even old men's eyes grew dim, this hand alone,
> Like some last courtier at a gypsy camping-place
> Babbling of fallen majesty, records what's gone.
>
> The lineaments, a heart that laughter has made sweet,
> These, these remain, but I record what's gone. A crowd
> Will gather, and not know it walks the very street
> Whereon a thing once walked that seemed a burning cloud.
>
> (P 123–24) [50]

---

3. On the male word's "murder" of woman or mother, see Sandra M. Gilbert and Susan Gubar, *The Madwoman in the Attic: The Woman Writer and the Nineteenth-Century Literary Imagination* (New Haven: Yale University Press, 1979), 14–25, and Margaret Homans, *Bearing the Word: Language and Female Experience in Nineteenth-Century Women's Writing* (Chicago: University of Chicago Press, 1986), 11. Ellmann aptly remarks that young men visited Maud Gonne because "they adored Yeats's images of her; and she died, rather unwillingly, into his poems, which she never greatly liked"; see *Yeats: The Man and the Masks*, xxi.

4. For example, Maurice Blanchot remarks: "For me to be able to say, 'This woman' I must somehow take her flesh and blood reality away from her, cause her to be absent, annihilate her. The word gives me the being, but it gives it to me deprived of being. The word is the absence of that being, its nothingness, what is left of it when it has lost being—the very fact that it does not exist. . . . Of course, my language does not kill anyone. And yet: when I say, 'This woman,' real death has been announced and is already present in my language" (*The Gaze of Orpheus, and Other Literary Essays*, ed. P. Adams Sitney, trans. Lydia Davis [Barrytown, N.Y.: Station Hill, 1981], 42). Regarding death and signification, see also Jacques Derrida, *Speech and Phenomena*, trans. David B. Allison (Evanston: Northwestern University Press, 1973), 40, 54, 93–96, 138, and *Of Grammatology*, trans. Gayatri Chakravorty Spivak (Baltimore: Johns Hopkins University Press, 1976), 69, 183–84.

5. W. B. Yeats, *Mythologies* (New York: Macmillan, 1959).

6. Freud recalls Schiller's lines: "What is to live immortal in song must perish in life" (*Was unsterblich im Gesang soll Leben, / Muss in Leben untergehen*); see *Moses and Monotheism, SE*, 23:101.

Although he confesses that something remains of her physical beauty, the Blakean and Paterian word he chooses for it, *lineaments*, is itself a figure for absence, suggestive of an out*line* that de*line*ates a void. What remains is almost irrelevant to the poet: "I record what's gone," he proudly declaims. As in "A Dream of Death," the beloved has lost her former "face," and the "hand" of the poet refigures her. The hand is now the agency of love and language, a last courtier, and the elaborate simile of the gypsy camping-place situates it in the belated and homeless realm of words.

The poem's effacement of the beloved is visible in the buried pun on her name, emphasized by its repetition. Unlike the Innominata in most love poetry, the nameless beloved is named in the lines that proclaim her absence: the hand "records what's gone"; "I record what's gone." The trace of the name remains in the word that excludes it. If a "last courtier," Yeats certainly is not the first to pun on his beloved's name, as we know from Petrarch, who celebrates his poetry (*l'aura, lauro*) in puns on Laura's name. Following Petrarch's example, Yeats's pun makes a proper name improper by detaching it from its referent and making of it a sign of the poetic process.[7] Yeats's pun may be even more revealing than Petrarch's, because the word that displaces the name of the beloved signifies her absence—gone—an absence apparently necessary for the poem's own presence. Striking out one letter from her name, the poet renames the beloved as absence. "Her Praise" opens with the pun, and goes on to describe the poet wishing he might find someone with whom he could "Manage the talk until her name come round" (P 150). Similarly, in "Fallen Majesty," the poet excludes the beloved's name, but through the pun makes us supply it, so that we become complicitous in reading the poem with a desire structured around a lack.

The famous early love poem "When You are Old" (1892) also elegizes the youth of the beloved, but this poem represents her loss of youth as the poet's fancy. Yeats revises Ronsard's sonnet by putting his own book instead of distaff in the hand of the beloved; and what she reads there is not simply her youth but her youth recast as the prelude to old age:

> When you are old and grey and full of sleep,
> And nodding by the fire, take down this book,
> And slowly read, and dream of the soft look
> Your eyes had once, and of their shadows deep . . . .
> (P 41) [17]

Yeats imagines her to be old, alienated from herself, with the book alone preserving what's gone. He wills away her present self so that he may create a love elegy for her youth. He opens a gap for his poetry between her actual and imaginary selves, and thus, in her hypothetical reading of this poem, she reaches her present self by the detour of reading his book in her old age. She now depends upon the mediation of the poet's language,

7. See John Freccero, "The Fig Tree and the Laurel: Petrarch's Poetics," rpt. in *Literary Theory / Renaissance Texts*, ed. Patricia Parker and David Quint (Baltimore: Johns Hopkins University Press, 1986), 20–32. Unlike Petrarch, Yeats puns on the beloved's real name. In English poetry, another precedent is John Donne's pun on his name (Donne/done) in "A Hymne to God the Father."

a mediation that cancels her externality and independence.[8] Once again a "love poem" turns out to be epitaphic, based on the forceful negation of the beloved. Tracing how his poems generate their constitutive desire, Yeats helps us to see more clearly an assumption shared by many poems of courtly love—poems that eclipse the beloved to produce their work of mourning. Even in his full-fledged elegies, where the death is not only imagined, Yeats still worries that he has contributed to the death he laments.

HAROLD BLOOM

The Wind Among the Reeds†

* * *

[F]ascinated self-repulsion, centered in a hieratic context, is one of the shifting moods recurrent in *The Wind Among the Reeds*, a volume of love's defeat, and of the lover's subsequent offering of his passion to supernal and occult powers. Ellmann's view of *The Wind Among the Reeds* is that it is "a poetry where one sinks down and down without finding bottom," a judgment fairly based on Yeats's own description of his mental state in writing this poetry: "I had sometimes when awake, but more often in sleep, moments of vision, a state very unlike dreaming, when these images took upon themselves what seemed an independent life and became a part of a mystic language, which seemed always as if it would bring me some strange revelation."[1]

However unsatisfactory the verse of *The Wind Among the Reeds* proved to Yeats, or to many Yeats critics, it is a highly finished collection and its rich lacquer seems now to have protected it against time's decay. Yeats's dream of a stylized love, of an emotion not less urgent for its *antithetical* discipline, is realized here with formidable skill, while the Irish mythological baggage is remarkably light in the actual movement of the poems, particularly when contrasted to the ornate and redundant explanatory notes Yeats felt obliged to write for them.

* * *

Probably the most important external information one can have about *The Wind Among the Reeds* is the date of its publication, the last year of a century, and in particular of a century in which the anguished sense of the moment had become a peculiarly acute element in art and in life. A comment by Ian Fletcher, the great authority on the Nineties, is relevant:

---

8. I draw here upon Hegel's master-slave dialectic; see G. W. F. Hegel, *The Phenomenology of Mind*, trans. J. B. Baillie (New York: Harper and Row, 1967), 233, 237.
† From *Yeats* by Harold Bloom. Copyright © 1972 by Oxford University Press, Inc. Used by permission of Oxford University Press, Inc.
1. Richard Ellmann, *Yeats: The Man and the Masks* (Oxford: Oxford University Press, 1948), 159. See *The Variorum Edition of the Poems of W. B. Yeats*, ed. Peter Allt and Russell K. Alspach (New York: Macmillan, 1966), 800.

It is in the nineteenth century that the sense of belonging to a dec-ade, to a generation, was developed. Not until the 1890s could Lord Henry Wotton have said to Dorian Gray "fin de siécle" and have re-ceived the antiphonal answer "fin du globe." Such tremors are com-mon to ends of centuries, but the 1890s have more in common with the year 1000—a year of perfect numbers—or with the year 1600, than with the shrugging dismissal of, say, Dryden's *Secular Masque*. As the blank zeros of the calendar figure approached, the temporal uncertain-ties of the century merged in a diffuse, an irrational chiliasm.[2]

The temporal uncertainties of the century must have had an effect on the century's many visions of timelessness and its various counter-visions of endless recurrence. Here we are all of us still in surmise, with little that is certain in our studies. Pater's central idea of style is an idea of freedom from time, and perhaps all of aestheticism was a desperate protest against the menace of time that Romanticism had failed to dispel. Yeats's wind among the reeds has both Irish mythological and occult sources, as usual, but its main source is in Shelley's winds of destruction-creation, which blow all through his poetry, and in Blake's wind of Beulah that uproots stones and trees. Indeed, the main source of Yeats's volume is the not very esoteric *Ode to the West Wind*. The two dozen and more references to the hair of Yeats's beloved or of the faeries, which so much exercised the puritanical P. E. More and a number of critics after him, all go back to the locks of the approaching storm in Shelley's *Ode*, the locks being at once fiery clouds and the hair uplifted from the head of the fierce Maenad, the West Wind, which comes to visit upon the poet either the fate of Orpheus, or an apocalyptic restoration.

Yeats begins the volume by a vision of the faery host riding the wind, *The Hosting of the Sidhe*. His own comment explains that "Sidhe is also Gaelic for wind, and certainly the Sidhe have much to do with the wind. They journey in whirling winds, the winds that were called the dance of the daughters of Herodias in the Middle Ages, Herodias doubtless taking the place of some old goddess."[3] But Yeats's host is hardly the traditional Sidhe, including as it does Caoilte, a warrior of the Fenian cycle, and Niamh, the enticing beauty of *The Wanderings of Oisin*. This odd place-ment of warrior and ideal beauty is a clue to the meaning of the poem. The courage and splendor of the world have been taken up into the faery host, and so the poem can resolve itself in the rhetorical question:

> The host is rushing 'twixt night and day,
> And where is there hope or deed as fair? [23]

Yeats has no answer, in this volume, but the odd strength of the volume is in his subtle, never quite spoken resistance to the "sweet everlasting Voices" that have appropriated all of human passion, and yet left a man suffering in and from time. *The Lover tells of the Rose in his Heart* and rejects "all things uncomely and broken"; the world is not shapely enough

2. Ian Fletcher, "Rhythm and Pattern in Autobiographies," in *An Honoured Guest*, ed. D. Donoghue and J. R. Mulryne (New York: St. Martin's Press, 1966), 177.
3. *Variorum Poems*, 800.

to provide fit context for his love, and he hungers to build a world more to the heart's desire. But this beautiful lyric tells against its singer, and our sympathies go out to everything he neglects; the cry of a child and the ploughman's steps, while we note how far this lover is from desiring a reality. He dreams of an image, and the image blossoms a rose in the heart's depths, and remains only an image. This is the condition of the "out-worn heart, in a time out-worn" of *Into the Twilight*, and it is expressed throughout the volume with a perfection that no lyrist in Romantic tradition had surpassed. * * *

HELEN VENDLER

Technique in the Earlier Poems of Yeats†

*   *   *

* * * Yeats's early poem "He wishes for the Cloths of Heaven" [is] an eight-line experiment in *rime riche* and internal rhyme:

> Had I the heavens' embroidered cloths,
> Enwrought with golden and silver light,
> The blue and the dim and the dark cloths
> Of night and light and the half-light,
> I would spread the cloths under your feet:
> But I, being poor, have only my dreams;
> I have spread my dreams under your feet;
> Tread softly because you tread on my dreams.
>
> (VP¹ 176) [29]

Here, as elsewhere in *The Wind Among the Reeds*, Yeats has departed from his earlier iambic habit in order to explore dactylic and anapaestic feet; this poem emphasises a dactylic beat in its first, counterfactual, unit, an anapaestic one in its second, narrative part. The yearning intensity of the counterfactual is borne by the ictus of the dactyl, the proud humility of the subsequent narrative being borne by the lapse, as it seems, into the gentleness of a largely anapaestic metre.

It would seem that Yeats thought, when he had finished this poem, that he had made something very beautiful. When we ask ourselves what he was working towards we see first of all the excessively foregrounded rhyme-words, three of which—*cloths, light,* and *dreams*—are repeated inside lines as well. We also see the internal rhymes *night/light* and *spread/tread,* the assonance of *being/feet/dreams* and of *embroidered/enwrought,* and the alliteration of *had/heaven/half.* In fact, the only significant word that dwells unattached in the poem is the word *poor:* it stands out unmoored, unmated, unwanted, awkward. Being poor, says the protagonist of the title,

---

† From *Yeats Annual* 8 (1991): 3–20. Reprinted by permission of Helen Vendler. Page references to this Norton Critical Edition are given in brackets after the author's original citations.
1. *The Variorum Edition of the Poems of W. B. Yeats,* ed. Peter Allt and Russell K. Alspach (New York: Macmillan, 1966).

he wishes. His wishes are fantasies of possession, as he dreams he has the fabric of the sky itself—the cloud-cloths, star-embroidered, wealthy in golden and silver lights—available to him for a courtier's gesture. The poem works by a substitution: when, in *l. 6*, the speaker says, "I have only my dreams", we mentally substitute those wishes and dreams he has told us of—the whole "Had I . . . I would" dream of the first five lines, with its gorgeous ennobling of the sky so as to make it worthy of the beloved. No non-lover would have the motivation so to elaborate the elemental round of sun, moon, and stars.

This poem is a good place to notice how Yeats has begun to define his stanza forms. Though defined by its rhymes as two quatrains, it is printed as a single octave, suggesting that for Yeats a "stanza" is not determined by rhymes alone. Here, the eight lines are printed as one stanza rather than two because the first sense-unit extends beyond the first quatrain. This sort of non-fit between sense-unit and rhyme-unit is one that Yeats exploited to the utmost, until he reached a height of perversity in which the last place he would put a sense-break was the point of rhyme-break.

In "He wishes for the Cloths of Heaven" the counterfactual takes up five lines, spilling over the end of the first quatrain and coming to an end at the colon; then comes the one-line present-tense factual counter-statement "But I, being poor, have only my dreams", ending in a semi-colon; then the narrative present perfect of continued action, again one line with a semicolon; and finally the injunction to the beloved, again a single line. This desperately asymmetrical shape—a five-line, long-breathed curve of the counterfactual followed by three one-liners of the factual ("I . . . have only dreams", "I have spread my dreams", "you tread on my dreams")—works by its evident singularity and irregularity against the static, even monotonous, circularity of the *rime riche*. We could say that the *rime riche* stands for the lover's fidelity, the irregular syntactic bursts for his hope, inadequacy, and nervousness. It is the emotional suggestive-ness of these formal properties that gives them their intimate interest for Yeats. He will continue, all his life, to counterpoint sense-units against rhyme-units, so that neither may become too predictable; a notable case in point is the ingenious variety of sense-units played against the *ottava rima* of "Among School Children", a contrapuntal variety which confers on the poem its air of spontaneous musing, inner hesitation, recalci-trance, and emotionality. In a later poem, the lady of "The Three Bushes" tells her lover that she hopes to hear "if we should kiss / A contrapuntal serpent hiss", and this contrapuntal principle of aesthetic tension, visible as early as "He wishes for the Cloths of Heaven", is never forsaken by Yeats.

While working closely on all sorts of structural formalisms—metres, rhymes, and stanza shapes—Yeats began almost at once to subvert that formality. In fact, his use of subtraction is one of his least-noticed elabo-rations. Though it may seem paradoxical to call subtraction a form of elaboration, it too is a way of foregrounding something, and becomes part of the Yeatsian stanzaic artifice as it calls attention to what is missing. This device is evident and formally satisfying in "The Lover mourns for the Loss of Love":

Pale brows, still hands and dim hair,	*a*
I had a beautiful friend	*b*
And dreamed that the old despair	*a*
Would end in love in the end:	*b*

She looked in my heart one day	*c*
And saw your image was there;	*a*
She has gone weeping away.	*c*
[. . . . .]	[*a*]

(VP 152) [25]

The first quatrain of this poem imposes itself solidly as it closes with a colon after the strong closing rhyme *end* of l. 4 (duplicated internally in the same line). We expect a second quatrain as conclusive as the first, and we seem to be finding it: *day/there/away/?* A blank occurs instead of a rhyme word to match *there*. The poem "needs" a line like "And I lack your love and her care". But the lover's double lack—of the loved woman unpossessed, of the kind friend unloved—is expressed more powerfully by the total absence of an eighth line. We notice that the poem is none the less formally complete, since the end word of the second line of quatrain two, *there*, matches the *a* rhymes (*hair/despair*) of the first quatrain, and so no line remains unrhymed.

Yeats never forgets what he has once invented, and a comparable deletion of a closing line turns up memorably (if at first invisibly) at the very end of the poem "The Tower". Part III of "The Tower" rhymes in trimeter quatrains *abab*, but the last "quatrain" has only three lines, as can be seen from this excerpting of the close:

Now I shall make my soul,	*a*
Compelling it to study	*b*
In a learned school	*a*
Till the wreck of body,	*b*

Slow decay of blood,	*a*
Testy delirium	*b*
Or dull decrepitude,	*a*
Or what worse evil come—	*b*

The death of friends, or death	*a*
Of every brilliant eye	*b*
That made a catch in the breath—	*a*
Seem but the clouds of the sky	*b*

When the horizon fades,	*a*
Or a bird's sleepy cry	*b*
Among the deepening shades.	*a*
[. . . . .]	[*b*]

(VP 416) [85–86]

We see in this late passage many persistences from early Yeats—the rhyme *eye/sky* of the vowel/consonant(s)-vowel sort, the monosyllabic similarly spelled rhymes *death/breath* and *fades/shades*. But we also find the slant rhymes so common in later Yeats, and the "modern" rhyme *delirium/come*, which is none the less reminiscent of the experiments in asymmetrical rhyme of early Yeats. As the shades deepen and the horizon fades, the last line vanishes with breath itself, and where we expected a conclusion we find a blank. As he did in "The Lover mourns for the Loss of Love", Yeats has once again anchored the second line of the last "deficient" quatrain by rhyming it with an anterior line, here with the *b* rhyme of the preceding quatrain, so that the poem sounds formally finished even though stanzaically it remains incomplete.

*   *   *

I cannot leave the topic of "missing" lines without citing the most famous instance, the line Yeats deleted from his epitaph at the end of "Under Ben Bulben". As we know from the drafts (L^2 913), the epitaph consisted originally of four lines, of which Yeats dropped the first:

> Draw rein; draw breath.
> Cast a cold eye
> On life, on death.
> Horseman, pass by.

The dimeters of this quatrain, combined into tetrameters, would make a couplet symmetrical with those composing the poem:

> Draw rein; draw breath. Cast a cold eye
> On life, on death. Horseman, pass by.

These lines are thus formally complete, whether considered as a true diameter quatrain or as an internally rhymed variant of the standard "Under Ben Bulben" tetrameter couplet. When Yeats decides to delete the first dimeter, he makes his inscription formally incomplete from both points of view, and thus emphasises the discrepancy of nonce dimeters occurring in a tetrameter poem; the deletion makes us read the epitaph as a quatrain that falls silent after its third line:

> *Cast a cold eye*   *b*
> *On life, on death.*   *b*
> *Horseman, pass by!*   *a*
> [. . . . .]   [*b*]
>   (VP 640) [125]

The original opening line, "Draw rein, draw breath", had inscribed Yeats's epitaph in the *Siste viator* tradition, and it is likely (given Yeats's debt in "Byzantium" to Coleridge's epitaph) that Yeats had in mind the Romantic and Christian formulations of Coleridge, from whom he borrowed the rhyme *death/breath*, as well as the passer-by and the exclamation point:

> Stop, Christian passer-by!—Stop, child of God . . .
> O, lift one thought in prayer for S. T. C.;

2. *The Letters of W. B. Yeats*, ed. Allan Wade (London: Rupert Hart-Davis, 1954; New York: Macmillan, 1955).

That he who many a year with toil of breath
Found death in life, may here find life in death![3]

By deleting the opening line of his epitaph, and commanding the (aristocratic, mounted) passer-by to pass by (rather than to draw rein to stop
and draw breath to pray), Yeats repudiates the Romantic and Christian
communion implored in piety by Coleridge, and substitutes for it a modernist and sceptical haughtiness, together with a modernist asymmetry. At
the same time, as Warwick Gould reminds me, we may suspect a debt,
noted by H. J. Oliver in the Arden *Timon of Athens*, to Timon's epitaph:

> Here lie I, Timon, who, alive, all living man did hate.
> Pass by and curse thy fill, but pass and stay not here thy gait.[4]

*   *   *

Yeats used profitably the uncertainty conferred on a poem by ambiguous
relations among its sense-units, its syntactic units, and its rhyme-units. The
most famous example of such ambiguity of relation in the early verse is
"Who Goes with Fergus?" The poem is composed of two six-line stanzas
rhyming *abcabc*. In the first stanza, the syntactic units—a question and a
set of injunctions—match the rhyme division exactly:

> Who will go drive with Fergus now,   *a*
> And pierce the deep wood's woven shade,   *b*
> And dance upon the level shore?   <u>c</u>
>
> Young man, lift up your russet brow,   *a*
> And lift your tender eyelids maid,   *b*
> And brood on hopes and fear no more.   *c*

But in the second stanza, the sense-break comes after two lines, not three.
This puts rhyme and sense at odds, or at least places them in an asymmetrical relation to each other, creating a "false quatrain" out of the last
four lines:

> And no more turn aside and brood   *a*
> Upon love's bitter mystery;   <u>*b*</u>
>
> For Fergus rules the brazen cars,   *c*
> And rules the shadows of the wood,   *a*
> And the white breast of the dim sea   *b*
> And all dishevelled wandering stars.   *c*
>   (VP 125–6) [18]

And, in the most complex move of the poem, the paired semiotic corre-
spondences between lines in stanza 1 and lines in stanza 2 come out
"wrongly", a pairing that leaves one piece unmatched:

3. Samuel Taylor Coleridge, "Epitaph", *Poems* (London: Oxford University Press, 1961) pp. 491–2.
4. William Shakespeare, *Timon of Athens*, ed. H. J. Oliver (London: Methuen, 1959); see the
   note on p. 140. The fact that Plutarch says that the last portion of the epitaph was written by
   Callimachus would also have recommended it to Yeats's attention.

Who . . . drive . . . Fergus	=	Fergus rules . . . cars
wood's woven shade	=	shadows of the wood
level shore	=	white breast of . . . dim sea
?	=	dishevelled wandering stars

There is nothing in stanza 1, or so it seems, to match the last line of the second sestet, "And all dishevelled wandering stars". The stars draw their very effect from their excessiveness, their "extra-ness" in the absence of any matching material. Because *ll.* 3, 4, and 5 of stanza 2 have echoed in exact order *ll.* 1, 2, and 3 of stanza 1, we expect line 6, in its turn, to match something (preferably *l.* 4 of stanza 1) to keep the order going. But the stars match nothing, surprising by their fine excess. We then see that the total poem has the form of a chiasmus:

Question	Negative injunction	Negative injunction	Conclusion
Fergus	Brood no more	Brood no more	Fergus

If the poem is broken at the end of *l.* 8 (" . . . mystery"), it becomes a "false" tetrameter sonnet, in which the octave is followed by a volta on "For" and an incomplete sestet.

Going off with Fergus is the alternative, for man and maid alike, to brooding on love's bitter mystery. It is suggested, I think, that Fergus is himself an erotic power, ruling the masculine brazen cars and the feminine breast of the sea. The woven shadows of the wood and the dishevelled wandering stars share so many common letters and phonemes (*shadows/ -shevelled, woven/wood/wandering*) that they suggest the expansiveness and continuity of a realm without borders or horizons. The lovers have exchanged love's bitter "mystery" (the one polysyllabic rhyme in the poem and therefore foregrounded) for an increasing expanse from wood to seashore to straying stars. The "expansion" beyond the matching lines to the unmatched stars gives the "extra" *l.* 6 a quasi-infinite dimension. We are left unsure whether we have read a poem of two six-line stanzas or a single twelve-line chiasmus; an incomplete tetrameter sonnet; a poem in tercets or a poem permitting a quatrain; a symmetrical poem in which lines are matched, or an asymmetrical poem with a leftover line at the end.

* * *

The "ambiguous" stanzas in this and other poems—are they sestets? are they octaves? are they quatrains?—are congruent with the frequently ambiguous rhythms of the early poetry. Yeats often aims at a "floating" formal undecidability of rhythm coincident with his attempt to reproduce meditative hovering. As I have said, I cannot take up Yeats's prosody here, but I want to point out that the odd alexandrines, pentameters (often in dactylic or anapaestic rhythms), and even trimeters of the early poetry will be found to have their descendants in the later verse—refined, more pointed, more sure of their intent.

At the other extreme from hovering, sensitivity, undecidability, lack, and ambiguity stand full power and command. It was to be some time before

Yeats could exert his full, even coercive, rhetorical strength. However, the early poetry does show signs of language used, I believe, with magical intent and confident will, without ambiguity of stanza form or rhythm. The most striking and beautiful example of what I would call poetry used as magic is "The Song of Wandering Aengus". Aengus, we are told, is the Irish Apollo, a god of poetry; and although he is here shown as a quester, he is also the chosen consort of a beckoning goddess, and his last words are words of powerful intent: "I will find out where she has gone / And kiss her lips and take her hands." Here is the poem, with the "magical" words and syllables in italics:

The Song of *Wandering* Aengus

I went *out* to the hazel wood,　　　　　*a*
Because a *fire* was in my *head*　　　　*b*
And cut and peeled a hazel *wand*,　　　*c*
And hooked a berry to a *thread*;　　　*b*
And when white *moths* were on the wi*ng*,
And *moth*-like stars were flickeri*ng* out,
I dropped the berry in a stream
And caught a little silver tr*out*.

When I had laid it on the *floor*
I went to blow the *fire* aflame;
But something rustled on the *floor*,
And some one *called me by my name*:
It had become a glimmeri*ng* girl
With *apple* blossom in her h*air*
Who *called me by my name* and ran
And faded through the brighteni*ng air*.

Though I am *old* with *wandering*
Through hol*low lands* and *hilly lands*,
I *will* find out where she has gone,
And kiss her lips and take her hands;
And walk among long d*apple*d grass,
And pluck *till* time and times are done
The silver *apples* of the moon,
The *golden* apples of the sun.　　　(VP 149–50) [24–25]

The poem is composed in alternately rhymed quatrains but printed in octaves, three of them. The story is simple: Aengus, using as bait a berry hooked by a thread to a hazel wand, catches a trout that turns into a girl who, after calling him by name, vanishes, leaving Aengus determined to continue pursuing her. But the way Yeats uses language in this poem suggests that he believes that language has powers of its own independent of the story it tells. It is no accident, I think, that the first thing *wand*-ering Aengus does is to cut a *wand*, or that his *head* finds a *thread*. Such pairings assert that magical, non-rational, non-etymological connections between words are as important to Yeats as logical, semantic, or etymological relations. Other magical connections are made in the rhymes and elsewhere:

just as the word *head* is contained in t*h*e*a*d, so *out* is contained in t*r*out,
air is contained in h*air*, *time* is contained in *times*, *though* is contained in
through, and *hollow lands and hilly lands* contains *low lands and hi[gh]
lands*. These linked words are foregrounded in various ways—*though* and
through, for instance, by being placed in the same initial position in suc-
cessive lines, and others by being placed in a rhyme position.

Other linkages are no less arbitrary. *Moths* on the *wing* are mysteriously
equated to *moth*-like stars flicke*ring*. The *fire* in Aengus's head is replicated
by the *fire* he blows aflame. The *rime riche* of *floor* and *floor*, and the
repetition of *called me by my name* are used, I think, to keep the setting
and action realistically constant while magical transformation occurs
creepingly in the nouns and pronouns:

> [I] caught a little silver *trout*.

> When I had laid *it* on the floor
> I went to blow the fire aflame,
> But *something* rustled on the floor,
> And *some one* called me by my name:
> *It* had become a glimmering *girl*
> With apple blossom in her hair
> Who called me by my name. . . .

The wande*ring* hero of the title, when moths were on the w*ing* and stars
were flicke*ring*, finds a glimme*ring* girl who fades through the brighten*ing*
air and makes him old with wande*ring*. These irrational -*ing* links connect
the title and the stanzas. Similar magical links cause the peculiar conclusiveness of the ending. Of course, as we read "the silver apples of the
moon, / The golden apples of the sun", we see the semantic reprise of
"silver" trout and "apple-blossom" in the girl's hair, but it is only by in-
spection that we see how the conclusiveness is also caused by the foreshadowing power of "*old*" for "*gold*en" and "*d*a*ppled*" for "*apples*". The
"out" words too—"I went *out* . . . when stars were . . . *out* . . . and caught
a tr*out*. . . . I will find *out* . . ."—are non-rational "magic" links in the
narrative. The very fabric of "The Song of Wandering Aengus" suggests
the reduplicative nature of spell-casting, full of anaphora and the repetition
of phrases, lines, and sounds. This sort of poetry enacts absolute
command—the magus's command of entirely mastered experience, or the
god's command over fate. The narrative is perfectly distributed in structural
equilibrium: a stanza for the trout, a stanza for the girl, and a stanza for
the quest.

But, in addition to perfectly mastered experience and language, this
performative poem promises, and gives, a paradise—the end of the quest
foreseen in Aengus's prophecy that he will attain the glimmering girl.
Many of the satisfactions of this paradise are foreshadowed, as I have said,
but we are I think surprised by the appearance of "the golden apples of
the sun". The silver trout had been caught at twilight and brought home
at evening; the silver apples of the moon therefore seem proper to it and
to the glimmering girl it became—but the golden apples of the sun burst
surprisingly upon this nocturne. They are perhaps forecast by the dawn

scene, the brightening air into which the girl fades in her paradoxical escape—"[She] ran / And faded through the brightening air". Aengus knows that she was silver and glimmering on this earth but will become golden, in the brightening sun, in eternity. We feel a foretaste of the Byzantium poems.

*   *   *

The incantatory power of reduplicative language (learned in part from Swinburne but not abused) served Yeats as an index of magical writing all his life. We hear it in the repetitions of "The Gyres":

> The gyres! the gyres! Old Rocky Face, look forth;
> Things thought too long can be no longer thought,
> For beauty dies of beauty, worth of worth. . . .
>
>   (VP 564) [114]

Repetition, by spell-casting, is the guarantee of revolution; and so transformative or revolutionary spells must be repetitive first, and then, with their unexpected golden apples or disinterments from broken sepulchres, revolutionary. The history of Yeats's style, as yet unwritten, will show how much, in the long run, the late style is a result of the early hard work—how, by those early experiments, the visual and auditory presence of individual words, rhymes, stanza schemes, and syntactic parallels took on for Yeats an almost palpable shape and solidity. The historian of Yeats's style will also want to speculate on the spiritual meaning certain practices of rhyme and metre and stanza form acquired for him over his lifetime.

*   *   *

MICHAEL J. SIDNELL

Yeats's "Written Speech": Writing, Hearing and Performance†

*   *   *

Yeats's concern that (written) poetry be rendered as speech is very much in evidence in the two essays that he composed, near the end of his life, by way of introduction to a collected edition that never appeared. In one of them, he says: "I have spent my life in clearing out of poetry every phrase written for the eye, and bringing all back to syntax that is for ear alone" (E&I¹ 529). The meaning of the first half of this statement is not self-evident. What is a "phrase written for the eye"? Doubtless whatever is picturesque or Pre-Raphaelite but also " 'vision', meaning by vision the intense realisation of a state of ecstatic emotion symbolised in a definite

---

† From *Yeats Annual* 11 (1995): 3–11. Reprinted by permission of Michael J. Sidnell. Page references to this Norton Critical Edition are given in brackets after the author's original citations.
1. W. B. Yeats, *Essays and Introductions* (London: Macmillan, 1961).

imagined region" (L² 583). More obviously, Yeats would exclude from poetry whatever in written language may be read silently for information, analysis, argument or conceptual content. Such reading might be accompanied by the pleasures that arise from the matched linguistic aptitudes and refinements of writer and reader—precision; etymological awareness; control, subtlety and variety of syntax; extensive and varied vocabulary; intertextuality and such—but such qualities would not be sufficient, in Yeats's poetics, to redeem whatever in language does not come in at the ear. It is clear, I think, that we are dealing with two tendencies rather than the sharp dichotomy that Yeats sets up and that, if what he means by language "written for the eye" is not so easy to pin down, what he has in mind when he speaks of "bringing all back to syntax that is for ear alone" should be evident from his actual practice.

A prime exhibit of Yeats's writing for the ear, partly because it talks about what it does, is "Adam's Curse", which is widely recognised as one of the very early manifestations of a startling stylistic revolution in Yeats's poetic language.

> We sat together at one summer's end,
> That beautiful mild woman, your close friend,
> And you and I, and talked of poetry.
> I said: 'A line will take us hours maybe;
> Yet if it does not seem a moment's thought,
> Our stitching and unstitching has been naught . . . .'
> (VP³ 204) [32]

Here, the effect of speech is doubled since, in the dramatic action of the poem, the poet directly quotes his own past words, and later the friend's. Congruent with this trope of speech within speech is that of the past occasion recalled on the present, equally particular, one. These tropes would become regular ones in Yeats. "The Fisherman", "The People", "The Municipal Gallery Revisited" are instances in which past speech and occasions are contained within those of the present, conveying effects of spontaneity and "the speech of a man" (YT⁴ 74). But, as he says in "Adam's Curse", with such superb confidence and candour, such effects are to be achieved only after a lot of drafting. Some of the characteristics of the resultant "written speech" in the case of "Adam's Curse" itself are: the use of appositional phrases; the creation of suspense by delaying the complement of the verb; a strong basic rhythm, secured by well-placed epithets; and, above all, the "contrapuntal" effect of colloquial phrases within a metrically regular form—in this case rhymed couplets. I say colloquial "phrases" because it is in them, rather than in the syntactical order of phrases that the effect mostly resides. In the anecdotal context, these features of direct speech and regular versification together constitute the acoustic representation of an elevated kind of conversation.

2. *The Letters of W. B. Yeats*, ed. Allan Wade (London: Rupert Hart-Davis, 1954; New York: Macmillan, 1955).
3. *The Variorum Edition of the Poems of W. B. Yeats*, ed. Peter Allt and Russell K. Alspach (New York: Macmillan, 1966).
4. *Yeats and the Theatre*, ed. Robert O'Driscoll and Lorna Reynolds (Toronto: Macmillan, 1975).

The opening of "Adam's Curse", which remained more or less unchanged after publication, is an example of Yeats's writing for the ear in 1902, while a revision of some succeeding lines—which has not been much noticed—shows him at work at a much later stage in his career, still revising for auditory effect. Let's look at this revision, briefly.

When Maud Gonne re-told the incident in which "Adam's Curse" germinated, she rendered her sister's remark with an authentic-sounding flatness: "It was on that occasion Kathleen remarked that it was hard work being beautiful, which Willie turned into his poem *Adam's Curse*."[5] Her sister's remark, as it happened, did not achieve its final verse form until about twenty years later. And this late revision is an example of Yeats' effort to rid his verse of everything not "for ear alone", and of some complications in his developing understanding of that process. The lines in question originally read:

> That woman then
> Murmured with her young voice for whose mild sake
> There's many a one shall find out all heartache
> In finding that it's young and mild and low.
> "There is one thing that all we women know
> Although we never heard of it at school,
> That we must labour to be beautiful."   (VP 205v.) [32]

If you recall their finished version, these lines will probably seem closer to normal speech and duller than they became. Here is the finished version:[6]

> And thereupon
> That beautiful mild woman for whose sake
> There's many a one shall find out all heartache
> On finding that her voice is sweet and low
> Replied: "To be born woman is to know—
> Although they do not talk of it at school—
> That we must labour to be beautiful."   (VP 205)

Some of the changes Yeats made to arrive at this version are these: the verb "murmured" is replaced with the dramatic and less self-effacing "replied"; and the verb, instead of being supplied immediately, is held in suspense for three lines—a display of virtuosity in the management of the period that is typical of the later Yeats. It brings into play a syntactical complexity that, in recitation, calls for careful placing of accents and pauses, variations of tempo and pitch, and breath control—and in silent reading, the equivalent mental representation of these effects.

Instead of "That woman then / Murmured . . .", the final version goes, "And thereupon / That beautiful mild woman . . .". "Thereupon" is a rather uncommonly used,[7] rather pedantic, adverb, mostly confined to

---

5. Maud Gonne MacBride, *A Servant of the Queen* (London: Victor Gollancz, 1938) p. 328.
6. Yeats's dissatisfaction with these lines is registered by the draft revisions (never printed) that he made of them in 1910 (W. B. Yeats, *Memoirs*, ed. Denis Donoghue [London: Macmillan, 1972] p. 244).
7. "Thereupon" occurs in a number of Yeats's major poems and sixteen times in all. It often indicates an epiphany or sudden change.

legal and poetic contexts, where it is intended to point to a moment with great precision.[8] Here, in association with the verb "replied" and the wording of that reply, it quite transforms the characterisation of the woman. Instead of a mousey murmurer she becomes an assertive dialectician— though it was the whole verbal texture (which expresses the personality of the poet) rather than the characterisation of the woman that was at stake.

The second of the lines in question, a rather feeble aggregate of monosyllables, contained a phrase that merely *tells* something about a voice: "Murmured with her young voice for whose mild sake". The "young voice" went, and also the first part of the line, which was replaced with a phrase already used—"That beautiful mild woman"—the repetition standing out as a deliberate rhetorical device for patterning and emphasis. The repeated line also happens to be syntactically structured in a way that Yeats particularly favoured: an appositional noun phrase beginning with the demonstrative determiner "that", demonstrating the speaker's own definiteness and implying a solid common ground of understanding with an interlocutor.

The last details I shall mention have to do with the couching of the woman's reply—as it has become. She no longer refers to what was passively *"heard"* in school but of what is actively *"talked of"* there—inserting the remark, moreover, as an interjection; and instead of the ordinary and rather prim "There is one thing that all we women know" Yeats now employs a sophisticated syntax: a pair of infinitives used as nouns, to epigrammatic effect: "To be born a woman is to know . . .".

This example of revision is a not untypical illustration of how the impression of speech develops in Yeats's poetry, becoming less "natural", more oratorical, more ideal and more intensely an effect depending on vocal self-dramatisation, whether inwardly or outwardly heard. In the instance in question, the late revision makes the linguistic texture of the poem more even. "She" becomes as eloquent as the poet and, in the process, the differentiation between the two voices is much diminished.

Yeats's adaptation of his poetry to the ear inscribes a particular voice rather than dramatised voices of various characters such as, to take named examples, Crazy Jane or John Kinsella. Yeats doesn't "do the police in different voices"[9] but projects a controlling, vocalised personality, who plays all the parts and pre-empts any performer's voice also. So, paradoxically enough, the inscription of personalised speech, which is a key poetic function in Yeats's lyric poetry, makes for difficulties in reciting it, if for no other reason than that reciters, too, have their own styles and can't imitate another without shifting the mode of performance from recitation to dramatic acting. * * *

8. The substitution of "On finding" for "In finding" also contributes to this effect in the poem.
9. T. S. Eliot, *The Waste Land: a facsimile and transcript of the original drafts including the annotations of Ezra Pound*, ed. Valerie Eliot (London: Faber & Faber, 1971) p. 16.

LUCY McDIARMID

Yeats and the Lettered Page†

Before men read, the ear and the tongue were subtle, and delighted one another with the little tunes that were in words. . . . They loved language, and all literature was then, whether in mouth of minstrels, players, or singers, but the perfection of an art that everybody practiced, a flower out of the stem of life. . . . (Ex¹ 212)

The title of this essay is meant to shock: why "lettered page," when Yeats devoted so much of his life to propaganda for the "living voice"? What about Florence Farr and her psaltery, and chants, Lady Gregory and the "popular theatre," and Yeats's many songs, ballads, and come-all-ye's? What about those "minstrels, players, or singers" whose spontaneous musical utterance Yeats professed to admire? What about the *fili*, those "wild-eyed men who spoke harmoniously to murmuring wires," and the "old world that sang and listened"?

Writing in 1922 about the enthusiasms of his Celtic Twilight days, Yeats referred to the "unrealities and half-truths propaganda had involved me in" (UPl² 34). His many (written) polemics against writing, and his defenses of the voice, constitute a large part of those "half-truths." I want to look afresh at the speech/writing dichotomy in Yeats's poems because it is so clearly a subject on which it is unwise to trust absolutely Yeats's prose assertions—and because the poems may tell the other "half" of the "truths."

Contemporary critics and theorists will have to erase from the tables of their memories all saws of *Writing and Difference* and *Of Grammatology*, because the terminology of Yeats's interest is simpler.³ Yeats inherited his terms and a concomitant set of values from Romanticism's preference for what was "primitive," "unspoiled," and "popular." Oral "literature" was only a fancier form of story-telling and singing, the "perfection of an art that everybody practiced," as Yeats wrote in 1906. To call it further a "flower out of the stem of life" suggests that such literature is little more than beautiful spontaneous utterance. Yeats emulated early folklorists like the Brothers Grimm, who (so legend had it) rescued from the mouths of their sources the uncontaminated versions of old stories.⁴ Talking with

---

† From *Yeats: An Annual of Critical and Textual Studies* 8 (1990): 100–11. Reprinted by permission of the University of Michigan Press. Page references to this Norton Critical Edition are given in brackets after the author's original citations.

1. W. B. Yeats, *Explorations* (New York: Macmillan, 1962).
2. *Uncollected Prose by W. B. Yeats*, vol. 1, ed. John P. Frayne (London: Macmillan, 1970).
3. Nevertheless, I shall refer interested readers to Jacques Derrida, "Freud and the Scene of Writing," *Writing and Difference*, trans. Alan Bass (Chicago: U of Chicago P, 1978) 196–231; to Paul de Man, "Autobiography as Defacement," *The Rhetoric of Romanticism* (New York: Columbia UP, 1984) 67–81; and to Fredric Jameson, *The Prison-House of Language* (Princeton: Princeton UP, 1972).
4. For a list and discussion of romantic collectors and the tradition in which they worked, see Walter J. Ong, *Orality and Literacy* (London: Methuen, 1982; New York: Methuen, 1983) Chapter 2.

peasants in County Galway at the turn of the century, Yeats and Lady Gregory sought folk-wisdom from similar conduits of tradition.

* * *

Yeats's two surges of involvement in propaganda for the "living voice" both ended in disillusion with his actual audience and recantation of his theories. The manifestoes for the National Theatre, which exhorted "Let us get back in everything to the spoken word" (Ex 95) and which noted that earlier literatures of a "whole people . . . found their way to men's minds without the mediation of print and paper" (Ex 209) were followed by Yeats's call for an "unpopular theatre" (Ex 254). Its audience would be "like a secret society," its music performed on drum, flute, and zither, and its verse artsy. Appropriate ticket-buyers would be found among those who "read poetry for their pleasure"—the literate well-to-do (Ex 255). This is the same retreat from voice implied in "The Fisherman," where the "people" are characterized by a coarse orality—"drunken cheer," "joke / Aimed at the commonest ear," "catch-cries of the clown"—and the ideal audience for whom Yeats *writes* that famous "cold / And passionate" poem is not a story-teller or a singer but a silent, solitary fisherman, imagined, and therefore incapable of disillusioning (VP⁵ 347–48) [63].

Yeats's second surge of interest in the living voice followed a similar pattern. Eager for immediate utility, Yeats in 1934 composed some marching songs for General O'Duffy's Blueshirts because he "wanted to write what some crowd in the street might understand and sing" (VP 543). But that crowd in the street mangled his words, transforming them into a vulgar "song that is all about shamrocks and harps. . . ." Yeats rewrote the songs (he said in a note) so "that no party might sing them" (VP 837).⁶

In none of his recantations of the living voice does Yeats explicitly praise the virtues of the written word. In lyric poems written after 1914, however, writing—particularly the physical activity of writing—begins to appear as a primary source of value. Particularly in the poems that describe and defend his metier, Yeats emerges as a cosmopolitan, lettered poet writing in a classical, European tradition, not a poet of the people.

Two kinds of poems from the second half of Yeats's career, inscriptions and poems describing the scene of their own composition, link Yeats with "Declamatory Epigrams" of the *Greek Anthology*. The first of these is a *genre* (discussed in some detail by Geoffrey Hartman in "Wordsworth, Inscriptions, and the Romantic Nature Poetry"); the second is a *topos* that Yeats turned into a major poetic subject.⁷ Although Yeats had not read the Greek originals, they were widely influential in European poetry beginning

5. *The Variorum Edition of the Poems of W. B. Yeats*, ed. Peter Allt and Russell K. Alspach (New York: Macmillan, 1966).
6. For an analysis of the changes Yeats made in these songs and for further discussion of Yeats's work in the light of his notions about speech and writing, see Lucy McDiarmid, "The Living Voice in the Thirtles," *Saving Civilization: Yeats, Eliot, and Auden between the Wars* (Cambridge: Cambridge UP, 1984).
7. See Geoffrey Hartman, "Wordsworth, Inscriptions, and Romantic Nature Poetry," *From Sensibility to Romanticism*, ed. F. W. Hilles and Harold Bloom (New York: Oxford UP, 1965) 389–413; hereafter cited in the text as Hartman.

in the Renaissance, and Yeats inherited their forms and concerns from English poets.[8] It was this classical tradition that provided Yeats with conventions for the lyrics most intimately focussed on the value of poetry, a poetry made up of lettered surfaces.

The inscription, according to Hartman, is "anything conscious of the place on which it was written" (Hartman 390). The *Greek Anthology* includes poems "to be inscribed on" wine bottles, pens, eggs, dishes, gates, and statues; it even includes three for a latrine (the same latrine).[9] English poetry numbers hundreds of poems from which Yeats could have absorbed the tradition, such as Lovelace's "Upon the Curtain of Lucasta's Picture," Dryden's "Line Printed under the Engraved Portrait of Milton," and Pope's famous couplet "Epigram. Engraved on the Collar of a Dog which I gave to his Royal Highness." (An *epigram*, originally identical to an inscription, became later the term used for any short, pithy poem. An *epitaph*, of which English poetry also includes countless examples, is a poem to be carved on a tombstone.)

In Yeats's work, such poems imply that the act of writing or inscribing is an act of consecration, an act of conferring or investing with value. The written words substitute for the poet himself, who is vicariously empowered by the very letters of the words of the poem. The ink on the page, or the carving in stone, represents the poet's meaningful imprint on raw matter. "Inscribing, naming, writing," notes Hartman, are "types of a commemorative and inherently elegiac act" (401). For Yeats, inscribing, naming and writing preclude the need for elegy: they constitute types of literary assertion and (on occasion) aggression. Yeats uses inscriptions to make the quintessentially Horatian statement, "Non omnis moriar," or the Shakespearean "So long lives this. . . ." In his contributions to this genre, Yeats is closer to the Renaissance bravado of Shakespeare's sonnets, or even the more conventional confidence of Herrick's weak Horatian echo at the end of *Hesperides* ("This pillar never shall / Decline or waste at all . . ."), than to the Romantic locodescriptive poetry discussed by Hartman.[1]

* * *

A more important contribution to the epigrammatic tradition is "To Be Carved on a Stone at Thoor Ballylee." The poem came only gradually to emphasize the inscription as much as the tower. In the original draft there was no reference to "these characters"; the poem simply laid a curse on Yeats's heirs if they changed anything architecturally:

> And on my heirs I lay a curse
> If they should alter for the worse,

8. The *locus classicus* for discussion of these traditions is the remarkable chapter "The Book as Symbol" in Ernst Robert Curtius, *European Literature and the Latin Middle Ages*, trans. Willard R. Trask (New York: Bollingen, 1953).
9. See *The Greek Anthology III*, trans. W. R. Paton (1917; Cambridge: Harvard UP, 1983) nos. 642–44; hereafter cited in the text as GA.
1. Robert Herrick, "The Pillar of Fame," *The Poems of Robert Herrick* (London: Oxford UP, 1902) 307.

From fashion or an empty mind,
What Raftery built and Scott designed.
(L² 651)

This version was closer to prototypes in the *Greek Anthology*, such as an epigram of Agathias Scholasticus titled "On a House in Constantinople":

Musonius built me with great labour, this large and imposing house, exposed to the north wind's blasts. Yet did he not avoid the dark house of Fate, but abandoning me he dwells underground. In a narrow bed of earth he lies, and I, his chiefest delight, am given up to strangers. (GA 376–77)

The subject of Yeats's poem in its final form is not the site of the inscription or the object inscribed but the struggle to shape matter into significant form: Yeats as builder makes his imprint on nature with boards and slates and iron; Yeats as poet makes his imprint with "characters" on the stone. The poem ends in a wish for its own immortality: even if the architectural resuscitation doesn't endure, Yeats wishes the commemorative poem about it may last: "And may these characters remain / When all is ruin once again."

But there are two ways for the inscription to last: the poem *as printed* lasts "so long as men can live breathe or eyes can see." The letters cut *in situ* "may" last even when the tower falls into ruin. The cut letters did in fact remain when all was ruin: after Yeat's death the tower fell into disrepair, but the stone with the "characters" lasted and is part of the re-rebuilt tower. The distinction is an important one, because the poem blends two traditions, the Horatian tradition of poem as metaphoric monument, and the epigrammatic tradition of poem on stone as metaphoric voice (prosopopeia).[3] Horace's poem is more lasting than bronze, and Yeats's poem more lasting than old millboards and sea-green slates. (In *Hesperides* Herrick plays on the distinction between the inscription as printed words and the inscription as inscribed words by composing "The Pillar of Fire" in the shape of a pillar, so that it is at least a printed, two-dimensional monument.)

In "To Be Carved on a Stone at Thoor Ballylee," the printed or chiseled letters stand in for the shaping, formative imagination of "I, the poet William Yeats." The act of inscribing the letters is equivalent to an act of consecration, and each reading of the poem, or even the mere endurance of the slab with the poem on it, unread, empowers the finite "I" of the poet, who begins his poem with the chest-thumping "I, the poet. . . ." Apparently indifferent to reader-response, Yeats expects value and meaning to reside exclusively *in the characters*, read or unread. (Less solipsistically, Shakespeare locates meaning in the interaction between print and reader —"So long as men can breathe or eyes can see, / So long lives this . . ." —making the life of "this" depend on breathing and seeing, and making

2. *The Letters of W. B. Yeats*, ed. Allan Wade (London: Rupert Hart-Davis, 1954; New York: Macmillan, 1955).
3. See Hartman 393 and de Man 77–78 for commentary on prosopopeia.

"thee" the beneficiary of the immortality conveyed through breathing and seeing.)

Yeats's other famous inscription is also the only other place I'm aware of where he mentions his own name in verse.[4] In the final lines of "Under Ben Bulben," the poem moves from the proper name, the finite self, to a transformed self, invested with permanent value as it becomes something written:

> Under bare Ben Bulben's head
> In Drumcliff churchyard Yeats is laid.
> An ancestor was rector there
> Long years ago, a church stands near,
> By the road an ancient cross.
> No marble, no conventional phrase;
> On limestone quarried near the spot
> By his command these words are cut:
>> *Cast a cold eye*
>> *On life, on death.*
>> *Horseman, pass by!*
>>   (VP 640) [124–25]

Here, the cut words testify not simply to their own endurance but to the power of the poet's personal authority. The poet's command ("By his command these words are cut") has obviously been carried out by some other writing hand: Yeats's written (and printed) words had sufficient authority to compel obedience.

The poem as read on the printed page informs you that Yeats wrote a poem containing an order. This is not prosopopeia; it is chutzpah. Yeats assumes that his (originally handwritten) word will be obeyed to the letter. The epitaph *in situ* reveals (to readers of "Under Ben Bulben," at least) the success of every order the poem gave: the epitaph is cut in limestone, in Drumcliff Churchyard, under bare Ben Bulben's head.

*   *   *

In Yeats's lyrics the *topos* of poems about the scene and materials of their own composition is less purely panegyric. Its presence signifies not the conferring of value but the weighing of value. The scene of poetic composition is for Yeats a locus of much ambivalence, and poems about it are occasions for meditation on the value of writing. Here there is less certainty, and less arrogance, than in the inscription poems.

A stanza in the second section of "Meditations in Time of Civil War" (1921–23), "My House," opens theatrically on the scene of writing:

> A winding stair, a chamber arched with stone,
> A grey stone fireplace with an open hearth,

4. Curtius discusses the author's use of her own name in medieval literature "for the purpose of intercession" or as an example of the modesty *topos*; apparently "pride of authorship" as a reason for use of one's name occurred primarily in the twelfth century (Curtius 515–18). Professor Kathleen Perry of Brandeis University has shown me two such examples: the beginning of *Erec et Enide*, in which Chrétien de Troyes refers proudly to himself by name, and the beginning of *Guiqemar*, in which Marie de France refers to herself by name.

A candle and written page.
Il Penseroso's Platonist toiled on
In some like chamber, shadowing forth
How the daemonic rage
Imagined everything.
Benighted travellers
From markets and from fairs
Have seen his midnight candle glimmering.
                         (VP 419–20) [87]

"Meditations in Time of Civil War" is an uncertain *apologia* for writing poetry. Questioning how poetry can be justified, it grows more dubious about poetry's value as it goes along. At this point in the poem, the answer is that it can be justified as work, particularly as vigorous work. Yeats has chosen this old Norman tower to work in

. . . that after me
My bodily heirs may find,
To exalt a lonely mind,
Befitting emblems of adversity.   (VP 420) [88]

They will keep strong and hardy, that is, unlike the effete, listless members of the declining family he imagines in the first section ("Ancestral Houses").

In this version of the *topos* Yeats emphasizes not a finished product, not a specific book or poems, but a scene of work. The example from Milton is an example of someone toiling. The only other people mentioned are not up late because they are reading, but because they have been engaged in more mundane work ("travellers / From markets and from fairs") and hence are "Benighted." Although Yeats is not busy in the market place, his apparent physical inactivity should not (the lines imply) be confused with the "slippered Contemplation" of the first section.

Here intellectual effort is associated with "rage," energy, and ascetic toil. Even the mention of the winding stair suggests effort. Yeats makes poetry-writing sound more physically demanding than the outdoors work of the poor benighted buyers and sellers. They may be outside walking and carrying heavy goods into the wee hours, but their only verb is "have seen." They are powerfully drawn to the sight of the poet's window, whereas the poet has climbed his winding stair and is now toiling.

In the concluding stanza of the final section of "Meditations in Time of Civil War" the same *topos* appears vestigially. After the nocturnal "tower-top" vision of unicorns and ladies, Yeats comments,

I turn away and shut the door, and on the stair
Wonder how many times I could have proved my worth
In something that all others understand or share;
But O! ambitious heart, had such a proof drawn forth
A company of friends, a conscience set at ease,
It had but made us pine the more. The abstract joy,
The half-read wisdom of daemonic images,
Suffice the ageing man as once the growing boy.
                         (VP 427) [91]

Once more the poet is envisaged alone in the tower, working and reading, separate from the world out there. But now the value of such endeavor is more doubtful; he is not calling non-poets "benighted." As the scene is introduced, he is on the stair, turning away, shutting the door, closing out the world and the war. The wisdom he remembers and will return to is "half-read"; there is less toil here, and the act of reading is perceived as a dreamy turning of pages.

What can be the value of half-read wisdom? Well, anything else, any other kind of life, would make him "pine," even a life with simple and familiar satisfactions—friends, a feeling of accomplishment—the kind of life that doesn't need continual justification. But *there is no writing going on here*. What is invoked is a scene of half-reading, an open but unfinished book. The "abstract joy" and wisdom that merely "suffice" do not offer permanence to the reader himself or signs of authority and durability to his heirs or audience.

Here Yeats no doubt feels a little closer to slippered Contemplation than he originally did. Why, after all, are his days "aimless" (as he describes them in the third section)? Uncertainty and ambivalence dominate. Daniel Harris has written of these final lines that they represent the retrieval of "constructive purpose from the debris of civil war," but acknowledges that "doubt qualifies every word."[5] The final passage comes close to undermining the poem's earlier self-justification. What value there is appears exclusively private at the end, merely "abstract," merely "images" that come into being through a turning away and a shutting out. No heirs, travellers, or readers are invoked to appreciate the ageing man's wisdom —how could they? Neither speaking nor writing, he is closing himself off from "something that all others understand or share"—and to study a wisdom that merely suffices.

"Nineteen Hundred and Nineteen" offers the same *topos* with a slightly different emphasis and in a more negative manifestation. In its second section, Yeats asks, should I finish writing this poem? He answers, implicitly, only that he is not yet ready to give it up. The first stanza introduces the swan that is just about to fly but is undecided "Whether to play, or to ride / Those winds that clamour of approaching night." In the following stanzas there are no candle and no night; but the solitude and solitary work, the man "in his own secret meditation," the "Platonist" and other signs of poetic composition are there, the "laborious life" and the "half-imagined, half-written page":

> A man in his own secret meditation
> Is lost amid the labyrinth that he has made
> In art or politics;
> Some Platonist affirms that in the station
> Where we should cast off body and trade
> The ancient habit sticks,
> And that if our works could
> But vanish with our breath

5. Daniel A. Harris, *Yeats: Coole Park and Ballylee* (Baltimore: Johns Hopkins UP, 1974) 184.

That were a lucky death,
For triumph can but mar our solitude.

The swan has leaped into the desolate heaven:
That image can bring wildness, bring a rage
To end all things, to end
What my laborious life imagined, even
The half-imagined, the half-written page:
O but we dreamed to mend
Whatever mischief seemed
To afflict mankind, but now
That winds of winter blow
Learn that we were crack-pated when we dreamed.

(VP 431) [93–94]

(In the nineteen-twenties, perhaps under the influence of A *Vision's* dichotomized world, everything with Yeats was halved: half-truths, half-read wisdom, half-imagined, half-written, halved soul.) This scene is that "chamber arched with stone" of "Meditations . . ." in its negative form. When you are working alone reading and writing, you do close out other things, and that exclusion can be seen as being "lost amid the labyrinth" you have made yourself. Here Yeats's concern is not about being closed off from the human community, that "company of friends," and "something that all others understand or share," but about being closed off from history; not isolation, but denial.

Perhaps the swan should leap into the desolate heaven—a possible choice for the speaker at the tower-top in "Meditations . . ." also. The beauty and freedom of the swan's hypothetical leap depend on a surrender of creative powers: the leap means ending all things, not finishing the "labor," not finishing the page. There is a long pause in that final stanza after the word "page." It is precisely a "half-written" stanza at that point: just in the middle of it Yeats pauses and decides whether or not to finish *this* page. Is it worth it? Why not just scrap the whole thing? What is the value of any page, half-written or fully written, once you see it as a prison, a labyrinth, a fancy useless structure?

Yeats does not answer his question. He undermines his own poem but continues it anyway, returning to what it felt like to believe that such a structure "in art or politics" had some utility. He finishes the poem because he has something more important to write about than himself-writing-the-poem. In a way, he breaks out of the labyrinth by acknowledging it: he has something more important to do than bemoan the uselessness of his own work. But briefly he pauses, paralyzed, in mid-*topos*, mid-stanza, to ask if it is worth finishing.

Sometimes, in fact, that "laborious nocturnal desk work" celebrated in the *Greek Anthology* becomes simple self-destruction. Sometimes writing is not (for Yeats) a source of value but a source of bad health—as it is, for instance, in the last stanza of "Among School Children":

Labour is blossoming or dancing where
The body is not bruised to pleasure soul,

Or beauty born out of its own despair,
Or blear-eyed wisdom out of midnight oil . . .
                                    (VP 445–46) [98]

In its ideal state labor is not a condition in which "blear-eyed wisdom" comes out of midnight oil, in which health and ordinary well-being are sacrificed for some remote, abstract "wisdom." In one line Yeats encapsulates a long tradition of English lyrics, the *topos* he has inherited through Shelley, Milton, the poets of the *Greek Anthology*, Plato and others—encapsulates it to suggest that the value built into the tradition, of pages, ink, volumes, back-breaking and eye-sight-ruining scholarly work, ought not to be an end in itself. The stanza sets out the positive definition of labor, blossoming or dancing, as only conditionally dependent on "laborious nocturnal desk work."

*   *   *

One of the central issues in Yeats's poetry is, "Is poetry valuable?" Yeats doesn't offer a simple answer. After all, his supernatural instructors identified "consciousness with conflict," and he gives different answers in different poems. But rarely is this poetry that may or may not be valuable conceived of as a voice, as direct speech that would be contaminated by print. Even when Yeats is asking himself "how many times I could have proved my worth / In something that all others understand or share," oral poetry is not an option: to be a poet is to be a solitary who reads and writes, whose tradition is a lettered tradition.

To assume that Yeats attributes anything like "absolute presence" to the creations of such a poet, inking letters on paper by lamplight, or having them cut in stone, is to misunderstand him: consciousness was not identified with absolutes. The heart of the issue for Yeats is not religious or philosophical but socioliterary: who is my audience? At the times when he appeared to privilege the oral, Yeats wanted a direct, immediate connection with his audience and had faith in the social usefulness of poetry as an instrument of nationalism for a colonized people or as a centripetal force in a disorderly society. Yeats's use of a lettered tradition for commentary on the value of poetry is not a privileging of the written but the strategic choice of a different kind of audience. As that master-strategist T. S. Eliot wrote in 1945, "It matters little whether a poet had a large audience in his own time. What matters is that there should always be at least a small audience for him in every generation."[6] So, in confidence, "I, the poet William Yeats" introduces himself to future visitors to Thoor Ballylee, those very few who have never heard of its most illustrious owner. And so, in uncertainty, questioning whether a life devoted to literature draws him away from "something that all others understand or share," questioning whether poetry is an evasion of truth, Yeats offers to another generation of readers the written word as paradigm of the contingent, the dubious, the unabsolute.

6. T. S. Eliot, "The Social Function of Poetry," *On Poetry and Poets* (New York: Farrar, 1961) 10–11.

R. F. FOSTER

The Taste of Salt 1902–1903†

In June 1902 [Maud Gonne] told her disapproving sister: '1st I am to become Catholic, 2nd I am to get married to Major MacBride, this last is not public yet.' She added, more defensively, that she was 'getting old and oh so tired and I have found a man who has a stronger will than myself and who at the same time is thoroughly honourable and who I trust . . . As for Willie Yeats I love him dearly as a friend but I could not for one minute imagine marrying him.'[1] None the less, she may have worried about his reaction. From this time, hints can be discerned in her letters to him—about her inclination to Catholicism, her meetings with MacBride's family in Mayo, her own increasing 'decrepitude' and rheumatism.[2] And through these very months of late 1902, she was also becoming more and more estranged from him on theatrical matters, perhaps a reflection of her deliberate desire to make a break.

But nothing could prepare him for this. Since December 1898 his great powers of rationalization had been directed towards convincing himself that their 'spiritual' relationship was the better part of passion. Time and time again his folklore stories concern a countryman (sometimes a 'poet') who is offered knowledge or pleasure by a fairy queen. When he chooses pleasure and becomes her lover, he is left bereft, making mournful songs until he dies.[3] Renunciation brought the reward of artistic achievement and continuing inspiration. Gonne was, however, about to shatter the understanding on which this compact was based.

Her alienation from WBY over theatre matters proceeded in step with this. In January 1903 she was in Dublin, complaining during rehearsals of the changes to Colum's play; 'Griffith declares it is spoiled from an artistic point of view & all openly say it is because Fay fears to vex the *respectable*.[4] But Fay by this point had lost all patience with the 'absolutely fossilized' approach of the nationalists.[5] She and WBY were on different sides in the dispute, though he remained in London. It was there he heard about her engagement, in early February. His later recollection of receiving a telegram just before addressing a public meeting probably refers to his lecture 'The Future of Irish Drama', given in London on 7 February.[6]

---

† From W. B. Yeats: A Life: I: The Apprentice Mage 1865–1914 (Oxford and New York: Oxford University Press, 1997), pp. 284–87. Copyright © 1997 by Oxford University Press. Used by permission of Oxford University Press, Inc.
1. The Gonne-Yeats Letters 1893–1938: Always Your Friend, ed. Anna MacBride White and A. Norman Jeffares (London: Hutchinson, 1992), 154.
2. E.g., ibid., 156.
3. See Uncollected Prose by W. B. Yeats, vol. 2, ed. John P. Frayne and Colton Johnson (London: Macmillan, 1975), 265, 269, and many other places.
4. The Gonne-Yeats Letters, 162.
5. Unpublished letter from William Fay to Yeats, 9 February 1903, University of Reading Library.
6. To 'Na Geadna Fiadhaine' ('The Wild Geese') at the Bijou Theatre, Bedford Street; Lady Gregory was present. Farr told Nevinson that Maud Gonne 'had not even told him about the engagement until the day before it became public' (Ronald Schuchard, "An Attendant Lord": H. W. Nevinson's Friendship with W. B. Yeats, Yeats Annual 7 [1990]: 104), which fits the dates: it was first published in Ireland in the Freeman's Journal on 9 February.

It was, for him, not only a private trauma but a public humiliation; his poems had solemnized their relationship before his reading public as well as his friends. Ricketts's reaction was probably fairly typical. 'Have you heard the news that Maud Gonne has gone and left Yeats and the future of Ireland for matrimony and comfortable Catholicism? Yeats is unconsolable in sonnets of the Oh thou! type to various little lilts and tunes.'[7]

The first three letters he sent her have been lost, but the fourth survived, a passionate plea to her to remain the inviolate self he had so often celebrated. 'In the name of 14 years of friendship', he implored her to think again. For all his anguish, his arguments were coherent and compelling. First, their ancient bond: he quoted from his diary of 12 December 1898, recalling their spiritual marriage in a dream and implicitly accusing her of a bigamous betrayal. 'I claim that this gives me the right to speak.' But his subsequent arguments stressed the danger of debasement—religious and social. Marriage with MacBride would make her 'fall into a lower order & do great injury to the religeon of free souls that is growing up in Ireland, it may be to enlighten the whole world.' 'The priests will exult over us.' 'You possess your influence in Ireland very largely because you come to the people from above. You represent a superior class, a class whose people are more independent, have a more beautiful life, a more refined life.' Above all, 'thrust down . . . to a lower order of faith' and society, she would destroy the *persona* she had created for herself. 'It was our work to teach a few strong aristocratic spirits that to believe the soul was immortal & that one prospered hereafter *if one laid upon oneself* an heroic discipline in living & [? to] send them to uplift the nation. You & I were chosen to begin this work & <just> just when <you> I come to understand it fully you go from me & seek to thrust the people <down> further into weakness further from self reliance.' She must not betray her pride, her solitude, her inspiration. He stressed the unworthiness of Catholicism rather than of MacBride himself—the priests had truckled under to the government over the Act of Union and had betrayed the Fenians. 'When the day of great hazard has come', they would tell the people, 'Be quiet, be good cristians, do not shed blood.'[8]

Thus he tried to show that revolution and mysticism, both essential to Gonne's being, were threatened by this *mésalliance*. What is not stated is the question: why him, and not me? His own position as lover (and MacBride's) went unmentioned, though it may have been expatiated upon in the earlier letters. Possibly it was too bitter an issue to be articulated, though it would powerfully affect WBY's self-image from now on. His hard-won confidence was jolted. As recently as December he had confided to Edith Craig, 'I seldom get credit for an absurd amount of timidity and shyness, which has a way, when I meet any body for the first time or practically for the first time, of hiding embarrassment under a brazen man-

7. J. G. P. Delaney, ' "Heirs of the Great Generation": Yeats's Friendship with Charles Ricketts and Charles Shannon,' *Yeats Annual* 4 (1986): 58 (letter to the Fields).
8. *The Gonne-Yeats Letters*, 164–66; *The Collected Letters of W. B. Yeats Volume III 1901–1904*, ed. John Kelly and Ronald Schuchard (Oxford: Clarendon Press, 1994), 315–17.

ner.'⁹ In the aftermath of Gonne's bombshell the brazen manner was shaken, but then adopted all the more resolutely.

In any case, she was unmoved. She had retired to a French convent for instruction; from there she replied soothingly that their friendship need not change. As to Catholicism, '<my> our nation looks at God or truth through one prism, The Catholic Religion'. In other words, to be Irish required being Catholic, the very conclusion WBY had devoted years of concentrated activity to disproving. And as for social superiority: 'You say I leave the few to mix myself with the crowd while Willie I have always told you I am the voice, the soul of the *crowd*.¹ This indeed was the kernel of the ancient difference between them. It was now exacerbated by her adoption of Catholicism. Farr's version to Nevinson put it tersely: '[Gonne] hates marriage & all sex. They had a sort of understanding to be together in old age. Now he contemplates an onslaught on the Church.'²

* * * As early as the honeymoon (in southern Spain, allegedly reconnoitring assassination arrangements for an impending royal visit to Gibraltar), the couple's incompatibility and MacBride's drunkenness were spectacularly evident. Gonne returned to Paris alone, and significantly headed for London, where WBY met her, as so often before, at Euston.³ Though a son (Seaghan, later Seán) was born the next year, there was little hope for the union; and by a terrible irony, the precipitating cause for its dissolution would be MacBride's molestation of his step-daughter Iseult, for whose protection Gonne had sought refuge in marriage. As for her attitude to WBY, they continued to quarrel about the theatre, to collaborate on Celtic rituals, and to disagree about religious philosophy ('*Neiche* [sic] *is not Celtic*,' she admonished him). She shrewdly chided him for manipulating the Celtic Rites to express his repugnance at her conversion to Catholicism, finding no difficulty in adapting their old symbols of spear, cauldron, stone and sword to Christian archetypes. 'Why Willie it was you yourself who taught me these things.' By early May, less than three months after the wedding ceremony, she was confessing that she had made a terrible mistake. As for him, his distant princess was now unattainable in a different way: a Catholic wife and mother of two children.

9. Letter of 18 December 1902, *The Collected Letters of W. B. Yeats Volume III 1901–1904*, 281.
1. *The Gonne-Yeats Letters*, 166.
2. Schuchard, " 'An Attendant Lord'," *Yeats Annual* 7 (1990): 104.
3. Interview with Maud Gonne, 27 June 1947, recorded in Richard Ellmann's interview book, Archives, Tulsa University, Oklahoma.

GEORGE BORNSTEIN

The Aesthetics of Antinomy†

"I have myself . . . begun . . . a movement downwards upon life, not upwards
out of life."

—*Yeats to Florence Farr, February 1906*

After 1903 Yeats moved from an Intellectual to an antinomial vision of
life. He built his new aesthetic upon the tension between balanced con-
traries rather than upon the intensity of exclusive devotion. Although in
the nineties he had forsaken social involvement for Shelleyan purity in his
verse, he now wanted to combine both in an art at once popular and
profound. "All things fall into a series of antinomies in human experience," he declared in a famous sentence from *A Vision*.[1] To reject any
part of experience was to reject the unity of the whole and, hence, to mar
the Unity of Being of the individual. The way to "ultimate reality" led not
merely upward with the spirit but also downward with the body. For Yeats,
Shelley represented the spiritual world of Intellectual Beauty. The more
Yeats laced his poetry with the other half of the antinomy—the actual
instead of the ideal—the more his enthusiasm for Shelley slackened. For
he had earlier identified himself with Shelley so fully that in order to
remake his art he had to reject not just his earlier work but also his earlier
model. To become Yeats, he had to repudiate Shelley. * * *
* * * Two descriptions of his own work in letters to friends, one from
1888 and the other from 1906, illustrate the change:

> 1888: I have noticed some things about my poetry I did not know
> before . . . it is almost all a flight into fairyland from the real
> world, and a summons to that flight . . . it is not the poetry of
> insight and knowledge, but of longing and complaint.
> 1906: I have myself . . . begun . . . a movement downwards upon
> life, not upwards our of life.[2]

Antinomial vision meant an inclusive vision based on the tension between
opposites like the ideal and the actual, whereas Intellectual vision is an
exclusive focus on the ideal at the expense of "life."[3] Yeats no longer
wanted to flee from the actual to the ideal, as he thought that Shelley had,
but instead sought to bring the ideal down into the actual for that instant
in which a terrible beauty could be born. He would move downward upon

---

† From *Yeats and Shelley* by George Bornstein (Chicago: University of Chicago Press, 1970), pp.
113, 116–121. Reprinted by permission of University of Chicago Press. Page references to this
Norton Critical Edition are given in brackets after the author's original citations.
1. W. B. Yeats, *A Vision* (London: Macmillan, 1937), 193.
2. *The Letters of W. B. Yeats*, ed. Allan Wade (London: Rupert Hart-Davis, 1954; New York: Macmillan, 1955), 63, 469.
3. After writing this I discovered that Frank Lentricchia has recently used a similar term, antinomic,
to describe something different: Yeats's separation from nineteenth century, principally Continental, aesthetics and his "ambiguous and contradictory motivations." See *The Gaiety of Language*:
An Essay on the Radical Politics of W. B. Yeats and Wallace Stevens (Berkeley: University of
California Press, 1968), 42 and passim.

life on his own, not upward out of it with Shelley. The downward movement required changes in the poet's subject, attitude, and style; let us
consider each of them in order.

The pressure of reality eventually crushed the imaginative Arcadia
which Yeats constructed under the guidance of Shelley. The Parnell controversy, the *Playboy* riots, the Lane pictures dispute, and the 1913 lockout
all dragged him back to the reality of prerevolutionary Ireland. To be sure,
in making Shelley the poet of idealized bowers of bliss Yeats distorted his
predecessor's work, for Shelley had condemned the Peterloo massacre in
The Masque of Anarchy, mocked George IV in *Swellfoot the Tyrant*, and
castigated most of the injustices of Europe in shorter pieces. But Yeats
does not mention those works and instead confines himself to the visionary
rhymes. It is his own early work that conforms to the pattern he ascribed
to Shelley, and his strictures on the difficulty of combining Shelley with
common life reflect his own uneasiness at the products of his youth and
at the remaking of his poetry.

Yeats chose Shelley to illustrate these changes in his own thought, particularly in his distinction between bird and market cart. In "Discoveries"
(1906) he wrote:

> There are two ways before literature—upward into ever-growing sub-
> tlety . . . or downward, taking the soul with us until all is simplified
> or solidified again. That is the choice of choices—the way of the bird
> until common eyes have lost us, or to the market carts; but we must
> see to it that the soul goes with us, for the bird's song is beautiful,
> and the traditions of modern imagination, growing always more mu-
> sical, more lyrical, more melancholy, casting up now a Shelley, now
> a Swinburne. . . . If the carts have hit our fancy we must have the
> soul tight within our bodies. . . . If it begin to slip away we must go
> after it, for Shelley's Chapel of the Morning Star is better than Burns's
> beerhouse . . . and it is always better than that uncomfortable place
> where there is no beer, the machine-shop of the realists.[4]

By 1906 the carts had clearly hit Yeats's fancy, and his problem became
to maintain his soul in the jostling marketplace which he had earlier fled.
He now sought just that mass audience which, directed by Hallam, he
had earlier condemned. The descent to life did not mean abandonment
of the ideal, however, for then at best he would become a habitué of
Burns's beerhouse and, at worst, of the realists' machine shop. Best of all
would be to be a bird perched on a market cart. Yeats's phrasing recalls
Shelley's "To a Skylark"—"the way of the bird until common eyes have
lost us." Yeats no longer wanted to ascend to the Intellectual with the
skylark, but to immerse himself in just that human world, the lusts of the
marketplace, which the skylark forsakes. His new symbol would be not a
skylark but the man-made golden bird. If the golden bird is out of nature,
man, not a Platonic idea, made it so. Shelley writes that the skylark

---

4. W. B. Yeats, *Essays and Introductions* (London: Macmillan, 1961), 266–67. Yeats's new attraction
   to the market cart during this period has been admirably elaborated by Edward Engelberg in his
   The Vast Design (Toronto: University of Toronto Press, 1974), chap. 2.

of death must deem
Things more true and deep
Than we mortals dream.[5]

Yeats located the source of the ideal in just those mortals whom the skylark surpassed. The former exponent of Plato and the Neoplatonists could write by 1927, despite continued attraction to his former masters:

And I declare my faith:
I mock Plotinus' thought
And cry in Plato's teeth,
Death and life were not
Till man made up the whole,
Made lock, stock and barrel
Out of his bitter soul,
Aye, sun and moon and star, all,
And further add to that
That, being dead, we rise,
Dream and so create
Translunar Paradise.[6]

Better than a choice between the ideal and the actual was a reconciliation, or at least a balance. Although he often tried to reconcile spirit and sense, Yeats could at times doubt their meeting and instead imagine only "change upon the instant."[7] Like the opposing kings Congal and Aedh in *The Herne's Egg*, the ideal and subtle were locked in a ritual combat with the actual and common from which neither side expected to emerge victorious. Instead, they were united into a whole maintained by the internecine warfare of its parts. Vision consisted in accepting the full dialectic, not merely half of it.

Yeats sometimes chose Dickens to represent the common life of the market cart. Celebrating the Unity of Being of the artist in the age of Homer, Yeats wrote, "A man of that unbroken day could have all the subtlety of Shelley and yet use no image unknown among the common people, and speak no thought that was not a deduction from common thought . . . we may never see again a Shelley and a Dickens in the one body, but be broken to the end."[8] Again, both halves of the antimony are necessary, Shelley without Dickens ascends into idiosyncratic subtlety, and

5. *The Poetical Works of Percy Bysshe Shelley*, ed. W. M. Rossetti (London: E. Moxon, 1870), 2: 305.
6. *The Variorum Edition of the Poems of W. B. Yeats*, ed. Peter Allt and Russell K. Alspach (New York: Macmillan, 1966), 414–15 [85]. Yeats conceded in a note that these lines were unfair to Plotinus.
7. W. B. Yeats, *Autobiographies* (London: Macmillan, 1955), 326.
8. Yeats, *Essays and Introductions*, 296. Yeats expresses the same idea in the preface to *The Unicorn from the Stars and Other Plays* (1908) where he describes the expression in his critical writings of the union of the "rough life of the road" and the "frenzy" of the poets as "a prophecy, as it were, of the time when it will be once again possible for a Dickens and a Shelley to be born in the one body." *The Variorum Edition of the Plays of W. B. Yeats*, ed. Russell K. Alspach (London: Macmillan, 1966), 1295–96.
   John Butler Yeats held a similar view. He wrote, "I have discovered Dickens; yes, here in my single room, I have discovered the great romancer and with it made another discovery, the people . . . I don't think Shelley discovered what I call the earthy. He was too much occupied with the soul and the imaginative reason." (*Further Letters of John Butler Yeats*, ed. Lennox Robinson [Dublin: Cuala Press, 1920], 37–38.)

Dickens without Shelley degenerates into soulless naturalism. The bird must pern around the cart.

Yeats's discussion of Shelley suggests the countertruth to Crazy Jane's famous lines: " 'Fair and foul are near of kin, / And fair needs foul,' I cried." If fair needs foul, foul also needs fair. The fair needs the foul to fasten it to reality and to keep the balloon of the mind from rising out of sight. Likewise, the foul needs the fair to transform it into something beyond mere fury and mire. The artist needs both, for otherwise he risks falsifying his object through failing to present it in tension with its opposite. In "September 1913" Yeats needs both O'Leary and the Paudeens, for each can be understood properly only in relation to the other, and apprehension of that relation guarantees a faithful rendering both of the hostility between bird and market cart in Irish life and, concomitantly, of the moral universe of which that life is but a part. Vision requires inclusive acceptance rather than exclusive rejection: the artist should condemn the Paudeens, but he should not banish them from his work.

The change in subject meant a change in attitude as well. The joy of antinomial vision replaced the sorrow of Intellectual vision. The unrestrained desire for beauty of Yeats's "Alastor" persona of the nineties led to suffering because of his necessary separation from the Rose. According to Yeats, consciousness of the antithesis of daily life" with the ideal "dream world" led to "intellectual suffering."[9] The melancholy of his solitary wanderers now appeared a morbid indulgence of their own fragmented sensibility. They could only further separate men from the life beyond themselves, whereas the purpose of modern art should be the reunion of mind, soul, and body "to the living world outside us."[1] To do that, to create Unity of Being in the individual and Unity of Culture in the age, meant abandoning the unidirectional quest of *Alastor*, which led only out of life.

To live fully was to accept both halves of the antithesis between the ideal and the actual, which Yeats also viewed as the conflict between reality and justice. In that conflict the ideal always lost, and the poet should simply witness its defeat rather than distort the outcome into a false victory of the good. Hence Yeats's famous aphorism, "We begin to live when we have conceived life as tragedy."[2] The cart would always defeat the skylark, but that tragedy no longer implied sorrow; like Blake, Yeats refused to consider the flowers of spring refuted simply because they were over. To see life Yeats's new way was to see it with antinomial vision and, hence, joyfully. The aged Chinese of "Lapis Lazuli," like the poet who describes them, possess the antinomial vision which the Yeats-"Alastor" of the nineties lacked: "Their eyes mid many wrinkles, their eyes, / Their ancient, glittering eyes, are gay."[3]

To present his new vision of life Yeats needed a new style. The Shelleyan cadences and diction of the Rose poems suited him so long as he wrote the kind of subjective poetry prescribed by Hallam, but they jarred

9. Yeats, *Autobiographies*, 142.
1. "Discoveries: Second Series" *Massachusetts Review* 5 (Winter 1964): 299.
2. Yeats, *Autobiographies*, 189 [221].
3. *The Variorum Edition of the Poems of W. B. Yeats*, 567 [116].

him when he turned to contemporary life for his subjects. He had described Aedth and Oisin in language learned from Shelley but could not do the same for the Easter martyrs, MacDonagh and MacBride, Connolly and Pearse. "It was years before I could rid myself of Shelley's Italian light," he admitted in 1901, "but now I think my style is myself."[4] He elaborated his reaction against Shelley's style in an essay called, significantly, "What is 'Popular Poetry'?" The problem affected him more deeply than his stoical cure—sleeping on a board—might suggest:

> I had a conviction, which indeed I have still, that one's verses should hold, as in a mirror, the colours of one's own climate and scenery in their right proportion; and, when I found my verses too full of the reds and yellows Shelley gathered in Italy, I thought for two days of setting things right, not as I should now by making the rhythms faint and nervous and filling my images with a certain coldness, a certain wintry wildness, but by eating little and sleeping on a board.[5]

*　*　*

4. Yeats, *Essays and Introductions*, 208.
5. Ibid., 5.

MICHAEL NORTH

W. B. Yeats: Cultural Nationalism†

* * *

Ideally, cultural nationalism should foster both unity and diversity, because it opposes a liberal system in which "uncontrolled individualism" divides individuals from one another while simultaneously removing local and national characteristics as a source of meaningful differentiation. In actual practice in Ireland, however, cultural nationalism proved both coercive and divisive. It led Yeats himself to two seemingly incompatible ends. He formulated cultural definitions of Irish nationality that proved, quite ironically in his own case, to be restrictive and arbitrary, so that he was forced, for sheer self-preservation, to fall back on liberal guarantees of individual rights. Yeats thus demonstrated as a personal contradiction the seemingly inevitable recreation of liberal dichotomies by the system that was supposed to overcome them.

Cullingford traces Yeats's cultural politics back to Davis's "conviction that Ireland's demand for political separation from England depended on her existence as a separate cultural unit. . . ."[1] If Ireland was to base its claims to independence on national uniqueness, it had somehow to define the culture that set it apart. Young Ireland had fostered the idea of the "Irish note," a concept whose power derived from its vagueness. Yet that vagueness became embarrassing in descriptions like this one from Yeats's friend Katharine Tynan:

> By the Irish note I mean that distinctive quality in Celtic poetry the charm of which is so much easier to feel than to explain. . . . Some of the parts which go to make up its whole are a simplicity which is *naive* — a freshness, an archness, a light touching of the cords as with fairy-finger tips; a shade of underlying melancholy as delicately evanescent as a breath upon glass, which yet gives its undertone and its shadow to all; fatalism side by side with buoyant hopefulness; laughter with tears; love with hatred; a rainbow of all colours where none conflict; a gamut of all notes which join to make perfect harmony.[2]

All this inept attempt makes clear is that the "Irish note" is called upon to unify a whole range of elements not naturally in union. In 1900, Yeats claimed, in response to an attack by D. P. Moran, that he had "avoided 'Celtic note' and 'Celtic renaissance' partly because both are vague and

---

† From *The Political Aesthetic of Yeats, Eliot, and Pound* (Cambridge: Cambridge University Press, 1991), pp. 29–37. Copyright © 1991. Reprinted with the permission of Cambridge University Press. Page references to this Norton Critical Edition are given in brackets after the author's original citations.
1. Elizabeth Cullingford, *Yeats, Ireland and Fascism* (London: Macmillan, 1981), p. 9.
2. Quoted in Philip L. Marcus, *Yeats and the Beginning of the Irish Renaissance* (Ithaca, NY: Cornell University Press, 1970), p. 2. See Marcus' discussion, pp. 1–34.

one is grandiloquent . . ." (UP,[3] 2:241). But he certainly believed in "certain ardent ideas and high attitudes of mind which were the nation to itself . . . " (E[4] p. 306). By means of these ideas and attitudes, Yeats felt he could distinguish "eternal and ancient Ireland" from "that passing and modern Ireland of prosaic cynicism and prosaic rivalries . . . " (UP, 2:141). Culture, in this analysis, serves as the "Irish note" does, to unify what seems superficially to be in rivalry or opposition.

In his early optimism, Yeats ignored a truth expressed best by F.S.L. Lyons. In Ireland, Lyons says, culture "has been a force that has worked against the evolution of a homogeneous society and in so doing has been an agent of anarchy rather than of unity."[5] The Irish cultural revival proved almost exactly the opposite of what Yeats set out to prove. Whatever it touched in its attempt to define Irish culture turned out to be a cause of division instead of unity. Most basic for an Anglo-Irish writer was, of course, the language question. In response to Douglas Hyde's famous address, "The Necessity for De-Anglicising Ireland," Yeats asked plaintively: "Can we not build up a national tradition, a national literature, which shall be none the less Irish in spirit from being English in language? Can we not keep the continuity of the nation's life, not by trying to do what Dr. Hyde has practically pronounced impossible, but by translating or retelling in English, which shall have an indefinable Irish quality of rythm [sic] and style, all that is best of the ancient literature?" (CL,[6] p. 338) Here, despite his denial, Yeats falls back on the "Irish note," that indefinable something that makes an alien language Irish after all. In groping for some common ground between English and Ireland, however, Yeats violated the principles of his own movement, which came to rely more and more on Irish "as the symbol of cultural difference."[7]

Race, of course, divides almost as surely as language. All his life, Yeats attempted to subordinate race to history, to argue that "certain native traditions" are passed on from father to son and "mould the foreign settler after the national type in a few years" (UP, 2:202). Of course, he had to flout history itself to argue that the Anglo-Irish Ascendancy had been assimilated into the indigenous culture it invaded. And though most scholars would agree that the word *Celtic* has virtually no meaning as a racial designation, Yeats created an even greater ambiguity in attempting to define a Celticism that is unified and yet not exclusive, pure even though it results from a mixture of races. Yeats argues that there is something peculiarly Irish that remains after the addition of Norman, Scottish, and English elements. The fact that "cosmopolitanism" became a common term of abuse during the Revival signifies his failure to convince many others.[8] It became increasingly difficult for Yeats himself to argue on one hand that Ireland was spiritually distinct, most especially from England,

3. *Uncollected Prose by W. B. Yeats*, vol. 2, ed. John P. Frayne and Colton Johnson (London: Macmillan, 1975).
4. W. B. Yeats, *Essays* (New York: Macmillan, 1924).
5. F. S. L. Lyons, *Culture and Anarchy in Ireland: 1890–1939* (Oxford: Clarendon Press, 1979), p. 2.
6. *The Collected Letters of W. B. Yeats Volume 1:1865–1895*, ed. John Kelly and Eric Domville (Oxford: Clarendon Press, 1986).
7. Lyons, *Culture and Anarchy*, p. 39.
8. Marcus, p. 15.

and to argue on the other that it could accommodate English elements without substantial alteration.

Religion would not even bear mention as an element of a unified Irish culture if Yeats had not insisted so strongly on a kind of folk religion, on a body of myth and superstition antedating and, he hoped, post-dating Christianity. The tremendous energy Yeats poured into projects associated with Irish folklore seems in proportion to the divisive power of the Christian sects within his country. Defining Irish spirituality in terms of folklore meant, as George Watson says, "that he did not have to consider the (for him) awkward fact of the peasant's devout Catholicism."[9] But there is another weakness in this project as well, for all of Yeats's attempts to connect the Irish folk tales and habits to a worldwide mystical tradition serve only to *lessen* the national character of Irish folklore.[1]

A good deal of Yeats's own patriotic feeling derived from his native geography, from his love for Sligo. But he apparently felt little sympathy for the desires of the landless to own what they had worked over generation after generation. Geography, in any case, could hardly unify when more than one group wanted the same plots of land. The most general cultural appeal of all is usually to history, but Ireland's is a history of discontinuity, of revolts and defeats. Commemoration in Ireland is the commemoration of strife and often its reenactment, as Yeats well knew when he planned the centennial of 1798 as a separatist coup. As Watson puts it, Ireland is such as deeply divided country there is "a total lack of a relatively steady tradition, like that of the English or French."[2]

This is precisely what the revival proved, that any conceivable definition of Irish culture led not to unity but to greater division. According to Denis Donoghue, "If there is a distinctive Irish experience, it is one of division, exacerbated by the fact that division in a country so small seems perverse."[3] Even more perverse, perhaps, is the fact that the very attempts to conceive of a unified Irish culture exacerbated the divisions that made such a culture impossible. In a relatively homogeneous society, according to Nicholas Mansergh, the concept of a nation is apt to be unifying, but "in a plural society the more explicitly that concept is formulated, the more likely it is to be divisive."[4] That Yeats's schemes for the Irish Literary Society almost immediately broke up in controversy and that his dreams of an Irish national theater brought riots instead of unity should not seem accidental. These conflicts are instead the logical products of Yeats's own plans. "Davis's ideal of a nationalism transcending differences of religion, class and ancestry, and appealing to Irishmen of all traditions, did not die with him," says J.C. Beckett. "But those who have professed to support this ideal have failed to recognize . . . that its realization would involve the negation, not the fulfilment, of the past history of Ireland."[5]

9. George Watson, *Irish Identity and the Literary Revival* (London: Croom Helm, 1979), p. 96.
1. See Marcus, p. 25.
2. Watson, p. 32.
3. Denis Donoghue, *We Irish: Essays on Irish Literature and Society* (New York: Knopf, 1986), p. 16.
4. Nicholas Mansergh, *The Irish Question 1840–1921*, 3rd ed. (London: Allen & Unwin, 1975), p. 23.
5. J. C. Beckett, *The Anglo-Irish Tradition* (London: Faber and Faber, 1976). p. 101.

Conflicts within the Irish Literary Revival dramatized the fact that culture cannot be confected. In the absence of common conceptions of culture, cultural arguments are both ahistorical, based as they must be on artificial, arbitrary notions, and coercive, because cultural unity is not an assumption but an imposition. Cultural nationalism failed to unify Ireland, but it did give one side the weapons it needed to coerce its opponents. Ironically for Yeats, that side was not his own. Yeats soon found himself being beaten with a stick he had been among the first to shake. In an 1898 letter to Lady Gregory, Yeats reports very proudly an incident at a "Masonic concert" to which he was taken by his uncle: "Somebody sang a stage Irishman song—the usual whiskey shallelagh kind of thing—and I hissed him and lest my hiss might be lost in the general applause waited till the applause was done and hissed again. This gave somebody else courage and we both hissed" (L,[6] p. 304). Nine years later, when the audience hissed and booed what it thought were stage Irishmen, Yeats was on the other side. The crowds arrayed against him were crowds he helped to bring into being, using ideas and even tactics he helped to make popular. The *Playboy* riots might be seen, then, not as Yeats's failure to make an audience for Irish national drama, but as the irony of his success.

* * *

The prudery Yeats confronted in the *Playboy* riots seems the very essence of small-mindedness. Yet this puritanism can hardly be separated from the myth of Irish moral superiority that Yeats himself helped to create. John Hutchinson describes the growth of this puritanism through the 1880s: "Gaelic Ireland gradually became the Catholic *insula sacra*: a unique spiritual haven of traditional folk simplicity, free from all the evils of modernity—a secular literature, alcoholism, sexual immorality, socialist agitations and materialist ideals."[7] Yeats, of course, had no desire to combat sexual immorality or alcoholism, or to make Ireland a *Catholic* sacred island, but he had celebrated "the Celt's futile revolt against the despotism of fact" and "against a political and moral materialism" (UP, 2:91).[8] Seamus Deane contends that Yeats's anti-materialism was easily turned against his own class, because the Anglo-Irish Ascendancy had been seen for so many years as holding its position of superiority through a purely material power, whereas its tenants and underlings had created in compensation a myth of their own moral superiority.[9]

On the other hand, Watson suggests that the rioters objected just as much to those characteristics Synge chose to idealize: "What the Anglo-Irishman chooses to celebrate—'wildness', 'savagery'—is so close to what the Englishman had for centuries chosen as the major denigratory feature

6. *The Letters of W. B. Yeats*, ed. Allan Wade (London: Rupert Hart-Davis, 1954; New York: Macmillan, 1955).
7. John Hutchinson, *The Dynamics of Cultural Nationalism: The Gaelic Revival and the Creation of the Irish Nation State* (London: Allen & Unwin, 1987), p. 140.
8. See Watson, p. 98.
9. Seamus Deane, "The Literary Myths of the Revival: A Case for their Abandonment," in *Myth and Reality in Irish Literature*, ed. Joseph Ronsley (Waterloo: Wilfred Laurie University Press, 1977), p. 320.

in his image of the Irish—violence, and another kind of savagery."[1] Dublin Catholics who were by no means crude and unlettered—Conor Cruise O'Brien lists his uncles Richard Sheehy and Francis Skeffington, the latter considered by James Joyce the second cleverest man at the Royal University, after Joyce himself—objected to the play because it idealized qualities the English had made a mockery.[2] In this respect, Yeats and Synge remain imprisoned in the Anglo-Irish predicament, their reaction against English stereotype nothing more than a reflex of English prejudice. Even in their love for the Irish they remained English, having simply reversed the emphasis of English stereotypes.

To Yeats, however, the riots proved just the opposite. The split he had seen between Ireland and England now became in his mind an internal split within Ireland itself. Resistance to Synge's plays and to his own, with the exception of *Cathleen ni Houlihan*, foot-dragging on the part of those who should have jumped at Hugh Lane's art collection, all seemed to reveal the penetration of English influence. The important word in Yeats's accounts of these controversies is *new*, suggesting both that something different has entered Irish life and that it is to be associated with the modern age that Ireland had successfully avoided until then. As early as 1902, he deplored the "new commonness / Upon the throne and crying about the streets . . . " (VP,[3] p. 198) [30]. In a journal passage of 1909, Yeats speaks of "the new class which is rising in Ireland" with its "thought made in some manufactory" (M,[4] p. 139). In his speech at the *Playboy* debate in 1907, he decried the national movement for making the mistakes of "the newly enfranchised everywhere . . . " (EX,[5] p. 227). Here Yeats charges democratic liberalism with the conflicts brought about by his own cultural nationalism; his opposition is not the democratic middle class but other cultural nationalists who see him as dangerously liberal and individualistic himself.

Consciously or not, Yeats turns against his antagonists exactly the weapons they used against him, and the fact that the same charges were hurled in both directions shows how close Yeats remains to his opposition. Though he had been under attack as dangerously cosmopolitan, he accused his opposition of being a "cosmopolitan and denationalised class" (UP, 2:155). Though he was himself suspect as more English than Irish, he attacks his opponents as bringing into Ireland modes of argument and behavior associated previously only with the English. In other words, the purity established as an ideal by cultural nationalism is used by both sides in the debate. The real conflict is about the terms by which that purity shall be defined. Though Yeats had done as much as anyone to promote the ideal, he stood to lose most from its implementation because of his Anglo-Irish background.

1. Watson, pp. 71–72.
2. Conor Cruise O'Brien, *States of Ireland* (London: Hutchinson, 1972), p. 73.
3. *The Variorum Edition of the Poems of W. B. Yeats*, ed. Peter Allt and Russell K. Alspach (New York: Macmillan, 1966).
4. W. B. Yeats, *Memoirs*, ed. Denis Donoghue (London: Macmillan, 1972).
5. W. B. Yeats, *Explorations* (New York: Macmillan, 1962).

Though Yeats attempted to remain consistent by using his old cultural arguments against the new foe, the conflict brought out in him a different argument as well. John Kelly maintains that attacks on Yeats's Anglo-Irish background made him "more wary of claiming a racial sanction for his ideas than he had been hitherto."[6] But such attacks also forced Yeats to find a new sanction in a different theory, that of individual civil rights. In these years, Yeats begins to defend the prerogatives of the individual with classically liberal arguments. He asserts "intellectual freedom" against "the hatred of ideas" (UP, 2:306–307). He decries the attack on the *Playboy* as "the annihilation of civil rights" (UP, 2:351). He defends over and over "the right of the individual mind to see the world in its own way, to cherish the thoughts which separate men from one another, and that are the creators of distinguished life, instead of those thoughts that had made one man like another . . . " (UP, 2:353). In 1905, he wrote John Quinn, "We will have a hard fight in Ireland before we get the right for every man to see the world in his own way admitted" (L, p. 447).

Yeats exposes the weakness of his cultural nationalism by implicitly admitting that liberalism provides the only model that can settle controversy without oppressing the losers. Yet this weakness propels Yeats into a major contradiction. On one hand, he bases his defense of himself and Synge on the doctrine of individual rights. His language makes clear the dependence of this doctrine on an opposition between individuals and the mass. The "thoughts which separate men from one another" are authentic, sincere, whereas those thoughts entertained by many alike are specious propaganda. The very notion of rights thus arises from the necessity to defend the individual from the rest of the world. On the other hand, Yeats attacks democracy and the "newly enfranchised," who are apparently unjust in asserting *their* rights. His cultural arguments depend on a notion of the Irish race radically incompatible with his individualism, because authenticity comes, in this analysis, from a common stock of memories, customs, and stories. Indeed, Yeats had based his arguments for the moral superiority of the Irish precisely on their cultural cohesiveness, on their difference from the atomized mass of the English, which was, of course, the product of the very individualism to which he now turned.

If cultural nationalism had simply recreated the tensions it was supposed to dissolve, if it had become both divisive and coercive, then Yeats needed a new alternative to give him hope for reconciliation. This he found in the aristocracy. Though Yeats had always felt that poets are "the most aristocratic of men" (UP, 2:131), he had begun his theater work by accepting what he called "the baptism of the gutter" (L, p. 339). He made common cause with "poverty against wealth," even with "the intellectual movement which has raised the cry that was heard in Russia in the seventies, the cry 'To the people' " (EX, p. 83). Here he chose sides, and he challenged other writers to choose "whether they will write as the upper classes have done, not to express but to exploit this country."

6. John Kelly, "Choosing and Inventing: Yeats and Ireland," in *Across A Roaring Hill: The Protestant Imagination in Ireland*, eds. Gerald Dawe and Edna Longley (Belfast and Dover, N.H.: Blackstaff, 1985), p. 20.

Yeats's dedication to the people did not survive the controversies over the Abbey Theater and Hugh Lane's pictures, and his antipathy to the upper classes began noticeably to fade. "Every day," he said in 1909, "I notice some new analogy between [the] long-established life of the well-born and the artist's life" (M, p. 156) [251]. Despite his friendship with Lady Gregory, this aristocracy was less an actual class than the resolution of a logical problem. For Yeats to continue voicing his cultural theories, based as they were on the spiritual unity of the Irish, while also standing on his rights as an individual, based as they were on a negation of public uniformity, he had to invent a minority that could serve to represent the whole. In 1904, Yeats speaks of "those few scattered people who have the right to call themselves the Irish race." Most Irish, apparently, are not really Irish. Yeats goes beyond this to assert a general rule: "It is only in the exceptions, in the few minds where the flame was burnt, as it were, that one can see the permanent character of a race" (EX, p. 147). This very odd brand of racialism, in which the race is epitomized precisely by those who do not fit comfortably into it, clearly comes from Yeats's immediate political situation. The aristocracy represents the conjuncture of two different political theories: the cultural nationalism of the 1890s and the liberal individualism that emerges as Yeats confronts his own nationalism rampant against him.

At the end of "J.M. Synge and the Ireland of His Time," published in 1910, Yeats meditates over the monastic brilliance of Mont Saint-Michel and longs for some such order for Ireland. Only from such an order "can we come upon those agreements, those separations from all else, that fasten men together lastingly . . . " (E, pp. 422–423). Unity, this formula suggests, comes from difference; only separation can truly fasten things together. Surely the aristocracy is the necessary social expression of this paradox, incarnating as it does for Yeats a national being out of its very difference from the common ruck. Thus Protestant landowners became the true Irish despite the growing claims of the Catholic masses to that status, precisely *because of* their difference from the mass. The Ascendancy becomes, in Hegelian terms, a universal class, a part that because of its very independence from the whole comes to represent it.

* * * But how can this part represent that which is its very antithesis, and what is to happen to the majority, which has to be removed somehow from "the whole"? Paul de Man points out that there is something logically unstable about "an ideal which is persistently referred to as Unity of Being, but most frequently expressed . . . by such terms as 'to reject' or 'to limit.' "[7] More dangerously, there is something politically unstable about a whole that exists in contradistinction to elements somehow outside the whole. Yeats's decision at this time that "the people are conquered by an ideal of life upheld by authority" (M, p. 180) shows in what direction that instability might lead.

---

7. Paul de Man, *The Rhetoric of Romanticism* (New York: Columbia University Press, 1984), p. 146.

JAHAN RAMAZANI

"Easter, 1916" and the Balladic Elegies†

In "To a Shade," "September 1913," "Easter, 1916," and "Parnell's Funeral," Yeats confronts his own imagined death through the historic occasion of loss, foreshadowing the public elegies of Robert Lowell and Geoffrey Hill. By bringing language to the horizon of death, his lyrics seek to wrest words from their entanglement with the market; they would prevent journalistic "idle talk" from concealing death as something that always happens to others and therefore to no one.[1] By means of this Romantic strategy—surely imbued with Romantic ideology—Yeats avoids in "Easter, 1916" the eulogistic cant that often clogs the public elegy. At the beginning of "Easter, 1916," much as in "September 1913," satire predominates; but now Yeats directs the satire at his own "polite meaningless words" (P,[2] 180). Robert Bly echoes Yeat's claim that we make out of "the quarrel with ourselves, poetry" (Myth,[3] 331) [285]: "A true political poem is a quarrel with ourselves. . . . The true political poem does not order us either to take any specific acts: like the personal poem, it moves to deepen awareness."[4] Though not relevant to all such poetry, Bly's statement can alert us to one political aim of "Easter, 1916": to fasten words to the human experience of death and history rather than to capitulate to formulas about the death of statesmen and the anonymous other. The discourse of the poem shifts from the first stanza's evocation of the monologic prattle that conceals death to the last's many-tongued confrontation with death in the language of mourning. The pressure of death discloses the collectivity within the poet's language and historical consciousness, so the nation is transformed from "a subject of knowledge" into "a dumb struggling thought seeking a mouth to utter it" (E&I,[5] 317). As Adorno writes of history and the lyric: "through the individual and his spontaneity, objective historical forces rouse themselves within the poem, forces which are propelling a restricted and restricting social condition beyond itself to a more

---

† From *Yeats and the Poetry of Death: Elegy, Self-Elegy, and the Sublime* by Jahan Ramazani (New Haven: Yale University Press, 1990), pp. 59–67. Reprinted by permission of Yale University Press. Page references to this Norton Critical Edition are given in brackets after the author's original citations.

1. See Martin Heidegger's discussion of "idle talk" (*Gerede*) and the concealment of death in *Being in Time*, trans. John Macquarrie and Edward Robinson (Oxford: Basil Blackwell, 1980), 211–14. Unfortunately, Heidegger's political affiliations suggest that he did not apply his potentially radical insights to the "idle talk" of nazism—a language that reduced the deaths of its victims to anonymous necessities. As Frank Kermode states, such racist scapegoating is a "fiction of escape which tells you nothing about death but projects it onto others" (*The Sense of an Ending* [Oxford: Oxford University Press, 1967], 39). Heidegger's and Yeats's views on death and "idle talk" are informed by the ideological notion that poetry "can transcend a corrupting 'world' of politics and money"; see Jerome J. McGann, *The Romantic Ideology: A Critical Investigation* (Chicago: University of Chicago Press, 1983), 13.

2. W. B. Yeats, *The Poems, Revised*, ed. Richard J. Finneran (New York: Macmillan, 1989).

3. W. B. Yeats, *Mythologies* (New York: Macmillan, 1959).

4. Robert Bly, "Leaping up into Political Poetry," in *Poetry and Politics*, ed. Richard Jones (New York: William Morrow, 1985), 133–34.

5. W. B. Yeats, *Essays and Introductions* (London: Macmillan, 1961).

humane one. . . . [V]arious levels of society's inner contradictory relationships manifest themselves in the poet's speaking."[6] "Easter, 1916" articulates the social and historical forces of revolution as an internal, polyvocalic debate about death.

To disclose the "quarrel with ourselves," Yeats must expunge the "idle talk" that Heidegger ascribes to "the everyday"—a talk so rigidly controlled by convention ("polite") and so mindlessly passed from one atomistic subject to another ("meaningless") that it can bespeak neither death nor historical transformation:

> I have passed with a nod of the head
> Or polite meaningless words,
> Or have lingered awhile and said
> Polite meaningless words . . .
>
> . . . .
>
> Being certain that they and I
> But lived where motley is worn:
> All changed, changed utterly:
> A terrible beauty is born.   (P 180–82) [73]

The stanza announces the historical shift by enacting it within its own language, leaping up several levels of discourse—from mechanical repetition to a sublime bewilderment before rupture. Because no *but* or other conjunction marks the transition, we seem to witness in the rhetorical break the birth of the terrible beauty.[7] Taking up an elegiac counterconvention that extends from Tennyson's "bald street" to Auden's "hundred cities," the poem opens with an urban setting—its "grey" houses as anonymous and interchangeable as the "faces" and "words."[8] Rising out of this public world's undifferentiated drabness, the nativity ode that is also a death song seems strange and inexplicable. To accentuate further the logical chasm between the new world, new consciousness, new language and the old, Yeats brilliantly formulates the crossing in the passive voice—"All changed" and "is born"—a formulation best explicated in the context of the next stanza.

An epistemological rift generates the poem: a rift between the knowledge that a change has occurred and the absence of an "efficient cause" to explain the change. The relation of the event to what precedes it is inorganic or "allegorical."[9] Thus, in the second stanza Yeats enumerates the

---

6. Theodor Adorno, "Lyric Poetry and Society" (1957), trans. Bruce Mayo, *Telos* 20 (1974).
7. For exhaustive analysis of the line "A terrible beauty is born" and a negative assessment of the poem's politics, see Terry Eagleton, *Against the Grain* (London: Verso, 1986), 173–80. For his early, sympathetic reading of the poem, see "History and Myth in Yeats's 'Easter 1916' " *Essays in Criticism* 21 (1971): 248–60.
8. Tennyson, *In Memoriam* 7, line 12; W. H. Auden, "In Memory of W. B. Yeats," *Collected Poems*, ed. Edward Mendelson (New York: Random House, 1976), 197.
9. My reading of the poem as allegorical and rhetorically discontinuous runs counter to interpretations of it in terms of symbol; see, e.g., Joseph Kishel, "Yeats's Elegies," *Yeats Eliot Review* 7 (1981): 87. I use *allegory* here in accordance with its meanings in Walter Benjamin, *The Origin of the German Tragic Drama*, trans. John Osborne (London: NLB, 1977), 159–235, and Paul de Man, "The Rhetoric of Temporality," *Blindness and Insight: Essays in the Rhetoric of Contemporary Criticism*, 2d ed. (Minneapolis: University of Minnesota Press, 1983), 187–228. For Yeats on allegory, see Yeats, *Essays and Introductions*, 147.

personal characteristics of the rebels only to show that these qualities cannot have brought about the historical transformation. Although his skepticism may be partly rooted in disagreement and animosity (against Maud Gonne's husband, for example), it develops into a powerful subversion of hero-historiography. Whereas an elegist like Davis would have marshaled personal attributes to explain heroic action, Yeats shows them to be almost irrelevant. As if the leaders were immediately before him and the verse merely pointing them out one by one, each portrait begins with a demonstrative adjective—"That," "This," "This," "This." The poet summons four rebels immediately before us to prove that, much as his own heightened awareness could not have been deduced from his earlier distraction, so too the heroic event could not have been predicted from the antiheroic participants. One had a sweet voice that grew shrill; another was a schoolkeeper who wrote poetry; his friend was sensitive and promising; the last seemed a "drunken, vainglorious lout." They hardly forebode terrible beauty, singly or together. Although Yeats allows them some responsibility for the change—the lout "has resigned" his former part—dropping out cannot explain the creation of new beauty. Yeats glories in the rhetorical disjunction: he implies that the lout and his compatriots had some role in creating the terrible beauty *and* that the beauty gave birth to itself:

> Yet I number him in the song;
> He, too, has resigned his part
> In the casual comedy;
> He, too, has been changed in his turn,
> Transformed utterly:
> A terrible beauty is born.

As the comedian leaves his former role, something larger than him transforms him. The agency of change remains unstated, because the verbs—"has been changed" and "Transformed"—are in the passive voice. Yeats is remembering and secularizing that earlier reflection on mutability included in his edition of Spenser: the "Mutability Cantos." In her final judgment Nature concedes that things "changed be," but when she repeats this verb with still more emphasis on the passive voice—"all shall changed bee"—she indicates the enormity of the final, apocalyptic change, a leap from time into eternity.[1] In Yeats's refrains, the passive mood suggests likewise that the change is definitive and inexplicable, but this poem's terms of reference are aesthetic rather than theological. Like Yeats, the patriots have left behind the "casual comedy" of the everyday. Their entry into a historical process larger than themselves engenders an unforeseeable event, just as the poet's surrender to a genre, a tradition, or a discourse occasions the birth of a work that transcends personality and intention (*E&I*, 509). For Yeats, the dislocations in history and writing are analogous.

The analogy may be more than an analogy and more than a mere aestheticizing of history, according to Blanchot: "The writer sees himself in the Revolution. It attracts him because it is the time during which

1. Spenser, "Two Cantos of Mutabilitie," 7.58.515, 7.59.525.

literature becomes history. It is his truth."[2] The strength of the elegy for the rebels is that Yeats sees himself in their revolutionary act, not only because they are analogues for his writing but because they concretize his writing in their historical actions. As Maud Gonne states: "Without Yeats there would have been no Literary Revival in Ireland. Without the inspiration of that Revival and the glorification of beauty and heroic virtue, I doubt if there would have been an Easter Week."[3] Over the years, Yeats worries about the historical enactment of his scripts, especially of an apparent script for martyrdom like *Cathleen ni Houlihan*, asking himself in "Man and the Echo":

> Did that play of mind send out
> Certain men the English shot?   (P 345) [127]

From this perspective the concession "Yet I number him in the song" has a darker meaning: the poet has numbered the "lout" and the other rebels not only in the song we read but also in the text of revolutionary action. The martyrs and history are not the only authors of the change; because of the poet too, all is transformed utterly.

In spite of the elegy's overall movement toward identification with the rebels, the next stanza distinguishes their work from the poet's. With their "one purpose alone," the rebels have become "a stone," the opposite of the running stream, the tumbling clouds, horse, rider, birds, moorhens, moorcocks—every "living" thing that "Changes" in the pastoral landscape. The stone cannot be an image of this poem's "lyric stasis," since there is nothing static about the lyric, except for the momentary pauses in the refrains, and even these are about metamorphosis.[4] Unlike such stilled elegies as "Her Courtesy" and "Beautiful Lofty Things," this restless lyric tries to *be* the transformation it describes.

If we need more evidence for this view of the poem, the final stanza is a dizzying spiral of changing responses to the dead—Yeats's derailing of the newspaper narrative of history from its "railway tracks of thought":

> Too long a sacrifice
> Can make a stone of the heart.
> O when may it suffice?
> That is Heaven's part, our part
> To murmur name upon name,
> As a mother names her child
> When sleep at last has come
> On limbs that had run wild.
> What is it but nightfall?

2. Maurice Blanchot, *The Gaze of Orpheus, and Other Literary Essays*, ed. P. Adams Sitney, trans. Lydia Davis (Barrytown, N.Y.: Station Hill, 1981), 40. "The writing of the poem becomes an analogue for the event which is its subject," observes C. K. Stead; but he sees the analogy differently, arguing that the stone in the third stanza is a metaphor for the poem and the Rising (*The New Poetic* [London: Hutchinson, 1964], 39).

3. Maud Gonne, "Yeats and Ireland," in *Scattering Branches*, ed. Stephen Gwynn (New York: Macmillan, 1940), 27 [332]. Elizabeth Cullingford discusses Yeats's influence on Pearse and MacDonagh in *Yeats, Ireland and Fascism* (New York: New York University Press, 1981), 91–95.

4. For the opposite view, see Stead, *New Poetic*, 39. External evidence, discounted by Stead, supports my reading of the stanza: Yeats used the stanza to implore Maud Gonne "to forget the stone and its inner fire for the flashing, changing joy of life"; see her "Yeats and Ireland," 31–32.

No, no, not night but death;
Was it needless death after all?
For England may keep faith
For all that is done and said.
We know their dream; enough
To know they dreamed and are dead;
And what if excess of love
Bewildered them till they died?

Assertion leads to question, question back to assertion, anger to acceptance, acceptance back to anger and then acceptance again; the rhetoric eddies back and forth; the mourning mind gropes between consolation and de-mystification. The poet's inner quarrel becomes a nation's quarrel: one voice says sacrifice hardens the heart, another that only heaven should judge, a third dallies with the false surmise that death is sleep, a fourth counters that death is death, a fifth adds that the sacrifice may have been unnecessary, and so on. The multiplicity of voices even brings about a momentary shift in gender, when the poet leaves behind the stern and judgmental voice of the paternal Minos for the loving murmur of the elegiac mother. Corrective distance alternates with identification, and the final embrace of the rebels assimilates their vision to the poet's "dream" and "love," as in "September 1913." Scorning his own "polite meaningless words," Yeats accuses himself in the first stanza of having nearly suffered what he calls elsewhere "the death of language"; but the renewed prox-imity to extra-linguistic death awakens his language to the "quarrel with ourselves" and within language itself—the quarrel that may be the Ro-mantic lyric's authentic grasp of history. The poet, in Adorno's words, "comes to full accord with the language itself," until "the voice of language itself is heard."[5] The deeply personal meditation before death oddly allows a nation's language, with its many conflicting voices, to be heard.

How can we explain the prominent role of proper names in effecting the elegy's linguistic shift? A review of naming in Yeats's other elegies might help us with this question. Elegists from Jonson to Yeats use names as if they were verbal switchboards, allowing or barring access to the dead. In some of the elegies, such as "On a Child's Death," "Mourn—And Then Onward!" "Upon a Dying Lady," and "Shepherd and Goatherd," Yeats obeys the elegiac convention of not naming the dead; similarly, he with-holds names in the brief portraits of this poem's second stanza. Apparently to protect Parnell from the jaws of the pack, "To a Shade" leaves him nameless, thinking him "safer in the tomb." In other elegies, such as "All Souls' Night," "Beautiful Lofty Things," and "The Municipal Gallery Re-visited," the poet names the dead with much pomp, as if this performative act would call them among us. Having summoned the dead in "All Souls' Night," he dismisses them with the disavowal, "But names are nothing" (P 229). In still other elegies, he skillfully uses names to organize the work; for example, he names Johnson, Synge, and Pollexfen in vignettes but sets Gregory apart by naming him only in the title, "In Memory of Major Robert Gregory." "September 1913" is closest to "Easter, 1916" in its

5. Adorno, "Lyric Poetry," 62.

pacing of names, withholding its roll call until the climactic moment when the martyrs are interfused with the poet's "delirium." Yeats claims that his use of names in "Easter, 1916" arose partly from the shame of hearing an old Irish member of Parliament recite a ballad, "repeating over his sacred names, Wolfe Tone, Emmer, and Owen Roe, and mourning that new poets and new movements should have taken something of their sacredness away"; in this elegy and in "September 1913," Yeats adopts this Irish tradition of repeating over the names of the dead (Au,[6] 299). Frazer and Freud discuss the taboo on the names of the dead, names whose utterance might bring the dead into one's presence; but for Yeats, such "contagious magic" or "omnipotence of thoughts" facilitates the desired contact.[7] In "Easter, 1916" he figures this communion as a mother's murmuring her child's name; the echoic verb *murmur*, unlike *say* or *speak*, helps to blur further the distinctions between signifier and signified, subject and object. But lest we think Yeats has given himself over to the dead, he reasserts the power of the namer, grasping in the name all that remains, conferring existence on the nonexistent dead:

> I write it out in a verse—
> MacDonagh and MacBride
> And Connolly and Pearse
> Now and in time to be,
> Wherever green is worn,
> Are changed, changed utterly:
> A terrible beauty is born.

Dramatizing his act of writing the names into a verse, the poet again suggests that it is he who has changed them utterly. By the synecdoche of a name, he inscribes each rebel into this lyric, "Now and in time to be." He reenacts a historical change as a perpetual linguistic event.

* * *

ELIZABETH BUTLER CULLINGFORD

Shrill Voices, Accursed Opinions†

"Easter 1916," a political elegy, is also a poem about love: the martyrs' love of Ireland, and Yeats's devotion to Gonne as the symbol of Ireland. Praising his countrymen for being good lovers, Yeats claimed they "had never served any abstract cause, except the one, and that we personified

6. W. B. Yeats, *Autobiographies* (London: Macmillan, 1955).
7. Sir James Frazer, *The Golden Bough*, abridged ed. (London: Macmillan, 1957), 331–38; Freud, *Totem and Taboo, The Standard Edition of the Complete Psychological Works of Sigmund Freud*, ed. James Strachey (London: Hogarth Press and the Institute of Psycho-Analysis, 1953–74), 13:54–59, 81–87. Yeats describes his magical use of names in *Autobiographies* (London: Macmillan, 1955), 247–48.
† From *Gender and History in Yeats's Love Poetry* (Syracuse, N.Y.: Syracuse University Press, 1996), pp. 52–54. Copyright © 1996. Reprinted by permission of Elizabeth Butler Cullingford. Page references to this Norton Critical Edition are given in brackets after the author's original citations.

by a woman" (Au[1] 545). "Easter 1916" evokes the personified "terrible beauty" or sacrificial queen while it examines the emotional costs of a political *Liebestod*. Yeats thought the patriot O'Leary "was like some man who serves a woman all his life without asking whether she be good or bad, wise or foolish" (Au 215), but he himself was ready to interrogate his images. "Easter 1916" was written before his marriage separated him from Gonne and enabled his hostile analysis of her in "A Prayer for my Daughter" (1919), where the "terrible beauty" is far more terrible than beautiful. The two poems, though written three years apart, are connected by more than their proximity in *Michael Robartes and the Dancer*: both thematize the destruction of "sweetness" by women's "shrill" devotion to "opinions." Both are related to Yeats's poem about the incarceration of Constance Markievicz, "On a Political Prisoner," and, like "Michael Robartes and the Dancer," both question the effect of participation in public and intellectual life upon the woman's role in love poetry as the aesthetic object of male contemplation, and in history as the inspiration of male political action.

Markievicz stands in for Gonne in "Easter 1916."[2] The Countess, condemned to death for her part in the Rising but reprieved because of her sex, offered a mirror image of Gonne's devotion to her country and of what might have been her fate had she stayed in Dublin. Yeats claimed that he had been the first to tell Markievicz about Gonne, "in imitation of whom, perhaps, she was to earn the life-sentence she is now serving" (Mem[3] 78). Gonne herself, who wrote after the Rising that "Constance Markievicz was like a sister to me,"[4] must have strengthened Yeats's identification of the two women. Once the very embodiment of "romantic political Ireland" (Mem 247), Gonne is mentioned in "Easter 1916" only as the victim of John MacBride, who had "done most bitter wrong / To some who are near my heart," but his ambivalence about their relationship informs the poem's hesitant judgments about the politics of love for one's country. The fact that not just one, but two beautiful women who could have moved in Ascendancy and Garrison circles had chosen to dedicate themselves to nationalist politics convinced Yeats that he was observing not an aberration, but a historical trend. The lines describing Markievicz are suggestively juxtaposed with the first articulation of the refrain, "A terrible beauty is born," so she appears as a concrete realization of that abstract oxymoron: her beauty in the distant past; her terrible fanaticism in the immediate past; her "change," in which both terms of the opposition are retained but transvalued, eternally present. Yeats was originally more generous in his assessment of her character:

> That woman at while would be shrill
> In aimless argument;
> Had ignorant good will,

1. W. B. Yeats, *Autobiographies* (London: Macmillan, 1955).
2. George Mayhew, "A Corrected Typescript of Yeats's 'Easter 1916'," *Huntington Library Quarterly* 7.1 (1963), 69–71.
3. W. B. Yeats, *Memoirs*, ed. Denis Donoghue (London: Macmillan, 1972).
4. Margaret Ward, *Maud Gonne: Ireland's Joan of Arc* (London: Pandora, 1990), 111.

> All that she got she spent,
> Her charity had no bounds.   (VP⁵ 392v)

Although the last two lines are weakly non-specific, reading like a pious obituary for some Lady Bountiful, in omitting them as he revised Yeats showed artistic judgment rather than tact. He kept the rhyme word "spent," but changed the nature of the Countess's spending from economic beneficence to ignorant time-wasting. Omitting the archaic phrase "at while," Yeats tightened the diction, but its absence suggests that Markievicz was not occasionally but always shrill. The loosely articulated "Had ignorant good will," is integrated into the syntax but strengthens the negative tone; "ignorant good-will" becomes her defining characteristic. In introducing the aesthetically pleasing verbal balance between "days" and "nights," Yeats improves the rhetorical frame around his picture; but the increased temporal precision leaves Markievicz no time for anything but ignorance and argument:

> That woman's days were spent
> In ignorant good-will,
> Her nights in argument
> Until her voice grew shrill.   (VP 392) [73]

In excising the reference to her generosity Yeats casts doubts upon his own. Did he sacrifice Markievicz's historical specificity to the exigencies of poetic economy, rhythmic balance, and formal closure; or did his view of her harden as, staying with Gonne in Normandy while he wrote the poem, he watched her uncompromising reaction to the Rising?

Markievicz was a prominent supporter of labor and a leading member of Connolly's socialist Citizen Army. Her work feeding hungry school children and striking workers hardly merits Yeats's patronizing dismissal of her "ignorant good-will."[6] As we have seen, the shrill-voiced woman was associated in popular culture with suffrage agitation, and Markievicz was a suffragist, though Republicanism and socialism dominated her political agenda. In 1896 she had asserted the need for militant women to be "shrill":

> John Stuart Mill said thirty years ago that the only forcible argument against giving women the suffrage was "that they did not demand it with sufficient force and noise". Now, one of the many sneers I have been accustomed to hear against women is that they make too much noise; and yet we are told the principal argument against our having votes is that we don't make noise enough.[7]

Yeats, however, declares that Markievicz's argumentativeness and social concern have destroyed both her youthful beauty and her "sweet" voice. She is no longer a pleasing object of aesthetic contemplation. Though she

---

5. *The Variorum Edition of the Poems of W. B. Yeats*, ed. Peter Allt and Russell K. Alspach (New York: Macmillan, 1966).
6. Anne Haverty, *Constance Markievicz: An Independent Life* (London: Pandora, 1988), 105–06, 110–11; C. L. Innes, "Yeats's Female Voices: Crazy Jane and Other Woman in *The Winding Stair and Other Poems*," *Text and Context* 3 (Autumn 1988), 57.
7. Quoted in Haverty, *Markievicz*, 41.

is not in fact dead, he elegizes her, as he was to do again in "On a Political Prisoner," through the class-specific image of the Anglo-Irish huntswoman:

> What voice more sweet than hers
> When, young and beautiful,
> She rode to harriers?   (VP 392) [73]

Much love poetry that celebrates the beloved as a (dead) aesthetic object adopts an elegiac tone. "In Memory of Eva Gore-Booth and Con Markievicz" (1927) elegizes not two sisters in the fullness of their intellectual and political commitment, one working with her companion Esther Roper for suffrage and the rights of trade unionists, the other a nationalist revolutionary, Minister for Labor in the first Dáil, and President of Cumann na mBan; but the apolitical Ascendancy "girls" they once were, both beautiful, one a "gazelle" (VP 475). Yeats could have been thinking of either of the sisters when he later wrote dismissively that he had known "A Helen of social welfare dream / Climb on a wagonette to scream" ("Why should not Old Men be Mad?" VP 626). Non-Helens may occupy themselves with social welfare, but the beautiful have their work cut out guarding their good looks.

The static, aesthetically attractive image of the two lovely young women, framed in their exotic silk kimonos by the great windows of the Big House,[8] is disfigured by the women's assumption of public voice: "a raving autumn shears / Blossom from the summer's wreath." (The word "wreath" ambiguously evokes both the garlands of a summer wedding and the metaphorical flowers brought to a grave by the writer of elegy: both love and death.) As Yeats searched for an image appropriate to his sense of loss, he returned to the identification of Ireland as a woman who resembles the sisters in their politicized old age. "Ireland is a hag," he wrote. Although the line was canceled, it fits with Stallworthy's reading of the "great gazebo" as Yeats's "early vision, more romantic than realistic, of a resurgent Ireland."[9] Ireland is a hag in Cathleen ni Houlihan and, as we have seen, Markievicz regarded Yeats's play as a gospel. Yeats deplored his own influence on her: the line originally read "I the great gazebo built."[1]

Aesthetics intersect with class snobbery as the former Ascendancy belle "drags out lonely years / Conspiring among the ignorant": the loss of beauty is accompanied by social descent. A canceled line in the drafts disparages her socialism as "Contagion of the popular breath,"[2] recalling his earlier condemnation of the "popular enmity" that governed her thought (VP 397) [75]. In asserting "the folly of a fight / With a common wrong or right," Yeats devalues the sisters' interventions in politics in favor of their status as "Pictures of the mind": his mind. To claim that "The innocent and the beautiful / Have no enemy but time" (VP 475–76) [102] is to echo the carpe diem mode and to dismiss the facts of history with a willful blindness that Yeats seldom shows elsewhere. Under the guise of

---

8. Innes, "Yeats's Female Voices," 56–58.
9. Jon Stallworthy, Between the Lines: Yeats's Poetry in the Making (Oxford: Clarendon Press, 1963), 172.
1. Stallworthy, Between the Lines, 172, 169, 171.
2. Stallworthy, Between the Lines, 168.

elegy Yeats revivifies the clichés of the love genre (obsession with the visual, the beautiful object framed in a window, emphasis on fine clothing, depiction of women as female deer or fragile blossoms, aristocratic pretensions, concern with the passing of time) in a vain attempt to cancel or reverse the processes of history.

"Easter 1916" does not question the right of male patriots to engage in argument: since men are not defined as aesthetic objects, their beauty cannot be spoiled by opinions. Yeats made the distinction clear when he wrote of Gonne in 1909:

> I fear for her any renewed devotion to an opinion. Women, because the main event of their lives has been a giving of themselves, give themselves to an opinion as if [it] were some terrible stone doll. We [men] take up an opinion lightly and are easily false to it, and when faithful keep the habit of many interests . . . the opinion becomes so much a part of them [women] that it is as though a part of their flesh becomes, as it were, stone. (*Mem* 192)

Although Yeats can see that the difference between the sexes is socially constructed by the fact that men have "many interests" while for women "the main event of their life has been a giving of themselves," he accepts this disparity as natural law.

The idea that a political woman's flesh turns to stone, however, is degendered in "Easter 1916." "September 1913" had explicitly linked the "delirium" of Irish male nationalist martyrs with sexual passion:

> "Some woman's yellow hair
> Has maddened every mother's son":
> They weighed so lightly what they gave. (*VP* 290) [45]

Here the trope is used approvingly: for men in the Irish national tradition, sexuality and politics are properly fused. "Easter 1916," however, while it celebrates the *hieros gamos* between the martyrs and their motherland, asks whether the sacrifice of change occasioned by obsessive love of country may not give political men as well as political women hearts of stone.

Yeats admitted after the Rising that " 'Romantic Ireland's dead and gone' sounds old-fashioned now" (*VP* 820). His reflections on the romantic gesture of the martyrs led him back to the Romantic model of his youth, Shelley, whose poem *Alastor* had helped to shape his approach to the subject of love.[3] In *Alastor* a young poet sees a dream-vision of ideal feminine perfection, before which "His strong heart sunk and sickened with excess / Of love." This "excess of love" drives him on a desperate search for the dream-woman, a search that can only end in death:

> Lost, lost, forever lost,
> In the wide pathless desert of dim sleep,
> That beautiful shape! Does the dark gate of death
> Conduct to thy mysterious paradise,
> O Sleep?

---

3. See George Bornstein, *Yeats and Shelley* (Chicago: University of Chicago Press, 1970), 29–66.

Worn out by his failure to find his dream-beloved, the poet descends "to an untimely grave." Shelley acknowledges the destructiveness of the poet's fatal passion, but he is contemptuous of those who have never felt the power of the dream:

> They . . . deluded by no generous error, instigated by no sacred thirst of doubtful knowledge, duped by no illustrious superstition, loving nothing on this earth . . . are morally dead. They are neither friends, nor lovers, nor fathers, nor citizens of the world, nor benefactors of their country.[4]

The same ambivalence about the passion that leads to death informs "Easter 1916," which affirms the political *Liebestod* only after numerous qualifications. Meditating on the dubious practical efficacy of the rebellion, Yeats remembers Shelley's Poet, whose heart "sickened with excess of love," who was deluded by a generous error, and who sought his vision of love first in dreams and then in the grave:

> Was it needless death after all?
> For England may keep faith
> For all that is done and said.
> We know their dream; enough
> To know they dreamed and are dead;
> And what if excess of love
> Bewildered them till they died?   (VP 394) [74]

"Excess of love" gives birth to a "terrible beauty": the romantic sacrifice and the woman for whom it is offered are dangerously fused. Dalton has suggested a source for Yeats's "terrible beauty" in Sheridan Le Fanu's long poem *The Legend of the Glaive*, where the sorceress Fionula, whom Dalton identifies with Eire, is described as "the Cruel, the brightest, the worst, / With a terrible beauty." She exemplifies her cruelty by sending a young man to die for her in battle.[5] Here the "terrible beauty" is not an ideal image of the miraculous transformation wrought by sacrifice, but an actual woman, a witch.

In "On the Medusa of Leonardo da Vinci in the Florentine Gallery," Shelley represents the Medusa's head as both alluring and repellent. He is fascinated by the fusion of female beauty, male violence, and pain; by

> Loveliness like a shadow, from which shine,
> Fiery and lurid, struggling underneath,
> The agonies of anguish and of death.

Throughout the poem Shelley repeatedly juxtaposes terror and beauty: "Its horror and its beauty are divine"; " 'Tis the tempestuous loveliness of terror"; "all the beauty and the terror there." Shelley's contention, that "it is less the horror than the grace / Which turns the gazer's spirit into stone,"[6]

4. Percy Bysshe Shelley, *The Complete Poetical Works*, ed. Thomas Hutchinson (London: Oxford University Press, 1969), 19, 15.
5. G. F. Dalton, "The Tradition of Blood Sacrifice to the Goddess Eire," *Studies* 63:252 (1974): 350–51. Yeats had a copy of Le Fanu's poems: Edward O'Shea, *A Descriptive Catalog of W. B. Yeats's Library* (New York: Garland, 1985), 150.
6. Shelley, *Poetical Works*, 582–83.

explains why Yeats's poem balances the beauty of a generous love against the terrible consequences of single-minded devotion:

> Hearts with one purpose alone
> Through summer and winter seem
> Enchanted to a stone
> To trouble the living stream.   (VP 393) [74]

"Too long a sacrifice" has the same effect as the glance of the Medusa: it makes a stone of the heart. Yeats criticizes the rebels for their singlemindedness, but if they have loved their country to excess, he has loved a female image of that country with the same persistency. Toomey has noted the sexual connotations of the word "trouble" in Yeats's work;[7] and the imagery of water in motion that represents the world of change in "Easter 1916" is linked with sexual fulfillment rather than sublimation, as Yeats's juxtaposition of male and female birds indicates:

> The long-legged moor-hens dive,
> And hens to moor-cocks call;
> Minute by minute they live:
> The stone's in the midst of all.   (VP 393) [74]

Gonne recorded that, as Yeats recited "Easter 1916" to her on the beach in Normandy, he made the connection between stifled sexuality and patriotic dedication explicit, begging her to "forget the stone and its inner fire for the flashing, changing joy of life." Adopting his metaphor, however, she said that her mind was "dull with the stone of the fixed idea of getting back to Ireland."[8] When he later sent her a completed draft she commented tartly, "No I don't like your poem . . . you who have studied philosophy & know something of history know quite well that sacrifice has never yet turned a heart to stone though it has immortalised many" (AYF[9] 384).

Composed at the same time as "Easter 1916," "Men improve with the Years" uses the same images of stone and stream, and in so doing constructs an intertexual analogy between love and patriotism. Yeats claims that his romantic "dreams," like the dreams of Ireland shared by the political martyrs, have also turned him into stone:

> But I grow old among dreams,
> A weather-worn, marble triton
> Among the streams.   (VP 329) [59]

The triton, like the patriots, troubles the living stream: "enchanted" to a stone by the terrible beauty, he cannot respond to "The Living Beauty" or "pay its tribute of wild tears" (VP 334) [59]. In "The Laugh of the Medusa" Cixous has pointed out that the "terrible beauty" is in the eye

7. Deirdre Toomey, "Labyrinths: Yeats and Maud Gonne" in Yeats and Women, ed. Deirdre Toomey Yeats Annual 9 (London: Macmillan, 1991), 103.
8. Maud Gonne MacBride, "Yeats and Ireland" in Scattering Branches, ed. Stephen Gwynn (New York: Macmillan, 1940), 32.
9. The Gonne-Yeats Letters 1893–1938: Always Your Friend, ed. Anna MacBride White and A. Norman Jeffares (London: Hutchinson, 1992).

of the male beholder. Women did not create the figure of the deadly woman or the mother who demands the blood of her children. Eire as a pre-Christian earth-goddess who demands human sacrifice[1] is an avatar of the "Great Mother," the feminine figured in tripartite form as life-giving womb, pleasure-giving vagina, and devouring grave. Yeats found anthropological authority in Frazer for the fertility myth that he called "the old ritual of the year . . . the mother goddess and the slain god" (VP 857), but the male creator of culture imposes upon himself this archetypal story of his infantilization and destruction by the mother. His incapacities as bearer and inadequacies as nurturer combine with childhood memories of total dependence to produce a figure of terror. Although she certainly needed and depended on him, and later even teasingly warned him against matrimony (AYF 320), Gonne did not compel Yeats's sacrifice; indeed she warned him against making it. She insisted that if the "absolutely *platonic friendship*" she offered "unsettles you & spoils your work then you must have the strength & courage at once to give up meeting me" (AYF 85). Though wanting him on her terms, she reminded him that he was always free to reject them. In 1899 she wrote, "my dear Friend I do not want you to make up your mind to sacrifice yourself for me. I know that just now, perhaps, it is useless my saying to you 'love some other woman'. All I want of you is not to make up your mind *not* to" (AYF 130). The sacrifice, like the Medusa complex, was self-imposed.[2]

"Easter 1916" does not challenge the poetic stereotype of the "terrible beauty," but presents it in both its negative and positive aspects. When Yeats wishes to claim bardic authority in immortalizing the dead heroes of 1916 he figures them as children, with himself and his audience as surrogates for Mother Ireland in her nurturing rather than destructive embodiment:

> our part
> To murmur name upon name,
> As a mother names her child
> When sleep at last has come
> On limbs that had run wild.   (VP 394) [74]

Even this move has been challenged: Kiberd argues that Yeats, in employing the old colonialist metaphor of parent and child, "has infantilized the fallen rebels in much the same way as they obligingly, if unconsciously, infantilized themselves in the opening sentence of their proclamation."[3] This judgment, however, neglects the psychological empowerment that the rebels must have felt in naming themselves the "children" of Mother Ireland, and that Yeats reflects in mourning them as such. So powerful, indeed, is the metaphor of the mother and the sleeping child that Yeats is forced to remind himself in a heavily stressed, grimly alliterative, and unmusical monosyllabic line that it is only a figure: "No, no, not night

1. Dalton, "Tradition of Blood Sacrifice," 343–45.
2. See John Harwood, *Olivia Shakespear and W. B. Yeats: After Long Silence* (London: Macmillan, 1989), 52, for a more negative reading of her motives.
3. Declan Kiberd, "The War Against the Past" in *The Uses of the Past: Essays on Irish Culture*, ed. Audrey S. Eyler and Robert F. Garratt (Newark: University of Delaware Press, 1988), 39.

but death" (*VP* 394) [74]. The image of the mother is evoked only to be canceled: unlike Pearse, Yeats distinguishes biological mothers from symbolic, sacrificial ones.

* * *

JOHN KELLY

"Friendship Is the Only House I Have": Lady Gregory and W. B. Yeats†

* * *

Barely three months after Yeats's marriage Robert Gregory was killed in Italy. A moving passage in *Seventy Years* gives an account of how Lady Gregory received the telegram and of her numbed journey to Galway to break the news to her daughter-in-law.[1] The fact that there were still grandchildren and, most importantly, a grandson helped to mitigate the dynastic consequences of the death, but she must have understood at once that the chances of a Gregory remaining at Coole into the middle part of the century were now drastically diminished. It seemed that the great ambition of her life since her widowing had come to nothing.

Yeats was not so affected. In some ways the death of Gregory fitted with his historical and personal perception of Coole: that it had reached the apogee of its cultural destiny by the beginning of the century and that inheritance could only mean dilution. He had registered his ambiguous attitude towards Gregory's character in a diary entry [in 1909][2] and although the absoluteness of death put his reservations into a different perspective the ambiguity could never be quite exorcised, not even in the great elegy.

That he should write an elegy was never in question; he learned of the death in a letter from Lady Gregory of 2 February which had the postscript, 'If you feel like it some time—write something down that we may keep— you understood him better than many.'[3] He would no doubt have written something in any case, but this was a command that he could not refuse, and, besides, she kept him up to the mark. A few days later she added Margaret's appeal to her own: 'If you would send even a paragraph—just some thing of what I know you are feeling—to the *Observer*—or failing that the *Nation*—she would feel it a comfort.'[4] Lest 'what I know you are feeling' should furnish insufficient copy, she also sent him 'typed notes

---

† From *Lady Gregory: Fifty Years After*, ed. Ann Saddlemyer and Colin Smythe (Gerrards Cross, Bucks, England: Colin Smythe, 1987), pp. 234–43. Copyright © Colin Smythe Ltd., on behalf of Anne de Winton and Catherine Kennedy. Page references to this Norton Critical Edition are given in brackets after the author's original citations.
1. *Seventy Years. Being the Autobiography of Lady Gregory*, ed. Colin Smythe (New York: Macmillan, 1974), pp. 553–4.
2. W. B. Yeats, *Memoirs*, ed. Denis Donoghue (London: Macmillan, 1972), p. 230.
3. Unpublished letter from Lady Gregory to Yeats, 2 February 1918.
4. Unpublished letter from Lady Gregory to Yeats, 5 February 1918.

. . . not to use but to waken your memory to different sides of him.'[5] As it turned out, these 'typed notes' were to be of great value; not only did they provide him with facts, but also, in wakening his memory 'to different sides' of Gregory's character, helped him to resolve some of the nagging questions about the nature of his achievement.

These questions and hesitations obtrude into his *Observer* article, and into letters he wrote to John Quinn and Iseult Gonne in the immediate aftermath of the death. He told both that he felt the loss more for Lady Gregory's sake than for Robert's, and tried to describe to them Robert's attributes:

> I think he had genius. Certainly no contemporary landscape moved me as much as two or three of his, except perhaps a certain landscape by Innes, from whom he had learned a good deal. His paintings had majesty and austerity, and at the same time sweetness. He was the most accomplished man I have ever known; he could do more things than any other.[6]

This does not quite take away as much as it gives, but it sounds like a man trying to convince himself. Yeats *thinks* Gregory has genius, and tries to justify this supposition by citing a few paintings, limited both as to genre ('contemporary landscape') and quantity ('two or three'); moreover, it appears that even these may perhaps be derivative of, and slightly inferior to, their model, the landscape of Innes. Writing to Iseult Gonne the following day, Yeats now credited Gregory with 'a strange pure genius, full of vast austere rhythms. I always felt that he had a luckless star and have expected the end'.[7] The descriptions (or are they qualifications?) of Gregory's genius, 'strange', 'pure', 'full of vast austere rhythms', hardly bring it into closer focus. The *Observer* article is more definite, but only by taking Lady Gregory's hint about 'the different sides':

> I have known no man accomplished in so many ways as Major Robert Gregory . . . His very accomplishment hid from many his genius. He had so many sides . . . that some among his friends were not sure what his work would be. To me he will always remain a great painter in the immaturity of his youth . . . Though he often seemed led away from his work by some other gift, his attitude to life and art never lost intensity—he was never the amateur.[8]

Rupert Brooke was twenty-eight when he was killed, Wilfrid Owen twenty-five; Robert Gregory was in his thirty-eight year, an age by which most great painters have gone well beyond the 'immaturity of . . . youth', and staked their claim to genius with more than two or three pictures. This Yeats knew, and the recurrent qualifications, 'hid from many', 'not sure what his work would be', 'immaturity of his youth', 'often seemed led away

5. Unpublished letter from Lady Gregory to Yeats, 10 February 1918.
6. *The Letters of W. B. Yeats*, ed. Allan Wade (London: Rupert Hart-Davis, 1954; New York: Macmillan, 1955), p. 646.
7. Unpublished letter from Yeats to Iseult Gonne, 9 February 1918.
8. "Major Robert Gregory." *The Observer*, 17 February 1918. Reprinted in *Uncollected Prose by W. B. Yeats*, vol. 2, ed. John P. Frayne and Colton Johnson (London: Macmillan, 1975), pp. 429–31.

from his work', indicate his lack of ease. Nor could the list of Gregory's other accomplishments have been very convincing to anyone who had known him. The Oxford Greats Examiners would have been amused to hear the young man upon whom they had conferred a third-class degree described as a 'classical scholar', and there is little evidence that his knowledge of art history or modern literature was in any way exceptional. Lady Gregory was all too aware of this. Her urgency in importuning Yeats to write an elegy arose from the very fact that without a poem so little would remain. In her letters she spoke of 'the cruel shortening of a life that was still so full of possibility . . .' and lamented that he 'had not built or planted or brought treasure, all he has left are those few beautiful pictures—& a good name'.[9]

The *Observer* paragraphs had been an immediate response, written at pressing request, and from the first he intended 'later on some fuller & more meaning thing'.[1] In addressing himself to a poem that would be fuller and more meaning, he had to review his attitude towards Gregory and to assess more exactly the achievements and meaning of his life. Given the relatively limited evidence of those achievements, and his ambivalence towards them, this was never going to be easy. One resource for avoiding a too intimate and problematic approach was to use a traditional form to distance and dignify the occasion. Thus when he first attempted 'to write something in verse about Robert' he found himself 'trying a poem in a manner like one that Spenser wrote for Sir Philip Sidney'.[2] * * *

Yeats probably showed Lady Gregory the [resulting] poem ["Shepherd and Goatherd"] for the first time when he went to stay at Coole with his bride in early April, and her reactions to it are unknown. It is hardly the poem she had expected, for she had looked for 'the intensity and crystallization of thought' that 'would go best into ones memory of him'. 'Shepherd and Goatherd' lacks both intensity and 'crystallization', and, almost certainly at her urging, he began another elegy during his visit. In this new poem Yeats developed lines of thought he had touched upon in his *Observer* comments and in the eclogue, and turned to poetic advantage the doubts he entertained about Gregory. In particular, he wanted to present Gregory's divided aims and plurality of interests as an illustration of a perfect identification of the man of action with the man of contemplation. Since this is a theme which much occupied Yeats, his imagination is more fully engaged in this poem than in 'Shepherd and Goatherd' and the 'true', under-achieving, biographical Gregory is transformed into a Paterian hero who has lived his life to its full intensity. Much of the success of the poem depends, as in many others where Yeats is attempting to mythologize his friends, upon its convincing the reader that this transformation is more than mere grandiloquence, more, that is, than a superior kind of poetic special pleading. Critics worried by possible objections on this score tend to point to Milton, and argue that the facts of Gregory's life are of no more interest to this poem than are those of that other lamented Anglo-

9. Unpublished letter from Lady Gregory to Yeats, 25 February 1918.
1. Unpublished letter from Yeats to Iseult Gonne, 9 February 1918.
2. *The Letters of W. B. Yeats*, p. 646.

Irishman, Edward King, to 'Lycidas'. Milton's relationship to King was, however, very different from that of Yeats to Gregory and, more importantly, to Lady Gregory. The poems about Robert were no mere exercises in the elegiac mode, but a written memorial in which a proud and grieving mother took a sometimes all too active interest:

> I have done nothing but . . . discuss with Lady Gregory the new stanza that is to commend Roberts courage in the hunting field. It has been a little thorny but we have settled a compromise. I have got from her a list of musical place-names where he has hunted & hope for a new representation of the place. I have firmly resisted all suggested eloquence about aero planes "& the blue Italian sky." It is pathetic for Lady Gregory constantly says it is his monument—"all that remains." I see that she feels that his pictures are as it were his thought but not himself.[3]

Yeats had, therefore, a more difficult task before him in writing this poem than had faced either Milton or Spenser: he was closer to Gregory than Milton had been to King, so that the historical presence cannot be so easily subsumed into the mythical; and, unlike Spenser's subject, Sidney, the historical presence had far less of the mythical in his achievements. Not only had Yeats to write a public celebration of a man about whom he had mixed feelings, but he had to do it in a way that, without compromising his own integrity, would satisfy a close friend and mother who was herself afraid that her son had failed to gain the worldly triumph that she thought was potentially his.

Once more Yeats turned to a traditional form, this time to Cowley's Ode on William Harvey. The ode proved a more congenial vehicle than pastoral blank verse, and in this poem tradition confers decorum without imposing conventionality; it distances the poet sufficiently from his raw material and yet enables him to sound the personal note all the more powerfully by allowing it to break through that very decorum. Following the practice of many of his mythologizing poems, Yeats begins with the here and now and establishes a rooted, domestic location in which to ground his later affirmations. In this case it is the turf fire and the ancient tower of Thoor Ballylee, Yeats's first house, and his first experience of settled married life with his new wife. Gregory himself does not enter the poem until Yeats has welcomed Johnson, Synge and George Pollexfen, three apparently random ghosts from his past but each illustrating in isolation gifts that Gregory is supposed to have combined. With Gregory's first appearance, almost half way through the poem, Yeats indicates at once the double nature of his role—as personal friend and yet also as a symbol of Renaissance man:

> my dear friend's dear son,
> Our Sidney and our perfect man[4]

3. Unpublished letter from Yeats to George Yeats, May 1918.
4. *The Variorum Edition of the Poems of W. B. Yeats*, ed. Peter Allt and Russell K. Alspach (New York: Macmillan, 1966), p. 325 [56].

One notices, as in 'Shepherd and Goatherd', how far Gregory's significance for Yeats is associated with his mother—that he was before all else 'my dear friend's dear son'. This gives the plural possessive pronouns, 'our', of the next line a measure of maternal as well as poetic license by allowing the hyperbolic comparison with Sidney to assume the tact of a mother's friend's overstatement. The following stanza establishes Gregory as a local man, a man to whom the flora and fauna of the Tower's landscape were actual experiences, and onto the immediacy of this physical presence Yeats begins to graft Gregory's mythical claims. He opens with the equestrian prowess he shared with George Pollexfen, and the names of the places where his exploits took place, insistently provided by Lady Gregory, help once more to underscore a physical, geographical and biographical presence. His ability as a horseman is attested in the naming of names; his ability as a painter was always in more doubt, and when Yeats turns to this aspect of his achievement he is more circumspect. The certainty of fact gives way to the tact of interpretation:

> We dreamed that a great painter had been born
> To cold Clare rock and Galway rock and thorn,
> To that stern colour and that delicate line
> That are our secret discipline
> Wherein the gazing heart doubles her might.[5]

'We *dreamed* that a great painter had been born' insists upon little more than a perhaps phantasmagoric hope, especially since the poem later indicates that dreams may come through the gates of horn as well as ivory ('What made us dream that he could comb grey hair?'), but the following lines absorb Gregory through the generosity of the plural pronouns into a tradition of visionary artists—stretching back to Blake and Palmer—among whom Yeats himself wished to be numbered. Without making any explicit claims for Gregory's talent as a painter Yeats has managed to confer importance upon him by association.

Thus far the poem has proceeded with tact and with a detailed texture that gives credence to the claims being advanced. Now Yeats moves into an assertive mode, proclaiming Gregory as

> Soldier, scholar, horseman, he,
> And yet he had the intensity
> To have published all to be a world's delight.[6]

We have had a stanza upon his horsemanship; his soldiering, scholarship and intensity we must, however, take on trust. It is significant that Yeats does not include 'painter' in the list of Gregory's proven abilities, so that his Paterian intensities are rather one-sided, more straightforwardly athletic than Pater would have thought strictly satisfying. Although Johnson and Synge have been invoked as examples of the choice that Gregory was to have made, there is little in the poem to convince us that he had Johnson's scholarly gifts, and even less to allow us to suppose that he partook of Synge's creative genius. For this reason, one must modify Frank Kermode's

5. Ibid., p. 326 [57].
6. Ibid., p. 327 [57].

brilliantly suggestive argument that the poem dramatizes the dilemma facing the Romantic artist of becoming a man of action or a man of contemplation. The theme seems more akin to the idea that those whom the gods
love die young, a notion close to that Lady Gregory advanced when she
described her son to Yeats as a bird which flies from tree to tree in the
knowledge of its early death.[7] Unease with the poem arises from the fact
that although, as Harold Bloom puts it, Gregory is more an Edward King
than a Sidney, Yeats insists on trying to pass him off as a Sidney. This
results in an unconvincing hyperbole: the overused 'all', in the unmediated
assertions 'all he did done perfectly', 'all life's epitome', and 'yet he had
the intensity / To have published all to be a world's delight' (which
prompts the question why by the age of thirty-seven he had 'published' so
little). The nagging doubt which this rhetoric tries to override also manifests itself in the curious image of the penultimate stanza

> Some burn damp faggots, others may consume
> The entire combustible world in one small room
> As though dried straw . . .[8]

Both Lady Gregory and Yeats had to agree that the compensation for
Gregory's under-achievement lay in the promise provided by his intensity,
intensity always being a privileged word in the Yeatsean lexicon. Intensity
is, of course, a primary Paterian virtue, but Pater commends his readers
to burn with a hard, gem-like flame, a persevering and all-but unquenchable energy, far different from the momentary flash of 'dried straw', which
can generate little heat and but brief illumination. Yeats must have been
aware of the limiting nature of his metaphor, and indeed, used it later
during an unsettled time to disparage his own lack of consistency.[9]

'In Memory of Major Robert Gregory' is a more unstable poem than is
often recognized, and a close reading shows how difficult it was for Yeats
to suppress the doubts and ambiguities he felt about its subject. The fact
that Lady Gregory was in constant attendance during the composition did
nothing to mitigate the problems that faced him, and yet it would be wrong
to see the desperate attempts at hyperbole as merely Yeats's deference to
her maternal insistences. Gregory's death, notwithstanding his children,
solved the problem of inheritance for Yeats. Nothing became Robert so
much as his untimely but military end; through it he could be drawn into
the myth of Coole from which Yeats had previously excluded him on
account of his lack of will. That lack of will, the plurality of interests that
it generated, was now turned to poetic account, and Gregory emerges as
a somewhat athletic Paterian hero who acts in accordance with a preordained fate. For once in a Coole poem Time becomes an accessory rather
than an enemy; in the poems about Lady Gregory, her memory is envisaged as defeating Time; in the poems about Robert, Time wins. They
invoke an unachieved Future: promise can be exuberantly celebrated for

---

7. Unpublished letter from Lady Gregory to Yeats, 25 February 1918.
8. *The Variorum Edition of the Poems of W. B. Yeats*, p. 327 [57].
9. Unpublished letter from Yeats to an unidentified correspondent, c. March 1923.

there is no longer the fear that promise will not be realized. Death, discourteous to the physical Gregory, enabled Yeats to be courteous to his memory.

* * *

THOMAS PARKINSON

The Passionate Syntax†

* * *

The proper ratio of naturalness to formality cannot be fixed in any rigorously systematic manner, but Yeats was constantly seeking the unique and intuitively felt ratio that would endow each poetic structure with its appropriate form. His rhymes reflect his preoccupation, for they are rhymes, clearly enough, but often very imperfect. One poem has the following rhyme pattern:

A	flare
A	ear
B	room
A	bore
B	womb
A	shows
A	knows
B	walk
A	clothes
B	talk
A	pains
A	sustains
B	stop
A	bones
B	up[1]

This is far from atypical of a rhyming habit that can produce such combinations as "gone–stone–sun," "intent–point," "house–luminous," "thought–begot," "on–man–Lane," all in one very formal poem ["Coole Park, 1929" (106–07)]. Because of his intent concern with meaning, and because his rhyme words often controlled meaning and established tone, his persistent assonance does not seem forced. Professor Wimsatt has discussed the novelty generated by Pope's refusal to rhyme noun with noun or verb with verb, so that the expected rhyming sound continued surprising

† From W. B. Yeats, *The Later Poetry*. Copyright © 1964 the Regents of the University of California, pp. 194–99. Reprinted by permission of University of California Press. Page references to this Norton Critical Edition are given in brackets after the author's original citations.
1. *The Variorum Edition of the Poems of W. B. Yeats*, ed. Peter Allt and Russell K. Alspach (New York: Macmillan, 1966), p. 499.

through centuries of couplets. Yeats achieved the opposite effect by upsetting the ear's expectancies and fulfilling the emotional currents of meaning:

> The light of evening, Lissadell,
> Great windows open to the south,
> Two girls in silk kimonos, both
> Beautiful, one a gazelle.[2]

Here the off-rhyme of "both" with "south" is rhetorically predictable by the antecedent "Two girls," and when the full rhyme comes, it does not clang heavily because the carryover of the preceding line holds the gazelle in its web. I do not mean by this that the rhymes are to be unnoticed, merely that they are to be seen as part of the line. The importance of this linear unity is engrossed by Yeats's tendency to present his matter in a long and overriding period. The result is a great deal of rhetorical repetition within a given stanza, fortified and at times undercut by the poetics, the insistence on linear form rather than periodic. In the reminiscent poems this is especially evident, and when in his commemorative poem for Eva Gore-Booth and Con Markiewicz he returns to the initial image of the two girls in silk kimonos, the repetition is qualified by the use of off-rhyme:

> Many a time I think to seek
> One or the other out and speak
> Of that old Georgian mansion, mix
> Pictures of the mind, recall
> That table and the talk of youth,
> Two girls in silk kimonos, both
> Beautiful, one a gazelle.[3]

As with all his refrains, this repetition is so changed by its context that its meaning has shifted, in this instance, from the original exaltation to muted sadness. The development of the poem has been a major force, and the rhyme of "recall–gazelle" merely fortifies the resigned imperfection of life so far presented. And since the initial image of the girls at the south window has been revised and qualified by the overlay of their later experience, the term "recall" implies effortfulness in evocation, and what was so sweetly and spontaneously present initially has by now become soiled and darkened by the irrelevancies of life. The imperfect rhyme is consonant with the imperfections of experience that have led from the prized recollection to this hesitant attempt to bring back to mind what had once occurred without conscious thought.

*   *   *

We do not, in reading Yeats's later poems, think of the off-rhymes as violations of perfection. They are too normal, too pervasive in the poetry's texture, to come as violations of expectation. When he rhymes, in "Sailing to Byzantium," "young" with "song" and "dress" with "magnificence" and "soul" with "animal," no principle is violated, no convention flaunted.

2. Ibid., p. 475 [102].
3. Ibid.

The rhymes require no more justification than do perfect rhymes, for they are striking only in their appropriateness.

With these provisos, it is still possible to see Yeats's off-rhymes as indices to his state of mind. In his early poems, the extremely rare off-rhymes asked to be forgiven, and this was easy enough to do on the infrequent occasions when charity required it. They were simply the sort of thing that is, at times, necessary. After the 1903 volume [*In the Seven Woods*], the frequency of off-rhyme increased until off-rhyme became a predictable part of the expectations of any reader of Yeats's verse. But like all the technical changes in Yeats's verse, this major shift was tightly bound up with the changes in the quality of experience that he took to be poetically admissible. The off-rhymes are comic not in the conventional sense but in the Yeatsean sense that they admit the presence of a world of divided imperfection, and the language of that world. They were part of his refusal to be ingratiating, and they were means of indicating the precedent claims of fullness. And these off-rhymes were not mere failures, second-best choices that he used only after he had tried unsuccessfully to make perfect rhymes. One of his habits in composing was to establish his possible rhymes and write to them, fill out the design thus offered. The rhyming of "bough" with "dew" in the second part of "Vacillation" was established early in the manuscript drafts, and when he wrote out a set of rhymes for this stanza, he accepted the rhyme without trouble:

> bough
> leaf
> dew
> chief
> anew
> belief
> grief[4]

And though he changed "anew" to "renew" and altered "leaf," "chief," and "belief," he accepted "bough" and "dew." He was not deterred by their obvious imperfection.

He did not say, "Well, let's rough it up a bit here and make it awkward there; that will make it seem mussed and *real*." The truth was that the off-rhymes were to his mind normal, not violations of convention but in effect the establishment of patterns that were in themselves valid. They made his already tightly linked—by internal sound pattern, by syntax—poems more linear. The assonant rhymes of Wilfred Owen, by contrast, do not make the poems linear but instead call attention, by their insistent harshness, to themselves. With Owen, we are always aware that the poems are rhyming very oddly; with Yeats, we know that they rhyme, but we see the rhyme, important as it is, as part of a general interweaving of sound and assertion. One virtue of his prosody is its insistence on the line as unit, and off-rhyme was a device strengthening this insistence.

* * *

---

4. Unpublished MS.

RONALD SCHUCHARD

Hawk and Butterfly: The Double Vision of
The Wild Swans at Coole (1917, 1919)†

There are two distinct volumes under the title *The Wild Swans at Coole*: the Cuala Press edition of 1917—its twenty-three lyrics swelled to volume size by the inclusion of *At the Hawk's Well*—and the Macmillan edition of 1919, which absorbed the former volume, minus the play, and added seventeen startlingly different poems.[1] Though they share the same title, they are the sun and the moon apart—the former a solar volume, mired in the emotional realities and intellectual hatreds of the objective world, the latter a lunar volume, lifted by the recovery of a subjective reality that leads the poet back to a lost visionary plane. In 1919, at the cost of obscuring the sequential nature of the volumes and the dramatic transformation that had taken place in the seventeen months that separate them, Yeats deliberately conflated the two groups of poems and distorted their chronology, evidently to prevent people from knowing "too much about his personal concerns".[2] Thus, in the *Collected Poems*, readers of the *The Wild Swans at Coole* have long encountered a lengthy, not-so-heady volume of very mixed wine. What I want to do is to pull apart these antithetical volumes, to take the reader, first, out of the *Collected Poems* and back to that dark-blue, linen-backed, paper-labelled volume that issued from the Cuala Press in November 1917, a volume "rhymed out in love's despair" (*VP*[3] 337) [60], and then to trace in the new poems of 1918 the liberation of Yeats's visionary imagination, the transference of rational thoughts into magical images, the recovery of a joy and an ecstacy that had abandoned his poems for over a decade.

It is merely coincidental that T. S. Eliot's *Prufrock and Other Observations* also appeared in 1917, some months earlier, but I would like to draw briefly on the audience's familiarity with the sensibility of Eliot's famous persona to suggest that the first issue of the *The Wild Swans at Coole* is Yeats's Prufrock volume—one in which the poetic sensibility is tormented by a growing consciousness of age, by his awareness of a higher plane of existence that is presently inaccessible to him, by an intense awareness of an intellectual and emotional predicament from which he is powerless to extricate himself, by the nightmarish figures of unnamed women who haunt the corridors and the stairways of his consciousness, by a self-mockery and a self-contempt that would make even Prufrock shudder. The exhaustion of mind and spirit leads to premature cries of age—"I am worn

† From *Yeats Annual* 10 (1993): 111–34. Reprinted by permission of Ronald Schuchard, Goodrich C. White Professor of English, Emory University. Page references to this Norton Critical Edition are given in brackets after the author's original citations.
1. An earlier version of this essay was presented at the Thirty-Second Yeats International Summer School, Sligo, Ireland, 15 August 1991.
2. See A. Norman Jeffares, *A New Commentary on the Poems of W. B. Yeats* (London: Macmillan, 1984) p. 129.
3. *The Variorum Edition of the Poems of W. B. Yeats*, ed. Peter Allt and Russell K. Alspach (New York: Macmillan, 1966).

out with dreams", he says—"A weather-worn, marble triton / Among the streams" (VP 329) [58]. But there are worse fears: for Prufrock, in distraction, the eternal dispossession of his unexamined soul; for Yeats, in dejection, the permanent loss of his visionary imagination and creative power. Even in his title poem that fear is subtly at work.

In "The Wild Swans at Coole" the suddenly departing swans leave behind their emphatic actuality, all "nine-and-fifty" rapidly taking on their "mysterious", symbolic attributes as unwearied emblems of supernatural beauty, as visitants from a cold, companionable world from which they make temporal incursions and returns. But as the poet follows these "brilliant creatures" the reader tends to leave the lake at Coole in its actual "autumn beauty", when in fact Yeats internalises the lake—for nineteen years a place of wondrous visitations—as a symbol of the divine imagination, of the mind of Nature. The lake is enfolded by illusions of stillness, just at twilight, that Yeatsian moment when wakefulness fades into dream. If you sound the poem for your auditory imagination, listen anew to the repetition of "twilight" and the quadruple repetition of "still", which describes the illusory state of the sky, the water and the immortal attributes of the swans themselves. The brimming water, held in a twilight stillness, trembles like the Veil of the Temple, and to confirm its symbolic nature we look only to a companion poem, "Broken Dreams", where we encounter again "that mysterious, always brimming lake / Where those that have obeyed the holy law / Paddle and are perfect" (VP 356) [65]. The swans, in alighting, metaphorically break the viscosity of the mysterious lake, which floods the poet's mind with images, and in that visionary moment the swans are seen to "drift on the still water", an image taken from the second edition of *The Celtic Twilight* (1902), where he added the stories collected at Coole:

> Images form themselves in our minds perpetually as if they were reflected in some pool. . . . We can make our minds so like still water that beings gather about us that they may see, it may be, their own images, and so live for a moment with a clearer, perhaps even with a fiercer life because of our quiet. (*Myth*[4] 80)

But it is clear in the poem that the poet has not obeyed the holy law of visionary ascent, that he has lost the fiercer life of passion derived from vision. Indeed, this is a poem of remembered vision only, a poem generated by a dejected sense of physical and imaginative change. "All's changed", laments the poet, who is ironically "asleep" in his heavy-hearted, solar reality from which he cannot awaken. His fear lies in awakening to a world without delight, to what he later calls the swan's "desolate heaven" (VP 431) [94].

> Among what rushes will they build,
> By what lake's edge or pool
> Delight men's eyes when I awake some day
> To find they have flown away?   (VP 323) [55]

4. W. B. Yeats, *Mythologies* (New York: Macmillan, 1959).

There are no impending arrivals; this is a poem darkened by departures.

This disturbed separation from a subjective plane dominates and determines the poet's relation to his, art in the volume. In "Lines Written in Dejection" he is first embittered by his entrapment in the social and political arms of a solar reality, "timid" to discover the harsh-lit, maddened objects in its surface-searching light. Shut out from contact with the elemental beings of a lunar world—the dark leopards, the wild witches, the holy centaurs, the magical images evoked in the vision-seeking mind—Yeats's bitterness over banishment turns to dejection over vanishment, his rich images having left him in a world of barren thoughts to be tormented by knaves, dolts, the mob:

> The holy centaurs of the hills are vanished;
> I have nothing but the embittered sun;
> Banished heroic mother moon and vanished,
> And now that I have come to fifty years
> I must endure the timid sun.   (VP 344) [61]

As his mind deflates in disgust and despair, so does his diction in those tossed-off quatrains and sestets of self-contempt, as in "The Balloon of the Mind", where the earth-skidding imagination is hauled back into its "narrow shed" because it "bellies and drags" in the solar wind (VP 358) [65]; as in "On Being Asked for a War Poem", where in declining the invitation he declares that the poetic act, described as an act of "meddling" (VP 359) [65], is sufficient if it please an indolent young girl or an infirm old man, thereby declaring his indulgent, sentimental art unworthy of its muse and of his distant visionary masters.

The other hook on the anchor of his mind is the "curse" of Maud Gonne, whose altered presence inhabits nine poems in the volume. Yeats's double depression is nowhere more dramatically expressed than in the appended play, At the Hawk's Well, where the Old Man, cut off from the immortal images of the well for fifty years by the vigilant Hawk of Thought, tells young Cuchulain not only of the futility of waiting, but of another curse that awaits him: "Never to win a woman's love and keep it; / Or always to mix hatred in the love" (VPl[5] 407) [165]. In "On Woman" we discover Maud Gonne curiously alluded to as the "Perverse creature of chance" (VP 346) [62] to whom his creative fate has been inexorably tied. Indeed, we have never seen Maud Gonne as we see her in this volume. We must look back to 1903, when she broke what he calls here her "deep-sworn vow" (VP 357), a vow to marry no one else, to have a spiritual marriage to him during their active lives, and to be together in old age. When she married John MacBride in that year, the worst year of Yeats's life, his cynical friend, the painter Charles Ricketts, wrote to Michael Field: "Have you heard the news that Maud Gonne has gone and left Yeats and the future of Ireland for matrimony and comfortable Catholi-

---

5. The Variorum Edition of the Plays of W. B. Yeats, ed. Russell K. Alspach (London: Macmillan, 1966).

cism? Yeats is unconsolable in sonnets of the Oh thou! type to various little lilts and tunes."[6] And that is cruelly characteristic of the poems that shortly made their way into *In the Seven Woods*: "O heart! O heart! if she'd but turn her head, / You'd know the folly of being comforted" (*VP* 200) [31].

During the next thirteen years, in *The Green Helmet and Other Poems* (1912) and in the two editions of *Responsibilities* (1914, 1916), Maud Gonne was elevated in the poetry to an heroic position on a mythological plane, "Helenised", we might say. But in 1908, three years after her separation from MacBride, she told Yeats in Paris that she had truly loved him all those years, and the consummation of their love then—in the Big Year—is recorded here in the guise of Solomon and Sheba in "On Woman":

> Harshness of their desire
> That made them stretch and yawn,
> Pleasure that comes with sleep,
> Shudder that made them one. (*VP* 345–6) [61–62]

The union in 1908 was for Yeats a brief incarnation of his long-held dream of an occult marriage,[7] and within months he was to embody the discipline and wisdom of such a marriage in the love of Solomon and Sheba, a love which "must have lasted for all the silence of the Scriptures" (*Mem*[8] 144–5). In such an ideal marriage, Yeats proclaimed in his diary, both lovers achieve their masks:

> In wise love each divines the high secret self of the other and, refusing to believe in the mere daily self, creates a mirror where the lover or the beloved sees an image to copy in daily life. Love also creates the mask. (*Mem* 145)

Yeats's belief that their occult, sexually-satisfying marriage would eventually materialise remained unbroken, but in "On Woman", written on 25 May 1914, just after investigating the miracle at Mirabeau with Maud Gonne and Everard Feilding, the fantasy of the Solomon/Sheba union was momentarily broken by his despairing, teeth-gnashing realisation that his "Perverse creature of chance" had failed to incarnate as Sheba to his Solomon. He continued to dream that part of the broken vow would be honoured—to be together in old age—but in July 1916, three months after the execution of MacBride, she refused his proposal for the last, devastating time. The wild distraction, the dispossession, weigh heavily on the poetry, but it must be seen that it was not until the 1919 edition of *The Wild Swans*, in "Solomon to Sheba", written in March 1918, and later in "Solomon and the Witch" (1921), also written in 1918, that Yeats trans-

---

6. Manuscript draft letter in Diary for 1903, British Library (*BL Add. MS.* 58088).
7. For a reconstruction of the earliest phase of that dream, see Warwick Gould and Deirdre Toomey, " 'Cycles Ago . . .': Maud Gonne and the Lyrics of 1891", *Yeats Annual* 7: 184–93.
8. W. B. Yeats, *Memoirs*, ed. Denis Donoghue (London: Macmillan, 1972).

ferred the Solomon/Sheba trope to what became his spiritistic marriage to Georgie Hyde-Lees.[9]

His impulse in 1916, of course, was to escape Maud Gonne's rejection, to set sail like Oisin for an untroubled country of the mind, where among the daughters of kings he would "learn that the best thing is / To change my loves while dancing / And pay but a kiss for a kiss", there to peer serenely through the collar-bone of a hare "At the old bitter world where they marry in churches" (VP 330). But Yeats was incapable of such passive detachment, and in *The Wild Swans at Coole* we can hear his idealised Helen plummet through clouds of myth to land in Dublin clay. In his frustrated desire to seize her in his physical world, he deliberately names her flaw in "Broken Dreams", named to prevent her swan-like departure into the symbolic imagination once again:

> You are more beautiful than any one,
> And yet your body had a flaw:
> Your small hands were not beautiful,
>   . . . Leave unchanged
> The hands that I have kissed,
> For old sake's sake.   (VP 356–7) [65]

Her grey hair, her fading beauty, which brings no catch in any young man's breath, make her in "Her Praise" "foremost of those that I would hear praised", as though by manipulating public praise of her past he can hold her in the present: "I have turned the talk by hook or crook / Until her praise should be the uppermost theme, / . . . I have found / Some beggar sheltering from the wind, and there / Manage the talk until her name come round" (VP 350–1). In other poems his vague, self-demeaning memories of her reduce him to "rambling talk with an image of air", make him live again old emotional pains: "I was abashed, and now

---

9. The confusion has been fostered by the fact that Yeats placed "Solomon to Sheba" before "On Woman" in the mixed arrangement of the 1919 edition. After Yeats married in October 1917, Maud Gonne remained Helen, and was still Helen when, as Richard Ellmann observed, Yeats recorded that unfading consummation again in "His Memories" (1926):

> My arms are like the twisted thorn
> And yet there beauty lay;
>
> The first of all the tribe lay there
> And did such pleasure take—
> She who had brought great Hector down
> And put all Troy to wreck—
> That she cried into this ear,
> "Strike me if I shriek."   (VP 455)

See Richard Ellmann, *Yeats: The Man and the Masks*, corrected edition with a new Preface (Oxford: Oxford University Press, 1979) pp. xxvi–xxvii; hereafter cited as *YMM* in the text.

A recently discovered Solomon/Sheba poem ("Am I a fool or a wise man?") is inserted undated among drafts for *The Wild Swans at Coole* in NLI [National Library of Ireland], but doubtless it is addressed in despair to Maud Gonne before his marriage to Georgie. The poet depicts himself as a folly-ridden Solomon who knows not whether his futile attempts to school himself in the closed "labyrinth" of Sheba's mind will prove him to be a wise man or "but a fool". See *Yeats Annual* 6: 211–13.

they [her words] come to mind / After nine years, I sink my head abashed" (VP 357, 353) [65, 64].[1] * * *

The folly of his first proposal, in August 1916, to Iseult Gonne (daughter of Maud and Millevoye, conceived in the vault of their first child, Georges, late in 1893) only redoubled the emotional exhaustion and desperation. If at forty-nine he lamented in ["*Pardon, Old Fathers*"] [42] the absence of a child in his name, at fifty-one he is haunted in memories and dreams by images and forms of women whose unwedded love has passed him by. * * *

As we thumb through these highly autobiographical poems we see Yeats fallen into the circle of himself, and the imprisoning self-pity over unrequited love can become so self-mocking that he traps in a quatrain a squirrel at Kyle-na-no, who flees the poet's outreached hand "When / all I would do / Is to scratch your head / And let you go" (VP 359).

* * * [W]here, we must ask, is the visionary Yeats of old, the poet of "*To Ireland in the Coming Times*", whose "*rhymes more than their rhyming tell / Of things discovered in the deep*", and whose "*elemental creatures . . . hurry from unmeasured mind / To rant and rage in flood and wind*" (VP 138) [21]? Since *The Wind Among the Reeds* (1899) the poems have been not a revelation of a hidden life but an Arnoldian "criticism of life", steeped in bitterness and love's despair. Where is the poet who prophesied a magical revolution, who proclaimed in apocalyptic language the coming of a supersensual apprehension of reality? The poet had not lost his lyric force—the poems mount in number—but he had lost his visionary power; he had lost access to his antithetical self. So profoundly self-absorbed is the first issue of *The Wild Swans at Coole*, and so successfully does its tone dominate the mixed arrangement of the 1919 volume, that we might look less impatiently at John Middleton Murry's review of the work as "a swan song. It is eloquent of final defeat; the following of a lonely path had ended in the poet's sinking exhausted in a wilderness of grey. Not even the regret is passionate; it is pitiful."[2] Where is the modern leader of what he had called "the processional order" (*EƠI*[3] 191) of visionary poets and painters—Titian, Blake, Shelley, Rossetti? Ah! he is there, slowly rising phoenix-like from his ashes in two of the earliest poems in the volume— "The Fisherman", written in June 1914, and "Ego Dominus Tuus", written in December 1915. These remarkable poems floated like swans over the despairing poetry until they alighted in the volume as harbingers of a visionary re-awakening. Even as the volume went to press he was silently writing *Per Amica Silentia Lunae* as "a kind of prose backing to my poetry"

---

1. The poem manifestly derives from a reproach of Maud Gonne's in a letter of 7 May 1907. She contrasted Yeats's "unjust" attitude to "our people at home" with her own situation, in which "the frauds who I had exposed, the publicans & drunkards I had driven out the cowards who I had made own their cowardice all join MacBride's party & whisper calumny against me—but in neither of our cases were the people generally to blame". See Anna MacBride White and A. Norman Jeffares (eds), *Always Your Friend: Letters between Maud Gonne and W. B. Yeats 1893–1938* (London: Hutchinson, 1992) pp. 240–1.
2. "Mr Yeats's Swan Song" appeared in *The Athenaeum* (4 April 1919), rpt. in *W. B. Yeats: The Critical Heritage*, edited by A. Norman Jeffares (London: Routledge & Kegan Paul, 1977) pp. 216–20, at p. 218.
3. W. B. Yeats, *Essays and Introductions* (London: Macmillan, 1961).

(L^4 625), a volume in which "Ego Dominus Tuus" would find its proper place as preface.

*   *   *

Maud Gonne's final refusal of marriage in the summer of 1916 led him to resume *Per Amica* as a body of support for the kind of visionary poetry he *hoped* to write even as he wrote the poems of despair. Its Preface, "Ego Dominus Tuus", is a dialogue between the Latinately impersonal *Hic* and *Ille* (but Ezra Pound tells us that they are *Hic* and *Willie* [*YMM* 197]). Here *"Willie"* dissociates himself from those raven-pecked poets deluded by the modern hope of finding the self. *Hic* might well be a Lionel Johnson or an Ernest Dowson, but he is also Yeats's other self, one who had fallen on "the gentle, sensitive mind / And lost the old nonchalance of the hand" (*VP* 368) [66]. As he wrote in *Per Amica*,

> Some years ago I began to believe that our culture, with its doctrine of sincerity and self-realisation, made us gentle and passive, and that the Middle Ages and the Renaissance were right to found theirs upon the imitation of Christ or of some classic hero. Saint Francis and Caesar Borgia made themselves overmastering, creative persons by turning from the mirror to meditation upon a mask. When I had this thought I could see nothing else in life.   (*Myth* 333–4)

All who turn to the mirror are, to *"Willie"*, "but critics, or but half create, / Timid, entangled, empty and abashed" ("abashed", right out of his previous poem to Maud Gonne). He asks impatiently of them all: "What portion in the world can the artist have / Who has awakened from the common dream / But dissipation and despair?" (*VP* 369) [67]. But our main interest is in his search for an image that will lead him to the "mysterious one", the anti-self who will disclose in vision all that is sought. The full importance of this confrontation to Yeats, however, is lost unless we return to the source of the poem in the opening passages of the *Vita Nuova*, where Dante meets his anti-self, the Lord of Terrible Aspect. Nine years had elapsed since Dante last beheld his "wonderful lady", and when she turned her eyes toward him he stood "sorely abashed". I quote from Rossetti's translation, used by Yeats:

> And betaking me to the loneliness of mine own room, I fell to thinking of this most courteous lady, thinking of whom I was overtaken by a pleasant slumber, wherein a marvellous vision was presented to me: for there appeared to be in my room a mist of the colour of fire, within the which I discerned the figure of a lord of terrible aspect to such as should gaze upon him, but who seemed there-withal to rejoice inwardly that it was a marvel to see. Speaking he said many things . . . and of these, this: *Ego dominus tuus* [I am thy master]. In his arms it seemed to me that a person was sleeping, covered only with a blood-coloured cloth; upon whom looking very attentively, I knew that it was the lady. . . . And he who held her held also in his hand a thing that was burning in flames; and he said to me, *Vide cor*

---

4. *The Letters of W. B. Yeats*, ed. Allan Wade (London: Rupert Hart-Davis, 1954; New York: Macmillan, 1955).

tuum [Behold thy heart]. But when he had remained with me a little while, I thought that he set himself to awaken her that slept; after the which he made her to eat that thing which flamed in his hand; and she ate as one fearing. Then, having waited again a space, all his joy was turned into most bitter weeping; and as he wept he gathered the lady into his arms, and it seemed to me that he went with her up towards heaven.[5]

* * * "Ego Dominus Tuus" describes Yeats's way of visionary liberation from a mourned Maud Gonne and the "blasphemous men" of the objective world. It brings a new "vision of reality" to his art, a new life to the poet. Its presence both appeases and intensifies the abiding pain in that first gathering of *The Wild Swans at Coole*.

At this same time Yeats was writing *At the Hawk's Well* as an allegory of his paralysing struggle with thought. The Old Man, his imagination long parched, looks painfully upon the young Cuchulain who, duped himself by the guardian hawk, comes out of his dream and leaves the immortal well to engage in illusory combat with the guardian's troops, "the fierce women of the hills". The musicians' song that closes the action underscores the imaginative desolation in the play:

> Come to me, human faces,
> Familiar memories;
> I have found hateful eyes
> Among the desolate places,
> Unfaltering, unmoistened eyes.
>
> . . . .
> O lamentable shadows,
> Obscurity of strife! . . .
> Wisdom must live a bitter life.
>
> (VPI 412–13) [168]

Between these works, Yeats appears as the forlorn Arnoldian figure, wandering between two worlds, or, to anticipate the coming imagery, pulled between the dark and the full of the moon. But in that terrible summer of refusals in 1916, Yeats was reading with Iseult the new French Catholic poets, and that experience pushed him closer to a full embrasure of the ancient revelation. * * *

But more bitterness and disappointment *were* at hand. In the summer of 1917 Iseult refused him for the second time. The poems rhymed out in despair to her—"The Living Beauty", "To a Young Beauty" and "To a Young Girl"—were too late for the first edition of *The Wild Swans at Coole* but are characteristic of it. The next month Georgie Hyde-Lees accepted him, and on 20 October they were married.

Yeats entered that marriage in a state of "great gloom", feeling that he had betrayed all three women—Maud, Iseult, George. A week into the marriage, perhaps to divert his mood, George Yeats surprised him by attempting automatic writing. On the 29th he wrote to Lady Gregory, who knew of his troubled state:

5. *The Early Italian Poets*, trans. D. G. Rossetti (London: George Newnes, 1904) pp. 173–4.

The last two days Georgie and I have been very happy . . . There has been something very like a miraculous intervention. . . . From being more miserable than I ever remember being since Maud Gonne's marriage I became extremely happy. That sense of happiness has lasted ever since.   (L 633)

The miraculous intervention that dispelled fourteen years of gloom took place on 27 October, when the spirit communicators announced that they had come to give him metaphors of poetry. The long struggle back to the spirit world that had been lost with Maud Gonne was over. With that intervention a dubious marriage was miraculously transformed into a spir-itistic union that Yeats would celebrate in "Solomon to Sheba":

> "There's not a man or woman
> Born under the skies
> Dare match in learning with us two,
> And all day long we have found
> There's not a thing but love can make
> The world a narrow pound."   (VP 333)

That union made, the spirit masters shook the ravens from the holy tree and the new poems came in abundance.[6]

* * *

Yeats had first used the butterfly as his symbol of non-rational wisdom in *The Hour Glass*, composed late in 1902 before the deep-sworn vow was broken, a play in which the "little winged thing" that flies from the Wise Man's mouth in death is caught in the hands of the Angel, who will release it again "in the Garden of Paradise" (VP1 638).[7] Disconnected allusions to the butterfly began to appear in the automatic script, particularly in the exhaustive session of 22 November 1917, and George later drew the figures of a butterfly and a hawk in an elaborate diagram dated 7 January 1919.[8] Evoking the image of the butterfly in *Per Amica Silentia Lunae*, Yeats wrote:

> But the passions, when we know that they cannot find fulfilment, become vision; and a vision, whether we wake or sleep, prolongs its power by rhythm and pattern, the wheel where the world is butterfly. We need no protection, but it does, for if we become interested in *ourselves*, in our *own* lives, we pass out of the vision. (*Myth* 341; emphasis added)

The passage, which plays upon Pope's satiric question in *Epistle to Dr Arbuthnot*, "Who breaks a butterfly upon a wheel?", points us to that

---

6. The first two poems to come from the intervention were "The Lover Speaks" and "The Heart Replies", sent to Lady Gregory for safekeeping and described as "among the best I have done" (L 633–4). They were not published until 1924 and were included in *The Tower* under the single title "Owen Aherne and his Dancers".
7. Yeats sharpened the image as "the white butterfly" in the 1914 version of *The Hour Glass* (VP 639).
8. See George Mills Harper, *The Making of Yeats's 'A Vision'*, vol. I (Carbondale and Edwardsville: Southern Illinois Univ. Press, 1987) p. 52; vol. II, p. 199. Professor Harper interprets the diagram as an illustration of "Another Song of a Fool", but the multiple symbols (eye, hand, book, butterfly, hawk, cross, tower) invite further interpretation.

distant, oddly titled volume of plays *Wheels and Butterflies* (1934), where the wheel is the gyre of the mind that enables it to seek the mask and prolong vision in rhythm and pattern, the butterfly the aimless but instinctive movement of image toward the mask. In the epigraph to that book he says, in pity for those writers in Garrets and Cellars who are disciples of the hawk:

> To Garret or Cellar a wheel I send,
> But every butterfly to a friend.   (p. v)

So crucial was the butterfly to his struggle with the hawk that he had a ring forged with the symbols. And when, in *The Tower*, he came to contemplate the coming emptiness of heart, in part VII of "Meditations in Time of Civil War", he inevitably saw the "musing eyes" of the ladies on magical unicorns "Give place to an indifferent multitude, give place / To brazen hawks" (*VP* 427) [91]. "I suppose", he wrote in a note to the poem; "that I must have put hawks into the fourth stanza because I have a ring with a hawk and a butterfly upon it, to symbolise the straight road of logic, and so of mechanism, and the crooked road of intuition: 'For wisdom is a butterfly and not a gloomy bird of prey'—1928" (*VP* 827).

Tom O'Roughley's lines had become Yeats's motto, the lines that he would most frequently inscribe in his books for the next twenty years.[9] And when, on 22 September 1934, William Force Stead wrote to Yeats for an interpretation of his own meditation on Wisdom, described as a series of images that changed in shape from a candle to a butterfly, making him think that he "had passed from wisdom to Folly", Stead wanted to know more about the symbolism of the butterfly. Yeats had already explained that "the Butterfly is the symbol of the highest Wisdom",[1] but in reiteration of his earlier statements he responded:

> The Butterfly is the main symbol in my ring—the ring I always wear. The other symbol is the Hawk. The Hawk is the straight road of logic, the Butterfly the crooked road of intuition—the Hawk pounces, the Butterfly flutters. . . . I suggest that your candle is knowledge, conscious effort, thought; & the butterfly the wisdom out of the unconscious that follows. A Japanese describes the attainment of nirvana in these words 'Something delightful has happened to the young man but he can only tell it to his sweetheart'.[2]

* * * There are critics who argue that Yeats was guilty of insincerity in his elegies to Robert Gregory, failing to see that he came to write them

---

9. On 6 July 1928 Yeats wrote to Thomas Sturge Moore: "when I sign a book for anybody I put a line of verse, very commonly 'For wisdom is a butterfly and not a gloomy bird of prey'. . . . Can you leave me space on that design for such a line?" Yeats wanted to print the line on a paper label that Sturge Moore had designed "to paste over the Ricketts endpaper in the Collected Edition", but additional volumes of the Collected Edition (Macmillan) were delayed and the label, reproduced in *Yeats Annual 4*, 180, was never used. See *W. B. Yeats and T. Sturge Moore: Their Correspondence, 1901–1937*, ed. Ursula Bridge (London: Routledge and Kegan Paul, 1953), 132, 140.

1. See George Mills Harper, "William Force Stead's Friendship with Yeats and Eliot", *Massachusetts Review*, 21 (Spring 1980) p. 22.

2. Unpublished letter (private) of 26 September 1934, quoted by permission of Michael B. Yeats and Anne Yeats.

in a brimming state of mind, heightened and exhilarated by the recovery of an ecstatic vision that he could not keep from the elegiac poems.[3]

* * *

Indeed, the persistent theme of these new poems is the necessary movement from knowledge to ignorance, from thought to image, to states of mind preparatory to vision. "I would be ignorant as the dawn", he writes in expectation. "I would be—for no knowledge is worth a straw— / Ignorant and wanton as the dawn" (VP 344). Even the Goatherd describes Robert Gregory's "dreaming back" at the moment of his death as a dream that carries him from knowledge to a "sweeter ignorance" that leads to rebirth:

> "Knowledge he shall unwind
> Through victories of the mind . . .
> All knowledge lost in trance
> Of sweeter ignorance."   (VP 343)

In "The Phases of the Moon" Aherne and Robartes mock the solitary poet in the tower who discovers "Mere images". When Aherne asks Robartes why he does not take his truths to the poet, Robartes recalls that the poet excluded him from consciousness years ago, that he "Said I was dead; and dead I choose to be". Out of the poet's hearing, Robartes describes the movement of phases toward complete subjectivity, and when Aherne asks him to sing out "The strange reward of all that discipline" Robartes declares that in the visionary moment "All thought becomes an image and the soul / Becomes a body" (VP 374). He goes on to describe that moment for "creatures of the full", who seek to embody the soul and behold in vision their beloved, indifferent objects:

> Caught up in contemplation, the mind's eye
> Fixed upon images that once were thought;
> For separate, perfect, and immovable
> Images can break the solitude
> Of lovely, satisfied, indifferent eyes.   (VP 375)

His lines recall not only Dante's vision of Beatrice in the arms of the Lord of Terrible Aspect, but "the mysterious one" who will disclose all that the poet seeks.

In the companion poem which fittingly concludes the new volume, "The Double Vision of Michael Robartes", Robartes, who has returned to the poet as persona once again, calls to the mind's eye the figures of a Sphinx and a Buddha, who gaze in thought and love upon all things known and unknown, loved and unloved. Between the two appears a second vision of a dancing girl who, in bodily perfection, "had outdanced thought". In the full moon of this "fifteenth night" (VP 383) [69], Robartes achieves "at last" an ecstatic vision of "That girl my unremembering nights

---

3. John S. Kelly makes a sustained case against the sincerity of the poems in " 'Friendship Is All the House I Have': Lady Gregory and W. B. Yeats", in *Lady Gregory, Fifty Years After* (Gerrards Cross, Bucks: Colin Smythe, 1987) pp. 234–45, arguing that "Gregory is being manipulated in ["An Irish Airman"] for Yeats's merely polemical purposes" (p. 245) [see pp. 407–13 in this volume].

hold fast" (*VP* 384) [70]. The nature and effect of that vision are described in *A Vision*, where the fifteenth night becomes phase fifteen:

> Now contemplation and desire, united into one, inhabit a world where every beloved image has bodily form, and every bodily form is loved. This love knows nothing of desire, for desire implies effort, and though there is still separation from the loved object, love accepts the separation as necessary to its own existence.   (*AV B*⁴ 136)

Only in the aftermath of that aimless joy, in the natural world of desire, does Robartes reveal the emotional wrenching that comes with recognition of the meaning of his vision. His association of the dancing girl with "Homer's Paragon", the indifferent figure of Helen, Maud Gonne, leads him once again into a demeaning "pitch of folly". Torn between the pull of the dark moon and the full, he recalls again the great antagonism, "The commonness of thought and images / That have the frenzy of our western seas". With a great "moan" Robartes mourns his lost object, but in his painful recognition there is both acceptance and gratitude. Out of that long personal conflict has come at last the transcendent poem to the patient poet who had ironically been ignorant of ignorance so long:

> Thereon I made my moan,
> And after kissed a stone,
>
> And after that arranged it in a song
> Seeing that I, ignorant for so long,
> Had been rewarded thus
> In Cormac's ruined house.
>   (*VP* 384) [70]

When the two antithetical gyres of the 1917 and 1919 volumes (see Figure 1) are allowed to interlock once again in the *Collected Poems*, we can see perning there the conflict of the objective and subjective selves: we can see a despairing poet achieve his joyous mask. Though Yeats did not name *The Wild Swans at Coole* among his strongest volumes, it stems from the most dramatic and productive period of his life. In fact, most of the poems collected in *Michael Robartes and the Dancer* (1921) were written between 1914 and 1919 and are late-published fragments of the former volume rather than sequential to it—including the title poem, the poems of the Easter Rebellion, "Solomon and the Witch" and "Demon and Beast", in which an "aimless joy" (*VP* 400) accompanies the poet's newfound freedom from hatred and desire. By 1919 Yeats had begun to redirect much of his poetic energy to completing the play whose abstract thought had tormented him since 1907, *The Player Queen* (1922), and to transforming the dialogue of Aherne and Robartes into *A Vision* (1925).

Looking back from a distance, Yeats saw his poetic strength gathered in the greater simplicity of *The Tower* (1928). "I can now", he wrote in his "Dedication" to *A Vision*, "if I have the energy, find the simplicity I have sought in vain. I need no longer write poems like 'The Phases of the Moon'

4. W. B. Yeats, *A Vision* (London: Macmillan, 1962).

nor 'Ego Dominus Tuus,' nor spend barren years . . . striving with abstractions that substituted themselves for the play that I had planned" (AV A[5] xii). But he must have sensed that *The Wild Swans at Coole* was the

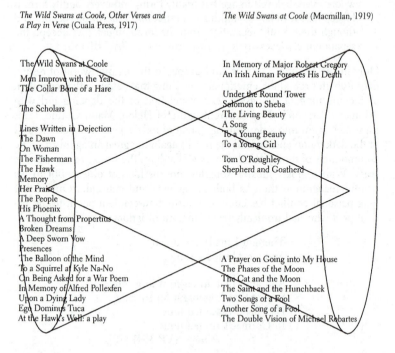

The Wild Swans at Coole, Other Verses and a Play in Verse (Cuala Press, 1917)

The Wild Swans at Coole (Macmillan, 1919)

The Wild Swans at Coole
Men Improve with the Years
The Collar Bone of a Hare

The Scholars

Lines Written in Dejection
The Dawn
On Woman
The Fisherman
The Hawk
Memory
Her Praise
The People
His Phoenix
A Thought from Propertius
Broken Dreams
A Deep Sworn Vow
Presences
The Balloon of the Mind
To a Squirrel at Kyle Na-No
On Being Asked for a War Poem
In Memory of Alfred Pollexfen
Upon a Dying Lady
Ego Dominus Tuca
At the Hawk's Well: a play

In Memory of Major Robert Gregory
An Irish Airman Foresees His Death

Under the Round Tower
Solomon to Sheba
The Living Beauty
A Song
To a Young Beauty
To a Young Girl

Tom O'Roughley
Shepherd and Goatherd

A Prayer on Going into My House
The Phases of the Moon
The Cat and the Moon
The Saint and the Hunchback
Two Songs of a Fool
Another Song of a Fool
The Double Vision of Michael Robartes

Figure 1   The gyres of *The Wild Swans at Coole*

watershed for the great work to come, for it was in that volume that his major battles as a visionary poet were fought and won. Hereafter, Maud Gonne, who had been de-Helenised and then resublimated in the two gatherings, would become increasingly an image from a past life. He had indeed wooed a proud woman not kindred of his soul, had, in pursuit of her love, "turned aside / From a great labyrinth out of pride" (VP 413) [84]. We must ask, at what cost to his life as a visionary poet had he wooed her? Had he not lost the magical gleam during those fourteen years, he would doubtless have been a quite different, perhaps a more abstract visionary, which he deeply feared. But would the poetry have had its human power? Yeats had no doubts: "only an aching heart / Conceives a changeless work of art" (VP 421) [88]—a declaration learned and earned in *The Wild Swans at Coole*.

✳   ✳   ✳

5. *A Critical Edition of Yeats's "A Vision"* (1925), ed. George Mills Harper and Walter Kelly Hood (London: Macmillan, 1978).

SEAMUS HEANEY

W. B. Yeats and Thoor Ballylee†

* * *

The usual assumption, when we speak of writers and place, is that the writer stands in some directly expressive or interpretative relationship to the milieu. He or she becomes a voice of the spirit of the region. The writing is infused with the atmosphere, physical and emotional, of a certain landscape or seascape, and while the writer's immediate purpose may not have any direct bearing upon the regional or national background, the background is sensed as a distinctive element in the work.

This filial relationship with region did indeed work for the young Yeats and the Sligo countryside should arguably be called the Young Yeats Country. But in this lecture I am concerned with the poet from the age of fifty onward, establishing an outpost of poetic reality in the shape of a physical landmark, a poet with a domineering rather than a grateful relation to place, one whose poems have created a country of the mind rather than the other way round, (and the more usual way) where the country has created the mind which in turn creates the poems.

* * *

Yeats admittedly spent most of his life in houses which were [merely] machines for living in. The house where he was born in Sandymount Avenue in Dublin remains the usual semi-detached, mid-Victorian, bay-windowed, steps and basement type of residence which would be hard to mythologize beyond its solid bourgeois respectability. The same is true of his apartments in Bloomsbury and the town house in Dublin's Merrion Square which was his main base during the very time when the later tower poems were being written. These addresses were not significant and would not be made to signify in terms of Yeats's imagining. They remained structures which would never become symbols. They were places where Yeats would remain his unwritten self.

But a Norman keep in the Barony of Kiltartan, dating from the thirteenth or fourteenth century, descending from the great line of the de Burgos, and registered in *The Booke of Connaught* at the end of the sixteenth century, this was a very different matter. Even though Yeats bought it for £35 from a government body called with an unromantic grimness The Congested Districts Board, it retained for him the aura of its historically resonant past and became a verifying force within his mind. It sponsored an attitude and a style, attained in his books a fabulous second dimension that would eventually transform its original status as a picturesque antiquity in the fields of Ballylee.

Mary Hanley and Liam Miller, whose pamphlet on the tower and its

† From *The Place of Writing* (Atlanta, GA: Scholars Press, 1989), pp. 20–35. Reprinted by permission of the publisher. Page references to this Norton Critical Edition are given in brackets.

history I am gratefully drawing upon here (*Thoor Ballylee*, Dolmen, 1965), have documented Yeats's negotiations thoroughly and shown that it is not just within the poetry that the tower's force and effect are registered. From the moment he began to make plans for its restoration, there is a sense of occasion in Yeats's letters. We recognize that a ceremonious action is being undertaken. His negotiations with builders and architects are heightened and solemnized by the tone, as though he were a Renaissance Pope or a Tuscan duke commissioning masters. A boozy professor of architecture becomes a genius. The adjective "great" begins to intone itself like a mantra. Here he is, writing to John Quinn on July 23, 1918:

> We are surrounded with plans. This morning designs arrived from the drunken man of genius, Scott, for two beds. The war is improving the work for, being unable to import anything, we have bought the whole contents of an old mill—great beams and three-inch planks, and old paving stones; and the local carpenter and mason and blacksmith are at work for us. On a great stone beside the front door will be inscribed these lines:
>
>> I, the poet, William Yeats,
>> With common sedge and broken slates
>> And smithy work from the Gort forge,
>> Restored this tower for my wife George;
>> And on my heirs I lay a curse
>> If they should alter for the worse,
>> From fashion or an empty mind,
>> What Raftery built and Scott designed.

Nothing Hardyesque about that. And all the while, William Scott was designing what his employer designated "great" chairs and tables, and "great" elmwood beds, and ceilings which would be painted with magical stars and angles, as befitted a castle. For a castle it was and a castle Yeats inclined to call it, as in the following letter to his father on July 16, 1919. By now his wife and young family have been able to move in, but the passage conjures up not so much a family home as a Homeric chamber: the word "hall," for example, gradually attains the legendary amplitude of Hrothgar's Heorot or Thomas Moore's Tara:

> I am writing in the great ground floor of the castle—pleasantest room I have yet seen, a great wide window opening over the river and a round arched door leading to the thatched hall. . . . There is a stone floor and a stone-roofed entrance-hall with the door to winding stair to left, and then a larger thatched hall, beyond which is a cottage and kitchen. In the thatched hall imagine a great copper hanging lantern (which is, however, not there yet but will be I hope, next week). I am writing at a great trestle table which George keeps covered with wild flowers.

A month before, Yeats had completed the mighty rhetoric of the poem he called "A Prayer for my Daughter," so it is no surprise to discover a similarity of tone in the letter and in the last stanza of the poem. Both conceive of a house as a ritually disposed and ceremoniously bedecked enclosure, and the final lines of the poem explicitly link the possibility of ample, innocent life to the dream of a house self-consciously high-mannered and liturgical:

> And may her bridegroom bring her to a house
> Where all's accustomed, ceremonious;
> For arrogance and hatred are the wares
> Peddled in the thoroughfares.
> How but in custom and in ceremony
> Are innocence and beauty born?
> Ceremony's a name for the rich horn,
> And custom for the spreading laurel tree. [78]

Wonderful melodies; and given the fact that Yeats himself was still a bridegroom of sorts when he wrote these lines—less than three years married—one could be forgiven for discerning in them as much a paean to the house he was preparing for his young wife as a prayer for his infant daughter.

Three years had passed between Yeats's purchase of the tower in 1916 and that summer of 1919 when he and George moved in; but even then, the residence was never to be permanent. Thoor Ballylee remained a kind of summer home, occupied occasionally by the family between 1919 and 1928, after which date their visits ceased altogether. By then, Yeats's health was beginning to fail. Moreover, in 1928 the volume of poems entitled *The Tower* appeared, and its sequel, *The Winding Stair* (1933), had been conceived. The tower had now entered so deeply into the prophetic strains of his voice that it could be invoked without being inhabited. He no longer needed to live in it since he had attained a state in which he lived *by* it.

To call it a summer home, then, is really slightly off the mark, since it is obvious that the tower's first function was not domestic. Here he was in the place of writing. It was one of his singing schools, one of the soul's monuments of its own magnificence. His other addresses were necessary shelters but Ballylee was a sacramental site, an outward sign of an inner grace. The grace here was poetry and the lonely tower was the poet's sign. Within it, he was within his own mind. The posture of the building corresponded to the posture he would attain. The stone in all its obstinacy and stillness, the plumb bulk and resistant profile of the keep, the dream form and the brute fact simultaneously impressed on mind and senses, all this transmission of sensation and symbolic aura made the actual building stones into touchstones for the work he would aspire to. And that work would have to be a holding action in the face of old age, death and the disintegrating civilization which he, "Heart smitten with emotion" [120], perceived in its decline.

One of the first functions of a poem, after all, is to satisfy a need in the poet. The achievement of a sufficient form and the release of a self-given music have a justifying effect within his life. And if the horizons inside which that life is being lived are menacing, the need for the steadying gift of finished art becomes all the more urgent. So it is in the light of just such a constantly flickering horizon of violence and breakdown that we must read the tower poems and much else of Yeats's work at this period.

The Easter Rising had occurred in Dublin a few months before his negotiations with the Congested Districts Board in 1916. The Battle of the Somme was fought that summer also. The Russian Revolution broke in 1917. From 1919 onwards, the War of Independence was in full swing in Ireland, and between 1922 and 1923, the Civil War got close enough to Ballylee for the builder, Thomas Rafferty, to get shot, for the bridge outside the tower to get blown up, and for the mind of this most public-spirited of poets to be darkened by a sense of personal danger and civic collapse.

So it is no wonder that the plough was set deeper into the emotional ground than ever before. If refuge within a medieval keep had given Yeats intimations of a new authoritativeness, the authoritativeness could not be credible to him until the poems were there like ramparts thrown up to prove that he had survived the onslaught of menacing circumstance. Richard Ellmann, for example, long ago noted how insistently the first person possessive figures in the subtitles of "Meditations in Time of Civil War": "My House," "My Table," "My Descendants," "The Road at My Door," "The Stare's Nest by My Window." With characteristic insight, he found in all this a symptom of the fully empowered imagination, Yeats as a man of means and position living in a microcosm where, in Ellmann's persuasive formulation, "life is condensed and controlled by the mechanism of symbolism." Yet I would want to add a corollary and suggest that this obsessive "my" is also conceivably a symptom of a last ditch stand. The poet, thrown back within the final personal ring of defense, is forced into single combat with old age and with history and can employ as weapons only those things which lie most nakedly to his hand or most indelibly inside his mind.

For example, "My House," the second poem in the sequence, begins and accumulates its force as a pile-up of nouns wrested from the air and placed like builder's blocks in a course of stonework, each block handled and fitted without the benefit of mortar, which is to say that the nouns function without the bonding action of a main verb. There are thirteen lines of dense affirmative word-chunks which convey an opaque feeling of constituted strength, of gathered, battened-down, self-absorbed power. This is writing which has, to be sure, an immediate covenant with the substantial world, yet the words operate perhaps more as a phonetic element than as a referential system.

> An ancient bridge, and a more ancient tower,
> A farmhouse that is sheltered by its wall,
> An acre of stony ground,
> Where the symbolic rose can break in flower,
> Old ragged elms, old thorns innumerable,
> The sound of the rain or sound
> Of every wind that blows;
> The stilted water-hen
> Crossing stream again
> Scared by the splashing of a dozen cows;
> A winding stair, a chamber arched with stone,

> A grey stone fireplace with an open hearth,
> A candle and written page. [87]

At this point the turn arrives: at the culmination of physical and linguistic density, enter a Platonist. Typically, Yeats's imagining could not repose for too long in the consolations of the material world. It is as if at the climax of solidarity, at the very apotheosis of body-strength and world-thickness, the language calls forth an antithetical mind-strength; as if the noun cores burst and erupt a magma of verb fire.

If this is to overdramatize the case, it is not misrepresent it. The visionary process that is sketched in "My House" when the wind changes its theme at line 14 is magnificently evoked in another tower poem, "Blood and the Moon:"

> The strength that gives our blood and state magnanimity of its
>   own desire;
> Everything that is not God consumed with intellectual fire.
>
> [106]

In that poem, after all, Yeats espouses Bishop Berkeley's conviction that if the mind changes its theme, then "this pragmatical, preposterous pig of a world, its farrow that so solid seem, / Must vanish." The world does not, of course, vanish in this section of "Meditations in Time of Civil War," nor is the apocalypse of "all things consumed in intellectual fire" attempted. Nevertheless, the poem does proceed to concentrate its focus inward so that the fortress of stone passing into the fortress of words becomes finally a manifestation of the fortified mind, besieged yet ablaze, exalted and incontrovertible:

> *Il Penseroso*'s Platonist toiled on
> In some like chamber, shadowing forth
> How the daemonic rage
> Imagined everything.
> Benighted travellers
> From markets and from fairs
> Have seen his midnight candle glimmering.
>
> Two men have founded here. A man-at-arms
> Gathered a score of horse and spent his days
> In this tumultuous spot,
> Where through long wars and sudden night alarms
> His dwindling score and he seemed castaways
> Forgetting and forgot;
> And I, that after me
> My bodily heirs may find,
> To exalt a lonely mind,
> Befitting emblems of adversity. [87–88]

This poem and the sequence of which it forms a part are ultimately about artistic faith, about trusting images and emblems rather than conventional readings of the world, about holding fast, living in a fastness, fastening the mind upon the certain tragedy of one's extinction and still refusing, even in the face of that extinction, to cede the value of what Yeats calls elsewhere "The spiritual intellect's great work" [128].

There is a transcendent imperative in the image of the tower. It is true that in Yeats's mind it was also linked to the Anglo-Irish tradition, and symbolized the historical bonds of ancestry and inheritance, but its virtue effectively released his consciousness from the exorbitance of the historical. For example, at the historical moment of "Meditations," Yeats's espoused caste, the Protestant Ascendancy, were being given notice that their influence and control were at an end in a newly independent, mainly Catholic Ireland. Outside his poems, Yeats would identify with them in an understandably partisan and political way, most notably in his Senate speech of 1925 when he spoke against a bill which was to make divorce illegal in the new Free State. Again it was Richard Ellmann, writing in *Yeats: The Man and the Masks* (1948), who acutely suggested that Yeats spoke on that occasion in the service of class rather than of principle. The speech reveals the nexus of haughty if not snobbish social attitudes which underlie his more exposed and existential stance as heroic solitary in a candle-lit cell. The famous lines are these:

> I think it tragic that within three years of this country gaining its independence we should be discussing a measure which a minority of this nation considers to be grossly oppressive. I am proud to consider myself a typical man of that minority. We against whom you have done this thing are no petty people. We are one of the great stocks of Europe. We are the people of Burke; we are the people of Grattan; we are the people of Swift, the people of Emmet, the people of Parnell. We have created the most of the modern literature of this country. We have created the best of its political intelligence. Yet I do not altogether regret what has happened. I shall be able to find out, if not I, my children will be able to find out whether we have lost our stamina or not.

What in these stung lines is combative and vindictive in a class-conscious way becomes visionary and stoical in the third section of "Meditations," the poem called "My Descendants." In it, the future into which Yeats's children must live is envisaged as non-chivalric and anti-aristocratic, the very antithesis of all that the poet cherishes; yet the poem, unlike the speech, attains a spirit of equanimity. It can bear to contemplate the affront which reality will offer his expectations. Here is not simply nostalgia for the vanished glories of the Anglo-Irish, not a jeremiad upon the filthy modern tide, but a steady gaze at the consequences of his own perception that "man is in love and loves what vanishes" [93].

> And what if my descendants lose the flower
> Through natural declension of the soul,
> Through too much business with the passing hour,
> Through too much play, or marriage with a fool?
> May this laborious stair and this stark tower
> Become a roofless ruin that the owl

May build in the cracked masonry and cry
Her desolation to the desolate sky.

The Primum Mobile that fashioned us
Has made the very owls in circles move;
And I, that count myself most prosperous,
Seeing that love and friendship are enough,
For an old neighbour's friendship chose the house
And decked and altered it for a girl's love,
And know whatever flourish and decline
These stones remain their monument and mine. [89]

Here the place of writing is essentially the stanza form itself, that strong-arched room of eight iambic pentameters rhyming *abababcc* which serves as a redoubt for the resurgent spirit in poems like "Sailing to Byzantium," the first section of "Nineteen Hundred and Nineteen," "Among School Children," "Coole Park and Ballylee, 1931" and several of his other definitive works. In these poems, the unshakably affirmative music of this *ottava rima* stanza is the formal correlative of the poet's indomitable spirit. The complete coincidence between period and stanza which he had begun to strive for compounds utterance with architecture, recalls Milton's figure of the poet as one who builds the lofty rhyme and also recalls Yeats's own stated desire to make the tower a permanent symbol of his poetic work, "plainly visible to the passer-by."

In the case of the poem we have just read, the tower calls him from propaganda towards prophecy. It would have him exalt vision rather than salt the historical wound. The tower may be crumbling into a destructive future, but that very crumbling is part of an inexorable reality which the mind must accept as truth. Yet the mind, once it has digested this knowledge, is still not permitted to renege on its challenge, not allowed to cave in to a passive acceptance of the deplorable. Its responsibility to its own affirmative project is not absolved by its perception of the foredoomed nature of that project.

All of this remains implicit in the pitch and roundedness of the poetry in "My Descendants," but it is proclaimed confidently and explicitly in a poem composed in 1926, the year after the Senate speech. In the title poem of *The Tower* volume, Thoor Ballylee is not just picturesque nor simply emblematical of the menaced splendours of a particular cultural heritage. It is rather a podium from which the spirit's voice can best be projected. In the third section of this poem, the tower's stoniness is repeated in the lean, clean-chiselled obelisk of the verse-form; its head-clearing airiness is present in the rise and enjambement of the three-stressed line. Indeed, the tower is now not just an embodied attitude or symbol of loyalties but also a pure discharge of energy. Inevitably, it continues to affiliate Yeats with his caste and casts him as its self-appointed panegyrist. But it also marks an original space where utterance and being are synonymous. This section of "The Tower" so strives to transcend its personal and historical occasion that it reminds us of the exultation and absolutism of another tower-dwelling visionary, Rainer Maria Rilke. It was

Rilke who declared in his third sonnet to Orpheus, written in 1922, only a few years before Yeats's poem, that *Gesang ist Dasein*, singing is being, or song is reality, phrases that could easily stand as epigraph to Yeats's superb peroration:

> Now shall I make my soul,
> Compelling it to study
> In a learned school
> Till the wreck of body,
> Slow decay of blood,
> Testy delirium
> Or dull decrepitude,
> Or what worse evil come—
> The death of friends, or death
> Of every brilliant eye
> That made a catch in the breath—
> Seem but the clouds of the sky
> When the horizon fades;
> Or a bird's sleepy cry
> Among the deepening shades. [85–86]

One brilliant eye which had made a catch in the breath in nineteenth-century Ballylee was the beauty Mary Hynes, celebrated in song by the blind poet Anthony Raftery. Both of them are invoked in an earlier part of "The Tower," but all through this period of his writing, Yeats was in the situation dramatized in another famous Raftery poem:

> *Mise Raifteiri an file,*
> *Lán dóchas 's grá,*
> *Dul siar ar mo thuras*
> *Le solus mo chroí.*
>
> *Féach anois mé*
> *Mo chúl le balla,*
> *Ag seinm ceoil*
> *Le póchaí folaimh.*

> I am Raftery the poet,
> Full of hope and love,
> Going westward on my journey
> By the light of my heart.
>
> Look at me now,
> My back to a wall,
> Playing music
> To empty pockets.

When he quartered himself and his poetry in Thoor Ballylee, Yeats was similarly backed into an extreme position. He was being compelled by his years and his times into a new awareness of himself as his own solitary protagonist out on the mortal arena, and suddenly in that needy space, a tower ascended. Not a tree, as in Rilke's first sonnet to Orpheus, not a natural given miracle but a built-up, lived-with, deliberately adhered-to tower. Yet by now that tower is as deep inside our hearing as the temple which Rilke imagines the god Orpheus building inside the listening consciousness of the creatures. * * * That sense of a temple inside the hearing, of an undeniable acoustic architecture, of a written vaulting, of the firmness and in-placeness and undislodgeableness of poetic form, that is one of Yeats's great gifts to our century; and his power to achieve it was due in no small measure to the "beckoning," the "new beginning," the "pure transcendence" of an old Norman castle in Ballylee, a place that was nowhere until it was a written place.

Yet we must go further, since Yeats himself went further. Another of his gifts was his own boldness to question the final value and trustworthiness of this powerfully composed tower in the ear—for it is a mark of the fully empowered imagination that it shirks none of the challenges that the fully awakened intelligence can offer it. The last stanza of "All Souls Night," for example, represents the positive force that Yeats's tower-schooled mind could command: his prayer for concentration is itself focused and shining with an inward, self-directed illumination:

> Such thought—such thought have I that hold it tight
> Till meditation master all its parts,
> Nothing can stay my glance
> Until that glance run in the world's despite
> To where the damned have howled away their hearts,
> And where the blessed dance;
> Such thought, that in it bound
> I need no other thing,
> Wound in mind's wandering
> As mummies in the mummy-cloth are wound. [101]

I have talked mostly about this kind of centered, purposeful writing because it is what we rejoice at most immediately in Yeats's poems. Here conviction has arisen out of the very words in which it is sought, and stamina has been conjured by the strong expression of his own need for it. But, as Richard Ellmann has insisted, the credibility of this art is ultimately guaranteed by Yeats's readiness to doubt its efficaciousness. The very power of his desire for foundedness should alert us to the fear of unfoundedness which might lurk beneath it, what Philip Larkin called "the solving emptiness / That lies just under all we do." It is Yeats's greatest triumph that he could acknowledge this possibility and yet maintain a resolute faith in the worth of artistic creation. In a late poem like "Man and the Echo," the much-vaunted insulation of the tower dweller—that quarantined, stone-kept otherness of the artist—is helpless against the unaccommodated cry of suffering nature. The man's composure is certainly assailed by the mocking echo of his own doubting mind, but it is finally most vulnerable to the yelp of pain in a hurt creature:

> But hush, for I have lost the theme
> Its joy or night seem but a dream;
> Up there some hawk or owl has struck

> Dropping out of sky or rock,
> A stricken rabbit is crying out
> And its cry distracts my thought. [128]

It is the triumph of this art to confront a despair at the very notion of art *as* triumph. Yet it also manages to wrest from the confrontation with such despair a margin of trust that makes the renewal of artistic effort contemplatable. Behind the large firm gestures of Yeats's last poems, where the humanist effort is racked upon a wheel that is a paradigm of hollowness, we can already make out the shuffling, unappeasable decrepitude of Beckett's heroes going on refusing to go on.

I will return to these concerns in the third lecture, since they constitute the theme from Ellmann that I wish to address. Here, in conclusion, I shall follow his lead to "The Black Tower," the last poem which Yeats composed. This poem dramatizes, with an almost scampish offhandedness, a dialectic between the spirit's indomitable, affirmative impulses and the mind's capacity to ironize and mock those impulses as self-serving fictions. The indomitable aspect is reflected in an ancient motif of warriors buried in a standing position, signifying their eternal vigilance and oath-bound fidelity to the cause that unified them during their lives. The ironist and questioner is their old cook, who represents a kind of unheroic life force, a scuttling principle of survival and self-preservation. He embodies all that Cuchulain had come to terms with in the poem "Cuchulain Comforted" when the hero goes to the underworld and must consort with "Convicted cowards . . . by kindred slain / 'Or driven from home and left to die in fear.' " Yet the cook's thoroughly creditable scepticism is resisted by the *comitatus*; they persist at their post even as they are pestered by his rumours and heckling. They are like T.S. Eliot's magi journeying towards an ambiguous epiphany with voices singing in their ears that this may be all folly:

> Say that the men of the old black tower
> Though they may but feed as the goatherd feeds,
> Their money spent, their wine gone sour,
> Lack nothing that a soldier needs,
> That all are oath-bound men;
> Those banners come not in.
>
> *There in the tomb stand the dead upright,*
> *But winds come up from the shore;*
> *They shake when the winds roar*
> *Old bones upon the mountain shake.* [125]

In this final appearance of Thoor Ballylee in Yeats's poetry, it stands fast and Yeats stands by it. Both tower and poet stand, as Macbeth and Macbeth's castle once stood, suspended in art time, ratified by a prophetic utterance. In Shakespeare's play, Macbeth's sense of inviolable sanctuary was based on oracles delivered to him when the witches prophesied that he would be safe until Birnam Wood should come to Dunsinane. Yeats, on the other hand, had written his own oracles to himself and created a fortified space within the rooms of many powerfully vaulted stanzas. But just as the witches equivocated and the world as a wood of trees moved unthinkably to dislodge Macbeth, so in the end the Yeatsian keep of tragic commitment and loyalty is assailed by mutinous doubts about the ultimate value of what there is to keep. Nevertheless, the Yeatsian drama ends with the poet as Macbeth, still pacing the battlements, just acknowledging the tremor on the fringes of Birnam but refusing to allow his chivalric countenance to quail. The tower as emblem of adversity, as the place of writing, has taken on a final aspect as icon of the absurd. And it is because of the way these manifold, extreme and unshirked recognitions are embodied in Yeats's poems that we know again that poetry is truly a vision of reality, and the creative imagination a truth-seeking and truth-augmenting faculty.

MARJORIE HOWES

In the Bedroom of the Big House†

* * *

In "A Prayer For My Daughter" (*VP*,[1] 403–6) [76], Yeats depicts the Anglo-Irish as a community constantly in crisis by representing them as a tradition whose continuity is both dependent on and threatened by female sexual choice. Yeats began the poem while staying at the tower during the Anglo-Irish war, two days after Anne's birth on February 26, 1919. It is clear that on a biographical level Yeat's prayer for his daughter is in part that she grow up to be like her mother rather than like [Maud] Gonne and the other women in Yeats's life. More important, however, is the way the poem structures these two alternatives. Similarly, while it is certainly true that the poem's speaker offers an obviously sexist prescription for his daughter's future life and development, that observation alone leaves much about the text unexplained. We need to read his prescription with two other points in mind. First, the poem relentlessly casts questions about female social and sexual development as, simultaneously, political questions about the survival of the Anglo-Irish aristocracy. Second, while the text initially depicts the Big House as threatened by violent forces from without, it blurs the boundaries between these forces and the internal threat posed by the potentially turbulent desires of aristocratic women.

The poem's opening stanzas function as a framing device, calling attention to the violence and chaos of the turbulent political scene of 1919, both in Ireland and in Europe, embodied by the storm,[2] and indicating

---

† From *Yeats's Nations: Gender, Class, and Irishness* (Cambridge: Cambridge University Press, 1996), pp. 115–20. Reprinted with the permission of Cambridge University Press. Page references to this Norton Critical Edition are given in brackets after the author's original citations.
1. *The Variorum Edition of the Poems of W. B. Yeats*, ed. Peter Allt and Russell K. Alspach (New York: Macmillan, 1966).
2. The drafts of the poem indicate that the roof-levelling wind embodies the forces of sterile Irish political opinion; the manuscripts refer to the storm as a "popular tempest," to the "bitterness" of political hatred, and to mob rule: "all must be with opinion driven wild." See Jon Stallworthy, *Between the Lines: Yeats's Poetry in the Making* (Oxford: Clarendon Press, 1971), pp. 29–30.

that the speaker's prescriptions for his daughter form part of his response
to a larger set of political issues and dangers:

> . . . There is no obstacle
> But Gregory's wood and one bare hill
> Whereby the haystack- and roof-levelling wind,
> Bred on the Atlantic, can be stayed.

These lines designate Anglo-Irish estates like Coole as crucial but tenuous
sites of resistance to such chaos; the screaming wind, ironically "bred" on
the Atlantic, can only be countered by those who have been bred to better things in the Big House. Yeats wrote "The Second Coming" (VP,
401–2) [76] just before Anne's birth, and he placed that poem just before
"A Prayer For My Daughter" in Michael Robartes and the Dancer to
highlight the connections between the public apocalypse of the one and
the private trauma of the other. Both are figured as crises of sexual reproduction. The "rough beast" that "slouches towards Bethlehem to be born"
in "The Second Coming" embodies history as driven by divine (or demonic) sexual acts or annunciations. Like the ill-bred screaming wind, its
monstrous birth figures destiny as the product of a kind of cosmic
miscegenation.

A number of critics have pointed out that the speaker's prayer is actually
a contradictory combination of two opposing prayers; the poem contains
a tension between the speaker's wish that his daughter become an auton-
omous individual and his wish that she become a custodian of traditional
sanctity and loveliness.[3] On one hand, the speaker wants her to be "self-
delighting," on the other, he wants her to "choose right," and marry into
an aristocratic house. The contrast between individual pleasure and properly educated desire corresponds to Yeat's two conflicting but inseparable
aristocratic modes, and the conflict between them embodies reproduction
(the sexual and social production of the next generation) as the repetition
of an original crisis. The speaker's explicit prayer for his daughter is that
she be granted the independent qualities which will enable her to be
happy despite the chaos around her. However, several aspects of the poem
emphasize that the outcome of her psycho-sexual development will determine whether she will counter or contribute to that chaos. As a woman,
the speaker's daughter must ultimately be relegated to embodying the feminine principle of continuity.

Female sexual identity is a subject for fatherly concern and management
because the continuity of traditional, aristocratic culture depends on
women, who, left to their own devices, may betray it by making improper
sexual choices. Venus, "Being fatherless could have her way," and chose
poorly. The negative examples of beautiful women who made unwise sexual choices combine public consequences with personal cost. Helen is

---

3. Elizabeth Cullingford's persuasive reading of the poem points out a similar conflict: "the poem
indeed contains an unresolved tension between female autonomy and female subordination, between chastity and matrimony" ("Yeats and Women: Michael Robartes and the Dancer," Yeats:
An Annual of Critical and Textual Studies, 4, p. 49), and Harris observes, "nowhere in his work
are the opposing claims of individual aristocratic freedom and the historical coherence of the
aristocratic order so unresolved as here" (Daniel Harris, Yeats, Coole Park and Ballylee [Baltimore
and London: Johns Hopkins University Press, 1974], p. 146).

probably Western culture's prime example of the catastrophic social consequences of private obsession, and the poem's laconic observation that she "later had much trouble with a fool" merely underscores this by understating it so arrestingly. The "Horn of Plenty," the cultured feminine principle of continuity and reproduction symbolized by Coole, can be "undone" from within by the appetites of fine women: "It's certain that fine women eat / A crazy salad with their meat / Whereby the Horn of Plenty is undone." The horn of plenty refers not only to the gracious fecundity of individual women, but also to the material wealth and cultured fertility of the aristocratic setting. Maud Gonne is another such woman whose desires endanger the tradition that produced her and that depends upon her for its continued existence:

> Have I not seen the loveliest woman born
> Out of the mouth of Plenty's horn,
> Because of her opinionated mind
> Barter that horn and every good
> By quiet natures understood
> For an old bellows full of angry wind? [78]

Gonne has betrayed, not merely (or even primarily) herself, but the horn of plenty which produced her and which she in turn must reproduce. She has sold away, not goods in her own eyes, but goods in the eyes of "quiet natures." The play on "goods" suggests that their sale might be more appropriate than the speaker wants to admit.

While an individual might find it natural and desirable to barter things intended for that purpose, following such inclinations threatens the continuity of the house or the nation/race. The poem reinforces the daughter's role as a potential danger to the very culture she is supposed to support by constructing a number of verbal parallels between the external threat of violent and commercial forces and the internal corruption of transgressive female desire. Does the screaming wind that threatens the horn of plenty originate, as the first stanza suggests, on the Atlantic, or in Gonne's choice of MacBride as a husband, "an old bellows full of angry wind?" The poem's last stanza claims that "arrogance and hatred are the wares / Peddled in the thoroughfares" outside the estate, but Gonne has fallen into commercial exchange and has "bartered" her rightful aristocratic existence. The speaker himself admits that his own mind has been choked with hatred; he knows "that to be choked with hate / May well be of all evil chances chief."[4] The external forces which threaten the Big House are mirrored by the dangerous desires of the women within it. The speaker's daughter can contribute to the resistance to the storm offered by the custom and ceremony of Coole, or she can succumb to those desires within her which ally her with the screaming wind.

The speaker ends by projecting his daughter's sexual maturity, a future in which she chooses the former course and embodies the correspondence between woman and house that illustrates the feminine principle of aris-

---

4. The drafts of the poem make it clearer that the speaker's knowledge of the evils of hatred comes out of his own experience; he says his mind "has grown half barren from much hate" (Stallworthy, *Between the Lines*, p. 35).

tocratic continuity. The first line of the last stanza illustrates her passivity, in sharp contrast to the emphasis on autonomy in the previous stanza. The values of custom and ceremony are first introduced as attributes of the house, and then transferred, not to the daughter herself, but to the symbols with which the poem associates her—the "rich horn" and "spreading laurel tree." The last stanza is dominated by the metonyms of aristocratic life and the adjectives the speaker associates with them, rather than by either the bride or the groom. In the original draft, Yeats did not even include the figure of a bridegroom, writing "and may she marry into some old house."[5]

In "A Prayer For My Daughter" the internal weaknesses of the Anglo-Irish are equivalent to the potentially "crazy" sexual identities and choices of "fine women." "Nineteen Hundred and Nineteen" (*VP*, 428–33) [92] also aligns the corruption of the public and private virtues Yeats attributed to the Anglo-Irish with female sexual depravity. Yeats's Big House poems connect the laudable aspects of Anglo-Irishness with integrity in public life, strong political leadership, and a vigorous cultural tradition; "Nineteen Hundred and Nineteen" laments the decline of all these things during the Anglo-Irish War. The end of the poem embodies the political, moral and cultural decay it chronicles in Lady Kyteler's perverse desire for the succubus Robert Artisson, the rough beast whose coming heralds the beginning of a new and barbarous age:

> But now the wind drops, dust settles; thereupon
> There lurches past, his great eyes without thought
> Under the shadow of stupid straw-pale locks,
> That insolent fiend Robert Artisson
> To whom the love-lorn Lady Kyteler brought
> Bronzed peacock feathers, red combs of her cocks. [95]

Like the corrupt erotic choices of the women in "A Prayer For My Daughter," Lady Kyteler's lust for the "insolent" fiend suggests a natural aristocrat's inappropriate desire for an unworthy and disrespectful inferior. In addition, the contrast between Artisson's lurching stupidity and lack of thought and Lady Kyteler's active and slightly pornographic gift-giving makes her appear as the real instigator of the historical rupture symbolized by Artisson, as does the fact that the poem ends with her.

"A Prayer For My Daughter" ends by projecting continuity rather than apocalyptic change. The poem's linking of female sexual development and the survival of the Anglo-Irish finds its corollary in the merging of woman and estate; in the final stanza, the speaker's daughter dissolves into the gracious house and atmosphere of the Anglo-Irish. The conflation of the daughter with her future house also constitutes the poem's acknowledgment that she can serve the communal goods of custom and ceremony only by surrendering herself as an individual. The poem constructs an Anglo-Irish community which maintains itself through victories over individual women. While one could read the poem's unresolved tension between autonomy and subordination for the daughter as a mark of in-

5. *Ibid.*, p. 43.

coherence, in the context of Yeats's definition of kindred as crisis, by refusing to resolve this tension the poem highlights the violence inherent in this conception of the family.

The ultimate embodiment of a kindred relation that involves coerced sexuality as the engine of history, familial or civilizational, is the rape of the daughter. "Leda and the Swan" (VP, 441) [96] presents such a rape. The poem emphasizes the helplessness of the "staggering girl," with her "helpless breast" and "terrified vague fingers." It also emphasizes the power and savagery of her attacker in the mimetic force of the opening—"A sudden blow"—and the descriptions of the swan's "great wings" and "feathered glory." Contemporary critics accused Yeats of eroticizing rape and glorifying violence, but in relation to most previous poetic treatments of Leda and the swan Yeats had put the violence back into a scene that was frequently figured more as a seduction than a rape. While the poem insists on Leda's violent subjugation it does not simply imagine her going gently into the night of her own violation. Instead, it raises the question of her subaltern subjectivity: "How can those terrified vague fingers push / The feathered glory from her loosening thighs? / And how can body, laid in that white rush, / But feel the strange heart beating where it lies?" The final question also posits Leda's experience as important but inaccessible: "Did she put on his knowledge with his power / Before the indifferent beak could let her drop?" These lines introduce the question of the relationship between power and knowledge; what kind of knowledge accrues to the woman whose only power lies in the fact that she is a vessel through which some large impersonal force actualizes itself? In "A Prayer For My Daughter" that force is dynastic continuity, while in "Leda and the Swan" it is the historical rupture implied by the destruction of Troy and the death of Agamemnon. In both cases, knowledge and power are divided from each other. In "A Prayer For My Daughter" the daughter's support for Anglo-Irish tradition coincides with her "innocence" rather than her knowledge. The question of Leda's knowledge is more complicated: the poem holds out the possibility that she acquires Jove's knowledge and power, but it balances that possibility with the suggestion that Leda's knowledge is merely the inarticulable knowledge of her own subordination. Yeats's Anglo-Irish meditations and related poems like "Leda and the Swan" enact the subordination of women to the particular imperatives of kindred reproduction.

* * *

MARJORIE PERLOFF

Between Hatred and Desire: Sexuality and Subterfuge in "A Prayer for my Daughter"†

* * *

* * * [S]o elaborately wrought is the mask worn in "A Prayer for my Daughter" [76–78] that readers have generally taken the poem at face value as a kind of Ode to Moderation, a Hymn to Balance and Restraint. * * *

As such, "A Prayer for my Daughter" has been read as heralding Yeats's "Jonsonian" phase, the excessive Romanticism of his youth now reputedly behind him. Charles Tomlinson, referring to the poem's fifth stanza ("In courtesy I'd have her chiefly learned;/Hearts are not had as a gift but hearts are earned/By those that are not entirely beautiful . . ."), comments,

> In the last line Yeats's aristocracy takes on its fullest humanity; whatever simplifying, fragmenting violence his ideal may seem in danger of, is purged away in this conception where love is something to be earned by a courtesy that is moral endeavour. . . . Within this conception Yeats has found a poetic style for domesticity, . . . one that bestows on its human subject the kind of more-than-individual importance which Jonson gives to his figure of the lady in "To Penshurst".[1]

And Donald Davie, in his commentary on *Michael Robartes and the Dancer*, takes this Jonsonian motif even further:

> "Ceremony" is Yeats's word for what he values most in an aristocratic organisation of society, as he envisaged it on the model of his own relationship with Lady Gregory . . . just as it is implied also in the many references to Urbino, and to Castiglione's record of the Renaissance court in such a city state. This was the relationship between poet and patron which Jonson celebrated in many of his verse-epistles . . . .[2]

Indeed, such seemingly hackneyed properties as the cornucopia and the laurel tree—both of them central images in "A Prayer for my Daughter" —provide the poem with a necessary sense of tradition, a needed "anonymity" in a poem "which celebrates above all the time-hallowed unwritten laws of social usage."[3]

Inevitably, the reading of "A Prayer for my Daughter" as a Jonsonian tribute to order and tradition, custom and ceremony—a reading of this and related poems that went largely unchallenged in the 1960s and early 1970s—has given Yeats a bad reputation in the socially conscious class-

† From *Yeats Annual* 7 (1990): 29–45. Reprinted by permission of Marjorie Perloff. Page references to this Norton Critical Edition are given in brackets after the author's original citations.
1. Charles Tomlinson, "Yeats and the Practising Poet", in *An Honoured Guest: New Essays on W. B. Yeats*, ed. Denis Donoghue and J. R. Mulryne (New York: St. Martin's Press, 1966) p. 6.
2. Donald Davie, "*Michael Robartes and the Dancer*", in *An Honoured Guest*, p. 83.
3. Ibid., p. 84.

rooms of the 1980s. Indeed, one need hardly be a radical Marxist or feminist to take exception to this modern father's prayer that his daughter grow up to be neither beautiful nor brilliant (these being qualities that get girls into trouble!) but rather that she live a life of decorous retirement ("may she live like some green laurel / Rooted in one dear perpetual place"), removed from worldly strife by her protective "bridegroom", who will "bring her to a house / Where all's accustomed, ceremonious". Joyce Carol Oates surely speaks for many contemporary readers when she declares, "This celebrated poet would have his daughter an object in nature for others'—which is to say male—delectation. She is not even an animal or a bird in his imagination, but a vegetable: immobile, unthinking, placid, 'hidden'." Indeed, "the poet's daughter is to be brainless and voiceless, *rooted*", her "thoughts" irritatingly compared to the "linnet with its modest brown plumage".[4] As for the "self-delighting, / Self-appeasing, self-affrighting" soul which the daughter must gradually "learn" to make hers, such soul-making, declares Oates, must involve "a kind of autism of the spirit".[5]

Anyone who teaches Yeats in the university today will have met with something like this reaction to "A Prayer for my Daughter" and related Yeats poems, the irony being that Oates never questions the traditional reading of the poem; she merely imputes negative value to what, say, Jeffares or Davie or Harris would see as positive. In neither case, however, has it been remarked that the title of "A Prayer for my Daughter" and its opening lines ("Once more the storm is howling, and half hid / Under this cradle-hood and coverlid / My child sleeps on") constitute no more than Coleridgean decor ("Frost at Midnight" being the obvious precursor text here),[6] the real focus throughout its ten stanzas being on Yeats's own relationship to Maud Gonne. Indeed, the "bridegroom" of the final stanza is, as Harold Bloom remarked, a "movingly archaic" image of "Yeats himself, making in a phantasmagoria the marriage he was denied in life, yet ironically marrying only his own soul".[7]

"Denied in life" is perhaps not quite accurate: the projected marriage is, I would argue, the one Yeats *thought he should make*, that, in a sense, he did make when, on the rebound from his proposal first to Maud Gonne and then to her daughter Iseult in 1917, he chose to marry a well-born and respectable young woman, who, as he wrote to Lady Gregory less than two months after his marriage and only three months after Iseult's final

4. Joyce Carol Oates, " 'At Least I Have Made a Woman of Her': Images of Women in Twentieth-Century Literature," *Georgia Review*, 37 (Spring 1983) 17.
5. Ibid., p. 18.
6. Archibald for example, devotes the entire first chapter of his *Yeats* to a comparison between "A Prayer for my Daughter" and "Frost at Midnight", noting that both poems begin "in an ordinary and, therefore important domestic situation", that "composition of an actual and specific scene", in which the father watches over his child sleeping in its cradle, moves the anxiety to prayer to a new-found serenity [Douglas Archibald, *Yeats* (Syracuse, NY: Syracuse University Press, 1983), pp. 1–2]. But, whereas Coleridge wants for his son Hartley what he himself never had—oneness with nature—the final epiphany of the icicles "Quietly shining to the quiet moon" reflecting the poet's discovery that Nature is the visible language of God (p. 10), Yeats's social prayer for his daughter is a little banal and not a little snobbish and escapist, "ridden by male chauvinism and reactionary nostalgia" (p. 8). Archibald, in other words, takes the poem's "prayer for the recovery of the soul's innocence" quite literally and hence is troubled by its sexism.
7. Harold Bloom, *Yeats* (New York: Oxford University Press, 1970) p. 326.

refusal, "is a perfect wife, kind, wise, and unselfish. . . . She has made my life serene and full of order" (L^8 634). The equation of perfection with kindness, serenity and order is one that the Daimonic Man (as the Yeats of *Per Amica Silentia Lunas* and *A Vision* perceived himself) could sustain only at his peril. Indeed, the "True Mask" Yeats assigned himself as a man of Phase 17 was that of "intellectual or sexual passion" ($AV B^9$ 141), and he remarks that Dante, the exemplary poet of this phase, "could never keep from politics, [and] was, according to a contemporary, such a partisan, that if a child, or a woman, spoke against his party he would pelt this child or woman with stones" ($AV B$ 143).

It is in the light of such statements that we should rethink that well-worn commonplace of Yeats criticism: the poet loved Maud Gonne for her great beauty but abhorred her "intellectual hatred" and "opinionated mind". Did Yeats in fact believe that "to be choked with hate / May well be of all evil chances chief", that "all hatred driven hence, / The soul recovers radical innocence"? And, if so, was the "radical innocence" of the "self-delighting" soul what Yeats was really after? Or was something else at stake?

* * *

Maud Gonne's rejection [of Yeats] in the summer of 1917 led, first, to the proposal to Maud's surrogate, her daughter Iseult, and then, when Iseult said no, to what we might call the shotgun courtship of Georgie Hyde-Lees. The despondency of Yeats on his honeymoon is a familiar story; equally familiar is the previously mentioned narrative of Yeats's delight in his wife's discovery that she could do automatic writing, a delight that supposedly brought the joys of marital happiness.[1]

Michael Robartes and the Dancer (1921), the first fruit of this "happiness", tells, however, a very different story, especially when read in the context of George Mills Harper's critical edition of the 1925 *A Vision* (1978) and his more recent publication of the automatic script itself, as recorded by Mrs Yeats and edited by her husband. We learn, for example, that an early section of the automatic script refers to Maud Gonne's placement at Phase 16 of the Great Wheel and of Iseult's at Phase 14, even as Michael Robartes says, "If a man has not loved a woman of the fourteenth or the sixteenth phase, he has not known the greatest earthly beauty" ($AV A^2$ nn. 19, 21). At this early stage, too, George Yeats is placed at Phase

8. *The Letters of W. B. Yeats*, ed. Allan Wade (London: Rupert Hart-Davis, 1954; New York: Macmillan, 1955).
9. W. B. Yeats, *A Vision* (London: Macmillan, 1962).
1. In his Preface to the second edition of *Yeats: The Man and the Masks* (Oxford: Oxford University Press, 1979), Ellmann notes that on the first few days of the "honeymoon" in Ashdown Forest, Mrs Yeats was so aware of her husband's depression, his conviction that he might have done the wrong thing in marrying her, that she "wondered whether to leave him. Casting about for some means of distraction, she thought of attempting automatic writing . . . . Her idea was to fake a sentence or two that would allay his anxieties over Iseult and herself, and after the session to own up to what she had done." But, when Yeats responded with excitement and enthusiasm, she herself began to believe that voices were speaking—or rather writing—through her, and so the project was born (pp. xii–xiii).
2. W. B. Yeats, *A Vision: An Explanation of Life Founded upon the Writings of Giraldus and upon certain Doctrines attributed to Kusta Ben Luka* (London: privately printed for subscribers only, T. Werner Laurie, Ltd, 1925).

18, the phase of Goethe and Arnold. "Goethe", writes Yeats in the 1937 *Vision*, "did not . . . marry his cook, but he certainly did not marry the woman he had desired, and his grief at her death showed that, unlike Phase 16 or Phase 17, which forget their broken toys, he could love what disillusionment gave" (*AV B* 146–7).

Does Yeats, via the mediumship of his wife, identify with Goethe here, thinking of himself as similarly coming to "love what disillusionment gave"? It seems likely, given the entries that fill the pages of automatic script throughout 1918. "What", Yeats asks at one point, "is the evil genius when Ego is at 16"? And the answer is contained in one word, "violence".[3] Or again, with reference to troubled relations with an unnamed woman:

37. Have I passed from such a relation?
37. Waves
38. Why have you written waves?
38. Cuchulain fighting the waves   (*MYV* I, 121)

That the "waves" had to be "fought" continually is a theme running through the automatic script. Questions about sexuality dominate the sessions, their tone being one of persistent anxiety, almost of voyeurism. Certainly, what Claude Rawson has described as "a sharp feeling for comedy, including sexual comedy" in the 1937 *A Vision*—its "readiness to allow ribaldry into a context normally associated with haughty sublimities of Romantic Agony"[4]—is not the mood of the automatic script that was its raw material. Even in the summer and fall of 1918, when Mrs Yeats, now pregnant, often complains of exhaustion and asks to be excused from the daily hour-long sessions of automatic writing, Yeats presses on, eager to learn this or that detail that has not yet emerged (see *MYV* 1, 242–3).

Indeed, the daily question-and-answer period becomes for Yeats an odd form of sublimation: clearly, this is where his energy, sexual as well as mental, seems to go during the first two years of his marriage. Subsequently, when the sessions stop, so does the poet's emphasis on "the marriage bed" as "solved antinomy" (*AV B* 52), this metaphor giving way to the poet's mounting rage at the old age that has deprived him (or his persona Crazy Jane) of the sexual fulfilment he craves.

But what about *Michael Robartes and the Dancer*, with its reference, in the witty "Solomon and the Witch", to "Chance being at one with Choice at last", to the moment of Unity of Being:

> When oil and wick are burned in one;
> Therefore a blessed moon last night
> Gave Sheba to her Solomon.   (*VP*[5] 388)

And what about the epitaph that closes *Michael Robartes*, with its straightforward homage to marriage and domestic stability:

3. See George Mills Harper, *The Making of Yeats's* A Vision: *A Study of the Automatic Script*, 2 vols (London: Macmillan; Carbondale: Southern Illinois University Press, 1984–5) II 103. Subsequently cited in the text as *MYV*.
4. Claude Rawson, "A Question of Potency" (review essay on Yeats), *The Times Literary Supplement*, 24 July 1987, p. 784.
5. *The Variorum Edition of the Poems of W. B. Yeats*, ed. Peter Allt and Russell K. Alspach (New York: Macmillan, 1957).

I, the poet William Yeats,
With old mill boards and sea-green slates,
And smithy work from the Gort forge,
Restored this tower for my wife George;
And may these characters remain
When all is ruin once again.   (VP 406) [79]

"What is new [in this volume]", Donald Davie asserts, "is that Yeats, freed at last from his passion for Maud Gonne with her distracting devotion to abstractions, is now able to see woman as peculiarly responsible for escaping from 'what Blake calls mathematic form, from every abstract thing . . . ' ".[6]

A closer look at the chronology of *Michael Robartes and the Dancer* (see COM[7] 217–50) raises some doubts about this reading. Of the fifteen poems in the volume, four ("Easter 1916", "Sixteen Dead Men", "The Rose Tree" and "A Meditation in Time of War") had been written before Yeats's marriage, whereas two important poems of 1919—"The Double Vision of Michael Robartes" and "Nineteen Hundred and Nineteen"— were published in *Wild Swans at Coole* and *The Tower* respectively. Neither the former, with its central image of the idealised dancer as observed by an enraptured poet, "Being caught between the pull / Of the dark moon and the full" [70], nor the latter, with its dark apocalyptic vision of the violent, turbulent present, point even marginally to the "marriage bed" as "solved antinomy". Those poems that do (e.g., "Solomon and the Witch") date from 1918, before the terrible quarrel with Maud Gonne. But, even before this crisis, Yeats wrote one poem that uncannily predicted the future. That poem is "Demon and Beast" of November 1918:

For certain minutes at the least
That crafty demon and that loud beast
That plague me day and night
Ran out of my sight;
Though I had long perned in the gyre,
Between my hatred and desire,
I saw my freedom won
And all laugh in the sun.   (VP 399–400)

The moment of respite in the ongoing battle between the demon of hatred and the beast of desire is a moment of blessedness, of laughter and joy. Watching an "absurd / Portly green-pated bird / [shake] off the water from his back", the poet can exult that "Being no more demoniac / A stupid happy creature / Could rouse my whole nature". But for Yeats such moments, sweet as they are, and longing as one does to make them "linger half a day", are inimical to creative energy:

Yet I am certain as can be
That every natural victory
Belongs to beast or demon,

---

6. Davie, in *An Honoured Guest*, p. 75.
7. A. N. Jeffares, *A Commentary on the Collected Poems of W. B. Yeats* (Stanford, Calif.: Stanford University Press, 1968).

> That never yet had freeman
> Right mastery of natural things . . . . (VP 401)

The "freedom" from "hatred and desire", in other words, can also be construed as the freedom of mere emptiness—of inaction and lassitude, whether mental or physical.

The return of Maud Gonne to Ireland with its attendant bitter quarrel, in any case, marked a decisive return of "That crafty demon and that loud beast / That plague me day and night". By January 1919 Yeats had written "The Second Coming," a poem whose "revelation" of the moment when "Things fall apart" is so generalised that we do not stop to wonder whom Yeats has in mind when he declares in a now celebrated aphorism, "The best lack all conviction, while the worst / Are full of passionate intensity" (VP 402) [76].

The drowning of the "ceremony of innocence" with its attendant loosing of "Mere anarchy . . . upon the world" recurs in the opening stanza ("Once more the storm is howling . . .") of "A Prayer for my Daughter"; indeed, as every reader knows, the imagery of the first, and especially the second, stanza is a direct offshoot of the earlier poem:

> I have walked and prayed for this young child an hour
> And heard the sea-wind scream upon the tower,
> And under the arches of the bridge, and scream
> In the elms above the flooded stream;
> Imagining in excited reverie
> That the future years had come,
> Dancing to a frenzied drum,
> Out of the murderous innocence of the sea. (VP 403) [77]

The storm, notes Daniel Harris,[8] may refer to the Russian Revolution of 1917, to the arrest of Con Markiewicz and Maud Gonne as conspirators in the "German plot" against conscription, to Sinn Fein's victory over the moderates in the election of December 1918, or to Britain's imposition of military rule in Ireland and the "retaliatory guerrilla campaign waged by the IRA".

* * *

But the gorgeous rhetoric of the passage should not blind us to the recognition that, if Yeats does indeed have the political situation of Ireland or the Russian Revolution in mind, as critics such as Harris have supposed, he says nothing meaningful about them. Chaos, crisis, storm, the terrible vision of a dreaded future: this "vast image out of *Spiritus Mundi*", as Yeats calls it in "The Second Coming", remains purposely incoherent, open to whatever interpretation we want to read into it; a prevision of the rise of Fascism, of the Irish Civil War, and so on.[9] Indeed, what Yeats has done

---

8. Daniel Harris, Yeats: *Coole Park and Ballylee* (Baltimore: Johns Hopkins University Press, 1974) p. 138.
9. Harold Bloom makes this point about "The Second Coming": "There is imagistic desperation in Yeats's closing rhetorical lunge. Has he earned his ironic reversal of his own arbitrary use of the Christian reference? And is his closing image coherent in itself? In what sense will the rough beast be 'born' at Bethlehem? Clearly, not literally, but is it legitimate then to use 'born' for what would actually be a demonic epiphany?" (*Yeats*, p. 323).

is to cover up, with superb artistry, the real subject of his "excited reverie", which is neither war in Europe nor, except quite indirectly, Sinn Fein's victory at home, but the more immediate storm that has triggered "the great gloom that is in [the poet's] mind." * * *

Surely one of the ironies of "A Prayer for my Daughter" is that the "woman won", who is the baby's mother, plays no role even as the "woman lost" takes centre stage. The manuscript drafts of the poem, reproduced by Jon Stallworthy in *Between the Lines*, are interesting in this regard. No rough draft of stanza 1 exists (although Stallworthy thinks there must have been one and that it was destroyed—*BL*[1] 29), but here is the first version of stanza 2:

> God grant my prayer
> Nor am I the first father that has stood
> > here
> And judged ~~the~~ here beside this cradle hood
> > ~~seeing~~ thinking that
> And ~~seeing that~~ a popular tempest blew
> > all
> As though to make things a ~~knew~~ new,
> ~~According to opinion, driven men wild~~
> ~~Decides that some (————————)~~
> As this opinion wound, had driven men wild
> And filled their hearts with bitterness
> ~~Feared for this child unless~~
> ~~For Had fear~~
> Had dread for his child's peace unless
> Heaven pour abounding sweetness on the child   (*BL* 29–30)

This stanza undergoes further drafts, all of them containing references to "opinion" that has "driven men wild" and to "hearts" "choked with dusty bitterness", as the third draft has it. In the revision, these references are saved for stanzas 7 and 8, with their explicit repudiation of "the loveliest woman born". But clearly "A Prayer for my Daughter" has its roots in the acute self-conflict which finds the poet "pern[ing] in the gyre, / Between my hatred and desire (*VP* 400). Indeed, "opinion" is the opening word of *Michael Robartes and the Dancer*: "Opinion is not worth a rush", Michael Robartes tells "the Dancer" in the title poem, thus opening the debate between "opinion" and "ceremony" that runs through the volume.

In the title poem, this *débat* is a light and witty sparring match, the lady (here Iseult Gonne[2]) bemusedly letting her male companion tell her to "bear in mind your lover's wage / Is what your looking-glass can show" (*VP* 385) [71] only to turn the tables on him by having the last word: "They say such different things at school". But in "A Prayer for my Daughter", the beloved has no such opportunity. Nameless and voiceless, she can only be, so to speak, shouted down:

---

1. Jon Stallworthy, *Between the Lines: Yeats's Poetry in the Making* (Oxford: Clarendon Press, 1963).
2. See, on this point, the excellent analysis in Elizabeth Cullingford, "Yeats and Women: *Michael Robartes and the Dancer*," *Yeats Annual* 4, pp. 30–33.

May she be granted beauty and yet not
Beauty to make a stranger's eye distraught,
Or hers before a looking-glass, for such,
Being made beautiful overmuch,
Consider beauty a sufficient end,
Lose natural kindness and maybe
The heart-revealing intimacy
That chooses right, and never find a friend. (VP 403–4) [77]

Beauty, it seems, cannot coexist with "natural kindness" and "heart-revealing intimacy"; indeed, beauty precludes wise choice and the finding of "a friend". In stanza 4, Yeats illustrates these truths, using Greek mythology to make his point: both Helen and Aphrodite chose badly and suffered the consequences.

Implicit in this "reasoning", which, incidentally, has little to do with Anne Butler Yeats's potential to become so beautiful that she would drive men crazy, and even less with Sinn Fein or Fascism, is the suggestion that Maud Gonne had made a fatal error in rejecting his proposal, that had she not done so, [things] might have been very different. Indeed, as the poet indirectly reminds her in stanza 5, "Hearts are not had as a gift but hearts are earned / By those that are not entirely beautiful". Maud Gonne having rejected his love, the poet, somewhat self-indulgently presented here as "many a poor man that has roved, / Loved and thought himself beloved", has opted for the "glad kindness" (note the echo from "Under Saturn") of the woman who *is* willing to "earn" his heart. This is the extent of the tribute Yeats pays to his wife in "A Prayer for my Daughter".

Having devoted three of the first five stanzas to the delineation of what his daughter should *not* be, the poet turns in stanza 6 to the positive side of the equation: the flourishing hidden tree, the linnet, the "magnanimities of sound", the rootedness of the green laurel in "one dear perpetual place". But, even here, the reference to "merriment" oddly brings to mind the idea of a "chase" (an allusion to Daphne, changed into the laurel tree and hence free from the advances of Apollo[3]), and then, even more oddly, a "quarrel". Why should there be quarrelling amid the "merriment" of this idyllic landscape of bird and tree? An earlier draft of the stanza provides a clue:

O let her live contented as a bird
That in the left hand bush a moment heard
A moment later on the right hand sings
And will not though it clap its wings
For the excitement of an unknown face
With customary faces quarrel
Or let her live like a green laurel
Rooted in one dear perpetual place. (BL 35)

3. Cullingford aptly comments, "Daphne, fleeing from the lustful Apollo, cried for help to her father, the river god Peneus. Peneus responded by turning her into a laurel tree, thus preserving her chastity at the expense of her humanity. Despite the last stanza, the prevailing tone of 'A Prayer for my Daughter' suggests that sexuality is troublesome, dangerous, and best avoided if possible" (*Yeats Annual* 4, p. 47).

The fear here is that the daughter might grow up to be the sort of woman who is easily distracted, a woman who "For the excitement of an unknown face"—perhaps a new lover?—"With customary faces [will] quarrel". And whose is the "customary face" but Yeats's own, rejected perhaps most notably in the "quarrel" that had taken place when Maud Gonne had arrived on his doorstep that winter? In revising the stanza, Yeats carefully expunged the topical, personal reference but retained the word "quarrel", the context making it possible to construe that word as a lover's quarrel— part and parcel of the merriment of the chase—that we might find in a conventional pastoral.

But the pastoral motif is dispelled in the next stanza:

> My mind, because the minds that I have loved,
> The sort of beauty that I have approved,
> Prosper but little, has dried up of late,
> Yet knows that to be choked with hate
> May well be of all evil chances chief.
> If there's no hatred in a mind
> Assault and battery of the wind
> Can never tear the linnet from the leaf.   (*VP* 405) [78]

Again, the rhetoric and sound structure of this famous stanza carry us along on a wave of conviction, without our worrying too much what the poem is really saying. To be "choked with hate / May well be of all evil chances chief": again and again, in the poems of *The Tower* and *The Winding Stair*, Yeats will make this moral statement, will insist on the need to cast out, not only hatred, but remorse. In "A Prayer for my Daughter", the opposition between courtesy and kindness on the one hand, and hatred and opinion on the other, seems to be what Joyce Carol Oates calls the "crude division between good girl and shrill (hysterical?) woman".[4] Even the rhythm is assertive: "linnet" and "leaf" being related by alliteration as well as by the emphatic iambic pentameter, with its stresses falling on "lin-" and "leaf", as if to say that no disagreement with what the poet says is possible.

Yet there is also desperation in Yeats's willed insistence on the expiation of hatred, in his recognition that his own mind "has dried up of late," or, as he puts it in the first draft, "Has grown half barren from much hate" (see *BL* 35). For why and how should hate—primarily an energising force in Yeats[5]—produce such barrenness? A decade later Yeats would have his old hermit Ribh declare,

> Why should I seek for love or study it?
> It is of God and passes human wit.
> I study hatred with great diligence,
> For that's a passion in my own control,

4. Oates, in *Georgia Review*, 37, p. 19.
5. There are two good discussions of hatred as a positive force in Yeats's poetry: Joseph M. Hassett's *Yeats and the Poetics of Hate* (Dublin: Gill and Macmillan; New York: St. Martin's Press, 1986); and Fahmy Farag, *The Opposing Virtues: Two Essays*, New Yeats Papers xv (Dublin: Dolmen Press, 1978). Both Hassett and Farag begin by noting that the word "hate" and its cognates seems to be used in opposite ways by Yeats, but they agree that ultimately the two are complementary'. Hassett's discussion of *Per Amica Silentia Lunae* in chapter 3 is especially useful.

A sort of besom that can clear the soul
Of everything that is not mind or sense.   (VP 558)

And A *Concordance to the Poems* cites fifty-three examples of "hate" and
its cognates,[6] the later appearances of the word coming back again and
again to the notion, put forward by Ribh, that "Hatred of God may bring
the soul to God" (VP 558), or that as Crazy Jane, watching the dancers
enact their passionate ritual of death, declares, "They had all that had their
hate" (VP 514).

Is it then only "intellectual hatred" as displayed by women that Yeats
rejects? Not even this, as we can see in "The Circus Animals' Desertion",
when the poet, recalling *The Countess Cathleen* (the play he had written
for and about Maud Gonne in the nineties, and in which she acted),
admits,

I thought my dear must her own soul destroy,
So did fanaticism and hate enslave it,
And this brought forth a dream and soon enough
This dream itself had all my thought and love.   (VP 630) [129]

"Fanaticism and hate", it is here implied, far from undercutting the poet's
"dream", actually triggered it, for great hatred produces conflict with the
anti-self and generates the passion necessary for the production of art. Thus
when, in "Remorse for Intemperate Speech", the poet recalls his attempt
to curb his hatred—"I sought my betters: though in each / Fine manners,
liberal speech, / Turn hatred into sport"—he quickly recognises that such
"sport" is not for him, that "Nothing said or done can reach / My fanatic
heart" (VP 506). Indeed, when hatred is dissipated, so, evidently, is sexual
potency. This is why the Yeats of *Last Poems* must repeatedly pose as Wild
Old Wicked Man, begging the gods to "Grant me an old man's frenzy, /
Myself must I remake" (VP 576).

It is against this larger backdrop that I wish to place the final stanza of
"A Prayer for my Daughter". The Yeats who wrote this poem knew that
it was his fate to have "long perned in the gyre, / Between [his] hatred
and desire". Accordingly, when he expresses the hope that his daughter's
future "bridegroom bring her to a house / Where all's accustomed, ceremonious; / For arrogance and hatred are the wares / Peddled in the thoroughfares", we must take the causal "For . . ." clause with a large grain
of salt. If hatred was a commodity to be "Peddled in the thoroughfares"
(the phrase recalls "No Second Troy", in which the poet is at once fascinated and appalled by Maud–Helen's "hurl[ing] the little streets upon
the great" [37]), Yeats may well have been one of its hawkers. As for
arrogance (see the "arrogant loveliness" of the "sweetheart from another
life" in "An Image from a Past Life", VP 390), consider what happens in
that great poem written just two years before Yeats's death, "Beautiful Lofty
Things", the poem in which, for the first time, Maud Gonne is called by
name:

6. See Stephen Maxwell Parrish (ed.), A *Concordance to the Poems of W. B. Yeats* (Ithaca, NY:
Cornell University Press, 1963) p. 363.

> . . . Maud Gonne at Howth station waiting a train,
> Pallas Athene in that straight back and arrogant head. . . .
>
> (VP 578) [117]

Not only does *arrogance* here have positive connotations for Yeats, but the particular prose in which he chooses to memorialise Maud Gonne is revealing. Why does the poet place his Pallas Athene "at Howth station waiting a train"? Jeffares suggests that "this memory goes back to their walks at Howth where Yeats first proposed to her" (COM 462), but "waiting a train" also points to Maud Gonne's potential for action rather than repose. Hers is emphatically *not* a life of being "Rooted in one dear perpetual place"; rather, she is remembered as "waiting a train" that will take her away from the poet. Indeed, the railway station is, so to speak, Maud Gonne's natural habitat;[7] she is always in transit or, as we would now say, "on the road", her beauty "like a tightened bow" (VP 256) [37], threatening all comers.

How, then, are we meant to take the ending of "A Prayer for my Daughter"? Having descried "arrogance and hatred", the poem's speaker concludes,

> How but in custom and in ceremony
> Are innocence and beauty born?
> Ceremony's a name for the rich horn,
> And custom for the spreading laurel tree.

These lines are characterised by a kind of willed regression, the linkage of the Horn of Plenty and "spreading" laurel tree with custom and ceremony having been firmly established in stanzas 4–6, and requiring no exposition here. Is the poem then merely spinning its wheels? Not really, if we read these lines as part of the poet's ongoing quarrel with his "sweetheart from another life", a quarrel in which Yeats tries to convince Maud Gonne that he no longer wants or adores her, that he has cast out hatred and remorse, opting for the antithetical virtues of courtesy and "radical innocence".

For a brief moment, the poet can achieve this state of what Ellmann calls, with reference to "A Dialogue of Self and Soul", a "secular blessedness".[8] In the words of "Demon and Beast", written just a few months earlier, "For certain minutes at the least / That crafty demon and that loud beast / That plague me day and night / Ran out of my sight" (VP 399). But before that poem is over, as I remarked earlier, its speaker has opted for the old conflict, knowing "That every natural victory / Belongs to beast or demon". Indeed, in an especially revealing line in this stanza, the poet concludes "that mere growing old, that brings / Chilled blood, this sweetness brought" (VP 401).

"Radical innocence", in other words, is for the old; only when our blood

---

7. "In the next few years I saw her always when she passed to and fro between Dublin and Paris, surrounded, no matter how rapid her journey and how brief her stay at either end of it, by cages full of birds, canaries, finches of all kinds, dogs, a parrot, and once a full-grown hawk from Donegal. Once when I saw her to her railway carriage I noticed how the cages obstructed racks and cushions and wondered what her fellow-travellers would say, but the carriage remained empty" (Yeats, *Autobiographies* [London: Macmillan, 1955] p. 123–4).
8. Richard Ellmann, *The Identity of Yeats* (New York: Oxford University Press, 1954) p. 9.

chills are we willing to assume the passivity of the "self-delighting" soul that is willing to let "its own sweet will [be] Heaven's will". Thus, try as the poet may to project such a "Self-appeasing, self-affrighting" soul as belonging to his infant daughter, to invent for that daughter a myth of custom and ceremony, of a happiness that ignores the "howl[ing]" of the "windy quarter" outside the gates, he himself knows that he can only function in that howling storm.

* * *

PAUL DE MAN

The Rhetorical Question: "Among School Children"†

* * * Yeats's poem "Among School Children" ends with the famous line: "How can we know the dancer from the dance?" Although there are some revealing inconsistencies within the commentaries, the line is usually interpreted as stating, with the increased emphasis of a rhetorical device, the potential unity between form and experience, between creator and creation. It could be said that it denies the discrepancy between the sign and the referent from which we started out. Many elements in the imagery and the dramatic development of the poem strengthen this traditional reading; without having to look any further than the immediately preceding lines, one finds powerful and consecrated images of the continuity from part to whole that makes synecdoche into the most seductive of metaphors: the organic beauty of the tree, stated in the parallel syntax of a similar rhetorical question, or the convergence, in the dance, of erotic desire with musical form:

> O chestnut-tree, great-rooted blossomer,
> Are you the leaf, the blossom or the bole?
> O body swayed to music, O brightening glance,
> How can we know the dancer from the dance? [98]

A more extended reading, always assuming that the final line is to be read as a rhetorical question, reveals that the thematic and rhetorical grammar of the poem yields a consistent reading that extends from the first line to the last and that can account for all the details in the text. It is equally possible, however, to read the last line literally rather than figuratively, as asking with some urgency the question we asked earlier within the context of contemporary criticism: *not* that sign and referent are so exquisitely fitted to each other that all difference between them is at times blotted out but, rather, since the two essentially different elements, sign and meaning, are so intricately intertwined in the imagined "presence" that the poem addresses, how can we possibly make the distinctions that would shelter us from the error of identifying what cannot be identified? The

† From Paul de Man, "Semiology and Rhetoric," in *Diacritics.* © The Johns Hopkins University Press. Page references in brackets are to this Norton Critical Edition.

clumsiness of the paraphrase reveals that it is not necessarily the literal reading which is simpler than the figurative one * * *; here, the figural reading, which assumes the question to be rhetorical, is perhaps naïve, whereas the literal reading leads to greater complication of theme and statement. For it turns out that the entire scheme set up by the first reading can be undermined, or deconstructed, in the terms of the second, in which the final line is read literally as meaning that, since the dancer and the dance are not the same, it might be useful, perhaps even desperately necessary—for the question can be given a ring of urgency, "Please tell me how *can* I know the dancer from the dance"—to tell them apart. But this will replace the reading of each symbolic detail by a divergent interpretation. The oneness of trunk, leaf, and blossom, for example, that would have appealed to Goethe, would find itself replaced by the much less reassuring Tree of Life from the Mabinogion that appears in the poem "Vacillation," in which the fiery blossom and the earthly leaf are held together, as well as apart, by the crucified and castrated God Attis [109], of whose body it can hardly be said that it is "not bruised to pleasure soul." This hint should suffice to suggest that two entirely coherent but entirely incompatible readings can be made to hinge on one line, whose grammatical structure is devoid of ambiguity, but whose rhetorical mode turns the mood as well as the mode of the entire poem upside down. Neither can we say, as was already the case in the first example, that the poem simply has two meanings that exist side by side. The two readings have to engage each other in direct confrontation, for the one reading is precisely the error denounced by the other and has to be undone by it. Nor can we in any way make a valid decision as to which of the readings can be given priority over the other; none can exist in the other's absence. There can be no dance without a dancer, no sign without a referent. On the other hand, the authority of the meaning engendered by the grammatical structure is fully obscured by the duplicity of a figure that cries out for the differentiation that it conceals.

Yeats's poem is not explicitly "about" rhetorical questions but about images or metaphors, and about the possibility of convergence between experiences of consciousness such as memory or emotions—what the poem calls passion, piety, and affection—and entities accessible to the senses such as bodies, persons, or icons. We return to the inside/outside model from which we started out and which the poem puts into question by means of a syntactical device (the question) made to operate on a grammatical as well as on a rhetorical level. The couple grammar/rhetoric, certainly not a binary opposition since they in no way exclude each other, disrupts and confuses the neat antithesis of the inside/outside pattern. We can transfer this scheme to the act of reading and interpretation. By reading we get, as we say, *inside* a text that was first something alien to us and which we now make our own by an act of understanding. But this understanding becomes at once the representation of an extra-textual meaning * * *

ANITA SOKOLSKY

The Resistance to Sentimentality: Yeats, de Man, and the Aesthetic Education†

* * *

* * * De Man's persuasive analysis[1] of the closing lines [of "Among School Children"] argues that the final question must be read both rhetorically and literally. Thus its irreconcilable meanings as triumphant assertion of unity and despairing uncertainty endlessly undo one another, putting meaning *en abyme*. If one looks more closely at the lines, the threat to a recuperation of the poem's erotics of unsatisfied desire extends itself further.

> O chestnut tree, great-rooted blossomer,
> Are you the leaf, the blossom, or the bole?
> O body swayed to music, O brightening glance,
> How can we know the dancer from the dance?

The final lines attempt to act out on a grammatical level the subsumption of part to whole they describe. The final question is customarily assumed to reformulate the former. The lines substitute, as by a natural logic, "O chestnut tree, great-rooted blossomer" with "O body swayed to music, O brightening glance"; the invocatory "O" enforces the analogy. The dancing body is but another version of the spreading chestnut tree; as the tree extends itself through its components, so the dancer emerges through the dance. Thus both the dancer and the analogy appear to unfold naturally. But in fact "O brightening glance" is no proper analogy to "great-rooted blossomer": the synecdochical relation of brightening glance to dancer makes it more like the leaf, blossom, or bole. The "dancer" is parallel in position to "the leaf, the blossom, or the bole"; and since these latter are subsidiary qualities of their antecedent whole, "O chestnut tree," the dancer in turn appears to be a synecdoche for "body" or "glance." Moreover, the lines offer a temptingly false derivation; if the dancer can be defined only as one who dances, then the great-rooted blossomer ought to be located in the blossom, as opposed to the leaf or bole.

Thus, there are several mutually disruptive questions being raised in the final lines. The first asks of the chestnut tree, Are you the sum of your parts, or does your identity inhere in any one of them? That is a different question from "How can we know the dancer from the dance?," which asks, How can we tell form from its performance? How can we conceive the artist's identity except as it emerges through his creation? The imperfect and misleading homology of the two final questions raises the implicit problem: how can we distinguish the essential nature of a thing from its subsidiary characteristics? How does the lover know precisely what he or

† Reprinted from *Yale Journal of Criticism* 1:1 (1988): 77–78. Reprinted by permission of the publisher.
1. See preceding selection [*Editor*].

she desires in the beloved, wherein inheres the essential lovableness of the lover? How is the poet to define his essential nature through his created image?

These problems are not merely of casual interest; they determine the way one reads "Among School Children." Most interpretations of the poem in effect fetishize its final lines, reading the whole poem as if its essence were condensed in them. The poem is understood teleologically; its interpretation rests on the synecdochical reliability of its culminating image. When, as in the final lines of "Among School Children," the image refuses such assimilative tactics, it also undoes the postulate of epistemology which Aristotle and Plato lay down, the subordination of part to whole. The final lines not only upset a conciliation of artist and creation, image and referent, but also disrupt the precarious status of the fetishized part-object. Not only is such subordination deranged, but the very distinction between part and whole is debilitated. An epistemological quest is undone by the lines in which that quest should culminate.

* * *

ELIZABETH BUTLER CULLINGFORD

Desire and Hunger in "Among School Children"†

Paul de Man's deconstructive reading of "Among School Children" posits the concluding question as real rather than rhetorical: he thinks the speaker wants to distinguish the dancer from the dance.[1] According to de Man, the poem enacts an "anguished" need to choose between "asceticism" (separation of dancer from dance) and the satisfactions of natural life (union of dancer and dance).[2] Syntactically one cannot determine whether a question is rhetorical: the context alone enables interpretation. In suggesting that "asceticism" was a valid option for Yeats's speaker de Man's ahistorical reading severs the poem's grammar from the material circumstances out of which it arose.

In resituating "Among School Children" in its historical context, however, I make no claim to objective truth. History too is created by perspective, made in answer to ideological pressures. For example, the "histories" studied by the children in Yeats's 1926 classroom are versions of the Irish past that are currently derided by revisionists as vulgar nationalism. As Ward has pointed out, women have been excluded from both the nationalist and the revisionist versions of the Irish story.[3] In reading

† From *Gender and History in Yeats's Love Poetry* (Syracuse, N.Y.: Syracuse University Press, 1996), pp. 185–87. Reprinted by permission of Elizabeth Butler Cullingford. Page references to this Norton Critical Edition are given in brackets after the author's original citations.
1. See pp. 455–56 [*Editor*].
2. Paul de Man, *The Rhetoric of Romanticism* (New York: Columbia University Press, 1984), 200–05.
3. Margaret Ward, *The Missing Sex: Putting Women into Irish History* (Dublin: Attic Press, 1991), 5–12.

the poem through the lens of Irish women's history I construct an alternative narrative, which resituates Gonne as social activist as well as hollow-cheeked Muse, writing subject as well as aesthetic object.

In Sonnet 71 of *Astrophil and Stella* Sidney voices the metaphorical connection between sexual appetite and physical hunger that is a commonplace of love poetry. Astrophil praises Stella's beauty in the approved platonic fashion because it leads the mind of her lover towards spiritual perfection: "So while thy beauty draws the heart to love, / As fast thy Virtue bends that love to good." Abruptly, however, Sidney interrupts the voice of platonic sublimation with the urgent cry of the body: "But ah, desire still cries: 'Give me some food.' "[4] Since we can live without sex but not without nourishment, the metaphor reinforces the sexual imperative by equating desire with necessity. It is a figure of speech that privileges the body over the spirit, consummated over platonic love. Arguing for the Irish right to divorce, Yeats used the familiar amatory trope, claiming that without sexual ties "the emotions and therefore the spiritual life may be perverted and starved" (SS[5] 159). The juxtaposition of literary metaphor with political fact demonstrates the complex matrix of genre and history out of which both Yeats's poetry and his political interventions were generated. As a love poet Yeats could not have left the issue of divorce uncontested, since the proposed ban infringed the free expression of desire that was the basis of his art; and his position as a Senator involved in public debate about sexual mores informed his twenties love poetry.

The Free State inherited from the Imperial parliament the power to dissolve marriages, a power it immediately sought to renounce. In March 1925 Yeats published an "Undelivered Speech" in favor of divorce. Grounding his argument in the civil rights of the Southern Anglo-Irish minority, he warned against alienating the Northern Protestants, but his strongest claim was for sexual happiness. Gonne's traumatic marriage informed his conviction that:

> Marriage is not to us a Sacrament, but, upon the other hand, the love of man and woman, and the inseparable physical desire, are sacred. This conviction has come to us through ancient philosophy and modern literature, and it seems to us a most sacrilegious thing to persuade two people who hate one another because of some unforgettable wrong, to live together. (SS 158–59)

The sacredness of physical desire, especially as sanctioned by "modern literature," was not a proposition calculated to appeal to Catholic sensibilities, especially in a culture that privileged celibacy. *The Catholic Bulletin* charged that Yeats's speech, a "pestilential effusion," was "on the same level, in regard to common decency and morality, as his notorious Swan Sonnet contributed to the filthy pages of the defunct Monthly called *To-morrow.*"[6] "Leda and the Swan," with its graphic depiction of the sexual act, was the poetic correlative of Yeats's political defense of desire. Rape

4. Sir Philip Sidney, *Sir Philip Sidney*, ed. Katharine Duncan-Jones (Oxford: Oxford University Press, 1989), 182.
5. *The Senate Speeches of W. B. Yeats*, ed. Donald R. Pearce (London: Faber and Faber, 1961).
6. *Catholic Bulletin* (Dublin) 15.6 (1925): 530.

(unsanctioned union) and divorce (unsanctioned putting asunder) were cognate expressions of transgressive sexuality.

When he finally spoke in the Senate, Yeats supplemented his written arguments with an attack on the interference of the Church in the affairs of State. Admitting that "In the long warfare of this country with England the Catholic clergy took the side of the people, and owing to that they possess here an influence that they do not possess anywhere else in Europe" (*SS* 92–93), he nevertheless deplored the petrifying influence of churchmen of all denominations upon "the living, changing, advancing human mind." He argued that "Among modern communities there is a demand for happiness, which increases with education" (*SS* 96), insinuating those who would stifle happiness in the interests of morality were under-educated.

Yeats's defense of sexual happiness against clerical asceticism is fused poetically with the question of education in "Among School Children," a poem that is historically situated in the debate over the School Attendance Bill (1925), which closely followed the divorce controversy.[7] In May 1926, two months after his last Senate speech on the School Attendance Bill, Yeats told [Olivia] Shakespear, "I am writing poetry . . . and as always happens, no matter how I begin, it becomes love poetry" (*L*[8] 714–15). "Among School Children," which Ellmann dates June 1926, opens as the discursive memoirs of an elderly school inspector, but swiftly "becomes love poetry." Controlled by the traditional generic trope of desire as hunger, "Among School Children" implicitly poises Gonne's starvation of Yeats's sexual appetite against her feeding of poor school children, and ends with Yeats's most complete and satisfying celebration of the unbruised, undeprived body: the body whose desires have been fed.

As education spokesman, Yeats sought "to prepare for an Ireland that will be healthy, vigorous, orderly, and above all, happy" (*SS* 174), but the dilapidated and filthy condition of Irish schools was not conducive to happiness. Sectarian monopolies impeded government assistance, so in a speech on "The Child and the State" Yeats suggested that physical improvements should be financed by a county rate and supervised by county committees, without infringing the religious managers' right to control the intellectual life of the school (*SS* 170). In a long and hostile analysis of Yeats's speech, however, the *Bulletin* reaffirmed the principle of sectarian control. Claiming that, "It is obvious that Yeats and the Mutual Boosters mean to advance into the Educational Arena in 1926" and that "Pollexfen Yeats begirds himself for his new campaign of literary penetration" (surely not an innocent pun, considering "Leda"), the *Bulletin* explicitly warned Yeats off the educational grass.[9]

Yeats was not deterred. Accused by the Catholics of moral filth, he retaliated by charging that the schools controlled by religious managers

---

7. See Donald Torchiana, " 'Among School Children' and the Education of the Irish Spirit," in *In Excited Reverie: A Centenary Tribute to W. B. Yeats*, ed. A. Norman Jeffares and K. G. W. Cross (New York: Macmillan, 1965), passim.

8. *The Letters of W. B. Yeats*, ed. Allan Wade (London: Rupert Hart-Davis, 1954; New York: Macmillan, 1955).

9. *Catholic Bulletin* (Dublin) 16.1 (1926): 7, 8.

were the sites of physical filth (*SS* 108). He became obsessed by cleanliness: George Yeats describes his interrogating the nuns at Waterford about how often the floors were washed.[1] School attendance, he argued, should not be compulsory unless the schools were likely to promote happiness as well as learning: "And if the children are going to be forced to school you must not only see that those schools are warm and clean and sanitary, but you must . . . see that children during school hours are neither half-naked nor starved" (*SS* 169). The children's food was as important as their cleanliness.

Yeats's work on the School Attendance Bill is a major political tribute to Gonne, though they had quarreled about his support for draconian Free State measures against Republicans.[2] Much of Gonne's earliest work in Ireland had taken place among the starving people of the West. During the 1898 famine in the Erris peninsula she and James Connolly drafted a pamphlet citing ecclesiastics on the right of the hungry to steal food. Yeats dedicated *The Countess Cathleen*, "the tale of a woman selling her soul to buy food for a starving people" (*Mem*[3] 47), to Gonne. Like her model, Cathleen claims that:

> learned theologians have laid down
> That he who has no food, offending no way,
> May take his meat and bread from too-full larders.
>
> (*VPL*[4] 67v, 69v)

Although the Countess refuses to gratify the erotic desires of her poet Aleel, she sacrifices herself to obtain food for her tenants.

Between 1910 and 1914 Gonne devoted herself to the private feeding of poor Irish school children while attempting to persuade municipal authorities to take up the burden. Her efforts to get the English School Meals Act (1906) extended to Ireland were opposed by some Catholic school managers, who feared that public control of the schools would endanger the sectarian monopoly. Gonne "tried to enlist the help of nuns to influence the Irish bishops on the matter, so that the 'secret opposition which we are meeting from some of the clergy in Ireland who seem to think it dangerous and subversive to feed starving school children' could be prevented."[5] The religious managers opposed humanitarian reform in the interests of spiritual control. Gonne hoped that nuns would be more responsive than bishops to the children's need for food, thus framing the dispute in gendered terms: female social compassion versus male religious intransigence, or love versus hate.

When during the Dublin Lock-Out of 1913 philanthropists proposed to send the starving children of the striking trade unionists to temporary fosterage in England, the Archbishop of Dublin condemned the scheme as

1. Ann Saddlemyer, "George Yeats," unpublished lecture, Modern Language Association Convention, Chicago, 1990.
2. Maud Gonne MacBride, "Yeats and Ireland," in *Scattering Branches*, ed. Stephen Gwynn (New York: Macmillan, 1940), 25.
3. W. B. Yeats, *Memoirs*, ed. Denis Donoghue (London: Macmillan, 1972).
4. *The Variorum Edition of the Plays of W. B. Yeats*, ed. Russell K. Alspach (London: Macmillan, 1966).
5. Margaret Ward, *Maud Gonne: Ireland's Joan of Arc* (London: Pandora, 1990), 98–99.

likely to damage the children's religious faith; and Dublin priests encouraged hostile crowds to prevent their departure. Both the Lock-Out and the School Meals Act controversies poised Gonne's attempts to feed the hungry bodies of children against the Church's insistence on the preservation of pure souls. In a gesture reminiscent of the Countess Cathleen, she sold her jewels to provide food for the trade unionists.[6] Sharing Gonne's passionate concern about feeding the children,[7] Yeats wrote to Connolly's *Irish Worker* an indignant letter that accused the priests of turning "the religion of Him who thought it hard for a rich man to enter into the Kingdom of Heaven into an oppression of the poor" (*UP2*[8] 407). In November 1913 Gonne thanked Yeats for a "generous subscription to the children's dinners" (*AYF*[9] 329), while in his turn Yeats celebrated her social compassion and work for the poor in a remarkable group of love poems written in 1915.

"Broken Dreams" balances the poet's obsession with his mistress against the love she elicits from the old and the poor:

> Young men no longer suddenly catch their breath
> When you are passing;
> But maybe some old gaffer mutters a blessing
> Because it was your prayer
> Recovered him upon the bed of death.   (*VP*[1] 355) [64]

The speaker recuperates her diminished beauty by remembering her work for the disadvantaged. In "Her Praise" he can find no one in his own intellectual or political circle willing to celebrate her, so he seeks out a beggar:

> If there be rags enough he will know her name
> And be well pleased remembering it, for in the old days,
> Though she had young men's praise and old men's blame,
> Among the poor both old and young gave her praise. (*VP* 351)

In "The People" she remembers how "Those I had served and some that I had fed" were turned against her by her enemies, but the speaker endorses her refusal to complain of "the people" (*VP* 352) [64]. All three love poems modify the individualism of the tradition through their celebration of her social labors, as opposed to her political ones. Writing to her in 1927, shortly after the composition of "Among School Children," Yeats connected her philanthropic work with an earlier occult vision in which

> the spirit showed you the circles of Heaven possible to you, of these the third & highest was "labour from devine [sic] love". Then in 1909 or 1910 when you were working on the feeding of school children I

---

6. Information from Deirdre Toomey.
7. "Meals for School Children," *Irish Times* 29 October 1913: 8; Torchiana, "Among School Children," 138.
8. *Uncollected Prose by W. B. Yeats*, vol. 2, ed. John P. Frayne and Colton Johnson (London: Macmillan, 1975).
9. *The Gonne-Yeats Letters 1893–1938: Always Your Friend*, ed. Anna MacBride White and A. Norman Jeffares (London: Hutchinson, 1992).
1. *The Variorum Edition of the Poems of W. B. Yeats*, ed. Peter Allt and Russell K. Alspach (New York: Macmillan, 1966).

met you in Paris & you told me that you were convinced that all the misfortunes of your life had come upon you because you had taken up movements which had hate for their motive power.

In Yeats's mind the concepts of heavenly "labour" and Gonne's feeding of school children were closely associated, and opposed to what he identified as "labour from hatred" (AYF 443–44).

Although the School Meals Act was extended to Ireland in 1914, Gonne had to continue working to see that it did not "remain a dead letter" (AYF 388). In 1921 she told Yeats of a White Cross school meals campaign during which she had to arrange for the feeding of 2,500 children in Donegal (AYF 426–27, 524). In his Senate speech five years later, therefore, Yeats argued correctly that the operation of the Act was inadequate: while there were some arrangements for school meals in the towns,

> There are none in the country, and judging by my own countryside, where I live during the summer months, it is needed. Children will start early in the morning. They will be the greater portion of the day in school and they will have no adequate meals. They come away hungry, and it seems, if not very necessary, at least very desirable that they should have food. (SS 110)

Informed by his experiences as a school inspector, "Among School Children" shows Yeats attempting to adjust the imbalance between spiritual virtue and physical happiness through the "very desirable" feeding of the body. When he conjures Gonne's image into the pleasant Montessori classroom at Waterford, therefore, her presence is politically as well as emotionally appropriate.

St. Otteran's, the convent school at Waterford that is the site of the poem, was run by nuns who clearly did not subscribe to The Catholic Bulletin nor starve their children or their visitors. George Yeats recounts the lavish hospitality of the sisters, who in deference to the supposed worldliness of their distinguished guest swamped every dish on the long menu in alcohol.[2] Not all nuns were so liberal: Yeats wrote that, "Mrs. Kevin O'Higgins told me that a few years ago she was at a Retreat and on the day she left she and the others were addressed by the Mother Superior. They were told that there were two men 'they must never know, must not even bow to in the streets'—Lennox Robinson and W. B. Yeats" (L 747). His poetic compliment to a Catholic school is therefore strategic: he deliberately sites himself, a "filthy" and "Cromwellian" member of the New Protestant Ascendancy, next to a "kind old nun" who does not regard him as an enemy of her faith, the sort of nun to whom Gonne had appealed in her struggle against the male clergy. In the second stanza he follows the nun with a "Ledaean body": a deliberate allusion to his controversial "Swan Sonnet." Indeed, the subtext of "Among School Children" is "Leda and the Swan." Helen/Gonne, inheritor of the "Ledaean body," is one of the "daughters of the swan," while the speaker, though "never of Ledaean kind / Had pretty plumage once" (VP 443–44) [97]. Written two years after the To-morrow controversy, "Among School Children" redefines the place

2. Saddlemyer, "George Yeats."

and nature of sexual love in the Catholic Free State through a meditation on desire, hunger, and the body.

Critics have contrasted the "masculine" volume *The Tower* with its "feminine" sequel *The Winding Stair*,[3] but "Among School Children," a poem dominated by representations of the feminine, fails to conform to this pattern. The children noticed by the speaker are all girls; the teacher is a nun; the poet remembers Gonne, evokes her mythical analogue Helen the daughter of Leda, and speculates about the feelings of a "youthful mother." The dancer, though grammatically ungendered (in the drafts there was once a "dancing couple"),[4] belongs to the tradition of the female performance artist represented by Jane Avril and Loie Fuller.[5] Only the philosophers and the poet are male, and the poet's masculinity is ambiguously figured. His alter ego is the nun, who has renounced sexuality. Her voluntary celibacy is linked with the comical impotence of her elderly questioner: Yeats enforces their relation by shared epithets: the nun is "kind" and "old"; while he is "A sixty-year old smiling public man" and "a comfortable kind of old scarecrow" (VP 443–44) [97].

The male philosopher with whom Yeats struggles in "Among School Children" is Plato, source of the dualistic separation of soul from body that Yeats sees as constitutive of Irish Catholic teaching on sexuality: "Plato thought nature but a spume that plays / Upon a ghostly paradigm of things" (VP 445) [98]. Gonne's insistence on "an absolutely *platonic friendship* which is all I can or ever will be able to give" (AYF 85) laid the foundations of Yeats's later antipathy to the idea of "platonic" love, a love that denied nature. In *A Vision* Michael Robartes remembers "my past loves, neither numerous nor happy, back to the platonic love of boyhood, the most impassioned of all, and was plunged into hopeless misery" (AV [B][6] 40).

Ironically, Plato's Aristophanes perpetrates the romantic myth of perfect union between lovers. In *The Symposium* he describes an original splitting or self-alienation that can be overcome only in the arms of the missing other half. Zeus divided spherical mankind into two halves "like eggs which are cut with a hair," and the separated halves strove desperately to reunite. Love is "simply the name for the desire and pursuit of the whole."[7] In "Among School Children" Yeats remembers an occasion when

> it seemed that our two natures blent
> Into a sphere from youthful sympathy,
> Or else, to alter Plato's parable,
> Into the yolk and white of the one shell. (VP 443) [97]

Yeats "alters" Plato's parable by replacing the originary sphere with Leda's egg, suggesting that he and his beloved, like Helen and Pollux in some versions of the story, may have issued from "the one shell." The image

3. See, for example, C. L. Innes, "Yeats's Female Voices: Crazy Jane and Other Women in *The Winding Stair and Other Poems*" *Text and Context* 3 (Autumn 1988): 56; Patrick J. Keane, *Yeats's Interactions with Tradition* (Columbia: University of Missouri Press, 1987), 286.
4. For the poem's genesis see Thomas Parkinson, *W. B. Yeats Self-Critic and The Later Poetry* (Berkeley: University of California Press, 1971), 92–103.
5. Frank Kermode, *Romantic Image* (London: Routledge, 1986), 70–72.
6. W. B. Yeats, *A Vision* (London: Macmillan, 1962).
7. Plato, *The Symposium*, trans. Walter Hamilton (Harmondsworth: Penguin, 1951), 60–64.

conflates their "youthful sympathy" with Gonne's 1908 vision of astral union: "your lips touched mine. We melted into one another till we formed only *one being, a being greater than ourselves* who felt all & knew all with double intensity" (*AYF* 257). In the poem, however, the word "seemed" qualifies the image of two people blending into a perfect whole: spiritual union cannot satisfy the body's hungers.

Yeats therefore contrasts his vision of his beloved as an imaginary "living child" with her present image as a skeletally thin old woman. The crucial lines, "Hollow of cheek as though it drank the wind / And took a mess of shadows for its meat" (*VP* 444) [97], suggest malnutrition as much as the ravages of time: wind and shadows are inadequate food and drink. Gonne had earlier described herself to Yeats as looking "thin & 'hungry' " (*AYF* 319). The "hollow" cheek, like the hollow moon of "Adam's Curse," evokes the emptiness of courtly frustration. The wind is Yeats's traditional image for unfulfilled desire; and he perhaps alludes to Hamlet's dissatisfactions: "I eat the air, promise-crammed. You cannot feed capons so."[8] The phrase "took a mess of shadows for its meat" (originally "mass of shadows" [*VP* 444v]), also suggests Esau, who because he was hungry sold his birthright for a "mess of pottage." Yeats implies that Gonne has received nothing in exchange for her birthright: like the prisoners in Plato's Cave she has mistaken "shadows" for substantial food. She, who left her own children alone in Paris while she labored in Dublin to feed the school children of the poor, remains afflicted by unsatisfied hungers, while he is a bodiless "old scarecrow" who denies food to the birds. In "The Circus Animals' Desertion" he reiterates the metaphor of hunger: he was "starved for the bosom of his faery bride" (*VP* 629) [129].

Gonne's letters to Yeats justifying her renunciation of the body after their brief affair in 1908[9] emphasize her deliberate suppression of physical desire:

> I have prayed so hard to have all earthly desire taken from my love for you & dearest, loving you as I do, I have prayed & I am praying still that the bodily desire for me may be taken from you too. I know how hard and rare a thing it is for a man to hold spiritual love when the bodily desire is gone & I have not made these prayers without a terrible struggle. (*AYF* 258)

At this time Yeats noted the reawakening of the dread of physical love to which she had admitted in 1898 (*Mem* 134), but it is pointless to speculate about what Toomey calls Gonne's "essential sexual coldness."[1] When she promised to pray that "suffering & temptation may be taken from you as they have from me & that we may gain spiritual union stronger than earthly union could ever be" (*AYF* 271), was she saving Yeats's feelings?

---

8. William Shakespeare, *The Complete Works*, ed. David Bevington, 4th edition (New York: Harper Collins, 1992), 1089.
9. Richard Ellmann, *Yeats: The Man and the Masks* (Oxford: Oxford University Press, 1979), xxii–xxiii; and Curtis Bradford, "Yeats and Maud Gonne" *Texas Studies in Language and Literature* 3 (1962): 464–66, have discussed this affair. See *The Gonne-Yeats Letters 1893–1938: Always Your Friend*, ed. Anna MacBride White and A. Norman Jeffares (London: Hutchinson, 1992), 255–83, for her letters between June 1908 and July 1909.
1. Deirdre Toomey, "Labyrinths: Yeats and Maud Gonne," in *Yeats and Women*, ed. Deirdre Toomey, *Yeats Annual* 9 (London: Macmillan, 1991), 96.

It is preferable to be renounced after a struggle with temptation than to suspect that you were never particularly tempting in the first place. Given the unreliability of contraception and the difficulties she had already endured in attempting to conceal the identity of her two illegitimate children, however, her physical withdrawal may have been warranted; and the theological register of her language also demonstrates a genuine, if relatively new, commitment to Catholic social teaching on sex. In May 1909 she wrote to Yeats in terms that anticipate the heroine of Graham Greene's *The End of The Affair*: "My loved one I belong to you more in this renunciation than if I came to you in sin." In November she added, "Willie I know we are doing the right thing. The love whose physical realization we deny here will unite us in another life—If we did the easy thing & yielded to it now, very likely it would *part us here* & after" (AYF 272, 283). Yeats's dislike of Catholic asceticism was strengthened by her theological justification of the deliberate starvation of desire. Her letters after 1908 sustain a running argument with him about the necessity of bodily fulfillment both to health and creativity. Yeats had obviously suggested that when "body is not bruised to pleasure soul" (*VP* 445) [98] artistic productivity increases, but she insisted that, "Raphael bowed down to sex till it killed him when he was only 30, his painting is the essence of prettiness. Michael Angelo denied the power of sex, *for a year* while he was painting the marvel of the Sistine Chapel" (AYF 261). In her emphasis on the virtue of self-denial and the sinfulness of carnality she resembles the nun in "Among School Children," worshipping heartbreaking images that "keep a marble or a bronze repose" (*VP* 445) [98].

Yeats occasionally uses the image of starvation to define left-wing activist women in negative terms: in "In Memory of Eva Gore-Booth and Con Markievicz" the "skeleton-gaunt" Eva Gore-Booth, trade-unionist, social worker, and suffragist, becomes "An image of such politics" (*VP* 475) [102]. The semiotics of hunger in the Irish context, however, are contradictory: connected both with the forced starvation of the Famine, image of England's genocidal colonial policies, and with the voluntary starvation of the hunger strike, an ancient Irish practice codified in the Brehon laws, and depicted approvingly by Yeats in his 1904 play *The King's Threshold*. The tactic was re-introduced by the suffragists and later adopted by the Republicans. Hannah Sheehy Skeffington wrote that in 1912 the hunger strike was "a new weapon—we were the first to try it out in Ireland—had we but known, we were the pioneers in a long line. At first Sinn Fein and its allies regarded the hunger strike as a womanish thing."[2] By 1926, however, many Republican prisoners, including Markievicz,[3] had followed the suffragist example. Gonne threatened to refuse food during her term of imprisonment in 1918 (AYF 395); she did not do so, but described herself to Yeats on her discharge as "*very thin*" (AYF 399). In 1920 Terence McSwiney, Republican Lord Mayor of Cork, died while on hunger strike against the British; and Yeats staged *The King's Threshold* in his honor,

2. Hanna Sheehy Skeffington, "Reminiscences of an Irish Suffragette," in *Votes for Women: Irish Women's Struggle for the Vote*, ed. A. D. Sheehy Skeffington and Rosemary Owens (Dublin: n.p., 1975), 32.

3. Anne Haverty, *Constance Markievicz: An Independent Life* (London: Pandora, 1988), 218–19.

changing Seanchan's previous literal triumph over the King to a moral victory in death.[4] He labored to secure Gonne's release when, jailed for disseminating anti-government publications, she went on hunger strike in 1923:[5] after twenty days in Kilmainham without food, her check was literally "hollow." Yeats later claimed disapprovingly that the hunger strike had made "deliberate suffering a chief instrument in our public life,"[6] yet in his poem the ambiguity of an image that, despite its hollowness, might have been fashioned by "Quattrocento finger," also suggests admiration: Cleanth Brooks argues that Gonne's cadaverous physiognomy is supposed to be "ideal."[7] Yeats compared Irishwomen favorably with Englishwomen, who tend to run to fat; in London,

> Certain old women's faces filled me with horror . . . the fat blotched faces, rising above double chins, of women who have drunk too much beer and eaten much meat. In Dublin I had often seen old women walking with erect heads and gaunt bodies, talking to themselves with loud voices, mad with drink and poverty, but they were different, they belonged to romance. Da Vinci had drawn women who looked so, and so carried their bodies. (*Au*[8] 155)

The image of the skeleton-gaunt woman, therefore, is a complex amalgam of forced and voluntary starvation: she may be obsessed by the wrong sort of activist politics, or she may be too poor to eat, but she is visually preferable to the over-fed one: she belongs to Leonardo and to romance.

The fifth stanza of the poem suggests that practical problems may attend the "feeding" of desire; for consuming the "Honey of generation" has material consequences in a culture without contraception. The child "betrayed" into the world (a strikingly negative word) by the sexual activity of its parents may not want to leave the pre-natal state of perfection; but the mother may feel equally "betrayed" by her pregnancy (Yeats's syntax is ambiguous at this point).[9] The stanza's representation of motherhood suggests unwillingness followed by disappointment. The baby son is no more than a somnolent or squalling "shape," the mother's "worship" given to an image of possibility rather than to the actuality of beloved flesh (*VP* 444–45) [98]. Yeats strongly advocated birth control as the liberator of desire. Arguing against that section of the Censorship of Publications Act that "forbids the sale or distribution of any 'appliances to be used for,' or any book or periodical which advocates . . . birth control,' " Yeats strategically produced St. Thomas Aquinas as his authority:

> Those who think it wrong to bring into the world children they cannot clothe and educate, and yet refuse to renounce that "on which the soul expands her wing," can say "no man knows whether the child is for love's sake, the fruit for the flower, or love for the child's

4. Elizabeth Cullingford, *Yeats, Ireland and Fascism* (London: Macmillan, 1981), 105–06.
5. Ward, *Maud Gonne*, 139–40.
6. W. B. Yeats, "Modern Ireland: An Address to American Audiences, 1932–33" *Massachusetts Review* 5.2 (1963–64): 266.
7. Cleanth Brooks, *The Well Wrought Urn: Studies in the Structure of Poetry* (New York: Reynal, 1947), 167.
8. W. B. Yeats, *Autobiographies* (London: Macmillan, 1955).
9. See Parkinson, *W. B. Yeats Self-Critic and The Later Poetry*, 102.

sake, the flower for the fruit"; or quote the words of St. Thomas: "Anima est in toto corpore." (*SS* 177–78)

Yeats had used a similar organic metaphor in "Among School Children": "Are you the leaf, the blossom or the bole?" (*VP* 446) [98]. If generation is not to be a "betrayal" of sexual love then the "labour" of childbirth must be a welcome "blossoming" rather than Eve's curse: "I will greatly multiply thy sorrow and thy conception; in sorrow thou shalt bring forth children."[1]

Yeats was pleased to marshall so respectable a Catholic authority as Aquinas in his defense of birth control. Gonne commented shrewdly on his strategy: "You hate the Catholic Church with the hate of the Daemon condemned by the old monk of the Mariotic Sea & when you take your stand on certain papal Encyclicals you always remind me of Satan rebuking Sin" (*AYF* 442). In "The Censorship and St. Thomas Aquinas" Yeats attacked the Censorship Bill's proposed definition of indecency as "calculated to excite sexual passion." Claiming that this definition "must be sacrilegious to a Thomist," he ironically expressed surprise that Catholic lawyers and ecclesiastics could make such a blunder as to call natural bodily desires indecent. He tendentiously referred to his opponent in the "Leda" controversy: "Had Professor Trench made it [the blunder] I would understand, for his sort of evangelical belief, whatever it owes to the ascetic Platonism of the seventeenth century, owes nothing to Aquinas." "Anima est in toto corpore" lines up Aquinas in defense of sexual passion, against Plato and Descartes, "who both consider the soul as a substance completely distinct from the body." The contentious definition of "indecency" became the focus of Yeats's opposition to the Censorship Bill, which he represented as the repression of "sexual passion" by "ascetic Platonism." Yeats's politically motivated debate with Plato and "the Platonizing theology of Byzantium" (*UP2* 477–78) informs both "Among School Children" and almost all his love poetry between 1926 and 1932.

St. Thomas's maxim "Anima est in toto corpore" also helped Yeats to avoid a simplistic binarism in his poetic representations of the body. The Church bruised the flesh to pleasure the soul, but Yeats resisted the temptation to banish soul in the interests of corporeal reality. The soul was too important to be left to priests or philosophers. In "Among School Children" Yeats remembers Plato's parable of the soul as a winged charioteer with two horses, one docile, the other (symbolizing physical appetite) wild and unruly. In the drafts he refers to "the souls horses";[2] in the finished work he echoes Plato's phrase "the soul's plumage" in his own former "pretty plumage" (*VP* 444) [97]. Through appetite, Plato's charioteer loses the feathers from his wings, and sinks down into the incarnate state, "the pollution of the walking sepulchre which we call a body."[3] Memory alone can rescue man: under the form of time it becomes Eros or love of beauty, which will enable the soul of the philosopher to "regain its wings" through

---

1. Genesis 3.16.
2. Parkinson, W. B. *Yeats Self-Critic and The Later Poetry*, 99.
3. Plato, *The Phaedrus and the Seventh and Eighth Letters*, trans. Walter Hamilton (Harmondsworth: Penguin, 1973), 57.

recollection of the heavenly vision.[4] Platonic Eros is thus not what we (or Yeats) would call erotic.

In *The Symposium* Plato distances Eros still further from sexual love: Diotima tells Socrates that the object of love is not beauty but "to procreate and bring forth in beauty" because "love is love of immortality as well as of the good."[5] The highest kind of procreation is not that of the youthful mother, but that of the celibate philosopher, whose issue is wisdom. Yeats, however, denies that the spiritual procreators, the philosophical lovers of wisdom, will succeed in growing wings again. Plato has despised the living beauty of the body in favor of abstraction, "a ghostly paradigm of things," while "Solider Aristotle played the taws / Upon the bottom of a king of kings" (*VP* 445) [98]. Like a dour Scottish schoolmaster, Aristotle has "bruised" the body of the young Alexander with the "taws." During debates on the School Attendance Bill Yeats argued that children should not be unjustly disciplined, and urged the scrupulous keeping of "punishment books" as a check on bad-tempered masters (*SS* 109). He sought to avoid the "harsh reproof" that turns "some childish day to tragedy." Plato and Aristotle, the philosophical founders of Western patriarchy, are scarecrows designed to keep Nature away from Culture: "Old clothes upon old sticks to scare a bird." They not only fail to regain their plumage; they drive away those who still have feathers from the food they desire. They are the agents of punishment and starvation.

Yeats sees Plato's teaching as having had a destructive influence both on Christian assumptions about sex and on the ideology of romantic love, since Platonic dualism informs our privileging of male over female, soul over body, heaven over earth. Platonic binary oppositions are always hierarchical. Decades before Derrida, Yeats attempted to hybridize them without discarding difference. *A Vision* is founded on the alternation and interpretation of oppositions: Yeats had "never thought with Hegel that the two ends of the see-saw are one another's negation, nor that the spring vegetables were refuted when over" (*AV[B]* 72–73). Plato's lover is committed to the metaphysical absolute, not the dialogical: "treating his beloved as if he were himself a god, he fashions and adorns an image, metaphorically speaking, and makes it the object of his honour and worship."[6] Or as Yeats puts it: "Both nuns and mothers worship images" (*VP* 445) [98]. The Platonic Presences represent absolute truth, "Yet even the truth into which Plato dies is a form of death, for when he separates the Eternal Ideas from Nature and shows them self-sustained he prepares the Christian desert and the stoic suicide" (*AV[A]*[7] 183). Those self-born images of unreachable perfection that inspire the "passion" of the lover, the "piety" of the nun, and the "affection" of the mother may symbolize heavenly glory, but in despising Nature they lead to frustration, celibacy, and despair: the body is not fed, but "bruised to pleasure soul."

---

4. Ibid., 55–66.
5. Plato, *Symposium*, 87.
6. Plato, *Phaedrus*, 60.
7. W. B. Yeats, *A Vision: An Explanation of Life Founded upon the Writings of Giraldus and upon certain Doctrines attributed to Kusta Ben Luka* (London: privately printed for subscribers only, T. Werner Laurie, Ltd., 1925).

* * * In "Among School Children" Yeats moved from Plato's sour asceticism towards his own "art of the body."

Yet he could not originally summon the energy to challenge Plato's "Presences." In earlier drafts the poem ended after stanza seven in a mood of despondency appropriate to Yeats's gloomy initial notes, which emphasize that children can never fulfill their teachers' hopes, and that all life is a preparation for something that never happens.[8] Yeats transformed the ending of his poem by deciding to apostrophize the "self-born mockers of man's enterprise." He rhetorically defies the heartbreak enforced by Platonic idealism in love and religion by employing a trope that foregrounds his own poetic and bodily presence in the poem. * * *

Yeats's apostrophes locate him not only as the speaking subject of the poem, but also as a spokesman for others: the school children of Ireland, Gonne's special care, whose bodies need food, warmth, and cleanliness before they can begin to acquire wisdom. Arguing in the Senate that "we ought to be able to give the child of the poor as good an education as we give to the child of the rich" (SS 111), Yeats upheld the rights of the voiceless and underprivileged. It is often assumed that by the last stanza of the poem Yeats has "transcended" the local and particular historical incident out of which it arose. On the contrary, we are never closer to the prosaic material details of the School Attendance Bill, and to Yeats's experiences (both good and bad) as a school inspector, than in the lines

> Labour is blossoming or dancing where
> The body is not bruised to pleasure soul,
> Nor beauty born out of its own despair,
> Nor blear-eyed wisdom out of midnight oil.   (VP 445–46) [98]

This evocation of unalienated labor and joyful learning can be read both as an impossible Utopia and as a plea for a humane and decent system of primary education. Yeats was certain that "for a child to spend all day in school with a stupid, ill-trained man under an ill-planned system, is less good for that child than that the child should be running through the fields and learning nothing" (SS 110). Amid the general "bitterness" (Yeats's word) of The Tower (L 742), "Among School Children" offers a romantic image of happiness and liberation comparable to the image of the child (a Wordsworthian child escaped momentarily from the prison house of learning) "running through the fields."

* * *

The last stanza affirms the unalienated bodies of tree and dancer. Two apostrophes combine with two rhetorical questions to produce a heightened coda in which the individualist "I" is replaced by the collective "we";

> O chestnut-tree, great-rooted blossomer,
> Are you the leaf, the blossom or the bole?
> O body swayed to music, O brightening glance,
> How can we know the dancer from the dance?   (VP 446) [98]

8. Parkinson, W. B. Yeats Self-Critic and The Later Poetry, 93–94, 104–05.

Yeat's choice of the dancer as a non-ascetic image of bodily sanity, grace, and wholeness is partly a product of his oppositional dialogue with the voices of Catholic Ireland. While Kermode reads her as an icon of the decadent tradition, a faintly sinister female symbol left over from the nineties,[9] Yeats's dancer also manifests a contemporary social combativeness. The Irish bishops were obsessed by "foreign corrupting dances," which were not "the clean, healthy, National Irish dances . . . [but] importations from the vilest dens of London, Paris and New York—direct and unmistakable incitements to evil thoughts, evil desires, and grossest acts of impurity."[1] Yeats's dancer, body sensuously "swayed to music," is certainly not performing a "healthy" Irish reel.

Sending Gonne a copy of *The Tower*, Yeats told her that she would find "a reference to your self in 'Among School Children,' " adding, "I do not think it will offend you." It did not: she thought it "kind" (*AYF* 445). "Among School Children" is Yeats's most Utopian poem. For him Utopia and femininity were related terms, although not always complimentary ones: he accused the social worker Eva Gore-Booth of dreaming "Some vague Utopia" (*VP* 475) [102]. In the historical speculations of *A Vision* he gendered the democratic politics of social concern: a primary civilization is "levelling, unifying, feminine, humane, peace its means and end" (*AV[B]* 263). Yeats's equation of femininity with humanity, democracy, unity, and peace is essentialist: women are stereotyped as caregivers and mediators. Essentialism, however, led to a progressive social praxis, and to a poem whose almost universal appeal lies precisely in what Yeats would call its "femininity": its celebration of the material body, informed but not dominated by the spirit.[2] * * *

JAMES L. PETHICA

Patronage and Creative Exchange: Yeats, Lady Gregory, and the Economy of Indebtedness[†]

* * *

As Lady Gregory's ever-increasing involvement in Yeats's personal and creative affairs became more permanent in the first years of the new century, the patterns of obligation in the relationship began to be a matter of public debate. Annie Horniman, whose own hopes of using her fortune to secure a relationship with Yeats had been permanently dashed, vented her bitterness in uncompromising terms, accusing Yeats of being "ceaselessly victimised by Lady Gregory on the score of your gratitude for her

9. Kermode, *Romantic Image*, 60–65.
1. *Irish Catholic Register* (Dublin), 1925: 562–63.
2. Innes, "Yeats's Female Voices," 56.
† From Deirdre Toomey, ed., *Yeats and Women*, 2nd ed. (London: Macmillan, 1997), pp. 186–96. Reprinted by permission of Deirdre Toomey. Page references to this Norton Critical Edition are given in brackets after the author's original citations.

kindness"[1] but also berating him to "make it quite clear" in the collected edition of his work what creative debts he owed her for help on his plays.[2] Lady Gregory, likewise, was alternately viewed as victim and as beneficiary of the partnership, earning resentment for her tenacious promotion of Yeats's interests at the Abbey but being criticised equally for pressuring him to support the production of her own work.[3] * * * By the last years of the decade, these public strains were mirrored in a gradual deterioration, and then ending of the close collaborative partnership between the friends. * * *

Yeats's first comprehensive effort to find a model for the relationship, coinciding closely with this [deterioration], deliberately addresses both public and private aspects of friendship and patronage. * * * On the surface, his celebration of Coole as a latter-day Urbino appears unequivocally complimentary. Castiglione's work depicts a court presided over by an aristocratic woman, Duchess Montefeltro, who acts as mediator in the debates of her courtiers, and is held up by them as a pattern of excellence and decorum. Her inspiring presence and example, and the forum of after-dinner conversation she has instituted, are the principal influences which allow the artistry of the court to manifest itself. But, while Castiglione's Urbino offered Yeats a model in which a dominant and respected woman is the organising principal, Duchess Montefeltro herself remains in equivocal relationship to that artistry. Though apparently a dominant personality within the scheme of The Courtier, her intellectual contribution to the debates is negligible, and she is both viewed and views herself as a muse figure rather than an initiator.[4] Even her authority over the court is provisional, for as Robert Hanning and David Rosand note, "she rules as much by knowing when not to exercise authority as when to do so".[5] In effect, her courtiers' idealisation of her deprives her of the freedom to be a truly active principal in their artistic and intellectual interplay. * * *

Yeats's parallels between the centrality of the Duchess at Urbino and that of Lady Gregory at Coole thus allowed him simultaneously to cele-

1. Letter to Yeats, quoted in Gerard Fay, The Abby Theatre, Cradle of Genius (New York: Macmillan, 1958) p. 109.
2. Letter of 7 July 1907, Letters to W. B. Yeats, ed. Richard J. Finneran, George Mills Harper, and William M. Murphy (London: Macmillan, 1977), I, 185. Miss Horniman also notes in this letter that she has relayed to Yeat's publisher, A. H. Bullen, "what you told me some time ago, that [Lady Gregory] considers that she has a certain claim on your disposal of your work because of the help she has given you".
3. Lady Gregory significantly damaged her relationship with Synge, for instance, by insisting that Yeats's work was the "chief distinction" at the Abbey: see Ann Saddlemyer (ed.), Theatre Business (Gerrards Cross, Bucks: Colin Smythe, 1982) p. 197. Synge was subsequently sceptical regarding his influence in the directorial triumvirate, and came to suspect the theatre of being a "Yeats–Gregory show": see The Collected Letters of John Millington Synge, ed. Ann Saddlemyer (Oxford: Oxford University Press, 1983) I, 318. Yeats addresses the general rumours that Lady Gregory was taking "advantage of her position as Director to put her own plays on the stage" in W. B. Yeats, Memoirs, ed. Denis Donoghue (London: Macmillan, 1972) p. 161. Hereafter referred to as Mem. In Two Flamboyant Fathers (London: Collins, 1968) p. 128, Nicolette Devas recalls that on a visit to Coole she was "shocked by the servile way" in which Lady Gregory waited on Yeats. Anecdotes abound to show that in other situations the roles were reversed.
4. Baldesar Castiglione, The Book of the Courtier, tr. L. Opdycke (New York: Charles Scribner's Sons, 1903), passim. The Duchess repeatedly uses a surrogate to speak for her, typically her friend Emilia Pia.
5. Robert Hanning and David Rosand (eds.), Preface to Castiglione: The Ideal and the Real in Renaissance Culture (New Haven, Conn.: Yale University Press, 1983) p. xiii.

brate her influence and to define it in circumscribed terms, thereby codifying a process begun considerably earlier. Just as the courtiers themselves (and the question of what makes the perfect courtier) are the true focus of Castiglione's work, so too, in Yeats's adoption of the Urbino model his principal interest was in the position of the artist and the conditions which make art possible. With its emphatic advocacy and celebration of court patronage as essential to the health of the arts, *The Courtier* provided him with a historical model which he had long sought, in which the artist is not only accorded a respected social role, but is also seen as part of a symbiotic relationship with his aristocratic patron that is necessary and fundamental to the creative vitality of court and country alike. This implication of necessity was clearly of crucial appeal. Drawing on Castiglione, Yeats progressively began to represent the small literary coterie centred on Coole as a heroic elite resisting the "contagious" mediocrity of the commercial classes.[6] His diary of 1909, which reflects his increasing preoccupation with his own ancestry and a growing bitterness over the state of contemporary Ireland, charts a deepening conviction that wealth and breeding are essential to personal and artistic excellence:

> In spite of myself my mind dwells more and more on ideas of class. Ireland has grown sterile, because power has passed to men who lack the training which requires a certain amount of wealth to ensure continuity from generation to generation, and to free the mind in part from other tasks. A gentleman is for one thing a man whose principal ideas are not connected with his personal needs and his personal success. In old days he was a clerk or a noble, that is to say, he had freedom because of inherited wealth and position, or because of a personal renunciation. The names are different today, and I would put the artist and the scholar in the category of the clerk. (*Mem* 178–9) [252].

His aestheticisation of Coole as a modern-day Urbino thus effects a massive displacement of material indebtedness. The artist is conceived as one who has to "renounce" the material world in associating himself with the traditions and breeding of the aristocratic class. Instead of being a mere dependant, he is part of a heroic attempt to redeem society at large from its vulgarities and cultural sterility. The bitter poems of *Responsibilities*, in which Urbino first features as an ideal of aristocratic and artistic excellence, mark the shift acutely in their open scorn of middle-class values. The poems repeatedly affect disdain for material considerations, and assert that art, and aristocratic patronage of the arts, are alone of redeeming value:

> What cared Duke Ercole, that bid
> His mummers to the market-place,
> What th'onion-sellers thought or did

---

6. See especially *Mem* 154: "Both Synge and Lady Gregory isolate themselves, Synge instinctively and Lady Gregory consciously from all contagious opinions of poorer minds: Synge so instinctively and naturally—helped by certain habits of an invalid—that no one is conscious of rejection. Lady Gregory's life is too energetic and complex for her rejections to be other than deliberate."

So that his Plautus set the pace
For the Italian comedies?
(*VP*[7] 287) [43]

The displacement is manifest in Yeats's celebration of Lady Gregory in *Autobiographies*—"If that influence were lacking, Ireland would be greatly impoverished"[8]—for, in the most literal sense, it is he himself who would have been impoverished. The aestheticisation of Coole in effect aligns and then conflates the material preconditions of art (which Yeats initially stresses as of paramount importance) with preconditions which are aesthetic: as in his notes for "Upon a House shaken by the Land Agitation", it is ultimately the "spacious forms"[9] that Coole provides, rather than its material support, which are accorded most value.

* * *

Yeats's continuing engagement with [his] remaining debt obligations surfaces throughout the record of his friendship with Lady Gregory in the years after 1914, and in his representations of her in his writing, but is nowhere clearer than in the drafts of "Coole Park, 1929". As a formal work of celebration the poem forced Yeats to decide not only what specific achievements he should praise her for but also how he should treat both his own presence and their partnership within its rhetorical scheme. The delicate value judgement involved in these decisions is reflected in the unusual extent and complexity of the drafts. As Jon Stallworthy observes in *Between the Lines*, the manuscripts comprise "thirty-eight pages of working—more than went to the making of any other poem I know".[1] From almost his first jottings, Yeats alleviated these difficulties to some extent by figuring Lady Gregory largely as an implied presence in the poem. His initial prose sketch signals an intention to "Describe Lady G.", but as his first stanza takes provisional shape it is Coole itself—"that intricate house"—which provides his focus (*BTL* 180, 182). The metonymy of house for owner simultaneously allowed Yeats a certain indirection in attributing creative influence and responsibility—in the final version, the "great works" achieved at Coole are figured as a "dance-like glory that those walls begot" (*VP* 488) [107]—and served to embody structurally in the poem the very interdependence of Lady Gregory's personal, material and creative influences on him, which it would have been most difficult to make explicit. While the trope was undoubtedly strategically useful, it was also of extreme personal force for Yeats. His essay "The Death of Lady Gregory" records his emotional response when Margaret Gough expressed surprise at his unconcern in remaining in the house alone with Lady Gregory's coffin in 1932: " 'I said it is not the coffin that [w]rings my heart but all this' pointing to the books and the paintings. She said 'Yes it is your home too that is broken up.' "[2] As the draft progresses, the metonymy

---

7. *The Variorum Edition of the Poems of W. B. Yeats*, ed. Peter A. and Russell K. Alspach (New York: Macmillan, 1966).
8. W. B. Yeats, *Autobiographies* (London: Macmillan, 1955) p. 381. Hereafter referred to as *Au*.
9. *Mem* p. 226.
1. Jon Stallworthy, *Between the Lines: Yeats's Poetry in the Making* (Oxford: Clarendon Press, 1963) p. 200. Hereafter referred to as *BTL*; references in text.
2. Lady Gregory, *The Journals*, ed. Daniel J. Murphy (Oxford: Oxford University Press, 1987) II, 634.

allows Yeats to resist any slippage into overly explicit claims, and he repeatedly deletes or abandons his most specific references to Lady Gregory and her creative influence. In a movement reminiscent of his draft of "Friends", for instance, the line "She had such intellect & character" is left undeveloped: Yeats turns his attention to his opening lines, and when he finally returns to the stanza, favours instead a more diffuse celebration of her "powerful character" (*BTL* 193–4)

Yeats had greater difficulty finding a perspective from which he could praise Lady Gregory and the Coole literary circle and simultaneously acknowledge his own presence and share in the "great works" (*VP* 488) [107] that he describes. In early stanzas of the drafts he includes himself readily amongst the summer guests who gathered—"We came like swallows & like swallows went"—and repeatedly uses the first person for himself: "Here I, under an embittered pose . . ." (*BTL* 188, 193). But by the first full draft he appears to have recognised the potential for seeming self-praise in these formulations, and figures himself more cryptically in the list of guests as "one that ruffled in a manly pose" (*BTL* 189), a change followed by a shift from "We" to "They" to describe the movement of the swallows (*BTL* 195). This distancing, though, offered an equally unsatisfactory perspective for praise, effectively absenting Yeats—and the friendship most central to Lady Gregory's fame—from the heart of the poem. The drafts show Yeats experimenting with the noncommittal form "All came" to describe the swallows (*BTL* 197), rejecting this as inadequate, and only finding his solution in the last stages of polishing. In the final versions a crucial shift in the poet's own location takes place within the movement of the poem. Hyde, Synge, the young Yeats and the rest are now imaged as "There" (*BTL* 199)—in a Coole of the remembered past, which is implicitly distanced from the poet's present location and which indeed, as the new opening line signals, exists only in his meditation. The last stanza effects a stunning compensatory movement as the poet belatedly inserts himself both in the Coole Park of the present—1929—and by extension in the derelict Coole of an imagined future: "Here traveller, scholar, poet take your stand / When all those rooms and passages are gone" (*VP* 489) [107]. The effect is an extraordinary movement of intimacy, in which the poem re-enacts its author's own movement from ruffling pose to poetic assertion, and declares the enduring permanence of his presence at Coole, thus linking poet and house—and hence Yeats and Lady Gregory herself—in what is past, passing and to come.

By contrast, the drafts show Yeats struggling at length with the matter of his collaborative work with Lady Gregory. Significantly, the collaboration forms the first subject of his workings in verse, in two rough stanzas in which he attempts to formulate a principal motive and theme for the poem:

> for the generation after us
> I ~~praise~~ sing miraculous intricacies
> ~~Old amities~~
> ~~Or amities~~
> Amities of skill, amities of kind thought (*BTL* 181)

The lines continue irresolutely, with their debate immediately centring on whether it is amity of friendship, or of skill, imagination and thought, which has allowed these "miraculous" intricacies to be produced:

> I sing miraculous intricacies
> ~~Old amities of skill, amities of thought~~
> ~~Made in friendship, & in skill~~
> ~~Friendship, imagination, or skillful skill~~
> ~~Skill & imagination, friendly thought~~
> ~~Imagination daring friendly thought~~
> Of new thoughts knitted to a common thought
>   (BTL 181)

What remains after the deletions is a retraction from the idea of two daring, skillful imaginations becoming combined: instead "new thoughts" have been blended with "a common thought". The associations underlying this new potential scheme for the poem are concisely glossed by a passage in *Autobiographies* in which Yeats, some years later, reviews Lady Gregory's creative achievement:

> When in later years her literary style became in my ears the best written by a woman, she had made the people a part of her soul; a phrase of Aristotle's had become her motto: "To think like a wise man, but to express oneself like the common people."   (*Au* 395)

The implication of the draft lines is not that the thought "knitted" to Yeats's own is "common" in the sense of being mundane or undistinguished, but that it represents the distillation into common speech of traditional ideas.[3] The scheme encapsulates with almost algebraic simplicity the rationalisations animating Yeats's accounts of his collaboration with Lady Gregory on *Cathleen ni Houlihan*, the folklore essays and all of their later joint works: in effect, he has added her "peasant talk" to the fertile material of his own imagination.

Having reached this configuration in his first draft lines, Yeats forcibly changes direction in a manner which suggests that he recognised its presence as problematic in a poem of celebration. In succeeding lines he casts about in search of an alternative source or location for the intricacy he wishes to praise—"I praise for pleasure that intricate house / Set among the wood's intricacies" (*BTL* 182)—while the status of the amities so confidently introduced at the outset is also suddenly thrown into question: they are successively figured as "unnatural", rejected in favour of "miraculous consanguinities", turned into "unnatural consanguinities", and then, finally, late in the compositional process, abandoned altogether. The final version of the poem enacts a neat swerve around the sticking-point as the "knitted thoughts" are used instead as a symbol of the Coole heritage— that aristocratic "continuity from generation to generation" which he had

---

3. In his notes to *The Unicorn from the Stars* Yeats formulates this joining of two forms of knowledge in a way that directly aligns the cultural continuities made possible by wealth and aristocracy with the "heredity" of the poetic tradition: "I have waited with impatience a linking . . . of the hereditary knowledge of the countryside . . . with our old [poetic] lyricism so full of ancient frenzies and hereditary wisdom" (*The Variorum Edition of the Plays of W. B. Yeats*, ed. Russell K. Alspach [London: Macmillan, 1966], p. 714).

praised in 1909—infusing the assembled individual talent with the necessary measure of tradition. The issue of direct collaboration has been dropped from the poem, with only an underlying metonymic force surviving in the finished lines to remind us of the contested act of begetting:

> Great works constructed there in nature's spite
> For scholars and for poets after us,
> Thoughts long knitted into a single thought,
> A dance-like glory that those walls begot.
>
> (VP 488) [107]

In textual terms, the encounter with indebtedness enacted in "Coole Park, 1929" provided Yeats with no full resolution of his continuing debate over his creative partnership with Lady Gregory, just as in its personal dimension that debate would continue until her death ended the dutiful vigil that he at Coole in her last months. But, like "Coole Park and Ballylee, 1931" and his other major celebrations of their association, "Coole Park, 1929" should be seen as providing, in its creation, a certain compensatory movement within the economy of their partnership. The drafts of "Coole Park, 1929" emphasise how the poem served as Yeats's reciprocal gift. Though he initially conceives it in the drafts as praise he has begun "for pleasure" and then "for my heart's sake" (BTL 182), as the poem emerges it becomes clear that Lady Gregory is both subject and recipient: "I praise for living ears that ancient house" (BTL 188). The poem was planned from the outset to form the frontispiece of Lady Gregory's Coole—her own elegy on the house, its guests and herself—in which position it served as a powerful advertisement for the book. By 1930, when the failing trajectory of her financial and personal fortunes had completely reversed Lady Gregory's position with respect to Yeats, she was acutely conscious of the worth of such bounty.[4] In its original setting in Coole, the poem provides a fitting image of collaboration and gift-exchange: two works together blending to form a greater whole; the binding power of old debts being augmented and modified by new exchanges.

DEIRDRE TOOMEY

Away[†]

*   *   *

By January 1889, Susan Yeats was gradually retreating from life and beginning a long descent into mutism. On 31 January, Yeats wrote to Katharine Tynan, ". . . you ask about my Mother. She is as usual, that is

---

4. Lady Gregory was by this point selling off personal possessions such as her books to raise money, and Yeats had long been a paying guest during his stays at Coole.
† From Deirdre Toomey, ed., Yeats and Women, 2nd ed. (London: Macmillan, 1997), pp. 145–56. Reprinted by permission of Deirdre Toomey. Page references to this Norton Critical Edition are given in brackets after the author's original citations.

to say feable and unable to go out of doors, or move about much" (CL1[1] 136). On the previous day Yeats's life had been transformed by his first meeting with Maud Gonne:

> I was twenty-three when the troubling of my life began. . . . she drove up to our house in Bedford Park with an introduction from John O'Leary to my father. I had never thought to see in a living woman so great beauty. It belonged to famous pictures, to poetry, to some legendary past. A complexion like the blossom of apples, and yet face and body had the beauty of lineaments which Blake calls the highest beauty because it changes least from youth to age, and a stature so great that she seemed of divine race.   (Mem[2] 40) [225–26]

What connects Yeats's romantic obsession with a tall, beautiful, independent, wealthy, cosmopolitan revolutionary and feminist with the fate of his mother, a slight, dependent, conventional, provincial woman? Explanations (as well as non-explanations) of the dynamics of Yeats's love for Maud Gonne abound. Many writers take Yeats's love as a *fait accompli*. It is, as it were, not worth analysis. He met her, she was very beautiful, they shared nationalist ideals, and that was that for the next twenty-five years. The most sophisticated analysis to date (that of John Harwood) argues that Yeats had created, over several years, an *imago* of a beautiful quasi-supernatural woman, and that Maud Gonne walked into a fully prepared role: yet, as he points out, it is not just that Maud Gonne steps "into Niamh's shoes", but that the " 'faery bride' subsequently assimilates the mortal woman".[3] From this point on, Harwood argues, Yeats worked with great intensity assimilating an *imago* of Maud Gonne into his imaginative world: "Maud Gonne did not overpower his imagination; his imagination overpowered 'Maud Gonne' and then he began, in life, to enter a relationship with 'the image he had made' " (YA 9 18). The word was made flesh—and then the flesh was made word again. The only thing missing from this astute analysis is the question "Why Maud Gonne, in January 1889?" She was probably the most beautiful woman whom Yeats had met, but it does seem remarkable that, after his adolescent infatuation with Laura Armstrong,[4] he had remained completely free of romantic or sexual attachments for nearly five years. Even given that his closest female friend of this period was Katharine Tynan, "a simple brightlooking Biddy",[5] to whom even under strong moral pressure he was unable to feel attracted, the hiatus is arresting.

1. *The Collected Letters of W. B. Yeats*, vol. 1: *1865–1895*, ed. John Kelly and Eric Domville (Oxford: Clarendon Press, 1986). Hereafter CL1.
2. W. B. Yeats, *Memoirs*, ed. Denis Donoghue (London: Macmillan, 1972).
3. See " 'Secret Communion': Yeats's Sexual Destiny," *Yeats Annual* [YA] 9 (London: Macmillan, 1991), 3–30, at p. 16. Martin Bergmann reports a similar strategy in the life of a patient: " 'When I fell in love I wrote the whole scenario myself and only later looked around for a list of characters.' " See "On the Intrapsychic Function of Falling in Love", *Psychoanalytic Quarterly* 49 (1980) pp. 56–76, at p. 67. However, this patient's "scenario" was not "The Wanderings of Oisin".
4. Dateable to c. 1883–4. See CL1 155. The sheer *normality* of Yeats's infatuation with Laura Armstrong forms a contrast to his later obsession with Maud Gonne.
5. So described by Gerard Manley Hopkins, who met her in 1886, See Claude Colleer Abbott (ed.), *Further Letters of Gerard Manley Hopkins including his Correspondence with Coventry Patmore* (London: Oxford University Press, 2nd edition, 1956) p. 373.

It has been argued that overwhelming romantic love is often a reaction to an "object loss", to a traumatic or distressing event in the lover's life,[6] a death, an illness, a separation, even a major disappointment. The distress is erased by "being in love" and by the consequent over-valuation of the beloved. Yeats had suffered bouts of anxiety and depression in 1887 and 1888, which are referred to in his letters to Katharine Tynan: "In bad spirits . . . I had one of my dreadful despondent moods on . . . like a burnt out taper . . . one of my 'collapses' " (CLI 75, 77, 92, 118). In January 1888 Yeats underwent a terrifying experience at a Dublin séance:

> . . . my whole body moved like a suddenly unrolled watch-spring, and I was thrown backward on the wall. . . . I was now struggling vainly with this force which compelled me to movements I had not willed, and my movements became so violent that the table was broken. I tried to pray. . . . For years afterwards I would not go to a séance . . . and would often ask myself what was that violent impulse that had run through my nerves. Was it a part of myself—something always to be a danger perhaps; or had it come from without, as it seemed?   (Au[7] 103–5)

These depressions and crises do not seem completely unconnected with his mother's illness and decline and an inevitable, if only half conscious, meditation by Yeats on the innumerable negative aspects of his parents' marriage. In the first period of his love for Maud Gonne, his feelings for her were symbiotic: "[s]he seemed to understand every subtlety of my own art and especially all my spiritual philosophy" (Mem 61). This sense of spiritual and emotional fusion, recalled in "Among School Children"

> . . . it seemed that our two natures blent
> Into a sphere from youthful sympathy,   (VP 443) [97]

presented an absolute antithesis to his parents' polarised, uncommunicative marriage.

A reflection of the link between the major love of his life and a "dead" mother is found in the first two drafts of The Speckled Bird, written between 1896 and 1898. In these early versions Michael's dead mother is identified by his father with the Virgin and remembered as a "star of beauty"; "his father had begun to talk a good deal about his dead wife and call her by the names of the Mother of God" (SB[8] 124). When Michael and his father hear that Margaret, daughter of the dead woman's sister, is a replica of the dead wife/mother both are deeply moved, although they have not seen the child:

> "She is like my wife. She is like my wife" . . . "Oh, father, do ask my cousin to come and stay with us, I never see anyone here and she is like my mother too."   (SB 126–7)

6. See Robert Bak, "Being in Love and Object Loss", International Journal of Psychoanalysis, 54 (1973) pp. 1–7.
7. W. B. Yeats, Autobiographies (London: Macmillan, 1955).
8. W. B. Yeats, The Speckled Bird, With Variant Versions, ed. William H. O'Donnell (Toronto: McLelland & Stewart, 1976).

So it is made clear that the hero is destined to fall in love with a young girl who exactly resembles his dead (and unknown) mother. This is a second fictional attempt to transform and idealise biographical material, with a father-son unit replacing the mother-son unit of *John Sherman*.[9]

* * *

In 1938, a ghostly mother destroyed by marriage returns to trouble *Purgatory*, presented, in the ordering of *Last Poems and Two Plays*, from beyond the grave. The play is extraordinary in its absolute rejection of catharsis, in its violence and apparent nihilism, and in its realisation of the primal scene on stage *via* the mechanism of a supernatural vision of an endlessly re-enacted past.[1] The central situation is that of *The Speckled Bird*, but the family romance is complicated by two generations of sons, and is brutally de-idealised.

The Old Man's desire is to end his mother's torment, her purgatorial re-enactment of her wedding night, which will endlessly result in the birth of a parricide;

> " . . . . O my God
> she does not understand—her agony, her agonised joy,
> or her remorse begin all over again . . .
>
> . . . .
> She did not [know] the worst because
> She died in giving birth to me
> But now [being] a soul in purgatory
> She knows it all . . .[2]

In the ruined house the ghostly mother must, like the ghosts in "Swedenborg, Mediums and the Desolate Places", relive her agony forever, unless her son's murder of *his* son will undo the cause by undoing the end. The Old Man sacrifices father and son to free his mother's soul:

9. The abandonment of the dead mother–beloved identification in the last two versions of the novel is probably linked to Maud Gonne's revelations to Yeats of December 1898. See my "Labyrinths: Yeats and Maud Gonne" (YA 9 95–191) at pp. 107, where I argue that Yeats's aversion to marriage and his shock when he discovered that Maud Gonne had had two children was linked to the depressing circumstances of his parents' marriage. André Green has discussed the problem of a symbolically dead mother in *On Private Madness* (London: The Hogarth Press and the Institute of Psycho-Analysis, 1986). In Chapter 7, "The Dead Mother", Green discusses the problem, not of an actual dead mother, but of a mother whose depression "brutally transforms a living object, which was a source of vitality . . . into a distant figure, toneless, practically inanimate' (p. 142) — a fair description of Susan Yeats for the last decade of her married life.

1. In *Purgatory*, Yeats dramatises the eternity of Karmic punishment, drawing on a work very important to him in his youth, Ráma Prasád's *The Science of Breath and the Philosophy of the Tatwas . . . with Fifteen Introductory & Explanatory Essays on nature's Finer Forces* (London: Theosophical Publishing Society, 1890). Prasád insists that evil or destructive acts done in one lifetime are reenacted in reverse in the next; the murderer endlessly suffers the terror of his victim in his next existence, "that picture of the ebbing life of the victim is now part and parcel of his constitution, the pain, the terror, and the feeling of despair. . . . His life is miserable; slowly but surely it wanes away. Let the curtain fall on this stage. The incarnated thief now comes on the stage. . . . He is doomed to a lonely house. The picture of somebody coming into the house . . . perhaps strangling him, makes its appearance with the fullest strength" (pp. 134–5). Prasád's central image of a cosmic gallery or Akashic record of images of all human acts of all times, being constantly projected back into human consciousness, is patently absorbed in the magic lantern realisation of the past in *Purgatory*; and Prasád's powerful representation of the murderer and the lonely house in the setting and *dramatis personae* of the play.

2. *Purgatory: Manuscript Materials Including the Author's Final Text*, edited by Sandra F. Siegel (Ithaca and London: Cornell University Press, 1986) pp. 53, 79, first and second drafts.

Study that tree.
It stands there like a purified soul,
All cold, sweet, glistening light.
Dear mother, the window is dark again,
But you are in the light because
I finished all that consequence.   (*VPL*[3] 1049) [174]

Yeats not only outdoes *Oedipus Rex* by representing parricide and infanticide by the same actor, but—and in Ireland—by presenting the primal scene on stage. The Old Man watches as the ghosts re-enact his conception;

.... They mount the stairs.
She brings him into her own chamber.
And that is the marriage-chamber now.
The window is dimly lit again

Do not let him touch you! . . .
    . . . she must live
Through everything in exact detail,
Driven to it by remorse, and yet
Can she renew the sexual act
And find no pleasure in it, and if not,
If pleasure and remorse must both be there
Which is the greater?   (*VPL* 1046) [172]

There is such a slaughtering of social taboos in *Purgatory* that it is inconceivable to construe these horrifying exhibitions as solely expressive of Yeats's fear of a degenerated Ireland.[4] The lullaby which the Old Man sings after killing his son

"Hush-a-bye baby, thy father's a knight,
Thy mother a lady, lovely and bright."
No, that is something I read in a book
And if I sing it must be to my mother
And I lack rhyme.   (*VPL* 1048) [174]

is, in its fusion of dead child and infant self in a recreation of the family romance, too disturbing and psychically primary to be a by-product of

3. *The Variorum Edition of the Plays of W. B. Yeats*, ed. Russell K. Alspach (London: Macmillan, 1966).
4. Yeats's "explanation" of his play in response to Father Terence Connolly's queries is deteriorationist and eugenic in its thrust: "In my play, a spirit suffers because of its share, when alive, in the destruction of an honoured house; that destruction is taking place all over Ireland today. Sometimes it is the result of poverty, but more often because a new individualistic generation has lost interest in the ancient sanctities. . . . I have founded my play on [mesalilance] partly because of my interest in certain problems of eugenics . . ." (*Irish Independent, Irish Times*, 13 August 1938). Of course a eugenic/deteriorationist argument is a part of the play's "meaning"; it was conceived in tandem with *On the Boiler*. Yeats's curtain speech had been, "I wish to say that I have put into this play not many thoughts that are picturesque, but my own beliefs about this world and the next" (*Irish Independent*, 11 August 1938). Yeats was wisely guarded in his "explanations": despite a good reception from puzzled but impressed audiences ("even to hardened playgoers the effect was uncanny" *Irish Independent*, 13 August 1938) a predictable controversy arose as to the legitimacy of Yeats's use of Catholic dogma, given his non-Christian belief-system (*Irish Times*, August 14, 16, 17, 18, 19, 20, 1938).

eugenic anxieties. The dénouement rejects catharsis for an eternal repetition:

> . . . . Dear God
> . . . .
> Her mind cannot hold up that dream.
> Twice a murderer and all for nothing,
> And she must animate that dead night
> Not once but many times!
>   O God!
> Release my mother's soul from its dream!
> Mankind can do no more. Appease
> The misery of the living and the remorse of the dead.
>   (VPL 1049) [174]

* * *

MARJORIE HOWES

The Rule of Kindred†

* * *

In *Purgatory*, kindred relations are those of violence, discontinuity and death. The cast of characters does not indicate that the old man and the boy are father and son; the reader learns this several pages into the play, indicating that the conventional relations between fathers and sons—affection, Oedipal rivalry—are purely incidental to their Yeatsian kindred relation. This version of family is the family of eugenic thinking, of "If I Were Four-and-Twenty" and "A Race Philosophy," a family founded on a vision of evil. In *Purgatory*, the antinomies of Yeats's race philosophy encounter each other violently and irresolvably. The mother's dream reenacts the conflict between the family/national imperatives which generate her remorse and the individual desires which drove her to seek transgressive pleasure. The old man represents the family struggle; the boy embodies the individual struggle. No reconciliation is possible, and the temporary triumph of one over the other does nothing to abate the crisis and conflict which structure their existence.

Purgatory performs a eugenic critique of the old man and his mother. The mother represents both the continuity of aristocratic tradition and its betrayal. She owned the house and embodied its virtues, and the old man reports that "some / Half-loved me for my half of her" (VPL,[1] 1044) [171]. On the other hand, the play focuses on her sexual choice as the cause of degeneration. Similarly, the old man, product of an aristocratic mother

---

† From *Yeats's Nations: Gender, Class, and Irishness* (Cambridge: Cambridge University Press, 1996), pp. 184–85. Reprinted with the permission of Cambridge University Press. Page references to this Norton Critical Edition are given in brackets after the author's original citations.

1. *The Variorum Edition of the Plays of W. B. Yeats*, ed. Russell K. Alspach (London: Macmillan, 1966).

and a lowly father, embodies kindred as both tradition and its crisis. While he claims kinship to his mother, he also admits "I am my father's son" (*VPL*, 1045) [171].

The old man stands for something else too—a particular inadequate way of confronting this crisis-ridden model of nationality, the way of nostalgia, self-pity and the utopian hope that such kindred aristocracies are founded on anything besides constant violence and struggle. This inadequacy makes the old man a degenerate symptom as well as a eugenic critic. His existential squeamishness and his inability to appropriate the scene imaginatively lead him to desire a release from conflict and repetition; he wants the antinomies to be resolved and the struggle to cease. This leads him in turn to murder his own son. Yeats structured *Purgatory* so that the denial of perennial conflict leads to murder, precisely the shape of his critique of utopian thought, particularly Marxism,[2] and of his assertion that the rule of kindred, organized around his race philosophy, would create, in its way, a more humane and individualistic society than democracy.

Yeats's race philosophy and the eugenic model of nationality that went along with it were certainly not fascism. But they were hardly more compatible with liberal democracy than fascism. Politically, such a model of nationality has few attractions. Analytically, however, it has several uses. The major achievement of this strand in the middle and late Yeats is that it does what *Purgatory*'s old man cannot do: through acts of creative will, it teases out, examines and come to terms with all the things that most conceptions of nationality work hardest to deny. Instead of secure and natural foundations, harmonious relations between the individual and the nation, and synthesis, Yeats's eugenic nationality and kindred politics offer arbitrariness, violence, and irresolvable conflict. In other words, they present, in exaggerated and explicit form the things that often lurk behind the facades of more attractive versions of the nation. They expose, by refiguring and refusing, the naturalizing work that conventional conceptions of gender, sexuality and the family often perform. Finally, they point to an important problem for contemporary scholarship on nationality and postcolonial theory: the need to find a way of confronting the crisis and potential violence that underlies all constructions of nationality without succumbing to the temptation to repeat the old man's murderous desire for synthesis, stasis and purity.

---

2. For an excellent discussion of Yeats critique of Marxism, see Elizabeth Cullingord, *Yeats, Ireland and Fascism* (London: Macmillan, 1981), chapter 8. Cullingford observes that Yeats saw his own philosophy of history as "more pessimistic but less bloodthirsty than Hegel's or Marx's" (p. 123).

DOUGLAS ARCHIBALD

Politics and Public Life†

* * *

[Yeats's] withdrawal from Fascism [from late 1933 onward], cagey and timely though it may be, is also sincere. As he realizes that he cannot and will not be an agent of a new, imposed order, he cultivates an anarchy of will, a determination to be no victim despite all the murderous forces gathering around him. He fondly recalls Blake's " 'And he his seventy disciples sent / Against religion and government,' " and adds, to Ethel Mannin, "I hate more than you do, for my hatred can have no expression in action. I am a forerunner of that horde that will some day come down the mountains."[1] He insists that programs and ideologies offer no salvation and turns instead to personal will, a new version of the "interior personality created out of the tradition of myself"[2] he had cultivated in *Estrangement*:

> When there is despair, public or private, when settled order seems lost, people look for strength within or without. Auden, Spender, all that seem the new movement, *look* for strength in Marxian Socialism, or in Major Douglas; they want marching feet. The lasting expression of our time is not this obvious choice but in a sense of something steel-like and cold within the will, something passionate and cold.[3]

At the same time he was reworking some bitter controversies. He read Harrison's *Parnell Vindicated*, which argued that Captain O'Shea had been bribed and Parnell betrayed by the Party and the clergy, and Maloney's *The Forged Casement Diaries*, which attacked as bogus the diaries circulated by the British in 1916 to justify the execution of Sir Roger Casement. Yeats must have remembered Lady Gregory's quiet, decisive remark, "I defy anyone to study Irish history without getting a dislike and distrust of England,"[4] and he published, during the winter of 1936–37, five furious, virulent, anti-English ballads about Casement, the O'Rahilly, killed in 1916, and Parnell. The ballads were political acts, as O'Brien says, as potentially explosive as *Cathleen ni Houlihan*; and they are far more serious than the "Marching Songs." The Casement ballads in particular would remind readers on both sides of the channel and in America that Sir Roger was executed for attempting to bring German support to Ireland's rebellion. The sea was no longer the old sea because "the nation from which Casement had tried to bring help now possessed a powerful

† From *Yeats* (Syracuse, N.Y.: Syracuse University Press, 1983), pp. 149–53. Reprinted by permission of Syracuse University Press. The notes have been edited, and page references to this Norton Critical edition are given in brackets after the author's original citations.
1. Letter to Ethel Mannin, December 11, 1938, *The Letters of W. B. Yeats*, ed. Allan Wade (London: Rupert Hart-Davis, 1954; New York: Macmillan, 1955), 873; hereafter cited as *L*.
2. W. B. Yeats, *Autobiographies* (London: Macmillan, 1955), 463.
3. *L*, 837.
4. Lady Gregory, *Our Irish Theatre: A Chapter of Autobiography* (New York: Putnam, 1913), 41.

airforce."[5] The ballads gave Yeats a measure of public popularity he had not enjoyed for some time, and they risked the loss of friends in England. They offered eccentric but clear support to deValera and his policy of neutrality. The ballads may have contributed to what became, in a year or so, the IRA "policy" of random bombings in England and declared intention of replacing, by whatever means necessary, Ireland's elected leaders. There is no positive evidence that the Republican extremists read Yeats or any poetry; he certainly did not write with them in mind; but the mood of the poems, their combination of rage and threat, is not wholly removed from acts of violence.

He is also feeling, once again and more fiercely, that other rage—against age and loneliness. AE died in 1935, and Yeats "had to use all my powers of intrigue and self-assertion to prevent a fanatical woman from making it a political demonstration by draping the coffin with the tricolour."[6] Olivia Shakespear went in 1938; "all other lovers being estranged or dead," she was the last contact with his youth.[7] He had written her, in one of the letters marking his disengagement from the Blueshirts, that he was working on a play "that I might write lyrics out of dramatic experience, all my personal experience having in some strange way come to an end."[8] For such a relentlessly autobiographical poet that is the recognition of a crisis. Institutions disappeared as friends died. The Irish Senate, where he had found a role, a platform, and some ideology, was abolished after a struggle in 1936, which must have seemed, like the destruction of Coole, the sacrifice of one more monument of the Old Order. The rage and lust he writes about to Dorothy Wellesley and Ethel Mannin constitute a half-apology for the Casement ballads; it is also part of a personal apocalypse, a sense of himself as "the first of the final destroying horde."[9] In the context of the letter in which it appears "The Spur" is not a playful poem:

> You think it horrible that Lust and Rage
> Should dance attendance upon my old age;
> They were not such a plague when I was young;
> What else have I to spur me into song?[1]

What has happened is a kind of internalization of fascism. It begins with the withdrawal, lasts for the rest of his life, and proceeds simultaneously with more healthy feelings and statements. A letter to Olivia Shakespear from the summer of 1934 illustrates the process:

> I had a Swedish compliment the other day, that has pleased me better than any I have ever had. Some Swede said to my wife "Our Royal Family liked your husband better than any other Nobel prize winner. They said he has the manners of a Courtier." I would like to think this true but I doubt—my kind of critical mind creates harshness and

5. *In Excited Reverie: A Centenary Tribute to William Butler Yeats. 1865–1939*, ed. A. Norman Jeffares and K. G. W. Cross (London: Macmillan, 1965), 266–70.
6. *L*, 838.
7. *The Variorum Edition of the Poems of W. B. Yeats*, ed. Peter Allt and Russell K. Alspach (New York: Macmillan, 1966), 523; hereafter cited as *VP*.
8. *L*, 819.
9. *L*, 869.
1. *L*, 872 [119].

toughness. Which somehow reminds me, have you read *Hadrian the Seventh* by Lionel's friend or acquaintance "Baron Corvo"?—it is quite cheap and nearly a great book, my sort of book, the love of the ruling mind, the ruling race. An imaginary Pope is the theme, with enough evil to be a great man. I hate the pale victims of modern fiction—that suffer that they may have minds like photographic plates.[2]

That sounds like an aristocratic pose descending through alienation into fascism, but it is attached to gossip and a book, not to a movement which Yeats has already judged and found insufficient. The Blueshirt song writer is becoming the "Wild Old Wicked Man." Yeats creates speakers who are directly autobiographical:

> I pray—for fashion's word is out
> And prayer comes round again—
> That I may seem, though I die old,
> A foolish, passionate man.[3]

and others, like Ribh in "Supernatural Songs," who dramatize his own needs:

> Why should I seek for love or study it?
> It is of God and passes human wit.
> I study hatred with great diligence,
> For that's a passion in my own control,
> A sort of besom that can clear the soul
> Of everything that is not mind or sense.[4]

The internalization is distressing—frequently repulsive, often hysterical, sometimes self-parodic—but it represents a fictive identity not a political program. The identity is problematical but so far removed from ordinary politics that it is not a public danger. It can provide an acid imaginative strength, as Yeats sees himself "ravening, raging, and uprooting that he may come / Into the desolation of reality" and cultivates "the brutality, the ill-breeding, the barbarism of truth" which he claimed for *On The Boiler*, his last prose work, "a *Fors Clavigera* of sorts—my advice to the youthful mind on all manner of things, and poems."[5] Yeats worked hard on the series of five tracts and his letters, written between the fall of 1937 and the following summer when he expected publication (it came posthumously), show an odd combination of motives and emotions. He hopes for commercial success to endow the Cuala Press so it will not be a burden on his family. He writes with some anxiety ("I wonder how many friends I will have left") but more gaiety about the ruckus he anticipates ("The boiler is going to very hot").[6] He delights in new sources of energy. The letters both tease and apologize, but finally come down on seriousness of purpose: "For the first time in my life I am saying what are my political

2. *L*, 827.
3. *VP*, 553 [113].
4. *VP*, 558.
5. *VP*, 563; *L*, 900, 903.
6. *L*, 912.

beliefs."[7] The results are depressing, except for those who want a stick with which to beat the old poet and his admirers, like Harold Bloom who advertises "that very late and grotesque tract all good Yeatsians should re-read once a year."[8] In fact, *On the Boiler* justifies neither the enthusiasm of Yeats's letters nor the pouncing of his detractors. It is a sad and silly document, repetitious, dull, an almost senile rehearsal of various Yeats doctrines on art, education, politics, and science:

> A City Father of a defeated Spanish town said that he could not understand it because their commander was not less well born than his opponent.
>
> Eugenical and psychical research are the revolutionary movements with that element of novelty and sensation which sooner or later stir men to action.
>
> Desire some just war, that big house and hovel, college and public-house, civil servant—his Gaelic certificate in his pocket—and international bride-playing woman, may know that they belong to one nation.[9]

That is not thought but a parody of thought, just as "Under Ben Bulben" ("Scorn the sort now growing up/ . . . Base-born products of base beds") is a parody of late Yeats, not "an old man's eagle mind,"[1] but an old man's self-indulgent rant, WBY as Cecil B. DeMille.

✻   ✻   ✻

7. *L*, 902.
8. Harold Bloom, *Yeats* (New York: Oxford University Press, 1970), 58.
9. W. B. Yeats, *On the Boiler* (Dublin: Cuala Press, 1939), passim.
1. *VP*, 639 [124], 575.

Yeats: A Chronology

1865 Born on June 13 at 1 George's Ville, Sandymount Avenue, Dublin, eldest child of John Butler Yeats (JBY) and Susan Mary Yeats (SMY).

1866 Yeats's sister Susan Mary (Lily) Yeats born. JBY is called to the Irish bar.

1867 JBY gives up the law to study art. The Yeats family moves to London.

1868 Yeats's sister Elizabeth Corbet (Lolly) Yeats born.

1871 Yeats's brother, John Butler (Jack) Yeats, born.

1872 SMY and children leave London for Sligo, where they spend two years.

1874 Family returns to London and settles in Kensington.

1877 Enrolls at the Godolphin School, Hammersmith.

1879 Family moves to Bedford Park. The Irish Land League founded.

1881 Leaves Godolphin School. As JBY's financial situation deteriorates, the family returns to Ireland, living at Howth, north of Dublin. Enrolls at Erasmus Smith High School, Dublin.

1882 Begins writing poetry, under the influence of Shelley. Falls in love with a cousin, Laura Armstrong.

1883 Hears Oscar Wilde lecture in Dublin. Leaves high school.

1884 Enrolls at the Metropolitan School of Art, Dublin.

1885 First poems published (in the *Dublin University Review*). Presides over first meeting of the Dublin Hermetic Society. Begins friendships with John O'Leary and Katherine Tynan.

1886 Stops attending art school. Meets William Morris. The long poem *Mosada* is published as a pamphlet. Attends his first séance. Gladstone's first Home Rule bill defeated.

1887 The Yeats family returns to live in London. Meets Madame Blavatsky. Finishes "The Wanderings of Oisin." SMY suffers a debilitating stroke.

1888 Meets Bernard Shaw at William Morris's house; gets to know Oscar Wilde. Publishes *Fairy and Folk Tales of the Irish Peasantry*. Writes "The Lake Isle of Innisfree." Joins the Esoteric Section of the Theosophical Society.

1889 *The Wanderings of Oisin and Other Poems* published. Meets Maud Gonne (MG) and falls in love with her. Begins *The Countess Kathleen*.

1890 Cofounds The Rhymers' Club with John Rhys. Initiated into the Hermetic Order of the Golden Dawn. Verdict in the

O'Shea divorce case splits the Irish Party and ends Parnell's leadership.

1891   *Representative Irish Tales* published. Proposes to MG for the first time. Parnell dies. *John Sherman and Dhoya* published.

1892   *Irish Fairy Tales* and *The Countess Kathleen and Various Legends and Lyrics* published. Organizes National Literary Society in Dublin with John O'Leary.

1893   *The Works of William Blake* (co-edited with Edwin Ellis) and *The Celtic Twilight* published. Gladstone's second Home Rule bill defeated. The Gaelic League is founded by Douglas Hyde.

1894   Sees Villiers de L'Isle Adams's symbolist play *Axël* during his first visit to Paris. Begins *The Shadowy Waters*. Meets Olivia Shakespear. *The Land of Heart's Desire* published and produced.

1895   *Poems* (1895) published. Leaves the family home to share lodgings with Arthur Symons in central London.

1896   Moves to his own rented lodgings at 18 Woburn Buildings, London. Begins affair with Olivia Shakespear. Travels with Symons in Ireland over the summer, where he visits the Aran Islands, stays with Edward Martyn, and meets Lady Gregory (AG). Meets J. M. Synge in Paris.

1897   Chairs committee celebrating the centenary of the 1798 Irish rebellion. Ends relationship with Olivia Shakespear. *The Secret Rose* published. Stays with Edward Martyn in Galway in early summer and then spends two months at Coole Park with AG. Lays plans for the "Celtic Theatre" (which became the Irish Literary Theatre) and issues appeal for funds. Collects folklore with AG.

1898   Publishes folklore articles based on his gatherings with AG. Lobbies successfully for changes in Dublin theater licensing laws so that the Celtic Theatre can go ahead. "Crisis" in December as MG tells Yeats of her affair with Millevoye; she and Yeats enter a "spiritual marriage." Spends much of the year working on occult rituals and evoking visions, sometimes under the influence of mescal or hashish.

1899   Visits Paris and again proposes to MG, but is again refused. *The Wind Among the Reeds* is published. First season of the Irish Literary Theatre is marked by public controversy over the religious orthodoxy of *The Countess Kathleen*.

1900   Proposes to MG in London. SMY dies. Protests Queen Victoria's visit to Ireland. Publishes *The Shadowy Waters*. Collaborates with George Moore on *Diarmuid and Grania*.

1901   Proposes to MG. *Diarmuid and Grania* is produced. Begins collaborative playwriting with AG.

1902   *Cathleen ni Houlihan* produced in Dublin with MG as the Old Woman. Dun Emer Press established. Meets James Joyce.

1903   MG marries John MacBride. *Ideas of Good and Evil* and *In the Seven Woods* published. Leaves in November for American lecture tour.

1904 Returns from America in spring. Abbey Theatre opens in December with Yeats as producer-manager.

1905 MG separates from MacBride. Abbey Theatre reorganized as a limited Company with Yeats, AG, and Synge as codirectors.

1906 *Poems, 1899–1905* published.

1907 Riots at the Abbey Theatre over Synge's *The Playboy of the Western World*. Travels to Italy with AG and her son Robert. *Discoveries* published. JBY leaves for America, where he would remain for the rest of his life.

1908 Liaison with Mabel Dickinson begins. *Collected Works* published by the Shakespeare Head Press in eight volumes. Briefly consummates sexual relationship with MG in summer.

1909 Synge dies. Controversy over Abbey Theatre's production of Shaw's *The Shewing-Up of Blanco Posnet*. Meets Ezra Pound.

1910 Abbey Theatre remains open after the death of King Edward VII, initiating a terminal row with Annie Horniman, whose subsidies had supported the theater. Yeats is granted a Civil List Pension of £150 per year by the British government. *The Green Helmet and Other Poems* is published.

1911 Goes to America in autumn with touring Abbey Theatre company.

1912 Third Home Rule bill is introduced. *The Cutting of an Agate* published. Controversy over Hugh Lane's plans for the Dublin Municipal Gallery of Modern Art.

1913 Ends liaison with Mabel Dickinson. *Poems Written in Discouragement* published. Spends winter at Stone Cottage, Sussex, with Ezra Pound acting as his secretary.

1914 Lectures in America, February to April. *Responsibilities* published. Home Rule bill passes but is suspended following the outbreak of World War I in August. Begins writing his autobiography.

1915 At Stone Cottage with Ezra and Dorothy Pound, January and February. Hugh Lane drowned in the sinking of the *Lusitania*. Yeats refuses a knighthood.

1916 At Stone Cottage with Ezra and Dorothy Pound, January to March. *Reveries Over Childhood and Youth* published. *At the Hawk's Well* privately performed in London. Easter Rising in Dublin. John MacBride is among the leaders executed in its aftermath. Yeats stays with MG in Normandy and proposes to her for the last time. Begins campaign with AG to have the Lane pictures returned to Dublin.

1917 Buys Thoor Ballylee, a Norman Tower in Galway. Spends summer with MG in Normandy. Proposes to her daughter, Iseult, but is refused. Proposes to Georgie Hyde-Lees in September and is accepted. Marries October 20th. Georgie begins automatic writing, which would become the basis for *A Vision*, soon afterward. *The Wild Swans at Coole* published.

1918 *Per Amica Silentia Lunae* published. Robert Gregory killed in action in Italy. Summer in Ireland supervising restoration of

Thoor Ballylee. Armistice signed, November 11. Sinn Fein wins elections, but candidates refuse to take their seats at Westminster.

1919 Sinn Fein forms independent Irish Parliament, Dáil Éireann. War of Independence begins. Anne Yeats born on February 26. Yeats returns to England in May. Ends lease of 18 Woburn Buildings and moves to 4 Broad Street, Oxford. Sinn Fein is outlawed. Guerrilla war breaks out in Ireland.

1920 Lectures in America, January to May. War in Ireland intensifies as Black and Tans, reinforcing the regular police, begin violent coercion of the civilian population. Government of Ireland Act allows six Ulster counties to devolve and form a separate Northern Ireland Parliament.

1921 *Michael Robartes and the Dancer* published. Michael Yeats born on August 22. *Four Plays for Dancers* and *Four Years* published. Anglo-Irish Treaty debated in the Dáil. Northern Irish Parliament opens at Stormont.

1922 Anglo-Irish Treaty is ratified by the Dáil, giving the twenty-six southern counties dominion status within the British Empire. Civil war breaks out between pro-treaty and Republican forces. Yeats buys 82 Merrion Square, Dublin. JBY dies in New York. The Yeatses live at Ballylee, March to September as civil war rages. Yeats becomes a senator in the Free State Government.

1923 De Valera orders Republican cease-fire, and the civil war ends. Yeats awarded Nobel Prize for Literature.

1924 *Essays*, "Meditations in Time of Civil War," and *The Cat and the Moon* published.

1925 Visits Sicily and Rome, January and February. Speaks in favor of divorce in Irish Senate. O'Casey's *The Plough and the Stars* causes riots at the Abbey Theatre.

1926 *A Vision* (dated 1925), *Estrangement*, and *Autobiographies* published.

1927 *October Blast* published. Seriously ill with congestion of the lungs, Yeats spends winter at Algeciras, Seville, and Cannes.

1928 *The Tower* published. Sells house in Merrion Square. Controversy over Abbey Theatre's refusal of Sean O'Casey's play *The Silver Tassie*. Resigns from the Senate. Goes to Rapallo for the winter in poor health.

1929 Hemorrhage of lungs, and then critically ill with Malta fever at Rapallo. *The Winding Stair* (1929) published.

1930 Convalesces slowly. Returns to Dublin, July. Meets Virginia Woolf, November.

1931 Prepares most of an "Edition de Luxe" for Macmillan. Stays at Coole from autumn on as AG declines.

1932 De Valera and Fianna Fáil win elections. AG dies, May 22, and Coole is emptied. Yeats leases house at Riversdale, Rathfarnham. Founds Irish Academy of Letters. Begins his last lecture tour in America, October.

1933 Returns from America, January. Flirts with O'Duffy's fascist

Blueshirt movement. *The Winding Stair and Other Poems* published.

1934   Undergoes Steinach rejuvenation operation. *Collected Plays* published.

1935   Invalided by renewed congestion of the lungs, January to March. Seventieth birthday celebrations. Winter in Majorca, collaborating with Shri Purohit Swami on a translation of the Upanishads. *A Full Moon in March* is published.

1936   Seriously ill with heart and kidney ailments. Edits controversial *Oxford Book of Modern Verse*.

1937   Announces retirement from public life. Revised edition of *A Vision* published.

1938   *New Poems* published. *Purgatory* causes controversy. Olivia Shakespear dies.

1939   Dies January 28 and is interred at Roquebrune in the south of France. *Last Poems and Two Plays* and *On the Boiler* appear posthumously. World War II begins, September.

1948   Yeats's body is reinterred at Drumcliff, Sligo, in September.

Bibliographical and Textual Appendix

Poems

From *Crossways*

Yeats first adopted the title "Crossways" in 1895 as the title for a group of poems he selected from *The Wanderings of Oisin and Other Poems* (1889; hereafter *WO*) and from *The Countess Kathleen and Various Legends and Lyrics* (1892; hereafter *CK*) because, he wrote, "in them he tried many pathways" (*Poems*, 1895). The collection was dedicated to "A.E.," Yeats's friend George Russell (1867–1935), writer and painter, and has as epigraph a line adapted from "Night the Ninth, Being the Last Judgement," in *Vala* by William Blake: "The stars are threshed, and the souls are threshed from their husks."

Copy-texts for the printings in this Norton Critical Edition are taken from *Poems* (1895), except for the 1889 version of "Ephemera," drawn from *WO*.

"The Song of the Happy Shepherd": First published in the *Dublin University Review*, October 1885, as "An Epilogue / To 'The Island of Statues' and 'The Seeker.'" Reprinted under the title "Song of the Last Arcadian" in *WO* (1889).

"The Sad Shepherd": First published in the *Dublin University Review*, October 1886, as "Miserrimus."

"The Cloak, the Boat, and the Shoes": First published in the *Dublin University Review*, March 1885, as "Voices." It was originally written as part of Yeats's Arcadian play *The Island of Statues*.

"The Indian to His Love": First published in the *Dublin University Review*, December 1886, as "An Indian Song."

"The Falling of the Leaves": First published in *WO* (1889), as "Falling of the Leaves."

"Ephemera": Written in 1884, and first published in *WO* (1889), as "Ephemera. An Autumn Idyl." Retitled and revised extensively for *Poems* (1895).

"The Stolen Child": First published in the *Irish Monthly*, December 1886. The printing error "hand and hand" in line 52 of the copy-text used for this Norton Critical Edition has been silently emended to "hand in hand," to accord with all printings after 1899.

"To an Isle in the Water": First published in *WO* (1889).

495

"Down by the Salley Gardens": First published in WO (1889), as "An Old
Song Re-Sung." Yeats's note accompanying the poem in that printing
reads: "This is an attempt to reconstruct an old song from three lines
imperfectly remembered by an old peasant woman in the village of
Ballysodare, Sligo, who often sings them to herself."
"The Meditation of the Old Fisherman": First published in the *Irish
Monthly*, October 1886. Substantively revised for *Poems* (1895).

From *The Rose*

Yeats dedicated this sequence to Lionel Johnson (1867–1902), poet and
critic, and it has as its epigraph a line from St. Augustine's *Confessions*:
"Sero te amavi, Pulchritudo tam antiqua et tam nova! Sero te amavi"
("Too late I loved you, Beauty so old and so new! Too late I loved you").
The title for the sequence was first adopted in 1895 as a heading for poems
selected from *CK* (1892). In *Poems* (1895), "The Rose" preceded "Crossways" despite the fact that its poems were written later, and Yeats retained
this order through the numerous editions of *Poems* between 1895 and
1929, before reversing them in *Early Poems and Stories* (1925; hereafter
EPS), in *Collected Poems* (1933), and then in all subsequent editions of
his work.
   Copy-texts for the printings in this Norton Critical Edition are taken
from *Poems* (1895), except for the later versions of "The Sorrow of Love,"
"The Dedication to a Book of Stories selected from the Irish Novelists,"
and "The Lamentation of the Old Pensioner" (for each of which, see notes
below).

"To the Rose upon the Rood of Time": First published in *CK* (1892).
"Fergus and the Druid": First published in the *National Observer*, May
1892.
"The Rose of the World": First published in the *National Observer*, Jan-
uary 1892, as "Rosa Mundi." Retitled and moderately revised for *CK*
(1892).
"The Lake Isle of Innisfree": First published in the *National Observer*,
December 1890.
"The Pity of Love": First published in *CK* (1892). Moderately revised for
Poems (1895), and with further incremental changes in some later
printings.
"The Sorrow of Love": First published in *CK* (1892). Substantively revised
for *EPS* (1925), which serves as copy-text for the later version printed
in this Norton Critical Edition.
"When You are Old": First published in *CK* (1892). Moderately revised
for *Poems* (1895).
"The White Birds": First published in the *National Observer*, May 1892.
Moderately revised for *Poems* (1895).
"[Who goes with Fergus?]": First published in Yeats's play *The Countess
Kathleen* in *CK* (1892) as an untitled lyric, and with its two stanzas sepa-
rated by several lines of dialogue. First included as a freestanding poem in
"The Rose" sequence in 1912, with the title "Who goes with Fergus?"

"The Dedication to a Book of Stories selected from the Irish Novelists": First published, as "Dedication," in *Representative Irish Tales* (1891). Substantively revised in the *Irish Statesman*, November 8, 1924, and incorporated as revised in subsequent printings of "The Rose" sequence. Copy-text for the later version printed in this Norton Critical Edition is taken from *EPS* (1925).

"The Lamentation of the Old Pensioner": First published in the *Scots Observer*, November 1890, as "The Old Pensioner." Substantively revised for *EPS* (1925), from which copy-text is taken for the later version printed in this Norton Critical Edition.

"To Ireland in the Coming Times": First published in *CK* (1892), as "Apologia addressed to Ireland in the coming days."

From *The Wind Among the Reeds*

The Wind Among the Reeds (hereafter WAR) was first published in 1899. In reprinting these poems in 1906, Yeats revised many of their titles, although he made relatively few changes to their texts.

Copy-texts for the printings in this Norton Critical Edition are taken from *The Poetical Works of William Butler Yeats, Vol. I, Lyrical Poems* (1906).

"The Hosting of the Sidhe": First published in the *National Observer*, October 1893, as "The Faery Host." Retitled "The Host" in *The Celtic Twilight* (1893), and as "The Hosting of the Sidhe" in WAR (1899).

"The Lover tells of the Rose in his Heart": First published in the *National Observer*, November 1892, as "The Rose in my Heart." Retitled "Aedh tells of the Rose in his Heart" in WAR (1899), and again as "The Lover tells of the Rose in his Heart" in 1906.

"The Fisherman" ["The Fish"]: First published in the *Cornish Magazine*, December 1898, as "Bressel the Fisherman." Retitled "Breasal the Fisherman" in WAR (1899), as "The Fisherman" from 1906 until 1933, and as "The Fish" thereafter.

"The Song of Wandering Aengus": First published in the *Sketch*, August 1897, as "A Mad Song." Retitled as "The Song of Wandering Aengus" in WAR (1899).

"The Lover mourns for the Loss of Love": First published in the *Dome*, May 1898, in a three-poem sequence entitled "Aedh to Dectora." Retitled "Aedh laments the Loss of Love" in WAR (1899), and as "The Lover mourns for the Loss of Love" in 1906.

"He reproves the Curlew": First published in the *Savoy*, November 1896, as "O'Sullivan Rua to the Curlew," in a two-poem sequence headed "Windle-straws." Retitled as "Hanrahan reproves the Curlew" in WAR (1899), and as "He reproves the Curlew" in 1906.

"He remembers Forgotten Beauty": First published in the *Savoy*, July 1896, as "O'Sullivan Rua to Mary Lavell." Retitled "Michael Robartes remembers Forgotten Beauty" in WAR (1899), and as "He remembers Forgotten Beauty" in 1906.

"A Poet to his Beloved": First published in the *Senate*, March 1896, as

"O'Sullivan the Red to Mary Lavell," in a two-poem sequence. Retitled "A Poet to his Beloved" in WAR (1899).

"He gives his Beloved certain Rhymes": First published in the *Savoy*, January 1896, untitled, in the short story "The Binding of the Hair." Retitled "Aedh gives his Beloved certain Rhymes" in WAR (1899) and as "He gives his Beloved certain Rhymes" in 1906.

"To my Heart, bidding it have no Fear" ["To his Heart, bidding it have no Fear"]: First published in the *Savoy*, November 1896, as "Out of the Old Days," in a two-poem sequence headed "Windle-straws." Retitled in WAR (1899) as "To my Heart, bidding it have no Fear." Finally retitled "To his Heart, bidding it have no Fear" in 1922.

"The Cap and Bells": First published in the *National Observer*, March 1894, as "Cap and Bell." Retitled "The Cap and Bells" in all subsequent printings.

"He hears the Cry of the Sedge": First published in the *Dome*, May 1898, in a three-poem sequence headed "Aodh to Dectora." Retitled "Aedh hears the Cry of the Sedge" in WAR (1899), and as "He hears the Cry of the Sedge" in 1906.

"He thinks of those who have Spoken Evil of his Beloved": First published in the *Dome*, May 1898, in a three-poem sequence headed "Aodh to Dectora." Retitled "Aedh thinks of those who have Spoken Evil of his Beloved" in WAR (1899), and as "He thinks of those who have Spoken Evil of his Beloved" in 1906.

"The Lover pleads with his Friend for Old Friends": First published in the *Saturday Review*, July 1897, as "Song." Retitled "The Poet pleads with his Friend for Old Friends" in WAR (1899), and as "The Lover pleads with his Friend for Old Friends" in 1906.

"He wishes his Beloved were Dead": First published in the *Sketch*, February 1898, as "Aodh to Dectora." Retitled "Aedh wishes his Beloved were Dead" in WAR (1899), and then as "He wishes his Beloved were Dead" in 1906.

"He wishes for the Cloths of Heaven": First published in WAR (1899), as "Aedh wishes for the Cloths of Heaven." Retitled "He wishes for the Cloths of Heaven" in 1906.

From *In the Seven Woods*

First published by the Dun Emer Press in August 1903, in a limited edition, *In the Seven Woods* (hereafter *ISW* 1903) was comprised of twelve poems and the play *On Baile's Strand*. A Macmillan trade edition with the same contents was also published that month. Three new poems were added to the sequence in *Poems, 1899–1905*; two long narrative poems ("The Old Age of Queen Maeve" and "Baile and Aillinn") were removed to become freestanding works in *The Poetical Works of William Butler Yeats, Vol. I, Lyrical Poems* (1906), and two additional new poems were added in *The Collected Works in Verse and Prose of William Butler Yeats* (1908).

Copy-texts for the printings in this Norton Critical Edition are taken from *Poems, 1899–1905* (1906) unless otherwise noted below.

"In the Seven Woods": First published in *ISW* (1903).

"The Arrow": First published in *ISW* (1903). Moderately revised in 1922.

"The Folly of Being Comforted": First published in the *Speaker*, January 1902. Minor revisions after 1903.

"Never Give all the Heart": First published in *McClure's Magazine*, December 1905, and added to *In the Seven Woods* in 1906.

"Adam's Curse": First published in the *Monthly Review*, December 1902. Moderate revisions after 1903.

"Red Hanrahan's Song about Ireland": First published, with no title and with a very different text, in the *National Observer*, August 1894, as part of Yeats's story "Kathleen-Ny-Hoolihan." Retitled "The Song of Red Hanrahan" in *ISW* (1903), and then as "Red Hanrahan's Song about Ireland" in *The Poetical Works of William Butler Yeats, Vol. I, Lyrical Poems* (1906), from which copy-text is taken for this Norton Critical Edition.

"The Old Men Admiring Themselves in the Water": First published in the *Pall Mall Magazine*, January 1903.

"O Do Not Love Too Long": First published in the *Acorn*, October 1905, as "Do Not Love Too Long." Added to the *In the Seven Woods* sequence in 1908. Copy-text for this Norton Critical Edition is taken from *The Collected Works in Verse and Prose of William Butler Yeats* (1908).

From *The Green Helmet and Other Poems*

First published by the Cuala Press in December 1910, in a limited edition, *The Green Helmet and Other Poems* (hereafter GH 1910) was comprised of nineteen poems and the play *The Green Helmet*. Six new poems were added to the sequence in the trade edition issued by Macmillan in 1912.

Copy-texts for the printings in this Norton Critical Edition are taken from *The Green Helmet and Other Poems* (London: Macmillan, 1912) unless otherwise noted below.

"His Dream": First published in the *Nation* (London), July 1908, as "A Dream." Included as "His Dream" in an eight-poem sequence with the general title "Raymond Lully and his wife Pernella" in GH (1910).

"A Woman Homer Sung": First published in GH (1910) in an eight-poem sequence with the general title "Raymond Lully and his wife Pernella."

"The Consolation" ["Words"]: First published in GH (1910) in an eight-poem sequence with the general title "Raymond Lully and his wife Pernella." Retitled "Words" in *Collected Poems* (1933).

"No Second Troy": First published in GH (1910) in an eight-poem sequence with the general title "Raymond Lully and his wife Pernella."

"Reconciliation": First published in GH (1910) in an eight-poem sequence with the general title "Raymond Lully and his wife Pernella."

"The Fascination of What's Difficult": First published in GH (1910) in an eleven-poem sequence with the general title "Momentary Thoughts."

"A Drinking Song": First published in GH (1910) in an eleven-poem sequence with the general title "Momentary Thoughts."

"The Coming of Wisdom with Time": First published in *McClure's Mag-*

azine, December 1910, as "Youth and Age." Retitled in *GH* (1910), where it was included in an eleven-poem sequence with the general title "Momentary Thoughts."

"On hearing that the Students of our New University have joined the Ancient Order of Hibernians and the Agitation against Immoral Literature": First published in *The Green Helmet and Other Poems* in 1912. Title revised to "On hearing that the Students of our New University have joined the Agitation against Immoral Literature" in 1922.

"To a Poet, who would have me Praise certain Bad Poets, Imitators of His and Mine": First published in *GH* (1910), as "To a Poet, who would have me Praise certain Bad Poets, Imitators of His and of Mine," in an eleven-poem sequence with the general title "Momentary Thoughts." Retitled in 1911.

"The Mask": First published in *GH* (1910), as "A Lyric from an Unpublished Play," in an eleven-poem sequence with the general title "Momentary Thoughts." Retitled as "The Mask" in *A Selection from the Love Poetry of William Butler Yeats* (Cuala Press, 1913), from which copy-text is taken for this Norton Critical Edition.

"Upon a House shaken by the Land Agitation": First published in *McClure's Magazine*, December 1910, as "To a Certain Country House in Time of Change." Retitled "Upon a Threatened House" in *GH* (1910), and included in an eleven-poem sequence with the general title "Momentary Thoughts." Retitled as "Upon a House shaken by the Land Agitation" in 1912.

"All Things can Tempt Me": First published in the *English Review*, February 1909, as "Distraction." Retitled as "All Things can Tempt me" in *GH* (1910), and included in an eleven-poem sequence with the general title "Momentary Thoughts."

"The Young Man's Song" ["Brown Penny"]: First published in *GH* (1910) in an eleven-poem sequence with the general title "Momentary Thoughts." Retitled "Brown Penny" in *Collected Poems* (1933).

From *Responsibilities*

First published by the Cuala Press in May 1914, in a limited edition, *Responsibilities: Poems and a Play* (hereafter *R* 1914) was comprised of thirty-one poems and a new version of the play *The Hour-Glass*. One new poem, "The Well and the Tree," was added in the trade edition issued by Macmillan in 1916, but it was subsequently removed from the sequence to become part of the play *At the Hawk's Well* [see p. 168].

Copy-texts for the printings in this Norton Critical Edition are taken from the British edition of *Responsibilities and Other Poems* (1916).

["Introductory Rhymes"]: First published, untitled, in *R* (1914). Titled "Introductory Rhymes" in table of contents, but untitled above poem, in all subsequent printings during Yeats's lifetime except *Collected Poems* (1933), in which it is again untitled above the poem but appears as "Introductory Rhyme" in the table of contents.

"To a Wealthy Man who promised a Second Subscription to the Dublin

Municipal Gallery if it were proved the People wanted Pictures": First published in the *Irish Times*, January 1913, under the title "The Gift / To a friend who promises a bigger subscription than his first to the Dublin Municipal Gallery if the amount collected proved that there is a considerable 'popular demand' for the pictures." Retitled "To a Wealthy Man, who promised a Second Subscription if it were proved the People wanted Pictures" in *Poems Written in Discouragement* (1913) and as "To a Wealthy Man who promised a Second Subscription if it were proved the People wanted Pictures" in *Poems Written in Discouragement* (1913) and as "To a Wealthy Man who promised a Second Subscription to the Dublin Municipal Gallery if it were proved the People wanted Pictures" in *R* (1914).

"September 1913": First published in the *Irish Times*, September 1913, under the title "Romance in Ireland / (On reading much of the correspondence against the Art Gallery.)" Retitled "Romantic Ireland / (September 1913)" in *Nine Poems* (1914), and as "September, 1913" in *R* (1914). Titled "September 1913" in all subsequent printings.

"To a Friend whose Work has come to Nothing": First published in *Poems Written in Discouragement* (1913).

"Paudeen": First published in *Poems Written in Discouragement* (1913).

"The Three Beggars": First published in *Harper's Weekly*, November 1913.

"Beggar to Beggar Cried": First published in *Poetry* (Chicago), May 1914.

"I. The Witch": First published in *Poetry* (Chicago), May 1914.

"II. The Peacock": First published in *Poetry* (Chicago), May 1914.

"To a Child Dancing in the Wind" / ["Two Years Later"]: Lines 1–12 first published in *Poetry* (Chicago), December 1912, as "To a Child dancing upon the Shore"; lines 13–24 first published in *Poetry* (Chicago), May 1914, as "To a Child Dancing in the Wind." From *R* (1914) until 1922 the two poems were presented under a single title as in this Norton Critical Edition; from 1922 onward, lines 1–12 were titled "I / To a Child Dancing in the Wind" and lines 13–24 as "II / Two Years Later."

"Fallen Majesty": First published in *Poetry* (Chicago), December 1912.

"Friends": First published in *The Green Helmet and Other Poems* (1912). Moderately revised in 1924 and again in 1933.

"The Cold Heaven": First published in *The Green Helmet and Other Poems* (1912).

"The Magi": First published in *Poetry* (Chicago), May 1914. Until 1933, the poem was printed in sequence with "The Dolls" in all book printings in which both appeared, with "The Magi" being numbered "I" and "The Dolls" numbered "II."

"The Dolls": First published in *Responsibilities* (1914). See note to "The Magi." The misspelling "balls" in line 2 of the poem in printings through 1916 has been silently corrected to "bawls" in this Norton Critical Edition.

"A Coat": First published in *Poetry* (Chicago), May 1914.

["Closing Rhymes"]: First published in the *New Statesman*, February 1914, under the title "Notoriety / (*Suggested by a recent magazine article*)." It is untitled above the text but titled "Closing Rhymes" in the tables of contents of all subsequent printings during Yeats's lifetime, except *Collected Poems* (1933), in which it is again untitled above the poem but appears as "Closing Rhyme" in the table of contents.

From *The Wild Swans at Coole*

First published by the Cuala Press in November 1917 in a limited edition, *The Wild Swans at Coole* (hereafter WSC 1917) was comprised of twenty-three poems, one being in seven parts, and the play *At the Hawk's Well*. Seventeen new poems were added in the Macmillan trade edition published in 1919 (hereafter WSC 1919).

Copy-texts for the printings in this Norton Critical Edition are taken from the British edition of WSC (1919) unless otherwise noted below.

"The Wild Swans at Coole": First published in the *Little Review*, June 1917. The positions of stanzas 2 and 6 were switched in all subsequent printings.

"In Memory of Major Robert Gregory": First published in the *English Review*, August 1918, as "In Memory of Robert Gregory." Title revised to "In Memory of Major Robert Gregory" in WSC (1919).

"An Irish Airman Foresees his Death": First published in WSC (1919). Copy-text for this Norton Critical Edition is taken from *The Wild Swans at Coole* (Macmillan, 1920).

"Men Improve with the Years": First published in the *Little Review*, June 1917.

"The Living Beauty": First published in the *Little Review*, October 1918. Substantially revised in 1933.

"A Song": First published in the *Little Review*, October 1918. Lines 5–6, 11–12, and 17–18 were italicized in printings from 1933 on.

"The Scholars": First published in the *Catholic Anthology* (1915). Significantly revised for *Selected Poems* in 1929, from which copy-text for the later version printed in this Norton Critical Edition is taken.

"Lines Written in Dejection": First published in WSC (1917). Copy-text for this Norton Critical Edition is taken from *The Wild Swans at Coole* (Macmillan, 1920), in which the poem was moderately revised.

"On Woman": First published in *Poetry* (Chicago) February 1916.

"The Fisherman": First published in *Poetry* (Chicago), February 1916.

"The People": First published in *Poetry* (Chicago), February 1916, as "The Phoenix." Retitled "The People" in WSC (1917).

"Broken Dreams": First published in the *Little Review*, June 1917.

"The Balloon of the Mind": First published in the *New Statesman*, September 29, 1917.

"On being asked for a War Poem": First published in *The Book of the Homeless*, ed. Edith Wharton (1916), under the title "A Reason for Keeping Silent." Retitled as "On being asked for a War Poem" in WSC (1917).

"Ego Dominus Tuus": First published in *Poetry* (Chicago), October 1917.

"The Double Vision of Michael Robartes": First published in WSC (1919).

From *Michael Robartes and the Dancer*

First published by the Cuala Press in February 1921 in a limited edition, *Michael Robartes and the Dancer* (hereafter MRD 1921) was comprised of fifteen poems.

Copy-texts for the printings in this Norton Critical Edition are taken from *Later Poems* (London: Macmillan, 1922) unless otherwise noted below.

"Michael Robartes and the Dancer": First published in the *Dial*, November 1920, from which copy-text is taken for this Norton Critical Edition. Yeats made minor revisions in MRD (1921).

"Easter, 1916": First issued in *Easter, 1916*, a privately distributed printing of only twenty-five copies, in 1916, and then not published commercially or otherwise until 1920, at which point Yeats incorporated modest revisions.

"On a Political Prisoner": First published in the *Dial*, November 1920.

"The Second Coming": First published in the *Dial*, November 1920.

"A Prayer for my Daughter": First published in *Poetry* (Chicago), November 1919.

"To be Carved on a Stone at Thoor Ballylee": First published in MRD (1921) under the title "To be Carved on a Stone at Ballylee." Title revised to "To be Carved on a Stone at Thoor Ballylee" in 1922.

From *The Tower*

First published by Macmillan (London) in February 1928. Copy-texts for the printings in this Norton Critical Edition are taken from that edition.

"Sailing to Byzantium": First published in *October Blast*, 1927.

"The Tower": First published in the *New Republic*, June 1927.

"Meditations in Time of Civil War": First published in the *Dial*, January 1923. Moderate revisions were made throughout for its printing in *The Tower* (1928), including the deletion of an entire stanza from "My House" (part II of the sequence) and the retitling of part VI as "The Stare's Nest by my Window," instead of "The Jay's Nest by my Window."

"Nineteen Hundred and Nineteen": First published in the *Dial*, September 1921, under the title "Thoughts upon the Present State of the Word." Retitled "Nineteen Hundred and Nineteen" in *The Tower* (1928).

"A Prayer for my Son": First published in *Seven Poems and a Fragment* (1922). Moderately revised in *The Tower* (1928).

"Leda and the Swan": First published in the *Dial*, June 1924, and significantly revised for inclusion in *A Vision* (1925).

"Among School Children": First published in the *Dial*, August 1927, under the title "Among Schoolchildren." Retitled "Among School Children" in *October Blast* (1927).

"All Souls' Night": First published in the *New Republic*, March 1921.

From *The Winding Stair and Other Poems*

First published by the Fountain Press, New York, in October 1929, as a signed limited edition, *The Winding Stair* (hereafter WS 1929) was comprised of five poems plus the eleven-poem sequence "A Woman Young and Old." Forty-six poems were added to the sequence in the Macmillan trade edition, *The Winding Stair*, in 1933 (hereafter WS 1933). Copy-texts for the printings in this Norton Critical Edition are taken from the British edition of this later volume.

"In Memory of Eva Gore-Booth and Con Markiewicz": First published in WS (1929) under the title "In Memory of Eva Gore Booth and Con Markiewicz." Title revised to "In Memory of Eva Gore-Booth and Con Markiewicz" in WS (1933).

"A Dialogue of Self and Soul": First published in WS (1929). Minor revisions made for its inclusion in WS (1933).

"Blood and the Moon": First published in the *Exile*, Spring 1928.

"Coole Park, 1929": First published in *Coole* (1931), by Lady Gregory, under the title "Coole Park." Retitled "Coole Park 1929" in *Words for Music Perhaps and Other Poems* (1932), and as "Coole Park, 1929" in WS (1933).

"The Choice": First printed in *Words for Music Perhaps and Other Poems* (1932), as the sixth stanza of the poem "Coole Park and Ballylee 1932." It was removed from that poem (which was later retitled "Coole Park and Ballylee, 1931") in WS (1933), and made into a freestanding poem under the title "The Choice."

"Byzantium": First printed in *Words for Music Perhaps and Other Poems* (1932).

"Vacillation": First printed in *Words for Music Perhaps and Other Poems* (1932), in which the poem's sections were titled as follows: I as "What is Joy," II and III (forming one section, with subsequent sections renumbered accordingly) as "The Burning Tree," IV as "Happiness," V as "Conscience," VI as "Conquerors," VII as "A Dialogue," and VIII as "Von Hügel."

"Crazy Jane talks with the Bishop": First published in WS (1933) as the sixth section of a twenty-five poem sequence given the collective title "Words for Music Perhaps."

"Father and Child": First published in WS (1929) as the first section of an eleven-poem sequence given the collective title "A Woman Young and Old."

From *A Full Moon in March*

Published by Macmillan, London, in November 1935. The volume was comprised of two plays (*A Full Moon in March* and a new version of *The King of the Great Clock Tower*) plus six poems and the twelve-part sequence "Supernatural Songs." Copy-texts for the printings in this Norton Critical Edition are taken from that volume.

"A Prayer for Old Age": First published in the *Spectator*, November 1934, under the title "Old Age."

"The Four Ages of Man": First published in *Poetry* (Chicago), December 1934, as the fifth poem in an eight-poem sequence given the collective title "Supernatural Songs." In *A Full Moon in March* (1935), this sequence was extended to twelve poems, of which "The Four Ages of Man" is the ninth poem.

From *New Poems*

New Poems (hereafter *NP*) was first published by the Cuala Press in May 1938, in a limited edition. Copy-texts for the printings in this Norton Critical Edition are taken from that volume.

"The Gyres": First published in *NP*.

"Lapis Lazuli": First published in the *London Mercury*, March 1938.

"Imitated from the Japanese": First published in *NP*.

"What Then?": First published in the *Erasmian* (Dublin), April 1937. The *NP* printing of the poem has no comma after "wife" in line 12 of the poem. The comma is present on Yeats's final corrected typescript and in the *Erasmian* printing, and it was reinserted by Yeats's widow in the posthumously printed volume *Last Poems and Plays* (1940). I have emended the text accordingly.

"Beautiful Lofty Things": First published in *NP*.

"Come Gather Round Me Parnellites": First published in *A Broadside* (ed. W. B. Yeats and F. R. Higgins), Number 1, January 1937.

"The Great Day": First published in the *London Mercury*, March 1938, as one of four poems under the general title "Fragments."

"Parnell": First published in the *London Mercury*, March 1938, as one of four poems under the general title "Fragments."

"The Spur": First published in the *London Mercury*, March 1938, as one of four poems under the general title "Fragments."

"The Municipal Gallery Re-visited": First published in *A Speech and Two Poems* (1937). Moderately revised for *NP*.

From *Last Poems*

Before his death in January 1939, Yeats completed much of the planning for a new volume to be issued by the Cuala Press, and he drew up a draft list of contents just a few days before he died, showing the proposed order for nineteen poems and two plays (*The Death of Cuchulain* and *Purgatory*). Yeats had corrected proof for journal printings of nearly half the nineteen poems for the proposed volume, but the remainder were extent only in typescripts (some of which were quite heavily revised) at the time of his death. Given his usual habits, even those poems that had been printed in journals would likely have received some emendation had he proofed them for the Cuala volume. The long-standing denotation of the nineteen poems as "Last Poems" has no clear authorial sanction, as the collection's title seems to have been devised by Yeats's widow after his death. Copy-texts for the printings given in this Norton Critical Edition are taken from journal printings known to have been proofed by Yeats or, in the case of poems not printed during his lifetime, from the latest-known surviving draft state. Details are given for each poem below. The surviving draft materials for *Last Poems* are presented in my edition of *W. B. Yeats: Last Poems: Manuscript Materials* (Cornell University Press, 1997); hereafter referred to as *YLP*.

"Under Ben Bulben": First published, posthumously, in the *Irish Times* and the *Irish Independent*, February 3, 1939. Copy-text for the printing here is taken from Yeats's typescript drafts in the National Library of Ireland (NLI 13,593). Yeats made late revisions to the poem on two differing states of the surviving typescripts, apparently unaware (in his declining health) of the resulting ambiguity as to which text he considered final. The text printed in this Norton Critical Edition consequently draws on the following typescripts: for lines 1–36 of the poem, NLI 13,593 (52), 16r, with the addition of the revisions to the title and lines 3 and 6 on NLI 13,593 (52), 15r, and with the spelling "Mariotic" emended to "Mareotic" to accord with Yeats's usual spelling of this word; for lines 37–67, NLI 13,593 (52), 19r, with the addition of a line apparently dropped accidentally from NLI 13,593 (52), 18r (lineated 55a in this edition); for lines 68–94, NLI 13,593 (52), 23r, but with the typist's error "Druncliffe" emended to "Drumcliff" to accord with Yeats's usual spelling of this word. For a transcription of the typescripts of the poem, and for a discussion of the ambiguities surrounding line 55a, see *YLP*, pp. xxxvi–xli and 36–47 (but note that the photo identified on pp. 42 and 44 as NLI 13,593 [52], 19r, is, in fact, NLI 13,593 [52], 20r).

"The Black Tower": First published, posthumously, in *Last Poems and Two Plays* (1939). Copy-text for this Norton Critical Edition is taken from Yeats's last typescript draft in the National Library of Ireland, NLI 30,200 (1); see *YLP* pp. 138–41.

"Long-legged Fly": First published in the *London Mercury*, March 1939, and the *Nation* April 15, 1939. Copy-text for this Norton Critical Edition is taken from Yeats's last typescript draft in the National Library of Ireland, NLI 13,593 (36), 3r; see *YLP* pp. 262–63.

"High Talk": First published in the *London Mercury*, December 1938. Copy-text for this Norton Critical Edition is taken from this printing, for which Yeats is known to have corrected the proofs, but with the misspelling "fench" in line 4 corrected to "fence" as in the final typescript and the *Nation* printing of December 1938.

"Man and the Echo": First published in the *London Mercury*, January 1939. Copy-text for this Norton Critical Edition is taken from this printing, for which Yeats is known to have corrected the proofs.

"The Circus Animals' Desertion": First published in the *London Mercury*, January 1939. Copy-text for this Norton Critical Edition is taken from this printing, for which Yeats is known to have corrected the proofs, but with the correction of "Animals'" for "Animal's" in the title.

"Politics": First published in the *London Mercury*, January 1939. Copy-text for this Norton Critical Edition is taken from this printing, for which Yeats is known to have corrected the proofs.

Plays

Cathleen ni Houlihan: First published in *Samhain* in October 1902, and incrementally revised (including a brief change in the spelling of its title) in *Cathleen ni Hoolihan* (1902), *The Hour-Glass and Other Plays* (1904), and *The Hour-Glass, Cathleen ni Houlihan, The Pot of Broth* (1904). Copy-text for this Norton Critical Edition is taken from *Cathleen ni Houlihan* (London: A. H. Bullen, 1906).

On Baile's Strand: First published in the Dun Emer Press volume *In the Seven Woods* (1903). Substantially revised in *Poems, 1899–1905* (1906), and with minor further revisions in *On Baile's Strand* (London: A. H. Bullen, 1907), from which printing copy-text for this Norton Critical Edition is taken.

At the Hawk's Well: First published in *Harper's Bazaar*, March 1917, and with minor variants in *To-Day* (London), June 1917, and *The Wild Swans at Coole* (1917). Copy-text for this Norton Critical Edition is taken from *Four Plays for Dancers* (1921), in which further revisions were incorporated.

Purgatory: First published by the Cuala Press, in the posthumously prepared volume *Last Poems and Two Plays* (1939), from which copy-text for this Norton Critical Edition is taken.

Prose Fiction and Folklore Writings

The Celtic Twilight: First published by T. Fisher Unwin (London) in 1893, comprising twenty short essays, three poems, and a preface. Most of this volume's contents had appeared in earlier journal printings, usually in variant forms. A revised and enlarged edition was issued by A. H. Bullen (London) in 1902, with eighteen new essays (most of which had likewise appeared in earlier journal printings), substantive revisions to most of the earlier essays, and with one essay dropped from the earlier volume. The enlarged edition reflects the influence of Lady Gregory's folklore researches with and for Yeats, and many of the new essays were written collaboratively with her. Copy-text for "This Book," "Belief and Unbelief," and "Drumcliff and Rosses" in this Norton Critical Edition is taken from *The Celtic Twilight* (1893), and for " 'Dust hath closed Helen's Eye,' " "Enchanted Woods," and "By the Roadside" from *The Celtic Twilight* (1902).

The Secret Rose: First published by Lawrence and Bullen (London) in 1897, comprising seventeen stories and one poem (all of which had previously been published in variant form in journals). Copy-texts for "The Crucifixion of the Outcast" and "The Old Men of the Twilight" in this Norton Critical Edition are taken from this volume.

Stories of Red Hanrahan: First published by the Dun Emer Press in May 1905 (although the title page reads 1904), in a limited edition comprising six stories, most of which were revised versions of stories included in *The Secret Rose* (1897). Copy-texts for "The Twisting of the Rope" and "The Death of Hanrahan" in this Norton Critical Edition are taken from the Dun Emer volume.

Autobiographical Writings

Reveries Over Childhood and Youth: First published in a limited edition by the Cuala Press in March 1915. Copy-text for this Norton Critical Edition is taken from this volume.

The Trembling of the Veil: First published as a book in a limited edition for subscribers only, issued by T. Werner Laurie in 1922. Book I: *Four Years: 1887–1891* had previously been issued as a separate volume by the Cuala Press in December 1921, and, in variant form (under the title "Four Years"), in the *London Mercury* and the *Dial* in June, July, and August 1921. Copy-text for this Norton Critical Edition is taken from the *Dial* printings. Book II: *Ireland After Parnell*, parts of Book III: *Hodos Chameliontos*, and Book IV: *The Tragic Generation* were first published, again in variant form, under the title "More Memories" in the *London Mercury* May to August 1922, and in the *Dial*, May to October 1922; copy-text for these sections in this Norton Critical Edition is taken from the *Dial* printings. Portions of Book V: *The Stirring of the Bones* were printed as "A Biographical Fragment, with some notes" in the *Criterion* and the *Dial*, July 1923. Copy-text in this Norton Critical Edition is taken from the *Dial* printing. Yeats made incremental minor alterations to the titles of the sectional "books" in *The Trembling of the Veil* after 1922, and the titles given in this Norton Critical Edition follow the forms he first adopted in *Autobiographies*.

"Autobiography": Yeats's draft manuscript "Autobiography," written in 1916–17, was first transcribed and edited by Denis Donoghue in *Memoirs* (London: Macmillan, 1972). Copy-text for this Norton Critical Edition is taken from that volume.

Dramatic Personae: First published in the *London Mercury*, November 1935 to January 1936, and as a limited edition by the Cuala Press, December 1935. Reprinted in *Dramatis Personae, 1896–1902* in a trade edition by Macmillan in 1936. Copy-text for this Norton Critical Edition is taken from the London printing of this latter volume.

"Journal": Yeats's manuscript "Journal," written mainly in 1909–10 (but with sporadic later entries though 1930) was first transcribed and edited by Denis Donoghue in *Memoirs* (London: Macmillan, 1972). Copy-text for this Norton Critical Edition is taken from that volume.

Pages from a Diary Written in Nineteen Hundred and Thirty: First published in a limited edition by the Cuala Press in November 1944, and reprinted in *Explorations* (London: Macmillan, 1962), from which latter volume copy-text for this Norton Critical Edition is taken.

Critical Writings

Copy-texts for the critical writings by Yeats in this Norton Critical Edition are from first printings unless otherwise noted.

"Hopes and Fears for Irish Literature": First published in *United Ireland*, October 15, 1892. The misspelling or compositor error "Decadents" has been silently corrected to "Decadence."

"The De-Anglicising of Ireland": First published in *United Ireland*, December 17, 1892. The misspelling or compositor error "rythm" has been silently corrected to "rhythm."

"The Message of the Folk-lorist": First published in the *Speaker*, August 19, 1893.

"The Celtic Element in Literature": First published in *Cosmopolis*, June 1898, and revised and extended in *Ideas of Good and Evil* (London, 1903), from which volume copy-text for this Norton Critical Edition is taken.

"The Irish Literary Theatre": First published in the *Daily Express* (Dublin), January 14, 1899.

"Irish Language and Irish Literature": First published in the *Leader*, September 1, 1900.

"The Symbolism of Poetry": First published in the *Dome*, April 1900, and reprinted in *Ideas of Good and Evil* (London, 1903), from which volume copy-text for this Norton Critical Edition is taken.

"Magic": First published in the *Monthly Review*, September 1901, and reprinted in *Ideas of Good and Evil* (London, 1903), from which volume copy-text for this Norton Critical Edition is taken.

"The Reform of the Theatre": First published in the *United Irishman*, April 4, 1903, and reprinted with additions in *Samhain*, September 1903, from which copy-text for this Norton Critical Edition is taken.

"On Taking 'The Playboy' to London": First published in the *Arrow*, June 1, 1907, under the title "Notes." Reprinted in part and retitled "On Taking 'The Playboy' to London" in *The Irish Dramatic Movement* in *Collected Works* (1908), from which copy-text for this Norton Critical Edition is taken.

"The Play of Modern Manners" and "A Tower on the Appenines": Both first published in *Discoveries* (Dublin: Cuala Press, 1907) and reprinted in *Collected Works* (1908) from which copy-texts for this Norton Critical Edition are taken. The title misspelling "Appenine" has been silently emended to "Appenines" in this Norton Critical Edition.

"Poetry and Tradition": First published in December 1908, under the title "Poetry and Patriotism" in *Poetry and Ireland* (Dublin Cuala Press), and, the same month, as "Poetry and Tradition" in *Collected Works* (1908), from which copy-text for this Norton Critical Edition is taken.

"First Principles": First published in *Samhain*, November 1908.

Per Amica Silentia Lunae: First published in January 1918 (London: Macmillan).

"A People's Theatre": First published in the *Irish Statesman* (November 29 and December 6, 1919) and reprinted in the *Dial* (April 1920), from which copy-text for this Norton Critical Edition is taken.

The Bounty of Sweden: First published by the Cuala Press in July 1925, and reprinted in *Dramatis Personae, 1896–1902* (Macmillan, 1936), from which copy-text for this Norton Critical Edition is taken.

Introduction to *The Oxford Book of Modern Verse 1892–1935*: First published in *The Oxford Book of Modern Verse 1892–1935* (Oxford: Clarendon Press, 1936).

A Vision: First published by Macmillan (London), October 1937. The earlier privately printed *A Vision*, issued for subscribers only by T. Werner Laurie in January 1926, is a substantially different book.

Essays for the Scribner Edition of Yeats's *Collected Works*: First published in *Essays and Introductions* (London: Macmillan, 1961), with "Introduction" under the title "A General Introduction for My Work," "Introduction to Essays" under the title "Introduction," and "Introduction to Plays" under the title "An Introduction for my Plays."

On the Boiler: First published by the Cuala Press in 1939. All but a few copies of the first printing were destroyed and replaced with a second issue published in August 1939, from which copy-text for this Norton Critical Edition is taken.

Selected Bibliography

● Indicates those works excerpted in this Norton Critical Edition.

I. BIBLIOGRAPHIES

Jochum, K. P. S. *W. B. Yeats: A Classified Bibliography of Criticism*. 2nd ed. Urbana and Chicago: U of Illinois P, 1990.

Wade, Allan. *A Bibliography of the Writings of W. B. Yeats*. 3rd ed., rev. Russell K. Alspach. London: Rupert Hart-Davis, 1968.

II. EDITIONS, CRITICAL EDITIONS, CONCORDANCES, AND TEXTUAL STUDIES

Adams, Steve L., Barbara Frieling, and Sandra Sprayberry, eds. *Yeats's "Vision" Papers*. vols. 1–2. Iowa: UP of Iowa, 1992.

Allt, Peter, and Russell K. Alspach, eds. *The Variorum Edition of the Poems of W. B. Yeats*. New York: Macmillan, 1966.

Alspach, Russell K. *The Variorum Edition of the Plays of W. B. Yeats*. London and New York: Macmillan, 1966.

Armstrong, Alison, ed. *The Herne's Egg: Manuscript Materials*. Ithaca and London: Cornell UP, 1994.

Bornstein, George, and Hugh Witemyer, eds. *Letters to the New Island: A New Edition*. London: Macmillan, 1989.

———, ed. *The Early Poetry, Volume I: "Mosada" and "The Island of Statues": Manuscript Materials*. Ithaca and London: Cornell UP, 1987.

———, ed. *The Early Poetry, Volume II: "The Wanderings of Oisin" and Other Early Poems to 1895: Manuscript Materials*. Ithaca and London: Cornell UP, 1994.

Bradford, Curtis. *Yeats at Work*. Carbondale and Edwardsville: Southern Illinois UP, 1965.

Bridge, Ursula. *W. B. Yeats and T. Sturge Moore: Their Correspondence, 1901–1937*. London: Routledge and Kegan Paul; New York: Oxford University Press, 1953.

Clark, David R., ed. *The Winding Stair (1929): Manuscript Materials*. Ithaca and London: Cornell UP, 1995.

Domville, Eric. *A Concordance to the Plays of W. B. Yeats*. 2 vols. Ithaca and London: Cornell UP, 1972.

● Donoghue, Denis, ed. *W. B. Yeats: Memoirs: Autobiography—First Draft: Journal*. London: Macmillan, 1972; New York: Macmillan, 1973.

Finneran, Richard J. *Editing Yeats's Poems: A Reconsideration*. New York: St. Martin's P, 1990.

———, ed. *The Correspondence of Robert Bridges and W. B. Yeats*. London: Macmillan, 1977.

———, ed. *W. B. Yeats: John Sherman and Dhoya*. New York: Macmillan, 1991.

———, ed. *The Collected Poems of W. B. Yeats: Revised Second Edition*. New York: Macmillan, 1996.

———, George Mills Harper, and William M. Murphy with the assistance of Alan B. Himber, eds. *Letters to W. B. Yeats*. 2 vols. London: Macmillan, 1977; New York: Columbia UP, 1977.

Frayne, John P., ed. *Uncollected Prose by W. B. Yeats*. Vol. I. London: Macmillan; New York: Columbia UP, 1970.

———, and Colton Johnson, eds. *Uncollected Prose by W. B. Yeats*. Vol. II. London: Macmillan, 1975; New York: Columbia UP, 1976.

Gould, Warwick, Phillip L. Marcus, and Michael J. Sidnell, eds. *The Secret Rose: A Variorum Edition*. 2nd ed., rev. and enl. London: Macmillan, 1992.

———, John Kelly, and Deirdre Toomey, eds. *The Collected Letters of W. B. Yeats, Volume II: 1865–1895*. Oxford: Clarendon Press, 1997.

Harper, George Mills, and Walter Kelly Hood, eds. *A Critical Edition of Yeats's "A Vision" (1925)*. London: Macmillan, 1978.

Holdsworth, Carolyn, ed. *The Wind Among the Reeds: Manuscript Materials*. Ithaca and London: Cornell UP, 1993.

Jeffares, A. Norman, ed., with an Appendix by Warwick Gould. *Yeats's Poems*. 2nd ed., rev. London: Macmillan, 1991.

Kelly, John, and Eric Domville, eds. *The Collected Letters of W. B. Yeats, Volume I: 1865–1895*. Oxford: Clarendon P, 1986.

——, and Ronald Schuchard, eds. *The Collected Letters of W. B. Yeats, Volume III: 1865–1895.* Oxford: Clarendon P, 1994.

Marcus, Phillip L., ed. *The Death of Cuchulain: Manuscript Materials.* Ithaca and London: Cornell UP, 1981.

Martinich, Robert A., and Margaret Mills Harper, eds. *Yeats's "Vision" Papers.* Vol. 3. Iowa City: U of Iowa P, 1992.

McHugh, Roger, ed. *"Ah, Sweet Dancer": W. B. Yeats/Margot Ruddock, A Correspondence.* London and New York: Macmillan, 1970.

O'Donnell, William H., ed. *The Speckled Bird, with Variant Versions.* Toronto: McClelland and Stewart, 1976.

——, ed. *Prefaces and Introductions: Uncollected Prefaces and Introductions by Yeats to Works by other Authors and to Anthologies edited by Yeats.* London: Macmillan, 1988.

——, ed., with assistance from Elizabeth Bergmann Loizeaux. *W. B. Yeats: Later Essays.* New York: Scribner, 1994.

——, and Douglas Archibald, eds., J. Fraser Cocks III and Gretchen Schwenker, asst. eds. *W. B. Yeats: Autobiographies.* New York: Scribner, 1999.

O'Shea, Edward. *A Descriptive Catalog of W. B. Yeats's Library.* New York and London: Garland, 1985.

Parkinson, Thomas, ed., with Anne Brannen. *Michael Robartes and the Dancer: Manuscript Materials.* Ithaca and London: Cornell UP, 1994.

Parrish, Stephen, and James Allan Painter. *A Concordance to the Poems of W. B. Yeats.* Ithaca and London: Cornell UP, 1963.

——, ed. *The Wild Swans at Coole: Manuscript Materials.* Ithaca and London: Cornell UP, 1994.

Pearce, Donald R., ed. *The Senate Speeches of W. B. Yeats.* Bloomington: Indiana UP, 1960; London: Faber and Faber, 1961.

Pethica, James, ed. *Last Poems: Manuscript Materials.* Ithaca and London: Cornell UP, 1997.

Phillips, Catherine, ed. *The Hour-Glass: Manuscript Materials.* Ithaca and London: Cornell UP, 1994.

Saddlemyer, Anne, ed. *Theatre Business: The Correspondence of the First Abbey Theatre Directors: William Butler Yeats, Lady Gregory and J. M. Synge.* Gerrards Cross: Colin Smythe, 1982.

Sidnell, Michael J., George Mayhew, and David R. Clark, eds. *Druid Craft: The Writing of "The Shadowy Waters."* Amherst: The U of Massachusetts P, 1971.

——, and Wayne Chapman, eds. *The Countess Cathleen: Manuscript Materials.* Ithaca and London: Cornell UP, 1999.

Siegel, Sandra, ed. *Purgatory: Manuscript Materials.* Ithaca and London: Cornell UP, 1986.

Stallworthy, Jon. *Between the Lines: Yeats's Poetry in the Making.* Oxford: Clarendon P, 1963.

——. *Vision and Revision in Yeats's "Last Poems."* Oxford: Clarendon P, 1969.

Wade, Allan. *The Letters of W. B. Yeats.* London: Rupert Hart-Davis, 1954; New York, Macmillan, 1955.

White, Anna MacBride, and A. Norman Jeffares, eds. *The Gonne-Yeats Letters, 1893–1938: Always Your Friend.* London: Hutchinson, 1992.

Yeats, William Butler, ed. *A Book of Irish Verse Selected from Modern Writers.* London: Methuen, 1895.

——. *Essays and Introductions.* London and New York: Macmillan, 1961.

——. *Explorations.* London and New York: Macmillan, 1962.

——. *Mythologies.* London and New York: Macmillan, 1959.

——. *The Oxford Book of Modern Verse, 1895–1935. Chosen by W. B. Yeats.* Oxford: Clarendon Press, 1936.

——, ed. *Fairy and Folk Tales of the Irish Peasantry.* London: Scott, 1888.

——, and Edwin Ellis, eds. *The Works of William Blake: Poetic, Symbolic, and Critical.* 3 vols. London: Quaritch, 1893.

III. BIOGRAPHIES AND BIOGRAPHICAL STUDIES

Brown, Terence. *The Life of W. B. Yeats: A Critical Biography.* Oxford: Blackwell, 1999.

Ellmann, Richard. *Eminent Domain: Yeats among Wilde, Joyce, Pound, Eliot and Auden.* New York: Oxford UP, 1967.

● ——. *Yeats: The Man and the Masks.* 2nd ed. Oxford: Oxford UP, 1979.

● Foster, R. F. *W. B. Yeats: A Life: I: The Apprentice Mage, 1865–1914.* Oxford and New York: Oxford UP, 1997.

Harwood, John. *Olivia Shakespear and W. B. Yeats: After Long Silence.* London: Macmillan, 1989.

Hone, Joseph. *W. B. Yeats, 1865–1939.* New York: St. Martin's P, 1962.

Jeffares, A. N. *W. B. Yeats: Man and Poet.* Rev. ed. London: Routledge and Kegan Paul, 1962.

Lewis, Gifford. *The Yeats Sisters and the Cuala.* Dublin: Irish Academic P, 1994.

MacBride, Maud Gonne. *A Servant of the Queen: Reminiscences.* A. Norman Jeffares and Anna MacBride White, eds. Gerrards Cross: Colin Smythe, 1994.

Maddox, Brenda. *Yeats's Ghosts: The Secret Life of W. B. Yeats.* New York: HarperCollins, 1999.

Murphy, William M. *Prodigal Father: The Life of John Butler Yeats (1839–1922).* Ithaca and London: Cornell UP, 1978.

IV. CRITICAL STUDIES AND COLLECTIONS OF CRITICAL ESSAYS

Adams, Hazard. *The Book of Yeats's Poems.* Tallahassee: Florida State UP, 1990.
●Albright, Daniel. *Quantum Poetics: Yeats, Pound, Eliot, and the Science of Modernism.* Cambridge: Cambridge UP, 1997.
Allison, Jonathan, ed. *Yeats's Political Identities: Selected Essays.* Ann Arbor: U of Michigan P, 1996.
●Archibald, Douglas. *Yeats.* Syracuse: Syracuse UP, 1983.
●Bloom, Harold. *Yeats.* New York: Oxford UP, 1970.
——, ed. *Modern Critical Views: William Butler Yeats.* New York and Philadelphia: Chelsea House, 1986.
●Bornstein, George. *Yeats and Shelley.* Chicago and London: U of Chicago P, 1970.
——. *Poetic Remaking: The Art of Browning, Yeats and Pound.* University Park and London: Pennsylvania State UP, 1988.
Chapman, Wayne. *Yeats and English Renaissance Literature.* New York: St. Martin's P, 1991.
Cullingford, Elizabeth Butler. *Yeats, Ireland and Fascism.* London: Macmillan, 1981.
——, ed. *Yeats: Poems, 1919–1935: A Casebook.* London: Macmillan, 1984.
●——. *Gender and History in Yeats's Love Poetry.* Cambridge: Cambridge UP, 1993; Syracuse: Syracuse UP, 1996.
Diggory, Terence. *Yeats and American Poetry: The Tradition of the Self.* Princeton: Princeton UP, 1983.
Donoghue, Denis, and J. R. Mulryne, eds. *An Honoured Guest: New Essays on W. B. Yeats.* London: Edward Arnold, 1965.
——. *William Butler Yeats.* New York: Viking, 1971.
Ellmann, Richard. *The Identity of Yeats.* 2nd ed. London: Faber and Faber, 1964.
——. *Yeats's Second Puberty.* Washington: Library of Congress, 1986.
Engleberg, Edward. *The Vast Design: Patterns in W. B. Yeats's Aesthetic.* Toronto: U of Toronto P, 1974.
Flannery, James W. *W. B. Yeats and the Idea of a Theatre: The Early Abbey Theatre in Theory and Practice.* New Haven and London: Yale UP, 1976.
Fletcher, Ian. *W. B. Yeats and His Contemporaries.* Brighton: Harvester, 1987.
Frazier, Adrien. *Behind the Scenes: Yeats, Horniman, and the Struggle for the Abbey Theatre.* Berkeley, Los Angeles, and London: U of California P, 1990.
Freyer, Grattan. *W. B. Yeats and the Anti-Democratic Tradition.* Dublin: Gill and Macmillan, 1981.
Harper, George Mills. *Yeats's Golden Dawn.* London: Macmillan, 1974.
——, ed. *Yeats and the Occult.* London: Macmillan, 1976.
Harris, Daniel. *Yeats: Coole Park and Ballylee.* Baltimore: Johns Hopkins UP, 1974.
Holdeman, David. *Much Labouring: The Texts and Authors of Yeats's First Modernist Books.* Ann Arbor: U of Michigan P, 1997.
●Howes, Marjorie. *Yeats's Nations: Gender, Class, and Irishness.* Cambridge: Cambridge UP, 1996.
Jeffares, A. Norman. *A New Commentary on the Poems of W. B. Yeats.* Stanford: Stanford UP, 1984.
——, ed. *Yeats the European.* Savage, Md.: Barnes and Noble, 1989.
Keane, Patrick J. *Yeats's Interactions with Tradition.* Columbia: U of Missouri P, 1987.
——. *Terrible Beauty: Yeats, Joyce, Ireland, and the Myth of the Devouring Female.* Columbia: U of Missouri P, 1988.
Kermode, Frank. *Romantic Image.* London: Routledge and Kegan Paul; New York: Macmillan, 1957.
●Kiberd, Declan. *Inventing Ireland.* Cambridge: Harvard UP, 1996.
Kinahan, Frank. *Yeats, Folklore and Occultism: Contexts of the Early Work and Thought.* London: Unwin and Hyman, 1988.
Loizeaux, Elizabeth Bergmann. *Yeats and the Visual Arts.* New Brunswick and London: Rutgers UP, 1986.
Longenbach, James. *Stone Cottage: Pound, Yeats, and Modernism.* Oxford: Oxford UP, 1988.
Lynch, David. *Yeats: The Poetics of the Self.* Chicago: U of Chicago P, 1979.
Marcus, Phillip L. *Yeats and the Beginning of the Irish Renaissance.* Ithaca and London: Cornell UP, 1970.
——. *Yeats and Artistic Power.* New York: New York UP, 1992.
●North, Michael. *The Political Aesthetic of Yeats, Eliot, and Pound.* Cambridge: Cambridge UP, 1991.
O'Donnell, William. *A Guide to the Prose Fiction of W. B. Yeats.* Ann Arbor, Mich.: UMI Research P, 1983.
Olney, James. *The Rhizome and the Flower: The Perennial Philosophy—Yeats and Jung.* Berkeley, Los Angeles, and London: U of California P, 1980.
Orr, Leonard, ed. *Yeats and Postmodernism.* Syracuse: Syracuse UP, 1991.
●Parkinson, Thomas. *W. B. Yeats, Self-Critic: A Study of His Early Verse.* Berkeley and Los Angeles: U of California P, 1951.
——. *W. B. Yeats: The Later Poetry.* Berkeley and Los Angeles: U of California P, 1965.
Pierce, David. *Yeats's Worlds: Ireland, England and the Poetic Imagination.* New Haven and London: Yale UP, 1995.
Putzel, Steven. *Reconstructing Yeats: The Secret Rose and The Wind Among the Reeds.* Dublin: Gill and Macmillan; Totowa, N.J.: Barnes and Noble, 1986.
Raine, Kathleen. *Yeats the Initiate: Essays on Certain Themes in the Work of W. B. Yeats.* Dublin: Dolmen Press; London: George Allen and Unwin, 1986.

● Ramazani, Jahan. *Yeats and the Poetry of Death: Elegy, Self-Elegy, and the Sublime.* New Haven and London: Yale UP, 1990.

Sidnell, Michael J. *Yeats's Poetry and Poetics.* London: St. Martin's P, 1996.

Stanfield, Paul Scott. *Yeats and Politics in the Nineteen-Thirties.* London: Macmillan, 1988.

Stead, C. K. *The New Poetic: Yeats to Eliot.* London: Hutchinson University Library, 1964.

———. *Pound, Yeats, Eliot, and the Modernist Movement.* London: Macmillan, 1986.

Thuente, Mary. *Yeats and Irish Folklore.* Dublin: Gill and Macmillan; Totowa, N.J.: Barnes and Noble, 1981.

● Toomey, Deirdre, ed. *Yeats and Women.* 2nd ed. London: Macmillan; New York: St. Martin's P, 1997.

Torchiana, Donald. *Yeats and Georgian Ireland.* Oxford: Oxford UP, 1966.

Vendler, Helen. *Yeats's "Vision" and the Later Plays.* Cambridge: Harvard UP, 1963.

Watson, George. *Irish Identity and the Literary Revival: Synge, Yeats, Joyce and O'Casey.* 2nd ed. Washington: Catholic U of America P, 1994.

V. CRITICAL JOURNALS

Yeats: An Annual of Critical and Textual Studies. Ithaca and London: Cornell UP, 1983–85; Ann Arbor and London: UMI Research P, 1986–.

Yeats Annual. London: Macmillan, 1982–.

Index of Titles and
First Lines of Poems

515